P9-DMU-189

The Gambia & Senegal

Katharina Kane

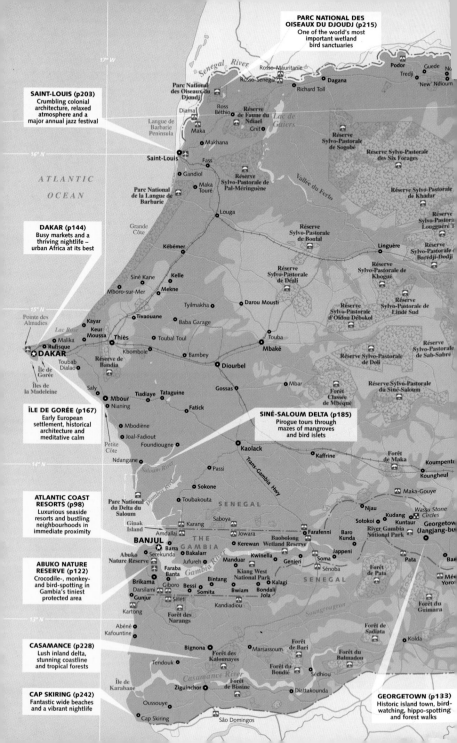

PARC NATIONAL DES OISEAUX DU DJOUDJ (p215)
One of the world's most important wetland bird sanctuaries

SAINT-LOUIS (p203)
Crumbling colonial architecture, relaxed atmosphere and a major annual jazz festival

DAKAR (p144)
Busy markets and a thriving nightlife – urban Africa at its best

ÎLE DE GORÉE (p167)
Early European settlement, historical architecture and meditative calm

SINÉ-SALOUM DELTA (p185)
Pirogue tours through mazes of mangroves and bird islets

ATLANTIC COAST RESORTS (p98)
Luxurious seaside resorts and bustling neighbourhoods in immediate proximity

ABUKO NATURE RESERVE (p122)
Crocodile-, monkey- and bird-spotting in Gambia's tiniest protected area

CASAMANCE (p228)
Lush inland delta, stunning coastline and tropical forests

CAP SKIRING (p242)
Fantastic wide beaches and a vibrant nightlife

GEORGETOWN (p133)
Historic island town, bird-watching, hippo-spotting and forest walks

ATLANTIC OCEAN

Senegal River

THE GAMBIA

SENEGAL

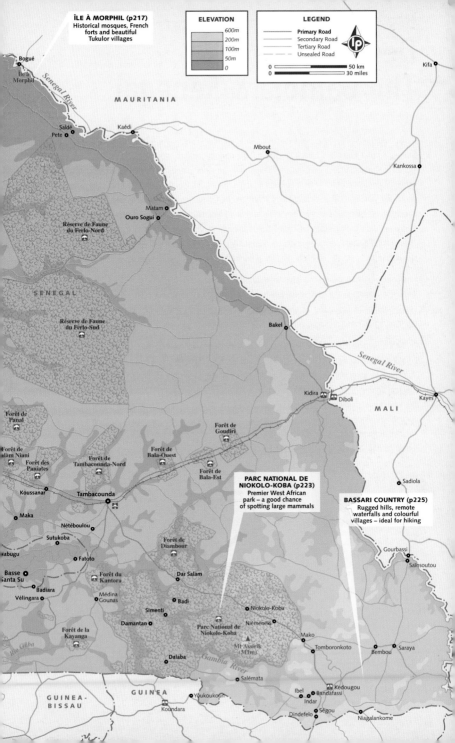

ÎLE À MORPHIL (p217)
ÎLE À MORPHIL (p217)
Historical mosques, French
forts and beautiful
Tukulor villages

ELEVATION

	600m
	200m
	100m
	50m
	0

LEGEND

Primary Road
Secondary Road
Tertiary Road
Unsealed Road

0   50 km
0   30 miles

Bogué
Île à
Morphil
Kifa

Senegal River

MAURITANIA

Saldé
Pete
Kaédi

Mbout

Kankossa

Matam
Ouro Sogui

Réserve de Faune
du Ferlo-Nord

SENEGAL

Réserve de Faune
du Ferlo-Sud

Bakel

Senegal River

Kidira
Diboli

MALI

Kayes

Forêt de
Panal

Forêt de
Goudiri

Forêt de
Salam Niani

Forêt des
Paniates

Forêt de
Tambacounda-Nord

Forêt de
Bala-Ouest

Forêt de
Bala-Est

Koussanar

Tambacounda

Sadiola

**PARC NATIONAL DE
NIOKOLO-KOBA (p223)**
Premier West African
park – a good chance
of spotting large mammals

Maka

Nétéboulou

Forêt de
Diambour

BASSARI COUNTRY (p225)
Rugged hills, remote
waterfalls and colourful
villages – ideal for hiking

Sutukoba

Dabugu

Fatoto

Gourbassi
Saïnsoutou

Basse
Santa Su

Forêt du
Kantora

Dar Salam

Badiara

Médina
Gounas

Badi

Niokolo-Koba

Vélingara

Simenti

Niéméniki

Mako

Tomboronkoto

Bembou

Saraya

Damantan

Parc National de
Niokolo-Koba

Forêt de la
Kayanga

Mt Assirik
(311m)

Dalaba

Gambia River

Kédougou

GUINEA-
BISSAU

GUINEA

Salémata

Ibel

Bandafassi

Indar

Ségou

Youkoukoun

Dindefelo

Rio Geba

Koundara

Niagalankome

Destination
The Gambia & Senegal

Couched between the arid desert lands of the north and lush tropical forests in the south, Senegal and Gambia boast a stunning array of sights, sounds and flavours. Perched on the tip of a beach-lined peninsula, Senegal's capital Dakar is composed elegance and shrewd street hustler rolled into one. Its busy streets, vibrant markets and glittering nightlife try to draw you into their relentless rhythm, but the escape route is always open – be it to the meditative calm of the historical Île de Gorée or the golden sand strands of Yoff and N'Gor on the Cap Vert peninsula. Or head for the calm sway of the architectural beauty of Saint-Louis, the first French settlement in West Africa, or Gambia's Banjul, the continent's most understated capital, which boasts a vibrant urban culture without the inner-city bustle.

Most visitors come to this region for its beaches, and for good reason. All along the Atlantic coast, wide strips of white sand invite you to swim and sunbathe – in the built-up resort zones a lazy day at the beach can be followed by a cocktail trail at night, the coast's charming fishing village beaches are dotted with hundreds of colourful wooden pirogues.

At the wide deltas of Senegal's Casamance and Saloum Rivers, the straight coastline is broken up into a maze of thick mangroves, tiny creeks, wide lagoons and shimmering plains. A pirogue trip through these striking zones reveals hundreds of bird species, from tiny, gleaming kingfishers to proudly poised pink flamingos. In the north, where hot desert sands blow across the land, the River Senegal forms the border between Senegal and Mauritania. Along its shore stand French forts and abandoned 19th-century warehouses and humble mud-brick mosques. Further south, the cries of over 300 species of birds will follow you as your pirogue charts a leisurely course along the Gambia River.

ERIC L WH

Rivers & Beaches

OTHER HIGHLIGHTS

- Immerse yourself in sun, sand and sea, either the resort or the village way, on Gambia's Atlantic coast (p98).
- Cruise the Senegal River in style on the historic, much-loved 1950s liner *Bou El Mogdad* (p209).

ANDREW BURKE

Lounge under traditional paillotes on the Kafountine beach (p247), Senegal

ANDREW BURKE

Spot birds galore along the waterways of Gambia's Baobolong Wetland Reserve (p131)

Track the telltale signs of horse and cart along the beach at Grande Côte (p176), Senegal

ANDREW BURKE

Village Life

ANDREW BURKE

Plunge into noise, action and atmosphere at Gambia's huge Serekunda market (p111)

OTHER HIGHLIGHTS

- Catch one of the hugely popular wrestling matches (p49) in Gambia or Senegal.
- Down a hot *ataaya*, West Africa's classic afternoon pick-me-up tea (p144), in Senegal.

ARIADNE VAN ZANDBERGEN

See a Bédik woman prepare a local brew in Bassari country (p225), Senegal

Bone up on traditional initiation ceremonies in Bassari country (p225), Senegal

ARIADNE VAN ZAND

Natural Beauty

ANDREW BURKE

Take a rustic pirogue past the mangroves in the Makasutu Culture Forest (p124), Gambia

ANDREW BURKE

Wander the beach at Cap Skiring (p242) in Casamance, Senegal's most beautiful region

OTHER HIGHLIGHTS

- Be awed by the colossal sand dunes of Senegal's Désert de Lompoul (p214).
- Go wild about nature in the wildlife-rich Petite Côte (p177) reserves, Senegal.

Experience Gambia's scenery at its best on a slow boat along the Gambia River (p288)

DAVID TIPLING

Wildlife

Smile at a Nile crocodile at the Kachikaly
Crocodile Pool (p103), Gambia

Shoot a portrait of a forest buffalo up to its neck in
water, Réserve de Bandia (p179), Senegal

OTHER HIGHLIGHTS

- Look out for crocs, monkeys and birds at
  Gambia's tiniest protected area, Abuko Nature
  Reserve (p122).
- Find all manner of African animals and birds
  at the vast biosphere reserve Parc National de
  Niokolo-Koba (p223), a World Heritage site.

Go where the antelope roam between the baobabs of Réserve de Bandia (p179), Senegal

Contents

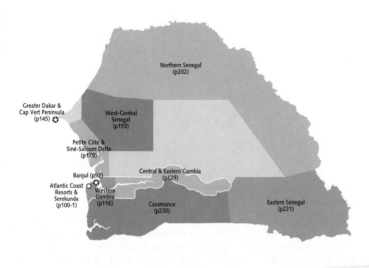

The Author

KATHARINA KANE

When Katharina heard the haunting sound of a Fula flute during a London concert, her fate was sealed. She headed straight to Guinea in West Africa, where she ended up studying the instrument for a year before writing a PhD on its origins. She then decamped to Senegal, a country that she'd fallen in love with during one of her many travels to West Africa in her role as a music journalist. Katharina has worked on other Lonely Planet titles, writes for various world-music magazines including *fRoots* and *Songlines*, and produces world-music features for radio stations including the BBC and WDR. She currently divides her time between Dakar, Cologne and London.

My Favourite Trip

Travelling for me has always been about music – which explains why I've settled in Senegal, one of West Africa's most buzzing music scenes. Dakar, with its dazzling live-music scene (p161), is hard to leave if you love music. Only in May does the northern town of Saint-Louis rival Dakar's nightlife with its spectacular jazz festival (p206). Podor (p217) in the north is the place to hear Fula music, perhaps during Baaba Maal's Festival du Fleuve. For the really rootsy stuff, Salémata (p226), with its vibrant Bassari culture, and Kartong (p119), site of a bustling festival, are my destinations of choice, while Ziguinchor in Casamance is best visited during its carnival (p235), and Abéné (p250) during its reggae-fuelled New Year's festival. And for a gentle comedown, Brikama is the place to indulge in some masterful kora playing (p124).

Getting Started

Whether it's a lazy beach holiday you're after or a solitary tour around remote villages, myriad mangrove swamps and endless savannah plains, you'll be well served in Gambia and Senegal.

For a brief stay in the built-up tourist zones – such as the Atlantic resorts in The Gambia, and Saly and Cap Skiring in Senegal – you won't need much advance preparation, next to none if you travel with an organised tour.

Independent travellers and those intending to venture far off the beaten track should spend a good amount of time crouched over maps and travel guides – if you know where you're hoping to stay, many of the isolated lodgings upcountry can help you with transport if you contact them in advance. Most tourists tend to visit either Senegal or Gambia – and they're all missing out. A trip to Casamance can boost a Gambia holiday enormously, and a tour along the Gambia River can make a visit to Senegal complete.

Apart from some tedious border formalities, it's relatively easy to combine a visit to both – don't let the language differences (French in Senegal and English in Gambia) scare you.

Both countries have a good choice of accommodation facilities, restaurants and travel options to suit most budgets. However, shoestring travellers will find Dakar a challenge, while those who prefer to travel like kings will find their choices limited when travelling inland.

WHEN TO GO

By far the most popular tourist season in Gambia and Senegal is the period from November to February, when conditions are dry and relatively cool. This is also the best time to watch wildlife and birds (including many European migratory species) in the countries' many national parks, and the season you're guaranteed best access to all regions, as the absence of rains makes even the remotest dirt road reasonably accessible. And if you want to party, the urban centre of Dakar is a great place to spend Christmas and New Year.

See Climate (p258) for more information.

Several of Senegal's famous dance and music festivals, however, tend to take place between March and June, when temperatures are higher and the climate still dry.

DON'T LEAVE HOME WITHOUT...

- your vaccination certificate with a yellow-fever stamp – Gambian officials love to check it
- checking the latest security situation in Casamance
- making copies of all official documents – it will make getting any necessary replacements much easier
- a torch (flashlight) – many remote places don't have electricity and cuts are frequent even in the urban zones
- binoculars – even those with no ornithological inclination whatsoever are likely to be converted in this region
- a set of smart clothes – don't be outdazzled by the impeccably dressed locals
- a warm jersey – January nights in Dakar can get wool-sweater chilly.

VISITS DURING RAMADAN

Ramadan, the holy month of the Islamic calendar, is a time of religious contemplation, dedicated to prayer and the study of the Quran. Most importantly, it's the fasting month – Muslims are not allowed to eat, drink, smoke or have sex from dawn until dusk.

The Ramadan fast completely changes the rhythm of life in the Muslim world. Many people wake around 5am for an early breakfast before sunrise, and some businesses cancel the usual lunch break and finish around 4.30pm, allowing their tired and hungry employees to return home.

It isn't an ideal month for travelling, even if you're not a Muslim. Many restaurants, bars and nightclubs close for the 30 days and there won't be many live concerts, as music and other worldly pleasures are frowned upon for its duration. Collective hunger also means that tempers tend to rise, especially towards the late afternoon. A Ramadan traffic jam before dusk is always a scene of loud arguments and occasional fist fights.

As a non-Muslim you won't be expected to fast, and people won't take offence if you eat in their presence. Just bear in mind that most others around you run on empty stomachs, and be considerate of their needs. If you use the services of a driver, allow for prayer stops and try to get back before the break of the fast. If that's impossible, make sure you put in a stop when the prayer is called after dusk, allowing him to take in a hot drink and a bite to eat. The fast is usually broken with a handful of dates, so you can offer the driver some if you're running late and want to show your appreciation. Generally, be patient with the occasional show of grumpiness. If you want to know what it's like, try to live the Ramadan rhythm for a while. You'll understand what most of the locals are experiencing.

The wet season (late June to late September) is the time most tourists avoid. The rains wash away some of the roads, rendering certain journeys upcountry impossible. Malaria is widespread, the humidity can become stifling and many national parks (and a few hotels) shut down. But there's a positive side to this, too. Everything is greener, independent travellers will enjoy the absence of large tourist groups, and many places (especially in The Gambia) reduce their prices by up to 50%.

October and November are again fairly dry, though very hot – but if you can take the temperatures, this is a great time to come. You can still enjoy the sight of lush greens, swelling rivers and large waterfalls, while staying dry yourself. The beaches aren't packed yet and you're bound to find a hotel room.

Since you're travelling to a predominantly Muslim region, it's worth checking the lunar calendar, particularly for the dates of the fasting month of Ramadan (above). Though it's perfectly possible to visit during Ramadan, and the month's special ambience is worth experiencing, many restaurants close and the entertainment scene goes into hibernation.

COSTS & MONEY

It's pretty much up to you how cheap or expensive you render your trip to Gambia and Senegal. Shoestringers can get by on a budget of around US$15 per day, but that means battered minibuses, dorms and street food. Spending US$30 to US$40 allows for some creature comforts. With US$50 you'll be at ease, and with US$100 there are few luxuries that aren't within reach.

Locally produced items (including food and beer) are much cheaper than in Europe or America, but as soon as you head for the supermarket for some French yogurt or a box of cornflakes, you pay twice the amount you would at home.

All around the region, you can get a generous platter of rice and sauce in a local-style restaurant for US$3 or even less, but a three-course meal for two at the smart restaurants of Dakar or the coastal resorts of Gambia will set you back US$30. In between, you get the whole range of quality and cost.

Hotel prices vary enormously between the urban centres and up-country villages. In Dakar even staying in a brothel might set you back US$20, while the same amount gets you a spacious, stunning double room (or two) in a *campement* (hostel accommodation in bungalows) outside the capital.

On average allow US$25 to US$50 for midrange hotels; top-notch establishments go for anything from US$75 and far, far above. Couples can save on accommodation costs, as double rooms are normally only 25% to 50% more than singles or don't cost extra at all. In most hotels, children sharing with their parents stay free of charge or for 10% to 50% of the full price.

It's in transport that differences in costs are most notable. Bush taxis are fairly cheap (US$1.50 to US$3 per 100km) but rough. For anything more comfortable you have to pay – around US$40 to US$60 per day for a private taxi, and US$80 or more per day for a 4WD with driver.

HOW MUCH?

French bread D8/CFA150

Newspaper D10/CFA200

Internet 1hr D30/CFA300

Soft drink D15/CFA300

Sandwich D50/CFA1000

READING UP

Very few travel books have been published about the region, but you can still read your way into the countries' culture through a whole range of related topics.

The most famous work relating to The Gambia is probably *Roots* by Alex Haley, which was written in 1976. A mix of fiction and historical fact, this hugely influential book describes the African-American author's search for his African origins.

For historical insights into the region, give Mungo Park's *Travels in the Interior of Africa* a try. The classic tome details the author's expeditions through Gambia and Senegal to the Niger River in the late 18th and early 19th centuries. His descriptions of the musical performances by griots could still apply to their timeless art today.

The stunning art book *Senegal behind Glass* (1994) by Anne-Marie Bouttianaux-Ndiaye contains reproductions of beautiful *sous-verre* paintings (p50), from historical to contemporary examples, thereby giving artistic insights into the country's religion, culture and arts scene.

A Saint in the City (2003) by Allen and Mary Roberts takes a similar approach, discussing Senegalese culture via the arts and the ubiquitous images of Senegal's great Sufi leader Cheikh Amadou Bamba (p197) around urban Dakar, which you're bound to see on your travels.

Most works on Senegal are written in French so if you're familiar with the language, *Sénégal* (2005), Christian Saglio's musings on the country, should be your first choice. The author, currently head of Dakar's Institut Français, has spent the greater part of his life in Senegal where, among other things, he helped conceive the fabulous network of *campements villageois* (p237) in Casamance in the 1970s.

For an easy-to-read and entertaining account of travels around West Africa's music scene, try Mark Hudson's *Our Grandmother's Drum* and the amusing *Music in My Head,* which describes the power, influence and everyday realities of modern African music set in a mythical city that is instantly recognisable as Dakar.

Overland travellers to the region must read *Sahara Overland – A Route & Planning Guide* by Chris Scott, which covers every tiny detail you might need to know. Published by Trailblazer in 2000, it can be 'upgraded' at Scott's website (www.sahara-overland.com).

TOP TENS

Top 10 Festivals

It's hard to come to Dakar and not find a festival in full swing. The country has a fantastically vibrant arts and music scene, as well as a population that loves a good party. Gambia is barely keeping up, though it's also got a couple of events that mustn't be missed.

- Ziguinchor Carnival (p235), Ziguinchor, late February or early March
- Kartong Festival (p120), Kartong, March
- Dak'Art Biennale (p156), Dakar, every two years in May
- Saint-Louis Jazz Festival (p206), Saint-Louis, May
- Kaay Fecc (p156), Dakar, June
- Roots Homecoming Festival, throughout Gambia, every two years in June
- Gorée Diaspora Festival (p167), Île de Gorée, November
- Festival International du Film de Quartier (p156), Dakar, December
- Abéné Festivalo (p247), Abéné, December
- Les Fanals de Saint-Louis (p207), Saint-Louis, December

Top 10 Albums

Look on any 'world music' shelf in your nearest record store and you'll find the Senegal section spilling over with a wide mix of styles, ranging from acoustic kora to heavy hip-hop. This country has brought forth a long chain of renowned artists including, of course, the best-known African singer of all – Youssou N'Dour. See p54 for more information on individual artists.

- *Dikaale*, Abdou Guité Seck
- *Djam Leeli*, Baaba Maal and Mansour Seck
- *Né la Thiass,* Cheikh Lô
- *Esperanza,* Daara J
- *Jaliology,* Dembo Konté and Kausu Kuyateh
- *Myamba,* Omar Pene
- *L'Itinéraire d'un Enfant Bronzé,* Sérigne Mbaye (Disiz La Peste)
- *Orientissimo,* Thione Seck
- *Viviane & Frères,* Viviane N'Dour
- *Immigrés,* Youssou N'Dour

Top 10 Bird-Watching Sites

Senegal and Gambia are among the world's major bird-watching destinations, and you never have to venture far to get some shiny feathers in front of your binoculars (see also p71).

- Abuko Nature Reserve (p122), Gambia
- Baobolong Wetland Reserve (p131), Gambia
- Îles de la Madeleine (p170), Senegal
- Footsteps Eco Lodge (p119), Gambia
- Kiang West National Park (p131), Gambia
- Marakissa (p124), Gambia
- Parc National des Oiseaux du Djoudj (p214), Senegal
- Réserve de Popenguine (p180), Senegal
- Tanji River Bird Reserve (p117), Gambia
- Toubakouta (p190), Senegal

INTERNET RESOURCES

ASSET (www.asset-gambia.com) The home page of the Gambian Association of Small Scale Enterprises in Tourism; lists plenty of interesting small businesses, from juice pressers and hotels to fashion designers and taxi drivers. The perfect guide for venturing off the beaten tourist trail and exploring the 'underground' of the travel scene.

Au-Senegal (www.au-senegal.com) Information overload – no detail of practical information, cultural historical aspects or news has been left out. You can book hotels online, get the latest updates on the political situation and much, much more.

Lonely Planet (www.lonelyplanet.com) Up-to-date information on travelling to the region and links to other good travel resources.

Senegal Tourist Office (www.senegal-tourism.com) Comprehensive tourist site that lists attractions and gives travel and accommodation tips.

Stanford Site Guide (www-sul.stanford.edu/depts/ssrg/africa/sene.html) Has links to hundreds of websites about Senegal, both in English and French.

The Gambia Tourism Authority (www.visitthegambia.gm) Gambia's official tourist website; covers the basics of travel information, though not in any great detail.

Itineraries

CLASSIC ROUTES

GAMBIA – COASTAL COMFORTS TO RURAL REMOTENESS

One to Two Weeks

The Gambia's compact size makes it an ideal destination for a one- or two-week visit. From Banjul airport, head for the **Atlantic coast** (p98), where you find the biggest choice of places to stay. Spend a couple of days at the beaches, and take the occasional day trip to the surrounding areas once the glamour of sea and sun alone has worn off. The busy market of **Serekunda** (p98) is close by, and the pretty museum and bird reserve of **Tanji** (p117), as well as the small fishing villages of **Gunjur** (p119) and **Kartong** (p119), are only a short hop further along the coast. You can spend the night in one of the villages, then visit the bustling junction town of **Brikama** (p123). Carry on to **Makasutu** (p124), visit the Culture Forest and head back to the coast.

Abuko Nature Reserve (p122), Gambia's smallest stretch of protected nature, is only a short drive away from the coast. A trip here can be combined with a meal at **Lamin Lodge** (p121), a creaking wooden restaurant that nestles in the mangroves.

The small and dusty capital of **Banjul** (p90) sits roughly 20km from the coastal resorts, and tempts with a lively market and colonial architecture. Take the ferry to the north bank for a visit to **Jufureh** (p126), and make time for the beautiful **Ginak Island** (p125).

If you have two weeks, take a journey upcountry. A river trip to **Georgetown** (p133) is an absolute treat. If that's beyond budget, you can follow the southern shore by road, stopping at Bintang for **Bintang Bolong** (p129), then carrying on to Georgetown, from where you can take pirogue and walking excursions to **Wassu** (p137), **River Gambia National Park** (p138) and **Basse Santa Su** (p138).

> This itinerary travels the entire country. It takes you to all the major sites of Gambia, from the beaches and fishing villages of the Atlantic coast to the most important national parks – from Ginak Island in the west to River Gambia National Park in Eastern Gambia. Approximate return length is 950km.

THE MANY FACES OF SENEGAL'S COAST   Two Weeks

Most flights go to **Dakar** (p145), and you shouldn't leave the vibrant capital without tasting its nightlife, checking out the arts and restaurant scenes and perusing the markets. From Dakar, day-trip to peaceful **Île de Gorée** (p167) and **Îles de la Madeleine** (p170).

Next, head north to historical **Saint-Louis** (p203) and from here day-trip to **Parc National des Oiseaux du Djoudj** (p214) and **Parc National de la Langue de Barbarie** (p214).

Return south, taking in the **Désert de Lompoul** (p214) on your way to the Petite Côte. Stop at the chilled-out fishing village of **Toubab Dialao** (p178), before following the shoreline south to **Mbour** (p183). If you're after low-key beach time, visit the seashell town of **Joal-Fadiout** (p184) or, if you're more at home in a holiday-resort zone, check out **Saly** (p181). From Mbour, trace the coastal road to **Palmarin** (p185), the stunning entry port to the Siné-Saloum Delta region, then head for **Toubakouta** (p190), one of the prettiest spots in the Delta.

Alternatively, head back to Dakar and take the plane or boat to Ziguinchor, for a few days in **Casamance** (p228), Senegal's most beautiful region.

Travel north from Dakar to Saint-Louis' nearby national parks for bird-watching then south past the dunes of Lompoul and along the Petite Côte. Culminate in the Siné-Saloum Delta. Starting and ending in Dakar, this tour is around 1050km.

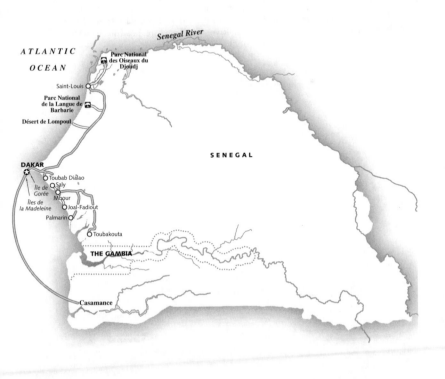

ROADS LESS TRAVELLED

THE CASAMANCE–GAMBIA TOUR

Two to Three Weeks

This is a perfect holiday – a tour around Senegal's beautiful Casamance, including the beaches of Cap Skiring, the surrounding mangroves and pretty villages, some major sights of Gambia – even a tour around Bassari country in Senegal. Starting in Cap Skiring and finishing in Dakar, it's 1700km.

It's perfectly possible to visit the Casamance for a chilled weekend at the beach only, but the region has so much to offer that it's best explored on a longer trip. Fly from Dakar to **Cap Skiring** (p242), the coastal area of the Casamance. Day-trip to **Diembéring** (p245), then take a pirogue to **Île de Karabane** (p240), stay at the calm island for a day, then visit **Elinkine** (p240) by wooden boat, before taking the road towards **Oussouye** (p239). On the road, you'll pass the impressive *cases à étage* (mudbrick houses) in **M'Lomp** (p240), and once in Oussouye, you can inhabit one, in the town's stunning Campement Villageois. Next, head eastwards to **Ziguinchor** (p232), the relaxed capital of the Casamance. Having spent a couple of days there, take the northbound road towards the chilled-out villages of **Kafountine** (p247) and **Abéné** (p250). Then it's off to Gambia, perhaps via the tiny crossing in **Darsilami** (p124). From here, join the pothole-troubled road eastwards, stopping at beautiful **Bintang Bolong** (p129), then braving the tired tarmac towards **Georgetown** (p133), a great place for river excursions and forest walks. **Basse** (p138), and the Senegalese border is only a few kilometres away. Head towards Vélingara, from where you get frequent transport towards **Tambacounda** (p221). If you've got time, add a trip to **Parc National de Niokolo-Koba** (p223) and the **Bassari country** (p225), as described in the Senegal River Tour, before heading to **Dakar** (p145) for a half-forgotten feel of city life.

THE SENEGAL RIVER ROUTE   Two to Three Weeks

This historical itinerary follows the Senegal River, the country's national border with Mauritania, tracing the route of French colonial incursion. Start in **Saint-Louis** (p203), the ancient capital of French West Africa, where you can learn about the town's unique history and culture on guided city tours and through independent exploration. From here you can either take the classic *Bou El Mogdad* upriver to Podor, or mirror the ship's journey on a trip by road. The town of **Richard Toll** (p216), home to the derelict Folie de Baron Roger, lies on the way. In **Podor** (p217) you visit the ancient fort and head on an off-road journey around the **Île à Morphil** (p218), which delights with classic Omarian mosques, stunning savannah countryside and Tukulor villages rooted in ancient times. Further along you'll reach **Matam** (p217), with its crumbling colonial architecture and **Bakel** (p218), which has another impressive fort and the René Caillié Pavilion. A short hop south, and you reach **Kidira** (p219) at the Malian border. If you're not crossing into Mali, head west for the junction town of **Tambacounda** (p221). If you have enough time, take a trip to the **Parc National de Niokolo-Koba** (p223), then keep going south towards **Kedougou** (p225) and **Bassari country** (p225). Here you can go for long hikes in the mountains, take in the strong traditional culture of the Bassari and Bédik people and see plateaux, waterfalls and forests.

From here, it's a long way back to Dakar. Put in another day's rest at Tambacounda, and, if you've got the time, a side-stop at the holy town of **Touba** (p196) before re-entering the capital.

This takes you along the rarely travelled road following the Senegal River, past the ancient forts of Podor, Matam and Bakel. You'll travel to the Parc National de Niokolo-Koba, Senegal's largest national park, and hike through the hills of Bassari country. Starting in Saint-Louis and finishing in Dakar, this tour is about 1800km.

TAILORED TRIPS

AS THE CROW FLIES

Senegal and Gambia are among the best destinations for bird-watching in West Africa.

In Gambia the chirping of hundreds of species greets you before you've even left your hotel, in the backyards of the Senegambia Hotel in

Kololi (p108) or the Ecolodge in **Gunjur** (p119). The **Abuko Nature Reserve** (p122) is a more 'official' bird-watching site, complete with guides and hides.

The nearby **Tanji River Bird Reserve** (p117) is a great place to spot a variety of wading and forest birds. Inland, **Marakissa** (p124) is worth a visit, as are **Baobolong Wetland Reserve** (p131) and **Kiang West National Park** (p131). **Georgetown** (p133) tempts with numerous bird-watching excursions, complete with trained guides based at various camps in town.

In Senegal, the *bolong* (creeks) of **Siné-Saloum** (p185) and **Casamance** (p228) are bird-watchers' dream destinations, with hundreds of sea birds and waders nesting on river islets and circling above thick mangrove forests. The bird-watcher's highlights in Senegal are the **Parc National des Oiseaux du Djoudj** (p214), the word's third-largest bird sanctuary, and the stunning peninsula of **Parc National de la Langue de Barbarie** (p214).

ARCHITECTURAL GEMS

You can almost trace the history of colonisation by following the architectural 'monuments' of Gambia and Senegal. If it's local culture you're after, you will have a fantastic time checking out the different building styles of the countries' various regions.

For colonial impact, **Île de Gorée** (p167) and **Saint-Louis** (p203) with their partly preserved French buildings, complete with wrought-iron balconies and leafy patios, are a must-see. **Rufisque** (p175) and **Banjul** (p90) have similar colonial houses, though in a less well-kept state.

Along the Senegal River, the Folie de Baron Roger in **Richard Toll** (p216) is a monument to the grand aspirations of colonialism, as are the Faidherbian forts of **Podor** (p217) and **Bakel** (p218). On **Île à Morphil** (p218), the Sudanese architecture of Omarian mosques reminds of local resistance to colonisation.

In Gambia, the British **Fort James** is partly preserved (p127), and **Georgetown** (p133) has a couple of crumbling colonial warehouses. In the Casamance, you can sleep in the old governor's house and mission on **Île de Karabane** (p240), and admire the *cases à étage* in **M'Lomp** (p240) and the *cases à impluvium* (round mud houses) in **Enampor** (p238) and **Affiniam** (p246).

THE JOURNEY IS THE DESTINATION

People often complain about how difficult it is to get around Gambia and Senegal, particularly if you rely on public transport. Well, they're right. But everything depends on attitude, and with the right sense of adventure (and humour) mastering the local transport system will be a trip indeed. Start in **Dakar** (p145) on a *car rapide* (a form of bush taxi, often decrepit) and tour around the inner city – stop whenever you want by tapping a coin on the roof. Take a *sept-place* taxi to **Saint-Louis** (p203), and explore the town by horse-drawn cart. Or, if you really want it rough, travel by *car mouride*, the large long-distance bus of the Mourides, to **Kaolack** (p197). Explore the city on the back of a *mobylette* (pedal-power moped) and watch pedestrians passing you by as you circle the local market. Then catch a Ndiaga Ndiaye (32-seater Mercedes minibus) to **Tambacounda** (p221), take a luxurious 4WD side-trip to **Parc National de Niokolo-Koba** (p223), and head for **Kedougou** (p225). Exploring the stunning villages of the Bassari region by public transport means waiting for the local market days, having an early start and enduring a bumpy ride. Just what you want! Alternatively, take a bush taxi from Kaolack to **Toubakouta** (p190), from where a combination of pirogue trips and donkey-cart rides gets you to the Siné-Saloum Delta. Head up the lonely dirt road (pick-up truck, anyone?) to **Foundiougne** (p189), from where it's a ferry ride and *sept-place* bush-taxi journey back to Dakar.

A MULTIFAITH PILGRIMAGE

Senegal is a country renowned for its religious tolerance, where Christians, Muslims and those following traditional beliefs live together in harmony. Take a trip around the major sacred sites of all these faiths. In **Dakar** (p152), the floodlit Grande Mosquée is a sight to behold, as is the Mosquée de la Divinité, perched on the steep coast of Les Mamelles. The Layen Mausoleum in **Yoff** (p172) is also worth a visit. Along the Petite Côte, the Pentecostal pilgrimage site of **Popenguine** (p180) has a large, modern cathedral while in **Joal-Fadiout** (p184) images of the Virgin Mary sit close to the mosque, and a Christian and Muslim cemetery is reached via a long wooden bridge leading to a seashell island. In the holy city of **Touba** (p196) an annual pilgrimage of the Mouride Brotherhood attracts millions to the town's gigantic mosque – one of the most impressive places of prayer in the whole of West Africa. The Omarian mosques along the **Île à Morphil** (p218) are far more humble in their Sudanese mud architecture. The cathedral in **Saint-Louis** (p206) is one of the oldest in West Africa, while the town's mosque features a churchlike clock tower.

Traditional faith doesn't require the construction of huge prayer sites, but you will observe ritual objects in many public places, such as the *campement* (hotel) in **Enampor** (p238).

History

PREHISTORY & EARLY SOCIETIES

The earliest evidence of human settlements in The Gambia and Senegal dates from around AD 500. In eastern Gambia, stone circles, such as the famous Wassu group, and shell mounds used for burial are evidence of the region's early inhabitants. A stunning example of early shell mounds is the Diorom Boumag near Toubakouta.

As the 1st millennium AD progressed, trade increased between the regions north and south of the Sahara. Goods transported across the desert included salt, gold, silver, ivory and slaves. Some settlements on the edge of the desert took advantage of the trade (eventually controlling it) and grew in size, wealth and power. Some of these settlements became city-states, and a few developed into powerful confederations with hierarchical structures, in which society was divided into groups such as rulers, administrators, traders, artisans, artists, commoners and captives.

KINGDOMS & EMPIRES

Precolonial history in West Africa is the story of the rise and fall of powerful empires, whose social structures and ethnic make-up determine life in the region today. The power of these often-wealthy states depended on the control of the trans-Saharan trade, and many a battle was fought to ascertain strategic positions.

The first major state established in the region was the Empire of Ghana. Founded in the 5th century AD, it flourished between the 8th and 11th centuries, covering much of what is now eastern Senegal and western Mali. The vast empire was eventually destroyed; in the late 11th century Berbers from the Almoravid empire (Mauritania and Morocco) moved into the region, bringing Islam. The Tekrur empire of northern Senegal, established by the Tukulor (a branch of the Fula ethnic group) and which thrived in the 9th and 10th centuries, was quickly Islamised and became an ally of the Almoravids in fighting the Ghanaian forces.

In the 13th century Sunjata Keita, the illustrious leader of the Malinké people, built the greatest West African kingdom of all – the Mali empire. By the 14th century its territory stretched from the Atlantic coast, encompassing the modern-day countries of Gambia and Senegal, across to today's Niger and Nigeria. It became a major centre of finance and Islamic learning, and was very wealthy. Evidence of this wealth was displayed when Mansa Musa, the then emperor of Mali, went on a pilgrimage to Mecca in the early 14th century: he took with him an entourage of 60,000 people and showered his hosts with gifts of gold.

> Ancient seashell mounds, which were traditional burial sites, can be found in mangrove swamps in Gambia and Senegal. More than 120 graves were found in the large manmade shell island of Diorom Boumag near Toubakouta, Senegal, which dates to between AD 730 and 1370.

THE GAMBIA

The Gambia's official name always includes 'The', but this is often omitted in everyday situations. In this book we have usually omitted 'The' for reasons of clarity and to ensure a smooth-flowing text.

TIMELINE

11th century	12th–14th centuries
The Tukulor empire of Tekrur spans the Senegal River valley	The Wolof people establish the Jolof empire

Mali's influence began to wane in the mid-15th century, when it was eclipsed by the more powerful Songhaï empire. Around the same time, in today's Senegal, the Wolof people established the empire of Jolof, which spread north and west to dominate the adjacent Tekrur and Serer kingdoms. However, in the mid-16th century the Jolof empire divided into a loose confederation of several separate kingdoms, including the Walo along the Senegal River and the Cayor north of the Cap Vert peninsula. This division was largely due to the growing power of the coastal states, including the kingdoms of Siné and Saloum in the area between the Saloum River and the present-day towns of Thiès and Kaolack.

Meanwhile, in northern Senegal, the Tekrur empire was invaded in the early 16th century by Fula people, under the leadership of Koli Tengela Ba. The new kingdom, Fouta Toro, expanded over the next century along the Senegal River and southwards into modern-day Guinea.

The disintegration of the Mali empire caused another migratory movement – that of the Malinké towards the valley of the Gambia River. The Malinké brought Islam with them, and became known as the Mandinka.

FIRST EUROPEAN INCURSIONS

Meanwhile, in Europe, interest in West Africa was growing. Much of the gold transported across the Sahara eventually reached the courts and treasuries of countries such as England, France, Spain and Portugal, and by the 14th century the financial stability of these European powers depended greatly on this supply. Along with the gold came hazy reports of the wealthy empires south of the Sahara, but at this time no European had ever visited the region. (It's been suggested that the metaphorical use of Timbuktu to describe faraway places dates from this time.)

In the early 15th century Prince Henry of Portugal (known as Henry the Navigator) encouraged explorers to sail down the coast of West Africa, hoping to bypass the Arab and Muslim domination of the trans-Saharan gold trade and reach the source by sea. In 1443, Portuguese ships reached the mouth of the Senegal River, and a year later they landed on the coast of Senegal at a peninsula they named Cabo Verde, meaning Green Cape. (It is now called Cap Vert, and is the site of Dakar; it is not to be confused with the Cape Verde Islands, some 600km west in the Atlantic.) The Portuguese made contact with local chiefs on the mainland and established a trading station on Île de Gorée, a short distance off the coast.

In a series of voyages, the Portuguese pushed further around the West African coast. By 1500 they had established trading stations on the coast and some distance upstream along the Senegal and Gambia Rivers, from which slaves and commodities such as gold were shipped back to Europe.

The Senegal and Gambia Rivers, along with the Saloum and Casamance Rivers, provided major routes into the interior of Africa, and grew in strategic importance. Explorers such as Scotsman Mungo Park and Frenchman René Caillé set forth in search of Timbuktu and its fabled riches along these waterways. As the years passed, the French, English and Dutch fought with the Portuguese for control of these rivers and the resulting trade, which was predominantly in slaves.

Ethnic Groups of the Senegambia by Patience Sonko-Godwin describes in great detail the stories of the main peoples of Gambia and Senegal, tracing their histories back to the era of the great West African empires or earlier. This small paperback is available locally.

1455	1588
The Portuguese establish trading stations along the Gambia River	The Dutch turn the trading station on Île de Gorée into a major slave port

THE SLAVE TRADE

Over the following centuries, West Africa's fate depended on developments in an entirely different part of the globe – the so-called New World, which included South America, the Caribbean and the south of what became the USA. Portugal had established settlements in Brazil by 1530, which grew into large commercial sugar estates between 1575 and 1600. Their expansion led to a demand for labourers, which the Portuguese met by importing slaves from West Africa – a development that was to have huge and serious repercussions throughout the continent.

Although local slavery had existed in West Africa for many centuries, the Portuguese developed the trade on a massive scale. By the 16th century other European powers became active in the trade. The French had been defying the Portuguese monopoly for some time and between 1500 and 1530 they captured hundreds of Portuguese vessels with their human cargo. England joined the trade in the mid-16th century and in 1617 Dutch traders took over the settlement on Île de Gorée. The French established La Compagnie du Cap Vert et Sénégal in 1633, one of several trading companies and the one responsible for their slave trade until 1791. In 1659 the French developed a trading station at Saint-Louis at the mouth of the Senegal River, and in 1677 took Gorée from the Dutch.

By the 1650s Portugal had been largely ousted from the coasts of present-day Gambia and Senegal. There was strong competition between the remaining traders, with frequent skirmishes over slaving stations. Fort James, on an island near the mouth of the Gambia River, was controlled by Latvian, French and Dutch traders, plus several independent 'privateers' (pirates), and changed hands eight times in 60 years before finally being secured by the English.

As the plantation economies in the New World expanded, the demand for slaves grew massively and a triangular trans-Atlantic trade route developed. Slaves were transported to the Americas, the raw materials they produced were taken to Europe, and finished goods were brought from Europe to Africa to be exchanged once again for slaves. European traders encouraged African chiefs in the coastal areas to invade neighbouring tribes and take captives, and their subsequent raids caused profound social and political change in the kingdoms of Fouta Toro, Walo and Cayor.

Between the 16th and 19th centuries, up to 20 million Africans were captured as slaves. Between a quarter and a half of this number died soon after capture, mostly during transportation, due to poor conditions and the length of the journey. Of the approximately 10 million slaves who reached the Americas, around 50% died within a few years as a result of malnourishment and inhuman working and living conditions. These figures are hotly debated by historians, as exact figures are impossible to gauge. But the debate sometimes obscures the main issue: whatever the numbers, the slave trade was undeniably cruel and inhuman, and its legacy in West Africa and many other parts of the world is still felt today.

The comprehensive website http://webworld.unesco.org/goree covers the history of Senegal's Île de Gorée, and includes a virtual tour of its infamous Maison des Esclaves.

THE EXPANSION OF ISLAMIC INFLUENCE

As European influences grew and their control of trade tightened, the power of the old empires declined, resulting in instability among the local population. Islam filled the vacuum. Muslim faith had been introduced to

The French found Saint-Louis on a strategic island in northern Senegal

Present boundaries of The Gambia set by agreement between Britain and France

West Africa as early as the 10th century, yet had for a long time remained the religion of the wealthy and the rulers, who tolerated the practice of traditional faiths among their subjects. Elements of ancient African religion gradually found their way into West African Islam, and this mixture characterises religious practice in the region today.

The Islamic practice that has expanded in today's Senegal and Gambia takes the form of Sufism, a belief system that emphasises mystical and spiritual attributes. It also allows for the influence of holy men called marabouts, many of whom are credited with having divine powers and the ability to communicate with Allah. With the rise of Islam, the marabouts became influential figures and counterforces to the European powers, whose worst fear was a universal spread of Islam.

Islamic expansionism led to two centuries of holy wars (jihads) fought under the leadership of marabouts against the 'nonbelievers' of the region. The most famous of these wars were led by the illustrious El Hajj Omar Tall, who created a vast Islamic empire that stretched from Timbuktu (in present-day Mali) to western Senegal. Tall was a Tukulor warrior who had fought under the marabout Suliman Bal against the descendants of Koli Tengela Ba in the Fouta Toro kingdom in the 1770s. In 1820 he undertook the haj (pilgrimage to Mecca), where he was initiated into the Tijaniya brotherhood. On his return, he began building his empire.

EUROPEAN EXPANSION

Although El Hajj Omar Tall's empire was vast, it didn't reach the coast; this region was firmly controlled by the French who now owned large settlements, notably Gorée and Saint-Louis. As the Portuguese had done before them, French settlers intermarried with the local population, and by the 1790s the considerable mixed-race population formed a veritable bourgeoisie. Saint-Louis is particularly famous for the *signares,* mixed-race women who married white traders, and to this day the town has a large mixed-race population.

Britain imposed a ban on slavery in 1807, and while Napoleon officially abolished the trade in 1815, it wasn't until 1848 that it finally stopped. This was also the time of the Napoleonic Wars (1799–1815) and tensions between Britain and France were high. The slavery ban gave Britain a good excuse to attack the old enemy – French ships off the coasts of Gambia and Senegal were frequently chased and captured by the British navy, and slaves were freed and resettled.

In 1816 Britain bought an island on the south side of the mouth of the Gambia River from a local chief. The local name was Banjul Island (meaning bamboo), but the British built a fort there and renamed it Bathurst. They declared the Gambia River and the area now known as The Gambia a British protectorate in 1820. The Gambia was administered from the British colony of Sierra Leone, further along the West African coast, which had been established as a haven for freed slaves in 1787. In 1826 Fort Bullen was built on the northern bank of the Gambia River, and in 1828 another fort was built about 200km upstream from the river mouth; this became Georgetown.

While the British built forts, the French introduced Catholic missions. However, with the slave trade at an end the colonists were forced to look for

'The considerable mixed-race population formed a veritable bourgeoisie'

1894	1895
Following the Berlin Conference, Gambia becomes a British colony	Senegal becomes part of the Afrique Occidentale Française (AOF; French West Africa)

new sources of wealth. In 1829 the British planted groundnuts (peanuts) along the Gambia River, in the hope that exports of this crop would provide an income for the fledgling protectorate.

Meanwhile the Royal Order, a French decree introduced in 1840, created administrative structures in France's West African colonies. Towns became self-governing communes with residents enjoying the same rights as their equals in France. Influence spread from Saint-Louis along the Senegal River and the governor, Baron Jacques Roger, tried to establish groundnut plantations and settlements (most notably at Richard Toll, where the ruins of his chateau can still be seen).

In the 1850s his successor, Louis Faidherbe, took a more direct approach by simply invading the lands of the Wolof (who until then had been uneasy allies of the French). He established large plantations and introduced forced labour. From the French point of view, this method was effective – he made the colonial administration self-financing within 10 years. To combat the forces of Omar Tall, who posed a threat from the north and east, Faidherbe established a chain of forts along the Senegal River (including Bakel, Matam, Podor and Kayes), which remain today. On the peninsula opposite Île de Gorée, Faidherbe established a settlement which was named after a local chief and later became Dakar.

The 19th century saw the egalitarian principles inspired by the French Revolution of 1789 gain prominence, and the inhabitants of Saint-Louis, Gorée, Rufisque and Dakar were awarded French citizenship in 1887.

THE MARABOUTS

Omar Tall's forces were finally defeated by the French in 1864, but his missionary zeal inspired followers to keep fighting jihads, the so-called Marabout Wars, for another three decades. By this time, the Wolof had fervently embraced Islam and now fought fiercely against French expansionism. Notable battles included those between the French army and the Cayor Wolof, led by Lat Dior, when the French built a railway line between Dakar and Saint-Louis. The last significant Wolof battle was in 1889 at Yang-Yang (near present-day Linguère, in Senegal), where the army of Alboury Ndiaye was defeated by the French. Eventually, superior French firepower, along with a divided marabout army, allowed the French to gain control of most of Senegal and Mali.

The British in Gambia experienced similar Marabout Wars, as local followers of Omar Tall attempted to overthrow their traditional Mandinka rulers. Some of the fiercest fighting took place in western Gambia, near the British outpost of Bathurst. When the Fula entered the fray from the north, the British and French became involved in some extremely touchy diplomatic incidents. The colonial powers finally decided to cooperate to overthrow the marabouts, although limited resistance by the tenacious leader Fodi Kabba continued into the early 1900s.

The final thorn in the French colonials' side was another marabout called Amadou Bamba. By 1887 he had gained a large following, and was exiled by the French until 1907. Today, Bamba remains an iconic figure, and the brotherhood he founded – the Mouride Brotherhood – is a major cultural, economic and political force in modern Senegal. (See p197 for more details.)

Donald Cruise O'Brien's book *The Mourides of Senegal* is one of the most comprehensive discussions of the origins of the powerful Senegalese brotherhoods. Though published in the 1980s, it's largely still relevant to an understanding of the force of religion in Senegal today.

1960	1965
Senegal gains independence under President Léopold Senghor	The Gambia becomes independent with David Jawara as prime minister

THE SCRAMBLE FOR AFRICA

The term 'Scramble for Africa' refers to the late-1870s 'land-grabbing' by several European powers, including France, Britain and Germany, which played out their battle for dominance in Europe on African soil. The scramble was triggered in 1879 when King Leopold of Belgium claimed the Congo (which later became Zaïre, and recently was renamed Congo). France responded by establishing a territory in the neighbouring area, which became known as French Congo (now Congo) and Gabon. Meanwhile, the British were increasing their influence in East Africa, as part of a strategy to control the headwaters of the Nile. Germany's leader, Otto von Bismarck, also wanted 'a place in the sun' and claimed various parts of Africa, including territories that later became Togo and Cameroon.

In 1883 Britain staked a claim to much of East Africa and to territories in West Africa – such as Gambia, Sierra Leone, Gold Coast (modern-day Ghana) and Nigeria. The claims of the European powers were settled at the Berlin Conference of 1884–85, when most of Africa was split neatly into colonies. In 1895 France established Afrique Occidentale Française (AOF; French West Africa), comprising most of the Sahel belt, which stretched eastwards from Senegal to parts of the Sahara and North African territories.

THE GAMBIA FALLS TO BRITAIN

Although Gambia was a British protectorate from 1820 and became a full British colony in 1886, the decision makers in London didn't really want this sliver of land surrounded by French territory. Attempts were made to exchange Gambia for land elsewhere – a common practice among the colonial powers of the time – but no matter how much the British talked up the qualities of the territory, no-one was interested. Thus Britain was lumbered with Gambia, and the little colony was almost forgotten as events in other parts of Africa and India dominated British colonial policy in the first half of the 20th century. Little wealth came out of Gambia and as a result very little 'development' was attempted – administration was limited to a few British district commissioners and the local chiefs they appointed.

In the 1950s Gambia's groundnut plantations were improved as a way to increase export earnings, and some other agricultural schemes were set up. There was little in the way of services, and by the early 1960s Gambia had fewer than 50 primary schools and only a handful of doctors. While the rest of West Africa was gaining independence, this seemed unlikely for Gambia; there was hardly any local political infrastructure and Britain was against the move. A federation with Senegal, which had just gained independence from France, was considered but came to nothing.

Around this time David Jawara, a Mandinka from the upcountry provinces, founded the People's Progressive Party (PPP). It was the first party to attract mass support from rural Mandinka Muslims, the overwhelming majority of Gambia's population. To prepare for at least partial self-government, a Gambian parliament – the House of Representatives – was instituted and elections were held in 1962, with prompt victory by Jawara's PPP.

'Little wealth came out of Gambia and as a result very little "development" was attempted'

1970	1981
The Gambia becomes a republic following a referendum; Jawara is elected as president and changes his first name to Dawda	Abdou Diouf becomes president of Senegal

FRANCE GRABS SENEGAL

The territory of Senegal formed part of the AOF. Saint-Louis, the first French settlement in West Africa, initially became capital of the entire region, before administration was shifted to Dakar in 1902 (although Saint-Louis remained capital of Senegal).

While the four largest towns (Dakar, Gorée, Saint-Louis and Rufisque) had been seen as part of France, and had sent delegates to the French National Assembly in Paris, these delegates had usually been white or of mixed race. In 1914 the colony sent the first black delegate – Blaise Diagne. That same year, the first political party in West Africa was established, and several Senegalese intellectuals went to France to study. Among them was Léopold Senghor; he became the first African secondary-school teacher in France. During this period, he began writing poems and founded *Présence Africaine*, a magazine promoting the values of African culture.

After WWII France continued to regard its overseas possessions (including Senegal, Mali and Côte d'Ivoire) as territories that were part of the mother country, rather than mere colonies. Though the French National Assembly in Paris was still the political centre, each territory was also granted its own assembly. Senghor returned from France and became the elected candidate in Dakar. At first he was regarded as an unlikely choice: as well as being young, Catholic and a member of the minority Serer group, he spoke little Wolof, was married to a white French woman and was somewhat aloof from his people. He was, however, remarkably astute, and went on to become one of Africa's most influential 20th-century politicians.

Despite initially being perceived as out of touch with his constituents, Senghor became known as a man of the people. He introduced social reforms such as the abolition of forced labour and improvements in education. In 1948 he founded the Bloc Démocratique Sénégalais. Meanwhile, the marabouts had become increasingly involved in politics, and through the 1950s Senghor made several deals with leading figures. He allowed them partial autonomy and control of the lucrative groundnut economy in return for their public support, which ensured safe votes from their followers in the rural areas.

FRANCE'S AFRICAN TERRITORIES – INDEPENDENCE OR FEDERATION?

In the 1950s the potential independence of France's African colonies became a major issue. Senghor was in favour of autonomy, but promoted the idea of a strong federal union of all French territories in Africa, to prevent them from being Balkanised – divided, weakened and at war with one another. His rival was Côte d'Ivoire's leader, Felix Houphouët-Boigny, who wanted French West Africa divided; Houphouët-Boigny feared that within a federal union the richer territories (such as Côte d'Ivoire) would have to subsidise the poorer ones.

In the late 1950s Senghor gained support from French Sudan (present-day Mali), Upper Volta (present-day Burkina Faso) and Dahomey (present-day Benin) to form a single union, the Mali Federation. But in 1958 General Charles de Gaulle came to power in France and offered

During WWI 13,339 Senegalese *tirailleurs* (soldiers) were recruited to fight in the French army against Germany. Many of these *tirailleurs* perished for their supposed 'motherland'. Sembéne Ousmane's moving film, *Camp de Thiaroye*, tells of an uprising of returned *tirailleurs*, whose request of due payment was violently quenched by the French.

1981	1982
Five hundred people are killed in The Gambia when Senegalese troops are called in to suppress a coup	The Gambia and Senegal form a loose confederation called Senegambia, which collapses seven years later

the overseas territories a stark choice: complete independence and a total break from France; or limited self-government within a union still controlled by France.

DE GAULLE'S SWITCH – INDEPENDENCE FOR SENEGAL

Upper Volta and Dahomey withdrew from the Mali Federation under pressure from both France and Côte d'Ivoire, leaving Senegal and Mali as the only members. In 1959 these two countries demanded complete independence, not as individual countries, but as an independent union. De Gaulle realised he stood to lose more than he might gain and switched tack suddenly. On 20 June 1960 Senegal and Mali, while remaining within the French union, became a completely independent federation. Only two months later, the Senegal-Mali union broke up. French West Africa had become nine separate republics.

Senghor became the first president of Senegal and, after initial problems with students and the labour unions, he managed to consolidate his position; throughout the 1970s, his party, now renamed Parti Socialiste (PS), remained in power. In 1980, after 20 years as president, he did what no other African head of state had done before – voluntarily stepped down. His hand-picked successor, Prime Minister Abdou Diouf, took over on 1 January 1981.

THROWING OFF THE BRITISH YOKE

In 1965 The Gambia became independent, with David Jawara as prime minister, although Britain's Queen Elizabeth II remained titular head of state. Bathurst, now renamed Banjul, became the country's capital. Although the tiny nation appeared to have no viable economic future, two events occurred that enabled it to survive and even prosper. For a decade after independence, the world price for groundnuts increased significantly, raising the country's GNP almost threefold. The second event had an even more resounding effect – Gambia became a tourist destination. In 1966 the number of tourists visiting Gambia was recorded as 300. By the end of the 1960s, this number had risen to several thousand; by 1976 it had reached 25,000 per year.

Economic growth translated into political confidence. In 1970 The Gambia became a fully independent republic. Prime Minister Jawara became president and changed his name from David to Dawda. Opposition parties were tolerated, and there was a relatively free press. Still, the PPP was deeply conservative and Jawara's opponents accused his government of benign neglect and financial corruption, claiming that the president, ministers and other PPP politicians retained power through a complex web of largesse and patronage, rather than through any genuine level of public support.

'The world price for groundnuts increased significantly, raising the country's GNP almost threefold'

THE DIOUF ERA

In 1980 and 1981 Dawda Jawara's leadership was threatened by two attempted coups. Both times, he clung onto power, thanks to military help from the Senegalese army. Senegalese president Abdou Diouf sent in troops and, after a considerable amount of bloodshed, Jawara's leadership was ensured. This cooperation was acknowledged and formalised when the Senegambia Confederation was established in early 1982.

1989	1989
In Senegal, the separatist Mouvement des Forces Démocratiques de la Casamance (MFDC) gains momentum	Conflict erupts between Senegal and Mauritania over grazing rights

In 1983 Diouf's PS won Senegal's national elections with over 83% of the vote. Yet only two years later, he felt his position was at risk when his major opponent, Abdoulaye Wade, attempted to unite various opposition parties. The result: Diouf banned the organisation. In 1988 Wade contested the presidency, but when violence erupted during the campaign Wade was arrested and charged with intent to subvert the government. Diouf won the election with 73% of the vote against Wade's 26%, but rumours of rigging were rampant. Wade was given a one-year suspended sentence and left for France.

By this time the Senegambia Confederation was in trouble and, in 1989, it was dissolved completely. But while Diouf was contending with this break-up and calls for political reform, he had two other major problems to deal with: one was a dispute with Mauritania, and the other was the separatist movement in the southern region of Casamance.

There had been periodic calls for independence in Casamance for many years, but they came to a head in 1989, when rebels from the Mouvement des Forces Démocratiques de la Casamance (MFDC) started attacking government installations (see p229 for further details).

Abdoulaye Wade returned from political exile in 1990. In response to his return, huge crowds took to the streets chanting for *sopi* (change). In an attempt at appeasement, Wade was made minister of state. He later resigned his position to stand against Diouf in the presidential election, and though Diouf won with 58% against Wade's 32%, Wade's popularity was on the rise. Yet in the following parliamentary elections, Diouf's PS still won over two-thirds of the seats. This led to violent protests in many parts of the country, particularly in Casamance where anti-Diouf feeling still ran high. Large numbers of troops were once again sent into the region. After long negotiations, another ceasefire was declared in June 1993 and further talks saw full peace return to Casamance – at least for the time being.

Antigovernment protest continued in other parts of the country, and Diouf responded with unpopular austerity measures. In 1993 Wade was arrested again. He was accused of conspiracy and was tried in March 1994 on charges relating to the murder of a state official. Charges were dismissed in 1995, and Wade was released and reinstated in government.

'After long negotiations, another ceasefire was declared in June 1993 and further talks saw full peace return to Casamance'

THE 1980S: GAMBIAN DISCONTENTS

The coup attempts of 1980 and 1981, staged by factions of the army, were major signs of discontent over the PPP's grip on Gambia. When both were thwarted with the help of Senegalese troops, Jawara acknowledged this debt by announcing that Gambian and Senegalese armed forces would be fully integrated. In 1982 the Senegambia Confederation came into effect. Under this agreement Senegal would provide military protection for Gambia (in other words, for Jawara), while Gambia made some noncommittal noises about an eventual united Senegambian country.

The confederation, however, lacked popular support. The Gambian Mandinka who formed the PPP's power base saw it as a Wolof takeover. Smuggling was another problem: high customs duties in Senegal made some imported goods there more expensive, while prices for groundnuts in the two countries varied.

1994	2000
After a military coup in Gambia, Yahya Jammeh becomes the new president	At least 12 people are shot dead in Gambia during student demonstrations against the alleged torture and murder of a student

The 1980s saw mounting discontent towards Jawara and his government, though this didn't endanger his victory in the 1982 and 1987 elections. Yet at the end of the 1980s, the tide began to turn. Groundnut prices continued to fall, and agricultural subsidies and spending on public services were cut as part of an International Monetary Fund (IMF) restructure. The government made few attempts to alleviate this situation, and was seen by many Gambians as being too far removed from the everyday problems faced by the populace.

In the political arena, there were a couple more coup attempts made, allegedly with support from Senegalese opposition figures, and in 1989 the Senegambia Confederation was dissolved. Both Gambia and Senegal imposed severe border restrictions, and tensions ran high well into 1990. After a year, relations between the countries improved again, and a treaty of friendship and cooperation was signed in 1991.

African Civilization Revisited: From Antiquity to Modern Times (1990) is only one of many accessible works on African history by the influential writer Basil Davidson.

TIME UP FOR JAWARA

Despite their many obvious failures, President Jawara and the PPP were re-elected for a sixth term in April 1992. To the outside world Jawara appeared to remain popular. It came as a surprise, therefore, when on 22 July 1994 a protest by soldiers over late salaries and harsh treatment by Nigerian officers (during peacekeeping duties in Liberia and Sierra Leone) turned into a coup d'état. The coup leader was Yahya Jammeh, a young lieutenant.

A new military government was hastily formed, headed by the Armed Forces Provisional Ruling Council (AFPRC). It was composed of senior military officers, most of whom had trained in Britain and the USA, and civilian ministers who had served under Jawara's government. Jammeh initially promised that the AFPRC would be back in the barracks within a few months, but in October 1994 he announced he would stay in power at least until 1998.

Despite international pressure, Jammeh was unrepentant. Although still only 29 years old and completely inexperienced, he remained firmly at the helm and from the start implemented a leadership style marked by stark hostility towards journalists and members of the opposition.

Following a decline in tourist numbers throughout the '90s, Jammeh pragmatically switched tack in 1995 and announced elections would be held the following year. In response to this in March 1995, the British Foreign Office advised tourists that Gambia was safe again, and tourism picked up.

JAMMEH TAKES CHARGE

Jammeh and the AFPRC remained in control and a new constitution ushering in the Second Republic was introduced in 1996.

Presidential elections were held in the same year, and four candidates competed for the post. Yahya Jammeh was one of them, representing the APRC (the former AFPRC, now neatly renamed the Alliance for Patriotic Reorientation and Construction). He emerged as the clear winner with 56% of the vote, completing his smooth transition from minor army officer to head of state in just over two years.

In January 1997 the APRC also dominated the election for Gambia's national assembly, consolidating President Jammeh's hold on power. His

2000	2002
Abdoulaye Wade becomes president of Senegal in democratic elections	Some 1863 passengers are killed when the Senegalese ferry MS *Joola* capsizes

'Claims of corruption, embezzlement of public funds and human-rights violations appeared in several international magazines'

opponents claimed the election and the constitution were manipulated to disadvantage the fledgling opposition parties. Despite these claims and other complaints from within the country and abroad, President Jammeh appeared to remain popular with the Gambian people. Most saw him as a fresh new force, keen to sweep away the lethargy and corruption of the old days. To consolidate this support, Jammeh announced a series of impressive schemes to rebuild the country's infrastructure and economy. A new airport was constructed and a national TV station opened. New clinics and schools were promised for the upcountry provinces.

But in the Gambian parliament, opposition members continued to question the new president's rule, and claims of corruption, embezzlement of public funds and human-rights violations appeared in several international magazines. Jammeh responded by intimidating political opponents and media organisations that dared to criticise – a reaction that characterises his rule to this day. Meanwhile, Jammeh quietly focused on building his personal fortune, acquiring a series of properties and businesses (including the Kairaba Hotel at Kololi and the Sindola Hotel near Kanilai), and becoming one of the richest men in Gambia.

In October 2001 Jammeh won his second five-year term as president, taking 53% of the vote against second-placed Ousainou Darboe's 33%. International observers proclaimed the elections to be free and fair, but Darboe's United Democratic Party (UDP) accused Jammeh of rigging the result. In response the UDP boycotted parliamentary elections held in January 2002. As a result, Jammeh's APRC won comfortably, with more than two-thirds of seats not even contested.

WADE'S SOPI CAMPAIGN

Senegal's political situation was similar to that of Gambia's when, in 1998, when the PS won parliamentary polls in a landslide, also amid accusations of election fraud. It was clear that opposition to Diouf's leadership was growing, partly fuelled by worries over the ongoing rebellion in the Casamance region. The pressure on Diouf was mounting and, in February 2000, he finally gave up his seat of power when Wade's spectacular *sopi* campaign gained him a historic victory.

If Senegal and the rest of the world were stunned by the electoral defeat of an African incumbent of such long standing, even more unusual was Diouf's acceptance of the result and the peaceful transfer of power. The people of Senegal were rightly proud of this affirmation of the strength of democracy in their country and, in January 2001, more than 90% voted for a new constitution which allowed the formation of opposition parties, gave enhanced status to the prime minister, and reduced the president's term of office from seven years to five.

SENEGAL TODAY

After such a monumental shift in the balance of power, change in Senegal was disappointingly slow. Another peace accord between separatist forces and the government, signed in 2001, failed to quench uprisings entirely, as divisions and leadership changes within the rebel movement fuelled renewed insurgences among some factions. In 2002 the country (and Casamance in particular) suffered a huge tragedy when the MS *Joola*, the

2004

New Gambian law allows the jailing of journalists found guilty of libel; days later a critic of the law is shot dead

2004

A peace deal is reached between the Senegalese government and the separatist forces of the MFDC in Casamance ferry connecting Dakar and the Casamance capital, Ziguinchor, capsized due to dangerous overloading, leaving almost 2000 people dead. The shock of the tragedy prompted the government to look seriously into issues of security in transport and at public events. It is also thought that Wade's subsequent dismissal of his entire government was related to their handling of the catastrophe.

In 2004 there was finally good news from the Casamance, when yet another peace deal between the MFDC and Wade's government started showing results. The situation in southern Senegal began to calm down. However, the president's controversial decision to arrest former prime minister Idrissa Seck sparked clashes between Seck's supporters and police and sent the country into a flurry of political debate. The former prime minister was accused of undermining state security and embezzling funds while working as mayor of the commune Thiès. In February 2006 Seck was released and all charges were dropped, probably in order to strengthen the Parti Démocratique Sénégalais (PDS; Senegalese Democratic Party) in good time before the next presidential and parliamentary elections in 2007.

> The name Senegal is thought to be derived from the Wolof term *'sunu gal'*, meaning 'boat'.

THE GAMBIA TODAY

While Senegal began to prepare for a peaceful election campaign, signs from Gambia were increasingly worrying.

Jammeh's government had always had an uneasy relationship with the press, but things reached an all-time low when, in December 2004, prominent journalist Deyda Hydara was assassinated only days after expressing his opposition to a controversial media law that granted the government powers to jail journalists accused of libel. Following the murder, an increasing climate of repression developed.

In December 2005 Senegal-Gambia relations suffered a new low, when Gambia decided to double the charges of the ferry service used by most Senegalese truck drivers to transport goods between the Casamance and northern Senegal. Senegal's drivers retaliated by blocking the borders and circumventing Gambia altogether. The economic effects were dramatic for both countries. Several attempts by Wade to resolve the issue were blocked by Gambia's head of state, and it was only when Nigerian president Olusegun Obasanjo brokered talks in October 2005 that tariffs were reduced to their former level and the borders were reopened.

In March 2006 international observers were once again alerted to the political situation in Gambia, when several high-ranking military officers were arrested on claims of an attempted coup d'état – one of several such claims made by Jammeh during his time in power. Occurring only a few months before the presidential polls, this was widely interpreted as a way of 'cleansing' the government of rivals, and seems indicative of the way elections might be handled in future.

2005	2006
Senegal's former prime minister Idrissa Seck is jailed, to be released a few months later	Gambia's government says a planned military coup has been foiled

The Culture

THE NATIONAL PSYCHE

Skimming any glossy holiday brochure about Senegal, you'll sooner or later stumble across the term *teranga,* meaning 'hospitality'. Senegal takes great pride in being the 'Land of Teranga', the national football team is called 'Lions of Teranga', and plenty of hotels and restaurants have adopted the name. Much of this is promotional hype, but as these things go, it's indeed rooted in that proverbial kernel of truth. The same goes for Gambia's colourful descriptions as the 'Smiling Coast'. In both countries, people tend to be open and welcoming towards visitors, and a stranded stranger will quickly be lent a helping hand, be invited for meals or offered a bed for the night.

However, in busy tourist areas it can be hard to tell the difference between true hospitality and a 'con job', devised to trick you into some unplanned spending. Tourism, and the power of the tourist dollar, has gradually eroded some of the original codes of conduct, and not every offer of *teranga* might come from the heart. The further you get away from the resort zones, the more 'real' society gets, and you can relax your shoulders and practise your rudimentary Wolof, Mandinka or French – people will be keen to teach you their language.

In Senegal and Gambia, conversation is the key to local culture, and the key to conversation is a great sense of humour and a quick-witted tongue. Especially in Senegal, people love talking, teasing, and testing you out, and the better you slide into the conversational game, the easier you'll get around. Someone mocks your habits? Don't tense up, retaliate with a clever remark, and you're likely to be on your way to an entertaining evening. You've gathered the courage to try your first feeble *mbalax* dance steps, and your humble attempts at 'going local' are greeted with noisy amusement? Don't blush and hide in the corner – join in the hilarity and keep copying the gyrating hips around you. People don't mean harm, and the ability to laugh at yourself is just as important an item to bring with you as your malaria pills and T-shirts.

Having mastered the art of conversation, there's only one other crucial ground rule: don't hurry. If you're on holiday, you're likely to be positively inclined towards the idea of turtle's pace; if you're on business, the slow speed of society can be frustrating – if you keep fighting it. Senegal and Gambia are governed by a great paradox of time – the more you relax, the quicker you'll get things done. Fit into the rhythm of the temporal tide, and you won't have quite such a rocky ride.

Anyone who has ever travelled by battered bush taxi and been entertained by the lively conversations of the local passengers will love Moussa Touré's hilarious movie *TGV*, which is set in one such clapped-out vehicle.

DAILY LIFE
The Extended Family

Visitors to Africa are often struck by the staggering size of most families, and the importance parental ties play in a person's life. While in the Western world the nuclear family is the usual unit of reference, in most African cultures individuals are closely tied to their extended family, including uncles, aunts, and distant cousins. This network widens even more in polygamous families, which still account for the majority of marriages in Senegal and Gambia (see p40).

Unmarried children, particularly women, stay at their parents' home until they wed, which is when men found their own household, and women join that of their husband. Marrying is an expensive business, and many men don't have the necessary means at their disposal to take this step until they are in their mid-20s. It's therefore not unusual (nor discreditable) for men of this age to still occupy a room in their parents' house. It's also common for a man who enjoys greater financial success than his parents to invite them to move into his home, thus bringing the whole big family back together.

In case of a divorce, the woman often rejoins her family, bringing her children with her. Single women, single-mother households or even the households of young female students that are common in the Western world are virtually unheard of in Gambia and Senegal.

Relationships between family members are clearly defined and govern a person's responsibilities towards another relative, his or her rights over someone else, and the respect one owes a next of kin. Generally, elder relatives are to be treated with the greatest deference, and aunts and uncles are to be respected like one's own mother and father. Children are expected to help in the house, and will interrupt recreation to run some errands for a family member.

Having to fulfil the expectations of a large group of relatives is an enormous responsibility – just ask any emigrant from Senegal or Gambia who lives abroad (many families in the region have at least one family member who has emigrated to Europe or America). The meagre earnings of an expatriate in the West never belong to him or her alone, but are to be shared with those who have stayed at home. This puts enormous strains on the émigré, and many are reluctant to return home as they feel they can't fulfil financial expectations.

On the other hand, family solidarity means that elderly people will always be looked after by kin, and children are raised in a family environment even if both parents work. Also, there is no alienation between generations, as the young and old are in permanent contact with one another.

These traditional family relations remain unchanged in rural regions more than in cities. However, as many young men leave their villages to seek work in the cities or abroad, some rural communities show a worrying absence of men.

Education

One of the much-hyped UN Millennium Goals for global development stated that by 2010, every child in the world should have access to education, at least at primary level. This seems a big ask in Gambia

---

JOKING COUSINS

Did this young man really just call his elder an uncivilised, bean-eating descendant of a lowlife? And how on earth did he get away with the insult? Just when you thought you understood the hierarchies of respect in Senegal and Gambia, along comes the 'joking cousin' and turns everything upside-down. All across West Africa, this social practice of mockery binds family members, such as cross cousins, and entire ethnic groups into an entertaining bond that allows, and even requires them to trade insults – offence taking is not allowed. And so you'll come across a Fula mocking the habits of his Serer neighbour, a member of the Ndiaye family dissing a stranger called Diop – no matter that he just met him – and a Diallo calling his brother-in-law of the Ba clan his slave. This sanctioned rudeness is hilarious and people get fantastically creative with their insults. Far more than just a game, these relationships can be a way of easing any real tension between neighbouring ethnic groups, and can thus prevent conflict. As a traveller, you can make a deep impression and ease your way into the culture by participating in the exchange – but it means 'adopting' a Senegalese family yourself first, otherwise you're just insulting people.

CODES OF INTERACTION

Greetings

Extended greetings are an important part of social interaction and many doors will open for you if you are capable of exchanging simple greeting phrases in the local language. Even a few words make a big difference. (Some basic words and phrases are provided on p305.)

Most areas are Islamic, and upon entering someone's home, announce your arrival with a confident 'Salaam aleikum' (peace be with you), and your presence will be acknowledged with 'Aleikum salaam' (and peace be with you).

This is followed by inquiries about your health, the health of your family, the state of your affairs and those of your children. You're never expected to give an honest answer at this point. In Gambia things are always fine; in Senegal the response is always 'Ça va'. Never mind the real troubles that might be plaguing you – these can be mentioned later in the conversation.

Although it's not necessary for foreigners to go through the whole routine, it's important to use greetings whenever possible. Even if you're just changing money, negotiating a taxi fee or asking directions, precede your request with a simple, 'Hello, how are you? Can you help me please?', rather than plunging right in.

Shaking Hands

You'll shake a lot of hands during your stay. Particularly for men it's important to shake hands with other men when entering and leaving a gathering. In social settings you are expected to go around the room, greet everyone and shake hands with those present, even if it takes a few minutes. Local women don't always greet their male peers with handshakes, and some Muslim elders prefer not to shake hands with women. Don't take offence if someone leaves your out-stretched arm unanswered – they're probably following religious principles.

Deference

In traditional societies, older people, those of superior social status and trained professionals are treated with deference. Thus, when you're travelling and you meet people in authority such as immigration officers, police and village chiefs, it is very important to be polite. Officials are normally courteous, but manners, patience and a friendly smile are essential to ensure a pleasant exchange. Undermining an official's authority or insulting their ego will only tie you up in red tape. When visiting small villages, it's polite to go and see the chief to announce yourself and ask for permission before setting up camp or wandering through the village. You will rarely be refused.

Eye contact is usually avoided, especially between men and women in the Sahel: if a local doesn't look you in the eye during a conversation, often they're being polite, not cold.

and Senegal. Both countries have state education systems established by their colonial powers, and in theory, primary education is available to all children. In reality, it's family income, rather than academic availability, that determines which children go to school and for how long. Low-income families may not be able to afford school fees or extra items such as uniforms and books (especially if children wish to go beyond primary school). Those who find themselves in the most drastic circumstances may also keep their children from entering school, as their help is needed to generate income. The lack of government funds for education compounds the problem. Classes are often large, sometimes holding up to 100 pupils in spaces intended for half the amount; teachers are underpaid; and resources, such as books, paper and pens usually need to be shared.

Boys generally continue their education to higher levels than girls. While numbers are fairly equal during the early years of primary school,

Giving Money

As a foreigner travelling to Africa, you're usually regarded as a rich person, and though you might be struggling to pay the bills at home, you are comparatively wealthy in a society where many live well under the breadline. You're likely to be met with frequent demands for money, and need to decide when to give and when to decline a request. Don't give upon any request. Some can be outright scams, and you don't want to establish yourself as a money-giver from the outset. But do be generous, especially if eliciting services. If you've been offered food or a bed for the night, you should repay the kindness, either by contributing food, or by handing the host some money when it's time for goodbyes. Just consider what you'd have paid for a similar meal or hotel room, and judge the amount you give from there.

Giving money is usually done discreetly, and sometimes without discussing amounts or even demanding payment upfront. If people help you out, they will usually expect to be paid something at the end. Consider if someone has had to pay their own transport to meet you – you should give them the amount before they go back home.

Especially in city areas, you're likely to see a lot of beggars. Dakar's streets in particular are full of *talibe* – boy students sent out to beg by their religious teachers – or street kids. You'll probably feel embarrassed by their demands, and certainly can't give to everyone. But giving loose change occasionally isn't a bad thing. In Islamic culture, making small gifts to the poor is part of religious practice, and you'll see plenty of locals who own a lot less spare some change, especially on Friday, the holy day.

If you visit families or remote villages, tobacco, tea and perfume are appreciated, as are kola nuts.

Dress

Especially on Fridays, the most important day of the week in Muslim countries, and on public holidays, you'll find the streets filled with people in shimmering, embroidered garments, often of stunning elegance. These billowing robes are called *boubous*. A *grand boubou* for men consists of a flowing robe that reaches to the ground. It's worn with baggy trousers and a shirt underneath. A woman's *boubou* is similar, though often more colourful, and worn with a wraparound skirt and matching headscarf. *Boubous* can be as simple or elaborate as occasion requires; one worn for a celebration such as a wedding should dazzle in the sunlight and rustle when you walk – it'll probably be made from a beaten, waxed, tie-dyed fabric.

In general, people in Gambia and Senegal place immense importance on appearance, and try to dress in the best clothes they can. Unless combined with a matching, tailored top, a wraparound skirt or sarong, so favoured by Western women travelling to Africa, is usually only worn around the house by local women. Travellers turning up in tatty clothes, shorts and simple T-shirts are frowned upon, especially in rural areas.

few girls complete their primary exams, and even fewer carry on to secondary level. This is largely due to family values. If there's not enough money to send every child to school, education is thought to benefit boys more, while the girls are valued in the home. At secondary or university level, girls often drop out if they are getting married or having children.

However, in both Gambia and Senegal several government initiatives try to redress the balance. In Gambia, efforts have been made to increase the number of schools, as well as proposals to offer free schooling to girls. In Senegal, there has been an additional focus on the preschool age, with a countrywide programme of building state-funded nurseries.

Despite recent initiatives, literacy rates in Gambia and Senegal remain low. Official figures from 2003 show Senegal has a literacy rate of 40.2%; Gambia's is 40.1%. For girls, rates are usually 15% to 20% lower than for boys.

Bitter irony: the valley of the Senegal River, where the French colonialists were strongly opposed by the armies of El Hajj Omar Tall, is today a region where entire male communities of villages have emigrated to France.

POLYGAMOUS MARRIAGES

When singer Youssou N'Dour married a second wife in 2006, in the private, hushed-up fashion that governs all of his personal affairs, he set Senegal's paparazzi machine in motion, the way only he can. In the following months, the debate about polygamy took up plenty of column space in Senegal's glossies. Young women were dismayed at the iconic singer's move, having seen his monogamous status as an influential example. The defenders of polygamy (mainly men) rejoiced, welcoming Youssou back into the more traditional fold.

The Holy Quran, which guides the lives of the vast Muslim majority of Gambia and Senegal, allows men to take up to four wives, normally on the condition that they can provide equally for and love all of them. And that's really the crux of the issue – can one equally love four women? Most women would say no, pointing an accusing finger at the many men who bring a pretty young wife into the family home once they've 'tired' of their first, aging, spouse.

Western women generally find it inconceivable to share their husband with another wife and, though Africa's women are generally resigned to this reality, few welcome it with joy, secretly praying that their partner will proudly spell the word 'monogamy' when asked about his choice at the civil wedding.

To the men who might dream of such rights, a word of warning: managing a polygamous household can be hard work. Wives can be jealous of one another, and resentment is often spread from the mothers to their children. All of this means a family home where tensions brew easily, and it's the head of the house who is expected to calm escalating situations.

Weddings

On a weekend stroll around the streets of Dakar, or any city in Senegal and Gambia, you are bound to pass groups of elegant women, decked out in their finest *boubous* and most delicate heels. They may be gathered in front of a house on rows of plastic chairs, or around amplifiers that carry the latest *mbalax* tunes or the sounds of a griot. These are wedding parties. There's always a wedding on somewhere, and the celebrations are mainly women's business. They meet and chat, dance and laugh, cook, serve food from huge pots, and eat, while the men go about the more serious business of 'tying the marriage' at the mosque. In the Muslim cultures of Senegal and Gambia, weddings are at least as much about the families as about the couple itself. The male relatives of the groom will offer kola nuts to the parents of the bride, demanding her in marriage. If the offer is accepted, they will convene at the mosque around 5pm, while the bride and groom remains elsewhere. Muslim religious marriages are sometimes performed without the husband-to-be. In fact, it's possible for parents to marry their son who is residing in Europe from home – a phone call will tell him about his new status.

Among the Tukulor, it's common for cousins to be married to one another, although incidences of this tradition are beginning to decline, particularly in urban settings, where children increasingly demand a choice in the arrangement of their marriage.

Gifts are important at weddings in the region and can become costly for the families involved. The groom's family should shower the bride and her parents with money, rolls of fabric and household items to display their social and economic status. The exchange of gifts is also a means of financial redistribution. If you receive large presents on your big day, you're supposed to double the expense when it's the donor's turn to celebrate. Women often form 'party circles', attending each other's weddings and keeping close track of the value of gifts.

For most of the day, the bride will wear a relatively simple dress, though especially in urban settings, she will change into the rustling folds of a white wedding dress for the reception, which is a Western-style celebration complete with wedding cake, drinks and music mainly attended by the younger generations. The elderly relatives remain in one of the houses, celebrating separately.

POPULATION

When travelling around The Gambia and Senegal, the different architecture, dress and customs make it easy to recognise that the countries' national boundaries are arbitrary, decided purely on a colonial drawing board. The territory was previously home to several indigenous empires that rose and fell throughout the centuries. To this day, the cultural and social practices that emerged in their wake, together with the ethnic groups associated with those empires, determine life in the region.

Ethnic Groups of The Gambia & Senegal

WOLOF

The Wolof, who are usually Muslim, are the dominant ethnic group of the region, accounting for 16% of the population in The Gambia and 43% in Senegal. Their language has become the lingua franca in both countries. Wolof culture was largely defined during the days of the 14th-century Jolof empire, which later split into several smaller kingdoms, including those of Walo and Cayor. Today, the Wolof are particularly concentrated in the regions of those ancient empires, notably in the central area to the north and east of Dakar, and along the coast. Traditionally farmers and traders, the Wolof today control a great deal of commerce, especially in Senegal. Smaller ethnic groups may sometimes complain about an increasing 'Wolofisation' of their culture, via music and language, yet few are the people that aren't glad for a unifying local tongue, or those that refuse the fever of the *mbalax*, a Wolof rhythm.

'The countries' national boundaries are arbitrary, decided purely on a colonial drawing board'

MANDINKA & MALINKÉ

The Mandinka live mainly in Gambia, where they constitute 42% of the population. Some are also at home in the Senegalese regions bordering The Gambia (such as the Casamance). The Mandinka form part of the Mande cultural groups, that also include the Malinké and Bambara in Mali. All Mande groups once belonged to the vast 13th-century Mali empire that spanned West Africa. Today, Mande surnames still tell of the social standing each family held in the days of their great ruler, Sunjata Keita. The Mande dialect of Gambia's Mandinka differs strongly from the Malinké spoken in Mali. The Mandinka are thought to have migrated to the Gambia region between the 13th and early 16th centuries, and to have brought Islam with them. The origin of the popular Mande kora instrument is believed to lie with the Gambian Mandinka.

FULA

The Fula (also known as Peul, Fulbe or Fulani) are an ethnic group consisting of various subgroups spread across West Africa, as far east as Sudan and as far south as Ghana and Nigeria. In Gambia around 18% of the population is Fula; in Senegal 24%. Their language, Pulaar (or Fulfulde), is the strongest unifying factor of the diverse groups that make up the Fula.

Traditionally the Fula were nomadic cattle herders, and the constant search for grazing land partly explains their wide dispersal across the region. The early adoption of Islam by some Fula branches also contributed to their dispersal. Converts spread the religion throughout West Africa and created several Muslim theocracies in northern Nigeria and Guinea. While most Fula groups have been sedentary for centuries, the majority maintain a strong attachment to cattle, and the presence of large cowherds is usually a sign of Fula residence.

In Senegal, Fula groups are mainly found around the Haute Casamance and Kedougou, as well as in Fouta Toro in the north, where the Tukulor, a sub-branch of the Fula is the dominant community.

Tukulor

The Tukulor people, constituting around 10% of the population in Senegal, are a culturally distinctive branch of the Fula. Their cultural roots date back to the Tekrur empire, a 9th-century kingdom that occupied a large area in the Senegal River zone (the Fouta Toro region). This is still where the largest concentration of Tukulor live. The Tukulor embraced Islam early, in the 10th or 11th century, when the religion was first carried south across the Sahara from Morocco, and played a major role in spreading the religion to other ethnic groups. The most famous Tukulor leader, El Hajj Omar Tall, built a vast Islamic empire in the mid-19th century that reached as far as Segou in Mali.

SERER

The Serer, representing around 14% of Senegal's population, are concentrated in the Siné-Saloum region of Senegal, in central Senegal, and just across the border in northwest Gambia. They are thought to have migrated from southern Senegal in the 16th century and in some areas they have intermarried with the Mandinka or Wolof people, or adopted their languages. The Serer refused Islamisation for a long time; their 11th-century refusal to succumb to the north African Almoravids led them to migrate to the regions of Baol, Siné and Saloum, where they established important small kingdoms. Today, many Serer have adopted Christian or Muslim faith, and their region is renowned for the peaceful cohabitation of both religious communities.

> 'The Siné-Saloum region is renowned for the peaceful cohabitation of both Christian and Muslim communities'

DIOLA

The Diola (also spelt Jola) live in southern Senegal, in the Casamance area, and in southwestern Senegal, from where they spread as far as Guinea-Bissau. In Gambia, around 10% of the population are Diola, compared with 5% in Senegal. The Diola preserve a strong spirit of independence, partly inspired by their differences from their neighbours. They are one of the few ethnic groups in the region whose society is not hierarchical but segmented and flexible, and they have largely rejected Islam, preferring either their own traditional beliefs or conversion to Christianity.

Due to the lack of a tradition in oral history present among the more hierarchically organised groups, their origins are slightly obscure. It is thought that they probably lived in the area for many centuries; their territory used to reach as far as the Gambia River but they were pushed south with the 13th- and 16th-century Mandinka migration.

SERAHULI

The Serahuli live in the eastern part of Senegal and far eastern Gambia. Almost exclusively Muslim, they are also known as Soninke, and live in several other countries in the Sahel including Mali and Burkina Faso. Soninke is also the Mandinka word for 'king', and the battles of the late 19th century between traditional Serahuli rulers and Islamic leaders were often called the Soninke-Marabout Wars. The origins of the Serahuli are

BUKUT: A DIOLA MASKING TRADITION   *John Graham*

The Diola people, who live in the Casamance region of Senegal and the southwestern parts of Gambia, have a long history of using masks made from plant fibre in a male initiation ceremony called the Bukut.

The Bukut takes place every 20 to 25 years and involves the gaining of knowledge and social status by a generation of young Diola men. Preparations for the Bukut start months in advance, as the celebrations entail huge feasts involving the sacrifice of many cattle. It is during these preparations that mothers compose songs that are sung by the initiated during a ritual involving the passing of cloth called Buyeet. Each youth has his own song, which will not be sung again in public until his death.

Distinctive woven-cane masks called Ejumbi, which have tubular eyes and are surmounted by a pair of massive cattle horns, are worn by some initiates when they return from the sacred forest. Not all initiates wear these masks – only those who are believed to possess special powers of clairvoyance. Other types of mask include the Fulundim, a cloth mask decorated with mirrors, beads, buttons and cowries, and the Gatombol, an abstract costume of plant material.

The masks are created by the initiates with the help of tribal elders and have retained their traditional form, although their construction can now incorporate the use of enamel paint and plastic fringing.

Though it has adapted to Christianity and Islam, the Bukut represents Diola identity and is still considered a very important event.

unclear. They may have migrated to this area after the break-up of the ancient Songhaï empire in present-day Mali at the end of the 15th century. Another theory has it that they have been in the region for longer, and are the descendants of the original Ghana Empire.

OTHER GROUPS

Minor groups in Senegal include the Bassari and the Bédik, largely animist or Christian, who live in the remote southeastern part of Senegal and have maintained a very strong, individual culture known for its impressive masked dances and initiation ceremonies.

The Lebu, Senegal's famous fishermen, are another distinct group, living almost exclusively around Yoff outside Dakar and along the coast. In Gambia, the Aku people (p44) are similar to the Krio found in other parts of West Africa.

Both Senegal and Gambia have significant Mauritanian and Lebanese communities, which are often involved in trade.

Social Structures

Most of the ancient West African empires were based on a clearly defined hierarchical system. Senegal's main cultural group the Wolof, as well as the Tukulor and Mandinka groups, are organised by such a pyramidal structure. Though economic success, education or relations abroad contribute, these traditional systems define social interaction to a large extent, and family surnames still largely reflect a person's place in society.

At the top of the pecking order sit the 'freeborn', ancient families of nobles and warriors that formed the traditional ruling elite. Slightly lower, though still freeborn, are farmers and traders. Lower down the scale are the artisans – blacksmiths, leather workers, woodcarvers and griots – occupational groups whose status is defined by their traditional profession. Though a child bearing a blacksmith's surname may never work metal, he is still a blacksmith by birth and in theory has the 'right' to exercise his parent's métier.

The Ceddo, Senegal's ancient dreadlocked, alcohol-drinking, grigri-wearing warriors – both fearless and fearsome – have a solid place in popular mythology. They represent precolonial strength and pre-Islamic ignorance. Their images are used in paintings, the classic griot song 'Ceddo' tells their story, and Sembene Ousmane has treated the subject in a film of the same name.

THE AKU

In The Gambia the Aku are a small but significant ethnic group, mostly descendants of freed slaves brought to the country in the early 19th century when the British established a protectorate here. Some came from plantations in the Americas, while others were released from slave ships leaving West Africa. Many also came from Sierra Leone, where a similar group of freed slaves settled (usually referred to as Krio people). The Aku language – a mix of 18th-century English and various indigenous tongues – is also similar to the Krio and pidgin spoken in other former British West African colonies.

Today there are still strong links between the Aku and Krio (sometimes the terms are used interchangeably) with many families having members in both Gambia and Sierra Leone. During the recent civil wars in Sierra Leone and Liberia, many Krio refugees settled in Banjul.

The Aku are mostly Christian and generally have names of British origin, such as Johnson or Thompson. Traditional Aku houses have steep tin roofs, gable windows and clapboard walls, a design thought to have originated in the southern states of the USA. They can still be seen in the old part of Banjul.

In colonial times, the administration often chose their civil servants among the Aku. The distinction between the former civil servants and other locals has its legacy in prejudices that prevail today.

At the bottom of the hierarchy were the captives, originally taken in wars or bought from traders, but kept in this position for many generations. Although this status no longer officially exists, many descendants of former captives still work as tenant farmers for the families of their former masters.

This is only a rough outline of a balanced system that is much more complex. Social status only explains part of a person's role in society, and supposedly inferior groups such as griots (*gewel* in Wolof, *gawlo* in Fula, and *jali* in Mande), have been able to exercise great influence, despite their relatively low rank. In song and poetry, griots recite oral tradition and maintain the histories of a particular family, village or clan, often going back for many centuries. Their praise song once confirmed the position and power of a ruler, and griots were historically also consulted as political advisers. Still today, you'll see people lavish gifts on griots in exchange for praise songs, and the most famous singers – those most capable of evoking nostalgia and pride in their listener by reciting his reputed ancestry – can sometimes achieve greater wealth than the person they are actually 'serving'. For more information about griots, see p54.

'Supposedly inferior groups such as griots have been able to exercise great influence, despite their relatively low rank'

RELIGION

In both Senegal and Gambia, Islam is the dominant religion – about 90% of the population is Muslim. The Wolof, Tukulor, Fula and Mandinka people are almost exclusively Muslim, while the Christian faith is most widespread among the Diola and to a lesser extent the Serer. Traditional religious forms (sometimes called animism) are most commonly practised in the predominantly Christian areas, and are often loosely combined with Christianity. Islam in Senegal and Gambia is also infused with elements of traditional religious practice.

Islam

Muslims across the world are united in their faith in God (Allah) and Mohammed, his Prophet. While some elements of religious practice, such as the submission to the Five Pillars of Islam (see opposite) and the study of the Holy Quran, are observed across the Islamic world, others differ from one Islamic culture to the next, depending on the religion's history in each region. Islam reached The Gambia and Senegal when the Almoravids (Berber warriors) conquered parts of today's northern Senegal in the 11th century. Regional practice evolved over the following centuries, and was refined in the 19th century, with the spread of the Muslim Sufi brotherhoods *(confréries)*. These brotherhoods follow the teachings of spiritual leaders called marabouts, who are deeply revered by the people, and hold enormous political and economic power. An understanding of Senegal's Muslim brotherhoods and their influence over society and culture is essential to gain an understanding of Senegal itself.

MARABOUTS & BROTHERHOODS

Take a tour around Dakar and you are bound to notice the images of two veiled men, one dressed in white the other in black, painted on numerous walls, cars and shop signs. They are the portraits of Cheikh Amadou Bamba, the 19th-century founder of the Mouride brotherhood, and Cheikh Ibra Fall, his illustrious follower and spiritual leader of the Baye Fall, a branch of Mouridism. *Télécentres* (privately owned telephone bureaus) and tailor shops are named after them, their names are written broadly across bush taxis and a vast number of pop songs, from *mbalax* to hip-hop, praise these two revered leaders.

'Muslim faith is more commonly channelled via saintly intermediaries (marabouts)'

While orthodox Islam holds that every believer is directly in touch with Allah, Muslim faith in Senegal and Gambia is more commonly channelled via saintly intermediaries (marabouts) who are ascribed divine powers and provide a link between God and the common populace. The concept of the marabout-led brotherhood was brought to Senegal from Morocco, where a spiritual leader is known as a *cheikh* or *caliph*, terms that are also used in Senegal. The earliest brotherhood established south of the Sahara was the 16th-century Qadiriya, which encouraged charity and humility and attracted followers throughout the northern Sahel. Today, most Qadiriya followers are Mandinka Muslims.

The Morocco-based Tijaniya brotherhood was introduced to Senegal by El Hajj Omar Tall in the mid-19th century, and remains powerful today, with large and important mosques in the towns of Tivaouane and Kaolack. Later in the 19th century, a smaller brotherhood called the Layen broke away from the Tijaniya under a marabout called Saidi Limamou Laye. Most Layen are Lebu people, who inhabit the town of Yoff, where you find the famous Layen Mausoleum.

With more than two million followers the Mouridiya, established by Cheikh Amadou Bamba, is by far the most important brotherhood (see the boxed text, p197), and its power has consistently grown since the mid-19th century. The rise of Mouridism is closely connected to colonial expansion,

---

THE FIVE PILLARS OF ISLAM

The five pillars of Islam are the basic tenets guiding Muslims in their daily lives:

Shahada (the profession of faith) 'There is no God but Allah, and Mohammed is his prophet' is the fundamental tenet of Islam.

Salat (prayer) Muslims must face Mecca and pray five times a day.

Zakat (alms) Muslims must give a portion of their income to the poor and needy.

Sawm (fasting) Ramadan is the month on the Muslim calendar when all Muslims must abstain from eating, drinking, smoking and sex from dawn to dusk.

Haj (pilgrimage) It is the duty of every Muslim who is fit and can afford it to make the pilgrimage to Mecca at least once.

and popular resistance to the measures imposed by the French. Colonial administration weakened, or completely disabled traditional structures of governance, rendering chiefs powerless and leaving their subjects without respect-worthy leaders. The evolving structures of the brotherhoods were remarkably close to the societal organisation that had been lost, which made them extremely attractive to a population that sought to preserve its autonomy and oppose the colonial power.

For many years Cheikh Amadou Bamba was merely a humble marabout, not more renowned than any other religious leaders of his time. Part of his remarkable rise to fame is due to the total adherence of his most famous *talibe* (student), Cheikh Ibra Fall. He was wholly devoted to the marabout, and demonstrated his profound commitment less through religious study than through hard, physical labour. 'Lamp' Fall, as he is often called, publicly renounced Quranic study, and refused the Ramadan fast, stating that in order to serve God, he required all his time and bodily force to work hard. He soon gathered his own, growing group of followers, the Baye Fall. Baye Fall adepts are traditionally recognisable by their long dreadlocks, heavy leather amulets containing pictures of their marabout, and patchwork clothing (though not all follow the dress code), and to this day, the Baye Fall tend to be the hardest workers in the region of Touba, building mosques and preparing fields for cultivation.

As the Mourides and Baye Fall gained in popularity, the French began to fear their impact, and forced Bamba into exile. His return from in 1907 is still celebrated by the annual Magal pilgrimage to Touba.

ISLAMIC HOLIDAYS

Below are the most important Islamic holidays, when commercial life in Gambia and Senegal comes to a stop:

Eid al-Moulid Birthday of the Prophet Mohammed.

Grand Magal Celebrated in the Senegalese town of Touba on the anniversary of the return from exile of Cheikh Amadou Bamba, the founder of the Mouride Islamic Brotherhood.

Korité (Eid al-Fitr) Celebrates the eagerly anticipated end of Ramadan, the month of the Muslim holy fast.

Tabaski (Eid al-Kebir) Commemorates Abraham's willingness to sacrifice his son on God's command. God rewarded Abraham by replacing the child with a ram, and Muslims across the world remember this by sacrificing a sheep.

Tamkharit The beginning of the Muslim New Year (though it's celebrated about 10 days later).

Since the Islamic calendar is based on 12 lunar months, Islamic holidays always fall about 11 days earlier than in the previous year. The exact dates depend on what hour the moon is seen, and by whom. To determine the exact beginning of the Ramadan fast, Muslims across the world are in theory supposed to take their cue from the astronomers at Mecca. Yet sometimes the spiritual leaders of the Senegalese brotherhoods determine the start of Ramadan a day before or after Mecca has spoken, and their followers will usually follow their announcement. This subsequently means that holidays such as Korité are celebrated one day by half the population, the next by the other, resulting in effect in a two-day holiday.

Forthcoming dates for major Muslim events (clouds withstanding):

Event	2006	2007	2008
Ramadan begins	24 Sep	13 Sep	2 Sep
Korité	24 Oct	13 Oct	2 Oct
Tabaski	31 Dec	20 Dec	9 Dec
Tamkharit	31 Jan	20 Jan	10 Jan
Eid al-Moulid	11 Apr	31 Mar	20 Mar

Today the Mourides, together with the ensemble of other brotherhoods, hold considerable power in politics and economics, particularly in Senegal. About a quarter of the population follow the words of the marabout of the Mourides – words that can thus easily decide the outcome of an election. The Mouride leaders also largely control the profitable groundnut trade, and their immense wealth swells further thanks to the donations they receive from their followers.

Christianity & Traditional Religions

Missionary zeal in Africa, the close companion of colonial expansionism, reached its high point in the mid-19th century, when the French and British established Catholic missions across their annexed territories. However, their impact wasn't as strong as desired, as Islam had already been successfully introduced to the region.

The roughly 10% of Christians in The Gambia and Senegal belong mainly to the Roman Catholic church; Pentecostal and Protestant churches also have minor followings. The Diola in Senegal's Casamance region constitute the largest Christian community. Along with the Bassari and Bédik of the Kedougou region, they are also the main group that still follows traditional religions, though these are often combined with Christian practice.

There are hundreds of traditional religions in West Africa, and while there are no written scriptures, beliefs and traditions have long been handed down by oral transmission. For outsiders, these beliefs and traditions can be complex and difficult to penetrate, as their practice commonly involves a high degree of secrecy. There are several factors common to these beliefs, although their descriptions here provide only an overview and are very simplified.

Almost all traditional religions are animist; that is, based on the attribution of life or consciousness to natural objects or phenomena. A certain tree, mountain, river or stone may be sacred, because it represents a spirit, or is home to a spirit, or simply is a spirit. Instead of 'spirit', some authorities use 'deity' or 'god'. The number of deities each religion accepts can vary, as can the phenomena that represent them.

Several traditional religions accept the existence of a supreme being or creator, a factor that largely facilitated the combination of Christianity, Islam and animist practices. In many African religions ancestors play a particularly strong role. Their principal function is to protect the community or family and they may, on occasion, show their pleasure or displeasure at the acts of their successors. Droughts, bad harvest or epidemic diseases can thus be interpreted at adversary acts of ancestral spirits. Many traditional religions hold that the ancestors are the real owners of the land, and while it can be enjoyed and used during the lifetime of descendants, it cannot be sold. Communication with ancestors or deities may take the form of prayer, offerings or sacrifice, possibly with the assistance of a holy man (or occasionally a holy woman).

'Fetishes' are an important feature of traditional religions. These are sacred objects (or charms) that can take many forms. The most common charms found throughout West Africa are small leather amulets – many containing a sacred object – worn around the neck, arm or waist. These are called grigri and are used to ward off evil or to bring good luck. Grigri are also worn by West African Muslims, for whom the amulet is empowered by a verse from the Quran enclosed in the leather wrap. This is only one example of the myriad connections between traditional religions and Islam or Christianity.

'There are hundreds of traditional religions in West Africa and traditions have long been handed down by oral transmission'

WOMEN IN GAMBIA & SENEGAL

The societies of Senegal and Gambia are predominantly Muslim and patriarchal, which means that women enjoy limited autonomy. Rare are women who live on their own – a woman usually only leaves her parental home to join that of her husband. Harshly put, this means that submission to her parents is immediately replaced by submission to her partner, and a woman's degree of independence depends largely on the open-mindedness *of* her spouse.

But this is only part of the story. Women have found various ways to assert themselves; women's cooperatives (*groupements de femmes* in Senegal) provide one arena in which women can affirm their identity. These associations function on the basis of a refined economic system – every associate pays a contribution, the sum of which is regularly given to one member who needs it most, perhaps to resolve a financial tight spot, prepare for a wedding or send a child to school. The cooperatives are often involved in community work, and can have an impressive impact. In the Senegalese Casamance region, for instance, one women's collective succeeded in persuading the local authority to tarmac the road to the local hospital, allowing for much safer journeys to the maternity unit. In some areas, these cooperatives have also played an important role in combating female circumcision – a practice that is still widespread in both Senegal and Gambia.

Although the majority of married women look after the house and children, many women in Senegal and Gambia do work, and some achieve high ranks in the political, economic or artistic arena. Even those who remain at home often engage in some form of commerce – perhaps a small street stall, or importing and selling jewellery and fabric – to boost their financial means.

Female confidence is also asserted in dress and make-up. Women tend to dress with an elegance that is hard to match. The dance floors of Dakar in particular are usually packed with stunningly (and daringly) clothed *disquettes* (stylish young girls), while the presence of successful, cosmopolitan businesswomen in their mid-40s (often referred to as *dirianké*) is amplified by billowing *boubous* and jingling gold jewellery. And breathtaking looks go hand in hand with a whole universe of uniquely female knowledge – that of the art of seduction. From tinkling, scented waist beads and arousing mixes of perfume, incense and soaps to culinary secrets, Senegalese women have an expansive and creative repertoire of how to prevent a husband from straying.

MEDIA
The Gambia

Senegal's most comprehensive cultural e-magazine, containing articles, dates of festivals and dozens of links, can be found at www.au-senegal.com/ciclo (in French).

Concerns about the freedom of press and safety of journalists in The Gambia have grown intensely recently. In 2004 a new press law was passed, giving the state powers to detain journalists if found guilty of libel. On 16 December 2004, only a few days after the law was instated, one of its main critics, the prominent journalist Deyda Hydara (editor of the independent newspaper the *Point* and correspondent of Agence France-Presse), was gunned down in Banjul while driving his car home. Investigations revealed that the journalist was under surveillance by the secret service at the time of the murder, yet the Gambian government has not allowed any independent investigations to take place. Quite the contrary: president Yahya Jammeh openly sent out further warnings to journalists expressing opinions contrary to governmental policy, and the reporters of the nation live in fear.

Senegal

Senegal isn't exactly a haven of independent, investigative journalism, but its range of print publications, private and state radios and two TV channels enjoy relative freedom of expression, with radio being a particularly lively and interesting medium. On 17 October 2005, the country's popular radio station Sud FM was closed after broadcasting an interview with a leader of the rebel movement in the Casamance. However, there were immediate protests, and the ban was lifted the same day.

SPORT
Football

There's no better time to get a break in Dakar's eternally gridlocked streets than when the national football (soccer) team is playing a televised match. The entire country will be grouped around TV sets, and businesses come to a virtual standstill. There's no worse time to sit in Dakar traffic than the moment after a victory – joyful masses will take to the streets, drowning the town in the national colours. Both Senegal and Gambia are football crazy – like most African nations – but the fever is more pronounced in Senegal, as the national team enjoys international renown ever since it balled its way into the quarter finals of the World Cup in 2002, having beaten the world champions France 1:0 in the opening match.

Most boys dream of becoming football stars and practise their kicks on improvised football grounds on the road, or, if they're lucky, on an actual terrain.

Larger towns and cities have stadiums where matches take place, most notably the Independence Stadium in Bakau near Banjul, and the Léopold Sédar Senghor Stadium on the northern side of Dakar. Games against sides from neighbouring countries are advertised and draw huge audiences.

Wrestling

Traditional wrestling (*la lutte* in French) is a hugely popular spectator sport in both Senegal and Gambia. In Senegal, it's mostly practised by the Serer and Diola, and you'll often find matches advertised around the Siné-Saloum and Casamance regions. If you do, go and watch. It's fascinating. In villages, you'll find the dust-filled terrain lit by oil lamps, while the repetitive wail of griots, wildly distorted by clattering amplifiers, tears the air. Groups of wrestlers, invariably dressed in a tied loincloth and wearing protective charms around arms and waist, warm up and prepare for their fights. An evening consists of a string of matches, culminating in the encounter of the most renowned fighters. Wrestlers will circle one another cautiously, carefully preparing the next rapid move. The winner is the one who manages to pin his opponent to the ground, shoulderblades touching the floor. He'll celebrate by performing a dance to furious drumming and the griots' praise song.

'The repetitive wail of griots, wildly distorted by clattering amplifiers, tears the air'

Matches can be held any time of year, but reach a peak in November and December. Senegal's most famous annual encounter takes place on 1 January in the national stadium. Urban settings are great, but if you can, try to see wrestling in rural surroundings for the full sensory experience.

ARTS
Music

The music of Senegal and Gambia alone is worth the money of a plane ticket. Senegal is home to some of Africa's most famous musicians, including singers such as Youssou N'Dour, Baaba Maal and Ismael Lô.

Gambia's star has slightly faded in recent years, though the country pro
duced some amazing groups in the post-independence years including th
Super Eagles. The beat to get people dancing in both countries is the fier
mbalax rhythm, originally created in Senegal though popular throughou
the entire region. See p54 for a more detailed discussion.

Painting & Sculpture

Judging by the amount of gaudy, spray-painted canvasses on sale in th
tourist centres of Gambia and Senegal, the countries seem to be veritabl
hothouses of visual artists. Well, not quite. Much of this stuff is quickl
churned out, and squarely aimed at tourists. The really good stuff is muc
harder to find, but it's there all the same. Senegal, in particular, has
vibrant contemporary arts scene.

The tradition of sculpture in Senegal and Gambia is primarily rooted i
the creation of wooden statues and masks originally produced for ritua
purposes, and today for sale en masse in tourist markets and boutiques
Some of these figures can be fascinating (Dakar's IFAN museum an
Banjul's national museum have some good examples on display), but th
countries have also produced some amazing contemporary sculptors.

The Senegalese sculptor Ousmane Sow, one of Africa's best-known art
ists, is still the reference in this field. He is famous for his gigantic ston
sculptures, which are particularly lifelike. Younger artists include Gabrie
Kemzo, whose beautiful metal works are on display around Île de Gorée
and Seni Awa Camara, who sells fantastical clay sculptures on the loca
market in Bignona, Casamance.

Senegal has brought forth some excellent painters, including well-know
artists such as Claire Goby, Souleymane Keita and Kambel Dieng. Beside
canvas painting, the country is particularly renowned for its unique tradi
tion of glass painting (*sous-verre*; below).

And don't forget to keep your eyes open for the everyday art tha
gives Dakar its particular character. The city's bush taxis are draped i
decorative writings and images. Reproductions of the portraits of Cheikh
Amadou Bamba and Cheikh Ibra Fall adorn walls around town, adding
spots of colour to ragged buildings.

Gifted photographer Mama Casset has created a series of memorable portraits depicting early-20th-century Senegalese styles. The booklet *Mama Casset*, published by Revue Noire, is in French, but the collection of images speaks for itself.

SOUS-VERRE – THE SENEGALESE ART OF GLASS PAINTING

Enter Moussa Sakho's charmingly chaotic atelier at the Institut Français in Dakar, and you're
greeted by a group of smiling faces looking out from a surface of colourfully painted glass.
Moussa Sakho is one of the leading contemporary artists of *sous-verre*, Senegal's distinctive art
of reverse-glass painting. In this special technique, images are drawn onto the back of a glass
surface, which lends them radiance and protection.

The origins of this tradition aren't entirely clear, but the practice reached an early highpoint
in the late 19th century, and its spread is thought to be connected with the expansion of Islam.
Islamic imagery was initially the most prominent theme of the *sous-verres*, something which
didn't please the French administration. Colonial governor William Ponty famously forbade their
creation, fearing that their wide distribution would aid the expansion of Islam. But his decree
didn't have the intended result. Quite the contrary – fearing for the few religious works they
possessed, painters started copying the works, and the art of *sous-verre* entered its most prolific
phase; it was now considered a counter-colonial force.

The most popular *sous-verres* today portray contemporary styles, fashions, and the minutiae
of daily life in Senegal. To find good-quality *sous-verre*, you have to look past the tourist stalls.
Moussa Sakho's workshop is a good place to start. Other artists of renown include Babacar Lô,
Andy Dolly, Séa Diallo, Mbida and Gora Mbengue.

OUMOU SY

When it comes to charting a fashionable course from ancient African cultures to downtown Dakar, few can do it with as much grace as Oumou Sy. If you're looking for an African haute couture, she's it. This ambitious lady has been one of the first to infuse universal wear with a healthy dose of Afrocentric styles. Musical instruments, calabash gourds, scrap materials and original prints all find their way into her daring catwalk creations. And there's more. Her design school, Leydi, has been the place many a young designer first learnt to wield scissors and thread, and the Carnival and International Fashion Week in Dakar she helped initiate are the places to see their imaginative cuts on display. And here's what really betrays the businesswoman in her: with the creation of her Web-connected cultural centre, Metissacana, she was also the person to launch cybercafé culture across Dakar.

Textile & Fashion Design

Classic techniques of textile design in Senegal and The Gambia include wax printing, tie-dye and *bazin* (dyed fabrics that are beaten to a shine with wooden clubs). You'll be able to admire *bazins* on any Friday in town, when people head to the mosque in their finest *boubous*. Watching traditional weavers at work is fascinating. They produce slim strips of roughly woven cloth on long and narrow looms, which are erected on footpaths in the artisans' quarters. The strips are then sown together to make a *pagne* (a length of colourful cloth worn as a skirt).

Contemporary artists and fashion designers take these traditional crafts in new directions. Senegalese artist Rackie Diankha has exhibited her fabulous oeuvres of textile internationally, and Baboucar Fall and Toimbo Laurens are shaping new directions in batik printing in Gambia.

Fashion conscious Senegal is also home to some of Africa's most re-nowned designers. Best known internationally is Oumou Sy, whose stunning Afrocentric creations have been exhibited in many international fashion shows. But there's a whole new generation of designers snapping at her heels. Colle Ardo Sow, nicknamed 'Queen of Woven Cloth', is fast becoming a reference, having given the humble *pagne* a new place of pride in modern cuts.

Another leading designer is Angélique Dhiedhiou, whose label Toolah proposes a new, contemporary elegance rooted in African styles. Her collections of stylish, wearable clothes combine shimmering woven cloth, silk and beads. The young label Sigil takes Afro-fashion to a cool street level, and is even affordable to the young generation it's intended for. You can purchase Sigel designs at its boutiques in Dakar.

For information on the creative underground in Senegal and Gambia, check www.greeneyezdesign .com, a comprehensive website featuring a number of emerging artists.

Literature
THE GAMBIA

Along with many countries of the Sahel, Gambia's literary tradition is partly based upon the family histories and epic poems told over the centuries by the griots (see Music of Senegal & Gambia, p54).

In more recent times, especially since independence, a number of contemporary writers have emerged, although compared with many other West African countries, Gambia does not have a major literary output. Gambia's best-known novelist is William Conton.

Conton's 1960s classic *The African* is a semi-autobiographical tale of an African student in Britain who experiences confusion and unhappiness there. He returns to his homeland, where he gets involved in nationalist politics and finally becomes president, still suffering from pangs of alienation and self-doubt. Published at a time when many former colonies were gaining independence, this book was an influential bestseller in many parts of Africa.

Whereas Conton has his roots in the colonial era, author Ebou Dibba is seen as part of the new Gambian generation, even though his first and best-known novel *Chaff on the Wind* (1986) is set in the pre-independence period. This book follows the fortunes of two rural boys – one keen and studious, the other looking only for a good time – who come to work in the capital city, both eventually suffering at the hands of fate, despite their attempts to control their own destinies. His most recent work is *Alhaji* (The Horse), published in 1992.

Another new-generation writer is Tijan Salleh. Primarily known as a poet – his main collection is *Kora Land,* published in 1989 – he has also written essays and short stories. His style has been described as blunt, abrasive, radical and confrontational. Common themes include the debunking of political hypocrisy and despair at the corruption and poverty endemic in African society.

SENEGAL

Senegal is one of the West African countries with the most prolific literary output; however, most works are published in French, and only a small number of works have been translated in other languages.

Filmmaker Ousmane Sembène was initially a writer, and is still among the country's best-known authors. His classic *God's Bits of Wood* (1970) is widely acclaimed. It tells of the struggles of strikers on the Dakar-Bamako train line in the late 1940s, and describes the emergence of a grassroots political consciousness in pre-independence Africa.

Senegal's most influential writer is probably Léopold Senghor, the country's first president. Studying in France during the 1930s, he coined the term 'negritude', which emphasised black African ideas and culture, countering the colonial policy of 'assimilation'. Naturally, these beliefs influenced Senghor's own political thought.

Karmen Geï sets the story of *Carmen* in a Senegalese context. Only the censored version of this controversial movie was shown in Senegal, as it portrayed a rape scene in a sacred Baye Fall setting.

The most famous female author is Mariama Ba, whose short but incisive novel *So Long a Letter* was first published in 1980 and won the Noma Award for publishing in Africa. It's one of the most sensitive, intimate and beautiful contemplations of female lives in a polygamous society. Her second novel, *The Scarlet Song,* is much lesser known, though equally outstanding. It's a tragic story about a failing marriage between a Senegalese man and a French woman.

Another woman writer is Aminata Sow-Fall. Her 1986 novel *The Beggars' Strike* is an ironic story highlighting the differences between rich and poor, and it questions the power of the political elite – two recurring themes in modern Senegalese literature.

The novel *An Ambiguous Adventure* by Cheikh Hamidou Kane has almost achieved the status of a Senegalese classic. It's a deeply philosophical discussion of issues of colonisation and religion, and the social transformations of early-20th-century Senegal.

Young author Fatou Diome's debut novel *Le Ventre de l'Atlantique* became an unexpected bestseller in 2004. The book, a brilliant treatment of the topic of emigration, sold thousands of copies in the Francophone world, and has since been translated into German. Perhaps her success will persuade publishing houses to work on an English translation, too.

Cinema

Senegal is one of the most prolific nations in African cinema, and while the scene was in its prime in the years following independence, today there's a resurgence of young filmmakers emerging against all financial odds, taking new approaches and addressing new themes. The doyen of Senegalese cinema is Ousmane Sembene. Born in 1923, he studied film in Russia, after hustling his way through '50s France as a seaman, dockworker and builder. He has used cinema to shed a critical eye onto Senegalese society, history and culture from his first 1962 realisation *Borom Saret* – a moving black-and-white tale about an inner-city horse-cart driver – through to the 2006 release *Moolaade,* which broaches the sensitive subject of female circumcision.

The illustrious filmmaker Djibril Diop Mambety surprised the movie world with daring, experimental works such as his 'Senegalese road movie' *Touki Bouki,* a surreal 1973 story of a young Dakar couple, and the 1992 oeuvre *Hyenas.*

Contemporary talents include Joseph Kamaka Gaye, whose acclaimed work *Karmen Geï* sets the classic story of *Carmen* in a Senegalese context. Dakar's annual Festival International du Film de Quartier (p156) is the place to spot the future big names.

'The illustrious filmmaker Djibril Diop Mambety surprised the movie world with daring, experimental works'

Architecture

The story of West Africa's ancient empires isn't easily traced by architectural styles, as the powerful rulers didn't enshrine their memory in monumental building work as did their counterparts in Europe. But what survives to this day are the contrasting architectures of ordinary housings, which differ greatly from region to region. In the north, the *banco* (mudbrick) constructions of Tukulor houses have much in common with Sudanese architecture. In the same region there are late-19th-century mosques, organic shapes built from mudbricks by the followers of El Hajj Omar Tall. The Kedougou region is home to the round stone huts typical of the Bassari, while in the area of Siné-Saloum, huts are made from thatch and mud.

Besides African building work, Senegal also has many examples of European architecture, some dating back to the Portuguese era.

The islands of Gorée and Saint-Louis, and the Senegal River settlements of Richard Toll, Podor, Matam and Bakel, are virtual time capsules of 18th- and 19th-century French architecture. Many of the buildings have seen better days, but some of the houses on Gorée and in Saint-Louis have been beautifully restored. The impact of Breton settlers on Île de Carabane at the remote mouth of the Casamance River is still plain to see in its large church and mission (now a hotel). In Gambia, Banjul is home to wide avenues of grand homes once occupied by the colonial elite, while, nearby stand small unpretentious Aku-style homes, some still occupied by the descendants of freed-slave families who moved to Banjul from Sierra Leone in the early 1800s. Fortifications were also important to the European colonists, and not far from Banjul you can see the remains of Fort James (James Island) and Fort Bullen (Barra).

For contemporary architecture, visit Arch 22 and Banjul Airport, both designed by Senegalese architect Pierre Goudiaby.

Music of The Gambia & Senegal

You don't have to search hard to find music in Senegal and Gambia – just step into a taxi and commence your search. The driver of your battered Peugeot is likely to have his stereo fully turned up, sweetening his endless tours around Dakar's sand-blown tarmac with the latest Youssou N'Dour or some homemade hip-hop. On a weekend, he'll probably pass several aching sound systems that carry the distorted voice of a griot or some local reggae through the bustling boroughs, entertaining radiant wedding parties or enticing tea-sipping youngsters to dance. If you're in Dakar, ask the driver to steer his cab straight into the impossibly crammed streets of Marché Sandaga, where scratchy stereos compete for attention, and where impatient car horns, clicking heels, rustling *boubous* (robes), shouts of bartering, and calls to prayer from the mosque mingle into a unique hymn to urban Dakar. This heaving downtown market is also home to several tiny stalls, stacked sky-high with cassettes and CDs that shift the latest local music releases to an eagerly waiting public – works they've probably just copied in the backrooms of their boutique. When it comes to music, no-one teaches West Africans anything. You'll be the one keen to learn the seductive hip swing of *mbalax* or the sensual sway of the latest zouk (a style of dance music, originally from Guadeloupe, that mixes African and Latin-American rhythms).

Mark Hudson's book *The Music in My Head* is an entertaining introduction to the world-music industry; it places the spotlight on the scenes of Gambia and Senegal.

A POTTED HISTORY OF GAMBIAN & SENEGALESE MUSIC

Even the most contemporary Senegalese and Gambian music trends evoke ancient roots, with its proud poise and soaring voice. The history of modern music in the region begins several centuries ago – in the days of the 13th-century Mali empire of the Malinké, the 15th-century Jolof empire established by the Wolof, and other influential kingdoms of pre-colonial Africa. The epic of Sunjata Keita, illustrious founder of the Mali empire, famously recounts the important role of his griot Bala Fasseke, and explains the establishment of a social hierarchy, in which musicians had a clearly defined place. Along with blacksmiths, woodcarvers and other artisans, griots occupied the place in society of professional groups, ranked lower than the 'freeborn' families of rulers and traders, and above the slaves. 'Griot' is a French word – local terms for this social group are *jali* in Mande, *gewel* in Wolof, and *gawlo* in Fula.

Griots are born musicians; they're born with the right to sing the praises of their rulers, act as political advisers, recite genealogies and, importantly, memorise and spread the region's oral history and pass it on to future generations. This is how the stories of Africa's ancient kingdoms have survived the centuries. It's also how the griots' classic repertoire has been transmitted from one generation to the next. Any accomplished griot today can still transport his listeners into past times, instilling pride in their family heritage – a gift that an appreciative audience awards with generous gifts of money or cloth.

One of the Mande griots' most famous instruments is the kora, icon of African music throughout the world; and its history is especially important in Gambia. This tiny country became a centre of kora playing when

Malinké groups settled in the region after the gradual collapse of the mighty Mali empire. Today Gambia proudly boasts a wide variety of kora styles, notably the dry patterns of the eastern regions around Bansang and Basse, and the softer style more common in the west of the country.

Take a time-machine ride from the precolonial era to the 1960s and you land directly on a swinging Cuban dance floor – right in the heart of Dakar. Cuban music was incredibly influential in the '60s and was first played in cosmopolitan dance clubs, such as the Miami in Dakar, to the affluent French and Senegalese elite. First brought over from France's fashionable dance floors, it quickly struck a chord with the Senegalese population. After all, Cuban rhythms were a 'New World' adaptation of musical styles originally brought to the Americas from Africa. Having now returned to their source, they once again became infused with African flavours.

Independence brought a whole new national consciousness, which left its traces in the music of the region. Inspired young musicians, notably Ibra Kasse and his Star Band, started to transform the imported Cuban beats, by infusing them with a uniquely Senegalese twist. Salsa sections were increasingly broken up with bursts of frenetic drumming, drawn from traditional ceremonies. Dancers went crazy on the floor, rotating hips, thrusting groins and spinning legs, spurring the drummers on to even faster playing. There was no going back. In this polyrhythmic marriage Senegal had found its own beat – the *mbalax*.

The birth of *mbalax* is mainly associated with one name, Youssou N'Dour, who proudly dons the epithet 'King of Mbalax'. In the late '70s, he was a young kid singing with the Etoile de Dakar, an offshoot of the Star Band. It was this group that took the novel Senegalese-Cuban sounds to a whole new immensely trendy level. The band's style of *mbalax* proved irresistible and launched N'Dour into superstardom. Its popularity hasn't abated to this day. *Mbalax* continues to evolve as it's combined with new sounds. Today the music is getting even faster yet its core sound, the rolling drumbeat called by the *sabar* and *tama* drums, hasn't changed.

If you enter any Gambian music shop today, you'll find about the same selection of music as in Senegal: Youssou N'Dour, Youssou N'Dour, Youssou N'Dour and a range of other Senegalese *mbalax* singers. Local artists are almost absent, with the exception of Jalibah Kouyateh and Tata Dindin Jobarteh. Other than that, popular Gambian music is largely ruled by Senegalese *mbalax*. But this hasn't always been the case. In the late '60s, the Afro-funky Super Eagles ruled the stages, and made a huge impact in Senegal, where they exerted a formative influence on the emerging *mbalax* scene. It's a contribution that has largely been forgotten today, together with most of Gambia's once flourishing artistic scene, which is now a shadow of its former vibrant self. Gambia's young generation has chosen an entirely different route – that of reggae. The lazy beat blasts from improvised sound systems around the country, each echoing bash proving that the nation's nickname 'Little Jamaica' is entirely deserved.

In Senegal, reggae is competing with a vibrant local hip-hop scene for youth attention. Senegalese hip-hop has been made famous worldwide by groups such as Positive Black Soul and Daara J, who sneer at the permanently overdressed, glittering *mbalax* audiences gathered in style at concerts of the likes of the R&B-influenced Viviane N'Dour, the streetwise Omar Pene and a host of excellent young singers. In the 30th year of his career, Youssou N'Dour is still unrivalled in popularity – neither the soft-voiced Thione Seck, Youssou's eternal challenger in Senegal, nor the nasally voiced Baaba Maal, the better-known name abroad, have ever been able to topple him from his throne.

Sunjata: Gambian Versions of the Mande Epic by Bamba Suso and Banna Kanute tells the story of the 13th-century ruler of the Mali empire in the words of two renowned Gambian griots. A great place to learn about history and Gambian kora styles at the same time.

TRADITIONAL MUSIC

Boundaries between traditional and modern music styles are fluid. During the day an artist (probably a griot) can recite the story of Sunjata and his warriors with soaring voice in a way that brings their tales of heroism truly to life. Yet in the evening, you might easily encounter the same artist backed by a full electric ensemble, experimenting with a kora-funk crossover. The difference between traditional and modern is perhaps best defined by context, rather than style. Music that's played for social occasions, such as weddings or naming ceremonies, is usually considered traditional, while a nightclub setting demands modernity and the scream of an amplified kora riff.

Established families often have their own griots, who perform praise songs and recite genealogies at celebrations and are usually showered with crumpled CFA or dalasi notes in return. But there's more to the traditional music of the region than the refined songs of the griots alone. Every ethnic group has its own rhythms, dances and instruments, and a tour around Gambia and Senegal will reveal the spectacular array of what's around – ranging from the flute and fiddle troupes of the Fula herders to stunning polyphonic Serer songs and the sky-high leaps that accompany Wolof *sabar* drumming. If you're serious about experiencing the region's variety of traditional music, head for the tiny villages. The best chance to see such music is at a family celebration, and if you approach the local wedding party respectfully, your presence is unlikely to offend.

Particularly spectacular are the masked dances and songs of the Bassari and Diola. These are mainly performed for initiation ceremonies, and the stunningly decorated dancers usually represent supernatural spirits that either protect or try to harm the newly circumcised boys. Masked shows have survived only in the non-Islamic regions of the country. Their deep connection to traditional religion, the spiritual associations of the drum and the representation of non-Islamic spirits via masks makes them incompatible with Muslim faith. There are some exceptions to this rule though: the dance of the Kankurang of the Malinké – where a spirit is represented by a rustling, grass-covered mask – has found its way into the region's Islamic culture, just as the protective amulets worn by followers of traditional religions are now worn by most Muslims.

> The stories of West Africa's great empires are kept alive to this day in the songs of the griots. The song 'Kelefa', for instance, tells the story of the ancient empire of Kaabu, while 'Tara' praises the heroism of El Hajj Omar Tall.

Traditional Instruments

DRUMS

The *tama* drum of the Wolof has gained much attention through its use in *mbalax*. The tiny size of this double-headed tension drum belies the frenzy it can cause among dancers. Watch out for the *tamakat* – the player of the drum – at any Youssou N'Dour gig. Once he gets up and starts pounding the stretched drum skin with a stick, women leap up from their chairs and dance until their shiny *pagnes* (skirts) and headscarves unravel.

Another Wolof drum is the *sabar*. This tall, thin drum is played in an ensemble and forms the clanging basis of the *mbalax* beat.

The ubiquitous *djembe* is probably the most popular of all African drums, and has an appeal that has reached beyond Africa and deep into Europe. The *djembe*-like *bougarabou* stems from the Casamance region.

There are plenty of drumming courses available all across Gambia and Senegal. **Batafon Arts** (☎ 4392517; www.batafonarts.co.uk) in Kololi enjoys a good reputation, and Kafountine and Abéné in the Casamance are Senegal's favourite destinations for aspiring *djembe* players, with plenty of informal drumming courses. In Dakar, try the **Centre Culturel Blaise Senghor** (Map p152; Rue 10, Dakar).

Famous Senegalese drummers:

Assane Thiam Youssou's famous *tama* player.

Doudou N'Diaye Rose Most renowned *bougarabou* player, who has spawned a diaspora of equally gifted sons.

Mbaye Dieye Faye Youssou N'Dour's equally famous *sabar* player.

STRINGED INSTRUMENTS

A variety of stringed instruments ranges from the Mandinka single-string *moolo* (plucked lute) and the *riti* (bowed fiddle) to the 21-string kora. The harp-lute kora is the classic instrument of the griots, and is arguably one of the most sophisticated instruments in sub-Saharan Africa. With its delicate tumble of shimmering notes, it has captured the souls of many listeners abroad, and been incorporated in a wide array of crossover works, ranging from jazz to Western classical music and even hip-hop.

Another important instrument of the griots is the *xalam* (a Wolof word pronounced kha-lam). It is known by a variety of names, including *konting* in Mandinka and *hoddu* in Fula, and has from three to five strings that are plucked to produce a dry, guitarlike sound; it's believed the banjo evolved from the *xalam*.

The best place to learn the kora playing is in Brikama, a dusty town in Gambia (see the boxed text, p124), where the famous griot families of Dembo Konté and Malamini reside.

Famous kora players:

Amadou Bansang Jobarteh The doyen of Gambia's dry, eastern style.

Dembo Konté One of the Brikama masters; has gained fame for his kora duets with the Casamance-born Kausu Kuyateh.

Jali Nyama Suso Outstanding Gambian kora player who wrote his country's national anthem.

Lamine Konté A kora player from the Casamance; one of Senegal's best.

Malamini Jobarteh Another member of the famous Brikama clan; his sons Pa and Tata Dindin Jobarteh are among Gambia's most popular musicians today.

WIND INSTRUMENTS

The Fula flute, with its husky call, is West Africa's most famous wind instrument. Flute musicians combine singing with playing sharp trills and tumbling descending patterns. The Fula flute stems from the Fouta Jallon in Guinea, but many flute players *(nyamakala)* have moved to Gambia and southern Senegal, where they often perform their hilarious, acrobatic shows for the entertainment of hotel guests. To learn the instrument properly, you should really go to Guinea. Otherwise, try Brikama (the Konté family can point you in the right direction; reach them on ☎ 7710015), or the Théâtre Daniel Sorano in Dakar.

Famous Fula flautists:

Ali Wague Based in Paris; plays on dozens of West African albums.

Issa Diao The flautist of Dakar's Théâtre National du Sénégal.

XYLOPHONES

The wooden *balafon,* whose dry tone is accompanied by the gentle buzz of vibrating gourds attached to each slab, is another typical griot instrument. It's most widespread in Guinea, but Malinké griots play it all across Gambia and Senegal. To take xylophone courses, try **Batafon Arts** (☎ 4392517; www.batafonarts.co.uk) in Kololi or, again, in Brikama.

El Hadj Sory Kouyate is a famous Guinean *balafon* player. His double CD, *Guinée: Anthologie du Balafon Mandingue,* is a great way to experience *balafon* music.

The children's film *Kirikou* may be created by a French cartoonist, but Senegalese star Youssou N'Dour created the music, and a member of the rap group PBS Radical provided Kirikou's voice. In the clever and cheeky *Kirikou,* West African children have found their first locally grounded cartoon hero.

POP MUSIC

Senegal's pop scene is thriving – find yourself in the epicentre of an exploding *mbalax* dance floor and you'll see how passionately people feel about their music. Dakar's contemporary music scene is fantastically varied. Anything, from hip-hop to reggae, salsa, folk, jazz and pop is available – all homemade and spiced with potent local flavours. The glitzy Senegalese scene compares to that of The Gambia the same way the two capitals do; the former is a vibrant party queen, the latter a sleepy backwater, only occasionally rippled by the bass drop of a reggae beat.

Dance Orchestras

In the 1970s, the pop-music scene in Senegal was dominated by large bands, complete with multipart horn sections, bass and rhythm guitar, and several singers and dancers. These mighty beasts are usually referred to as 'dance orchestras', an apt name considering their football-team size. The most famous of these, Orchestra Baobab, was the undisputed leader of the Senegalese scene throughout the '70s, before a young generation snatched its audiences away with cheek and a healthy dose of rebellious innovation. Right now the grand Baobab is living its second spring. It reformed in 2001 and now tours regularly, luring audiences worldwide on the dance floors, thanks to the members' inimitable grandfather charm.

The father of the Senegalese dance orchestra style, however, is an artist who is lesser known today. Ibra Kasse was a reputed tyrant when it came to working with talented musicians, and was the leader of a fantastically gifted group called the Star Band de Dakar. In the line-up were Pape Seck and the illustrious Gambian-born lead singer Labah Sosseh. When the star band divided into glittering pieces Etoile de Dakar emerged, proving the rocket shooter for Senegalese uberstar Youssou N'Dour.

Salsa

In the '60s the Senegalese scene was all about Cuban music. It was about conga rhythms and Spanish lyrics so perfectly reproduced that they almost passed for the original. And today Cuban bands still draw huge audiences – mainly among the middle-aged middle class. Just put a record of 'El Guantanamero' on in any classy club, and the couples will start turning on the dance floor. Internationally, the most famous band is currently the all-star orchestra Africando. In Senegal itself the charming orchestra Pape Fall & l'African Salsa tends to steal the crowds.

Mbalax

Mbalax is the heart and soul of Senegalese music – and the legs, thighs, hips and backsides, too. Several Gambian artists of the '60s created the fiery beat from a mixture of Cuban beats and traditional *sabar* drumming. *Mbalax* was made famous by Youssou N'Dour, who is still the unrivalled leader of the scene. He is also one of the biggest names in world music, a shrewd businessman, a cultural icon – and then some.

Since its inception, *mbalax* has evolved by adapting to changing fashions, without ever losing its essence. One example of the genre's versatility is the *mbalax* by impeccably suited-and-tied Thione Seck, who has married the beat with Indian-style vocals. In 1974, Senegal's 'street kid' Omar Pene and his band Super Diamono were the first to replace the congas of a standard *mbalax* outfit with a drum kit – a move that has been copied by every artist since.

Youssou N'Dour's sister-in-law Viviane N'Dour is one of Senegal's major style icons, mixing sexy *mbalax* beats with breathy, R&B-inspired

The most comprehensive website discussing releases of African urban music is www .africanhiphop.com. The related www.senerap .com tells you all about the Dakar scene.

Find out all about Gambia's vibrant reggae scene on www.onegambia.com, which comes complete with its own radio station, West Coast Radio.

vocals. Emerging *mbalax* artists causing havoc on the region's dance floors include Abdou Guité Seck, Ablaye Mbaye, Aliou Mbaye N'Der and Titi.

Afro-Jazz, Folk & Fusion

Senegal has a long tradition of jazz, usually called 'Afro' in the country itself. In the '80s, the group Xalam, which proposed a unique African-flavoured rock, went to such heights as to play support for the Rolling Stones. In Senegal itself, they never achieved nearly as much fame, though singer Souleymane Faye is still a renowned solo performer. Around the same time, the band of brothers known as Touré Kunda set out from its Casamance home to conquer the world – with some success. The new sound was embraced first by France, where the band went all the way into the national charts. Touré Kunda was one of the few Afro-jazz bands also appreciated at home – something most groups of the scene can only dream of. The many folk performers Senegal has produced – including artists such as the Frères Guisse, Daby Balde and Diogal Sakho – face a similar situation: the Western world loves them; the locals find them bland.

Although Baaba Maal's acoustic works are sometimes classed as folk, it's hard to categorise his music. He has produced a spectacularly varied catalogue, toying with hip-hop and dance beats among plenty of other styles. And Cheikh Lô, another well-known name in the West, stormed onto the scene with a moving blend of Latin rhythms, subtle hints of *mbalax* and praise lyrics to the Cheikh Amadou Bamba, spiritual leader of the Baye Fall.

Senegal is one of Africa's most vibrant hip-hop nations, with globally successful groups such as Daara J, PBS and Pee Froiss. If you're in the country, don't miss the annual hip-hop awards ceremony, featuring concerts by rappers from all across West Africa.

Hip-Hop & Reggae

Senegal has the most exciting hip-hop scene in West Africa, or the second-largest Francophone hip-hop scene worldwide. Since the mid-'80s, when the brash young trio PBS (Positive Black Soul) stormed the international scene, Sene-rap has simply refused to disappear. Dakar's kids have coupled the American beats with local rhymes and sounds, turning the music into a powerful tool of voicing discontent. The scene enjoyed a revival in 2004, when Daara J sold unexpected numbers of records, shifting the global spotlight right onto the urban youth culture of Senegal. Other leading hip-hop artists in Senegal include the witty Pee Froiss, soul-voiced Carlou D, and the slick crew Chronik 2H.

Gambia is more Kingston than New York, a country where reggae artists such as Egalitarian, Rebellion the Recaller and Dancehall Masters transfer Jamaican swagger into a Gambian context.

RESOURCES
Music Magazines

fRoots (www.frootsmag.com) Monthly magazine, a good source for reviews and articles that look beneath the surface of the music scene.

Songlines (www.songlines.co.uk) Quarterly, with a large reviews sections and a good variety of features.

Music Shops

The following Western stores stock West African music:

Blue Moon (☎ 03-9415 1157; fax 9415 1220; 54 Johnston St, Fitzroy, Victoria 3065) Try this address in Australia.

Stern's (☎ 020-7387 5550; fax 7388 2756; 74 Warren St, London W1P 5PA, UK) The best place in Britain for African music.

Stern's (☎ 212-964 5455; fax 964 5955; 71 Warren St, New York, NY 10007, USA) The best place in the USA for African music.

Environment

THE LAND

The Gambia and Senegal lie within the Sahel, the semidesert or savannah region that forms a broad band across Africa between the Sahara desert to the north and the forested countries of the south. The landscape is largely flat, the only peaks looking out over the land in Senegal's far southeastern corner.

The Gambia

The shape and position of Gambia epitomise the absurdity of the national boundaries carved by the European colonial powers at the end of the 20th century. About 300km long, but averaging only 35km wide, The Gambia, at only 11,300 sq km, is Africa's smallest country and is entirely surrounded by Senegal, with the small exception of an 80km coastline. This makes it half the size of Wales.

The country's territory, and its very existence, is determined by the Gambia River, which flows into the Atlantic Ocean, dividing Gambia's coastline into northern and southern sections. Banjul, the capital, is on the southern side of the mouth of the Gambia River. West of Banjul, on the Atlantic coast, are the holiday resorts of Bakau, Fajara, Kotu and Kololi. These constantly expanding tourist towns range in character from the more traditionally Gambian to generic sun-and-sea fare, and together form the centre of Gambia's tourist industry. Nearby is the town of Serekunda – a hub of commercial activity. Further up the river are many more villages, but the only towns of any size are Farafenni, Georgetown and Basse Santa Su.

Gambia has no hills or mountains or any other major topographical features. In fact, the country is so flat that the Gambia River drops less than 10m in around 450km between the far eastern border of the country near Fatoto and the mouth of the river at Banjul. The majority of travellers head directly to the 80km coastline in the west, where most of the tourist industry is concentrated. Upcountry, national parks such as the Baobolong Wetland Reserve and Kiang West are major attractions.

Senegal

Senegal is Africa's westernmost country. The continent's western tip, Pointe des Almadies, lies just north of Dakar. The country comprises an area of just under 200,000 sq km, which compares in size to England and Scotland combined.

Senegal is largely flat, with a natural vegetation of dry savannah woodland. The country's western border, some 600km in length, is marked

---

CANNONBALL RUN

The boundaries of Gambia largely follow the course of the Gambia River. From about 50km upstream, every meander of the river is echoed by a precise twist or turn in the borders, which run parallel to the river, less than 20km to the north and south. Local legend tells that the border was established by a British gunship sailing up the river and firing cannonballs as far as possible onto each bank. The points where the balls fell were then joined up to become the border. While this may not be strictly true, Gambia was initially established as a protectorate, and in the 19th century protection could be most easily administered by gunship.

HARMATTAN HAZE

The harmattan is a dry wind that blows from the north, usually from December to February. During this period the skies of most West African countries are grey from Sahara sand carried by the wind, and even when the wind stops blowing, skies remain hazy until the first rains fall. The effects are more noticeable away from the coast, and generally travel isn't too badly affected. Photographers can expect hazy results, while people with contact lenses should be prepared for problems.

---

by the shore of the Atlantic Ocean. About halfway down the coast, the large Cap Vert peninsula juts out west into the ocean and at the tip of its triangle lies Dakar, one of the largest cities in West Africa.

To the north of the Cap Vert peninsula, the coast faces northwest and is known as the Grande Côte (Great Coast), stretching unbroken almost to Senegal's border with Mauritania. South of the peninsula, the Petite Côte (Small Coast) faces southwest, an orientation that makes weather conditions more agreeable and the beaches safer, which is why it has become Senegal's prime tourist spot.

Senegal has four major rivers, which all flow east to west from the Fouta Jallon highlands in neighbouring Guinea to the Atlantic Ocean. In the north, the Senegal River flows through arid lands, and forms the border with Mauritania. Saint-Louis, the old capital, is at this river's mouth. In southeastern Senegal, the Gambia River flows through Senegal's only mountainous area – the lands surrounding Kedougou – and through the adjacent Parc National de Niokolo-Koba before entering Gambia itself. In the far south is the Casamance River, which irrigates the lush Casamance region. Tropical forests make this fertile zone one of Senegal's most stunning natural areas. Senegal's most beautiful beaches are also here, around Cap Skiring. The Saloum River enters the ocean via a large delta to the south of the Petite Côte. This is a zone of labyrinthine mangrove swamps, salty plains, lagoons, small creeks and river islands.

The website www .chimprehab.com gives excellent background information on the chimpanzee rehabilitation project in River Gambia National Park. You can even adopt your own chimp.

WILDLIFE
Animals

Senegal and Gambia aren't the kinds of countries that tempt tourists with huge safari parks. There is some wildlife to be seen, but it's much more humble than the herds of zebras and giraffes you can observe in other parts of Africa.

However, if the region can't show off with mighty elephants or rhinos, it beats most other destinations when it comes to birds. The Parc National des Oiseaux du Djoudj in Senegal, for instance, is the world's third-largest bird sanctuary, while tiny Gambia attracts large numbers of bird-watchers with hundreds of species and a well-organised system of birding tours. See p71 for more information.

Mammals are more a pleasant sideline of tourism to the region than a reason for travelling here. Popular and easily recognised animal species in forested areas include baboons and three types of monkeys (vervet, patas and red colobus). Abuko Nature Reserve in Gambia is one of the best places to see these monkey species. Chimpanzee populations occur naturally in Senegal's Parc National de Niokolo-Koba and also inhabit the River Gambia National Park, their northernmost outpost in Africa.

In the forested areas you also may see oribi and duikers (small members of the antelope family). In the drier grassland areas antelope species include cobs, roans, waterbucks and derby elands. The best place to see these is in Niokolo-Koba; in most other parts of Senegal and Gambia they are rare or extinct. Other animals found in this type of habitat include warthogs.

Niokolo-Koba is home to a few 'classic' African animals, including imported lions and elephants, but your chances of spotting them are minimal. The Réserve de Bandia (southeast of Dakar) has a whole range of large mammals, including rhinos, buffalos and giraffes, but these are not indigenous to Senegal and have been brought here as a tourist attraction.

Hyenas are relatively numerous in Niokolo-Koba and parts of the Siné-Saloum Delta. In the park, you might lucky enough to spot them, but around the delta you'll probably only hear their distinctive cries at night and see their tracks in the morning.

You'll also be able to see hippos (p138) in the Gambia River, but beware: this peaceful-looking creature can be very aggressive, so don't get too close. Creeks and lagoons are also home to other mammals, including manatees (sea cows), while dolphins can sometimes be seen where large rivers enter the sea. Another river inhabitant in Senegal and Gambia is the crocodile, both the more common Nile species and the very rare dwarf crocodile.

Other reptiles to watch out for (but that shouldn't inspire bush paranoia) are snakes. Gambia and Senegal have their complement of both venomous and harmless snakes (including pythons, cobras and mambas), but most fear humans and you'll be lucky to even see one. One snake worth a special mention is the puff adder, which reaches about 1m in length and, like all reptiles, enjoys sunning itself. Take care when hiking in bush areas, especially in the early morning when this snake is at its most lethargic and most likely to be lazing in open areas. Other reptiles include lizards (such as the large monitor lizard), geckos and tortoises.

Plants

Vegetation in the Sahel region consists primarily of well-dispersed trees and low scrub. Only the southern Casamance region, which receives more rainfall and is traversed by the Casamance River, could be defined as

---

THE VERSATILE BAOBAB

The mighty baobab (Adansonia digitata) is probably Africa's most characteristic tree and an instantly recognisable symbol of the continent. Its thick, sturdy trunk and stunted rootlike branches are featured on countless postcards, logos and even fashion designs. Baobabs grow in most parts of Gambia and Senegal; the flat savannah lands between Dakar and Kaolack in particular are richly covered with baobabs of all sizes and ages.

In many cultures, legend has it that a displeased deity plucked a tree in anger and thrust it back into the ground upside down – hence the thick, sprawling branches. Despite the alleged misdemeanours of its ancestor, the baobab is held in high regard by local people. Its wizened appearance, combined with an ability to survive great droughts and live for many hundreds of years, means the baobab is often deemed to be sacred and is believed to have magical powers. Very old trees develop cavities, and in ancient times these were sometimes used as burial places for griots, the praise singers and oral historians common to many West African societies.

The baobab has many practical uses too. The hollow trunk can hold rainwater, which may have percolated in from cracks higher up in the tree, forming a useful reservoir in times of drought. The tree's large pods (sometimes called 'monkey bread') contain seeds encased in a sherbetlike substance that can be eaten or made into a drink, and the leaves of the baobab can be chopped, boiled and made into a sauce. They can also be dried and ground into a paste to use as a poultice for skin infections and sore joints.

MANGROVES

The mangrove, a tropical evergreen plant, is typically found in the tidal mud flats and inlets of areas such as the Siné-Saloum Delta and the mouth of the Casamance – zones where large rivers spill into the ocean. It plays a vital role for both the local population and wildlife and has a fascinating reproductive system, perfectly adapted to its watery environment. It is one of very few plants that thrive in salt water, and this allows rapid colonisation of areas where no other plant would have a chance.

Two types of mangrove – the white and red mangrove – can be seen and easily identified. The latter is most prominent and is easily recognised by its leathery leaves and dense tangle of stiltlike buttress roots. The seeds germinate in the fruit while still hanging on the tree, growing a long stem called a 'radical'. When the fruit drops, the radical lodges in the mud and becomes a ready-made root for the new seedling.

The white mangrove is less common and found mainly on ground that is only covered by water when there are particularly high tides. It does not have stilt roots; its most recognisable characteristic is its breathing roots, which have circular pores and grow out of the mud from the base of the tree.

Mangrove trees catch silt, vegetation and other floating debris in their root systems, including their own falling leaves. As this mire becomes waterlogged and consolidated, it forms an ideal breeding ground for young mangroves. In this way, the mangrove creates new land. As the stands expand on the seaward side, the older growth on the landward side gradually gets further from the water. Eventually the trees die, leaving behind a rich soil perfect for cultivation.

The mangrove has many other uses. Oysters and shellfish cling to the roots as the tide comes in. When the tide retreats, they are left exposed and are easily gathered by local people.

woodland, while its vast networks of estuaries and mangroves also make a welcome change from the typical Sahel landscape – parts of northern Senegal come very close to being desert.

Trees characteristic of the Sahel include various flat-topped species of acacia, which usually have small thorny leaves. Other notable species include the baobab (see the boxed text, opposite) and the kapok, which is also known as the *Bombax* or silk-cotton tree. The kapok's most recognisable features are its yellowish bark, large podlike fruit and exposed roots, which form a maze around the base of the trunk. In Senegal this tree is called the *fromager* (from *fromage*, the French word for cheese) because the wood of the trunk is so soft and light. It is used in some areas to make the base of pirogues (traditional canoes) after being saturated, straightened and dried to the required shape. (For more information on pirogue building, see the boxed text, p154.)

In Gambia and southern Senegal many villages are built around an ancient kapok tree because the trees are believed to have special significance, harbouring spirits who protect the inhabitants from bad luck. The men of the village use the tree as a *bantaba* (meeting place), and the exposed roots often make comfortable benches.

The palm is another common tree of the region. Species include the doum palm, which grows to about 15m in height and produces an orange fruit called a drupe; the Senegal date palm, which grows to about 8m and produces small red berries; and the coconut palm, which can grow to 35m.

The dry, sparse landscape of the Sahel is interrupted by ribbons of dense gallery forest that occur along watercourses, most notably along the Gambia and Casamance Rivers. Gallery forest is quite similar to rainforest but is fed primarily by ground water, so many of the vines and epiphytes that are characteristic of rainforest are absent.

If you're considering purchasing a *djembe* drum, think twice. The *dimb* tree used to manufacture this much-loved percussion instrument has almost become extinct in the region, due to the staggering increase in European demand for *djembes*.

NATIONAL PARKS

The best time to visit the national parks of Senegal and Gambia is during the dry season (from November to February), when they are accessible and rich in bird life. The national parks and reserves listed in the table are the main ones in Senegal and Gambia, but there are numerous other small forest parks and community reserves. The Abuko Nature Reserve in Gambia is a good place to find out about Gambia's protected areas; in Senegal, try the **Océanium** (☎ 822 2441; www.oceanium.org; Rte de la Corniche-Est) in Dakar.

The Gambia

Six national parks and reserves cover 3.7% of the national land area of The Gambia, and it has several forest parks. The national parks and reserves are administered by the Department of Parks & Wildlife Management and have been set aside to protect representative samples of main habitat types and their associated fauna.

The forest parks have been established to preserve existing forest or provide renewable timber stocks.

All the parks and reserves listed here (except River Gambia National Park) are open to the public and between them provide a good cross-section of the different types of habitat in the country.

Abuko Nature Reserve is Gambia's oldest protected area. It covers 105 hectares in western Gambia near the holiday resorts on the Atlantic coast and is well touristed. The reserve protects a large tract of gallery forest and is particularly noted for its bird and monkey populations.

Baobolong Wetland Reserve is on the northern bank of the Gambia River in central Gambia, opposite Kiang West National Park. Its 22,000 hectares stretch inland almost to the Senegal border. This wetland was designated as Gambia's first Ramsar site (the convention on wetlands of international importance).

On the southern bank of the Gambia River, Kiang West National Park comprises 11,000 hectares dominated by dry woodland vegetation, with areas of mangrove and mud flats.

River Gambia National Park is more commonly known as Baboon Island. This 580-hectare park covers five midriver islands near Georgetown in eastern Gambia and was established mainly as a rehabilitation sanctuary for chimpanzees. Visitors are not permitted to enter the islands, but it's possible to take boat tours around the islands, and with some luck you can spot the chimps from there.

Niumi National Park is in the northwest of Gambia, contiguous with the Parc National du Delta du Saloum in neighbouring Senegal, and incorporates the coastal island of Ginak. It covers 5000 hectares and features dry woodland, sand dunes, mangroves, salt marshes and lagoons.

Other, smaller reserves include the Tanji River Bird Reserve, the Tanbi Wetland Complex.

For comprehensive information on Gambia's nature reserves, or to volunteer at the Abuko Nature Reserve near Banjul, check www .darwingambia.gm.

Senegal

Senegal has six national parks, and several other areas where natural habitats are protected. The most popular parks are Parc National de Niokolo-Koba (the country's largest) in southeast Senegal, with a wide range of habitat types and large numbers of birds and mammals; Parc National du Delta du Saloum, an area of coastal lagoons, mangroves, sandy islands and a section of dry woodland in the coastal area just north of Guinea; Îles de la Madeleine, a couple of small islands near Dakar;

NATIONAL PARKS OF THE GAMBIA & SENEGAL

Park	Features	Activities
Abuko Nature Reserve (p122)	gallery forest: bushbucks, monkeys, crocodiles, turacos	walks, bird-watching trail with hides
Aire Marine Protégée de Bamboung (p67)	mangrove swamps, savannah woodland: sea birds, waders, warthogs, hyenas	walks through mangroves, pirogue tours
Baobolong Wetland Reserve (p131)	wetland, marshes: herons, egrets, sunbirds manatees	pirogue tours
Bijilo Forest Park (p103)	woodland: monkeys, birds	guided walks
Kiang West National Park (p131)	mangrove creeks, woodland: bushbucks, birds of prey, warthogs	pirogue tours, guided walks
Parc National des Îles de la Madeleine (p170)	islet, rock pool: black kites, cormorants, dolphins, turtles	pirogue tours, swimming
Parc National de la Langue de Barbarie (p214)	sandbank, river: sea birds, waders	pirogue & kayak tours, walks, swimming
*Parc National de Niokolo-Koba (p223)	savannah woodland & gallery forest: porcupines, lions, hyenas, monkeys, elephants	guided 4WD tours, hides at waterholes
*Parc National des Oiseaux du Djoudj (p214)	woodland, creeks, mud flats: sea birds, waders, crocodiles	pirogue tours
Réserve de Popenguine (p180)	gallery forest: sea birds, sunbirds, rollers, birds of prey	guided walks through forest & lagoon
River Gambia National Park (p138)	islands, woodland: chimpanzees, hippos, birds	pirogue tours
Tanji River Bird Reserve (p117)	woodland, islands: Caspian terns, turtles	walks, pirogue tours

* denotes a World Heritage–listed site

Parc National des Oiseaux du Djoudj and Parc National de la Langue de Barbarie, near Saint-Louis in northern Senegal, both especially noted for their bird life. The Parc National de Basse-Casamance, an area of forest and mangrove in the Casamance region, has been closed for years because of rebel activity.

Other protected areas include the Ferlo wildlife reserves in the north-central part of Senegal, the Réserve de Bandia near the Petite Côte, the community-run Réserves de Popenguine and de la Somone, and the Aire Marine Protégée de Bamboung.

ENVIRONMENTAL ISSUES

The main environmental issues currently faced by Gambia and Senegal are overfishing, deforestation, desertification and coastal erosion.

Coastal Erosion

Coastal erosion has gone from being an unsightly inconvenience to a very serious problem, particularly in Gambia. Driven by the ever-increasing need for sand as a building material, illegal mining on the coast has soared massively.

The result is rather ironic: the very attraction that made Gambia a tourist destination – the wide sandy beaches of the Atlantic coast – also poses the greatest long-term threat to the businesses upon which so many Gambians survive. In order to accommodate those hordes, developers have dug thousands of tonnes of sand out of the coastline to be used in the construction of roads, hotels, resorts and just about any other of the building sites you see on Kairaba Ave and elsewhere.

The problem reached a climax in the late '90s, when some beaches around Cape St Mary and Kololi literally started disappearing. A US$20 million beach rejuvenation project, using Dutch technology to trap sand near the shore as it was washed in on the tide, brought some temporary relief. Yet sand mining continued apace, and only a few years after the beaches had been 'sprayed back on', they are once again diminishing at a rapid pace.

Senegal faces similar issues. Due to the country's longer coastline, however, the problems have taken longer to show, though they can now no longer be ignored. The areas near Malika and Rufisque in the north of the Cap Vert peninsula are the ones most hit by illegal mining. Endless lines of trucks collect full loads of sand every day. The results are now becoming obvious, with lines of trees and the first tourist venues being claimed by the sea.

In another bitter twist, the sand mined isn't even particularly suitable for building, as its high salt content ruins the metal skeletons of concrete constructions.

Overfishing

Overfishing off the coast of Senegal and Gambia is becoming a major environmental and economic issue. For many centuries local fishermen have harvested the seas off the Atlantic coast but, until the middle of the 20th century, fishing was a sustainable industry. However, since this time, there has been a significant increase in demand (from a growing local population and to supply the export market) and a big increase in the number of boats engaged in fishing.

Fish stocks near the coast have not kept up with the increased catches, so the boats have to go further out to sea to find new fishing areas. As these areas in turn become depleted, the fishermen have to go further still, sometimes spending many days at sea. The extra money spent on petrol eats into the earnings from the catch, reducing profit margins and contributing to increased poverty levels.

Unsustainable fishing methods exacerbate the problem. Netting the fish in the traditional way is seen as too slow, so in some areas the fishermen also use dynamite, simply throwing the explosive into a shoal of fish and collecting the dead ones that float to the surface. Apart from being an abhorrent practice, only a quarter of the fish killed are 'caught' – the rest sink.

Adding to the problem are large factory ships from Europe and East Asia that operate in the fishing grounds off the coast of Gambia and Senegal. These ships use large nets and highly efficient methods, landing catches far beyond the ability of local fishermen. Most of these factory ships have negotiated fishing rights with the governments of Gambia or

Dakar's U-shaped Plage de Hann, once one of the most stunning palm-lined beaches of the world, is now one of Senegal's biggest environmental catastrophes, ever since the industrial area behind the beach expanded massively and factories started dumping their sewage and waste directly into the sea.

AIRE MARINE PROTÉGÉE DE BAMBOUNG

Observing the colourfully painted pirogues of the Lebou, Serer or Diola fishermen going out to sea, it's hard to imagine that these small, pretty boats could be contributing to overfishing. To combat the problem, Senegal has established a number of protected sea zones, but only one of them, the Aire Marine Protégée du Bamboung (AMP; Maritime Reserve of Bamboung), near Toubakouta, has proven effective. There's a simple reason for this. The protected area is primarily managed and supervised by the 14 villages located on the periphery. These local communities are also the primary beneficiaries of the project.

Every day, motorised pirogues patrol the strikingly beautiful area of tidal mangrove swamps, *bolongs* (small creeks) and wood savannah, preventing attempts at illegal fishing, whether by the large hotels nearby, who take tourists on angling excursions, or by local fishermen.

The results have been overwhelming. Fish species such as the *thiof*, Senegal's most emblematic fish, have started recovering from a point of near extinction. The proliferation of this and other fish has given such a boost to the ecosystem that the area has become home to rare animals such as the sea cow, and attracted far greater numbers of birds including the goliath heron, pink-backed pelican, flamingo and pied kingfisher.

But the boat patrols that keep watch over the zone are hugely expensive and cannot be paid for by the villages or grants alone. This is how Bamboung became home to one of Senegal's most fully realised ecolodges, the *campement* Keur Bamboung, at the southern edge of the reserve.

Great care has been taken to prevent tourism from upsetting this new-found natural balance. With solar power, a water-filtering system and small vegetable gardens, the humble camp tries to remain as respectfully integrated in its surroundings as possible. It's a base for walks or pirogue tours through thick mangrove forests, bird-watching excursions or early-morning trips to a drinking pool for wild boars. At night, the cackle of hyenas accompanies the dreams of visitors, and during the day it's the monkeys that have a laugh at the 'intruders'.

Most importantly, all the profits of the *campement* go directly to the villages, which then use the money to finance the ongoing protection of the reserve.

Senegal and provide a vital source of income for the country. However, the frequency with which ships exceed their agreed quotas, or fish without any licence at all, is so great that the UN has entered the argument. But UN or no UN, making a living from the sea for the local fishermen in their traditional boats has become increasingly precarious.

Deforestation

Away from the coast, deforestation is another major environmental issue faced by both Gambia and Senegal. Woodland is partly cleared to match a growing demand for farmland, but trees are also felled to make firewood and charcoal, much of which is used to smoke fish. On a larger scale, wooded areas are cleared to make room for cash crops, notably groundnuts (peanuts). In Gambia, one of the major causes of deforestation is bushfires started by local farmers to promote new growth for livestock, to control pests such as the tsetse fly, and to flush out wild animals for hunting.

Whatever the reason, this clearing of natural woodland leads to soil erosion, and eventually the reduction of cultivable areas. More immediately, the loss of woodland also means reduced water catchment and a decrease in the availability of traditional building materials, foodstuffs and medicines. The destruction of wooded areas also leads to the loss of vital habitats for many of the region's bird and animal species.

In Gambia, this type of situation is being addressed by the Central Division Forestry Project (CDFP), which aims to manage the remaining natural woodland. Rather than fencing off the forest and keeping the locals out, the resident community reaps the benefits from helping to sustain the woodland. For example dead wood can be used for timber, fruits and edible leaves can be collected, and grasses can be harvested for thatch. These products can be used by the local people or sold, but all the activities take place without destroying the forest itself. In this way the local people see the forest as a source of income or employment, both now and in the future, and have a real incentive to protect and manage it in a sustainable way.

The Groundnut Economy

It may be a humble plant, but the groundnut is one of the principal sources of revenue for both Senegal and Gambia.

Groundnuts were introduced into Senegal in the early 19th century and, by 1860, the Senegal River area was lined with large plantations, established under the governance of Louis Faidherbe. By the early 20th century, groundnuts had become a major cash crop in Senegal and Gambia, and this situation remained unchanged through the colonial period and the first decades of independence.

Today in Senegal, the annual groundnut production is around 600,000 tonnes, which represents about 20% of export earnings. Groundnut plantations cover about one million hectares (around 40% of the country's arable land) and the industry employs about a million people. The main groundnut-growing region is east of Dakar, around the towns of Diourbel, Touba and Kaolack (sometimes called the 'groundnut triangle'). These are centres of the powerful Muslim brotherhoods whose marabouts dominate much of Senegal's political and economic life. Gambia is even more reliant on groundnuts, which make up more than 80% of total exports but account for only 27% of foreign earnings.

Océanium is Senegal's fantastically active environmental agency; its website, www.oceanium.org, contains plenty of general information and even allows you to book ecofriendly diving holidays.

Although groundnuts contribute to the economy, the large plantations have a devastating effect on the environment. The crop absorbs nutrients from the soil but replaces very little, and other parts of the crop (such as leaves and stems) are used as animal fodder rather than ploughed back into the ground after harvest. When the crop is harvested, the whole plant – roots and all – is picked, leaving the loose, dry soil exposed and subject to erosion by wind, rain, or goats that come to feed on any discarded remnants. Particularly in areas with marginal rainfall, the soil is soon exhausted or simply blown away and new plantations have to be established in other areas. The abandoned fields are slow to recover and the erosion continues.

Grassland, bush or other natural vegetation has to be cleared as new plantations are established, limiting habitats for wildlife and cattle-grazing land for pastoralists. This has become a major issue in central Senegal, where groundnut farmers expand with government approval ever eastward into grazing reserves supposedly set aside for seminomadic people such as the pastoral Fula.

Maka Diama Dam

The Maka Diama Dam was built across the Senegal River estuary in the late 1980s. The dam's principal purpose was to stop salt water coming upstream (the Senegal River is tidal). This way, more land on the riverbank could be irrigated for crop-growing, as rainfall in the area has always been unreliable and insufficient. While this may have been an admirable reason, crops now grown include groundnuts, which quickly exhaust nutrients in the soil and ultimately lead to erosion. The Maka Diama Dam has created several other problems. Following the decrease in salinity, thick water weeds now cover the surface of many channels and creeks along this stretch of the main river. These cut out light and reduce oxygen

RESPONSIBLE TRAVEL

Tourism relies on rich cultural traditions and natural resources such as healthy wildlife populations and clean rivers, but quite often does little to maintain, sustain or restore them and may even degrade them. Travellers intending to minimise the negative impact of their holiday often choose companies that promote so-called ecotourism.

However, there are no watertight definitions for this term, and some travel companies claim to be practising 'ecotourism' just because they do things outdoors.

In reality activities such as desert driving, hiking, camping, boating, wildlife-watching and sight-seeing trips to remote and fragile areas can be more environmentally or culturally harmful than a conventional holiday in a developed resort.

The growing number of 'ecolodges' is equally unregulated. Some are genuinely ecofriendly, with solar panels, compost toilets and water-filtering systems, while others adopt the term simply because of token acts, such as using biodegradable soap to wash the sheets.

If you would like to support tour companies with a good environmental record, look beyond the glossy brochures and vague 'ecofriendly' claims and ask what they are doing to protect or support the environment.

This includes not only animals and plants but, most importantly, the local community. Tourism can have an extremely damaging effect on traditional social structures and cultural practices; responsible tourism involves respecting existing lifestyles rather than interfering, and supporting initiatives that benefit and involve the local population, rather than channelling precious tourist dollars into a company's overseas account.

The following are some suggestions for responsible travel:

- Support local enterprise where possible by patronising locally owned hotels, restaurants, tour companies and shops.
- Don't buy items made from endangered species.
- Ask permission before photographing people. If they refuse, respect their wishes.
- Dress conservatively and, in particular, cover your legs.
- Stay in community-run hotels, such as the *campements villageois* in the Casamance.
- Stay in environmentally friendly hotels, and ask specific questions about ecofriendly practices before making your choice.
- Don't eat young *thiof* (a type of fish), which frequently features on menus in Senegal – you'll be contributing to the gradual extinction of the species.
- Don't participate in hunting activities organised by big hotels – despite their claims, many of them don't only go shooting in the legal zones.
- Be economical in your use of water and electricity – although you won't necessarily feel the cuts in these resources if you're staying in a tourist zone, the local population will.
- Don't buy a *djembe* (drum), as this will contribute to deforestation.

A number of organisations offer online advice on how to travel responsibly.

The British organisation **Tourism Concern** (www.tourismconcern.org.uk; membership per yr UK£24) runs numerous educational campaigns that you can support (and benefit from) by becoming a member.

To find out more about tour operators that are involved in responsible travel, check the website www.responsibletravel.com.

In Gambia, the Association of Small Scale Enterprises in Tourism (ASSET) has been awarded first prize in poverty reduction from the First Choice Responsible Tourism Awards for its support of small, local businesses. Check the website for businesses you might want to support during your travels.

In Senegal, the **Océanium** (☎ 822 24 41; www.oceanium.org; Rte de la Corniche-Est, Dakar) does amazing work in furthering environmentally friendly tourism, which includes running an ecolodge and responsible-diving courses.

levels, decreasing fish populations – a real disaster for local people who rely on fish for food or small-scale trade, and also for the many thousands of birds who feed in this area. On top of all this, the new freshwater areas now harbour malarial mosquitoes and the snails that carry schistosomes, so local people have to deal with an increase in these diseases, both of which are potentially fatal.

Community-Based Conservation

Africa's national parks, so treasured by tourists and environmentalists, haven't always been so appreciated by the people living in their proximity. And their creation not only upset the hunters and poachers, but in some cases also led to the forced removal of villagers who had inhabited those areas for a long time, disrupting their lifestyles and traditions and endangering their livelihood. But views of conservation are gradually beginning to change, and local populations are increasingly being involved in the planning and management of nature reserves. This change in tack is mainly due to the recognition that parks only flourish in the long term if the local communities participate in the process and can share in the benefits.

Such community-run schemes allow the local populace to continue living in a traditional manner, while also deriving an income from the jobs that wildlife tourism creates.

In Senegal's Parc National de Niokolo-Koba, local men from the surrounding villages have been trained as tourist guides, while in Parc National des Oiseaux du Djoudj various projects instigated by European conservation organisations ensure that park staff cooperates with local people in the surrounding villages. The tiny Réserve de Popenguine in Senegal is mainly maintained by a local women's cooperative that runs a small *campement* on the edge of the reserve and is largely self-financing. And a few kilometres further south, the Réserve de la Somone has been set up and is entirely run by the local community.

In Gambia, some of the most encouraging work has been done by the German-funded Central Division Forestry Project, which has created protected forests, employed villagers as tourist guides, and run ambitious educational programmes about the threat of deforestation. At Kiang West and Niumi National Parks, community groups have been established to give the local people a voice in the park management structure – ideally so they can benefit from the sustainable use of natural resources within the park.

For information on responsible tourism and how to minimise its impact on the environment, see p69.

Birds of The Gambia & Senegal

The Gambia and Senegal are important sites for a diverse range of birds in West Africa. The region is at an ecological crossroads between the rich fauna of equatorial Africa, the arid vastness of the Sahara, the bulk of continental Africa and the Atlantic coast. This important transition zone, especially vital for migratory birds, supports a mosaic of habitats in which some 660 species of birds have been recorded.

The bird diversity of Gambia reaches a concentration that seems out of all proportion to the tiny size of the country itself. Over 560 species have been recorded – just 80 fewer than in Senegal, which is almost 20 times larger – and the country's unique shape makes many good bird-watching sites easily accessible.

The region's proximity to Western Europe further enhances its popularity as a bird-watching holiday destination, and Gambia in particular draws a great number of ornithologists every year.

BIRD HABITATS

Many birds are wide ranging, but the vast majority have feeding, breeding or other biological requirements that restrict them to one habitat or group of habitats. Following is a brief rundown of bird habitats in Gambia and Senegal.

Cities, Towns & Villages

Since a city, town or village will be the first stop for nearly all visitors, it is worth mentioning a few birds that will be seen around towns and villages. The grey-headed sparrow will be the main representative of this cosmopolitan group; the red-billed firefinch frequents grain stores and village compounds; and swifts, swallows and martins nest under the eaves of buildings. Many travellers have their first introduction to the region's birds in a hotel garden. Look out for the gorgeous little cordon-bleu flitting among the vegetation and for starlings and the brilliant yellow-crowned gonolek feeding on lawns; weavers make their presence felt in noisy colonies. The piapiac, a long-tailed member of the crow family, can also be seen around towns.

Ocean Shore & Estuaries

The coastlines of the region are rich habitats for creatures such as crustaceans and molluscs, attracting humans and animals alike to feast on them. Birds likely to be seen feeding in these habitats include waders such as oystercatchers and plovers, and the reef egret, which stalks fish and crabs.

The Gambia and Casamance Rivers both have extensive mangrove-lined estuaries. Historically they have been dismissed as 'swamps', but mangroves are now recognised as an important ecological resource. At low tide the fine mud floor is exposed and makes a rich feeding ground for migratory waders such as curlews, sandpipers, stints, godwits and plovers. Small birds such as sunbirds feed in the mangrove canopy, while larger water birds, such as ibises, herons and spoonbills, roost and nest among the larger stands.

While there have as yet been no cases of avian flu in Gambia or Senegal, it has been much discussed, particularly as the region attracts huge numbers of migratory birds. Regular checks are now being conducted in some areas, most notably the Parc National des Oiseaux du Djoudj.

Waterways

The major river systems of Gambia and Senegal – and the associated fringing forests, grasslands and swamps – support an astonishing variety of birds. Some hunt along the shoreline or probe the soft mud at the water's edge, whereas long-legged species stride into deeper water to seek prey. Some kingfishers dive from overhanging branches into the water, while warblers and flycatchers hunt insects in riverside vegetation. For the beginner and expert birder alike, freshwater habitats provide some of the best viewing opportunities.

Low-lying areas may flood after the rains to create extensive ephemeral swamps, which are often superb for bird-watching. Egrets, herons and other wading birds stalk the shallows; dainty African jacanas walk across floating vegetation on their bizarre long splayed toes; and rails skulk in reed beds.

'There can be rich pickings for bird-watchers from the perplexing cisticolas to huge birds of prey'

Savannah & Woodland

Large swaths of central and southeastern Senegal, plus adjoining parts of Gambia, are characterised by savannah vegetation dominated by a mixture of small trees. There can be rich pickings for bird-watchers in this habitat, from the perplexing cisticolas to huge birds of prey, plus weavers, finches, starlings, rollers and many more.

The southern part of the region once supported extensive woodland, and though most of this has now been cleared or modified by human activities, patches of it still remain in the Parc National de Basse-Casamance and Abuko Nature Reserve. A number of rare birds, such as the African pied hornbill, the grey-headed bristlebill and the little greenbul, are found only in these protected areas.

Arid Areas

The northern part of Senegal is sub-Saharan semidesert, a sparsely vegetated landscape that has been shaped by the low rainfall inherent in this area. This habitat is seldom visited by bird-watchers but supports a few interesting species, including wheatears, desert finches and migratory birds stopping on their way to or from the northern hemisphere.

THE BIRDS

The Senegal parrot is the most famous bird of Senegal. It's known in French as *youyou* and scientifically as *Poicephalus senegalus*.

The following is a group-by-group description of some of the diverse birds visitors will possibly see during a trip to Gambia or Senegal. This is not a comprehensive list – refer to one of the guides (p77) for further information.

Many birds have been left out: for example, a peculiarly African group known as flufftails are so hard to spot as to be virtually invisible.

Barbets & Tinkerbirds

Barbets are closely related to woodpeckers but, rather than drilling into bark after grubs, they have strong, broad bills adapted to eating fruit and a variety of insect prey. Most of the region's seven species are found in Senegal. Barbets are often brightly coloured and perch in conspicuous locations; tinkerbirds are noisy but tiny and are sometimes difficult to see.

Bee-Eaters & Rollers

One of the pleasures of bird-watching in Africa is that beautiful and spectacular species aren't always rare. The various bee-eaters are often brilliant and always watchable; eight members of this colourful family are found in the region. Bee-eaters are commonly seen perched on fences and branches – sometimes in mixed flocks – from which they pursue flying insects, particularly, as their name suggests, bees and wasps. They may congregate in thousands – you won't quickly forget seeing a flock of stunning carmine bee-eaters.

Rollers are closely related to bee-eaters but not as gaudy, decked out usually in blues and mauves; the Abyssinian roller sports two long tail feathers. Most of the five species are common to the region.

Birds of Prey

Hawks, eagles, vultures and falcons number more than 50 species in the region. Their presence is almost ubiquitous and travellers will soon notice a few species, from soaring flocks of scavenging vultures to the stately bateleur eagle watching for prey. Several have specialised prey or habitat requirements. The osprey and striking African fish-eagle, for instance, feed almost exclusively on fish.

Cisticolas

These drab little warblers are common and widespread but sometimes difficult to see and even harder to identify. Many are so similar that they are most easily separated by their call, a characteristic that has led to common names such as singing, croaking, siffling and zitting cisticolas. Many of the region's 12 species are typically found in long grass and riverside vegetation.

Cranes

These graceful birds resemble storks and herons but are typically grassland-dwelling birds. The one species found in the region – the black-crowned crane – is eccentrically adorned with a colourful crest.

Finches, Weavers & Widows

This large group includes many small but colourful examples. They are readily seen in flocks along Gambian and Senegalese roads and wherever long grass is found in the region. All are seed eaters and while some, such as the various sparrows, are not spectacular, others develop showy courtship plumage and tail plumes of extraordinary size. A finch typical of the region is the crimson-coloured red-billed firefinch.

Weavers are usually yellow with varying amounts of black in the plumage and, as seed eaters, can become voracious pests of agriculture. The village weaver often forms big nesting colonies right in the centre of towns. Widows, like sparrows, typically come in shades of brown and grey while not breeding, but males moult to reveal black plumage with red or yellow highlights when courting. The whydah, a type of weaver, develops striking tail plumes during courtship; the enormous tail of the exclamatory paradise whydah can be more than twice the bird's body length.

'The enormous tail of the exclamatory paradise whydah can be more than twice the bird's body length'

Honeyguides

Displaying some of the most remarkable behaviours of any bird, honeyguides seek out the help of mammals such as the ratel (aka honey badger), or even humans, in order to 'guide' them to a beehive. Once it has attracted the attention of a 'helper', a honeyguide flies a short way ahead then waits to see if it is being followed. In this way it leads the helper to the hive (and its next meal), which the obliging creature breaks open and robs, while the honeyguide feeds on wax and bees' larvae and eggs.

Hornbills

Found in forests and woodland, hornbills are medium-sized birds that sport massive, down-curved bills. The African grey and red-billed hornbills are reasonably common; the rarer black Abyssinian ground hornbill is an extraordinary bird that stands about 1m high. It rarely flies, instead moving about in small groups along the ground.

Kingfishers

Colourful and active, the nine species of kingfishers found in Gambia and Senegal can be divided into two groups: those that typically dive into water after fish and tadpoles (and as a consequence are found along waterways), and those less dependent on water because they generally prey on lizards and large insects. Of the former, the giant kingfisher reaches 46cm in size while the jewel-like malachite kingfisher is a mere 14cm. Forest-dwelling kingfishers are generally less colourful than their water-diving relatives. The blue-breasted kingfisher, however, is a boldly patterned example.

Mention should also be made of the hoopoe, a black-and-white bird with a salmon-pink head and neck and a prominent crest.

Nightjars

Few nature films have images of birds in flight as stunning as Jaques Perrin's acclaimed *Winged Migration* (2001). It features a long extract about pelicans and other migratory birds, filmed in Senegal's Parc National des Oiseaux du Djoudj.

These small birds are another nocturnal group but are not related to owls, although their plumage is soft and their flight also silent. Nightjars roost on the ground by day, their subtle colouration making a perfect camouflage among the leaves and twigs. At dusk, they take flight and catch insects. Although they are not uncommon, you may be oblivious to their presence until one takes off near your feet. The identification of several species is difficult and often relies on their call, but when spotted during the day nightjars typically perch on a nearby branch, allowing a closer look. The standard-winged nightjar is the region's most spectacular example; with two feathers unadorned except at the ends, the bird seems to be flying flags to herald its flight.

Owls

These nocturnal birds of prey have soft feathers (which make their flight inaudible) and exceptional hearing, and can turn their heads in a 180-degree arc to locate their prey. Owls have inspired fear and superstition in many cultures, but their elusiveness makes them eagerly sought after by bird-watchers. There are 12 species in the region, ranging from the diminutive scops owl to the massive eagle owl, which measures up to 65cm in length. Their prey varies according to the species, with insects, mice and lizards eaten by the smaller species, and roosting birds and small mammals favoured by others. Pel's fishing owl hunts along rivers and feeds exclusively on fish.

Pigeons & Doves

Familiar to city and country dwellers alike, members of this family have managed to adapt to virtually every habitat. For example, the various turtledoves and the tiny Namaqua dove feed on the ground while the African green pigeon leads a nomadic life following the seasonal fruiting of trees. Two of the dove species, the cosmopolitan rock dove and the laughing dove, are common inhabitants of gardens and human settlements.

Sea Birds

Into this broad category can be grouped a number of bird families that hunt over the open sea. They include the various petrels and shearwaters, which usually live far out to sea and return to land only to breed; beautiful gannets, which plunge into the sea from a great height to feed on fish; and fish-eating cormorants (shags), which also live in brackish and freshwater habitats.

Starlings

Africa is the stronghold of these gregarious and intelligent birds, and there are 11 species found in Gambia and Senegal. Several species of the so-called glossy starlings, including purple, long-tailed and blue-eared varieties, may be seen in fast-flying, noisy flocks around the region. All are magnificent birds in iridescent blues and purples, although they may prove an identification challenge when they occur in mixed flocks. The yellow-billed oxpecker is another member of this family and can be seen clinging to livestock, from which it prises parasitic ticks and insects.

Sunbirds

Sunbirds are small, delicate nectar-feeders with sharp down-curved bills. The males of most species are brilliantly iridescent while the females are more drab. Spectacular species include the pygmy sunbird, whose slender tail plumes are almost double its 9cm length, the copper sunbird and the violet-backed sunbird.

Swifts & Swallows

Although unrelated, these two groups are superficially similar and can be seen chasing flying insects just about anywhere. Both groups have long wings and streamlined bodies adapted to lives in the air; both fly with grace and agility after insects; and both are usually dark in colouration. Swallows, however, differ in one major aspect: they can perch on twigs, fences or even the ground while swifts have weak legs and rarely land except at the nest. In fact, swifts are so adapted to life in the air that some are even known to roost on the wing. There are many examples of the swallow family in Gambia and Senegal; two often seen around towns and villages are the red-rumped and mosque swallows.

'Swifts are so adapted to life in the air that some are even known to roost on the wing'

Turacos

These often beautifully coloured, medium-sized forest birds can be difficult to see because they tend to remain hidden in the canopy, but three species (the violet turaco, green turaco and western grey plantain-eater) are common in the region. The violet turaco is a stunning bird, although you may only be lucky enough to catch a tantalising view when it flies across a clearing, showing its deep-violet wing patches.

Waders

Resident waders include the odd dikkops and the boldly marked lapwings – lanky, nocturnal species with grey spotted wings and weird wailing cries.

LONG-LEGGED WADERS

Virtually any waterway will have its complement of herons, egrets, storks, spoonbills and ibises. All have long legs and necks, and bills adapted to specific feeding strategies: herons and egrets have daggerlike bills for spearing fish and frogs; spoonbills have peculiar, flattened bills that they swish from side to side in the water to gather small creatures; ibises have long bills, curved down to probe in soft earth and seize insects; and storks have large, powerful beaks to snap up small animals and fish. Members of this group range from the tiny, secretive bittern and the enormous goliath heron, which stands 1.4m tall, to the ugly marabou stork, which feeds, along with vultures, on carrion. An unusual member of this group is the little hamerkop (aka hammerhead), which makes an enormous nest of twigs and grass.

MIGRATORY WADERS

Every year migrating shore birds leave their breeding grounds in the northern hemisphere and fly to their wintering grounds south of the Sahara. Generally nondescript in their winter plumage, these migratory 'waders' provide an identification challenge for the keen bird-watcher. They're usually found near waterways, feeding along the shore on small creatures or probing intertidal mud for worms. The migrants include the long-distance champions, sandpipers and plovers.

Waterfowl

As their collective name suggests, this large group is found almost exclusively around waterways, and includes the familiar ducks and geese. Waterfowl are strong flyers and can move vast distances in response to rainfall. The increased availability of food after the rains means they may be more easily seen at this time. In particular, the large, black-and-white spur-winged goose is often abundant at such times. Despite the significance of water as a habitat in Senegal and Gambia, there are comparatively few species of ducks and geese in the region.

WHERE TO LOOK

You will encounter birds virtually everywhere in your travels, although weather and temperature can affect bird activity. Both Gambia and Senegal have a number of reserves set up for the protection of wildlife and habitat, and these are good places to concentrate your bird-watching efforts, although some nonprotected areas can also be rewarding. Following is a brief rundown of popular sites; for more details see the relevant destinations in this book.

In Gambia, Abuko Nature Reserve is closest to Banjul and hosts a surprising diversity within its 105 hectares. Many forest species are easier to see here than in other parts of the country and conveniently located observation hides have been set up. Tanji River Bird Reserve, on the coast, protects a patchwork of habitat on the fly way for migrating birds. More than 300 species have been recorded in the park's 612 hectares. Kiang West National Park is one of the country's largest protected areas and a good spot to see a variety of wildlife, including birds. The adjacent Baobolong Wetland Reserve is also very rewarding. Other recommended areas include Niumi National Park, an extension of the Parc National du Delta du Saloum in neighbouring Senegal, and Bijilo Forest Park, which is easy to reach from the Atlantic coast resorts.

Senegal has six national parks, as well as several other areas set aside as reserves to protect wildlife. Near the mouth of the Senegal River in the north of the country are the Parc National de la Langue de Barbarie and Parc National des Oiseaux du Djoudj – both superb sites famous for flocks of pelicans and flamingos, and Djoudj is a Unesco World Heritage site where some 400 bird species have been recorded. In the southeast, the magnificent Parc National de Niokolo-Koba protects more than 9000 sq km of savannah and associated habitats; about 350 bird species have been recorded and this is also the last stronghold of Senegal's large mammal populations. Near Dakar, the Îles de la Madeleine are an excellent spot for spotting sea birds, while the small reserves of Popenguine and La Somone

For some of the best bird sightings in Gambia, you don't even have to leave your hotel. The Senegambia Hotel in Kotu, the Footsteps Eco Lodge in Gunjur and the Marakissa River Camp in Marakissa are only three lodgings where large varieties of species are regularly spotted.

are interesting to visit. Absolutely worth exploring are the beautiful Siné-Saloum Delta, an accessible area of coastal lagoons, mangroves, sandy islands and dry woodland, and the delta of the Casamance River, which boasts the Sanctuaire Ornithologique de la Pointe de Kalissaye and the highly rated Sanctuaire Ornithologique de Kassel. Both deltas are easily reached from Gambia.

BIRD-WATCHING TIPS

A pair of binoculars will reveal subtleties of form and plumage not usually detected by the naked eye. Be warned – once you've seen the shimmering iridescence of a glossy starling or the brash hues of a bee-eater through binoculars you may get hooked! Binoculars will also considerably aid identification and help you nut out the subtle differences between species. They are also useful for spotting shy mammals in areas such as the Parc National de Niokolo-Koba.

Basic binoculars can be purchased quite cheaply from duty-free outlets. If you like to keep baggage weight down, there are some very light and compact models available that will still help you get much more from your trip. If you get really serious about bird-watching you may want to invest in better-quality optics; expensive brands such as Leica, Zeiss and Swarovski should last a lifetime and offer unrivalled quality. You might also consider purchasing a spotting scope, which can give you stunning views with a magnification usually at least twice that of binoculars. The drawback is their size and the fact that they must be mounted on a tripod to obtain the best results. On the other hand, some models can be attached to a camera and double as a telephoto lens.

To help you get the most out of bird-watching, bear the following in mind:

'Once you've seen the brash hues of a bee-eater through binoculars you may get hooked!'

- Try to get an early start because most birds are generally active during the cooler hours of the day. This is particularly so in arid regions and during hot weather.
- Many species are quite approachable and will allow observation and photography if you approach slowly and avoid sudden movements or loud noises.
- If you're on foot, try to dress in drab clothing so as not to stand out. Birds are not usually too concerned about people in a vehicle or boat and stunning views can often be obtained from the roadside. Cruises on rivers and through mangroves are rewarding and great fun.
- Water birds and waders respond to tidal movements. As tides go out, more food is available and larger flocks are attracted but the birds are spread out; as the tide comes in the birds may be 'pushed' closer to your observation position.
- Do not disturb birds unnecessarily and never handle eggs or young birds in a nest. Adults will readily desert a nest that has been visited, leaving their young to perish.
- Remember that weather and wind can adversely affect viewing conditions and you should not expect to see everything at your first attempt.

RESOURCES
Books

Gambia's popularity as a bird-watching destination has inspired a number of illustrated books and other publications. *A Field Guide to the Birds of The Gambia & Senegal* by leading ornithologists Clive Barlow and Tim Wacher, with illustrations by award-winning artist Tony Disley, is undeniably the best. It lists over 660 species (illustrating 570), with colour plates, detailed descriptions and in-depth background information. This 400-page hardback is no featherweight, though, and costs UK£28 in Britain (US$42 in the US), but it's as essential as a pair of binoculars for any serious bird-watcher. It is also available in Gambia.

More portable is *Birds of The Gambia* by M Gore (UK£22) – an annotated checklist with extra information on habitat, distribution and vegetation, illustrated with photographs; it can be hard to find, though.

Another useful guide is *A Birdwatchers' Guide to The Gambia* by Rod Ward, a finely researched book concentrating on birding sites and likely sightings, rather than detailed species descriptions; it includes 28 maps.

A Field Guide to the Birds of West Africa by W Serle and GJ Morel is part of the long-running Collins field-guide series, though with a broader ambit than is usual for this series.

For more detailed information – plus excellent illustrations – on all African birds, refer to the six-volume *The Birds of Africa* by EK Urban, CH Fry and S Keith. The newest option is *Birds of Western Africa* by Nik Borrow and Ron Demey, a UK£55, 784-page monster that was released in 2002.

Websites

The Internet is a rich resource of information on birds, with databases of birds and their geographic distribution, tour booking sites, trip reports and forums.

African Bird Club (www.africanbirdclub.org) Set up by a charity aimed at the conservation of bird habitats, this site has features on both Gambia and Senegal and regular bulletins and updates.

Birds of the Gambia (www.birdsofthegambia.com) Home page of ornithologist Clive Barlow, with a virtual birding tour; you can also book trips to Gambia.

Gambia Birding (www.gambiabirding.org) This is an excellent site for bird-watchers, with reports on what birds are found where, how to find a guide, and links to birding tours.

Birding Guides

Gambia has a well-developed network of professional birding guides, as well as tour operators that specialise in bird-watching excursions. It's often recommended that you go with a good, local guide – if they know the region well, they'll be able to help you see many more species than you would on your own. Choose your guide carefully and get recommendations in the country if you can. It's best to do this in one of the nature reserves, in particular the **Abuko Nature Reserve** (☎ 7782633; www.darwingambia.gm; admission D31; ◷ 8am-7pm). Less formally, the bridge over Kotu Stream, near the Novotel in the Atlantic coast resort of Kotu, is a good bird-watching site and a traditional place to meet other birders and local guides looking for work. Unfortunately, there is no equivalent setup in Senegal, and visiting bird-watchers are pretty much on their own. Following is a brief list of recommended places offering bird tours and guides.

Bird Safari Camp (☎ 676108; www.bsc.gm/guides.htm; Georgetown) This camp has good birding facilities on site, and an informative website that can direct you to a good guide before you start your trip.

Habitat (Solomon Jallow ☎ 9907694; habitatafrica@hotmail.com) This established network of Gambian guides organises itineraries, transport and accommodation.

Hidden Gambia (in UK ☎ 01527 576239; www.hiddengambia.com) This UK-based group organises river trips, with stays at ecofriendly places equipped for birding.

Wally Faal (☎ 3372103; www.geocities.com/birdinggambia) Based in Gambia's Atlantic coast resorts, this local birding guide runs tours that have been highly recommended by travellers over the years.

To look up the names of birds, with translations in several European languages, check www.bsc-eoc.org/avibase /avibase.jsp, a seemingly unlimited resource.

Food & Drink

By West African standards Gambia and Senegal form a veritable culinary paradise. You could quite easily spend a couple of weeks here testing the myriad flavours of fish, meat and vegetable dishes. Two words summarise the basics of cooking in the region: rice and sauce. Along the coast, fish tends to be the main ingredient, while meat is more common in the inland (for those who can afford it). And those with a taste for delicacies should head directly for Senegal's Petite Côte, where you can suck freshly shucked oysters for breakfast.

STAPLES & SPECIALITIES

Breakfast local-style is a steaming cup of milky instant coffee, accompanied by French bread and butter. If you're from a part of the world where breakfast is a big deal or good coffee is essential to staying alive, Dakar in particular offers plenty choice: just locate your nearest patisserie and you're well on your way to a *café au lait* (coffee with milk) and croissants. Lunch and dinner usually consist of generous rice dishes, and if you're invited to anyone's home you're expected to dig in.

Any discussion of cooked food in the region has to start with the queen of all dishes – the *thiéboudienne* (spelt in myriad different ways, and pronounced chey-bou-jen), in Gambia called *benechin*. *Thiéboudienne* means fish and rice but is so much more than that. A platter of this delicious meal is quite a sight – carefully arranged chunks of fish, often stuffed with a parsley-garlic paste, carrots, cassava and other vegetables, served on a bed of red rice, which owes its colour to the tomato sauce it's cooked in. The festive version of this national dish is *thiébouyape* (or *riz yollof*), where fish is replaced by meat.

Another favourite is *yassa poulet*, grilled chicken marinated in a thick onion-and-lemon sauce. It features on the menu of every Senegalese restaurant, and after a two-week holiday you'll probably have tasted it often enough to know the subtle differences involved in spicing a *yassa*. Occasionally chicken is replaced by fish or meat, in which case it's called *yassa poisson* (fish) or *yassa bœuf* (beef), but it's just not the same. *Yassa* on its own is understood to mean the original chicken variety.

Rice is the staple food of The Gambia and Senegal. If you really want to thank people for their hospitality, such as inviting you for a meal, purchase a sack of rice at the end of your stay – your kindness won't be forgotten quickly.

TRAVEL YOUR TASTEBUDS

You've been in the region for a while? A simple *thiéboudienne* must by now be far too normal for you. Put your tastebuds to the test with a plate of *soupoukandia* – a slippery stew of okra and vegetables – which is definitely not for the fainthearted. But if the taste gets too much, you can always drown it in homemade chilli sauce, an obligatory addition to every Senegalese meal. If you're ever invited to someone's home, ask the women in charge of the cooking to show you how to make the sorrel sauce *bissap* (not to be confused with the sweet juice of the same name), which is usually offered with a plate of *thiéboudienne*. This humble accompaniment tastes sweet and sour, spicy and fresh at the same time, and once you've learnt the secret of its preparation your home cooking will never taste the same again.

If dairy products are your thing, head for the cooler shelves in your nearest Banjul or Dakar supermarket. They bend with small pots of *chakri* (a sugary millet mix covered with rich, sweet yogurt), and small pots of *lait caillé* (sweetened sour milk), which is eaten on its own or with cereal. For really fresh flavour, visit the Fula regions, where locals prepare the creamiest milk products of all.

The *thiof* is Senegal's best-loved fish, almost something of a national emblem. It's so appreciated that Senegalese women refer to a good-looking (or tasty?) young man or lover as their *thiof* (or super-*thiof*, but only if they're being served really top quality…).

In either country, if you're in the mood for something rich, ask for some *mafé* or *domodah* – you'll be served a platter of rice covered with a thick, smooth groundnut sauce with fried meat and vegetables.

At the house of a Fula or Tukulor family, chances are you'll be served a steaming plate of steamed millet couscous (it's darker than couscous made with semolina), either prepared with a vegetable sauce *(haako)* or meat sauce. Couscous served cold with sour or fresh milk *(lacciri e kosan)* is the delicious speciality of the Fula. The milk is served in a separate bowl or calabash and then poured over the couscous before eating. Show your appreciation for this dish and you'll be welcomed with open arms.

Lunch and dinner in Gambia and Senegal usually consist of a main course – though one heavy enough to quench any desire for dessert.

DRINKS
Nonalcoholic Drinks

Gambia and Senegal have a rich array of locally produced juices that are sold in many restaurants and along the beaches of the Gambian coast. Steer clear of the ones sold in plastic bags on the street, as you don't know what conditions they've been prepared under. The most famous drink, *bissap*, is made from hibiscus, sugar and water and is instantly recognisable by its deep purple colour. Ginger beer (*gingembre* in local French) is common, as is *bouyi*, a thick, sweet drink made from the fruits of the baobab tree. Despite the fantastic range of local stuff, the most widely consumed soft drink is Coca-Cola, on sale in even the tiniest, remotest boutique in the bush.

In the hot-drinks department, instant coffee (usually just called Nescafé) rules the game, though real coffee is available at better restaurants in both countries. Worth trying is the Senegalese *café touba*, a spicy brew served in small cups at roadside stalls. For teas, you can either get the tea-bag variety (Lipton is the going name, even if it's another brand), or capture the sweet flavour of home-brewed *kinkiliba*, a herbal tea that is supposed to have a whole host of healthy effects, from boosting energy to clearing skin conditions. And for a real caffeine punch, try a glass

---

TEA TIME

You see them everywhere in Senegal, from midafternoon to midnight – groups of boys and men, sometimes joined by women, grouped around a tiny chipped enamel kettle, a steaming stove and a tray holding a few tiny glasses. They're brewing *ataaya*, West Africa's classic pick-me-up. This is a punchy, bittersweet brew made from fistfuls of green tea leaves and a generous amount of sugar. While its high caffeine content does help you to stay awake in the suffocating midday heat, brewing *ataaya* is really about whiling away a hot afternoon people-watching, about meeting old friends and making new ones, about gossip, stories, jokes and football matches.

Brewing *ataaya* is a social ritual that follows a precise set of tiny, immutable laws that are repeated precisely all across the Sahel region. The main rule: making tea shall never be rushed. The leaves are left to infuse with a little water and plenty of sugar for hours. The tea-maker in charge has to watch the kettle and take it off the heat when the lid starts rattling; the first infusion is usually ready after an hour or so. The tea-maker blends the concoction by pouring it into the glasses from an impressive height to create the perfect froth, then back into the kettle and finally back into the glasses, which are now heated and covered in sweet froth.

The first infusion is a pungent wake-up call, usually offered to the men who dare. The second one is strong, sugary perfection; the third is 'sweet as love' (as the locals would have it). You down your hot tea as fast as your throat permits; the tea-maker will be waiting to collect the glass so it can be refilled and passed to the next in line.

COLLECTING PALM WINE

As you travel along the back roads of Gambia and southern Senegal, you'll almost certainly see men perched precariously on oil-palm trees, collecting the plant's precious sap. Palm wine is a much-loved drink and, once you've grown used to the yeasty flavour, you'll probably agree with the locals.

Watching the collectors climb the trees is an impressive sight. They use a simple loop of handmade rope (called a *kandab* in Diola) that fits like a large belt around the man and the tree, holding him close to the trunk. Just below the point where the palm fronds sprout from the tree, the collector punches a hole through the soft bark until he reaches the sap. The liquid drips slowly through a funnel (traditionally made from leaves, although these days it's usually a piece of plastic) into a container (once a natural gourd, today more likely to be a plastic bottle). At the end of the day, the collector comes back to pick up the bottle, filled with sweet, thick, white sap. At this stage, the alcohol content is still minimal – some say it's nonexistent, others say it's the strength of beer. But leave the palm wine to ferment overnight or a few days and you'll get a pretty strong brew. It's mainly a man's thing, but especially in non-Muslim areas women drink it, too.

---

of *ataaya* (see opposite), served with the free offer of an afternoon's socialising.

Although tap water is supposed to be safe to drink in some areas (the capital cities in particular), it's strongly advisable to rely on mineral water. This also means avoiding ice cubes in drinks – one of the most frequent sources of stomach aches. Definitely steer clear of the tap in Senegal's Petite Côte and Siné-Saloum areas and along Gambia's Atlantic coast. These regions are renowned for problems with the drinking water, ranging from pollution to a high salt content that destroys teeth at a frighteningly fast rate.

Alcoholic Drinks

Though Gambia and Senegal are Muslim regions, beer is widely available, and consumed in bars and restaurants. The main Senegalese brands are the watery Gazelle and the more upmarket Flag. In Gambia, Julbrew is the local brew. Buying a good wine can be something of an expensive mission, even in Senegal, despite all its French influence. As for liqueurs, you'll have plenty of choice in the cities and can always get a whisky or gin behind the stained curtains of a village drinking hole. Drinking is strictly a bar activity, and very few people drink at home. Open displays of drunkenness are very much frowned upon in both countries. Remember, you're in a predominantly Muslim region, and though many Muslims do drink, they tend to do it in a discreet fashion – drinking yourself to a stupor is not a way to gain 'cool' points in this part of the world. Palm wine (see above) is a popular home-brew, particularly in Gambia and Casamance, and the sweet-sour liquid is worth a try.

Legend has it that the island of Banjul, now the site of Gambia's capital, was purchased by the British from indigenous rulers for two bottles of brandy.

CELEBRATIONS

Celebrations here, as elsewhere in the world, put the focus firmly on food. Weddings, baptisms and other family celebrations are always on the large side in this region. They are occasions to get the whole extended family together as well as an opportunity to eat really well. At a medium-sized wedding, the eating budget can easily reach US$1000, and this in countries where basic foodstuffs aren't all that expensive. The meals served are more refined versions of the usual staples – with the addition of extra meat, a more expensive sauce or any other way to make a difference.

During naming ceremonies in Senegal, *lakh,* a delicious millet porridge served with sweet yogurt, is typically served in large bowls – taste it and you'll understand why people don't miss these parties.

Small fried doughnuts, usually given to guests in small plastic bags, are also obligatory at naming ceremonies and weddings.

For most celebrations, some animal has to give up its life – a sheep in most cases or a cow if the family is really big or immensely wealthy. At Tabaski (see p46), sheep are slaughtered in the homes of all Muslim families. Several days before the event, rams as big as cows line all major roads. On the day of Tabaski, only their droppings on the pavement and suspicious clouds of smoke created by multiple wood fires tell of their former presence.

WHERE TO EAT & DRINK

For an exhaustive report on Senegalese cuisine, complete with recipes and links to Dakar's restaurants, go to www.au-senegal.com (English version), click on 'Noon and Evening' and then on 'Cooking'.

Dakar and the urban zones along Gambia's Atlantic coast are blessed with an excellent restaurant scene. Here you'll find refined local and international cuisine, beach restaurants with sunbeds and terraced places with spectacular views, though these plush venues charge for the spoils.

If you're on a budget, hunt out the tiny local eateries, called *chop shops* in Gambia and *gargottes* in Senegal. Many are nameless but can usually be identified by the coloured plastic strips hanging in their doorways. Most of these places have only one dish available at any given time, so just ask what's on offer rather than asking for the menu. They are rarely open all day and only serve food during lunch and dinner – when the pots are empty at night, the place simply shuts or serves beers only. Choose your *chop shop* carefully – some have rather dubious standards of hygiene.

Also on the tiny side are the Senegalese *tangana* (literally meaning 'hot stuff'), where you get your *café touba* and perhaps a sandwich with sauce. A *dibiterie* in Senegal or *afra* in Gambia is a grilled-meat stall (open from evening until early morning); it's the place people head to before a night out on the town or when returning home after dancing the night away. Senegal has some fantastic patisseries where you can indulge in cakes and croissants; they're also a good postnightclub alternative to *dibiteries* for those who only leave parties at breakfast time.

Quick Eats

For food on the go, the trusted hamburger will be a good travel companion, though the more popular alternative is the Lebanese *shwarma,* a kebab-style sandwich made from thin, grilled slices of lamb or chicken wrapped in thin bread. They are sold in small eateries throughout the

---

CULTURAL KOLA NUTS

Any West African market has a stall trading kola nuts – white, pink and purple varieties, about half the size of a golf ball, sold with soil still clinging to them.

The nuts are chewed for their mildly narcotic effects, but their cultural significance goes far beyond their caffeine-type stimulation.

They are often presented as gifts, particularly in situations that demand the highest respect. If family elders ask for the hand of someone's daughter in marriage, they traditionally present their in-laws-to-be with kola nuts.

By extension, the term 'kola' is used to refer to a symbolic sum of money that changes hands at weddings, and is applied to small financial gifts bestowed on someone who has rendered a service.

LE MENU

In Senegal's smarter restaurants, the *menu du jour* (often shortened to *le menu*) is the meal of the day – usually comprising a starter, a main course and a dessert – at a set price. If you want to see the menu (ie the list of dishes available), ask for *la carte* instead. This may include the *plat du jour* (the dish of the day), usually at a special price too. It is often a good idea to go for *le menu* or *plat du jour* – any other choice may take much longer to prepare.

---

two countries. Sandwiches tend to be intimidating affairs, with fries, meat, mayonnaise and a few lettuce leaves all squeezed into a stick of French bread.

Selling food on the street is a way for many local women to add to the household income, and you'll see stalls all along busy market streets and near bus and taxi stops. Typically selling *brochettes* (skewered meat or fish), grilled fish, fried plantain – even plates of rice and sauce – they get busy over lunchtime and even more so in the evenings. Leave any nightclub and you'll see a street stall tempting you with something hot and grilled.

If you want to consume your street food sitting down, try an informal coffee stall, where traders, drivers and other working folk stop for milky coffee or *café touba* and bread and butter in the mornings or at lunch.

These roadside places charge only a handful of dalasi or CFA francs and, while eating there can save money, it's also the quickest way of catching a stomach bug. Hygiene in many of these ultrainformal places isn't exactly a primary concern. The interior of a place can tell you a lot – ramshackle doesn't necessarily mean bad quality, but food leftovers that haven't been cleaned up, dirty tablecloths and, well, stray cockroaches definitely do.

There's no end to the commercial ventures of Senegal's superstar musician Youssou N'Dour. In 2004 he coauthored the cookery book *La Cuisine de Ma Mère*, containing recipes for some of Senegal's most popular dishes.

VEGETARIANS & VEGANS

For vegetarians, this region can be a challenge.

If you eat fish, you'll be fine, but prepare for hard times if you follow a strict vegetarian diet. Vegetarian food is hard to find in restaurants and there's little understanding as to why someone who can afford meat won't eat it – vegetables are for the poor. This means that often when you order a dish without meat, you'll still notice a suspicious chicken or fish flavour, just no 'bits'.

The easiest way to get your message across is to say you have an allergy or that your beliefs don't allow you to touch meat. Still, prepare for a rather limited variety of food choices during your stay.

HABITS & CUSTOMS

If you get invited to share a meal with a local family or group of friends, there are a few customs to observe. You'll probably sit or squat with your hosts on the floor in a circle around the food, which will be served in one or two large bowls – usually one with rice, and the other with a sauce of palm oil, peanuts, vegetables, fish or meat. It is considered polite to take off your shoes, so do this if your hosts do.

The food is eaten with either the hand or a spoon. If you do use your hand, make sure it's the right one – the left is strictly reserved for personal hygiene.

As an honoured guest you might be passed chunks of meat or other choice morsels by the head of the household. It's usually polite to finish eating while there's still food in the bowl to show you have had enough.

TOP FIVE RESTAURANTS

■ Butcher's Shop (p108; Fajara, Gambia) Has the best steak and local fruit juices in the region.

■ Just 4 U (p161; Dakar, Senegal) Spectacular live music and a great ambience every night.

■ La Fourchette (p160; Dakar, Senegal) Imaginative, global cuisine in ice-cool surroundings.

■ La Linguère (p211; Saint-Louis, Senegal) A little run-down but still serving the best *yassa*.

■ Mama's Restaurant (p109; Fajara, Gambia) A bustling local place with scrumptious evening buffets.

The shocked comments of 'You haven't eaten anything, dig in' are more an acceptance of your finishing, rather than an invitation to eat more The same goes for invitations to eat whenever you pass someone about to take a meal – it's polite to invite, but you're not always expected to take it up.

EAT YOUR WORDS

For English speakers, dining in Gambia is no problem. However, a few words and phrases in French will come in handy in Senegal.

For tips on pronunciation, see p305.

Useful Phrases

Do you know a good restaurant?
ko·nay·say·voo un bon re·sto·ran — *Connaissez-vous un bon restaurant?*

What time does this restaurant open/close?
a kel·er oo·vrer/fairm ler res·to·ron — *À quelle heure ouvre/ferme le restaurant?*

I've just eaten.
zher vyen zhoost der mon·zhay — *Je viens juste de manger.*

Can I have the menu please?
es·ker zher per a·vwa la kart — *Est-ce que je peux avoir la carte?*

Do you have a menu in English?
es·ker voo·za vay ewn kart on·non·glay — *Est-ce que vous avez une carte en anglais?*

How much is the meal of the day?
kom·byun koot ler pla dew zhoor — *Combien coute le plat du jour?*

I'm a vegetarian.
zher swee vay·zhay·ta·ryun/ryen — *Je suis végétarien/végétarienne.*

I don't eat meat.
zher ner monzh pa de vyond — *Je ne mange pas de viande.*

I'm allergic to (meat/seafood).
zher swee·za·lair·zheek — *Je suis allergique.*
(a la vyond/o frwee der mair) — *(à la viande/aux fruits de mer)*

Can I have this dish without meat?
es·ker zher per a·vwa ser pla son vyond — *Est-ce que je peux avoir ce plat sans viande?*

Do you have any Senegalese dishes?
es·ker voo·za·vay day say·nay·ga·lay — *Est-ce que vous avez des plats sénégalais?*

What's your speciality?
kel ay vo·trer spay·sya·lee·tay — *Quelle est votre spécialité?*

Is this dish very spicy?
es·ker ser pla e·tray ay·pee·say — *Est-ce que ce plat est très épicé?*

Do you have any dishes for children?
es·ker voo·za·vay day pla poor lay·zon·fon — *Est-ce que vous avez des plats pour les enfants?*

A juice without ice cubes, please.
un zhew son gla·son seel voo play — *Un jus sans glaçons, s'il vous plaît.*

Thank you, I'm full.
mair·see zhay a·say mon·zhay   *Merci, j'ai assez mangé.*

Excuse me, I ordered quite some time ago.
ek·skew·zay·mwa zhay ko·mon·day ler   *Excusez-moi, j'ai commandé il*
day eel ya long·tom   *y a assez de temps.*

Can I have the bill please?
la·dee·syon seel voo play   *L'addition, s'il vous plaît?*

Food Glossary

DAIRY

le beurre	*ler ber*	butter
le fromage	*ler fro·mazh*	cheese
le lait	*ler lay*	milk
le lait caillé	*ler lay kay·yay*	sour milk
le yaourt	*ler ya·oort*	yogurt

FISH & SEAFOOD

le calmar	*ler kal·mar*	squid
les crevettes	*lay krer·vet*	prawns
les fruits de mer	*lay frwee der mair*	seafood
la langouste	*ler long·goost*	lobster
le poisson	*ler pwa·son*	fish
le poisson fumé	*ler pwa·son few·may*	smoked fish

FRUIT

l'ananas	*la·na·nas*	pineapple
la banane	*la ba·nan*	banana
le fruit	*ler frwee*	fruit
la mangue	*la mon·ger*	mango
la noix de coco	*la nwa de ko·ko*	coconut
la papaye	*la pa·pa·yer*	papaya

VEGETABLES, NUTS & GRAINS

fufu	*foo·foo*	mashed casssava
les arachides	*layz a·ra·sheed*	groundnuts/peanuts
les légumes	*lay lay·gewm*	vegetables
les pommes de terre	*lay pom der tair*	potatoes
le riz (thieb in Wolof)	*ler ree*	rice

EATERIES

Here are some useful words to know when you're hungry. Terms marked 'G' or 'S' are used only in Gambia or Senegal respectively.

afra – grilled-meat stall (G), or grilled meat
boulangerie – a bakery that only sells bread (usually French bread)
chop – meal, usually local-style (G)
chop shop – basic local-style eating house or restaurant (G)
dibiterie – grilled-meat stall (S)
patisserie – a bakery selling bread, croissants and cakes
salon de thé – tea shop (S)
snack – a place where you can get light meals and sandwiches; it does not refer to the food itself (S)
tangana – a roadside café serving hot drinks and snacks
terminus – a popular place to eat and mingle after a night out, usually a *dibiterie* or a *patisserie*

OTHER FOOD

les frîtes	*lay freet*	fries
le pain	*ler pun*	bread (usually French bread)
le piment	*ler pee·mon*	small red pepper
le sel	*ler sel*	salt
le sucre	*ler sew·krer*	sugar

DRINKS

bissap	*bis·sap*	a purple-coloured drink made of water, sugar and hibiscus leaves
bouyi	*boo·yee*	sweet, thick juice made from the fruits of the baobab tree
(un) café au lait	*(un) ka·fay o lay*	(a) coffee with milk/cream
(un) café touba	*(un) ka·fay too·ba*	(a) spiced, black coffee
corossol	*ko·ro·sol*	thick, white juice, made from the fruits of the soursop tree
jus de pomme	*zhew der pom*	apple juice
jus d'orange	*zhew do·ronzh*	orange juice
kinkiliba	*kin·ki·lee·ba*	local herbal tea
l'eau minérale	*lo·mee·nay·ral*	mineral water
(un) petit café	*(un) pe·tee ka·fay*	(an) espresso
pression	*pray·syon*	draught beer
(un) thé	*(un) tay*	(a) tea (usually black)
vin du palme	*vun der pal·mer*	palm wine

The Gambia

Snapshot The Gambia

Take a shared taxi along the coastal road from Bakau to Kartong. Keep your eyes on the beachfront and your ears open for the keen conversations of your fellow passengers. Outside you'll notice a string of new multistar palaces, restaurants and houses extending Gambia's coastal resort zone further south. In the car, a verbal commentary on their construction will run like a subtitle to the holiday movie you are watching.

Tourism is big business in The Gambia, and everyone, from the biggest hotel owner to the souvenir-selling hustler, wants their share in this, the country's largest industry. The debate about the woes and wonders of tourism is eagerly pursued. It brings more hard currency into the country – great. It threatens to transform tranquil fishing villages into busy holiday parks – not so great. It gives youngsters a chance to find work, yet might also turn them into beach-roaming 'bumsters'.

Upcountry, away from the beehive activity of the coast, conversations are more likely to revolve around feelings of 'benign neglect' rather than excitement about the latest hotel opening. According to the latest government plans, tourism is going to remain a beach-bound business that only makes a few sideward glances upriver towards sleepy Jangjang-bureh and Basse.

And yet it's inland, in the slightly more remote regions, that Gambia's most beautiful national parks lie, as well as a steadily growing number of community-managed forest parks. These forest parks are areas of protected woodland that are looked after by a small number of dedicated people, keen to promote their impressive range of wildlife and protect those fragile areas from deforestation – one of the major environmental problems Gambia faces.

Try to get any in-depth information on these issues, or on the troubles of tourist enterprises – even on things like music festivals and other cultural

FAST FACTS

Population: 1.6 million

Population under 15: 45%

Size: 11,300 sq km

Waterways: 1300 sq km

GDP per capita: US$1900

Inflation rate: 8.8%

Economic ranking: 188 out of 231 countries

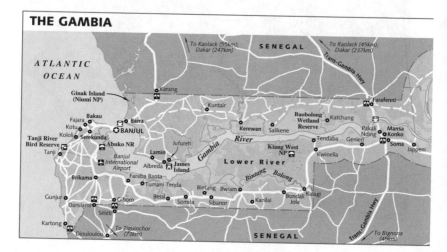

THE GAMBIA

events – and you might find that such curiosity doesn't necessarily lead to answers, but more often to feelings of suspicion from those you speak to.

Gambia is a country that has lived with restrictions to civil liberties for a long time, and it's a country where conversations are conducted with care – you just never know who might be listening. And if talks are somewhat hushed, so is the media.

Gambia's press is something of a journalistic equivalent of the 'Smiling Coast' – it cushions critical frowns carefully between column inches of confident celebration. For 'real news', for a deeper sense of national concerns, you usually have to read between the lines, to learn to listen to what isn't said out loud.

Gambia has never exactly been a haven for freedom of speech or press, but in recent years things have taken a turn for the worse.

They reached a tragic climax when in December 2004, the country's most prominent journalist, Deyda Hydara, was shot by unnamed assassins while driving home in his car. It later emerged that the distinguished reporter had been under surveillance by secret-service agents at the time of the shooting, and while this should have prompted the government to give an explanation – or at least launch an investigation – the answer from the head of state was increased pressure on, and barely veiled threats to, any potential voices of dissent.

When we visited Gambia in 2006, the country was preparing for elections. Few people had any doubt that current president Yahya Jammeh will once again emerge victorious, with most believing the elections to be little more than a token sign of democracy in an authoritarian state.

The government's already-firm grip on the country is getting even tighter, and it remains to be seen which direction Africa's tiniest nation will take.

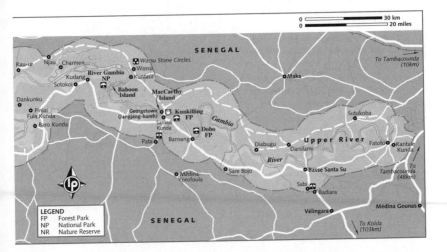

Banjul

It's hard to imagine a more unlikely, more consistently ignored capital city than the sleepy seaport of Banjul. People aren't flocking here, no new buildings are rising to the skies and the old ones are gradually crumbling to dust.

Just 30 minutes from the thriving tourist zones of the Atlantic coast, Banjul sits on its island like a sulking little sister who's stopped vying for attention. But despite the shadow of abandon that haunts its sand-blown streets, Banjul is truly worth a visit. Lively Albert Market, at the heart of the city, is one of Gambia's best places to snare a souvenir bargain and soak up the atmosphere of eager buying, selling and bartering that makes the narrow alleyways and ramshackle stalls hum with excitement. Down the road from the market, Banjul's hectic harbour is another vibrant slice of inner-city Africa. This is where Gambia's main ferry – a rusty old metal tub – chugs back and forth between the north and south banks of the river, heaving huge trucks, traders bearing wares, hustlers and travellers across the mouth of the Gambia River. The constant comings and goings and the bustle that accompanies the urban ritual are worth taking in, especially from one of the makeshift roadside cafés.

Banjul's 'old town', a mile of fading colonial structures, is imbued with a sense of history that the plush seaside resorts are lacking, and the National Museum, a charming institution with dusty exhibits, reinforces this atmosphere of a precious, though slightly neglected, past.

HIGHLIGHTS

- Soak up history and gritty reality wandering through the backstreets of Banjul's **old town** (p94)

- Find everything from spices to souvenirs in the colourful, chaotic **Albert Market** (p96)

- Check out what's changed in the city with a look at the dusty photos in the **National Museum** (p94)

- Enjoy the views across the capital, the ocean and the Gambia River from the massive construction that is **Arch 22** (p94)

- POPULATION: 50,000

HISTORY

Founded in 1816 by Captain Alexander Grant, Banjul was initially named Bathurst, after Henry Bathurst, the secretary of the British Colonial Office. Like many other colonial settlements, including Saint-Louis in Senegal, the town was strategically placed on an island (Banjul Island). However, while most of these seaports were built to facilitate the slave trade, Banjul was founded as an operational base from which to prevent the traffic of humans, after the British Abolition Act of 1807 prohibited the trading of slaves (at least on paper).

The town's regular street pattern was also laid down during this time and grew over the years from the area of today's State House and the old town, to the area it covers today. This is where you can still find examples of 19th-century architecture, the so-called Krio- or Aku-style houses, reminiscent of the adaptations of early Victorian architecture found in Freetown, Sierra Leone.

When Gambia achieved independence in 1965, Bathurst was granted city status, and became the capital of the young nation. It wasn't renamed Banjul (the Mandinka word for 'bamboo' and the island's original name) until 1973.

With the growth of Gambia's coastal towns into major tourist areas, Banjul experienced a strong decline, reflected in a shrinking population and the move of major businesses towards the coast. Today it's mainly an administrative centre, while a capital-worthy lifestyle is found in the resort zones.

ORIENTATION

Located on an island, Banjul is one of those cities that doesn't really have space to expand. Not that the town is attempting to grow – in fact, the capital continues to lose many of its offices, restaurants and shops to the flourishing coastal area. And so the city remains small enough to walk around without too much trouble. The centre is July 22 Sq, an unkempt public park from which several main streets run south, including Russell St, which leads past the bustling Albert Market into Liberation St. West of the October 17 Roundabout is the old part of Banjul – a maze of narrow streets and ramshackle houses rarely visited by tourists.

July 22 Dr runs northwest from July 22 Sq, becoming the main road out of Banjul. On the edge of the city it goes under the vast structure of Arch 22 and turns into a dual carriageway that after about 3km west crosses Oyster Creek on Denton Bridge to reach the mainland proper. Remember: only the president is allowed to drive under Arch 22 – everyone else must go around it.

Another 2km further west, the road splits: the right fork goes to Bakau, Fajara and the other Atlantic coast resorts; straight on it leads to Serekunda, the airport, and everywhere else along the southern bank of the Gambia River.

Maps

We didn't come across any maps whatsover while there, and no-one seemed to know of any that were available.

STREET NAME CHANGES

The town's streets, first named after the English heroes of the Battle of Waterloo, were given new designations in the late 1990s. They now carry the names of Gambia's heroes of independence. However, most people (including taxi drivers) are still more familiar with the old names, so you'll usually get a more reliable answer if you ask for directions using the old street names. We've included a list of some of the streets and their old names, but if you're still stuck, look for the addresses painted on the front of shops and businesses.

Old name	New name
Bund Rd	Kankujeri Rd
Clarkson St	Rene Blain St
Cotton St	Cherno Adamah Bah St
Dobson St	Ma Cumba Jallow St
Grant St	Rev William Cole St
Hagan St	Daniel Goddard St
Hill St	Imam Lamin Bah St
Hope St	Jallow Jallow St
Independence Dr	July 22 Dr
MacCarthy Sq	July 22 Sq
Marina Pde	Muammar al Gadhafi Ave
Orange St	Tafsir Ebou Samba St
Picton St	Davidson Carrol St
Wellington St	Liberation St

BANJUL

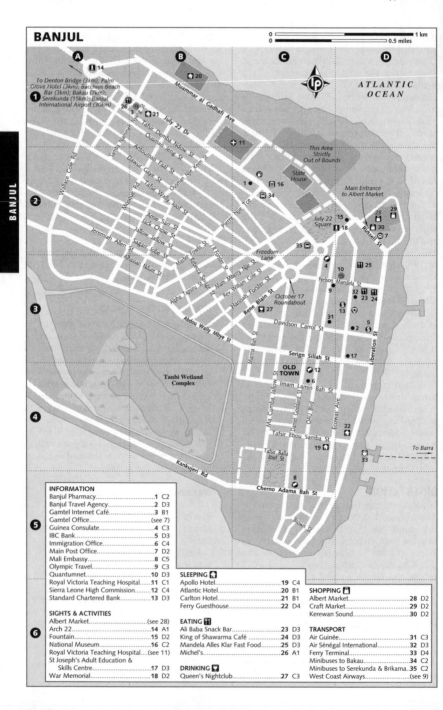

INFORMATION

Internet Access

Gamtel Internet Café (July 22 Dr; per hr D30; ☉ 8am-midnight)

Quantumnet (Nelson Mandela St; per hr D30; ☉ 9am-10pm)

Medical Services

Banjul Pharmacy (☎ 4227470; ☉ 9am-8.30pm) Across the road from the hospital.

Royal Victoria Teaching Hospital (☎ 4228223; July 22 Dr) Though renovated in 1993, its quality still lags behind that of the private establishment on the Atlantic coast, which is better for treating minor illnesses and injuries and doing malaria tests (see p99). The RVTH has an Accidents & Emergencies (A&E) department.

Money

Banks in Banjul city are open from 8am to 1.30pm Monday to Thursday, and from 8am to 11am Friday. These banks change travellers cheques and have ATMs that accept Visa cards:

IBC Bank (☎ 4428145; Liberation St)

Standard Chartered Bank (☎ 4222081; Ecowas Ave)

Post

Main post office (Russell St; ☉ 8am-4pm Mon-Sat) Near Albert Market. You can buy postcards, paper or envelopes from the hawkers outside.

Telephone

Gamtel Office (Russell St; ☉ 8am-11.30pm) Next door to the post office.

Travel Agencies

Most of the main travel agencies have decamped to Fajara, Kotu or Kololi (see p102). Among the remaining ones, these seem to be the most efficient:

Banjul Travel Agency (☎ 4228813; bta@qanet.gm; Ecowas Ave)

Olympic Travel (☎ 4223370; Nelson Mandela St)

DANGERS & ANNOYANCES

Violent crime is rare in Banjul, but there are plenty of pickpockets. Their favourite hunting ground is the Barra ferry, but you should also be vigilant around the ferry terminal and Albert Market.

Banjul turns its lights off after 8pm, and most streets in the centre drown in darkness, making the place feel quite unsafe. However, it's not armed bandits that represent nocturnal danger, but the

---

SUSPICIOUS SOCIETY

Be aware that just because you're excited about being in Gambia, the authorities may not be. Our experience was that there was a climate of distrust in the country – perhaps linked to the imminent electoral campaign, or perhaps a more permanent feature of Gambian society. Bear the power of the state in mind: too many questions, in particular about politically sensitive topics, may arouse suspicion, and obviously using maps may not only alert tricksters to your ignorance about the place, but present an excuse to a government official to hassle you with the powerful backing of the state.

---

maze of open sewers that crisscross the streets.

Don't enter the area behind the State House (marked 'Strictly Out of Bounds' on the map), or you risk difficulties with the military and police.

This researcher was asked to leave town by secret-service agents, who didn't like the sight of a map-wielding, question-asking visitor. If you experience similar hassles from the top, remain calm and polite, without giving in to any dubious requests too readily.

SIGHTS & ACTIVITIES

Banjul feels more like a very large village than a national capital, and this sleepy atmosphere has a quaint kind of charm. If you've come to The Gambia to experience Africa, rather than a slice of Europe laid down on a tropical beach, you might enjoy a day here more than at the nearby Atlantic coast resorts. The city's attraction lies not in grand sights but in intimate details – best taken in on a casual stroll around town.

Ferry Terminal

The terminal for the ferry to Barra, with its endless queues of lorries, the industrious hum of cargo being loaded and discharged, passengers boarding and disembarking and the continuous chatter of patiently waiting customers, is worth experiencing. Directly opposite, the warehouses, clothes stalls and grocery wholesalers that line Liberation St resound with animated bartering that mingles with the clamour.

BANJUL

BANJUL IN ONE DAY

Thanks to Banjul's manageable size, you can take in the town's sights in a relaxed one-day visit.

Get your energy levels up with a freshly pressed fruit juice at the **King of Shawarma Café** (p96), then head south for a visit to the inspirational, peaceful **St Joseph's Adult Education & Skills Centre** (opposite).

Change tempo by diving into the feverish bustle of **Albert Market** (below), then stroll past **July 22 Square** (p93), taking in the **War Memorial** and **fountain**. Walk along July 22 Dr and put in a stop at the **National Museum** (right) to enjoy the curious collection of historical artefacts.

Participate in a tour of the **Royal Victoria Teaching Hospital** (right), then head towards the gigantic **Arch 22** (right) to take in the sight of the city from above.

Weave your way back through the rarely visited backstreets of Banjul's pleasant **old town** (below), and finish your day with a meal and a drink at **Michel's** (p96).

Old Town

Head west from the ferry terminal, towards the wide Ma Cumba Jallow St (Dobson St) and beyond, and explore the **old town**, a chaotic assembly of decrepit colonial buildings and Krio-style clapboard houses – steep-roofed structures with wrought-iron balconies and corrugated roofs (see the boxed text, p44). It's no coincidence that they resemble the inner-city architecture of Freetown, Sierra Leone, as many of them still belong to families who came to Banjul from Freetown, some as early as the 1820s.

Albert Market

Since its creation in the mid-19th century, this **market**, an area of frenzied buying, bartering and bargaining, has been Banjul's hub of activity. From shimmering fabrics and false plaits, fresh fruits and dried fish to tourist-tempting souvenirs at the Craft Market, you can find almost anything here and then some.

Give yourself a good couple of hours to wander around Albert Market; long enough to take in the smells, sounds and sights, and get your haggling skills up to scratch. There are several drinks stalls and *chop shops* (basic

eateries) in the market to pacify shopped-out bellies. Albert Market is never a calm spot, but if you want to avoid the keenest hours, come early in the morning or late in the afternoon.

July 22 Square

A recently greened colonial creation, **July 22 Square** (MacCarthy Sq) was once the site of cricket matches but is now mainly used for governmental pomp and public celebrations. Look out for the **War Memorial** and the (now dried-up) **fountain** 'erected by public subscription' to commemorate the coronation of King George VI of Britain in 1937.

National Museum

The **National Museum** (July 22 Dr; admission D25; ☯ 8am-4pm Mon-Thu, to 1pm Fri & Sat) has some dog-eared and dated exhibits (including, rather bizarrely, the dress worn by Miss Gambia in 1984) that are still worth a look. Explanations are generally good, and there's a fascinating, if dusty, display of photos, maps and historical papers.

Arch 22

Designed by the Senegalese architect Pierre Goudiaby, **Arch 22** (July 22 Dr; admission D35; ☯ 9am-11pm) is an enormous gateway built to celebrate the military coup of 22 July 1994 (p33). At 35m high, it's by far the tallest building in The Gambia, and its publicly accessible balcony grants excellent views over the city and coast. There's also a cosy café, a souvenir shop and a small museum that enlightens visitors about the coup d'état.

Royal Victoria Teaching Hospital

Gambia's main health facility, the **Royal Victoria Teaching Hospital** (☎ 4226152; www.rvth .dosh.gm; July 22 Dr) not only offers emergency treatment, but also conducts tours of its complex of late-19th-century and modern buildings. This might indicate how wholly the country is devoted to and dependent upon the tourist dollar, or how ingenious even the health sector has to be in order to maintain public services. A hospital visit might not sound like a seductive holiday idea, but the daily two-hour tours (free, though donations are welcome) are surprisingly interesting. This offers excellent explanations of the hospital's international teaching programmes and research projects into malaria and hepatitis, and a worthwhile, though painful, insight into the dire situation medical services face in The Gambia.

St Joseph's Adult Education & Skills Centre

Tucked away in an ancient Portuguese building, **St Joseph's Adult Education & Skills Centre** (☎ 4228836; stjskills@qanet.com; Ecowas Ave; ꙮ 9am-2pm Mon-Thu, to noon Fri) has provided training to disadvantaged women for the last 20 years. Visitors can take a free tour of sewing, crafts and tie-dye classes, and purchase reasonably priced items such as patchwork products, embroidered purses and cute children's clothes at the on-site boutique.

Pirogue Trips

The quiet, mangrove-lined waterways of Oyster Creek, the main waterway separating Banjul Island from the mainland, and its minor tributaries are brilliant for bird-watching, sport fishing and wonderfully lazy afternoons relaxing in a pirogue to the sound of the waves. Most hotels organise pirogue trips, though you can also book your tour independently at the Sportsfishing Centre (p103) at **Denton Bridge**, which crosses Oyster Creek some 3km west from Banjul city centre.

To reach Denton Bridge by public transport, take any minibus running between Banjul and Bakau or Serekunda and ask the driver to let you off at the bridge. The Sportsfishing Centre is well signposted. It's best to phone first and explain which activity you're interested in, though you can probably also be put in touch with a pirogue or boat owner on the spot.

Tanbi Wetland Complex

If you like bird-watching but don't fancy travelling by pirogue, Kankujeri Rd might be more your scene.

The stretch of mangrove on either side of the road forms part of the Tanbi Wetland Complex, a large wetland area that stretches all the way to Oyster Creek and Lamin. The Banjul part of this wetland is commonly known as 'Bund Road', the former name of Kankujeri Road. It's something of a classic

on the Gambian bird-watching map, due to its accessibility and the large number of birds that can be observed here.

SLEEPING

Not many tourists stay in Banjul city, preferring instead the beach and comforts of the Atlantic coast. However, if you want a more African environment you're more likely to find it here. None of the budget options take credit cards.

Budget & Midrange

Ferry Guesthouse (Ami's Guesthouse; ☎ 4222028; 28 Liberation St; s/d/tr D350/500/610; ꙮ) Above a busy shop and up some gloomy stairs, this guesthouse is surprisingly acceptable. It's not glamorous, but it is your best budget bet, and the balcony is great for watching the busy trading stalls and ferry terminal. Single-room prices double if you want air-con.

Apollo Hotel (☎ 4228184; Tafsir Ebou Samba St; s/d with fan D450/550, with air-con D750/1000; ꙮ) Room prices in this shoddy guesthouse have doubled while standards have slipped towards the grimy bottom end. You want to pay a lot for very little? This is your place.

Carlton Hotel (☎ 228670; fax 4227214; 25 July 22 Dr; s/d D500/550, with air-con D800/850; ꙮ) This is a little more upmarket than the basic guesthouse lot, with luxuries such as running water and indoor toilets. A good-value option.

Top End

Atlantic Hotel (☎ 4228601; www.corinthiahotels.com; Muammar al Gadhafi Ave; s/d D3007/3937; P ꙮ ▯ ꙮ) This vast, plush resort hotel has numerous bars, restaurants and plenty of leisure facilities, including a nightclub, massage centre and a garden created by ornithologist Clive Barlow to please the bird-watchers. Rooms are bright and pleasant, with modern, unobtrusive décor and all the facilities you want to make you entirely comfortable, including minibar and satellite TV.

Palm Grove Hotel (☎ 4201620; www.gambia-palm grovehotel.com; s/d with breakfast D1150/1840; ꙮ ꙮ) About 3km out of Banjul towards Serekunda, this hotel is smaller, more personal and better value than the Atlantic. It has a decent swimming beach and all the usual activities you'd expect from a resort, including wind-surfing, canoeing and tennis.

EATING

The shift from Banjul to the coast has taken with it most of Banjul's decent eateries. Only a couple of the remaining places could reasonably be described as restaurants, most of the rest being fast-food joints. Around Albert Market and the north end of Liberation St are several cheap *chop shops* and streets stalls where plates of rice and sauce start at about D25. Breakfast at the ferry terminal – skewered beef on fresh bread rolls with sweet coffee – is highly recommended.

Ali Baba Snack Bar (☎ 4224055; Nelson Mandela St; ☽ 9am-5pm) More than just a kebab shop, this place is an institution with a deserved reputation for the best *shwarmas* (sliced, grilled meat and salad in pita bread) and falafel sandwiches in the country.

Michel's (☎ 4223108; 29 July 22 Dr; ☽ 8am-11pm) This is about the only restaurant in town that can be called classy. From the breakfast menu through to after-dinner drinks, this place offers excellent choices at decent rates.

Mandela Alles Klar Fast Food (Ecowas Ave; ☽ 10am-10pm) The name is as great as the food is greasy. But sometimes nothing but a grilled burger will do, right?

King of Shawarma Café (☎ 4229799; Nelson Mandela St; ☽ 9am-5pm Mon-Sat) This friendly place serves excellent Lebanese food, both the wrapped-up and sit-down varieties, and what's even better, large glasses of freshly squeezed fruit juice.

DRINKING & ENTERTAINMENT

The best places to drink in style are the bars at the Atlantic Hotel, Palm Grove Hotel and Michel's.

Bacchius Beach Bar (☎ 4227948; ☽ 10am-8pm) Next to the Palm Grove Hotel, this busy little beach bar is a great place to while away a day or an evening, sipping a drink and digging into a platter of grilled fish.

Queen's Nightclub (Rene Blain St; admission from D35; ☽ 9pm-2am) If you want a night out moving to an African beat, this is the only regularly operating option in the capital. This is a pretty raw scene, where women without male company are very likely to feel leering looks lingering on them. It gets busy after midnight.

Golden Palace (☎ 9925087; 10A Nelson Mandela St; ☽ 11am-1am) If you feel like gambling your holiday budget away, try this place. It gets

pretty sleazy at times, as seems to be the nature with these jackpot places.

SHOPPING

In Banjul, the best place to go shopping is Albert Market, which is also a sight in itself. If you enter via the main entrance you'll pass stalls stacked with shimmering fabrics, hair extensions, shoes, household and electrical wares and just about everything else you can imagine. Keep going and you'll reach the myriad colours and flavours of the fruit and vegetable market. Beyond here is the area usually called the Craft Market, with stalls selling tourist-tempting souvenirs (see p271 for information about the sorts of items you're likely to find here).

Near the main entrance, you'll also find **Kerewan Sound** (Russell St), Gambia's best place to buy CDs and cassettes, and one of the very few places that sells recordings by Gambian artists.

GETTING THERE & AWAY

Air

For details of international flights to/from Banjul see p279. To confirm reservations on a flight you've already booked, it's easiest to deal directly with the airline offices.

Air Guinée (☎ 4223296; 72 OAU Blvd)

Air Sénégal International (☎ 4472095; Ecowas Ave)

SN Brussels Airlines (Map pp100-1; ☎ 4496301/2; www.brussels-airlines.com; Badala Park Way, Fajara)

West Coast Airways (☎ 4201954; 7 Nelson Mandela St)

Boat

Ferries (☎ 4228205; Liberation St) run between Banjul and Barra, on the northern bank of the river. Two boats chug slowly back and forth, and though they are supposed to run every one to two hours, officially from 7am until 7pm, delays are frequent. The trip is supposed to take 45 minutes, but can take more than an hour if the tide is strong. Passengers pay D10, while cars cost D150 to D200.

The ferries take vehicles, but car space is limited so you might have to wait for a couple of hours (if it's any consolation, trucks can sometimes be there for days). You buy your ticket before going through to the waiting area and keep it until you get off; it will be checked on the other side. If you're coming from the north side by car, you need to purchase your ticket at the office near the border (just after the junction where the northbank road to Farafenni turns off), about 3km northeast from Barra.

There are open seating areas upstairs from which you get a good view over the river. Dolphins are occasionally spotted on the passage, so keep your camera handy (but safe – this is a pickpocketing hot spot).

If the wait for the ferry is too long, you could also jump onto one of the large pirogues that do the same journey (D50 for a seat on a public pirogue or around D600 if you hire the whole boat). Be warned though: they can get dangerously overloaded. Fares rise sharply after dark (as does the risk) and negotiating passage at this time will be the acid test of your bargaining skills.

Bus

Gambia's once-exceptional bus network, the state-owned Gambia Public Transport Corporation (GPTC), has almost completely vanished in recent years. Most vehicles have been worn out by the disastrous state of the upcountry roads, and the few remaining buses are in poor condition. Nor do they leave with any reliable regularity. You'll save yourself a lot of time and hassle by taking a bush taxi upcountry, and it doesn't cost much more either.

Bush Taxi

Yellow taxis and minibuses to Brikama and upcountry towns, as well as to places in southern Senegal, all go from the Serekunda garage near the market (see p113). For details about bush taxis to Senegal, see p287.

GETTING AROUND
To/From the Airport

Arriving at the airport, you'll find green tourist taxis waiting – the yellow ones aren't allowed a place in the queue. A tourist taxi from Banjul International Airport to Banjul, Serekunda, Kairaba Ave or the Atlantic coast resorts (Bakau, Fajara, Kotu and Kololi) costs around D300 to D400.

There is a cheaper way, though. Fend off the tourist-taxi drivers (no mean feat) and walk

straight ahead out of the terminal. Beyond the initial row of cars is a secondary car park and you'll probably find a few yellow taxis parked here. These drivers are not allowed into or even near the terminal, but they are allowed to take passengers if you seek them out. With a bit of bargaining you should be able to hitch a ride for D150 to D200.

Fares are the same whether you come from or head towards the airport.

Minibus & Shared Taxi

Minibuses run between Banjul, Serekunda and the other coastal towns, while shared taxis run between Serekunda, Fajara and Bakau. Both shared taxis and minibuses serve the route between Serekunda, Kotu and Kololi.

From Banjul, minibuses to Bakau (D6) leave from the stand diagonally opposite the Shell station on July 22 Dr. If you're going to Fajara, take a minibus to Bakau and either walk from there (30 minutes) or take an onward shared taxi to Serekunda and hop off in Fajara. Minibuses to Serekunda (D6) and Brikama (D15) leave from a roadside corner one block northwest of July 22 Sq. Add a further D2 for baggage. For more details see p114.

Private Taxi

A short ride across Banjul city centre (known as a 'town trip') in a private taxi will cost about D50, though you'll need to negotiate to get this. From Banjul it costs about D150 to D200 to go to Bakau, Serekunda, Fajara, Kotu or Kololi. Check the price with the driver before getting in.

Hiring a taxi for the day costs around D1000 to D1500, although this only applies for tours around Banjul and the coastal resorts. For a tour out of the city most drivers charge by the destination – the worse the roads they'll have to drive on, the steeper the price.

Private taxis are plentiful during the day but difficult to find at night in Banjul. The best place to find one is at the Atlantic Hotel.

BANJUL

Atlantic Coast Resorts & Serekunda

The 10km stretch of coast from Bakau and Fajara to Kotu and Kololi is the beating heart of Gambia's tourist industry. It's where almost everyone heads straight from Banjul airport, whether they're travelling by local cab or air-conditioned tour bus. The bustling area has all the makings of a thriving holiday zone: rows of hotels and guesthouses, a wide selection of restaurants, a vibrant nightlife and packed beaches.

Compared with the rest of Gambia the area is blindingly busy, though measured against sun-and-sea resorts worldwide it passes as low-key. Fields, lagoons and palm groves stand between the concrete, and most buildings are no more than a couple of storeys high.

Bakau has retained the strongest local character of the four places. The 'old town', a lively concentration of clapboard, corrugated iron and colourful market stalls, begins only a few steps away from the gleaming hotel fronts. Following the coast westwards you reach relaxed Fajara, home to some of the zone's best restaurants, and the place to breathe in deeply before hitting the tourist miles of Kotu and Kololi (the latter is known to most Gambians as 'Senegambia').

Once a small village, Serekunda has become the largest town in Gambia, absorbing the overspill from Banjul and attracting people from the rural areas who come in search of work. It's a hot and heaving market town, bursting at the seams with traffic and people. It's also the local transport hub. From here, taxis take you to the rest of the country, or along Kairaba Ave, a busy pipeline framed by supermarkets and restaurants that stretches back to Fajara.

HIGHLIGHTS

- Get a close-up view of the sacred crocdiles of **Kachikaly Crocodile Pool** (p103)
- Gibber with the monkeys or just sit and watch the birds at **Bijilo Forest Park** (p103)
- Track down one of the batik factories in **Serekunda** (p113) for a personalised batik item
- Leave the crowds behind in Bakau's peaceful **Botanic Gardens** (p103) – a perfect spot for bird-watching

★ Botanic Gardens

★ Kachikaly Crocodile Pool

★ Serekunda

★ Bijilo Forest Park

- POPULATION: 350,000

ORIENTATION

The main road in from Gambia's upcountry towns leads past Banjul International Airport and reaches the busy town of Serekunda. After passing through Serekunda this road divides: straight ahead is the dual carriageway leading to Banjul; to the left is Kairaba Ave, which leads to Fajara; Bakau is to the northeast, while Kotu and Kololi are to the southwest.

In Bakau and Fajara the main drag is Atlantic Rd, which runs parallel to the coast, linking Kairaba Ave and Old Cape Rd. Just south of Atlantic Rd, and running parallel to it, is Garba Jahumpa Rd (formerly, and still better known as, New Town Rd). Badala Park Way branches off Kairaba Ave at the Fajara end and leads to the hotel and beach areas of Kotu and Kololi and onto the airport and the south coast. (The busiest mile of the Atlantic resort zone is the part of Kololi leading from Badala Park Way to the Senegambia Hotel. Named after the hotel, it's known locally as the Senegambia strip.) Badala Park Way meets Kairaba Ave at the country's only set of traffic lights and links with Saitmatty Rd to the west, thus avoiding the bottleneck of Westfield Junction. The latter leads into Serekunda and spreads west from here along the town's busy market road.

INFORMATION

Bookshops

Most supermarkets stock magazines and postcards, and informal bookstalls in Serekunda (sometimes simply spread out on the roadside) invite rummaging.

Timbooktoo (☎ 4494345; cnr Kairaba Ave & Garba Jahumpa Rd, Fajara; ⏱ 10am-7pm Mon-Thu, to 1pm & 3-7pm Fri, 10am-8pm Sat) An excellent shop with a good range of fiction and nonfiction, maps and local and international papers.

Cultural Centre

Alliance Franco-Gambienne (☎ 4375418; www .alliancefrance.gm; Kairaba Ave, Serekunda; ⏱ 9.30am-5pm Mon-Fri) At the southern end of Kairaba Ave. It runs language courses (in French and Wolof) as well as regular concerts, films, shows and exhibitions. And it has a good and cheap restaurant at the back, perfect for lunch.

Internet Access

Getting online isn't a problem on this well-organised part of the coast. Many of the large hotels have Internet cafés, or head to

THE KOMBOS

The four Atlantic coast resorts of Bakau, Fajara, Kotu and Kololi, along with Serekunda and other nearby suburbs of Sukuta, Kanifeng, Faji Kunda and Dippa Kunda are sometimes known collectively as the Kombos. This is because the area around Banjul is divided into several local administrative districts called Kombo North, Kombo South, Kombo Central and Kombo St Mary.

Kairaba Ave. The following usually have good connections:

Bonacta Internet Café (Fajara; ⏱ 8am-11pm) Off Kairaba Ave.

Gamtel (☎ 4229999; gen-info@gamtel.gm; Westfield Junction, Serekunda; ⏱ 8am-11pm)

Gamtel Kololi (☎ 4377878; Senegambia Strip; ⏱ 9am-11pm)

Quantumnet (☎ 4494514; Kairaba Ave, Fajara; ⏱ 8.30am-10pm) Next to Timbooktoo bookshop.

Rainbow Café & Business Centre (Mannjai Kunda; ⏱ 9am-8pm)

Medical Services

If you are involved in an accident you may well be taken to the Royal Victoria Teaching Hospital in Banjul (p93).

Malak Chemist (☎ 4376087; Kairaba Ave, Serekunda; ⏱ 9am-midnight Mon-Sat, to 10pm Sun)

Medical Research Council (MRC; ☎ 4495446; Fajara) If you have a potentially serious illness, head for this British-run clinic off Atlantic Rd.

Stop Steps Pharmacy (☎ 4371344; Kairaba Ave, Fajara; ⏱ 9am-10pm Mon-Sat) One of the best-stocked pharmacy chains around, with branches all along the coast.

Westfield Clinic (☎ 4398448; Westfield Junction, Serekunda)

Money

The main banks – Standard Chartered, Trust Bank and IBC – have branches in Bakau, Serekunda and Kololi. Banks open in the morning (usually from 8.30am or 9am to noon or 2pm), as well as in the afternoon (from 4pm to 6pm) and for a few hours on Saturday morning. There are also a few exchange bureaus scattered around the busy tourist miles, but you're unlikely to get a better rate.

Police have seriously cracked down on Gambia's once-flourishing black market,

ATLANTIC COAST RESORTS & SEREKUNDA

INFORMATION
Afri-Swiss Travels.................................**1** F4
Africa Adventure Tours....................**2** F4
Alliance Franco-Gambienne.........**3** G5
Bonacta Internet Café.....................**4** F4
Cotton Club......................................(see 93)
French Embassy.................................**5** H2
Gambia River Experience...............**6** F3
Gamtel Office....................................**7** B6
Gamtel Office....................................**8** C6
Guinea Bissau Embassy...............(see 17)
IBC Bank Serekunda........................**9** G6
Main Post Office..............................**10** G5
Malak Chemist...................................**11** G5
Mauritanian Consulate...................**12** C6
Medical Research Council..............**13** F3
Official Tourist Guides.................(see 47)
Olympic Travel...............................(see 20)
Quantumnet....................................**14** F4
Rainbow Café Business Centre.....**15** E5
Senegalese High Commission........**16** F4
Standard Chartered Bank Bakau....**17** G2
Standard Chartered Bank Serekunda..**18** A5
Stop Steps Pharmacy....................(see 79)
Swedish & Norwegian Consuls.......**19** G3
Timbooktoo Bookshop...................**20** F3
Tropical Tour & Souvenirs...........(see 47)
Trust Bank Bakau..............................**21** G2
Trust Bank Kololi...............................**22** C6
UK High Commission........................**23** E3
US Embassy..**24** F4
Westfield Clinic.................................**25** B6

SIGHTS & ACTIVITIES
African Living Art Centre...............**26** F3
Batafon Arts......................................**27** G5
Bijilo Forest Park Headquarters.....**28** C6
Botanic Gardens...............................**29** G2
Fajara Golf Club.................................**30** E4
Kachikaly Crocodile Pool................**31** H3

SLEEPING
African Heritage Centre.............(see 106)
African Village Hotel.......................**32** G2
Badala Park Hotel.............................**33** D4
Bakau Guesthouse........................(see 106)
Bakau Lodge......................................**34** G2
Bakotu Hotel.....................................**35** E4
Balmoral Appartments....................**36** C6
Bungalow Beach Hotel....................**37** E4
Cape Point Hotel.........................(see 55)
Coconut Residence..........................**38** C6
Douniya Hotel...................................**39** G6
Effu's Villa...**40** G3
Fajara Guesthouse...........................**41** E3
Fajara Hotel.......................................**42** E3
Francisco's Hotel..............................**43** E3

Friendship Hotel...............................**44** G3
Holiday Beach Club Hotel...............**45** C6
Jabo Guest House.............................**46** H2
Kairaba Hotel....................................**47** C6
Kanifeng YMCA................................**48** G4
Kombo Beach Hotel.........................**49** D4
Kotu East Lodge...............................**50** E5
Kunta Kinteh Guesthouse...............**51** D5
Leybato..**52** E3
Mannjai Lodge..................................**53** E5
Ngala Lodge......................................**54** F3
Ocean Bay Hotel & Resort.............**55** H2
Praia Motel.......................................**56** G6
Roc Height's Lodge..........................**57** H2
Romana Hotel...................................**58** G2
Safari Garden Hotel.........................**59** E3
Sarge's Hotel....................................**60** C6
Seaview Gardens Hotel...................**61** D4
Senegambia Hotel........................(see 98)
Sunbeach Hotel & Resort...............**62** H2
Sunset Beach Hotel.........................**63** D4
Teranga Suites..................................**64** D5

EATING
Aisa Marie Cinema...........................**65** F6
Al Basha...**66** C6
Ali Baba's..**67** C6
Amber's Nest....................................**68** C6
Atlantic Bar & Restaurant...............**69** G2
Butcher's Shop.................................**70** C6
Chapman's..**71** G2
Clay Oven..**72** F3
Come Inn...**73** F5
Crystals Ice Cream Parlour &
   Gallery..(see 82)
Dutch Whale..................................(see 82)
Eddie's Bar & Restaurant................**74** E3
Esporta...**75** F3
Flavours..(see 59)
Francisco's Restaurant..................(see 43)
GTS Restaurant.................................**76** C6
Harry's Supermarket........................**77** F4
Italian Connection............................**78** H2
Kairaba Supermarket.......................**79** F5
Kora..**80** C6
La Pailotte.......................................(see 3)
La Rive Gauche..............................(see 49)
Le Palais du Chocolat......................**81** F4
Luigi's Italian Restaurant................**82** D5
Mama's Restaurant..........................**83** E3
Maroun's..**84** A6

Ngala Lodge..................................(see 54)
Ocean Clipper................................(see 55)
Pepper's Tropical Restaurant.....(see 105)
Ritz...**85** E3
Safe Way Afra King..........................**86** F5
Sailor's Beach Bar............................**87** E4
St Mary's Food & Wine....................**88** F4
St Mary's Food & Wine....................**89** H2
Sambou's...**90** G2
Scala Restaurant...........................(see 60)
Solomon's Beach Bar....................(see 92)
Sunshine Bar.....................................**91** H2
Teranga Beach Club.........................**92** C5
Weezo's..(see 26)
Yok...**93** E3
Youth Monument Bar & Restaurant..**94** B6

DRINKING
Aquarius..(see 80)
Chapman's......................................(see 71)
Churchill's.......................................(see 82)
Come Inn...(see 73)
Lana's Bar..**95** F6
Paparazzi...(see 66)
Queen's Head....................................**96** E6
Totties Nightclub..........................(see 105)
Weezo's...(see 93)

Kotu
Point

Kololi
Point

Kololi

Badala Park Way

Kololi Rd

Senegambia Rd

Bijilo Forest
Park

To Gambia Tours (1km);
Baobab Lodge (1km);
Bijilo Beach Hotel (1km);
Tanji (8km); Kartong (38km)

0   200 m
0   0.1 miles

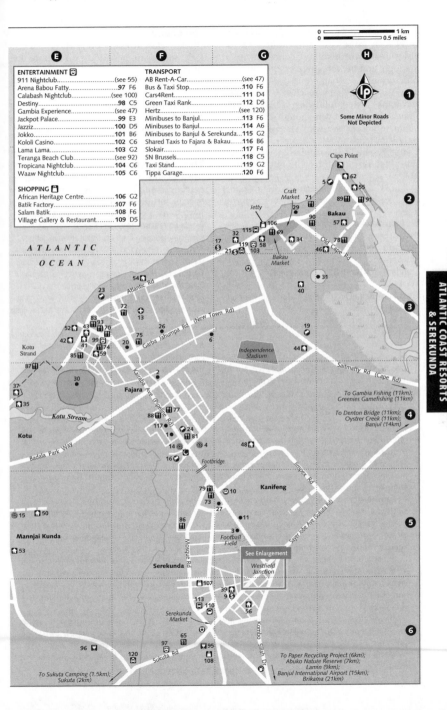

ENTERTAINMENT
911 Nightclub.........................(see 55)
Arena Babou Fatty....................**97** F6
Calabash Nightclub................(see 100)
Destiny....................................**98** C5
Gambia Experience..................(see 47)
Jackpot Palace.........................**99** E3
Jazziz...................................**100** D5
Jokko.....................................**101** B6
Kololi Casino..........................**102** C6
Lama Lama..............................**103** G2
Teranga Beach Club...............(see 92)
Tropicana Nightclub.................**104** C6
Waaw Nightclub......................**105** C6

SHOPPING
African Heritage Centre...........**106** G2
Batik Factory..........................**107** F6
Salam Batik.............................**108** F6
Village Gallery & Restaurant.........**109** D5

TRANSPORT
AB Rent-A-Car.......................(see 47)
Bus & Taxi Stop.....................**110** F6
Cars4Rent.............................**111** D4
Green Taxi Rank.....................**112** D5
Hertz..................................(see 120)
Minibuses to Banjul................**113** F6
Minibuses to Banjul................**114** A6
Minibuses to Banjul & Serekunda...**115** G2
Shared Taxis to Fajara & Bakau...**116** B6
Slokair.................................**117** F4
SN Brussels...........................**118** C5
Taxi Stand............................**119** G2
Tippa Garage.........................**120** F6

Some Minor Roads
Not Depicted

ATLANTIC
OCEAN

Cape Point

Craft
Market

Jetty

Bakau

Bakau
Market

Kotu
Strand

Independence
Stadium

Fajara

Kotu Stream

Kotu

Badala Park Way

Mannjai Kunda

Kanifeng

Footbridge

Serekunda

Football
Field

See Enlargement

Westfield
Junction

Serekunda
Market

To Gambia Fishing (11km);
Greenies Gamefishing (11km)

To Denton Bridge (11km);
Oyster Creek (11km);
Banjul (14km)

To Paper Recycling Project (6km);
Abuko Nature Reserve (7km);
Lamin (9km);
Banjul International Airport (15km);
Brikama (21km)

To Sukuta Camping (1.5km);
Sukuta (2km)

ATLANTIC COAST RESORTS
& SEREKUNDA

and though you can usually find someone to change some cash after hours, it's too risky to be worthwhile. Chances of fraud are high, and the rates aren't better than the official ones.

ATMs have finally reached Gambia and the banks listed following all have withdrawal facilities. Even though they might claim to accept the whole range of cards, only Visa tends to work. Unless things have changed, you'll also find that withdrawal limits are very tight, usually not exceeding D2000.

The Gambia Experience office (right) gives cash advances on MasterCards for a fee.

IBC Bank Serekunda (☎ 4377878; Sukuta Rd) Next to the Shell petrol station.

Standard Chartered Bank Bakau (☎ 4495046; Atlantic Rd)

Standard Chartered Bank Serekunda (☎ 4396102; Kairaba Ave)

Trust Bank Bakau (☎ 4495486; Atlantic Rd) Opposite Standard Chartered.

Trust Bank Kololi (☎ 4465303; Wilmon Company Bldg, Badala Park Way)

Post

The main post office is off Kairaba Ave, about halfway between Fajara and Serekunda.

Telephone

Private telecentres are everywhere, particularly in Serekunda and just off Kairaba Ave in Fajara.

Gamtel (Westfield Junction, Serekunda; ⏰ 8am-11pm)

Tourist Information

Tropical Tour & Souvenirs (☎ 4460536; tropicaltour@gamtel.gm; Kairaba Hotel, Kololi) The best place for information materials, maps, books and insightful advice.

Travel Agencies

Most agents are on Kairaba Ave between Serekunda and Fajara. They tend to represent specific airlines and operators so you might have to try a couple to get the best deal.

Africa Adventure Tours (off Kairaba Ave) Mainly deals with tours, including *Roots* tours with an overnight stay.

Afri-Swiss Travels (☎ 4371762/4; Kairaba Ave) A long-standing operator with good reports. Also does ticketing.

Gambia Experience (www.gambia.co.uk; Senegambia Hotel, Kololi) Gambia's biggest tour operator.

Gambia River Experience (☎ 4494360; www.gambiariver.com; Bakau New Town) Off Kairaba Ave; has excellent river tours.

Gambia Tours (☎ 4462601/2; www.gambiatours.gm) A large, independent operator off the coastal road, near Baobab Lodge.

Hidden Gambia (in UK ☎ 015-2757 6239; www.hiddengambia.com) Great for tours upriver and birding trips.

BUMSTERS & OTGS

Many visitors complain about local 'bumsters' or 'beach boys' who loiter in the resort areas and offer tourists everything from postcards to drugs and sex. As annoying as their presence can be to travellers, the fact is that they exist because of tourism. High unemployment and no welfare system in Gambia mean that many young men see their only hope of making an income in hustling or providing sexual favours to tourists. Bumsters can also earn commissions from tour companies and restaurants.

Bumsters can be very pushy, hard to shake off, and spoil a perfectly good holiday by clinging a little too closely to their 'victims'. Lone women travellers in particular might feel intimidated by their advances. If you don't want their services it's best to be polite but firm in declining their offers. If you get an angry response, just ignore it, and feel safe in the knowledge that violence against tourists is almost unheard of.

In 2001, with bumsters being blamed for huge numbers of visitors deciding not to return, the local Association of Small Scale Enterprises in Tourism (Asset) selected 66 bumsters and, in a six-week training camp, taught them how to deal better with tourists. Hotel managers, restaurateurs and other industry representatives explained how one could go from being an annoying bumster to a more respectable (and more acceptable) guide.

The result is a team of Official Tourist Guides (OTGs). The OTGs wear grey uniforms and can be found in an open shelter outside the Senegambia Hotel at Kololi, or on the beaches. They charge set rates: D100/160 for a half-/full day. Most importantly, while still keen to win your business, they will not walk kilometres along the beach bothering you until you break. So if you choose to hire a guide, choose an OTG.

Olympic Travel (☎ 4497204; Garba Jahumpa Rd) A good place for booking tickets and tours, and for all general inquiries.

Dangers & Annoyances

Petty thefts and muggings are always a possibility but incidents are few. There are a few hot spots: be careful on the path around Fajara golf course between Fajara and Kotu.

There's a good chance you'll be approached in the street by marijuana sellers – note that smoking weed is illegal and punished with heavy fines, and falling in the hands of Gambian police while engaging in illegal activities is really not something you want to do. Be careful when participating in street sound clashes (Jamaican-style parties with competing sound systems). These are also illegal, occasionally subject to police raids, and always places where violence quickly spirals out of control.

One of the major annoyances in this area is the constant hustling of tourists by 'bumsters'. See the boxed text, opposite. Single women should be careful on deserted beaches, especially after dark; several female readers have reported being hassled.

SIGHTS
Kachikaly Crocodile Pool

In the heart of Bakau village, the **Kachikaly Crocodile Pool** (admission D25; ☙ 9am-6pm), is a popular tourist attraction. For locals, it's a sacred site. It's a place of prayer for those with traditional beliefs, as the crocodiles represent the power of fertility. Success rates are apparently high (many children in this area are called Kachikaly) and the 80 fully grown crocodiles and 'countless' smaller ones remain protected and are easily seen. The reptiles are believed to have mystic powers, and legend has it that taking photographs can provoke their wrath and an early death for the picture taker. Most tourists are unperturbed by this, and the crocs seem resigned to basking on the bank, floating in the pool and enduring the camera flashes.

At the entrance to the pool, there's a collection of musical instruments and various other artefacts on display.

Botanic Gardens

Also in Bakau, at the northeastern end of Atlantic Rd, the **Botanic Gardens** (☎ 7774482; adult/child D50/free; ☙ 8am-4pm) are worth a look. They were established in 1924 and are peaceful with plenty of shade and good bird-spotting chances.

Not far away, a road turns north off Atlantic Rd and leads down to the **jetty**, where fishing boats come and go while thousands of fish dry in the sun. Morning and late afternoon are the best times to watch this spectacle.

Bijilo Forest Park

On the coast, just a short walk from Kololi, this small **wildlife reserve** (admission D30; ☙ 8am-6pm) is a beautiful place to visit, either on your own or on a guided walk (4.5km, one to two hours). Like all of Gambia's natural reserves, it has little funding but manages to run educational campaigns about the risks of deforestation. A well-maintained series of trails leads through the lush vegetation, and you'll see monkeys and numerous birds (mainly on the coast side).

The dunes near the beach are covered in grass and low bush, with tall stands of palm just behind. Further back, away from the dunes, the trees are large and dense and covered in creepers. Many trees are labelled, and you can buy a small booklet (D30) that tells you a little about their natural history and traditional uses.

ACTIVITIES
Fishing

The Sportsfishing Centre at Denton Bridge (Map p92) is the place to organise your fishing tours. The following two companies are based there.

Gambia Fishing (☎ 7721228; www.gambiafishing.com; Denton Bridge) This brilliant little business run by Mark and Tracey specialises in lure and anchored-bottom fishing. They're very professional and able to accommodate experienced anglers and those new to the game.

Greenies Gamefishing (☎ 9907073; greenies@gambia fishing.freeserve.co.uk; Denton Bridge) Malcolm 'Greenie' Green specialises in deep-sea fishing.

Golf

Fajara Golf Club (☎ 4495456) is the country's main golf course. Smooth grass is hard to grow here, so the holes are surrounded by well maintained 'browns', not greens! The club also has a pool and courts for tennis, squash and badminton. Temporary membership is available by the day. Inquire about rates.

Swimming

Most beaches in this area are relatively safe for swimming, but currents can sometimes get strong. Care should be taken along the beach in Fajara (near Leybato Hotel), where there's a strong undertow. Always check conditions before plunging in – people do drown every year on the Atlantic coast.

The entire coastline suffers badly from erosion, and the sand strands that lure tourists here are gradually disappearing (see p66). The best sand strands are in Fajara and Kotu.

If the Atlantic doesn't appeal, all the major hotels have swimming pools. If you're not a guest, you might have to pay or buy your swim with a sandwich and a drink.

Other Water Sports

Some of the large hotels – notably Ocean Bay, Atlantic and Combo Beach – offer various water sports to guests. Most of their activities are run by the **Watersports Centre** (Map p92; ☎ 7765765) at Denton Bridge, so go straight there to organise your jet skiing, parasailing, windsurfing or catamaran trip.

AFRICAN LIVING ART CENTRE

So you've seen 1000 wooden carvings, countless masks and a variety of other stuff that's impossible to classify, but have no clue about what it all means. You might like to head to the **African Living Art Centre** (☎ 4495131), where Suelle Nachif runs classes (by appointment only) in the appreciation of African art. Suelle is something of an artist himself and one of his greatest works is this centre at the Fajara end of Garba Jahumpa Rd. The centre is part gallery, part café, part orchid garden, part home and (wait for it ladies) the best full-service hair salon in West Africa. Admittedly, this last function seems hard to credit in Gambia, but before returning to his birthplace in 1995 Suelle spent most of the previous two decades cutting and styling for Vidal Sassoon in London and Elizabeth Arden in New York. Even if you don't want to know more about African art and don't need a cut, the centre is a great place to just relax with a cocktail in the fantastic Asian restaurant Yok (p109) on the top floor.

COURSES

Several of the hotels and guesthouses in this area run courses in traditional dance, singing and drumming. The courses run by the Safari Garden Hotel are recommended. It has African Dance on Tuesdays (per person D50, 6pm to 7pm) and African Drumming on Wednesdays (per person D150, 5.30pm to 6.30pm). Half- or all-day batik courses (D400) can be arranged on request.

Batafon Arts (☎ UK 01273 605791, Gambia 4392517; www.batafonarts.co.uk; Kairaba Ave, Serekunda) offers excellent African percussion and dance tuition. To book an entire musical holiday (from US$390 including half-board and tuition) call the UK number. If it's just a few lessons you're after, drop by and discuss what suits best. Accommodation is available on-site.

ATLANTIC COAST RESORTS & SEREKUNDA FOR CHILDREN

The Atlantic coast attracts plenty of family holidaymakers, and is well equipped for young people. Most of the large resort hotels offer high chairs, cots and even baby-sitting services, and some of the self-contained apartments gear themselves towards family visitors. (This is often the best set-up for people with children, as you have several connected apartment rooms and cooking facilities available.) Nappies and other baby items are available at all the larger supermarkets along Kairaba Ave.

When it comes to children's entertainment you'll need to be creative, unless your offspring is the kind that's perfectly content with two weeks at the hotel's paddling pool and sandpit. The **Kachikaly Crocodile Pool** (p103) is great to visit with children, and monkey-spotting at **Abuko Nature Reserve** (p122) and **Bijilo Forest Park** (p103) usually goes down a storm. Further away, the **Tanji Village Museum** (p118) is surprisingly interesting for children, with lively exhibits and an area where you can watch artisans at work. Near the village museum, you can also take your kids camel riding on the beach (see p117). Or try a good old pirogue tour, either around **Oyster Creek** (p95) or **Kartong** (p119).

TOURS

Organised excursions in the immediate area usually take in Bijilo Forest Park and Kachikaly Crocodile Pool at Bakau, or they go to Banjul city for a visit to Albert Market and the museum. All of these places are easily reached by taxi, public transport or hired bicycle, but if you prefer a tour contact the companies listed in the Transport chapter (p290) or the travel agencies listed earlier this chapter (p102).

Boat tours through the mangroves of Oyster Creek between Banjul and the mainland or as far as Lamin Lodge (p121) are highly recommended. Gambia River Experience (p102) runs excellent excursions, as does the Sportsfishing Centre at Denton Bridge (Map p92). Both operators' tours depart from Denton Bridge.

SLEEPING

You'll find everything from plush resorts to grotty dives on the Atlantic coast. Competition is so intense that if you're here out of the peak season you'll almost always be able to negotiate a better deal, even at the top places.

The list here is not exhaustive, but gives a good cross-section of options, especially for independent travellers. All rooms have bathroom unless otherwise specified.

Budget

BAKAU

Bakau Lodge (☎ /fax 4496103; www.thomasson.org .uk/gambia; d from D650; 🏊) This small place with spotless, two-room bungalows set around a swimming pool comes as a real surprise, off Atlantic Rd and right in the heart of the Bakau 'hood. Excellent value.

Jabo Guest House (☎ 4494906, 7777082; 9 Old Cape Rd; d D500) You wouldn't guess it from the high wall surrounding the Bakau compound, but this down-to-earth place has surprisingly large and clean rooms. The biggest have good self-catering facilities, and the location near Bakau market provides the right mix of relaxed beach life and urban Africa. Great value.

African Heritage Centre (☎ 4496778; Bakau; r D600) Sometimes the best accommodation is found not in hotels but in unexpected places, such as this art gallery-cum-restaurant near the ferry jetty. At the back are a couple of decent, well-furnished rooms.

Effu's Villa (☎ 4494699; d/apt D600/650) Lovely Effu has turned a few rooms in her compound into quite impressive self-contained lodgings. Rooms are spacious, clean, and even have hot water, and the kitchen has

a fridge stacked with drinks (for purchase) and fruits (free breakfast treats). Run by a woman and in a hassle-free zone, this is perfect for lone female travellers. Find your way to Tina's Grill (below the Swedish Consul) and ask for directions; it's five minutes from there.

Romana Hotel (☎ 4495127; aframsromanahotel@ yahoo.co.uk; Atlantic Rd; r D350) Rooms are basic, and some have portraits of African presidents painted on the walls. But if you close the door and sit in the pretty garden space, you'll probably make your peace with this place.

Bakau Guesthouse (☎ 4495059, 9921854; Atlantic Rd; s/d D600/800) Guesthouses don't come stranger than this. On the crumbling walls of this three-storey balconied building, odd artworks fight for space, while most of the structure is under some sort of construction. Rooms are enormous and have great potential, but this is still waiting to be exploited, so furnishings are rather shabby.

FAJARA & KANIFENG

Friendship Hotel (☎ 4495830; ifh@qanet.gm; Saitmatty Rd; s/d D300/400) Next to Independence Stadium, this drab hotel was built at the same time as the stadium and was a gift from China. Someone described it as 'the place that houses anybody', but the shoddiness of the rooms is slightly compensated by the range of sports facilities available on-site, which include tennis, basketball and football grounds.

Kanifeng YMCA (☎ 4392647; www.ymca.gm; B&B D175; 🖳) In the suburb of Kanifeng, this huge building has passable rooms for the budget-bound. Ask for the self-contained ones on the top floor. The Internet facilities are a big plus.

KOTU

Tourism is such big business on the Atlantic coast, and many private households have converted parts of their compound into self-contained apartments. There are too many to mention here, but they're all well signposted. They are worth checking out – many are better maintained than your average budget hotel.

Kunta Kinteh Guesthouse (☎ 4464314; r per person D550) This small, clean guesthouse has a friendly ambience and sits at breathing distance from the tourist hassles. Rooms are adequate and the manager, Mr Camara, is very forthcoming, but if you don't speak Fula his attempts at friendly explanations will be lost on you.

Kotu East Lodge (☎ 44262550; s/d D300/400) Off Kololi Rd, this converted home has attractively large, self-contained rooms. It's a basic, no-frills affair on the fringes of the tourist zone, but fair value for what it offers.

SEREKUNDA

Sukuta Camping (☎ 9917786; www.campingsukuta.de; camping per person D100, per vehicle D14, s/d D235/340, d with bathroom D465) This exceptionally well-organised camping ground in Sukuta (southwest of Serekunda) has long been a favourite with overlanders but now offers comfortable rooms as well. Friendly owners Joe and Claudia are experienced overland travellers themselves, and have thought of everything a desert driver might need, including long-term parking, repair shops, car sales advice and facilities and cheap return flights for those who leave their car here. Guests (and guests only) can also hire cars and 4WDs at bargain rates. The place is on the road towards Gunjur; head towards Brufut by taxi or minibus and follow the signs.

Praia Motel (☎ 4394887; Mame Jout St; r D300; [⚡]) A few minutes' walk off Sayer Jobe Ave, these simple but clean rooms in a very residential part of Serekunda are worth your consideration. Amiable manager Mr Ceesay is full of advice and serves cheap beer too.

Douniya Hotel (☎ 4370741/2; s D300) Just off the north side of Sayer Jobe Ave, this no-frills-at-all place is borderline cheap. The management operates a strict one-person-per-room rule, which is probably supposed to imply some particular decency that the rest of the facilities certainly lack. It's not necessarily a good option for lone women travellers, as the place usually teems with young men.

Midrange

Several of the hotels in this range are small, owner-managed, and more used to dealing with individual travellers than the larger top-end establishments. All rooms have their own bathroom and most hotels accept credit cards.

BAKAU

Cape Point Hotel (☎ 4495005; Atlantic Rd; d D1000; [⚡] [⚡]) At the east end of Atlantic Rd, this

family-run place is set in attractive gardens, and is pleasantly low-key compared to the mighty tourist palaces next door.

Roc Height's Lodge (☎ 4495428; www.rocheightslodge.com; Samba Breku Rd; s/d D1000/1500) Places this nice are a rare treat anywhere in the world. This three-storey villa sits in a quiet garden and has stylish rooms as well as apartments with fully equipped kitchen, and the forthcoming management does everything to make you feel at home.

African Village Hotel (☎ 4495384; Atlantic Rd; s/d from D650/1200; [⚡]) This unassuming hotel fills the gap between the dusty budget places and the slick palaces at the top. It's pretty enough, the more expensive sea-view apartments are particularly nice, and it offers a range of services including bicycle hire.

FAJARA

Leybato (☎ 4497186; www.leybato.abc.gm; d D800-900, with kitchen D1200) Hidden behind a small hill off Atlantic Rd, this calm and cosy guesthouse and its relaxed restaurant overlook the ocean from one of the best locations anywhere on the coast. Rooms vary in quality (the ones with kitchens tend to be better), but you're unlikely to find better beachfront value.

Fajara Guesthouse (☎ 4496122; fax 4494365; r incl breakfast D650-950; [⚡]) This cosy place, five minutes from Safari Garden Hotel, exudes family vibes with its leafy courtyard and welcoming lounge. Rooms are basic but clean, and some are big enough to house couples with children.

Francisco's Hotel (☎ /fax 4495332; Atlantic Rd; s/d D650/850; **P** **⊠**) Francisco's is mainly known for its leafy restaurant – an atmospheric place that has plenty more character than the rather ordinary rooms. They're still decent value and the location is right, too: it's just a short hike up the hill to Fajara's finest beach.

KOTU

Teranga Suites (☎ 4461961; s/d/ste D500/750/1000; **⊠**) This jewel of a guesthouse off Kololi Rd has airy rooms and large self-contained suites with bright, wooden decor and that rarity of really comfortable mattresses. Perfect for families (cots can be arranged).

Bakotu Hotel (☎ 4465555; fax 4465959; s/d D1250/1500; **⊠** **⊠**) Compared with its resort neighbours this hotel, in the strip between Fajara Golf Club and Kotu Stream, is pleasantly understated, and has comfy terrace apartments in a pleasant garden. It's particularly popular with young people and, like the whole of Kotu Beach, can get pretty noisy.

Other midrange options in Kotu:

Badala Park Hotel (☎ 4460400/1; www.badalapark -gambia.nl; s/d D900/1100; **⊠** **⊠**) West of Badala Park Way; rooms aren't as great as the façade suggests, and it can get pretty noisy here once the tourist buses have rolled in.

Mannjai Lodge (☎ 4463414; manlodge@gamtel.gm; s/d/apt from D500/750/1000, all incl breakfast; **⊡** **⊠**) This pretty-in-pink place in the heart of Mannjai Kunda, off Kololi Rd, has large rooms and self-contained apartments grouped around a lively bar and a dodgy pool.

KOLOLI

Balmoral Apartments (☎ 4461079; www.balmoral -apartments.com; s/d D925/1680; **⊠** **⊠**) Opposite the Senegambia mile in Kololi, east of Badala Park Way, these slick self-contained apartments are excellent value.

Holiday Beach Club Hotel (☎ 4460418; www .holidaybeachclubgambia.com; Senegambia Strip; s/d 1500/2000; **⊠** **⊠**) Slightly removed from the busiest hectare of the tourist mile, this place has comfortable bungalows set in a lush tropical garden.

Sarge's Hotel (Tafbel; ☎ 4460510; www.sargeshotel .gm; Senegambia Strip; s/d incl breakfast D1260/1750; **⊠** **⊠**) This well-equipped hotel is something of a classic on the Gambian scene. It sits right in the heart of Kololi, so don't expect much sleep at night.

Baobab Lodge (☎ /fax 4461270; lnbn@qanet.gm; s/d D900/1200; **⊠**) About 2km south of the Senegambia tourist mile in Kololi, this friendly family-style place has good-quality apartments with cooking facilities, TV and fridge – perfect for self-caterers. The beach lies just a few metres across the road.

Bijilo Beach Hotel (☎ 4462701; www.bijilohotel .com; s/d D1800/2200) On the main road between Kololi and Brufut, this is a fairly tranquil place set right near a nice stretch of beach.

Top End

If some of these seem too pricey for your budget, try negotiating. During the low season, many of these places are willing to offer sizable reductions in rates. Most of the following are near the beach, accept credit cards and deal mainly with tour groups.

BAKAU

Ocean Bay Hotel & Resort (☎ 4494265; www.oceanbay hotel.com; s/d D3105/3425; **P** **⊠** **⊡** **⊠**) Just like its sister, the Kairaba Hotel, this is government owned and one of Gambia's newest and plushest luxury hotels. Near Cape Point, this sparkling palace has all the amenities you'd expect, including an on-site clinic, baby-sitting and car rental; however, service doesn't live up to its five-star rating.

Sunbeach Hotel & Resort (☎ 4497190; www.sun beachhotel.com; s/d D2600/3000; **⊠** **⊡** **⊠**) At the tip of Cape Point, this vast hotel offers relaxed comfort in attractive, spacious rooms and a beachside terrain. Still, it's another resort hotel clone. That's fine if it's a beach holiday you're after, but disappointing if you like your stay spiced with a dose of originality.

FAJARA

Fajara Hotel (☎ 495605; fax 495339; Atlantic Rd; s/d D1250/1500; **⊠** **⊡** **⊠**) With its long, intimidating corridors and bland rooms, this old establishment looks more '60s communist concrete than the charming resort hotel it really wants to be.

Ngala Lodge (☎ 4494045; www.ngalalodge.com; 64 Atlantic Blvd; ste D3750; **⊠** **⊡** **⊠**) This stylish red-clay structure houses lovingly decorated rooms; think African materials and sculptures teased into modern designs. Your best chance of staying here – perhaps even in the glass-domed penthouse – is during low season; peak times are usually booked up by Gambia Experience clients.

KOTU

Several hotels are packed into the strip of beach between Fajara Golf Club and Kotu Stream and tend to attract young people on package holidays. The following are three such hotels:

Bungalow Beach Hotel (☎ 4465288; bbhotel@ganet .gm; Kotu Beach; s/d from D1600/2600; ❄ 🖳 🐾) Despite the name, this family-friendly place consists of dozens of self-contained apartments in two-storey long-houses.

Kombo Beach Hotel (☎ 4465466; info@kombobeach hotel.gm; Kotu Beach; s/d from D1530/2040; ❄ 🖳 🐾) A favourite with sexy young Europeans on group tours, facilities here include a clinic and nightclub, and one of the most renowned (and most expensive) restaurants around. The upstairs rooms are particularly nice.

Sunset Beach Hotel (☎ 4466397; www.sunsetbeach hotel.gm; Kotu Beach; s/d from D2000/2500; ❄ 🐾) It's a touch soulless, but pretty enough. Overpriced though, for what it offers. The suites housing four are great for families.

KOLOLI

Coconut Residence (☎ 4463377; info@coconutresidence .com; Badala Park Way; ste from D5500; ❄ 🐾) There isn't a nicer hotel in the country than this classy five-star palace. It's one of the few top hotels where luxury hasn't been traded for soul. All amenities and services come wrapped in a sophisticated chic that extends to the lush tropical gardens and carefully designed rooms. If you've got the money, this is where you want to spend it.

Seaview Gardens Hotel (☎ 4466660; www.seaview gardens-hotel.co.uk; s/d D2000/2500; ❄ 🖳 🐾) This tries hard to be a top-class place but lacks that stylish final touch. Not a bad option though.

Kairaba Hotel (☎ 4462940; www.kairabahotel .com; Senegambia Strip; s/d D4352/5235; 🅿 ❄ 🖳 🐾) This government-owned hotel is the kind of vast, labyrinthine, anything-can-be-arranged place you might be tempted never to leave during your whole holiday. It claims to be the best hotel in Gambia and might just be right. It has more facilities than you can probably think of, including massage parlours, sports studios, a nightclub and a babysitting service. This is the right address for a holiday break wrapped in cotton wool.

Senegambia Hotel (☎ 4462717; www.senegambia .com; Senegambia Strip; s/d D2205/2695; 🅿 ❄ 🖳 🐾) Next to the Kairaba, the Senegambia Hotel pales a little in comparison, but in less glamorous surroundings it would be considered the top of tops. The setting, on a beautiful stretch of beach, is this hotel's big winner – bird-watchers love it for the large numbers of species the hotel's tropical garden attracts.

EATING

Mass tourism has made the Atlantic coast resorts area one of the best areas to dine in West Africa; there is no shortage of places to eat. The strip near the Kairaba Hotel in Kololi has the highest density of restaurants, but for quality and character you're better off in Fajara and Bakau. Plenty of places offer a very similar menu, composed of a handful of dishes from all four corners of the globe plus some local flavours. But between the culinary grey, you find some real gems to tickle your tastebuds.

Bakau

Sambou's (☎ 4495237; Old Cape Rd; dishes from D100) This small, cheapish place has been around for years. Few restaurants last that long in this ever-changing region, and something is certainly right about the simple but tasty Gambian and European meals served here.

Atlantic Bar & Restaurant (☎ 4494083; Atlantic Rd; dishes from D60; ☉ 10am-2pm) This local-style place, run by a couple of enterprising youngsters, was just starting out when we visited. Gambian meals and snacks were as decent as they were cheap, and the kitchen is spotless.

THE AUTHOR'S CHOICE

Butcher's Shop (☎ 4495069; www.thebutchers shopgambia.com; Kairaba Ave, Fajara; dishes D169-285; ☉ 8am-11pm) This stunning Moroccan place has gradually morphed from being one of the best butchers in the area into one of the best butchers with *the* best restaurant on the Atlantic coast. The enthusiastic owner, Driss, is a celebrity chef complete with his own cable TV show, and is very very good at what he does. Everything here is given that crucial finishing touch – from rich local juices to light lunches and flavour-dripping three-course dinners. The pepper steak we had here was the best we've tasted anywhere, and the range of desserts and cocktails will prompt you to sell your calorie counter. Butcher's Shop also does a mean Sunday brunch from 10am to 4pm (D200). Go on, become a regular.

Other goodies in Bakau:

Sunshine Bar (☎ 9931800; dishes D75-150; ☺ until 8pm) This simple, relaxed bar right on the beach near Cape Point often gets lively with a young bikini-clad crowd.

Italian Connection (☎ 9956343; Kofi Annan Rd; meals around D150-300; ☺ lunch & dinner) The name does not deceive – this is indeed Bakau's main pizza and pasta joint. Standard Italian fare.

Chapman's (☎ 4495252; Atlantic Rd; meals around D150-250; ☺ 11am-10pm Thu-Tue) People call this 'the place where everyone seems to go'. It's usually packed with a mixed crowd, the menu is varied and drinks flow.

Ocean Clipper (☎ 4494265; meals around D200-300; ☺ 6pm-midnight) Part of the Ocean Bay Hotel & Resort complex, this lush place serves Mediterranean and Asian food with a dose of exclusivity.

For self-catering options, try **St Mary's Food & Wine** (Cape Point Rd) or any of the other small supermarkets in the heart of Bakau.

Fajara

Mama's Restaurant (☎ 4497640; cnr Atlantic Rd & Kairaba Ave; dishes around D100; ☺ 11am-10pm Tue-Sun) One of the most established places serving Gambian food, this vibrant restaurant is as much renowned for its delicious buffet dinners as for the raw charm of 'Mama' the manager.

Yok (☎ 4495131; African Living Arts Centre; Garba Jahumpa Rd; meals around D250; ☺ 12.30pm-midnight) No-one should visit Fajara without eating at Yok, which is locally better known as the Salon. Pass through the leafy, glass-roofed alleyway behind an impressively stacked antique and arts shop, and you'll find this striking Asian restaurant. It serves excellent Singaporean, Thai and Chinese fusion cuisine against a backdrop of gently flowing waterfalls and rustling palm trees. Oh, and it has the best cocktails on the coast. You'll feel like an actor in a classic East Asian movie and be treated like a star – indulge!

Clay Oven (☎ 4496600; meals D175-195; ☺ 7-11pm) For Indian food, this place off Atlantic Rd is one of the best in the whole of West Africa. No exaggeration. And with its scrubbed white walls, leafy garden and personalised service, the surroundings are right, too.

Eddie's Bar & Restaurant (dishes D60-100; ☺ 8am-2am) This tiny restaurant off Kairaba Ave can look a little desolate during the day, but is often full of locals at night. It's good for *afra* (grilled meat) and other Gambian dishes.

Flavours (dishes from D150; ☺ 8am-midnight) It's a hotel restaurant all right (it's part of the Safari Garden Hotel), but it's definitely one of the better ones. A range of imaginative dishes will appeal to carnivores and vegetarians alike, and meals taste as great as they look. A dip in the pool gets thrown in free with a drink or a meal (otherwise it's D75).

Ritz (☎ 4496754; meals from D150-250; ☺ 8am-midnight) The standard European fare of this small place near the Safari Garden Hotel doesn't live up to the restaurant's aspirational name, nor to its prices.

Francisco's Restaurant (☎ 4495332; cnr Atlantic Rd & Kairaba Ave; grills D150-300; ☺ lunch & dinner) There are few places where mixed seafood platters and grills taste better than in the tranquil setting of Francisco's garden.

Leybato (☎ 4497186; Fajara Beach; dishes around D100-150; ☺ 11am-11pm) The food here isn't exceptional (think a standard fish and steak menu), but it tastes better than elsewhere thanks to breathtaking views. Time your dinner to coincide with sunset.

Cotton Club (☎ 7777877; Kairaba Ave, Fajara; ☺ 9am-midnight) This place has about three different names displayed outside – signs of frequently changing ownership. At the time we visited, it had recently been taken up by a Portuguese owner and hopes among expats were set on some good Mediterranean cuisine.

Ngala Lodge (☎ 497672; Atlantic Rd; meals around D300; ☺ 11.30am-3pm & 7.30-11pm Mon-Sat) It doesn't get much better than Ngala Lodge, where Belgian chef Peter specialises in wonderful fish dishes while the manager keeps everything in a state of calm under the swaying palm trees that look down on the ocean. A jazz band plays every Friday.

Weezo's (☎ 4496918; 132 Kairaba Ave; mains around D250-350; ☺ 11am-3.30pm & 7pm-3am) This was once one of the classiest places in town, serving a range of excellent food, snacks and tapas all day, and cocktails in a trendy setting in the evenings. It was taking a slight downhill slope when we visited – check if it's recovered.

Le Palais du Chocolat (☎ 4395397; 19 Kairaba Ave; cakes around D30, ☺ lunch & dinner) It's all in the name – a chocolate palace. With a whole range of temptations for those with a sweet tooth, this is the perfect place for an indulgent breakfast. The cakes and pastries are particularly recommended.

La Paillote (☎ 4375418; www.alliancefrance.gm; dishes from D25; ☺ noon-4pm) The meal choice at the restaurant of the Alliance Franco-Gambienne is between the African dish at a mind-boggling D25 and the European three-course meal at D90. Both are usually delicious – you'd have to try very hard indeed to find better value anywhere.

Esporta (☎ 4494316; Garba Jahumpa Rd; sandwiches around D75) One of the better fast-food joints around, this is a good place to come for sandwiches – even jerk chicken – and the excellent natural juices bottled by Gamjuice.

Come Inn (☎ 4391464; ☾ 10am-2am) For a hearty meal, a good draught beer and a solid dose of local gossip, there's no better place than this German-style beer garden. It's popular with overlanders and pretty much anyone else who likes big portions at decent rates.

For supermarkets, head for Kairaba Ave where there's plenty of choice. Kairaba Supermarket is usually well stocked, while **Harry's Supermarket** (☾ 9am-10pm Mon-Sat) has the best hours. **St Mary's Food & Wine** (☾ 9am-7.30pm Mon-Sat, 10am-1.30pm Sun) has a branch here as well as in Bakau.

Kotu

Most restaurants in Kotu are unremarkable, but at the northern end of the resort strip there are some notable exceptions.

Sailor's Beach Bar (☎ 4464078; Kotu Beach; meals D100-200; ☾ 9am-midnight) One of the coast's better beach bars. A whole range of foods is available, from cheesy pizza to grilled barracuda, and drinks can be sipped lounging on sun beds (free for customers).

La Rive Gauche (☎ 4465466; Kotu Beach; dishes from D250) So what if it's a hotel restaurant! This stately eatery at the Kombo Beach Hotel enjoys a reputation for serving some of the most refined cuisine in town. It's a place for celebratory meals, though all this succulent luxury has its price, of course.

Kololi

There are plenty of generic tourist restaurants in Kololi; following is a selection of the more interesting ones.

PALMA RIMA AREA

Solomon's Beach Bar (☎ 4460716; Ralma Rima Rd; meals D100-200; ☾ 10am-midnight) At the northern end of Kololi beach, this cute round-house with a light reggae feel is famous for its grilled fish and youthful atmosphere.

Teranga Beach Club (☎ 7014581; Palma Rima Rd; ☾ 11am-3am) This relaxed place sits on a usually hassle-free part of the beach. It's the place to boost your vitamin intake – just try one of the gigantic bowls of fruit salad (D75 to D150).

Luigi's Italian Restaurant (☎ 4460280; Palma Rima Rd; dishes D200-300; ☾ lunch & dinner) Luigi knows his job – the pasta is al dente and the pizzas are crisp. Above the shiny restaurant are also a couple of excellent self-contained apartments and an Internet café.

Crystals Ice Cream Parlour & Gallery (☎ 7774567; Palma Rima Rd; snacks around D50-150; ☾ 11am-7pm Tue-Sun) A tranquil patio and colourful gallery invite to you linger over delicious ice creams, homemade from local ingredients and seasonal fruit. Cocktails, pancakes and panini are also on the menu, making this the coast's high point if you're after snacks.

Dutch Whale (☎ 4464804; Palma Rima Rd) This unpretentious small restaurant serves (surprise, surprise) Dutch specialities such as croquettes with frikadelle (meatballs), and also organises fishing trips.

SENEGAMBIA STRIP

Amber's Nest (☎ 4464181; Badala Park Way; meals around D150-200; ☾ lunch & dinner) This tiny, Gambian-run place serves excellent local dishes, discreetly infused with imaginative flavours. The Saturday buffets are a treat – perfect for tasting the breadth of chef Amber's culinary skills and listening to Gambian music.

Ali Baba's (☎ 4461030; Senegambia Strip; meals around D200; ☾ 11am-2am) Pretty much everyone knows Ali Baba's, so it's as much a useful meeting point as a commendable restaurant. The menu consists of a fairly uninspired international mix, though the Lebanese food and snacks get good reviews. It sometimes has live music in the garden.

Peppers Tropical Restaurant (☎ 4464792; Senegambia Strip; meals around D150-250; ☾ 24hr) In the heart of the Senegambia strip, this is where you find the best Caribbean food, as well as excellent Gambian dishes accompanied by local juices or cocktails. On Fridays and Saturdays, there's a live salsa band.

Al Basha (☎ 4463300; Senegambia Rd; meals from D300; ☾ 11am-2am) At the time we visited, this was an ice-cool Lebanese place with suit-'n'-tie attitude and occasional belly-dancing shows, but management was about to change. Check it out.

Kora (☎ 462727; Senegambia Strip; dishes D200-375; 🕙 lunch & dinner) This lush place does a tasty range of meals from around the world. Its enormous mixed platters for four people (per person D500) seemingly contain something of everything on the menu.

Scala Restaurant (☎ 4460813; Bijilo Park Rd; meals from D150; 🕙 10am-midnight) If you are looking for a night out in your best holiday clothes, this place on the Senegambia strip is for you.

GTS Restaurant (☎ 4462476; Bijilo Park Rd; meals around D150; 🕙 lunch & dinner) Meals are standard Gambian fare here, but surroundings are pretty and the concept is excellent; this is a local initiative trying to help youngsters get employment, and find an alternative to bumsterism in the tourism industry. Worthy of your support!

Serekunda

There are several cheap eateries around the market and taxi-station entrance, and several others scattered through the streets of Serekunda. Also popular is Aisa Marie Cinema, where you can sip a beer and buy a snack in a great people-watching zone while waiting for your B-grade movie to start.

Youth Monument Bar & Restaurant (Westfield Junction; meals around D100; 🕙 lunch & dinner) This impressively named eatery is a favourite with the locals and it is as much loved for cheap food and drinks as for the sports matches on screen. It's a great place to meet the locals.

For years shoestringers have descended on the following cheapies:

Safe Way Afra King (dishes D50-150; 🕙 5pm-midnight) Off the Mosque road; it's the place for *afra*, sandwiches, *fufu* (mashed cassava), 'cowfoot' and other African dishes.

Maroun's (Westfield Junction; 🕙 9am-7.30pm Mon-Sat, 10am-1.30pm Sun) The local supermarket with basics such as local and imported food, and toiletries.

DRINKING

All the major hotels have bars; some are large and nondescript, others are more personal and a few are in breathtaking locations. Most restaurants also turn the lights down and the music on at night. Gambia's sizable British and German community also means a range of pub-style places, ranging from brash to sleazy. The bars in Serekunda are more local in character.

Weezo's (☎ 4496918; Atlantic Rd) This enduring place in Fajara undergoes a fascinating transformation around sunset, from chic restaurant to atmospheric in-bar. It has a well-deserved reputation for serving some of the best cocktails on the coast.

Come Inn (☎ 4391464; Kairaba Ave; 🕙 10am-2am) For a draught beer, a hearty meal and a dose of raw pub humour, there's hardly a better place than this German beer garden. It's popular with anyone who knows how to handle a few beers.

Lana's Bar (☎ 395424) A small affair on a corner of Sukuta Rd, this slightly run-down but hugely entertaining café-bar sits right on Serekunda's busy market mile – a fabulous spot for people-watching at any time of day.

Aquarius (☎ 4460247; Bijilo Forest Park Rd, Senegambia Strip; 🕙 10am-3am) A smart café during the day, Aquarius turns into a glittering dance floor at night – a place where the dance beats are heavy and the crowds touristy. The drinks are expensive and the atmosphere is strict party-vibe – no place for a quiet drink.

In Bakau **Chapman's** (☎ 4495252; Atlantic Rd) is the best beer option. **Churchill's** (Palma Rima Rd) is the pub reference near Kololi beach, and **Queen's Head** (Kololi Rd) is the beer address in Kotu.

Around the tourist miles of Kotu and Kololi you find several upmarket bars, including **Paparazzi** (Senegambia Strip; 🕙 10pm-3am), a smart wine bar. It turns up the dance beats after 10pm.

ENTERTAINMENT
Live Music

The busy hotel miles always attract local Fula acrobats, Malinké griots and other musicians who busk outside the hotels or are invited to perform in the restaurants. Though these are often very tourist-tailored affairs, artists are often very good, even if the hotel lobby setting may not be the ideal place to experience them.

Actual live-music venues are surprisingly rare.

Teranga Beach Club (☎ 9982669; abdulkabirr@hotmail.com; Palma Rima Rd) A strange structure stranded between unfinished and falling down, it holds occasional jazz afternoons, large-scale concerts by visiting artists, and full-moon beach parties with seafood buffet and acoustic music (D100).

Jazziz (☎ 4462175; Palma Rima Rd; 🕙 10pm-late) Despite its name, Jazziz is not a jazz bar but a young and colourful salsa place that gets

---

SEX TOURISM

Like many developing countries, Gambia has become popular with wealthy white tourists looking for sexual thrills they don't get at home. But unlike Pattaya in Thailand or Manila in the Philippines, in Gambia it's not middle-aged men preying on young girls who constitute the majority of sex tourists, but middle-aged women looking for fit, young African men.

While the root of prostitution – poverty – remains the same whoever is involved, sex tourism in Gambia has its own set of peculiarities. The women usually travel in groups, and can be found in beach chairs and hammocks outside the hotels. The 'sex workers' spend all day working out on the beach. When the woman decides on her man, he will usually stay with her for the rest of her holiday, acting as guide and translator as well as sex partner. Some women return annually, or more often, and meet their man at the airport.

Some argue that these 'arrangements' benefit all parties involved – the women get their kicks, the men get a chance to obtain that hotly desired European visa, and with it an opening into what they hope to become a better life. But as with all forms of sex tourism, there is an obvious element of exploitation that stems from the unequal power relations involved. And in the case of West Africa, this smacks so bitterly of a continuation of colonial practices that it renders observers of the scenes extremely uneasy.

---

swinging on Fridays and Saturdays. The music is live and the atmosphere usually unbeatable.

Several of the nightclubs listed next also feature occasional live bands on weekends.

Nightclubs

You don't have to search too hard to find a heaving dance floor on the Atlantic coast, whether it's a rootsy, rowdy shack or a slick temple of dance you're after. The former are mostly found in Serekunda (and best explored with a Gambian mate), the latter are either attached to hotels, or set in the popular tourist miles.

Party spaces tend to fall quickly in and out of favour, so it's best to ask around about what's currently 'in' before heading out. Just like Gambia's restaurants, the nightclubs present punters with a global mix that tries to cater to everyone – a mixture of hip-hop, R&B, *mbalax* (a mixture of Cuban beats and traditional, fiery *sabar* drumming), reggae and a whole lot more.

Clubs usually open their doors around 9pm – don't even think about arriving before 11pm.

Lama Lama (☎ 4494747; Atlantic Rd, Bakau) At the time of writing, this was Bakau's club of choice for the dance-floor creatures who determine club popularity.

Calabash (☎ 4462263; Palma Rima Rd) In Kololi, this place is free for the ladies and anyone who dines at Jazziz – which makes for a great combination of evening dinner, late-

night salsa and some bursts of dancing in the early-morning hours.

Other popular options:

911 Club (Cape Point, Bakau) Near the Cape Point Hotel; attracts a mixed crowd every weekend.

Tropicana Nightclub (off Badala Park Way) Hugely popular. Still known (and mostly referred to) by locals as Spy Bar; gets sweaty late at night.

Waaw Nightclub (☎ 4460668; Senegambia Strip) Dance beats and generic global disco sounds.

Totties Nightclub (Senegambia Strip) New, with a gleaming dance floor. Strong competition for next-door Waaw.

Jokko (Westfield Junction) This open-air club in Serekunda is a raucous local affair, and makes a convincing claim at being the most entertaining club of all.

Destiny (off Badala Park Way, Kololi) Sparkling new at the time of research; draws glittering crowds on weekends.

Casinos

Kololi Casino (☎ 4460226; Senegambia Strip; ⏰ from 9pm) Near the Senegambia Hotel, this casino is reckoned by most to be the best in the country. The casino offers roulette, poker, blackjack and jackpot machines (from 4pm), plus a bar and coffee shop. There's a restaurant attached.

Slot-machine fans can find relief at **Jackpot Palace** (Kairaba Ave), or a host of similar places in Serekunda.

Sport
FOOTBALL

The Gambia's main stadium is Independence Stadium in Bakau; this is the site for major football matches and other sporting events, which are advertised locally on posters. Major matches are impossible to miss, as seemingly the entire population of Gambia heads for the stadium, many dressed in national colours or carrying flags. The atmosphere at times like this is electric, and it's well worth going along just for this, even if you don't actually see the match.

TRADITIONAL WRESTLING
Another spectator sport popular with locals and visitors is traditional wrestling (see p49). This occasionally takes place at Independence Stadium in Bakau but it's more interesting, and much more fun, to see the matches at one of several smaller 'arenas' (open patches of ground) in Serekunda. These include **Arena Babou Fatty** (off Sukuta Rd) – ask around outside Lana's Bar.

Matches take place in the late afternoon, usually on Sunday (less frequently in the dry season, and not during Ramadan). The entrance fee is usually about D30 for tourists. If you arrange a tour through a large hotel the cost is about D500. Taxis do this trip for a bit less, including waiting time. Or you can get to Serekunda by shared taxi for about D5, and follow the crowds to whichever arena is the venue that day.

SHOPPING
Bakau Market sells fruit and vegetables, and has an adjacent handicrafts section stuffed to the rims with carvings, traditional cloth and other souvenirs. Serekunda is the place to hunt for good-quality batiks.

African Heritage Centre (☎ 4496778) Opposite the market, next to the church, near the ferry jetty in Bakau, you find this beautiful boutique with a range of original sculptures, batiks, paintings and souvenirs (as well as a good restaurant and a few rooms that you can stay in down the back).

Tropical Tour & Souvenirs (☎ 4460536; Senegambia Strip, Kololi) In the Kairaba Hotel, this hassle-free place has a good range of information, books, maps, arts and fashion. While there, ask about its Tropical Gardens project, which had just taken off at the time of research, and is likely to grow into an impressive business.

Village Gallery & Restaurant (☎ 4463646; Kololi; 10am-midnight) Finding your way here is a little tricky: best take a left off Badala Park Way, then ask someone to show you – it's

absolutely worth the effort. This gallery sells original works by renowned and upcoming local artists. It also has a small café where a busy chef tries hard to match the exquisiteness of his food to that of the works on display.

Batik Factory (☎ 4392258) This is the workshop of Musu Kebba Drammeh. It's hidden deep in the backstreets of Serekunda, and tracking it down is almost as much fun as watching the batiks being made (taxi drivers and locals can give you directions).

Salam Batik (☎ Amadou Jallow 4395103, Sheikh Tijan Secka 9820125; London Corner, Serekunda) Forget about the mass-produced batik wares on display at various tourist markets. This inspiring, Gambian-owned enterprise is the place to get your personalised clothes, bags, bed throw or curtains dyed and tailored. You'll be the proud owner of a unique and beautiful item, while supporting local industry.

Paper Recycling Project (☎ 7776692, 7793358; may_roone@hotmail.com) A short drive out of Serekunda, this is a stunningly situated workshop where locally trained workers turn recycled paper, cloth and other scrap materials into beautiful gift items and schoolbooks. It's en route to Abuko and is well signposted.

For music, your best choice is Kerewan Sound in Banjul (see p96).

GETTING THERE & AWAY
Bush taxis depart from the garages of Serekunda, the country's main transport hub. Serekunda to Soma is D60, to Farafenni D75.

For the south coast, you can get bush taxis to Brufut (D12), Tanji (D15) and Sanyang (D18). A bush taxi to Gunjur is D30, either via Brikama or directly along the coastal road. Direct bush taxis to the south of the river leave from Serekunda's **Tippa Garage** (Bakoteh Junction, Serekunda) or from the Senegambia strip in Kololi, while vehicles for Brikama leave from Westfield Junction. Bush taxis (mainly *sept-place*) go from Serekunda to Kafountine and Ziguinchor in southern Senegal via the border at Séléti. See p287 for more details.

GETTING AROUND
To/From the Airport
A green tourist taxi from Banjul International Airport to Serekunda is D300, and to

any Atlantic coast resort it's D400. Yellow taxis cost about D150 or even less, depending upon your powers of negotiation.

There isn't any public transport to the airport, but minibuses between Brikama and Serekunda can drop you at the turn-off 3km from the airport.

Bicycle

Mountain bikes and traditional roadsters (of varying quality) can be hired from several hotels in Bakau, Kotu and Kololi, or from private outfits nearby. The Senegambia Hotel in Kololi and African Village Hotel in Bakau are good addresses. Expect to pay around D40 per hour, D160 for a half-day and D200 for a full day. Bargain hunters can probably negotiate these rates down by half.

Car & Motorcycle

All rates given here are exclusive of mileage and 15% sales tax. Drivers must be 23 years or over. Refundable deposits are required (around D25,000) and discounted rates are available for seven days or more.

AB Rent-a-Car (☎ 4460926; abrentacar@gamtel.gm; Senegambia Hotel, Kololi) Standard rates for the smallest cars start at D870 per day, going up to D1890 for a Pajero 4WD. Add D200 to D400 for the all-inclusive option, which includes insurance and mileage. Motorcycles are D1000 and discounts are available for seven-day rental.

Cars4Rent (☎ 7782848; cars4rentgambia@hotmail.com; Elton Badala Oasis, Kotu) This much smaller operation charges D1219 for a small car, D1665 for a 4WD.

Hertz (☎ 4390041; airport ☎ /fax 4473156; hertz@ gamtel.gm; Tippa Garage) Standard rates range from D520 for a small car to D1290 for a Toyota Land Cruiser. Beware, all-inclusive rates are about double that. Four-wheel drives can only be hired with a driver.

There are also a few local one-man-and-his-car operations that advertise in hotels, shops and supermarkets. These certainly offer cheaper rates, but make sure the cars are in good condition, particularly if you're travelling upcountry.

Private Taxi

In the Atlantic coast resorts there are hundreds of green 'tourist taxis'. These are privately owned cars, particularly designed for tourist comfort. In some of the dense tourist strips, such as the Senegambia strip, they are the only taxis that have permission to enter.

You can pick up a tourist taxi from most of the large hotels; just ask at the reception – sometimes drivers are waiting for clients outside. Their fares are fixed by the drivers syndicates and are advertised on large boards outside the hotels, as well as in the cars.

They are usually in a better condition than the yellow taxis and are safe and hassle-free, but you have to pay for the luxury. Prices are often three times the rate for yellow taxis. For example, a tourist taxi from Kololi to Kartong will cost you D3000, while you can probably negotiate your way down to D1000 or even D700 in a privately hired yellow taxi. From Fajara to Banjul, you'll pay around D350 by tourist taxi, D150 in a yellow cab.

Yellow taxis generally don't have fixed rates, except the 'town trip' (any trip between Bakau, Fajara, Kololi and Kotu) usually charged at D25. Hiring a taxi for a day to go around the Atlantic resorts and Banjul should cost around D1000 to D1500.

Shared Taxi

Shared taxis around the Atlantic coast resorts cost D5, or D6 to Banjul. From Bakau, at the junction of Saitmatty and Atlantic Rds, you can get shared taxis and minibuses to Banjul city centre or Serekunda. From Fajara, some shared taxis go from near the junction of Kairaba Ave and Atlantic Rd, but you usually have to walk to the junction of Garba Jahumpa Rd and Kairaba Ave, where you can pick up one coming from Bakau.

From Serekunda, you can get shared taxis to Bakau from outside the Gamtel office at Westfield Junction. For Fajara, it's usually necessary to be dropped at the Garba Jahumpa Rd junction on Kairaba Ave.

From the Serekunda taxi stop minibuses or shared taxis go to Kololi (drivers call the Kololi taxi park 'Senegambia'). They leave from near the market's northwest corner (ask anyone) and mostly go via the junction near Badala Park Hotel (where you can get off and walk to Kotu), but sometimes via the junction near Palma Rima Hotel. Minibuses run to Serekunda from Kololi taxi park.

In Serekunda, minibuses to Banjul city, or shared taxis up Kairaba Ave to Fajara and Bakau, leave from near Westfield Junction.

If you want to go directly from Kololi or Kotu to Fajara, there's no regular minibus service along Badala Park Way so you'll have to walk or wait for a taxi to come by.

Western Gambia

Heading inland or southward from the bustling tourist zones, big-business tourism gives way to a more intimate experience of Gambian nature and culture. Small fishing villages line the southern strip of white-sand coast, inviting visitors to experience local life.

Further inland, the clamorous junction town of Brikama lures you to more distant destinations. Though the town itself spells dusty discomfort, it is in fact a great artistic centre, being home to some of Gambia's most renowned families of kora players. Music-lovers should definitely put a stop in here. Those with a penchant for nature are probably better off at Abuko Nature Reserve, a tiny park that features a stunning range of wildlife on a stretch of land so small that it's easily explored on foot. For bird-watchers in particular, this is a dream destination – over 250 species have been spotted. West of here, the Makasutu Culture Forest is the place to experience a glossier-than-life version of Gambian nature and culture; treat yourself to a night in the adjacent luxury ecolodge.

On the north bank, the villages Jufureh and Albreda tempt with a fictionalised slice of history. Ever since Alex Haley's work *Roots* traced the author's ancestral lineage back to the Kinte family of Jufureh, the village has turned into a symbolic destination for those in search of answers to their past. While actual links between the Kintes of Jufureh and Haley are disputed, James Island off Jufureh's shore allows for no such ambiguities; the crumbling walls of its ancient slaving station remain a stark reminder of the cruel trade in humans that once took place here.

HIGHLIGHTS

- Walk around the beautifully conserved landscape of **Abuko Nature Reserve** (p122), spotting crocodiles, monkeys and hundreds of bird species
- Glimpse local culture and see artisans at work at **Tanji Village Museum** (p118)
- Enjoy a leisurely day hammock-lounging, boat-riding and artwork-gazing in the tranquil river village of **Kartong** (p119)
- Indulge in the calm atmosphere of **Makasutu Culture Forest** (p124), Gambia's cultural 'theme park'
- Motor up the Gambia River to **Jufureh** (p126), the village featured in Alex Haley's novel, *Roots*

- POPULATION: 600,000

WESTERN GAMBIA

SOUTH COAST

South from Serekunda and Kololi, a smooth tarred road takes you past the calm villages of the south coast, right to the Senegalese border at the Allahein River, some 50km away. This area is more peaceful than the crowded Atlantic resorts area of Kololi, Kotu, Fajara and Bakau, though the tourist industry is fast elbowing its way into the region, gradually transforming fishing beaches into sea resorts. Still, plenty of small-scale initiatives are springing up across the zone, proposing forms of tourism that align more with local interests and sensitivities.

BRUFUT

Brufut is a rapidly expanding village 17km south of Serekunda. It's famous for its fishing centre and a busy working beach, whose rhythm depends entirely on the tide. Boats roll in and out of the sea, and sell their still-jumping catch to dealers from Serekunda. Most of the fishing is done by Ghanaians who live in nearby Ghana Town, their pirogues identified by the coloured flags on their bows.

Tourism is trying hard to outdo fishing as a source of income; two gigantic multistar hotels were almost completed on the beach at the time of research, and in some areas, the sea view is already being obstructed by unimaginative rows of terraced housing.

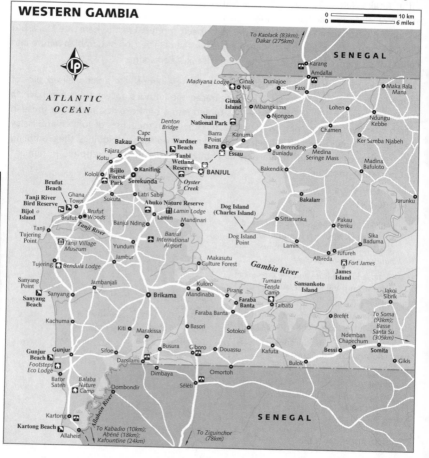

WESTERN GAMBIA

TWITCHER TIPS: BRUFUT WOODS

A short but hard-to-follow track leads from Brufut town to Brufut Woods, a small forest and well-known haunt of bird-lovers.

Over the years the area's woodland has permanently decreased in size due to deforestation, putting at risk one of Gambia's primary sanctuaries for species such as Verreaux's eagle owls, woodland and malachite kingfishers and various species of sunbirds.

Thanks to an enduring local initiative, the remaining area has now been fenced in and equipped with a drinking pool and hide. Initially managed by the West African Bird Study Association (Wabsa), it is now looked after by the village of Brufut and is an excellent destination for birders, as long as the expansion of tourism in the region doesn't put the area at risk once more.

About 50m back from the sea is **Texas Beach Bar** (meals around D100; ☽ 11am-9pm), which serves meals, drinks and snacks, and even has a couple of improvised guestrooms (D300). Brufut lies on the coastal road, just south of the Atlantic resorts. You reach the beach via dirt tracks from the main road.

TANJI RIVER BIRD RESERVE

About 5km south of Brufut Beach is the small village of Tanji. The area between these two points is called Karinti by locals, and is the site of the **Tanji River Bird Reserve** (adult/child D31.50; ☽ 8am-6pm). An area of dunes, lagoons, dry woodland and coastal scrub, the reserve also incorporates the mangrove creeks and estuary of the Tanji River, and the offshore Bijol Island with its surrounding reefs and islets.

The wide range of habitats here attracts an excellent selection of birds, including indigenous species and European migrants; more than 300 species have been recorded. Although waders and water birds are the most prolific, there are also 34 raptor species. The Bijol Island section of the reserve is an important area for the breeding of green turtles, the Caspian tern and grey-headed gull. This is a bird-protection area, and any visit means a disturbance to the fragile breeding project. The only legal tours (around D500) are organised by the wildlife department; these are run only outside breeding season.

Other people will probably offer to take you there – respect the breeding project and stick to the official tour. Even if you don't visit Bijol, a guided walk (per hour D200) around Tanji Reserve will have you spotting plenty of birds.

If you're already at Brufut Beach, a 2km walk along the road takes you to the reserve office, signposted on the right (western) side of the road, where you pay your entry fee. Otherwise, stay in the bush taxi from Serekunda and go directly to the office.

TANJI

About 3km south of the reserve office, the road crosses a small bridge to reach the village of Tanji. You can walk along the beach or through the reserve to get to this point.

If a dromedary tour along the beach is your idea of a good holiday, then you'll be well looked after by **Pepe's Camel Safaris** (☎ 4461083) on the coastal road, a tour-group favourite for camel rides along the Tanji coast. Right opposite, **Nyanya's Safari Lodge** (☎ 9822627; s/d D400/500) can put up any aspiring camel 'drivers' in simple but adequate rooms.

Those who prefer a sheltered mangrove setting to a busy beach, and watching birds to crouching on camels, are better off at the stunning **Paradise Inn Lodge** (☎ 8800209; www .paradiseinngarden.com; r per person incl breakfast D660) This has a well-deserved reputation for organising excellent bird-watching excursions in the surrounding mangroves and the Tanji reserve. Most rooms in this lush garden setting are enormous, and they also have bikes for hire and organise kora and drumming courses.

In Tanji village, **Kairoh Garden** (☎ 4414019; d with/without bathroom D500/400) is a spacious, palm-shaded place with good-value, clean rooms. It mainly attracts local visitors and the *chef de cuisine* claims to excel at Asian, African and vegetarian meals (meals around D150). Give him a try, or head for the cluster of local restaurants at the south end of Tanji Beach.

Tanji lies on the coastal road; a bush taxi from Serekunda is around D10.

TUJERING

About 3km south of Tanji, this tiny village is home to **Bendula Lodge** (☎ 7717481; www.bendula .com; s/d D510/680), a great place for some remote relaxing. Accommodation is in simple, pretty huts huddled on green terrain

---

TANJI VILLAGE MUSEUM

On the southern side of Tanji, about 2km from the centre, is the fascinating **Tanji Village Museum** (☎ 9926618; tanje@dds.nl; admission adult/child D100/25; ☻ 9am-5pm). It was planned, developed and built largely due to the vision of Abdulie Bayo, who worked for 20 years at the National Museum in Banjul before establishing this museum at Tanji, free of government bureaucracy.

The museum's centrepiece is a traditional Mandinka compound, made up of various round-houses that contain a carefully assembled selection of traditional furniture and artefacts. But it's beyond the compound walls that things get really interesting. A tranquil nature trail teaches you about Gambia's flora and fauna, and birds chirp in the tops of the many local trees. Further along the path, you can watch craftsmen such as weavers and woodcarvers, and buy the products of their work at the nearby shop.

There's also a good collection of traditional instruments including drums, koras, *balafon* (xylophone) and *simbingo* (a string instrument, similar to the kora), and resident artists who show you how they are played. Their playing usually accompanies your meals in the picnic area or small on-site restaurant.

Lovingly maintained and continuously expanded, the museum is one of the best in the region, and doesn't have any of the stuffiness that weighs down most of the state-owned exhibitions. And if you're still looking for a quiet place to stay – in traditional style, of course – there are a few comfortable self-contained huts round the back (per person D250). The museum lies on the coastal road, a 15-minute walk from Tanji village.

---

surrounded by lush forests. A long stretch of white beach is in walking distance. It's the perfect place to do very little at all, but if your energy flows over you can take up drumming or dancing, watch batik makers and weavers in the village, or even produce your own herbal tea and medicine together with a local healer. Don't forget your torch (flashlight) – there was no electricity at the time of research.

You can take any bush taxi that goes along the coastal road and ask to be dropped off at the turn-off to the lodge. From there, it's a 10-minute walk to Bendula. Or you hire a taxi (around D1000 to D1500) and get dropped directly at the lodge.

SANYANG BEACH

The small fishing village Sanyang, 20km south of Serekunda, lies on an attractive stretch of beach. The locals are so proud of it they call it paradise beach. It's a notch quieter than the coastal stretches further up, though mushrooming beach bars signal the increasing impact of mass tourism.

Sleeping & Eating

All along the sand strand, beach restaurants compete for customers.

Sanyang Nature Camp (☎ 9902408; per person incl breakfast D400) About 1km inland from the beach is this secluded and slightly neglected

place run by the people from Leybato in Fajara. It is almost eerily quiet, but might get livelier once the huge terrace restaurant is completed.

Kobokoto Lodge (☎ 9984838; www.salla.se/kkl; r per person D250) This is by far the prettiest option in Sayang. Rooms are simple but attractive, and the restaurant upstairs is a stunning place to have a meal (meals around D150, open for lunch and dinner). Don't confuse it with the similarly named beach bar (following).

Kobokoto (☎ 7005511; d D300) Far more basic than Kobokoto Lodge, this beach bar and popular picnic space has simple rooms. Bathrooms are shared.

Rainbow Beach Bar (☎ 9827790; dishes D150-500; ☻ 11am-9pm) This is one of the better beach restaurants, with a good selection of seafood dishes including such delicacies as grilled king prawns and lobster. Crucially, it's also got an enticing reputation for using fresh ingredients. The 8pm to 9pm happy hour is particularly popular.

Osprey (☎ 9924010; meals D100-550; ☻ 11am-8pm) This place serves similar food to the Rainbow Beach Bar, but seems to be a little less sheltered from hustlers and bumsters.

Both Jungle Resort Bar and Pelican had just started out when we visited. Several of the restaurants listed also had plans to expand into small hotels.

Getting There & Away

To get to the beach, follow the coastal road towards Sanyang, then take the dirt road that branches off towards the beach about 2km before reaching Sanyang village.

GUNJUR & GUNJUR BEACH

Some 30km south of Serekunda, Gunjur still seems a little lost between the holiday hype of the Atlantic resorts and the emerging tourism of Kartong. Tiny as it is, it's one of Gambia's largest fishing centres, and absorbing daily life at the bustling Gunjur Beach (a 3km walk or D5 taxi ride from town) is one of the nicest things to do here. Boats go in and out or rock on the waves, nets are being mended, and fish gutted, sold and dried. A couple of drinks in one of the beach bars is not a bad way to pass a day. Scantily dressed sun seekers, however, are better off a little bit further on, away from the nets, guts and disapproving eyes of the locals.

Sleeping & Eating

Footsteps Eco Lodge (☎ 7706830; www.naturesway gambia.com; camping D250, d D1750) If you can afford it, stay here. This is the only place in Gambia that truly deserves the title ecolodge. Compost toilets, solar power, a freshwater pool and an extensive garden producing a large part of the restaurant's fresh ingredients make this something of a self-sustaining eco-island. And the birds love it, too; 100 species or more have been counted in its vast garden terrain. Of course there's vegetarian food, and you can hire bikes for D100 to D300 per day.

Balaba Nature Camp (☎ 9919012; huts per person D550/700) A 5km drive from Gunjur down the coastal road will take you to this laid-back camp, set amid dense savannah woodland. It's deservedly proud of its efforts at operating an environmentally friendly business, and runs a host of activities from drumming and dancing to bird-watching excursions, boat trips and basket weaving.

African Lodge (☎ 4486143; fax 4486026; r per person incl breakfast D400) This peaceful, low-key hotel sits right in the heart of Gunjur village – perfect for a feel of 'real life' away from the tourist zones. What seems to be a tiny lodge turns out to be a well-kept maze of lush gardens, restaurant and bar corners and spread-out bungalows that invite relaxation.

Wulaba Madina (d D600) On the way to the beach from town, you pass this simple camp with clean huts and a spacious terrace restaurant serving standard European fare for lunch and dinner (meals around D175). For most of the day the place seems too quiet, but the restaurant can get lively in the evenings.

Dalaba Lodge (☎ 9815865; d D800; 🐕) For a place as tiny and humble as Gunjur, this hotel is surprisingly upmarket. It tempts with spacious, apartment-style bungalows and a pool. It's quite a trek to the beach, though – the lodge sits 2km from Gunjur on the road inland to Brikama.

Gunjur Beach Motel (☎ 7788283) Gunjur's former place of pride was closed at the time of our visit, and people couldn't agree whether it just hadn't opened for the season or folded for good.

Most of the camps provide food; the imaginative menu of Footsteps Eco Lodge is particularly good. For something cheaper and more local, try the African Lodge (order in advance), or the small food stalls behind the fishing centre. The spacious beach restaurant Sankule once enjoyed a reputation as a great place for food, music soirées and even camping, until the volatile owner started throwing clients out and locking himself in. It could have hit better times again, and even if it hasn't, the area surrounding it gives great views of ocean and beach life.

Getting There & Away

The quickest way to reach Gunjur is by direct bush taxis, which depart from Tippa Garage in Serekunda. The longer route via Brikama is also still frequently used by drivers; taxis leave from the main garage in Serekunda and you have to change in Brikama. Both options cost about D25. From Gunjur village to the beach, you'll pay about D5.

KARTONG

Kartong is a calm little village that sits 10km south of Gunjur and only a short pirogue journey north of Senegal. It's one of Gambia's best-kept secrets, a picture-postcard village where gigantic palm trees sway over women with children on their backs and old men on wobbly bicycles.

Kartong lies close to the coast, and most turn-offs leading from the main road to the holiday camps also take you to the shore.

WESTERN GAMBIA

The main beach, mainly used by fishermen but suitable for bathing, is a couple of kilometres further south, past the army and customs post. Take a right at the fork (2km from the village), and after a pleasant 1km walk through grassy dunes you'll be rewarded with a wide sand strand. If you turn left instead, the road meets the Allahein River marking the border of The Gambia and Senegal. There's a small harbour here, plus the Kartong Fishing Centre and several pirogues that ferry between the Gambian and Senegalese sides of the river.

Like elsewhere on the coast, things are changing here too, and several ambitious hotel projects are likely to put an end to Kartong's sleepiness. The good news is that the local community is active in trying to determine the direction of tourist development. The humble offices of **KART** (Kartong Association for Responsible Tourism; ☎ 4495887; www .safarigarden.com) in the heart of town are absolutely worth a visit – they can tell you how to best support their endeavours, as well as organise a variety of activities, ranging from bird-watching tours and apiary visits to pirogue, bicycle and walking tours.

KART also organises the rootsy **Kartong Festival** (☎ 8900411, 7730535), an annual dance and music event featuring a stunning array of dancing, drumming troupes and orchestras from the region. The first event happened in March 2006; inquire about future dates.

Sights & Activities

Kartong is a great place to lean back and enjoy the slow pace of African village life, and most activities here fit right into this lazy holiday scheme. Bird-watchers don't have to go far to spot numerous species, and the area is great for walking and bicycle tours (the KART office and Boboi Beach Lodge have a few wonky bikes for hire). A pirogue tour on the Allahein River is another great way of getting birds in front of your binoculars, or just to enjoy the picturesque surroundings. The **Riverside Café** (☎ 9957694) – which is a couple of plastic chairs and a cool box with drinks next to the Italian Restaurant – organises a range of river tours (D500 for one hour; D800 for two hours). Otherwise, you can practise your negotiating skills with the fishermen at the Fishing Centre.

Tours to the local **Reptile Farm** (admission D100) consist of guided walks, complete with tape-recorded information, around some small cages with snakes and lizards. If you like your reptiles in the wild, ask your hotel or KART for tours to the sacred **crocodile pool** of Mama Bambo Folonko. You'll need guidance; it's tricky to find.

Kartong is home to the pretty **Lemon Fish Art Gallery** (☎ 4394586; www.lemonfish.gm), well signposted on the main road. It has an excellent exhibition of contemporary paintings, sculptures and batiks by Gambian artists and it also runs art workshops. There's a boutique where you can purchase art, jewellery and fashion at fixed prices, and you can even rent rooms here.

Sleeping

Boboi Beach Lodge (☎ 7776736; www.gambia-adventure.com; camping per person D150, tree house D250, d incl breakfast D600) With bungalows set in a lush tropical garden, giant palm trees lending shade to hammocks, an invitation to sleep under a starlit sky (and a provided mosquito net), and 10-step access to the beach, this place is hard to beat as far as settings go. If it just sorted out its shared showers, too, this would be a dream destination.

Lemon Fish Art Gallery (☎ 4394586; www.lemon fish.gm) This pretty gallery overlooking the ocean has five excellent, colourfully decorated rooms to rent. They're intended for conference guests and friends of the gallery, but if there's space the friendly manager will no doubt accommodate you. Rates are negotiable; around D600 is appropriate.

Stiching Stala (☎ 9915604; www.stala-adventures .com) This Dutch-run bird-watching and fishing camp was getting ready to open when we visited – if no financial or other disaster has occurred, it should by now be a cosy ecolodge, driven by solar and wind power, and set in a breathtaking location right on the river. Prices weren't available yet at the time of research, so call to find out.

Tamba Kuruba (☎ 9851857; r per person D350) This place consists of six huts spread across a wide area – the beach is only a few metres past the dune. It's basic, but very friendly, and all profits go to the local hospital.

Country Edge Lodge (☎ 9933193; per person D350) This tranquil, solar-powered camp has clean, though uninspiring bungalows spread across a wide, and slightly barren terrain. The beach is in tempting proximity, possibly a good enough reason to stay here.

Sandele Eco-Retreat (☎ 4495887; geri@gamspirit .com) Another work in progress, this was about to become Kartong's first luxury hotel when we passed. The ambitious plans envisaged an ecolodge, but with attention paid to the minute details that add up to total comfort. The first beach bungalows nearing completion were as stylish as they were enormous – check if they're inhabitable yet. Prices weren't available at the time of research – but you can expect a top-end rate.

Eating

Eating options are limited, and self-catering isn't a bad idea. Most of the camps provide food, though you'll have to let them know if you intend to eat.

Italian Restaurant (☎ 9957694, 00221 616 43 82; 🕑 11am-midnight) Right on the river, past the Fishing Centre, you find this curious gem. It really is Italian, from the management and the chef (with his scooter parked outside), to *the al dente* spaghetti and the perfect espresso. Absolutely worth a visit – though you'll need a taxi or the leisure for a 3km walk to get there.

Morgan's Grocery (snacks & meals D50-200; 🕑 lunch & dinner) About 300m west of the village along a sandy track, Morgan's stands atop a sandy hill from where it's an easy walk to the crocodile pool. The African and European meals served here are simple but good, and taste even better in the friendly company of the well-informed management.

Umpacola Bar (☎ 4419111; silwia_barke@web.de; meals around D150; 🕑 lunch & dinner) In the heart of Kartong, Umpacola serves generous, hearty meals. The name means 'meeting place', and for making contact with locals the restaurant's central location is unbeatable.

Getting There & Away

There are two ways of getting to Kartong by public minibus from Serekunda; either the longer journey via Brikama to Gunjur where you change to another minibus to Kartong, or the more direct route from the Tippa Garage in Serekunda, which follows the coastal road. You also have to change in Gunjur if you take the coastal road. Both journeys should cost around D36. Note that waiting times for transport from Gunjur to Kartong can be discouragingly long. Hiring a bush taxi from Gunjur will cost around D200, and many of Kartong's camps offer

a pick-up service. Or take a bike with you from Serekunda and cycle the remaining few picturesque kilometres between Gunjur and Kartong. Hiring a taxi all the way from Serekunda should cost around D400; from Brikama it's D250.

On the map, Kartong seems like the perfect launch pad for a trip to Casamance, but with no regular transport, a river to cross, no border post and a 10km hike on the Senegal side, this is just an illusion. The police point at the southern exit of Kartong can normally stamp your passport, provided someone's there to do so. If not, don't cross the border without the stamp, as you'll run into difficulties on the Senegalese side.

If you can get that all-important stamp in Kartong and wish to attempt travelling into Senegal from here, you can cross the Allaheim River border by negotiating a pirogue at the Fishing Centre. Don't count on motorised traffic on the Senegalese side; you might have to walk about 10km to reach Kabadio. From Kabadio regular taxis depart to Abéné or Kafountine, where you'll need to have your passport stamped by Senegalese officials to complete your border crossing. See the boxed text, p251 for details.

If boat trips are for you, you might be able to negotiate a pirogue straight to Kafountine; ask at the Fishing Centre.

SOUTH BANK & INLAND

There's plenty besides beach tourism in Gambia, and you don't even have to step far beyond the sand's end to find it. The following four places can all be reached in day trips from the coast. The tiny village of Lamin on the main road southeast of Serekunda is worth visiting for the impressive river-set Lamin Lodge and Abuko Nature Reserve, which lies just around the corner. A few kilometres further south is dust-blown Brikama, the first 'upcountry' town on the route to the interior. And on the route to Casamance, the birders' paradise Marakissa and border town Darsilami make for peaceful stops.

LAMIN LODGE

This quirky **lodge** (☎ 4497603; www.gambiariver .com; 🕑 9am-11pm, meals around D200) looks like a little boy's dream; it's a rugged, handmade log cabin on stilts, overlooking a mangrove creek. It's one of the most ingenious restaurant ideas around – so treasured that the owner rebuilt and expanded it after it burnt to the ground a few years back. Most tour groups stop at this place, and for good reason. The food, mainly European cuisine with a seafood touch, is delicious and tastes best on the creaking 3rd floor at sunset.

The eccentric owner is also head of the **Gambia River Experience** (☎ 4494360; www.gambia river.com), an inspired little company that organises plenty of imaginative boat trips on the Gambia River. At the lodge, you can hire pirogues and small motorboats for trips by the day (D10,000), by the hour (D700), or you can arrange drop-offs to Denton Bridge (D1600) and Banjul (D1500). Best-loved of all is its famous birders' breakfast trip – think oysters and pancakes, with binoculars.

Getting There & Away

Most people get here by an organised boat tour. By road it's best to hire a taxi (D150 from Serekunda), or combine Lamin Lodge with time at Abuko Nature Reserve (D300 to D400 from Serekunda, including two to three hours' waiting time.). Alternatively, from Banjul or Serekunda you can take any minibus towards Brikama (D10), get off in Lamin village and then follow the dirt road for about 3km to the lodge.

ABUKO NATURE RESERVE

Despite its tiny size – 105 hectares, less than 1/8000th the size of Senegal's main national park Niokolo-Koba – **Abuko Nature Reserve** (☎ 7782633; www.darwingambia.gm; admission D31; ☑ 8am-7pm) is the mightiest force of Gambia's national parks.

The gallery forest, open woodlands and Guinea savannah of Abuko are home to myriad species of flora and fauna. The Lamin Stream runs through part of the reserve and is integral in attracting many of the more than 250 bird species regularly seen here; Abuko is one of the best places in West Africa for bird-watching.

Among the 52 mammal species calling Abuko home are bushbucks, duikers, porcupines, bushbabies and ground squirrels as well as three monkey types: green or vervet monkeys, endangered western red colobus monkeys and patas monkeys.

The reserve is particularly famous for its Nile crocodiles. Unlike those found in

the various sacred pools, the crocodiles of Abuko are completely wild and often enormous – you don't want to get too close, and certainly do *not* try patting them.

Crocs aren't the only reptiles here; they have the company of more than 30 other species including an impressive array of snakes such as pythons, puff adders, green mambas and forest cobras. They can sometimes be seen sunning themselves on the paths, but usually make for the undergrowth at the slightest approach – no incidents of snake-bite have been recorded by the park staff.

Assuming that the mamba you've spied does decamp into the bush, it could be sliding off underneath any one of more than 115 species of plants, many of which are labelled.

At the far end of Abuko is a small animal orphanage. Most of the animals staying here will be returned to the wild when ready, but there are also a few permanent residents, including hyenas and various monkeys. A few years back, the orphanage also famously housed a lion, but it was tragically shot by military when it was thought to be at risk of escaping.

Abuko is a great place to visit, but like all of Gambia's national parks, it's not having an easy time. It's fighting to preserve its area in its entirety, as well as its amazing biodiversity. Right at the heart of the reserve's amazing preservation work is the **Makasutu Wildlife Trust** (www.darwingambia.gm), a busy research centre that studies Gambia's biodiversity, trains wildlife guides and runs various education projects. The trust also takes on volunteers and can provide them with accommodation next to the reserve. Contact them for details.

Information

Even if you're not an early-rising birder, the morning hours before the midday heat are the best time to visit Abuko, although the reserve gets quieter as the sun rises.

There are several photo hides near Darwin Field Station by the crocodile pools and behind the animal orphanage (the latter is private and costs D50). You'll get the best pictures at the west-facing hides in the morning, when you've got the sun behind you.

The longest bird trail takes about two hours. If you're pressed for time, check the map at the main gate for shorter options.

> **TWITCHER TIPS: BIRD-WATCHING AT ABUKO NATURE RESERVE**
>
> Compact Abuko teems with birds, but the best places to spot the feathered creatures are an area of open Guinea savannah woodland, the bird extension behind the orphanage, and the main pool, where you can hope to view from photo hides collared sunbirds, green hylias, African goshawks, oriole warblers, yellowbills and leafloves. Abuko is about the only place in Gambia where you can observe green and violet turacos, white-spotted flufftails, ahanta francolins and western bluebills. The private hide near the animal orphanage is a good place to try your luck.
>
> Early morning is the best time to observe bird activity; the gates open at 6.30am for keen spotters. You will get the opportunity to see plenty of species by following the trail through the gallery forest, then along the extension walk with stops at the hides.

A thin book about the reserve can be bought at the ticket office, and several publications on the reserve and Gambian flora and fauna are for sale at the **Darwin Field Station** (🕓 8am-4pm).

Sleeping & Eating
African Zoo Rest & Lodge (☎ 4473414; s/d D500/600) Most people come to Abuko as part of a day trip. But if you want to explore the area for a bit longer you can stay here, opposite the reserve's entrance. It's a simple affair with shared bathrooms, and the restaurant usually serves no-frills meals during lunch and dinner hours (around D100 to D200). Management is friendly and welcoming.

Getting There & Away
A private taxi to Abuko from the Atlantic coast resorts costs about D300 to D400, including two hours of waiting time. Alternatively, you can take a minibus from Serekunda towards Brikama (D10). The reserve entrance is on the right (west) of the main road (you pass the exit about 200m before reaching the entrance).

BRIKAMA
Brikama, Gambia's third-largest settlement, is a typical junction town: extensive, noisy and busy. People and goods moving in and out, and up and down the country pass through this dusty upcountry place, though few choose to stay here.

There's little to see here, apart from the bustle itself, and the famous **craft market** (also known as Woodcarvers' Market, open 9am to 6pm daily) at the edge of town on the right as you come in from Banjul or Serekunda. It's a hectic corner of covered stalls crammed with souvenir-style sculptures, improvised ateliers and hordes of eager salesmen. It's the perfect place to acquire some tat and practise your negotiation skills.

Information
There's a hospital, Western Union branch, post office, a couple of Internet cafés (the best ones are Bojank K Net and the Gamtel office), and a Trust Bank branch that's supposed to take Visa cards, though you shouldn't rely on it.

Sleeping & Eating
Brikama's hotels are certainly no enticement to stay here.

Domor Deema (☎ 903302; Mosque Rd; r D200) Located about 300m from the taxi park, this place has never been great, and is rapidly getting worse. At least the plates are clean; the restaurant serves generous platters of the local classics *benechin* (fish with vegetables on a bed of rice) or *domodah* (rice, fried meat and vegetables covered with a groundnut sauce).

Bojang & Kawinkel Fast Food & Guest House (☎ 7700123; r D200) This place is only for the desperate or very brave-hearted. The rooms are shoddy and the shared toilets almost frighteningly filthy. Only a last resort.

Chief's Place (☎ 9845959; off Basse Hwy; r D200) 'Chief's Place' is what the locals call this surprisingly decent but hard-to-find nameless lodging, right behind the mayor's home. Ask for chief Bojang's house and you'll be led to an iron compound door that hides a cluster of well-maintained bungalows.

Food options are mainly limited to greasy local eateries. The Lucky Palace is a fairly decent option, the Kambeng Restaurant has a pretty garden, and the **Gilanka Restaurant** (☎ 9851857; meals D15) serves enormous bowls of tasty rice and fish. More exotic things such as chicken and chips are slightly pricier (D40).

KORA COURSES

For anybody interested in African music, Brikama should be an obligatory stop on the itinerary. The dusty town is home to one of the most renowned families of kora players in the country, a griot clan that reaches back several generations and has brought forth such mighty talents as Dembo Konté, his son Bakari Konté, and Malamini Jobarteh and his sons Pa and Tata Dindin Jobarteh. Forget about the 'instant drumming courses' on the coast, this is one of Gambia's best places to learn traditional instruments – such as kora, *djembe* (a short, goat hide–covered drum), *bolonbolong* (a three-string bass harp), *balafon* or *sabar* (a tall, thin, hourglass drum) – from brilliant players and teachers. You can also watch the instruments being made, and get an introduction into the griot's métier. Prices are entirely negotiable, depend on duration, and whether you stay and eat in your teacher's compound (which is possible). If you can't get the **musicians** (☎ 7710015; www.kairakundaarts.org) on the phone, ask any kid in town to show you the way to their home.

Getting There & Away

Brikama is easily reached by public transport as minibuses go up and down the main road between Banjul and Brikama, via Serekunda, about once every 10 minutes during the day. The fare both to and from Banjul and Serekunda is D10.

If you're headed east, there is frequent transport to Soma (D80), where you change for any other upcountry destination. The road between Brikama and Soma is probably the worst stretch of tarmac in the country – be prepared for a rocky ride, delays and punctures.

There are frequent bush taxis to Gunjur (D10), where you change for transport to Kartong.

Brikama is the junction from which it's best to reach the Casamance region in Senegal. A bush taxi to the Senegalese border in Séléti costs D40 (CFA800); Séléti to Ziguinchor is CFA2200. A direct taxi from Brikama to Kafountine is D60, and a bush taxi from Brikama to the tiny border post in Darsilami is D8 (see the boxed text, p251).

DARSILAMI

The tiny border village of Darsilami sees only the occasional tourist en route to Kafountine in Casamance. This is a shame, because it's a very pretty place, and a great birding site to boot. The best thing though is Sow Jallow Jeeri, the local NGO (nongovernmental organisation) that produces the best yogurt anywhere in the country. And yes, it is worth seeking out a small village for the sake of its dairy products, especially if the journey there is as beautiful as the scenic route from Sanyang via Sifoe, a rarely travelled but stunning stretch of tropical landscape. (There's no public transport, so you'll need to hire a taxi, which will cost around D400 to D500 from the coastal resorts.)

There's also a very nice place to stay, the friendly (and ecofriendly) **Timberland** (☎ 9946981; www.senegam.net; r incl full board per person D510). The simple rooms are nicely furnished, the restaurant serves excellent African and European meals (around D150), and you won't find friendlier management than that of the Dutch-Gambian couple running the place.

MARAKISSA

The peaceful quiet of this tiny village on the route from Darsilami to Brikama is only disturbed by the chirping of countless birds. This is a favourite spot for bird-watchers, who come to see white-breasted cuckoo shrikes, sunbirds, blue-breasted kingfishers, African darters and dozens of other species in the woodlands surrounding a calm river. Just spending a day on the terrace of the friendly **Marakissa River Camp** (☎ 9905852; marakissa@planet .nl; r per person incl breakfast D380; ▣) you will see several types of birds. Or you can always take part in one the river camp's excursions on foot or by pirogue (from D200).

MAKASUTU CULTURE FOREST

Makasutu means 'sacred forest' in Mandinka, or 'cultural theme park' in the language of tourist enterprise. Not far outside Brikama, the **Makasutu Culture Forest** (☎ 4483335; www .makasutu.com; admission per adult/child D700/400) occupies about 1000 hectares of land along Mandina Bolong; it's land that's dedicated to displaying a pretty, lush and smiling Gambia – just that little bit more pristine than the pristine environment beyond the forest boundaries.

A day in the forest includes a mangrove tour by pirogue; guided walks through a range of habitats including a palm forest where you can watch palm wine being tapped; and a visit to a crafts centre and demonstrations of traditional dancing. For a half-day visit take D200 off the price and the food out of the programme. The tours are well organised and make for a nice day out, though they'll appeal more to those who like their adventures with safety-net than those out to experience the 'real' Gambia.

Next to the forest is the **Mandina River Lodge** (☎/fax 4484100; www.makasutu.com; r per person incl half-board D5440), one of the most extravagant places to stay in the entire country. This exclusive ecoretreat is known for its successful marriage of lavishness and respect for nature, as well as for its stunning architecture. Its four solar-powered luxury lodges float on the river, and intimate dining areas are tucked away in the mangroves. Bookings are made through Gambia Experience (p102) or the Makasutu website, and if you're not a guest, you're not allowed to visit the lodge.

Getting There & Away

Most people come on a tour arranged through one of the tour operators. Most people come here on an organised tour. If you're making your own way, it's best to hire a taxi (D250 from Serekunda). Alternatively, you can ask a bush taxi to drop you at Tuti Falls Rd (D12 from Serekunda) and walk the last 3km. The place isn't well signposted, but any local can help you out.

TUMANI TENDA CAMP

This **camp** (☎ 9903662; tumanitenda@hotmail.com; per person D200) is another ecotourism venture situated about an hour from the coast on a *bolong* (creek) near the Gambia River. It's owned and operated by the residents of the neighbouring Taibatu village, who use the profits to fund community projects within the village. There are five traditional-style huts, each maintained by a different family from the village; rates include breakfast and other meals are D30. This is basic living, but for a taste of village life in a great location it's hard to beat. Bird-watchers venture here to try their luck spotting rare brown-necked parrots. With the help of a guide from the camp, you should also be able to observe porcupines from a hide.

Take a bush taxi from Brikama (D10) and ask to be dropped off at the turn-off to Taibatu (look for the sign). From here the camp's a 2.5km walk.

NORTH BANK

Gambia's north coast is even smaller than its south coast, stretching all of 10km from Barra at the mouth of the Gambia River to the island of Ginak, which marks the border with Senegal. Upriver from Barra are the historical sites of Albreda and James Island and the village of Jufureh, made famous by Alex Haley's book *Roots*.

BARRA

Barra lies on the northern bank of the Gambia River, opposite Banjul, and ferries regularly chug between the two towns (see p96). Most travellers pass through Barra as quickly as they can, taking transport to/from Senegal, but those with an interest in history may want to have a look at **Fort Bullen** (admission D25; 🕘 9am-5pm). Built by the British in the 1820s and '30s to complement the fort in Bathurst (now Banjul) and to control slave shipping on the Gambia River, the fort was abandoned in the 1870s. It was rearmed briefly during WWII before falling into disuse again. In 1996 the fort was renovated as part of the International Roots Festival, and today is open to visitors. The large, rectangular fort has low round bastions at each corner, and you can walk along the battlements overlooking the river mouth. An informative leaflet on the fort's history is available from Banjul's National Museum (p94).

GINAK ISLAND (NIUMI NATIONAL PARK)

Niumi National Park spreads across a small corner of northwest Gambia, including the long, narrow island of Ginak (also spelt Jinak). The island is separated from the mainland by a narrow creek, and is contiguous with the Parc National du Delta du Saloum in neighbouring Senegal.

A dead-straight border dating from colonial times runs through the island, and its northern section is in Senegalese territory. There are three main villages on the island. The two in Gambia are Ginak Kajata and Ginak Niji and the one in Senegal is Djinakh

Diatako, but the locals are all of the same Mandinka-speaking Serer clan and ignore the international boundary. This doesn't seem to matter as very few government officials from other countries ever venture onto Ginak.

The island has a good range of habitats in a very small area – beach, mud flats, salt marsh, dunes, mangrove swamps, lagoons, grassland and dry woodland – and is very good for bird-watching; waders and water birds are the main residents, but many other species can be seen, including birds of prey. Dolphins are occasionally spotted from the shore, and turtles nest on the beach. In theory, the park protects small populations of manatees, crocodiles, clawless otters, hyenas, bushbucks and duikers, plus various monkey species, but many animals have been hunted down, making the chances of spotting them slim.

Ginak is a pretty stretch of land, by all means, though claims to celestial beauty made by various tour operators are a touch exaggerated. Over the last few years, the heart of Niumi National Park has been eroded and replaced by large marijuana fields, which aren't quite as fascinating as the lush tropical forest that used to grow here. To see the remaining beautiful spots and not get lost in the illegal plantations, it's best to join an organised excursion.

Sleeping

Madiyana Lodge (☎ 4494088, 9920201; r per person D600) This modest place on the western seafront was privately built in close cooperation with the local population and the national park authorities. Accommodation is in simple huts, lighting is by kerosene lamp and toilets are shared. There's also a breezy bar-restaurant serving excellent Gambian and European food (meals D150).

Getting There & Away

If you phone Madiyana Lodge before arrival, you can organise pick-up from your front door. For CFA1500 (one way) you'll be driven to Banjul, and then taken to the lodge by boat. Another good option is joining an organised tour. The trips by the small operator **Hidden Gambia** (☎ in UK 01527 576239; www.hiddengambia.com) get consistently good reviews. For D3000 they include transport, accommodation at Madiyana Lodge and full board.

If you insist on independence, take the ferry from Banjul to Barra, and then hire a taxi to Ginak Niji (around D400). To get to Ginak Niji, take the main road north for a few kilometres to the village of Kanuma, then turn left and follow the sandy track northwest to reach the lagoon opposite the village of Ginak Niji. From there you need to negotiate a canoe across the river, and once on the other side it's a 20-minute walk directly west across the island to reach the lodge.

JUFUREH & ALBREDA

Jufureh (also spelt Juffure or Juffereh) is a small village on the Gambia River's northern bank about 25km upstream from Barra.

It became world famous in the 1970s following the publication of *Roots,* in which African-American writer Alex Haley describes how Kunta Kinte, his ancestor, was captured here and taken as a slave to America 200 years ago. His story turned the tiny community into a popular tourist destination, though there's little to see except the overblown village action when tourist boats arrive. Women pound millet at strategic points, babies are produced to be admired and filmed, the artisans in the craft market crank into gear and one of Haley's supposed relatives, an old lady (sister of the deceased Binde Kinte) makes a guest appearance. Photos are displayed of Alex Haley and the family, and tourists give money to take photos of the photos.

Albreda village is very close to Jufureh (a 500m walk) and is usually visited at the same time. It's a peaceful place, with huts and houses between baobabs, palms and kapok trees. The main thing to see is the ruined 'factory' (fortified slaving station) built by French traders in the late 17th century. It's on the river's edge near the quay where the tour boats land. Nearby is a large British cannon dating from the same period.

Between Jufureh and Albreda is a small **museum** (☎ 4710276, 7710276; admission D100; ☒ 10am-5pm Mon-Sat) with a simple but striking exhibition tracing the history of slavery on the Gambia River.

Sleeping & Eating

Jufureh Resthouse (☎ 5710276; amadou.juffure@yahoo.fr; r per person incl breakfast D300) This is mainly a rootsy, slightly lethargic drumming camp that works with French groups, but can

---

THE ROOTS DEBATE

Alex Haley based his research for his novel *Roots* on recollections of elder relatives who knew their African forebear's name was Kinte and that he'd been captured by slavers while chopping wood for a drum outside his village. This later tied in with a story Haley was told by a griot at Jufureh.

Critics have pointed out (quite reasonably) that the story is flawed in many areas. Kinte is a common clan name throughout West Africa, and the griot's story of Kunta Kinte's capture would hardly have been unique. Also, as the slave stations of Albreda and James Island had been very close to Jufureh for some decades, it's unlikely that a villager from here would have been taken by surprise in this way. While the story of Alex Haley's ancestor is almost certainly true, it's exceedingly unlikely that he actually came from Jufureh. Despite the inconsistencies, Haley seemed happy to believe he was descended from the Kintes of Jufureh, and the myth remains largely intact.

Detractors may delight in exposing fabrication, but there is a danger that the debate on the accuracy of Haley's story may obscure a much more serious and undeniable fact: the slave trade was immoral and inhuman, and had a devastating effect on Africa. Millions of men and women were captured by European traders, or by other Africans paid by Europeans, and taken to plantations in the Americas. Many historians hold that their labour, and the slave trade itself, was fundamental to the economic development of Europe and the USA in the 18th and 19th centuries.

---

accommodate independent travellers if there's space in the shabby bungalows.

Kunta Kinte Roots Camp (☎ 9905322; baboucarr lo@hotmail.com; s/d D500/1000) Down the road from the Rising Sun Restaurant, this ambitiously sized hotel has spotless accommodation in colourfully decorated bungalows. If you phone before arriving, staff can organise excellent meals. For groups, African buffet lunches are D125 per head.

Rising Sun Restaurant (meals D100-200; ☺ lunch & dinner) Right on the beach, you get a good view over the river from this unpretentious place. Meals aren't particularly inspiring, and there are lot of hasslesome freelance guides lurking around, but it's one of the very few food options in town.

Getting There & Away

The usual and easiest way to visit Jufureh and Albreda is by organised river tour (p290). All the tour operators along the Atlantic coast and several hotels have the 'Roots Tour' in their catalogue. If you go independently, it's cheaper to travel here by taxi. Take the ferry from Banjul to Barra and find a shared taxi to Jufureh, which costs around D50.

Hiring a private taxi for a day trip is best done in Barra rather than Banjul, so that you avoid paying the steep ferry car fee. From Barra you should pay around D400 there, up to D1000 if you ask the driver to wait and drive you back too. There are only a few shared taxis per day on this route, so if you want to do the trip in a day you'll

have to catch the first ferry. But if you are making the effort to come all this way, you should consider staying overnight; both Jufureh and Albreda are at their best in the evening, when the tourist groups have left.

JAMES ISLAND

This island in the middle of the Gambia River is about 2km south of Jufureh and Albreda. On it are the remains of Fort James (1650s), the site of numerous skirmishes in the following centuries. The fort was held variously by British, French and Dutch traders, as well as a couple of privateers (pirates), and was completely destroyed at least three times (twice by the French, and once by accident when a gunpowder store exploded). It was used as a slave collection point by British traders until slaving was outlawed, and finally abandoned in 1829.

The ruins of the fort are quite extensive, although the only intact room is a food store, which is often called the slave dungeon because it sounds more interesting. The island is rapidly being eroded, and at some points the water laps around the battlements. Only the sturdy baobab trees seem to be holding the island together.

Most people take in James Island as part of a Banjul–Jufureh boat trip, but you might be able to arrange a pirogue to take you over from Albreda, especially if you overnight in the village. Island admission including a visit to the museum of Jufureh costs D100; the pirogue costs D300 to D400.

Central & Eastern Gambia

Gambia being such a tiny sliver of land, nothing is really remote – yet once you've spent 12 hours on the tyre-busting road that leads upcountry, you'll probably feel as though you've crossed the continent. The route winds through crop fields, rice paddies, palm groves and patches of natural forest. Every 10km or so there's a junction where a dirt track leads north towards the Gambia River, which is never far away, but always frustratingly out of view.

If you want to see the waterway or maybe even go on a pirogue trip, just hop off the taxi and put in a couple of overnight stops at the few brilliantly located camps that are sprinkled along the riverside. Most of these are well equipped for ardent bird-watchers, for whom a trip upcountry is a must. Numerous national parks – including the River Gambia and Kiang West National Parks and the Baobolong Wetland Reserves – feature such a stunning array of birds (and other wildlife) that nature lovers might be tempted to camp out here for days.

Gambia's inland is best explored in leisure mode – there's plenty to see, and most places are tucked away in the country's remote corners. By far the most enjoyable way of travelling here is by boat – hardly surprising, as the narrow strip that is Gambia consists largely of waterway. Chugging slowly upriver, past mangrove-lined creeks, tiny islands and wide wetlands might easily be the unexpected highlight of your entire trip.

HIGHLIGHTS

- Wake up to the lapping of the waves and the calls of the birds at **Bintang Bolong** (opposite), where huts stand on stilts in the river

- Take a pirogue from Tendaba to the maze of mangroves in the **Baobolong Wetland Reserve** (p131)

- Follow in the footsteps of histories old and new at **Georgetown** (Jangjang-bureh; p133), where relics of ancient African and modern European cultures document different eras

- Try your luck at spotting hippos and chimpanzees on a boat tour to **River Gambia National Park** (p138)

- POPULATION: 450,000

CENTRAL GAMBIA

BINTANG BOLONG

A large, meandering tributary of the Gambia River, Bintang Bolong rises in Senegal and joins the river about 50km upstream from Banjul. The banks of the tidal river are lined with mangroves, and tucked away among the maze of shrubs near Bintang is the spectacular **Bintang Bolong Lodge** (☎ 4488035, 9867615; www.bintang-bolong.com; r per person D400; 🍴), an intimate, ecofriendly camp made from local mangrove, and clay bricks. It was renovated in 2004 and now houses up to 16 people in stunning huts that sit on stilts on the river. If the tide is high, you can almost leap from your bedroom into a canoe and go bird-watching or fishing in the mangroves. The lodge offers boat trips (D800 per hour per boat), as well as plenty of other activities (visits to the local crocodile pool where you can get close-up views of baby crocs are a favourite). It can also arrange a pick-up from Brikama (D750), Banjul or Serekunda (D1200) or Soma (D2000).

This is a great, family-friendly place to explore the natural surroundings of central Gambia, and catch a glimpse of rural life – the camp is closely integrated with the local community, employing villagers and investing in schools and hospitals.

Getting There & Away

Twice a day there's a bus from Brikama to Bintang (D25, one hour). If you can't face the wait for the bus to fill up, you can hire a private taxi (around D1700 to D2000). The driver needs to follow the main road east through the village of Somita, and at Killy turn left (north) along the dirt road to reach Bintang village and the lodge. Or just phone the place and arrange to be picked up.

KANILAI

A small village near the Senegalese border, Kanilai is the hometown of President Jammeh. He's honoured his birthplace and put it on the tourist map through the construction of the **Sindola Safari Lodge** (☎ 4483415/6; kairaba@gamtel.gm; hut D1020, ste D2040; ❌ 🍴), a most luxurious upcountry lodging.

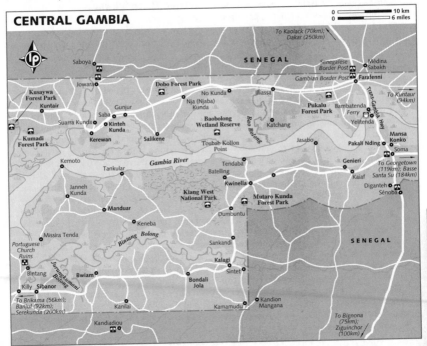

CENTRAL GAMBIA

Sindola offers the whole dazzling range of tourist facilities, from tennis and volley-ball courts to massage parlours and several bars and restaurants, spread out across a vast terrain of 30,000 sq metres. Birding trips and river fishing can be organised, too. The place owes its name 'Safari Lodge' to an adjoining wildlife park, a rather sad story of animals in cages. Several large mammals, including a couple of lions, were acquired to be 'put on display', but died before the park was completed.

To get here from the coast, you could take an all-inclusive tour from the Kairaba Hotel (p108), or hire a private taxi (around D3000). On public transport, take a bush taxi from Brikama and get off at the police checkpoint where the highway and the road to Kanilai meet. Kanilai is 6km further south.

TENDABA

On the southern bank of the Gambia River, the small village of Tendaba is 165km upstream from Banjul. The village occupies a place of honour in the upriver itineraries of many travellers, thanks to the enduringly attractive **Tendaba Camp** (☎ 4541024, 4465288; tendaba@qanet.gm; bungalows with/without bathroom from D245/225, VIP r D270). Established in the 1970s as a hunting camp, the hotel is something of a classic on the travellers scene, providing consistently good accommodation, service and a range of excursions. Tendaba's attraction lies in its position – opposite the Baobolong Wetland Reserve and in close proximity to Kiang West National Park – in short, it's a bird-watcher's dream destination.

Accommodation ranges from small bungalows to VIP rooms, fully equipped with a river-edge veranda and TV. The restaurant gets consistently good reviews – great news, as there's hardly anywhere else to go for a meal in the near surroundings. The bush pig in pepper sauce is a treat, and the evening buffets leave you spoilt for choice The camp frequently organises dance and drumming shows (donations always welcome).

From Tendaba, you can arrange 4WD excursions to Kiang West National Park and boat rides around the creeks of the Baobolong Wetland Reserve. If you don't want to take a vehicle trip, there are lots of options for **walking** in this area. A good destination for the day is Toubab Kollon Point, about 7km from the camp (see opposite for details).

Getting There & Away

Many people come to Tendaba Camp as part of a tour, and most large hotels and tour operators offer two-day excursions or

---

THE STATE OF THE ROADS

Two main arteries connect the eastern and western parts of Gambia – the north-bank road, on the upper side of the river, and the south-bank road, which parallels the Gambia River in the south. Both roads have been in a terrible state for years, the northern route being a washed-out dirt road, the southern a potholed stretch of tarred road. The southern connection used to be the better choice of two dire options, and the route used by most public transport. Yet continuous neglect has meant that the artery is now so rundown that it's even worse to drive on than the north-bank road. Bush taxis frequently drive on improvised dirt tracks beside the road, and Gambia's formerly proud bus network has literally been ground to a halt by the sand and stones.

If you're in your own car take the ferry from Banjul to Barra and travel via the north bank; your tyres and gearbox will be forever grateful. If you're travelling by bush taxi, you probably don't have much choice but to go via the southern route. From the coast to Brikama the tarred road is smooth, but the holes start only a few kilometres further down. The stretch from there to Soma is the worst, and things only really get better shortly before Georgetown. Georgetown to Basse is miraculously paved, raising hopes that the rest of the artery might be blessed with a new layer of asphalt, too, though no immediate works had been announced when we visited. The northern road, by contrast, is supposed to benefit from some fairly imminent improvements – ask around when you're there (and let us know!).

Whether you're going via the northern or southern connection, allow at least 12 hours for the tedious journey from the coast to Basse Santa Su. And if you want to eschew the treacherous potholes altogether and experience the scenery at its best, take the boat along Gambia's smoothest east–west connection – the Gambia River.

longer trips. A river tour is a particularly good idea (see p290). Prices differ widely – it's worth doing some phoning around before making your booking. Tours typically include transport, accommodation, food and side trips.

Another option is to come from the Atlantic Coast resorts by green tourist taxi (about D4000 for the car, carrying up to four people) and pay for your own room, food and day trips directly to the camp.

Independent travellers on public transport should take a bush taxi from Banjul or Serekunda along the main road towards Soma. Get off at the village of Kwinella; the camp (signposted) is 5km north along the dirt road. There are no regular minibuses, but camp manager Saja Touray promises to collect anyone from Kwinella for free. Otherwise it's a walk or trip by donkey cart.

KIANG WEST NATIONAL PARK

South of the river, and to the west of Tendaba Camp, **Kiang West National Park** (admission D31.50) is one of the largest protected areas in Gambia, and boasts its biggest and most diverse animal population. Habitats include mangrove creeks and mud flats (the river is still tidal this far upstream), plus large areas of dry woodland and grassland. A major natural feature is an escarpment, which runs parallel to the riverbank. We're not talking Rift Valley here, but even 20m is significant in a country as flat as Gambia, and from this high point you can look over the narrow plain between the escarpment foot and the river itself. Animals are often seen here, especially at the three water holes.

Kiang is one of the best places in Gambia to get a close-up look at cute bushbabies. Other frequently observed mammals include baboons, colobus monkeys, warthogs, marsh mongooses and bushbucks. You may see an antelope called a roan – it's large and horselike (hence the name), and migrates into the area from Casamance. Making very rare appearances are sitatungas, a larger relative of the bushbuck that are aquatic and adept at swimming and moving through river vegetation using their wide hooves.

Other rarely sighted species include hyenas, leopard, manatees, dolphins and crocodiles. Birds are also plentiful, with more than 300 species recorded (see right for birdwatching tips).

> ### TWITCHER TIPS: KIANG WEST NATIONAL PARK
>
> With more than 300 recorded species, Kiang West National Park is one of the richest birding areas in Gambia, and something of a pilgrimage site for keen watchers. Even visitors with little interest in the feathered creatures have been converted to binocular-wielding bird spotters, attracted by the sight of the large Abyssinian ground hornbill, ospreys, fish eagles, martial eagles and bateleur eagles. While raptor species are particularly common here, many other varieties, including the rare brown-necked parrot and the more common white-rumped swift are found here. Tendaba Camp has regular excursions to Kiang West, though for expert birding advice, you should consider coming with a specialist guide, and exploring the area on your own.

A popular place for viewing wildlife is **Toubab Kollon Point**, a river promontory in the northeast of the park. Behind the point, the escarpment runs close to the riverbank, and 2km west is a viewing hide overlooking a water hole, which attracts a good range of animals, especially in the dry season. November to January are the best months to visit, but wear pants to avoid being bitten by tsetse flies. The admission fee is payable at the park headquarters in Dumbuntu, although this is included in the price if you're on a tour from Tendaba.

BAOBOLONG WETLAND RESERVE

A tributary of the Gambia River, **Bao Bolong** rises in Senegal and enters the main river on the northern side, upstream from Tendaba. It contains several other *bolongs* (creeks), as well as mangroves and salt marshes, which together with the surrounding dry savannah woods and grassland make Baobolong Wetland Reserve of international importance. Baobolong is a Ramsar (the international wetlands convention) site.

The mangroves in this area are some of the largest in the region, growing over 20m high in places and forming a virtual forest. Birds are a major attraction – marshlands attract large numbers of herons (including the white-backed night heron) and egrets, the rare Pel's fishing owls and mouse-brown sunbirds. The reserve also protects various aquatic mammal species such as manatees, clawless otters and marshbucks.

The best way to experience this wonderful maze of islands and waterways is by boat, which is most easily arranged at Tendaba Camp.

SOMA & MANSA KONKO

Soma is a junction town where the main road crosses the Trans-Gambia Hwy, and is where you change transport if you're heading upcountry by bush taxi or, crucially, fill up the tank before continuing your journey east, where service stations are rare.

Soma is a dusty, flyblown place, with the main street full of trucks and rubbish, and nothing in the way of attractions. The border is only a few kilometres to the south, and the Gambian customs and immigration post is on the eastern edge of town. About 10km north of Soma is Yelitenda, where you catch the ferry across the Gambia River to Bambatenda, and then continue to Farafenni.

Near Soma is Mansa Konko, originally an important local chief's capital (the name means 'king's hill'), and then an administrative centre during the colonial era. Today it's a sleepy ghost town with a few reminders of the glory days, such as the **district commissioner's residence** and the crumbling **colonial villa**.

Sleeping & Eating

Moses Guesthouse (☎ 4531462; r per person D125) If you get stuck in Soma, this lively place on the north side of the main junction is the best option. Since it's the most popular place in a busy junction town, it can get quite noisy, but then again, it comes with the added attraction of 24-hour electricity.

Government Resthouse (s/d D150/250) This place in Mansa Konko is officially for government staff only, but desperate travellers can stay in the usually clean rooms. It's 2.5km from the main road near the old district commissioner's residence, which is the highest point for several kilometres around with some fine views over the Gambia River valley; the residence is also where to go if there's no-one around at the resthouse.

Getting There & Away

Most bush taxis from Serekunda terminate at the bush-taxi park in Soma's centre (the fare is D90) or go on to Farafenni (D100

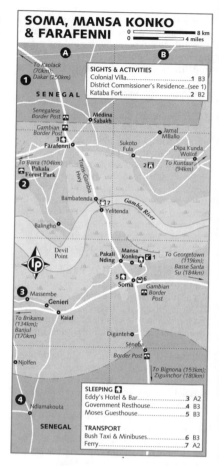

SOMA, MANSA KONKO & FARAFENNI

SIGHTS & ACTIVITIES	
Colonial Villa	1 B3
District Commissioner's Residence	(see 1)
Kataba Fort	2 B2

SLEEPING ⌂	
Eddy's Hotel & Bar	3 A2
Government Resthouse	4 B3
Moses Guesthouse	5 B3

TRANSPORT	
Bush Taxi & Minibuses	6 B3
Ferry	7 A2

from Serekunda). Transport to Georgetown (D80) and Basse Santa Su (D90) leaves from the same park. Heading south, you can also get bush taxis from the border to Bignona and Ziguinchor in southern Senegal.

If you're heading north from Soma, take a local bush taxi to the Gambia River ferry at Yelitenda (D6), go across as a foot passenger (D5), and take one of the vehicles waiting on the northern bank at Bambatenda to Farafenni (D6), where you can find transport to Kaolack or Dakar. The ferry service operates between 8am and 9pm, usually every half-hour, though waits can be longer, and the ferry suffers fairly frequent breakdowns. Tickets can be bought about 1km before you reach the ferry – anyone can indicate the office to you. Taking your own car across will cost around D65 – exact rates often depend on the mood of the official you happen to encounter on the day. You'll probably have to wait a while for a place, but it's not as bad as the Banjul to Barra ferry.

If you're on foot, you can also jump onto a pirogue (D4). Pirogues leave when they're full. You'll have pay another D4 for access to the port. A private pirogue should cost about D80.

FARAFENNI

Situated on the Trans-Gambia Hwy north of the Gambia River, Farafenni is a busy little town and much more pleasant than Soma. People come from surrounding villages and merchants come from as far as Mauritania and Guinea to sell their wares at the main Sunday *lumo* (market). This is a good place to sample upcountry life, although it feels more like Senegal than Gambia: CFA francs are used more than dalasi, and more French is spoken than English. If you're low on cash visit the **Trust Bank** (☎ 5735238; fax 5735007); it's the only bank for many kilometres. The Senegal border, 2km to the north, is open from 7am to midnight.

If you do get stuck here, it's worth taking the dirt road 10km east to **Kataba Fort**. Though reduced to its dusty foundations, this 1841 Wolof construction tells a half-forgotten story of old African kingdoms.

Sleeping & Eating

Eddy's Hotel & Bar (☎ 7735225; s/d with bathroom D200/250;) This place has been a popular travellers' meeting point for many years. You can eat chicken and chips or *benechin* (rice in a thick sauce of meat and vegetables) for in the shady garden courtyard (D35 to D45) while the apparently carefree Eddy shoots (unsuccessfully) at small birds with an air gun. Self-contained rooms come with either twin or double beds; note that room rates nearly double if you request air-con. There's also safe parking, cold beer and a disco at weekends.

For cheap food, there are several *chop shops* (local restaurants) on the main street, south of the junction.

Getting There & Away

If you're heading for Banjul, direct minibuses from Farafenni go to Serekunda most mornings for D90. If you're heading south

or anywhere upcountry on the southern bank, you have to go to Soma and change. If you're heading for Dakar there are bush taxis for CFA4000; some go from Farafenni itself, but most go from the Senegal side of the border. A minibus from the bush taxi stop in Farafenni to the Senegal border post is D5.

EASTERN GAMBIA

Beyond Farafenni is the Gambia River's transition zone – the area where it changes from saline to fresh water. The character of the river is also different: the tidal change is less noticeable, the mangroves thin out and thick forest grows down to the water's edge. And you'll increasingly notice islands on the river, the most famous being Baboon Island, which is part of the River Gambia National Park. As you head up the river there are several colonial-era towns. Georgetown and Basse Santa Su are both well worth visiting, as are the Wassu Stone Circles, enigmatic relics of an entirely different era.

GEORGETOWN (JANGJANG-BUREH)

Under the British, Georgetown was a busy administrative centre and trading hub full of grand buildings. Today it has a new (or should that be old?) name, a host of crumbling monuments to history and the sort of sluggish atmosphere that discourages all but the most necessary work – it's the perfect place to relax for a couple of days.

Located on the northern edge of Mac-Carthy Island in the Gambia River, about 300km by road from Banjul, the traditional and now officially reintroduced name for the town and island is Jangjang-bureh, but most people still call it Georgetown. The island is 10km long and 2.5km wide, covered with fields of rice and groundnuts, and has ferry links to both riverbanks. There is little in terms of infrastructure – no banks, no hospital – but there's an **Internet café** (per hr D25; 9am-6pm) for those who feel they need a connection beyond the island.

While in Georgetown, or even on the ferry taking you there, you'll undoubtedly be approached by persistent local youths offering their services as guides. Unless you're very directionally challenged you won't need their help; don't be afraid to say no.

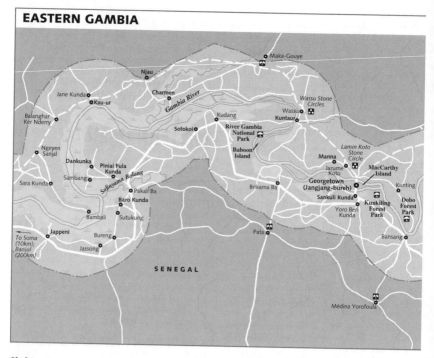

EASTERN GAMBIA

Sights

It may only take you a couple of hours to wander around Georgetown, but there is probably more to see here and in the surrounding area than in almost any other town in Gambia. Most of the 'sights' have a historical bent; two of the most interesting are crumbling **late-Victorian warehouses** situated on the waterfront either side of the northern ferry landing. Enterprising local youths have created a local 'Roots industry' from the structures. It started with one of the warehouses being referred to as 'Slave House', which was then changed to 'Slave Prison'; the place was then decorated with lit candles and a matching story was created. A 'Freedom Tree', claimed to guarantee liberation to any slave who touched it, another 'Slave House' and finally a 'Slave Market' joined the scene. Although records show slaves were transported through Georgetown, it is unlikely that the buildings were used in this trade as they were built well after slavery was abolished in British colonies in 1807. You might find this profitable rewriting of history an insult to the victims of slavery, or think of it as entertainment. Your choice – but be aware of the 'Visitors Book', encouraging incredibly generous donations in the memory of slavery.

Nearby is the old **Commissioner's Quarters** now inhabited by the district governor, and a **monument to Fort George** outside the police station. The fort was built by the British in 1823 after the local king asked for their protection against a neighbouring tribe. West of town is the **Armitage High School**, a historical building of vague interest to anyone keen on colonial architecture.

Those with a penchant for ancient historical features should take a trip to **Lamin Koto Stone Circle**. It's a smaller and less impressive monument than the famous Wassu Stone Circles, but sitting only 1.7km away from the north bank, it's closer and thus in good reach for those who can't make it to Wassu. The circle is on the right (northeast) side of the road, under a big tree.

Tours

Georgetown is an excellent base for pirogue tours and birding trips as well as for day

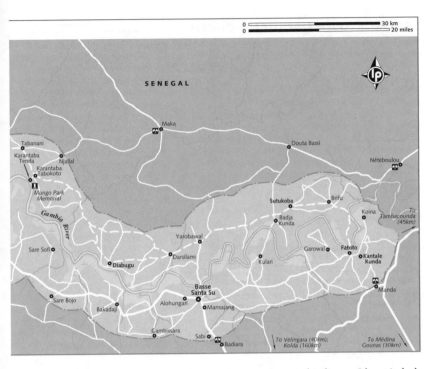

visits to the Mungo Park memorial at Karantaba Tenda, the River Gambia National Park, the Wassu Stone Circles and the Dobo and Kunkilling Forest Parks.

Most of the camps in Georgetown organise tours, and prices are roughly the same. Expect to pay D3500 per pirogue for day trips to the River Gambia National Park and D4000 for the double deal of a visit to Wassu and the River Gambia National Park. Baobolong Camp offers two-day boat trips to Karantaba Tenda (including on-board accommodation, D8000). Circumnavigations of MacCarthy Island also make for a good day out (per pirogue D1300).

Georgetown sees a lot of visitors interested in bird life, and most camps run birding excursions. The ones offered by the Bird Safari Camp are particularly recommended. Bird Safari Camp and Jangjang-bureh Camp are the best providers for river excursions.

Sleeping

Baobolong Camp (☎ 5676133; fax 5676120; Owens St; s/d D300/400) This is the best-functioning place in Jangjang-bureh itself – the luxury of a generator is a good indicator. It's set in lush gardens near the river at the eastern end of town. The camp attracts plenty of birds, and some of the various pirogue tours on offer are particularly geared towards twitchers.

Bird Safari Camp (☎ 5676108; fax 5674004; www.bsc.gm; r with half board per person D1000; 🖳) Some 2.5km west of a tiny island town, this place is about as secluded as it gets. Accommodation is in bungalows or luxury tents with bathroom. It has a generator, which you'll appreciate after dark. A resident ornithologist, private hides and guided walks make it a favourite with bird-watchers. To get here from central Georgetown, you can either hire a taxi or call to arrange a pick-up. This camp is on the itinerary of Hidden Gambia river trips (see p290), and can be reached by river as part of its tour.

Jangjang-bureh Camp (☎ /fax 5676182, 9920618; www.gambiariver.com; r per person D200) This rootsy place on the north bank of the Gambia River consists of an eclectic collection of rustic bungalows set in a mazelike garden. Lighting is by oil lamps, and a drink at the bar overlooking the river is a fine way to

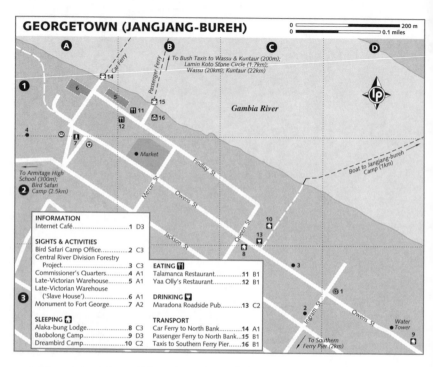

GEORGETOWN (JANGJANG-BUREH)

0-200 m
0-0.1 miles

To Bush Taxis to Wassu & Kuntaur (200m);
Lamin Koto Stone Circle (1.7km);
Wassu (20km); Kuntaur (22km)

Gambia River

Boat to Jangjang-bureh Camp (1km)

Market

To Armitage High
School (300m);
Bird Safari
Camp (2.5km)

Findlay St

Mercer St

Owens St

Jackson St

Queen St

Ingram St

Owens St

Water
Tower

To Southern
Ferry Pier (2km)

INFORMATION	
Internet Café	1 D3

SIGHTS & ACTIVITIES	
Bird Safari Camp Office	2 C3
Central River Division Forestry Project	3 C3
Commissioner's Quarters	4 A1
Late-Victorian Warehouse	5 A1
Late-Victorian Warehouse ('Slave House')	6 A1
Monument to Fort George	7 A2

SLEEPING	
Alaka-bung Lodge	8 C3
Baobolong Camp	9 D3
Dreambird Camp	10 C2

EATING	
Talamanca Restaurant	11 B1
Yaa Olly's Restaurant	12 B1

DRINKING	
Maradona Roadside Pub	13 C2

TRANSPORT	
Car Ferry to North Bank	14 A1
Passenger Ferry to North Bank	15 B1
Taxis to Southern Ferry Pier	16 B1

spend the evening. It's an old favourite with travellers and belongs to the Gambia River Experience – naturally, there's an enticing range of boat trips on offer.

Dreambird Camp (☎ /fax 5676182; r per person D200) This is mainly the embarkation point for the transfer boat to Jangjang-bureh Camp (free to guests and diners). It also has a few rooms, but these had collapsed when we visited. It was hard to tell whether they would be open again soon; no-one seemed inclined to make any specific statements – not a good sign...

Alaka-bung Lodge (☎ 5676123; alakabung@qanet .gm; Owens St; r per person D100) This low-key hostel, Georgetown's cheap and cheerful option, attracts a local clientele and has email access (but not always reliable generator power).

Eating & Drinking

Few options exist outside the camps and lodges, especially after dark, when Georgetown drowns in darkness and life retreats behind compound walls.

Talamanca Restaurant (☎ 9921100; Findlay St, meals from D100; ⏲ 11am-8pm) A relaxed spot run by the enterprising young Banna Kongira,

who's so keen he'll open after hours if hungry guests knock on his door. He also seems to be growing his humble restaurant into a 'hotel', having added a low-key, mosquito net–fitted bungalow. Inquire about rates.

There are a couple of cheap eateries around the market, as well as the following:
Maradona Roadside Pub (Owens St; snacks from D75; ⏲ lunch & dinner) Opposite Alaka-bung Lodge; a good place for snacks. Has a cheap bar.
Yaa Olly's Restaurant (Findlay St; meals D100-150; ⏲ lunch & dinner) An unpretentious address for cheap local meals.

Getting There & Away

Ferries reach MacCarthy Island from either the southern or northern bank of the river. The northern ferry operates from 8am to 7pm. The ferry connecting the island to the southern shore seems to run until demand dries up. We crossed onto the island at 11pm, while other travellers report the service inoperative after 6pm. Best to get there early. The main road between Banjul and Basse Santa Su does not go directly past the southern ferry ramp, but bush taxis turn off to drop off or pick up passengers here if you ask them. Ferry crossing costs D50/5 for cars/passengers. On the island, pick-ups take people to Georgetown for D10.

When leaving Georgetown, take a local pick-up to the southern ferry, and cross over to the southern bank. You may find a direct minibus to Basse Santa Su for D10. Alternatively, take a local minibus or bush taxi to Bansang (D5) and change here for transport to Basse Santa Su (D5). If you're heading west, go to Bansang or just to the main road. From there you can get to Soma, then change for Banjul and other destinations.

WASSU STONE CIRCLES

The area between the Gambia River and the Saloum River in southern Senegal is noted for its concentration of stone circles; the group at Wassu, 20km by road northwest of Georgetown and about 2km north of Kuntaur, is a particularly good example.

There are several **circles** (admission D30) each consisting of between 10 and 24 reddish-brown, massive stones, 1m to 2.5m high and weighing several tonnes. Most of the region's circles date from AD 500 to AD 1000, before the Mandinka people migrated to this area. Excavations have unearthed human bones and artefacts at the centre of many circles, indicating that they were burial sites,

although dating techniques show that bodies may have been buried after the circles were constructed. Little else is known about the people who built these structures. Theories suggest they were farmers because all the sites are near rivers; but some are buried with spears, suggesting they were hunters.

The caretaker will show you to a small but well-presented **museum** with exhibits discussing the possible origins of the circles. It has to be said that not everyone will find them a major attraction. Go if you want to see evidence of ancient African cultures, but not if you're expecting Stonehenge.

Getting There & Away

The stone circles are about 500m before the village of Wassu, coming from Georgetown. In theory Wassu can be reached from Farafenni, but transport can be hard to come by; most people come from Georgetown. A bush taxi to Wassu (D25) waits most mornings at the north-bank ferry ramp, but this goes only when full (which can take several hours), and even if you reach Wassu in time there might be nothing coming back. Bush taxis are only an option on Monday, the day of Wassu's colourful *lumo*, when they are more frequent. Otherwise it's safer to hire a private taxi for the day (around D700), or jump on a tour with a Georgetown camp.

THE CENTRAL RIVER DIVISION FORESTRY PROJECT

Deforestation is one of the greatest environmental dangers in Gambia, so it's encouraging to hear of the initiatives of the **Central River Division Forestry Project** (CRDFP; ☎ 5676198; www.crdfp.org). This inspiring environmental programme has been active in educating the local population about the importance of keeping forests intact, and has in the process created a series of excellent ecotrails through the remaining woods of central and eastern Gambia. One of these leads through the tiny **Dobo Forest Park**, a 34.5-hectare gallery forest that winds along the north bank of the Gambia River, not far from Bansang, and boasts an array of wildlife, including crocodiles, antelopes, bushbucks, hippos and bushbabies, as well as various bird species such as eagles, kingfishers, bee-eaters, rollers and woodpeckers.

The **Kunkilling Forest Park** on the south bank near Bansang is a much larger affair, and can either be walked through or explored by donkey cart. Its 200 hectares of riparian canopy forest are jointly managed by four neighbouring villages. Four ecotrails wind through rich woodlands (where more than 40 types of trees have been counted) inhabited by more than 185 bird species (among them African finfoots, white-backed vultures, adamawa turtle doves, shining-blue kingfishers and nightjars), monkeys, manatees and hippos. A guided visit will also take a brief historical detour, past the tomb of the 19th-century king of Fouladou, Musa Molo.

The CRDFP in Georgetown arranges highly recommended guided tours to these parks. And if a one-day exploration isn't enough for you, you can stay in one of the CRDFP's well-equipped rooms, and get more deeply involved in their preservation work. (The CRDFP is funded by GTZ and KfW. The DFS is the commissioned consultancy company for implementing the project.)

HIGHLY STRUNG HIPPOS

The best time to see hippos is at low tide, when the shallower water cannot hide them so well. If you see a hippo, admire it from afar. These giants of the river are notoriously cantankerous creatures. Forget lions, leopards and snakes – hippos are responsible for more deaths in Africa than any other animal. Despite being vegetarian, they frequently kill animals and people with their enormous jaws and 60cm-long teeth – not to eat them, but to protect their living space. Hippos are very territorial and short-sighted, and will plough into anything they consider a threat, including, unfortunately, the occasional boat with camera-wielding tourists. Keep a respectful distance and, naturally, don't try to feed them by throwing food towards their chomping jaws.

RIVER GAMBIA NATIONAL PARK

South of Kuntaur, five islands in the Gambia River are protected as a national park. Its heart is so-called Baboon Island – the name is sometimes used to refer to the entire park – the site of a project (privately initiated but now government-owned) that takes chimpanzees captured by illegal traders and rehabilitates them to live in the wild. Boat trips are available, but visitors are not allowed to land or get close to the islands. This is partly because it interferes with the rehabilitation process, but mainly because the chimps (there are more than 60) are nervous about humans getting too close. While females and young ones may be docile, the males can be quick to attack. Having lost their fear of people, they are more aggressive than 'wild' chimps and, being several times stronger than humans, they're capable of awesome deeds when riled. If they are not able to get at the object of their frustration, they will often vent their spleen on the females and youngsters of their own troop. Because of the dense cloak of gallery forest on the banks of the island, it is difficult to see chimps, and getting in close might result in your boat being boarded by a bristling alpha male.

If you visit the area, it's best to go with the aim of having a good day out on this beautiful stretch of river. You'll quite likely see baboons and monkeys, and possibly crocs and hippos too, plus an excellent selection of birds. And if you do happen to see any chimps – while keeping a responsible distance – it will be a bonus.

Getting There & Away

You can take a boat tour from Georgetown; several camps there have boats for hire at D1000 per day. Alternatively, you can go to Kuntaur by road and hire a boat from there. Several people provide the service; the going rate is about D250 for a three- or four-hour trip (after some bargaining). Boats are only permitted on the main channel between the islands and the east bank of the mainland, and are not allowed to approach the islands nearer than midstream. Boatmen often try to please their passengers by getting closer, but this should be discouraged.

MUNGO PARK MEMORIAL

Historians may want to head for Karantaba Tenda, about 20km east of Georgetown. Near this village, on the river bank, is the memorial pillar marking where the Scottish explorer Mungo Park set off into the interior to trace the course of the Niger River.

A bush taxi comes here most mornings from the north-bank ferry ramp opposite Georgetown but if your time is limited, hiring a private taxi may be the only certain way of getting there and back in a day (around D250). The pillar is outside the village, but local boys will guide you there for a small fee. Another option is to go by boat. You can hire one for the day from places in Georgetown from about D1000.

BANSANG

Music-lovers may know Bansang as the middle name of one of Gambia's greatest kora players – Amadu Bansang Jobarteh hails from here. A pilgrimage to his birthplace will introduce you to a large town spread out between the river and the main road. It's a calm area that invites walking, particularly if you're a keen bird-watcher – spectacular red-throated bee-eaters nest in a nearby quarry. And, quite importantly, Bansang also has the largest upcountry hospital.

BASSE SANTA SU

Set on a beautiful waterfront, Gambia's easternmost main town is the last major ferry-crossing point on the Gambia River and an area transport hub. It's a traditional trading centre, as crammed, busy, run-down and enterprising as any West African junction town, especially if you come on a Thursday, when the market is in full swing.

Both **Trust Bank** (☎ 5668907; fax: 5668907) and, opposite, **Standard Chartered Bank** (☎ 4668218) are in the town centre, on the road to Georgetown. They have branches in Basse that can advance money to Visa cardholders. You can make calls at the **Gamtel Office** (☎ 4229999; gen-info@gamtel.gm), opposite the post office, and possibly connect to the Internet, too, by the time you visit.

Sights & Activities

Most of Basse can be explored in an afternoon stroll, which should definitely include the town's bustling **market** and a walk along the waterfront. Heading for the ferry terminal, you'll see an imposing colonial warehouse on the riverside. A couple converted this building several years ago into the cultural centre and café **Traditions** (☎ 5668533; sulaymanjallowtraditions@yahoo.com; ☾ 9am-6pm). They exhibited and sold locally fabricated crafts including handmade clothes, mats and wall hangings, sewn from beautiful indigo, tie-dyed and mud-dyed cloth. Since they have left, the place has started gathering dust; the café as well as the display spaces were neglected when we visited. But the staff is still immensely enthusiastic and optimistic that this major stopping point of any tour to Basse will shine once again.

Even if you find Traditions devoid of activity, a trip here is rewarding. The balcony gives a great view across the river and ferry station, and, between June and February, it's also one of the best places in Gambia to see the Egyptian plover, a rare species, known locally as the crocodile bird. This small wader might be missed when standing quietly on the riverbank, but it is instantly recognised in flight by its swept-back wings and beautiful black-and-white markings.

Boat rides to see this and other birds (with a chance of spotting hippos or crocodiles) can be arranged with local boatmen on the waterfront, but rates are fiercely negotiable. Expect to pay about D300 an hour for a motorboat (although a lot depends on how much time the engine is actually running) or less for a paddled canoe.

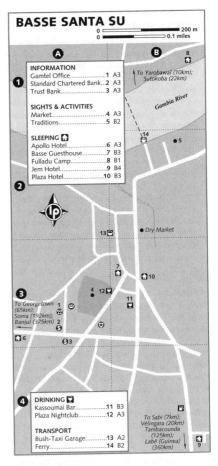

BASSE SANTA SU

INFORMATION	
Gamtel Office................1	A3
Standard Chartered Bank..2	A3
Trust Bank...................3	A3

SIGHTS & ACTIVITIES	
Market.......................4	A3
Traditions...................5	B2

SLEEPING 🏠	
Apollo Hotel.................6	A3
Basse Guesthouse............7	B3
Fulladu Camp................8	B1
Jem Hotel...................9	B4
Plaza Hotel.................10	B3

To Yarobawai (10km); Sutokoba (22km)

Gambia River

To Georgetown (65km); Soma (192km); Banjul (375km)

Dry Market

DRINKING 🍷	
Kassoumai Bar...............11	B3
Plaza Nightclub.............12	A3

TRANSPORT	
Bush-Taxi Garage...........13	A2
Ferry.......................14	B2

To Sabi (7km); Vélingara (20km); Tambacounda (125km); Labé (Guinea) (360km)

Sleeping & Eating

Staying the night in Basse can feel like a punishment if you're not used to roughing it a bit. Places that were once acceptable are now barely inhabitable – the end of the national bus service has meant that Basse has been almost totally deserted by tourists.

Fulladu Camp (☎ 5668743; r per person D300) On the north bank of the Gambia River this is undoubtedly the best place to stay. It sits about 100m from the ferry landing on a large terrain and has accommodation in comfortable bungalows. The management organises pirogue trips (prices negotiable) and shuttles you across the river if you call in advance. The restaurant here regularly gets good reviews, and is the best bet for eating in town.

MUNGO PARK

By the end of the 18th century, the incentive for exploring the interior of West Africa had switched from being commercial to 'scientific' (and evangelical – to convert 'heathens' to Christianity). Scientific exploration was based on solving two main puzzles: the position of Timbuktu (the mysterious 'city of gold') and the route of the Niger River. Although the Niger's existence was well known, its source and mouth, and even the direction of its flow, were a mystery.

In 1795 the London-based Association for Promoting the Discovery of the Interior Parts of Africa sent a young Scotsman called Mungo Park to the Gambia River. Park followed the river upstream by boat, sailing between British trading stations. He based himself near present-day Georgetown, where he learnt several local languages, and then set off across the plains, with just two servants and three donkeys. He travelled northeast, crossing the Senegal River, getting captured and escaping, and eventually reached the Niger at Ségou, confirming that it flowed in a northerly direction. After more adventures and incredible hardships, he eventually managed to return to the Gambia River and to Britain, where he wrote *Travels in the Interior of Africa*.

In 1801 Park returned to the Gambia River and again set out for the Niger. This time he took a larger support crew, although most of the men were army deserters and completely unprepared for the rigours of the expedition. By the time the group reached the Niger River, many had died, and even more perished either from disease or attacks by local people as they took a boat downstream. Park and the few remaining members of his party all died under attack at the Bussa Rapids, in the east of present-day Nigeria.

Jem Hotel (☎ 5668356; s/d D300/600) When we visited, the manager of this place off the road to Vélingara was a boy who's been in charge since his father's death and is doing a good job, though running this hotel-restaurant-nightclub is clearly tough. It's still one of the cleaner Basse options and the restaurant (open for lunch and dinner with meals around D100 to D150) is a bright spot. Phone in advance for meals.

Basse Guesthouse (☎ 5668283; r D150) Has dingy rooms with shared toilets, but you can spend hours people-watching from the 1st-floor balcony above a tailor shop.

The **Apollo Hotel** (☎ 57000852; r D100), west of the market, and **Plaza Hotel** (r D100), east of Basse Guesthouse, are run (and largely inhabited) by young men. Neither place is ideal for women; they're equally shoddy.

Traditions (☎ 5668533; r D250) can dust off the apartment of the former manager for unexpected visitors (D250). It also serves food; announce your eating plans in advance.

The state of hotels apart from those mentioned often indicates the standard of restaurants. You guessed it, there aren't many options in Basse. For local meals, you're pretty well served at the *chop shops* around the taxi park. If you arrive late at night they might be closed, and you'll be grateful for the roast-meat stalls that line the main road west of the market.

Drinking & Entertainment

The Jem Hotel nightclub promises 'London sounds', but the manager admitted that the sign was old. Still, it gets busy with youngsters bopping to reggae, hip-hop and African music on occasional weekends. The Kassoumai Bar opposite the market used to be a busy weekend spot; it's still active, though the quality has since declined. The Plaza Nightclub near the market gets packed on weekends. Otherwise it's back to the street meat stalls, beer in hand, where you can count on the company of locals.

Getting There & Away

Bush taxis go to the eastern outpost of Fatoto (D20, 40 minutes), the ferry ramp for Georgetown (D75, one hour); Soma (D150, four hours) and Serekunda (D300, eight hours).

The ferry to the Gambia River's northern bank takes one car at a time, and the journey is quick. The charge for a car is D50; passengers are D5. There are smaller boats taking passengers across; the fare is D10.

If you're heading for Senegal, you can go by bush taxi to Tambacounda via Vélingara. If your horizons are even further afield a *sept-place* taxi goes more or less daily (passengers depending) to Labé in northern Guinea. The fare is CFA30,000 and the trip takes at least 24 hours (or longer if there are delays at roadblocks).

Senegal

ARIADNE VAN ZANDBERGEN

Snapshot Senegal

Dakar's battered *cars rapides* (a form of bush taxi, often decrepit), ani
ated bars and packed restaurants buzz with eager conversation on the
latest political developments. The Senegalese love nothing better than a
political debate, weighing up the pros and cons of governmental policies
and gauging the future direction of their country. And they certainly
don't hold back with any criticisms of the current regime. When current
president Abdoulaye Wade won what were perhaps the calmest and least
disputed democratic elections in any African country and moved his
party, the Parti Démocratique Sénégalais (PDS; Senegalese Democratic
Party), into the strongest political position, the country was dizzy with
hope for a new era. Wade had promised *sopi* (change; p34), an end to
corruption, transparency in politics and economic progress.

In 2006, the country is still waiting for many of his ambitious goals to
materialise, and patience is beginning to wear thin. An estimated 48% of
the population is still without work, trying to make a living in the vast
sprawl that is the informal employment sector – the hazy money channels
of the *baol baol* (small traders).

To make matters worse, large parts of the population felt their high
hopes in democratic change betrayed when Idrissa Seck (p34), former
prime minister and potential rival of the 80-year-old Wade, was put
behind bars in July 2005, accused of embezzling substantial public funds
while working as mayor of Thiès – though he was released some seven
months later and the charges dropped in February 2006, and both he and
the president went to great lengths to portray an image of reconciliation,
probably to unite their now deeply divided party in the light of looming
2007 presidential elections of president and parliament.

There weren't any straightforward predictions of the outcome – certainly
the sign of a functioning democracy – but one thing was certain: the most
likely winner will be the one who succeeds in uniting the country's real
forces of influence behind him, the powerful marabouts of Senegal's Sufi
brotherhoods. Idrissa Seck's prominent participation in the 2006 Grand
Magal, a religious pilgrimage attracting over two million believers, indicates the importance of rallying the spiritual leaders, particularly the caliph
of the Mouride *confrérie* (brotherhood) in support. In 2005 the caliph of
the Mouridiya determined a date for the Muslim Ramadan fast that dif-
fered from the official announcement made in Mecca by a day, and large
parts of Muslim Senegal's population chose to ignore the Mecca declar-
ation, following their marabouts instead – an indication of the enormous
influence these religious leaders enjoy.

The mighty marabouts have also financed several construction and
transport projects, adding to the sense of relentless motion that characterises Senegal in the first decade of the 21st century.

President Abdoulaye Wade has coined the phrase of the land, 'en
chantier' (building site), and the feverish construction won't escape any
visitor, not least because of the traffic congestion all this intense activity
creates, particularly in Dakar. A new airport is being planned, and there's
even talk of moving the entire capital in order to allow the expansion it
can't enjoy within the confines of the narrow Cap Vert peninsula.

And thus the first impression that Dakar is likely to present you
with is that of a booming capital, a place where opportunities are up
for grabs.

FAST FACTS

Population: 11.1 million

Number of Senegalese
living abroad: 3 million

Population of greater
Dakar: 3 million

Population under 15: 42%

Size: 196,190 sq km

GDP per capita: US$1800

Literacy rate: 35%

Life expectancy: 51 years

Inflation rate: 1.7%

Economic ranking: 188th
out of 231 countries

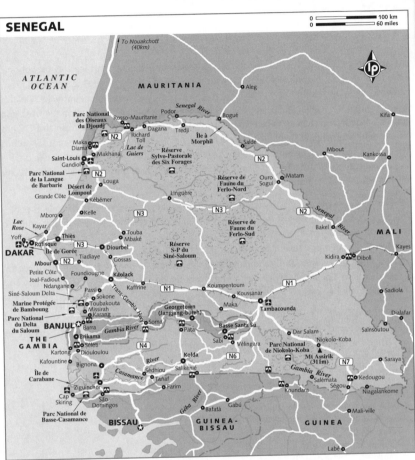

SENEGAL

0 — 100 km
0 — 60 miles

Senegal's creative scenes certainly aren't missing any chances. In Dakar hardly a week goes by without a music festival, a fashion show by another upcoming designer or a major exhibition.

And even in the rural areas, a major celebration seems never far away. The lively carnival celebrations of Ziguinchor and Kafountine are part of a thriving regional arts scene – but they're more than that. They also point to a new time of hope for lasting peace in the Casamance – a peace that took its cautious first steps in 2004, and in 2006 was still showing promising signs of lasting.

It is this sense that is gradually drawing many of the three million Senegalese emigrants back into the country.

Greater Dakar & Cap Vert Peninsula

If Dakar only could, it would burst its beaches, leap into the sea and lead its cacophonic parade of furious drumbeats, screeching traffic, exuberant nightlife, teeming markets, street hustling and boundless creativity in ever-wider circles across the country. But Dakar's frontiers are not negotiable. The vibrant city is limited by a long, sandy coast in the west, and a tight bottleneck in the east, which connects the Cap Vert peninsula to the mainland. Dakar's astounding energy can't flow over, and so it piles up sky-high on the few square kilometres the city occupies. This means you'll rarely have a boring day in Dakar, whether you're browsing through the city's markets, strolling around tiny boutiques and arts galleries or relaxing on the beaches of Yoff and N'Gor, two suburbs on the western edge of the peninsula.

The only moments you're likely to curse Dakar's enduring popularity, and certainly its peninsula setting, is in all those lost hours you're condemned to patience by yet another gridlock, wedged into a battered *car rapide* (colourfully decorated blue-and-yellow minibus) with dozens of fellow passengers and several bags of rice. But if the fumes, noise and intensity get too much, make a quick getaway to the tranquil Île de Gorée, only a 20-minute ferry ride from central Dakar, or spend a peaceful day enjoying African church music at Keur Moussa Monastery and glimpsing the pink shimmer of Lac Rose. Both lie an hour's drive east of the city.

Dakar is a feverish town that brims with life. It's got some of the best nightclubs, live-music venues and arts festivals in West Africa. And it only charges an occasional fee in unwanted hassle and sly con-jobs – easily negotiated once you've learnt a few tricks.

HIGHLIGHTS

- Put on your most glittering robes, hit the vibrant nightclub scene in **Dakar** (p162) and get a bout of *mbalax* fever
- Soak up the calm ambience and significance of the historical buildings and leafy alleyways on **Île de Gorée** (p167)
- Indulge in a day of sea, sand and sun at the beaches of **N'Gor** (p171)
- Get in the Sunday morning spirit at **Keur Moussa Monastery** (p176)
- Try to catch a glimpse of the **Lac Rose** (p174) shimmer on the way back to town

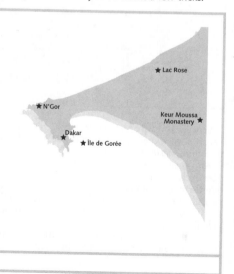

★ Lac Rose

★ N'Gor

Keur Moussa Monastery ★

Dakar ★

★ Île de Gorée

- POPULATION: 2.5 MILLION

DAKAR

HISTORY

Dakar was founded in 1857 and grew around an increasingly important trading port. By 1871, its importance had grown so much that the French granted it the special status of a self-governing community, together with Rufisque, Saint-Louis and Gorée. When the famous Dakar–Saint-Louis railway was opened in 1885, Dakar's role as an economic hub was strengthened further – so much that in 1902 the town became the capital of French West Africa. With Senegal's independence, it was chosen as capital of the newborn nation, and has since expanded so much that plans have been made to move the capital to a new location – one that can accommodate the growth in size and population that Dakar's peninsula setting doesn't permit.

ORIENTATION

Once a tiny settlement in the south of Cap Vert peninsula, Dakar now spreads almost across its entire triangle, from the southernmost tip of Cap Manuel to the northwestern end, the Pointe des Almadies, then east to N'Gor and Yoff beaches.

Dakar's heart is Place de l'Indépendance, from which Av Léopold Senghor heads south in the direction of the Palais Présidentiel and the Hôpital Principal. Av Pompidou (still known to most as Av Ponty) heads west, with the city's largest and busiest market,

Marché Sandaga, at its western end. These are Dakar's most hectic streets, with a vast selection of shops, restaurants, cafés, bars and street hustlers. At the time of research, plans to move the market out of the city were eagerly debated; you might find it already settled in a different part of town.

Leading from the eastern side of Place de l'Indépendance is the more upmarket Av Albert Sarraut, a major shopping street with another market, Marché Kermel, near its eastern end. The eastern edge of the city is marked by the ocean and the Rte de la Corniche-Est (Petite Corniche), which winds above cliffs and small beaches, linking to the main port to the north.

At the southwestern edge of the city are Place de Soweto, the IFAN Museum, the Assemblée Nationale and many embassies. From Place de Soweto you can head north along Av du Président Lamine Guèye, eventually reaching the Gare Routière Pompiers and the main autoroute (motorway) out of the city, which ends at the junction Patte d'Oie. From here, you can turn northwest towards the airport or take the eastern route towards Rufisque.

Av Blaise Diagne heads northwest from the centre, passing near the Grande Mosquée and Médina to become Av Cheikh Anta Diop (known to locals as Rte de Ouakam). This road runs between Fann and Point E, a pretty middle-class *quartier* (neighbourhood) before reaching Mermoz, Ouakam, and finally Pointe des Almadies and N'Gor.

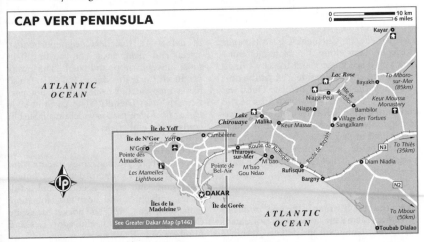

CAP VERT PENINSULA

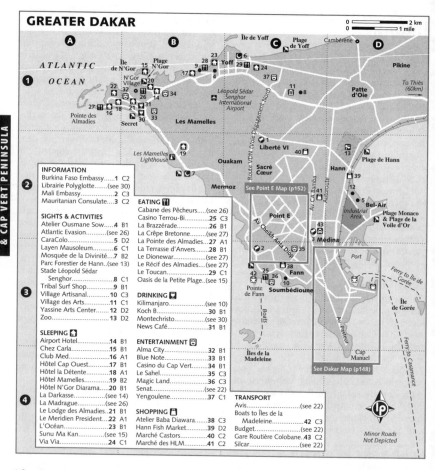

GREATER DAKAR

0 ____ 2 km
0 ____ 1 mile

GREATER DAKAR & CAP VERT PENINSULA

INFORMATION
Burkina Faso Embassy......1 C2
Librairie Polyglotte......(see 30)
Mali Embassy...............2 C3
Mauritanian Consulate......3 C2

SIGHTS & ACTIVITIES
Atelier Ousmane Sow......4 B1
Atlantic Evasion..........(see 26)
CaraColo..................5 D2
Layen Mausoleum...........6 C1
Mosquée de la Divinité....7 B2
Parc Forestier de Hann...(see 13)
Stade Léopold Sédar
  Senghor..................8 C1
Tribal Surf Shop..........9 B1
Village Artisanal.........10 C3
Village des Arts..........11 C1
Yassine Arts Center.......12 D2
Zoo......................13 D2

SLEEPING
Airport Hotel.............14 B1
Chez Carla................15 B1
Club Med..................16 A1
Hôtel Cap Ouest...........17 B1
Hôtel la Détente..........18 A1
Hôtel Mamelles............19 B2
Hôtel N'Gor Diarama.......20 B1
La Darkasse..............(see 14)
La Madrague..............(see 26)
Le Lodge des Almadies....21 B1
Le Meridien President....22 A1
L'Océan...................23 B1
Sunu Ma Kan.............(see 15)
Via Via...................24 C1

EATING
Cabane des Pêcheurs......(see 26)
Casino Terrou-Bi..........25 C3
La Brazzérade.............26 B1
La Crêpe Bretonne........(see 27)
La Pointe des Almadies....27 A1
La Terrasse d'Anvers......28 B1
Le Dionewar.............(see 27)
Le Récif des Almadies....(see 27)
Le Toucan.................29 C1
Oasis de la Petite Plage..(see 15)

DRINKING
Kilimanjaro..............(see 10)
Koch B....................30 B1
Montechristo............(see 30)
News Café.................31 B1

ENTERTAINMENT
Alma City.................32 B1
Blue Note.................33 B1
Casino du Cap Vert........34 B1
Le Sahel..................35 C3
Magic Land................36 C3
Senat...................(see 22)
Yengoulene................37 C1

SHOPPING
Atelier Baba Diawara......38 C3
Hann Fish Market..........39 D2
Marché Castors............40 C2
Marché des HLM............41 C2

TRANSPORT
Avis....................(see 22)
Boats to Îles de la
  Madeleine..............42 C3
Budget..................(see 22)
Gare Routière Colobane....43 C2
Silcar..................(see 22)

Minor Roads
Not Depicted

The Rte de la Corniche-Ouest (Grande Corniche) runs along the Atlantic Ocean – here you'll see joggers and the city's finest homes and embassy residences. At the time of writing, the Rte de la Corniche-Ouest was closed for construction works, planned to continue until 2008. Information on alternative routes to the centre of town is widely distributed in Dakar.

The Rte de la Corniche runs roughly parallel to Av Cheikh Anta Diop – the most direct access to Yoff Airport.

Maps

By far the best city map is the one produced by **Editions Laure Kane** (www.editionslaurekane.com; maps CFA3500). Colourful and detailed, it shows the names of all *quartiers* (neighbourhoods), streets and major sites. You can find it in most souvenir shops and hotels. The locally produced *Carte du Sénégal* (CFA3500) also has a map on the back, but it's not particularly user-friendly. The cartoon-style *Dakar Bird View* map is widely available but contains several errors.

INFORMATION

The free listings magazines *Dakar Tam Tam* and *L'Avis* contain details of hotels, restaurants and travel agencies and a full list of embassies and hospitals (for some embassies, see p262). The pocket magazine *Clin d'Œil* contains useful addresses and numbers as well as articles.

DAKAR IN...

Two Days

Start your day with croissants and coffee at the leafy **Institut Français** (below), then dive right into city life with a stroll around the historical buildings of the centre and a visit to the **IFAN Museum** (p153). Have a sumptuous lunch at **Le Sarraut** (p159), then spend the afternoon strolling around the historical alleyways of **Île de Gorée** (p167). Treat yourself to dinner at **La Fourchette** (p160), then hit the club scene, not missing **Le Seven** (p161) and the dance floors of **Kilimanjaro** (p161) and **Thiossane** (p161). Start the next day with breakfast at the beach on **Île de N'Gor** (p171). Enjoy the waves, then return by pirogue to the mainland and have lunch at the **Cabane des Pêcheurs** (p171). Visit the **Village des Arts** (p172) and the art gallery-cum–hairdressing salon, **Salon Michèle Ka** (p153). Round the day off with some brilliant live music at **Just 4 U** (p161).

Four Days

Start your visit as for the two-day itinerary, then add a day at the **markets** (p164) and admire the view across town from the lighthouse at **Les Mamelles** (p153). On day four, start early and travel to **Lac Rose** (p174). Go horse riding and take the pirogue across the lake for lunch at **Bonaba Café** (p174). Head back to Dakar for a sunset drink at the relaxed beach bar of the **Hôtel Cap Ouest** (p173) or gaze across the ocean from Africa's westernmost tip, the **Pointe des Almadies** (p171) before settling into an evening in style at **Koch B.** (p170).

The excellent pocket-sized glossy *221* (CFA500) contains plenty of interesting write-ups and events listings for music, arts and sports around the country, with a particular focus on Dakar. It's available at newsagents, shops, restaurants and hotels.

Bookshops

All of the following bookshops have a good range of books, magazines and maps, though there's little in English. The secondhand street stalls around the Marché Sandaga don't offer much choice, but you might find the occasional dog-eared curiosity among last season's women's magazines and outdated school books.

Librairie Clairafrique Central Dakar (Map p150; ☎ 822 2169; Rue C; ☒ 8.45am-12.30pm & 3-6.45pm Mon-Sat); Point E (Map p152; ☎ 864 4429; University Campus, Av Cheikh Anta Diop)

Librairie aux Quatre Vents (Map p150; ☎ 821 8083; Rue Félix Faure; ☒ 8.45am-12.30pm & 3-6.45pm)

Cultural Centres

British Council (Map p152; ☎ 869 2700; www.british council.org/senegal; Rue AAB-68, Amitié Zone A-B) Having moved to a nicer and calmer part of town, the office now has a pretty café (lunch around CFA1500), frequent exhibitions and a small library with a good selection of English-language books, magazines and DVDs.

British-Senegalese Institute (Map p148; ☎ 822 4023; Rue 18 Juin) Near Place de Soweto; has a library and frequently shows British, African and American films.

Goethe Institute (Map p150; ☎ 823 0407; www.goethe .de/dakar; 2 Av Albert Sarraut) The German Cultural Centre has frequent exhibitions and shows German, African and other films with French subtitles.

Institut Français Léopold Šédar Senghor (Map p150; ☎ 823 0320; www.institutfr-dakar.org; 89 Rue Joseph Gomis) This spacious centre occupying a whole block is the driving force behind many of Dakar's artistic and cultural endeavours. It produces a regular guide to upcoming events, houses an excellent café and a glass-painter's workshop in a small park, and has a performance arena that frequently hosts excellent live concerts and films.

Emergency

There's no general emergency number. The Hôpital Principal has the best accident and emergency department, followed by Hôpital Le Dantec. Outside the centre, **Suma Urgences** (Map p152; ☎ 824 2418; Fann Résidence, Av Cheikh Anta Diop) gives emergency assistance.

Internet Access

There are plenty of Internet cafés in Dakar, some fully equipped with scanners, Web cams etc; even those that aren't offer a good service for around CFA300 to CFA500 an hour. The university area is well covered with cybercafés (invariably crowded with chattering students). Wi-fi is becoming popular, with many hotels and restaurants becoming wi-fi spaces. At the time of research, the Novotel (p157) and Pen'Art jazz club (see p161) both had free wi-fi access.

GREATER DAKAR & CAP VERT PENINSULA

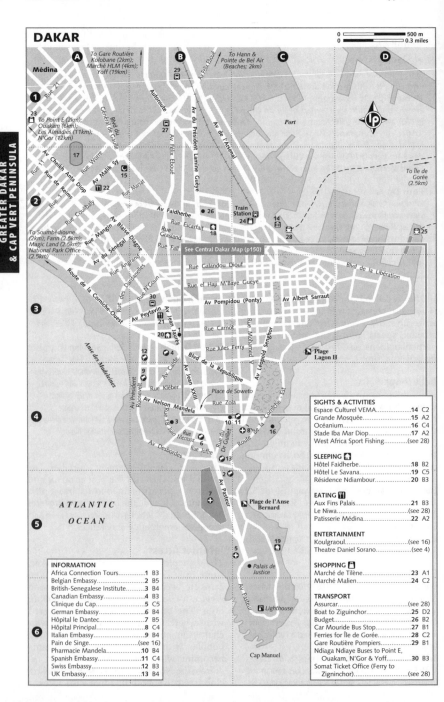

DAKAR

0 ————— 500 m
0 ————— 0.3 miles

GREATER DAKAR & CAP VERT PENINSULA

SIGHTS & ACTIVITIES
Espace Culturel VEMA	**14** C2
Grande Mosquée	**15** A2
Océanium	**16** C4
Stade Iba Mar Diop	**17** A2
West Africa Sport Fishing	(see 28)

SLEEPING
Hôtel Faidherbe	**18** B2
Hôtel Le Savana	**19** C5
Résidence Ndiambour	**20** B3

EATING
Aux Fins Palais	**21** B3
Le Niwa	(see 28)
Patisserie Médina	**22** A2

ENTERTAINMENT
Koulgraoul	(see 16)
Theatre Daniel Sorano	(see 4)

SHOPPING
Marché de Tilène	**23** A1
Marché Malien	**24** C2

TRANSPORT
Assurcar	(see 28)
Boat to Ziguinchor	**25** D2
Budget	**26** B2
Car Mouride Bus Stop	**27** B1
Ferries for Île de Gorée	**28** C2
Gare Routière Pompiers	**29** B1
Ndiaga Ndiaye Buses to Point E, Ouakam, N'Gor & Yoff	**30** B3
Somat Ticket Office (Ferry to Zigninchor)	(see 28)

INFORMATION
Africa Connection Tours	**1** B3
Belgian Embassy	**2** B5
British-Senegalese Institute	**3** B4
Canadian Embassy	**4** B3
Clinique du Cap	**5** C5
German Embassy	**6** B4
Hôpital le Dantec	**7** B5
Hôpital Principal	**8** C4
Italian Embassy	**9** B4
Pain de Singe	(see 16)
Pharmacie Mandela	**10** B4
Spanish Embassy	**11** C4
Swiss Embassy	**12** B3
UK Embassy	**13** B4

See Central Dakar Map (p150)

ATLANTIC OCEAN

Cap Manuel

Business Centre (Map p152; Blvd du Sud; ⌚ 8am-10pm) Opposite the Jardin Thaïlandais.
Cyber-Business Centre (Map p150; ☎ 823 3223; Av Léopold Senghor; ⌚ 8am-midnight)
Espace Sentoo (Map p150; Place de l'Indépendance; ⌚ 9.30am-8pm)
Espacetel Plus (Map p150; ☎ 822 9062; Blvd de la République; ⌚ 8am-midnight)

Medical Services

Most embassies have a list of doctors used to dealing with nonresidents, and can direct you to a doctor who speaks your language. Following are some of the best clinics and hospitals in Dakar.
Clinique du Cap (Map p148; ☎ 821 3627) Just south of Hôpital Le Dantec, this privately run clinic is good for treating minor illnesses and injuries.
Clinique Pasteur (Map p150; ☎ 839 9200; 50 Rue Carnot) West of Place de l'Indépendance, this is another comfortable, privately run clinic. Not best for emergencies, but a good place to go if you're after a malaria blood test.
Hôpital Le Dantec (Map p148; ☎ 889 3800; Av Pasteur) This hospital has a reputation for having the best-trained staff, but is terribly neglected in terms of infrastructure.
Hôpital Principal (Map p148; ☎ 839 5050; Av Léopold Senghor) Run by military staff, this is the best-organised hospital in Dakar and the one with the most effective emergency service.

Dakar has many pharmacies. Most open from 8am to 11pm, and there's a rotational 24-hour standby system; you'll find details of the current 24-hour place outside every pharmacy door.
Pharmacie Guigon (Map p150; ☎ 823 0333; Av du Président Lamine Guèye)
Pharmacie Mandela (Map p148; ☎ 821 2172; Av Nelson Mandela) Near the Hôpital Principal.

Money

Bicis, CBAO, Citibank and SGBS (Map p150) have offices on and around Place de l'Indépendance. They all change money, though sometimes are reluctant to change travellers cheques. All except Citibank have security-guarded ATMs. You can usually withdraw up to CFA250,000. There's a **Western Union** (Map p150; Rue du Docteur Thèze; ⌚ 7.30am-5.30pm Mon-Sat) in CBAO's Pompidou branch.

The suburbs are equally well served with ATM-enhanced banks and petrol stations. In Point E, the **SGBS** (Map p152; Blvd de l'Est) and the **Bicis** (Map p152; Place OMVS) ATM at the Station Mobil Relais are reliable options.

Opening hours vary from bank to bank, but they all tend to be open from around 8am to noon, and in the afternoon from around 2.30pm to 4pm. Some also open on Saturday morning, and you can get cash around the clock from ATMs.

Photography

Clic Numérique (Map p150; Rue Jules Ferry) The best place in town for digital prints.
Passport Photos (Map p150; Place de l'Indépendance) A good place to get your pictures developed.

Post

DHL (Map p150; ☎ 823 1394; 2 Av Albert Sarraut; ⌚ 8am-6.30pm Mon-Thu, to 7pm Fri, 8am-noon Sat) The Senegal agent for all express mail.
Main post office (Map p150; Blvd el Haji Djily Mbaye; ⌚ 7am-7pm Mon-Fri, 8am-5pm Sat) Near Marché Kermel. This is where you'll find poste restante. Letters are held for up to 30 days; the cost per item is CFA250.
Post office (Map p150; Av Pompidou) At the eastern end of Av Pompidou, this smaller office seems to run more smoothly than the main post office. It's got a small *télécentre* (privately owned telephone bureau) and a Western Union service.

Telephone

There are dozens of *télécentres* in Dakar, mostly with similar rates. A few recommended central ones are indicated on the Central Dakar map. Post offices and Internet cafés often also have telephone facilities.
Espace Sentoo (Map p150; Place de l'Indépendance) This established Internet café is also a good place for international calls.
Post office (Map p150; Av Pompidou)

Tourist Information

There is no official tourist information office in Dakar, but the travel agencies listed below will be able to help with enquiries.

Travel Agencies

For reconfirming flights, most airlines have offices in central Dakar (p280). For a ticket, a travel agency can save a lot of shopping around. Agencies' fares are standardised and are usually the same as the airline (or cheaper), although special deals are sometimes available, particularly to/from Paris. Most agencies also offer good rates on trips around the country from Dakar.
Africa Connection Tours (Map p148; ☎ 821 8316; 32 Rue Mass Diokhané) A tiny agency that caters particularly to English-speaking travellers.

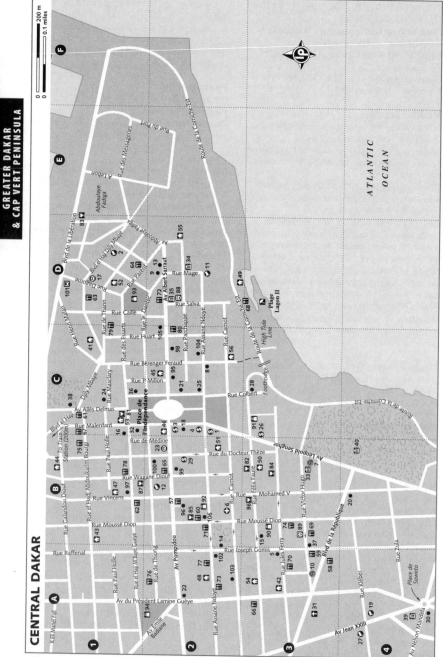

CENTRAL DAKAR

Dakar Voyages (Map p150; ☎ 823 3704; dakarvoyages@sentoo.sn; 28 Rue Assane Ndoye) Tends to have the best ticket deals.

Nouvelles Frontières (Map p150; ☎ 823 3434; fax 822 2817; 3 Blvd de la République) Sometimes has cheap seats to Paris on charter flights.

ONITS (Map p152; ☎ 516 3293; onits2005@yahoo.fr) This umbrella organisation for small-scale, Senegalese tourist enterprises can put you in touch with guesthouses and hostels around the country, as well as recommend itineraries.

Planète Tours Voyages (Map p150; ☎ 823 7423) Next to the Hôtel de l'Indépendance.

SDV Voyages (Map p150; ☎ 839 0081; dkrsdvagv@ sdvsen.net; 51 Av Albert Sarraut) The Diners Club agent.

Universities

Dakar's sprawling **Université Cheikh Anta Diop** (Map p152) occupies most of the Fann suburb, south of Point E.

It's like a vibrant city within itself, with plenty of little eateries, Internet cafés and copy shops catering to students. When we visited, clashes between students and police were frequent – stay well clear of the area if this is the case.

DANGERS & ANNOYANCES

The inner city of Dakar is a pickpocket's paradise – especially the crammed streets around Av Pompidou and Marché Sandaga.

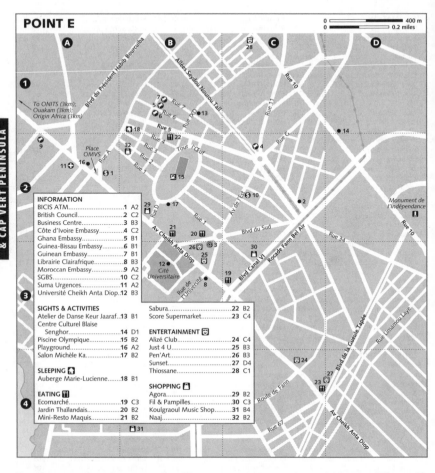

POINT E

0 _____ 400 m
0 _____ 0.2 miles

GREATER DAKAR & CAP VERT PENINSULA

To ONITS (3km);
Ouakam (3km);
Origin Africa (3km)

Blvd du Président Habib Bourguiba

Allées Seydou Nourou Tall

Rue 7
Rue 6
Rue 5
Rue 4
Rue 3
Rue 2
Rue 1

Place
OMVS

Tour / Œuf

Rue D
Av Cheikh Anta Diop

Cité
Universitaire

Rue de l'Université

Blvd du Sud

Blvd Canal VI

Rocade Fann Bel Air

Rue 34

Monument de
l'Indépendance

Rue 10

Blvd de la Gueule Tapée

Rue Limamou Laye

Route de Fann

Av Cheikh Anta Diop

Rue 67

INFORMATION
BICIS ATM.....................................1 A2
British Council..............................2 C2
Business Centre...........................3 B3
Côte d'Ivoire Embassy................4 C2
Ghana Embassy............................5 B1
Guinea-Bissau Embassy.............6 B1
Guinean Embassy........................7 B1
Librairie Clairafrique...................8 B3
Moroccan Embassy......................9 A2
SGBS..10 C2
Suma Urgences..........................11 A2
Université Cheikh Anta Diop.12 B3

SIGHTS & ACTIVITIES
Atelier de Danse Keur Jaaraf..13 B1
Centre Culturel Blaise
    Senghor..................................14 D1
Piscine Olympique....................15 B2
Playground.................................16 A2
Salon Michèle Ka.......................17 B2

SLEEPING 🛏
Auberge Marie-Lucienne.......18 B1

EATING 🍴
Ecomarché..................................19 C3
Jardin Thaïlandais......................20 B2
Mini-Resto Maquis....................21 B2

Sabura...22 B2
Score Supermarket....................23 C4

ENTERTAINMENT 📺
Alizé Club...................................24 C4
Just 4 U......................................25 B3
Pen'Art.......................................26 B3
Sunset..27 D4
Thiossane...................................28 C1

SHOPPING 🛍
Agora..29 B2
Fil & Pampilles...........................30 C3
Koulgraoul Music Shop.............31 B4
Naaj...32 B2

Avoid carrying large bags around and be on your guard. Less worrying, but potentially very annoying, are the street traders and hustlers. For ideas on how to shake them off, see p259.

Other pickpocketing hotspots are the beaches and the port, including the jetties for the Gorée Ferry and *Le Willis*, the boat to Ziguinchor. Stay alert and clutch your credit card. In the inner city, the 'Remember me?' scam is particularly popular (see Scams, p261). The remedy: don't respond to random calls of '*mon ami,* long time no see!' If someone doesn't know your name, chances are they don't know you; being rude to someone you do know is still preferable to having your passport and purse snatched.

As in most inner cities around the world, women should avoid walking around alone after dark or waiting for taxis in empty areas.

Some vigilance and common sense should help you get around unharmed – inner-city Dakar can be a pain to walk around, but Lagos it ain't, and none of the areas mentioned are no-go zones.

SIGHTS
Historical Buildings
The **cathedral** (Map p150; Blvd de la République) is a large but fairly unspectacular 1920s building. It's still worth a glimpse, being the main cathedral of the capital city, and the adjacent garden has a leafy children's playground – your kids will no doubt

Fishing pirogues (p154) near the mouth of the Senegal River, Senegal

DAVID ELSE

ANDREW BURKE

A wooden bridge linking the twin villages of Joal and Fadiout (p184), Senegal

Wassu stone circles (p137), Gambia

DAVID ELSE

Saint-Louis (p203), the former capital of Senegal

Mediterranean-style architecture, Île de Gorée (p167), Senegal

One of Dakar's old and colourful *car rapides* (p166), Senegal

Traditional weaving techniques at the Tanji Village Museum (p118), Gambia

prefer to staying there rather than take a tour of Dakar's impressive colonial buildings. There's the **Gouvernance** (Map p150) and the **Chambre de Commerce** (Map p150) on either side of Place de l'Indépendance, a remarkable space itself because it is huge, wide, lined by grand buildings and symmetrically laid out. The stately **Hôtel de Ville** (town hall; Map p150; Blvd el Hajj Djily Mbaye) sits north of the *place*. A short walk further north takes you to the **train station** (Map p148; Blvd de la Libération), whose elegant façade inspires ideas of romantic train journeys (quickly wiped away once you enter the bleak interior).

A short walk east from Place de l'Indépendance takes you to the cute round house of **Marché Kermel** (Map p150; see p164). Heading southwest, the awe-inspiring **Palais Présidentiel** (Map p150; Ave Léopold Senghor) is surrounded by sumptuous gardens and guards in colonial-style uniforms. It was originally built in 1907 for the governor of the time, General Roume, who used to lend his title to the street outside. The road has since been renamed Av Léopold Senghor, although most locals still refer to it by its old name. The **Assemblée Nationale** (Parliament; Map p150; Place de Soweto), with its modern glass façade, is easy to reach from here.

Dakar's most interesting mosques are slightly out of town. The **Grande Mosquée** (Map p148; Av Malik Sy), built in 1964, is impressive for its sheer size and landmark minaret. The building is closed to the public, but it's worth coming here anyway because the surrounding neighbourhood, **Médina**, is a bustling popular *quartier* with tiny tailor shops, a busy market (see p164) and streets brimming with life. It was built as a township for the local populace by the French, and is the birthplace of Senegalese superstar Youssou N'Dour.

Taking the coastal road northwards, you'll see the stunning **Mosqué de la Divinité** (Map p146; Rte de la Corniche-Ouest) perched on the coast near Les Mamelles *quartier*. **Les Mamelles Lighthouse** (Map p146), off Rte de la Corniche-Ouest, is just a 25-minute walk or 1km drive north from here, on a small volcanic hill. You get an excellent view across Dakar from the 1864 building; visits are best made during the day and are free of charge.

Museums & Art Galleries

A testament to former President Senghor's interest in promoting African art and culture, Dakar's **IFAN Museum** (Map p150; Place de Soweto; adult/child CFA2000/200; 8am-12.30pm & 2-6.30pm) compares well to the national museums of other West African nations. Yes, exhibits are gathering dust, but there are imaginative displays of masks and traditional dress from the whole region (including Mali, Guinea-Bissau, Benin and Nigeria), as well as fabrics and carvings, musical instruments and agricultural tools.

Dakar has a vibrant contemporary arts scene to be discovered in the cluster of small art galleries and ateliers hidden in the city's side streets. The leafy garden of the **Institut Français** (823 0320; 89 Rue Joseph Gomis) is a hub of creativity. The scrap-metal bird sculptures by Mamadou Tall Dhiedhiou and charmingly chaotic workshop of the famous *sous-verre* (reverse-glass painting) artist Moussa Sakho alone are worth a visit. The brilliant little **Galerie Le Manège** (Map p150; 821 0822; 3 Rue Parchappe; 9am-5pm Tue-Sat), in a beautifully restored 19th-century building, is also part of the French cultural complex. The space of the **Galerie Nationale** (Map p150; 821 2511; 19 Av Albert Sarraut; admission free; 9am-6pm) is slightly less enticing, but its frequently changing exhibitions of photography or paintings are usually very good. **Galerie Arte** (Map p150; 821 9556; www.arte.sn; 5 Rue Victor Hugo) looks more like a shop than a gallery, and though all items are for sale, there's no pressure to buy. The **Espace Culturel VEMA** (Map p148; 821 7026; Embarcadère de Gorée; 9am-1pm & 3-7pm) is a ray of hope in the dreary industrial lands near the Île de Gorée ferry. Its spiced-up warehouse frequently houses exhibitions and events, but you need to phone first to see if anything's on.

In Point E, the **Salon Michèle Ka** (Map p152; 824 7033; Tour de l'Œuf) is not only the funkiest hairdressing salon in town, but also one of the most original art galleries. The whole salon, from styling tables to wall displays, is decorated with urban *sous-verre* motifs à la *car rapide*. It's an absolute must-see – you don't need to get a new hairstyle to visit.

The Hann neighbourhood, Dakar's 'lost corner', squeezed between a polluted beach and impossibly jammed roads, is in fact a thriving place for the arts. You can't miss the gargantuan, lion-shaped entry to the **Yassine Arts Center** (Map p146; 832 2611; info@yassinearts .com; Baie de Hann). Exhibitions here have a habit of spilling over into the hotel, theatre, restaurant and even the fitness centre that form part of the complex. The fantastic **Cara-Colo** (Map p146; ☎ 832 1590; www.caracolo.com; 7 Allée Marinas) gallery is within walking distance of here. This original arts space exhibits and sells works made by local artists and artisans using materials found in the immediate creative space. Their metal, fabric and wooden objects are incredibly beautiful and, needless to say, unique.

Beaches

Beaches within easy reach of the city centre include the private Plage Lagon II (Map p150), near Hôtel Lagon II, and **Plage de l'Anse Bernard** (Map p148) near Hôtel Le Savana. Those along the Rte de la Corniche-Ouest are popular with local joggers, picnic parties and Sai-Sais (p277). Strong currents make them less suitable for swimming.

The **Plage de Hann** (Map p146), once one of Dakar's finest strands, is now an environmental catastrophe due to illegal sewage disposal by the adjacent industrial zone. South of here, in the shelter of Pointe de Bel-Air, are the private beaches **Plage de la Voile d'Or** (Map p146; admission CFA650) and the adjacent **Plage Monaco** (Map p146; admission CFA650), where occasional beach concerts take place year-round.

On the route towards Les Almadies, the so-called **Secret** (Map p146) is a favourite surfing spot, while further north, Dakar's finest sand stretches along the coast of **N'Gor** (p171), where beach access costs CFA500, and **Yoff** (p172). Strong currents make Yoff's beaches largely unsuitable for swimming, but most beach-lovers head there anyway, or to Île de Gorée (p167).

ACTIVITIES
Diving

Good scuba-diving (plongée sous-marine) sites include the rocky reefs and islets around the Pointe des Almadies and the islands of Gorée, N'Gor and La Madeleine. By far the best address for diving excursions is the **Océanium** (Map p148; ☎ 822 2441; www .oceanium.org; Rte de la Corniche-Est; ☺ Mon-Sat). It offers half-day dives as well as longer excursions and also has introductory courses for beginners. The Océanium also houses a very active and effective environmental protection agency, so its courses come with eco-awareness and as much extra environmental input as you like. Divers can stay at the Océa-

---

SOUMBÉDIOUNE PIROGUE CONSTRUCTION

Behind Soumbédioune beach is an area where fishing pirogues are constructed, usually by and for the Lebu, the ethnic group mainly involved in the fishing industry. The base of a pirogue is usually made from the hollowed-out trunk of a kapok tree (known locally as a fromager). This light, spongy wood is left outside to absorb water during the rainy season for up to eight months, after which it can be beaten perfectly straight to form the base of the boat. The sides are then built up around it using long planks of a harder wood such as kola, and finally the inside of the bottom half is coated with tar. When treated like this, the fromager base lasts for years; when the pirogue finally reaches the end of its life, the base may be reused several times in new boats.

Large pirogues take months to build and sell for around CFA12 million (about US$17,000). This is beyond the reach of most fishermen, so many large boats are owned by local businesspeople. They may lease their boat to a team of fishermen or simply employ them. Either way, they take up to 60% of the profits from each catch.

---

nium for more than reasonable rates; don't forget to ask about its tours to the Aire Marine Protégée de Bamboung (see p67).

Fishing

You can arrange deep-sea fishing at **West Africa Sport Fishing** (Map p148; ☎ 823 2858; fffs@sentoo .sn), next to the Île de Gorée ferry terminal, or at the **Océanium** (Map p148; ☎ 822 2441; www .oceanium.org; Rte de la Corniche-Est). The restaurant **Lagon I** (Map p150; ☎ 821 5322; Rte de la Corniche-Est) arranges deep-sea fishing trips and boasts several world-record catches.

Swimming

Dakar is surrounded by beaches, but not all of them are safe for swimming (see left). Other than that, there's always the chlorine option.

Dakar's best swimming pool is the sublime **Piscine Olympique** (Map p152; ☎ 869 0606; piscine olymp@sentoo.sn; Tour de l'Œuf). It's part of a huge sports complex, known locally as 'l'œuf' (the egg), housing other (smaller) pools, fitness centres, basketball courts and football grounds, plus restaurants and even rooms to spend the night. Sports courses are also available.

In town, most top-end hotels have swimming pools that are open to nonguests for a small fee. The Sofitel Teranga has a pool overlooking the ocean, which is free if you eat at the adjoining restaurant, otherwise it will cost you CFA4500 (CFA7000 on Sunday). The Hôtel de l'Indépendance charges CFA3000 for its rooftop pool with a great view of Dakar (free if you have a meal). At Hôtel Faidherbe, you get a dive, a drink and a sandwich for CFA2000.

Surfing

A swimmer's disappointment is a surfer's dream – the wave-beaten beaches around Dakar aren't always suitable for bathing, but make excellent surfer haunts. Any aspiring or experienced surfer should pass through the **Tribal Surf Shop** (Map p146; ☎ 646 0914, 820 5400; tribal@arc.sn; Yoff Virage), the best place to rent boards (CFA10,000 per day), take courses, buy gear, get your board repaired and find out about the best spots.

Exercise

The **Piscine Olympique** (☎ 869 0606; Tour de l'Œuf) in Point E has excellent fitness facilities. In town, **Héliopolis** (Map p150; ☎ 823 8686; Rue V Hugo; ☒ 7.30am-9.30pm Mon-Sat) is brilliantly equipped with state-of-the art machines and weights, and offers a range of classes from aerobics to yoga. Otherwise, try the large hotels. Many of them have gymnasiums that nonguests can use for a fee.

Wrestling

Dakar's main arena for traditional wrestling is in Médina, near the large **Stade Iba Mar Diop** (Map p148; Av Cheikh Anta Diop). Fights of big-name wrestlers are national sports events, held in **Stade Léopold Sédar Senghor** (Map p146), Dakar's main stadium in Yoff. Senegal's entire population awaits the results of the traditional star match held on 1 January.

Most matches are announced only on the radio, but important ones will be advertised by posters around town and talked about incessantly by the locals. Saturday and/or Sunday are the usual days for the fights, starting around 4.30pm or 5pm.

COURSES
Language

If you're spending more than a brief holiday in Senegal, a Wolof course is a good investment. The linguistic branch of the Institut Français, **Pôle Linguistique de l'Institut Français** (Map p150; ☎ 823 84 83; 3 Rue Parchappe; ☒ Oct-May) runs recommended courses (four hours per week for 12 weeks, CFA90,000). It's also a good place to brush up on your French.

Dance

For dance courses, try the **Centre Culturel Blaise Senghor** (Map p152; Rue 10). Its bleak facade doesn't do justice to the creative bustle going on inside. In Point E, the **Atelier de Danse Keur Jaaraf** (Map p152; ☎ 574 4056; Rue 1XD) is an inspiring little dance company that runs courses for adults and children, covering most major styles of dance.

DAKAR FOR CHILDREN

As a big, brash city, Dakar probably doesn't feature highly on a parent's list of must-sees. But the locals' overwhelmingly friendly attitude towards children, the surrounding beaches and a few child-focused activities make it surprisingly family-friendly – as long as you avoid the inner city.

Dakar's affluent citizens love taking their kids out to **Magic Land** (Map p146; ☎ 842 7307; Rte de la Corniche-Ouest;; adult/child under 2 CFA2500/free; ☒ 5-10pm Tue & Thu, 4-10pm Wed & Fri, 2-10pm Sat & Sun), a trendy theme park fully equipped with merry-go-rounds, Ferris wheels and other attractions. For something smaller, try **Sun Park** (Map p150; Jardin de la Cathédrale; adult/child CFA500/300; ☒ 4-10pm), a cute little playground in the garden of the cathedral. Another good **playground** (Map p152; Av Cheikh Anta Diop) is in a leafy park in Point E.

If your children are older than five, the glass-painting workshops by master Moussa Sakho in the **Institut Français** (Map p150; ☎ 823 0320; 89 Rue Joseph Gomis) are a must. And if you're lucky, you might be able to catch a show by the theatre troupe **Côte Jardin** (☎ 636 5497), a brilliant two-woman team that specialises in children's entertainment. Both women speak English and their shows take place in various venues around town; you can even invite them to your home for kids entertainment. Phone to see what's happening.

Other than that, a ferry trip to **Île de Gorée** (p167) and a pirogue tour to the **Îles de la**

Madeleine (p170) make for good family escapes from hectic Dakar.

With kids, you're better off staying in a hotel around Yoff or N'Gor rather than in town, both for the sake of sanity and space. You'll be close to the beaches, which is always good news with kids (N'Gor beach is by far the safest – keep a close eye on them, though, as the northern beaches aren't always safe).

Hann Zoo (Map p146) is supposed to be a kids attraction, but the sight of caged, neglected animals is more likely to make them cry. Stick to the adjacent **Parc Forestier de Hann** (Map p146) – a peaceful woodland area with paths, benches and a couple of snack bars that's popular with weekend picnic parties.

Note: it's next to impossible to push a pram around anywhere in Dakar. In the inner city you're fighting a losing battle against parked cars, and on the beaches, well, there's sand. Nappies, baby food and other baby products are readily available in all big supermarkets.

TOURS

The following agencies offer a good range of tours around the country.

Mboup Voyages (Map p150; ☎ 821 8163; mboup@telecomplus.sn; Place de l'Indépendance) One of the most enduring agencies for tours.

Origin Africa (Map p152; ☎ 860 1578; origin@sentoo .sn; Cité Africa, Ouakam) This is one of the more interesting tour operators in Senegal, with plenty of tours around Senegal on offer. It's well signposted.

Pain de Singe (Map p150; ☎ 824 2484; paindesinge@ arc.sn) Unbeatable for ecotourism, off-the-beaten-track and original itineraries. They are based in the suburb Sacré Cœur, but you can contact them at the **Océanium** (Map p148; ☎ 822 2441; Rte de la Corniche-Est).

Sahel Découverte Bassari (Map p150; ☎ 842 8751; carresahel@sentoo.sn; 7 Rue Masclary) Near Av Allés Delmas; has a range of inspired tours on offer and caters equally well to English, French and Spanish speakers. It offers tours to destinations all around Senegal, including an excellent hiking tour around Bassari Country.

Senegal Tours (Map p150; ☎ 839 9900; fax 823 2644; 5 Place de l'Indépendance) One of the largest operators with a reputation for reliability.

VIA Sénégal Voyages (Map p150; ☎ 823 3300; www .viavoyages.sn; 13 Rue Colbert) A fairly new oeprator owned by Hertz Car Hire; its catalogue is pretty standard.

FESTIVALS & EVENTS

Dakar's cultural calendar is packed, and outside the wettest months (July and August) you're almost bound to stumble across a festival, awards ceremony or concert series of some sort.

Dak'Art Biennale (☎ 823 0918; www.dakart.org; May) This biennial festival of painting and sculpture is the queen of Dakar's festivals. It drowns the town in colour for the whole of May, with exhibitions all across Dakar. Unmissable.

Kaay Fecc (☎ 826 4950; www.ausenegal.com/kaayfecc; early Jun) One of Africa's best dance festivals, Kaay Fecc features contemporary and traditional choreography from all across Africa and beyond.

Festival International du Film de Quartier (www .festivaldufilmdequartier.com) Film lovers shouldn't miss this annual showcasing of Senegal's best contemporary film work. For the duration of the festival many cultural centres, restaurants and other spaces mount screens to show films.

Afrikakeur (☎ 860 3116; early Jun) This comedy and music festival is held annually at venues all across Dakar.

SLEEPING

Dakar has a wide range of accommodation, from dodgy dosshouses to palatial hotels. Although everything is expensive, the steadily increasing prices are only justified in a few places.

Don't concentrate your room search only on the crammed city centre of Dakar. The suburbs of Yoff (close to the airport) and N'Gor are only a 30-minute taxi ride away and have plenty of hotels sitting right next to some of Dakar's finest beaches.

Budget

There's hardly such a thing as a budget hotel in Dakar. Like most West African cities, the town doesn't cater particularly well to backpackers. The cheapest places are usually brothels where there's a high chance of theft, so even travellers on a shoestring budget might be persuaded to dig a little deeper for a decent room (and the added luxury of undisturbed sleep).

Hôtel Continental (Map p150; ☎ 822 1083; 10 Rue Galandou Diouf; s/d from CFA13,000/15,000; 🛜) The best of the cheapest, with prices that have remained virtually unchanged over the last few years. The basic rooms even have a touch of character. For your own bathroom and air-conditioning you pay some CFA5000 more.

Hôtel Provençal (Map p150; ☎ 822 1069; 17 Rue Malenfant; s/d CFA14,400/16,800) This place isn't too bad for a part-time brothel. Just make sure you get a room upstairs to avoid most of the noise.

Midrange

All hotels in this price range have rooms with private bathrooms. Prices do not include tax (CFA600 per person). Most places accept credit and charge cards.

Hôtel Saint-Louis Sun (Map p150; ☎ 822 2570; fax 822 4651; Rue Félix Faure; s/d/tr CFA23,000/29,500/35,500; **P** **✗**) Pretty rooms with beach-house doors open onto a peaceful, green courtyard. Right in the heart of Dakar, this long-standing favourite with independent tourists allows for a mental escape from the crowds and car fumes that wash past it.

Hôtel Ganalé (Map p150; ☎ 889 4444; hganale@ sentoo.sn; 38 Rue Assane Ndoye; s/d CFA28,000/35,000, apt CFA38,000-48,000) This place is a gem. Never mind the sinister-looking lobby – the rooms are bright, tastefully decorated and come equipped with TV and telephone. The management is friendly and helpful, and the restaurant is a popular place with tourists and locals. You'll be hard pressed to find better value for your precious CFAs in this price range.

Hôtel Mamelles (Map p146; ☎ 860 0000; contact@ lesmamelles.com; s with/without bathroom CFA14,500/ 10,000, d with/without bathroom CFA19,500/15,000) Tucked away in a side street off Rte de la Corniche-Ouest in Les Mamelles *quartier*, this a hugely popular place, and for good reason. The colourfully decorated rooms are excellent value, and its small size and leafy patio give it a great ambience.

Hôtel Océanic (Map p150; ☎ 822 2044; www.hotel oceanicdakar.com; 9 Rue de Thann; s/d/tr/q CFA 21,600/ 25,800/33,000/36,800; **✗**) Just north of Marché Kermel, this pleasant old-style place has spotless rooms and larger apartments – fair value for Dakar. A relaxed bar-restaurant with a pretty courtyard offers a good *menu du jour* (meal of the day) for CFA4800.

Hôtel Faidherbe (Map p148; ☎ 889 1750; faid herbe@sentoo.sn; Av Faidherbe; s/d/ste CFA36,000/42,000/ 70,000) This place has plenty of the niceties of a top-end place: broadband connection in each of the pretty rooms, swimming pool, an ATM, a cosy bar and a popular restaurant – all for a much better rate than the grand hotels.

Hôtel Le Miramar (Map p150; ☎ 849 2929; miramard @hotmail.com; 25 Rue Félix Faure; s/d with breakfast CFA25,600/31,200; **✗**) Some call it funky, some call it scruffy. It has great ambience, although a concerted renovating effort wouldn't be lost on this gaudily coloured place.

Dakar Résidences (Map p150; ☎ 821 9568; dakar resid@sentoo.sn; Blvd el Haji Djily Mbaye; apt CFA35,000-45,000) Behind a humble entrance hide nicely maintained and neatly equipped apartments; good value for self-caterers.

Hôtel Farid (Map p150; ☎ 821 6127; www.hotelfarid .com; 51 Rue Vincens; s/d from CFA26,500/29,000) It looks modest, and is half-hidden in a side street, but here are some of the best-maintained rooms in central Dakar. And the restaurant is something you could get addicted to.

Auberge Marie-Lucienne (Map p152; ☎ 869 0090; Rue A, Point E; s/d CFA28,920/36,000; **🖳**) In Senegal, auberge often refers to something extremely basic. Though not exactly a glossy address, this one is nicer than many of its namesakes. Rooms have TV and hot water, and there's free Internet access in the reception area.

Also recommended:

Hôtel Al Baraka (Map p150; ☎ 822 5532; halbaraka@ arc.sn; 35 Rue el Hadj Abdoukarim Bourgi; s/d CFA28,000/ 33,000; **✗**) Large, modern rooms with TV, fridge and phone, but not exactly in a nice corner of Dakar – close to Marché Sandaga, so full of street hustlers.

Hôtel Nina (Map p150; ☎ 889 0120; hotelnina@sentoo .sn; 43 Rue du Docteur Thèze; s/d CFA28,000/35,000; **✗**) Recently renovated, but still feels stuffy.

Top End

All hotels in this range have rooms with private bathrooms, accept major credit/charge cards and have a tour desk where you can arrange excursions, car hire and so on.

Hôtel Al Afifa (Map p150; ☎ 889 9090; gmbafifa@ telecomplus.sn; 46 Rue Jules Ferry; s/d/ste CFA37,000/ 40,000/45,000; **✗**) This place is ageing a little but still retains some of its lustre. Ask for room 103 – the only one with a terrace. The bar, restaurant and disco downstairs offer plenty of nightlife within minimum staggering distance.

Sofitel Teranga (Map p150; ☎ 889 2200; fax 823 5001; Place de l'Indépendance; r from CFA136,000; **P** **✗** **🖳** **🖳**) Part of the Accor Hotel group, this is exactly what you would expect from a luxury, over-equipped businessperson's favourite hotel. Facilities include tennis courts, sauna, shops and nightclub. It's really very nice – but is a sea view worth CFA136,000 a night? Plenty think so.

Novotel (Map p150; ☎ 849 6161; novotel@sentoo .sn; Av Abdoulaye Fadiga; r CFA85,000; **✗** **🖳** **🖳**) It's a Novotel all right. Smooth standards, good service, bland character. Sea views cost an extra CFA5000.

Hôtel Lagon II (Map p150; ☎ 889 2525; www.lagon .sn; Rte de la Corniche-Est; s/d/ste CFA72,000/80,000/120,000; ☒ ☐) If you can bear the kitsch seafarers decor, this is a great place to view the ocean from cabin-style rooms perched on stilts at the edge of the ocean. A favourite address for those interested in deep-sea fishing.

Hôtel Savana (Map p148; ☎ 849 4242; www.savana .sn; Rte de la Corniche-Est; s/d CFA74,000/80,000; ☒ ☐ ☒) If you really want to relax in style, this ingenious construction overlooking the ocean is the place to go. Facilities include business centre, fishing deck, private jetty, tennis courts, nightclub, sauna and gym. For a right royal treatment, book one of the villas for a small briefcase of CFA (CFA 4.3 million per week).

Other options:

Hôtel de l'Indépendance (Map p150; ☎ 823 1019; www.hotel-independance.com; Place de l'Indépendance; s/d CFA50,000/55,000; ☒) The shine may have worn off this place but there are good views from the rooftop bar.

Hôtel Croix du Sud (Map p150; ☎ 889 7878; 20 Av Albert Sarraut; s/d CFA55,000/60,000) Overpriced hide-out for old-fashioned, armchair-lounging cigar smokers. The restaurant is excellent though, and renowned for its quality French cuisine.

Résidence Ndiambour (Map p148; ☎ 823 6111; ndiambour@sentoo.sn; 121 Rue Carnot; studio/ste CFA45,000/95,000) Spacious but unspectacular apartments.

EATING

Dakar's restaurant scene is definitely one of the capital's highlights. There are about 100 eateries in the town centre alone, and that's before you've even headed for the suburbs, where chic new restaurants open all the time.

French cuisine, a hangover from the colonial past, is a particular highlight, but there's more to Dakar than *entrecôte* (rib steak) and *crème brûlée* (cream dessert covered in caramelised sugar). Cape Verdean, Vietnamese, Thai, Lebanese, Italian, Korean and Mexican, along with a remarkable array of seafood restaurants, are also available. Almost every place will also be able to offer you some decent *yassa poulet* (grilled chicken marinated in a thick onion and lemon sauce) and *thiéboudienne* (Senegal's national dish; rice cooked in a thick sauce of fish and vegetables), though for the best taste of classic Senegalese dishes you're often better off trying one of the small, unremarkable places frequented by the locals.

Restaurants

Restaurants are listed here according to the cuisine they mainly serve, although there's a lot of overlap. Seafood is served in all Dakar restaurants.

Restaurants usually open from 11am to 2pm and 6pm to midnight or later. (Many only close when the last guest has staggered out). Some open all day, but might only serve food at lunch and dinner hours. Note that most Dakar restaurants are closed on Sunday.

AFRICAN

There are dozens of African restaurants in Dakar; most of the ones listed here have achieved near-classic status.

Keur N'Deye (Map p150; ☎ 821 4973; 68 Rue Vincens; dishes from CFA1500) Highly recommended, this place offers well-prepared Senegalese specialities and a reasonable range of vegetarian dishes including large bowls of salad. At most times, the tinkling of the kora accompanies the eager clattering of cutlery.

Restaurant Ali Baba (Map p150; ☎ 822 0172; 7 Rue El Haji M'Baye Gueye; dishes around CFA1500; ☒ 8am-midnight) Extremely packed during lunchtime, this is a favourite with Dakar's downtown workers. Huge portions of local and European food are served with a slice of real Dakar life.

Chez Loutcha (Map p150; ☎ 821 0302; 101 Rue Moussé Diop; dishes CFA2500-3500; ☒ noon-3pm & 7-11pm Mon-Sat) Ignore the air-conditioned front room and head out back to the fan-conditioned garden, where fountains embellish the aquatic theme. The Cape Verdean and 'Eur-African' cuisine is excellent and comes in enormous serves.

Point d'Interrogation (Map p150; ☎ 822 5072; Rue Assane Ndoye; dishes CFA1500-2500) This small eatery filling and seriously scrumptious Senegalese dishes for reasonable prices. Its *thiebouthienne* is divine.

Restaurant VSD (Map p150; ☎ 661 3333; 91 Rue Moussé Diop; mains CFA3500; ☒ 7am-midnight) There's not much jazz at this intimate place any more, but the West African and international dishes are still good value. Home delivery is also available.

EUROPEAN

Senegal's cultural heritage means Dakar has a wide choice of bars, bistros, cafés and restaurants doing French food.

Casino Terrou-Bi (Map p146; ☎ 839 9039; Rte de la Corniche-Ouest; meals around CFA5000-8000) Right on the sea, this chic garden restaurant serves highly recommended French cuisine. It's a favourite with Dakar's monied classes, and the perfect place to sip cocktails near the pool before blowing the holiday budget in the adjacent casino.

Le Sarraut (Map p150; ☎ 822 5523; Av Albert Sarraut; ⏱ 8am-midnight Mon-Sat) This place is a Dakar institution. It's not cheap – but is a great place to invest in a rounded culinary experience. The tasty French and international cuisine in this calm, central place is hard to beat – the scrumptious seafood spaghetti is enough to persuade you to return.

Café Restaurant de l'Institut (Map p150; ☎ / fax 823 1909, ☎ Institute 823 0320; 89 Rue Joseph Gomis; ⏱ 9am-11pm; dishes around CFA3000) In the cool shade of the Institut Français' mighty *fromager* tree, this oasis of calm has an excellent range of simple meals, delicious desserts and great coffee.

Le Méléa (Map p150; ☎ 502 8293; 90 Rue Moussé Diop; dishes around CFA5000) This tiny French restaurant is all simple elegance, and the food tastes divine (we enjoyed a gigantic bowl of Moroccan couscous, spiced to flavoursome perfection). The catch: it can get a little smoky.

Lagon I (Map p150; ☎ 821 5831; Rte de la Corniche-Est; mains around CFA7000) In this expensive restaurant the nautical theme is consistently pursued, from cruise-ship decor and cabin-style toilets to the terrace suspended on stilts in the ocean and scrumptious platters of seafood.

Ozio (Map p150; ☎ 823 8787; 21 Rue Victor Hugo; meals around CFA5000-9000) This ubertrendy restaurant has been a favourite of the glitterati for years. The food is great and is served with the ego-tickling sense of belonging to the in-crowd.

Le Bambou (Map p150; ☎ 822 0645; 19 Rue Victor Hugo; mains CFA6000-10,000) If money is not a concern, head to Le Bambou, the culinary equivalent of a day's pampering.

Café de Rome (Map p150; ☎ 823 2610; Blvd de la République) You want to mingle with Dakar's jet set? This is the place. So pretentious it borders on hilarious.

La Villa Chez Yannick (Map p150; ☎ 823 2197; 4 Rue Malenfant; mains CFA5000; ⏱ 11am-3pm & 7-11pm) French food and a few miscellaneous international dishes are served in an airy outdoor setting.

La Palmeraie (Map p150; ☎ 821 1594; 20 Av Pompidou; meals CFA4000-6000) This place is usually

buzzing – but that's got to be due to the central location. It can't be the ordinary food, nor the gloomy setting. The service? Disgruntled. Still, for a quick bite in the centre of town it's a reasonable option.

Le Niwa (Map p148; ☎ 822 2029; dishes CFA3000-6000; ⏱ 8am-9pm) Right above the Île de Gorée ferry departure hall, this usually crowded place is the 'waiting lounge' if you've missed your boat. Its seafood is recommended.

ASIAN

Dakar being the cosmopolitan lady it is, it also has the best range of Asian food for thousands of kilometres – we dare suggest.

Jardin Thaïlandais (Map p152; ☎ 825 5833; 10 Blvd du Sud; meals around CFA8000; ⏱ lunch & dinner Mon-Sat) There's no better Thai, perhaps no better Asian food altogether, in the whole of Senegal than that served at this pretty place in Point E. Prices are a bit steep, but every bite is worth it.

Le Dragon (Map p150; ☎ 821 6676; 35 Rue Jules Ferry; mains CFA3000-5000; ⏱ 6-11pm Mon-Sat) This is one of Dakar's oldest Vietnamese restaurants, and the one that started the popularity of Asian food in the city.

Saveur d'Asie (Map p150; ☎ 821 4774; 21 Rue de Thann; dishes around CFA5000) Hugely popular, this takeaway restaurant makes an enticing promise of serving Senegalese-Asian cuisine. It sells almost the complete works of Youssou N'Dour in its adjacent boutique.

Le Seoul (Map p150; ☎ 822 9000; 75 Rue Assane Ndoye; dishes CFA5000-8000; ⏱ noon-3pm & 7.30-11pm) The leafy courtyard setting is a welcome respite from the inner-city streets, and the Korean food is carefully prepared and subtly spiced.

INTERNATIONAL

Dakar's most original restaurants find themselves united under this globe-spanning heading.

Restaurant Farid (Map p150; ☎ 821 6127; 51 Rue Vincens; dishes CFA2500-4000; ⏱ Mon-Sat) Forget for a minute that this is a hotel restaurant. The Lebanese food here is probably the best in town.

La Casa Créole (Map p150; ☎ 823 4081; Blvd Djily Mbaye; meals around CFA4000-6000; ⏱ Mon-Sat) Don't be put off by the busy pub at the front – walk right through and you'll find a marvellous garden terrace where French and Creole food are served with a sprinkling of live jazz.

La Fourchette (Map p150; ☎ 821 8887; 4 Rue Parent; meals around CFA6000-10,000; ☺ Mon-Sat) The humble exterior betrays nothing of the polished food temple that hides within. Impeccable sushi and dishes from around the world prepared by two of Dakar's most renowned chefs attract expats and the trendiest Senegalese folks. The set lunch for CFA5500 must be the best value for money in Dakar – and don't leave without indulging in the heavenly roti *au chocolat*.

Le Toukouleur (Map p150; ☎ 821 5193; 122 Rue Moussé Diop; ☺ Mon-Sat) It's all about tasteful African chic in this mud-red painted, patio-adorned restaurant *de classe*. The food fits its environment, too; a refined mix of international flavours.

Sabura (Map p152; ☎ 641 1072; Av Birago Diop, Point E; meals CFA3000-5000) This Bissau-Guinean restaurant serves excellent Cape Verdean, Portuguese and Creole cuisine. If you want a royally prepared *catchoupa* – Cape Verde's porky answer to paella – this is your place. The many Cape Verdean and Guinean regulars are the best quality indicator.

Cafés & Patisseries

In Dakar, a patisserie is not somewhere to buy your bread but a place to take your date if you really want to make an impression. Patisseries are springing up all over the place, most of them air-conditioned to freezing point and scrubbed till they shine.

La Royaltine (Map p150; ☎ 821 9994; Av du Président Lamine Gueye) Guarded by a uniformed porter and drenched in soft, golden lighting, Dakar's most polished patisserie oozes class. Affluent Dakarois swagger in here for tasty cakes, desserts and chocolates.

La Galette (Map p150; ☎ 821 3340; 16 Av Pompidou) This patisserie is slightly more down-to-earth, though still floating way above a simple bakery.

Aux Fins Palais (Map p148; ☎ 823 4445; 97 Av André Petyavin) It's easy to tire of French bread in Dakar. This is one of the few places that serve an excellent range of wholemeal breads.

Pâtisserie Médina (Map p148; Av Faidherbe; ☺ 24hr) Dakar's 'terminus'. Every night out ends here at 5am, with coffee and croissants. With some luck, you'll even see some of Senegal's biggest music and football stars huddled around cups of hot chocolate.

Metissacana (Map p150; ☎ 822 2043; Rue de Thiong) This is a haven of peace in the inner city –

a leafy patio where you can enjoy a coffee and simple meals. And best of all – you can browse through the original creations by internationally acclaimed fashion designer Oumou Sy and her students in the adjacent boutique.

Quick Eats

All across Dakar you'll see women stirring pots of *mafé* (rice covered with a thick, smooth groundnut sauce with fried meat and vegetables) and grilling fish in the street and in makeshift *tanganas* (cafés literally meaning 'hot stuff') and selling steaming glasses of *café touba* (a spicy coffee) with a slice of bread and butter. A fast-food favourite is the *shwarma* (CFA800), sold in snack bars and restaurants.

Ali Baba Snack Bar (Map p150; ☎ 822 5297; Av Pompidou; ☺ 8am-2am) Dakar's classic fast-food haunt keeps turning thanks to the undying love of the Senegalese. Serves the whole fast-food range: kebabs, *shwarmas* and other quick snacks.

Caesar's (Map p150; ☎ 842 7879; 27 Blvd de la République) Sometimes only fried chicken wings, burgers and fries will do, and for those moments Caesar's is your place. Come here regularly and you'll gain precious insights into the complexities of teenage love life.

Les Grilladins (Map p150; ☎ 821 3839; 4 Rue el Hadj Abdoukarim Bourgi) This is a good address for pizzas and crêpes. Food here isn't fancy but its reliable, and even served relatively speedily. It also does home delivery.

Self-Catering

Corner shops stacked sky-high are scattered all across Dakar. They tend to have a standard selection of local foodstuffs. Supermarkets have a bigger, more expensive and French-oriented selection of foods. For Western-style supplies such as cornflakes, juice and pasta, you're better off at the shops at petrol stations, or you could head straight for one of the big supermarkets where the selection is good, but prices steep.

The best-stocked supermarkets in Dakar are those of the Score chain. There are two main branches: the **Score Supermarket** (Map p150; 31 Av Albert Sarraut) in the town centre and the giant one (Map p152) on Blvd de la Gueule Tapée in Point E. Both are good for imported items and food, sanitary and baby products and plenty of other nonfood items.

Fili Fili Supermarket (Map p150; Av Allés Delmas) three blocks north of Place de l'Indépendance is a dusty little place with slightly cheaper prices but a much smaller range of stock. In Point E, the **Ecomarché** (Map p152; Av Cheikh Anta Diop, Point E) is pretty good.

DRINKING

Dakar by night can be almost as busy as Dakar by day. The town centre has a scattering of good bars all within easy reach for an increasingly entertaining pub crawl. But the scene is getting bigger, and some of the best places are now in the suburbs rather than in the centre.

Le Mex (Map p150; ☎ 823 6717; 91 Rue Moussé Diop; ☺ noon-2am) Firmly on the rise when we visited, this colourful Mexican place transforms from a restaurant into a lively bar once the sun has set. It's popular with the French military and their obligatory female following, but can still be fun.

Le Seven (Map p150; ☎ 842 6911; seven_dkr@yahoo .fr; 25 Rue Mohamed V) This is the glittering queen of Dakar's bars. Think champagne bubbles, tiny tank tops, the latest hits. So *branché* (literally 'plugged in') that you risk electrocution, this is where the in-crowd parties.

Snooker Palace (Map p150; ☎ 822 9487; 44 Rue Wagane Diouf) This polished snooker hall starts early and gets hotter by the hour. Giant plasma screens ooze class and are perfect for watching football matches.

Café Indigo (Map p150; ☎ 842 2607; 26 Rue Félix Faure; ☺ 7am-midnight) Somewhere between a restaurant, a café and a bar, this is a relaxed place to start your night out.

Iguane Café (Map p150; 26 Rue Jules Ferry) This tiny place is draped in mock-military decor, but despite the strict camouflage colours of the surroundings its surprisingly easy-going.

Chez Grenelles (Map p150; ☎ 889 4444; 38 Rue Assane Ndoye) Classy and imaginatively decorated, this place in the Hôtel Ganalé gets crowded with a predominantly French and Lebanese crowd.

Also worth trying:

Bar L'Impérial (Map p150; ☎ 822 2663; Place de l'Indépendance) For those who like their bars nice and calm.

Bar de l'Hôtel de l'Indépendance (Map p150; ☎ 823 1019; Place de l'Indépendance) An uninspired setting, but the views across Dakar are brilliant.

Casino du Port (Map p150; ☎ 842 5311; Blvd de la Libération) Lose your money in luxurious surroundings.

ENTERTAINMENT

For a fun night out, don't even get your kit on before midnight. Leaving the house around 1am shows impeccable timing; returning home before 4am is a sign of weakness. Now go party.

Live Music

Dakar's live-music scene is booming. More and more restaurants and bars are opening small stages, and many nightclubs feature live gigs. In restaurants, admission is often free, while clubs charge between CFA3000 and CFA5000.

Pen'Art (Map p152; ☎ 864 5131; Blvd du Sud) Around the corner from Just 4 U, this is a cosy jazz club with good bands in a relaxed atmosphere. It's also a wi-fi space, which is great if you're trying to get online for free, but does affect the atmosphere – half the crowd hides behind their laptops.

Kilimanjaro (Map p146; Village Artisanal, Soumbédioune) The mighty Thione Seck plays here, at his personal club, every weekend. Fabulous. Men – don't forget your suit and tie…

Thiossane (Map p152; ☎ 824 6046; Rue 10) Youssou N'Dour's nightclub was once the hottest place in town but is now frequently closed when the world-music star is out of town. And even if he's there, he rarely appears on stage before 3am. Still, it's a hub of the glittering, hip-swaying, high-heeled *mbalax* scene.

THE AUTHOR'S CHOICE

Just 4 U (Map p152; ☎ 824 3250, 634 4801; just 4u@sentoo.sn; Av Cheikh Anta Diop; ☺ 11am-3am) There are few places where a platter of grilled fish is served in more welcoming surroundings than in the lovingly decorated open-air space of this restaurant-cum-bar. But that's not even the point. People flock to Just 4 U because it's by far the best address for live music in Dakar. There's a concert on every night, sometimes even two, and Senegalese greats such as Cheikh Lô, Souleymane Faye and Orchestra Baobab perform regularly on the small stage. This is usually the first stop for visiting stars, and with a bit of luck you might just take in a performance by the likes of Salif Keita, Philip Monteiro, Viviane N'Dour or Omar Pene while enjoying a sumptuous three-course meal.

GREATER DAKAR & CAP VERT PENINSULA

Alizé Club (Map p152; Av Cheikh Anta Diop) You want to master the *mbalax*? The informal environment of this live-music club is a good place to practise that seductive hip swing.

Sunset (Map p146; ☎ 821 2118; Centre Commercial Sahm) Similarly popular with the Dakarois, this club is on the northeastern corner of the intersection of Av Blaise Diagne and Blvd de la Gueule-Tapée, about 3km northwest of Marché Sandaga.

Nightclubs

Playclub (Map p150; 46 Rue Jules Ferry) The club of the Hôtel Al Afifa is a classy affair for the over 30s, so the music is smooth and comes spiced with salsa beats.

Koulgraoul (Map p148; ☎ 505 6969; Rte de la Corniche-Est; admission CFA2500) This relaxed club night held once a month in the garden of the Océanium (behind the Palais Présidentiel) attracts a mixed, laid-back crowd. Relief – a less dressed-up affair than most of Dakar's clubs.

King's Club (Map p150; 32 Rue Victor Hugo) This inner-city club is hugely popular for its heavy dance beats and good vibes.

Theatre

Théâtre Daniel Sorano (Map p148; ☎ 822 1715; Blvd de la République) This is Dakar's proudest theatre. The Ensemble Instrumental, the Ballet National du Sénégal and the Théâtre National du Sénégal perform here on occasion. Check listings magazines and posters for event updates.

Cinemas

Kadjinol Station (Map p150; ☎ 842 8662; www.kadjinol-edu.com; ❤ 11am-3am) This lounge bar and global-food restaurant off Rue Sarraut also has the most interesting film selection in town, with a strong focus on world cinema, as well as Hollywood classics and recent hits. Film viewings are free with purchase of drinks and/or food.

SHOPPING
Central Dakar

Dakar isn't really the place for a relaxed shopping stroll. You'll be too busy clutching your purse, shaking off hustlers and dodging parked cars to appreciate a relaxed promenade around the inner city. Still, there are a few places worth venturing into town for, most of them in the side streets between Av Pompidou and Blvd de la République. The **Institut Français** (Map p150; ☎ 823 0320; www.institutfr-dakar.org; 89 Rue Joseph Gomis) is one of Senegal's major outlets of the Maam Samba label, which is known for its simply cut clothes made from rich, stunningly coloured cottons. All ingredients are natural, and the fabrics are woven, dyed and sewn locally by the women of Ndem village, and sold fairtrade.

For children's clothes, two boutiques on Rue Assane Ndoye have cute, African-style cuts: **Garmy's Confection** (Map p150; ☎ 822 6126) and **Cajou** (Map p150) right next door, which also has a lovely range of toys and bags made from African fabrics. The spacious **Cocktail du Sénégal** (Map p150; ☎ 823 5315; 108 Rue Moussé Diop)

MBALAX FEVER

It's Saturday night, you're all decked out in your gladdest rags, and ready for a night on the dance floor. You're in Dakar, you're in the right place. Enter any one of the city's fancy clubs and you'll be greeted by the familiar sight of mirrors, showy lighting, huge amps and, yes, spinning disco balls. But that's where the comfort zone stops. Time to hit the dance floor and put your suppleness to the test. Already you feel underdressed among the glittering crowds – the curve-hugging dresses, sparkling heels and perfectly fitted shirts of the Senegalese. And now the *mbalax* beat kicks in, that uniquely Senegalese rhythm that sends legs spinning and provokes the most outrageously sensual hip gyrations. Keen dancers form small circles, urging each other on with laughter and hand claps to ever more daring moves. The beat gets faster, the air-conditioning loses against the body heat. Pearls of sweat appear on your forehead and that strapless top seems too much to wear. That's when the DJ switches. The lights go down, the music slows to a sensual *zouk,* and the clusters of dancers dissolve into tightly glued couples. As the night wears on, you'll swing your way through the latest R&B, heavy hip-hop from the USA and Senegal, and a few pounding techno tracks – enough to throw off any shyness and loosen up for the next round of *mbalax*.

TAILOR MADE

Dakar isn't normally included in the list of the world's capitals of style, but that's a serious omission. Dakar emanates chic. At any time of day, the city's sandy pavements are dotted with a dazzling range of colours, fabrics designed to reflect the sunlight in shimmering sparks, and myriad imaginative versions of the classic *boubou* (elaborate robe-like outfit worn by men and women) cut. Your holiday wardrobe will have a hard time competing. But worry not, the Senegalese love for all things elegant has brought with it a multitude of tailor shops. Time to get your own tailor-made gown.

First step: find your designer of choice. Dakar has everything, from the ateliers of world-famous designers such as Oumou Sy to numerous tiny shacks in all the major markets, where tailors churn out garments to meet local demand.

The best place by far to rummage for material is the Marché HLM in the lively neighbourhood HLM – every taxi driver knows it. Stroll along the countless boutiques and roughly constructed stalls, look, feel, negotiate hard and take your pick. Then take your precious wares to a tailor shop, dig up the artisan from under the pile of neatly folded fabrics, half-finished ensembles, threads, needles and sewing-machine oils, and explain the design you've got in mind. Just take along any drawings or clothes that will help explain your ideas. In less than a week, your item could be ready, and you ready to be seen.

At the smaller tailor shops you can have an item made for CFA10,000 to CFA20,000. At the more established places prices go up to about CFA40,000, much higher at the designers' showrooms. To find a good tailor, best ask the locals – everyone has their 'house favourite'.

also has a very good selection of clothes, both for children and adults, along with a great variety of original gifts, souvenirs and jewellery.

For quality African art and craftwork, try **Galerie Antenna** (Map p150; ☎ 822 1751; 9 Rue Félix Faure) near the Sofitel Teranga. The 'Moroccan mile' on Rue Mohamed V, between Av Pompidou and Rue Assane Ndoye, has a line of small shops with masks, carvings and other objects from all over West and central Africa. On the same street you will find shops selling Moroccan or Algerian-style carpets, leatherwork, pottery, Maghreb clothing and shoemakers that can produce stylish, made-to-measure footwear.

Point E

The leafy suburb of Point E is home to several chic boutiques – it's the place to rummage for souvenirs beyond the obvious. **Naaj** (Map p152; ☎ 825 7546; Rue 1) sells elegant tableware, decorated using Senegal's traditional *sous-verre* technique. **Fil & Pampilles** (Map p152; ☎ 824 0931; Blvd Canal IV) is the place to rummage for unique, contemporary craftwork, ranging from gaudily painted furniture and woven handbags to silver jewellery and classy *sous-verre* art. The airy patio setting of **Agora** (Map p152; ☎ 864 1448; Rue D) displays beautiful Moroccan artwork and

homewares and furnishings at steep prices. For music, the **Koulgraoul Music Shop** (Map p152; Fann; ☼ 9am-11pm) near the university has a great range of African and international CDs and cassettes, both new and used. And, here comes the real gem, the **Atelier Baba Diawara** (Map p146; Rte de la Corniche-Ouest) opposite Marché Soumbédioune is a magic corner selling bags, toys, CD stands, lamps and various other objects from recycled cans. A cool alternative to the usual touristy masks and batiks.

GETTING THERE & AWAY
Air

The Léopold Sédar Senghor International Airport is in Yoff. For details of flights between Dakar and international or regional destinations, see p279. Within Senegal, Dakar is connected to Saint-Louis, Cap Skiring, Ziguinchor and Tambacounda, though some upcountry airports are only served seasonally. For further information, see p291.

The following airline offices in Dakar can answer international flight inquiries, confirm flights and make reservations.

Air Algérie (Map p150; ☎ 823 5548; 2 Place de l'Indépendance)
Air France (Map p150; ☎ 829 7777; 47 Av Albert Sarraut)

MARKET-HOPPING

Dakar's markets are among the city's most fantastic features, and you can have a hugely entertaining time spending a day or two market-hopping. Just take plenty of energy and some money (best hidden in your pockets, as it's not advisable to carry bags or large wallets around the crammed market streets) and prepare for some hard negotiating with the shrewd traders.

If you want to plunge in headfirst, start at **Marché Sandaga** (Map p150; Av Pompidou), Dakar's largest, busiest and most central market (and the one where you're most likely to have your purse stolen). The market lies at the intersection of Av du Président Lamine Guèye and Av Émile Badiane. There's little you won't find here, and eager traders will try to satisfy even the most extraordinary requests. Hi-fi systems, folds of fabric, clothes and pirate videos are sold at stalls and hang off the shoulders of walking merchants. In Av Émile Badiane you'll find some of Dakar's best choices of CDs and cassettes, and a massive, Sudanese-inspired construction that houses plenty of grocery, meat and fish stalls.

At the Hôtel de l'Indépendance, the **Touareg jewellery market** (Map p150; Place de l'Indépendance) has a shining selection of beautifully decorated rings, earrings and necklaces – if it's around, that is. The traders occasionally dismantle their mobile stalls for exhibitions elsewhere.

The **Marché Malien** (Map p148; Av Faidherbe), near the station, is the place for women who are keen to learn the Senegalese art of seduction. All the ingredients, including incense, the earthenware you need to burn it in, mixed perfumes and jingling waist beads, are sold here.

The covered **Marché Kermel** (Map p150), behind Av Sarraut and within walking distance of Marché Sandaga, sells a mixture of foodstuffs and souvenirs. It's mainly worth visiting for the beautiful building that shelters its busy stalls. The original 1860 construction burnt down in 1994, but the 1997 reconstruction has been closely modelled on the building's initial structure and decoration.

Then it's time to head out of the city centre and into the heart of the Médina (a hire taxi there will cost around CFA1000). Created in colonial days, as a 'township' for African residents, this is still a popular and slightly deprived *quartier,* though one that buzzes with sights, sounds and smells. The bustling **Marché de Tilène** (Map p148; Av Blaise Diagne) mainly sells fruit, vegetables and daily household objects. The *quartier* itself has plenty of tiny tailor shops, perfect to get your clothing of choice made at a fraction of the retail price.

The Village Artisanal market of **Soumbédioune** (Map p146) on the Rte de la Corniche-Ouest, is one of the most popular places to buy woodcarvings, metalwork, ivory and batiks. It's squarely aimed at tourists, so prepare for some serious bargaining. Soumbédioune is also home to a busy fish market. Come in the late afternoon to catch sight of colourful pirogues rolling in to unload stacks of fish, prawns and crabs. You can buy the fish directly from the local women, who sort, prepare and sell it at the market.

Across town, you can observe the same spectacular event at the **Hann Fish Market** (Map p146).

The fabulous **Marché des HLM** (Map p146; Av CA Bamba) is the best place to buy African fabrics. Hundreds of rolls of wax-dyed *bazin* (dyed fabrics beaten to a shine with wooden clubs), vibrant prints, embroidered cloth, lace and silk lend colour to the ramshackle stalls and dusty streets of this popular *quartier.* You can get matching shoes, bags and jewellery at the same place, and even have your new ensemble sewn here.

A little further north is the relaxed **Marché Castors** (Map p146) in the residential suburb of the same name. Here it's all about fruit, vegetables, spices and cooking ingredients.

Air Guinée (Map p150; ☎ 821 4442; 25 Av Pompidou)
Air Ivoire (Map p146; ☎ 889 0280; www.airivoire.com; 31 Rue Abdul Karim Bourgi)
Air Mali (Map p150; ☎ 823 2461; 14 Rue El Haji M'Baye Gueye)
Air Mauritanie (Map p150; ☎ 822 8188; 2 Place de l'Indépendance)

Air Sénégal International (Map p150; ☎ 804 0404; 45 Av Albert Sarraut)
Alitalia (Map p150; ☎ 823 3874; 5 Av Pompidou)
Iberia (Map p150; ☎ 823 3477; 2 Place de l'Indépendance)
Royal Air Maroc (Map p150; ☎ 849 4747; 1 Place de l'Indépendance)

SN Brussels (Map p150; ☎ 823 0460; Rue Amadou Assane Ndoye)
South African Airways (Map p150; ☎ 823 0151; 12 Av Albert Sarraut)
TACV Cabo Verde Airlines (Map p150; ☎ 821 3968; 105 Rue Moussé Diop)
TAP Air Portugal (Map p150; ☎ 821 0065; Rue Amadou Assane Ndoye)

Boat
The excellent ferry boat *Le Wilis* (brand new in 2005) travels between Dakar and Ziguinchor twice weekly in each direction. For more details see p231.

Bush Taxi & Minibus
Ndiaga Ndiayes (white Mercedes bus, used as public transport in Senegal) and bush taxis for long-distance destinations leave from Gare Routière Pompiers (Map p148), at the junction of the autoroute and Av Malick Sy (3km north of Place de l'Indépendance) or from Gare Routière Colobane (Map p146).

Journey durations are impossible to quote with certainty, as they depend on tyre punctures, the number of people and the time it takes to get out of Dakar.

Taxis and minibuses only leave when they're full, and most people travel early. To get a quick start, be at the station well before 9am. (The only way to avoid Dakar's gridlock is to get out of town before 7am).

Sept-place taxis are slightly more expensive, but preferable to minibuses. They are safer, fill up quicker and arrive faster as there are fewer people to drop off on the way. You almost always have to pay extra for luggage (generally CFA100 per item).

Driving in Dakar can be a real nightmare – the city is almost permanently gridlocked. At the time of research, the Rte de la Corniche-Ouest and the Rond-Point de Kolobane had been blocked off due to huge roadwork projects, designed to improve traffic flow in the future. Until those have finished, expect traffic chaos.

Car & Motorcycle
There are several major car-rental agencies in Dakar:
Avis (Map p146; ☎ 849 7757; www.cfaogroup.com) At the airport.
Budget (Map p148; ☎ 822 2513) Has branches on the corner of Av du Président Lamine Guèye and Av Faidherbe, and agents at the airport.

Hertz (Map p150; ☎ 820 1174; www.hertz.sn) Has branches at the airport and on Rue Joseph Gomis in central Dakar.

Independent car-hire companies include the following:
Afrique Location (Map p150; ☎ 823 8801; 28 Rue Assane Ndoye)
Assurcar (Map p148; ☎ 823 7251; www.assurcar.sn) Near the Île de Gorée ferry terminal.
Dakar Location (Map p150; ☎ 823 8610; 7 Rue de Thiong)
Noprola (Map p150; ☎ 821 7311; 29 Rue Assane Ndoye)
Senecartours (Map p150; ☎ 889 7777; www.senecartours.sn; 64 Rue Carnot)
Silcar (Map p146; ☎ 859 0086; silcar@silcar.sn) Car hire is possible at the airport.

For a list of all operators see www.au-senegal.com; in the English version click Travel & Transport, then on Where to Rent a Car.

Car Mouride
This long-distance bus service is financed by the Sufi brotherhood of the Mourides (hence the name). Most buses are clean and safe, and the service is fairly reliable. Still, they are generally much slower than bush taxis and not particularly comfortable.

Book your seat ahead of travel (a couple of days notice is usually enough) at the office of the **Gare Routière Pompiers** (Map p148; ☎ 821 8585), off Av Lamine Gueye. It's always safer to go there in person. Most buses leave in the middle of the night (check exact departure times at the office), and thanks to the booking system they don't take too long to fill up.

Buses leave from a petrol station that doubles as a bus stop at an intersection of Malik Sy and Av Félix Eboué, near the Gare Routière Pompiers. Incoming transport sometimes terminates at Gare Routière Kolobane, about 2km north of Gare Routière Pompiers.

Train
Only one of Senegal's train lines survives – the train that goes from Dakar to Bamako (Mali) via important towns, including Thiès, Diourbel and Tambacounda. The service is completely unreliable and derailments are frequent. If you're keen on the adventure (which it certainly is), check the latest state of the service at Dakar's train station. If you

PUBLIC TRANSPORT FROM DAKAR

Following are public-transport costs for various destinations. Note that the prices given here are an indication only. Minor variations may be due to a luggage charge and, most likely, the rising cost of petrol.

Destination	Sept-place	Minibus	Ndiaga Ndiaye
Bakel	11,500	9500	9000
Kaolack	2600	1650	1350
Karang (Gambia)	5500	4500	3500
Mbour	1300	1000	670
Rosso	5510	3880	3440
Saint-Louis	3500	2600	2200
Tambacounda	7500	6000	5000
Thiès	1200	900	800
Touba	3200	1900	1500
Ziguinchor	7500	5500	5000

really want to get somewhere, take a bush taxi. For details of the train to Bamako, see p283.

GETTING AROUND
To/From the Airport

The journey from the airport to town is the only one with a fixed rate (CFA3000), though prices may well have risen by the time you read this. You can change money or use the ATM inside the terminal. Yoff and N'Gor are a lot closer, and should be cheaper (around CFA2000), though you might have to pay the full rate depending on how well you negotiate.

If you want to save a couple of hundred CFA, walk out of the airport onto the main road and flag down a taxi there.

Bus

Dakar's DDD (Dakar Dem Dikk, or 'Dakar going and returning') bus service is surprisingly good, and the large, blue DDD buses go and come back regularly – every 10 to 15 minutes during the day. They have fixed stops (some clearly visible, with small waiting cubicles, others simply marked by a tiny DDD sign stuck in the ground) and theoretically go every 10 minutes, depending on how tight the gridlock is. Short distances cost CFA150, longer ones range from

CFA175 to CFA250, with prices conforming to a system of zones. Pay for your ticket at the conductor's booth on the bus.

You can view the full network, complete with maps and prices, at www.demdikk.com. Some useful circuits:

No 1 Parcelles Assainies–Place Leclerc From the heart of town via the suburbs all the way up the peninsula.
No 7 Ouakam–Palais de Justice Travels the length of Ave Cheikh Anta Diop into the centre of town.
No 8 Aéroport (Yoff)–Palais de Justice The direct bus route from the airport to the centre of town.
No 11 Keur Massar–Palais 1 Takes you from Keur Massar, en route to Keur Moussa and Lac Rose right through to the centre of town.
No 16 Malika–Palais A direct connection between the village Malika and the town centre.

Car Rapide

These colourfully decorated, blue-and-yellow minibuses are Dakar icons, and while travelling in these pretty (though battered) vehicles is certainly an experience, the routes they follow are hard to understand if you don't know the city well. Destinations aren't marked, and the assistants perched dangerously on the back shout directions so fast that untrained ears won't understand a thing. If you approach to ask, chances are you'll be ushered in before you can protest, as the assistants are always keen to fill up a bus. *Car rapide* drivers have a reputation for driving dangerously, and stop frequently and randomly. When you want to get off, just tap a coin on the roof or window. Journeys cost between CFA50 and CFA100.

Ndiaga Ndiaye

This is another one for Dakar insiders. These privately owned, white 30-seater minibuses adorned with colourful decorations (most with *Alhamdoulilai* – meaning 'Thank God' – across the front) roughly follow the same routes as the DDD buses. Fares are between CFA100 and CFA150 depending on the length of your trip. Destinations and routes are not marked, so you'll have to ask or listen for the call from the apprentice.

Senbus

These white minibuses are made in Senegal. They were newly introduced in 2006 and are eventually supposed to replace the battered *cars rapides*. That's a little sad, seeing that the *cars rapides* are such an integral and typical part of Dakar street life, but it's good news for travellers. They are much more comfortable and infinitely more user-friendly, with clearly marked destinations and fairly fixed stops. Rates are the same as for *cars rapides*.

Taxi

Going by taxi is definitely the easiest way to get around Dakar, and the one most travellers rely on. You simply negotiate your fare and get dropped off exactly where you want. Dakar taxis are equipped with dusty old meters, but it's been years since any of them worked, so prices are up for discussion.

For a short ride across the city centre, the fare should be around CFA500. From Place de l'Indépendance to Gare Routière Pompiers is around CFA750, and Dakar Centre to Point E is around CFA1000. Rates go up at night and on public holidays. Hiring a taxi for day trips around Dakar should cost around CFA25,000.

CAP VERT PENINSULA

The Cap Vert peninsula stretches away beyond downtown Dakar, punctuated by a series of satellite towns and fishing villages that have expanded with the city and now blur into what has become greater Dakar. But these suburbs and settlements are far from uniform.

To the east of the city centre, about 3km offshore, is Île de Gorée (Gorée Island), one of the earliest European settlements along this part of the coast, and today a haven of history and peace within easy reach of the frenetic activity of Dakar. To the west are the Îles de la Madeleine, a national park with not a single historic site but plenty to see and a great place to just chill out in the rock pool.

North of the city centre, at the western tip of the Cap Vert peninsula, is Pointe Almadie – the African continent's westernmost tip. Along the coast from here are N'Gor and Yoff – the former an untidy mix of fishing village and seaside resort favoured at weekends by escapees from the crowded city, and the latter a compact traditional town with a fascinating cultural heritage but little in the way of tourist facilities.

East of here is the vast sprawling settlement of Pikine, stretching across the neck of the peninsula and almost connecting the north and south coasts. Pikine is technically a separate entity, but in reality it's a working-class suburb of Dakar that has expanded so rapidly it now has a larger population than the capital itself. Many of Senegal's famous wrestlers, rappers and other streetwise, self-made heroes stem from this vast sprawl of clapboard housing and crammed streets.

Beyond Pikine, the Cap Vert peninsula begins to widen and merge with the mainland. Within easy reach of Dakar are several more interesting places to visit, including the beaches at Malika, the monastery of Keur Moussa, and the great pink lagoon of Lac Rose (also called Lac Retba).

ÎLE DE GORÉE

It's only a 30-minute ferry ride from Dakar's hectic port to Gorée Island – 23 hectares of almost complete stillness. Where Dakar is all traffic noise, car fumes and beeping horns, Gorée is enveloped by an almost eerie calm, only disturbed by breaking waves, rustling leaves and voices. There are no tar roads and no cars on this island, just narrow alleyways filled with trailing bougainvillea and colonial brick structures whose wrought-iron balconies suggest Mediterranean love stories.

But Gorée's calm is not so much romantic as meditative. Ancient buildings bear witness to the island's role in the Atlantic slave trade. They attract visitors in search of historical truth, and have given rise to plenty of cultural initiatives like the **Gorée Diaspora Festival** (☎ 823 9177; www.goreediasporafestival.org; Mairie de Gorée), an annual celebration of music from Africa and the African diaspora. If you visit Gorée in May or June, you might be so lucky as to catch the annual 'Day of the open doors', when the island's many artists' workshops and some private homes are open to the public.

Information

Any tourist entering Gorée needs to pay a tourist tax of CFA500. You pay this at the tourist information booth near the ferry landing. You can also hire tourist guides here or at the **Syndicat d'Initiative** (Map p168; ☎ 823 9177; Rue du Port; ⏰ 9am-1pm & 2.30-5pm

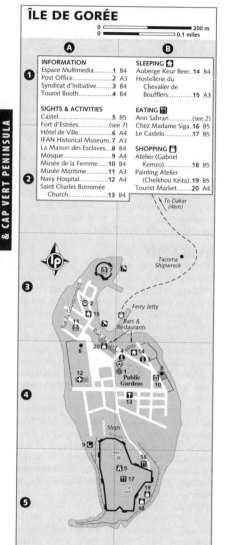

ÎLE DE GORÉE

0   200 m
0   0.1 miles

INFORMATION
Espace Multimedia..........1 B4
Post Office....................2 A3
Syndicat d'Initiative.......3 B4
Tourist Booth................4 B4

SIGHTS & ACTIVITIES
Castel.............................5 B5
Fort d'Estrées.............(see 7)
Hôtel de Ville.................6 A4
IFAN Historical Museum.7 A3
La Maison des Esclaves...8 B4
Mosque..........................9 A4
Musée de la Femme.....10 B4
Musée Maritime...........11 A3
Navy Hospital...............12 A4
Saint Charles Borromée
   Church....................13 B4

SLEEPING
Auberge Keur Beer..14 B4
Hostellerie du
   Chevalier de
   Boufflers.............15 A3

EATING
Ann Sabran.............(see 2)
Chez Madame Siga..16 B5
Le Castelo..............17 B5

SHOPPING
Atelier (Gabriel
   Kemzo)...............18 B5
Painting Atelier
   (Cheikhou Keita).19 B5
Tourist Market........20 A4

To Dakar
(4km)

Tacoma
Shipwreck

Rue du Gouvernement

Ferry Jetty

Bars &
Restaurants

Rue du Port

Public
Gardens

Steps

GREATER DAKAR
& CAP VERT PENINSULA

Tue-Sun), rather than using one of the free-lancers lurking around the ferry jetty. But Gorée is tiny and can easily be explored independently.

For leaflets and books, including the excellent *Gorée – The Island and the Historical Museum*, the Syndicat d'Initiative is a good address. For some on-the-spot information,

try the small tourist booth near the police station.

Gorée has a post office and an Internet café, **Espace Multimedia** (per hr CFA500; ☼ 10am-1pm & 3-10pm), both near the ferry jetty.

Sights

There's plenty to see on the island to fill a day, but don't come on a Monday, as all the museums and historical buildings will be closed.

The island's most famous building is **La Maison des Esclaves** (admission CFA500; ☼ Tue-Sun 10.30am-noon & 2.30-6pm). No trip to the island is complete without a visit to this 1776 Dutch construction, whose arched staircase opening to the ocean has become a symbolic image of the horrors of slavery. For more details see the boxed text, opposite.

The base of the **Castel** at the southern tip of the island is another Dutch building, though one that was erected in the 17th century, well before the slave house was built. Over the centuries other fortifications were added, including massive WWII guns, which sank a British warship in the harbour. You can walk up on its rocky plateau, from where you get excellent views over the island and across the water to Dakar. Today, the Castel is inhabited by a group of Baye Fall disciples (for more information on them, see the boxed text, p45).

Gorée's two sacred buildings are also worth seeing. The 1830 **Saint Charles Borromée Church** is an imposing building that's usually open to visitors, while the **mosque** (Castel), built in 1892, is one of the oldest stone mosques in Senegal.

There are several museums on the island. The **IFAN Historical Museum** (Fort d'Estrées; admission CFA200; ☼ 10am-1pm & 2.30-6pm Tue-Sat) has interesting pictures and artefacts portraying Senegalese history up to the present day. It's also worth visiting for its building, the ancient French **Fort d'Estrées** (1850). The permanent exhibition at the **Musée de la Femme** (Rue du Port; admission CFA500; ☼ 10am-5pm Tue-Sun), dedicated to the role of Senegalese women throughout history, is at least as interesting and really comes to life in the tour (CFA350) given by the enthusiastic museum guide. The **Musée Maritime** (admission CFA500), in an 18th-century West Indies company building, isn't quite as scintillating as the building it's housed in. Both the

LA MAISON DES ESCLAVES

Île de Gorée was a busy slave- and goods-trading centre during the 18th and 19th centuries, and many merchants built houses in which they would live or work in the upper storey and store their cargoes on the lower floor.

The Maison des Esclaves (Slave House) is one of the last remaining 18th-century buildings of this type on Gorée. It was built in 1786 and renovated in 1990 with French assistance. With its famous doorway opening directly from the storeroom onto the sea, this building has enormous spiritual significance for some visitors, particularly African-Americans whose ancestors were brought from Africa as slaves.

Walking around the dimly lit dungeons, particularly after a visit to the historical museum, you will begin to imagine the suffering of the people held here. This is reinforced by the gruesome details provided by the Slave House curator. The Maison des Esclaves is an important symbol and reminder of the horrors of the slave trade. However, although an important slave-trading culture did exist in Gorée, the island's role as a major slave-shipment point is sometimes overstated. Of the 20 million slaves that were taken from Africa, only 300 per year may have gone through Gorée and, even then, the famous doorway would not have been used – ships could not get near the dangerous rocks and the town had a jetty a short distance away.

But the number of slaves transported from here isn't necessarily what matters in the debate around Gorée. The island, and particularly the Maison des Esclaves, stands as a terrible reminder of the immense suffering inflicted on African people as a result of the Atlantic slave trade.

old **Navy Hospital** and the **Hôtel de Ville**, just north of the hospital, are interesting historical buildings.

Sleeping

Gorée's hotels rarely get booked up, but if you find them full, you can always inquire at some of the bars and restaurants facing the ferry jetty about a room in a private home. Rates start at CFA7500 per room per night.

Auberge Keur Beer (☎ /fax 821 3801; keurbeergie@ yahoo.fr; Rue du Port; s/d CFA20,000/25,000) Gorée's most popular place has pristine rooms. Management is full of useful information and can even arrange accommodation in private homes should the auberge be full.

Hostellerie du Chevalier de Boufflers (☎ 822 5364; www.boufflers.com; r from CFA18,000) Best known for its terrace restaurant overlooking the harbour, this place in the northern part of Gorée has several rooms spread across a whole block. Prices vary depending on the view and the floor. Best are the enormous, tastefully decorated rooms upstairs that sleep up to five.

Eating

For food, try the two hotels, or any of the stretch of restaurants opposite the ferry jetty. At the post office, **Ann Sabran** (☎ 826 9429; dishes around CFA2500) is a cosy port-side restaurant where the meals are simple and the sandwiches filling. At the Castel, your choice is between the local *gargotte* (basic eatery) Chez Madame Siga or **Le Castelo** (dishes around CFA2500), superbly located on top of the plateau.

Shopping

Just behind the row of bars and restaurants facing the ferry jetty is a little tourist market that's crammed full of crafts and batiks. The countless stalls that line the ascent to the Castel sell similar souvenirs and cheap paintings.

If you really want to invest in some artwork, it's best to go directly to the workshop of one of several artists who have made Gorée their home. The brilliant sculptor Gabriel Kemzo has his atelier in a beautiful spot near the Castel, formerly the workshop of his teacher, the renowned Moustapha Dimé. Cheikhou Keita, one of Senegal's most outstanding painters, also lives nearby. His home and atelier can be visited.

Getting There & Away

A **ferry** (☎ 849 7961, 24hr infoline 628 1111) runs regularly from the wharf in Dakar, just north of Place de l'Indépendance, to Île de Gorée. The trip across takes 20 minutes and costs CFA5000 return for foreigners. For the ferry timetable phone the infoline or check www .ausenegal.com.

> **TWITCHER TIPS: ÎLES DE LA MADELEINE**
>
> The 45-hectare park of the Îles de la Madeleine is home to an impressive number of birds. The black kite, the islands' emblem, is only one species to be observed here. There are also breeding colonies of common cormorants, northern gannets, bridled terns, ospreys and red-billed tropical birds – the latter a beautiful specimen with narrow, swept-back wings, and long tail streamers in the breeding season.

ÎLES DE LA MADELEINE

Declared a national park in 1985, the Îles de la Madeleine are west of central Dakar, about 4km off the mainland. Consisting of a main island called Sarpan and two other islets – plus several lumps of volcanic rock that stick out of the water at low tide – they are not inhabited, which makes their nature very interesting. Sarpan's dwarf baobab trees are worth looking at, and with a bit of luck you might spot dolphins or turtles. The best thing to do on the Madeleines is bird-watch (see above). If small trees and big birds don't make your heart beat faster, you can come here for some snorkelling, diving or swimming in the rock pool.

Remember to bring all the food and water you'll need as well as a hat, as there's virtually no shade.

Getting There & Away

To reach the Îles de la Madeleine, go to the well-signposted **National Park Office** (☎ 821 8182) on Rte de la Corniche-Ouest, just a few metres north of Casino Terrou-Bi and Magic Land; ask for park rangers Mr Seck or Mr Mbaye. A park ranger will organise your trip to the islands (admission adult/child under 10 CFA1000/free; pirogue 20 minutes, CFA3000). Groups of three to 10 people get a CFA1000 discount per person.

Alternatively, the **Océanium** (Map p148; ☎ 822 2441; www.oceanium.org; Rte de la Corniche-Est) runs diving trips to the islands.

LES ALMADIES

Les Almadies is Dakar's *quartier chic*, a plush neighbourhood where the polished villas of Senegal's richest look out onto private beaches. It's also home to the city's best

hotel, a string of lively bars and restaurants, and a great popular ambience that brews behind the luxury dwellings in the streetside food stalls and secret surfer spots at the Pointe des Almadies.

Route des Almadies & Route de N'Gor

The Route des Almadies, the northern continuation of the Rte de la Corniche-Ouest, is the area's lifeline. It's lined with several restaurants, bars and hotels and there will probably be plenty more by the time you visit. The major banks have branches with ATMs, and there's **Librairie Polyglotte** (Map p146; ☎ 820 8887; polyglotte@sentoo.sn; Rte de N'Gor, Les Almadies), a friendly little bookstore with a good selection of English-language books and magazines.

SLEEPING & EATING

The only cheapie in this realm of the affluent is **La Darkasse** (Map p146; ☎ 820 0353; Rte de N'Gor; CFA15,100/17,100), which somewhat resembles a bleak office block, but has decent rooms for the price you pay. The **Airport Hotel** (Map p146; ☎ 820 0480; Rte de N'Gor; s/d CFA39,000/43,000; ✕ ⌘), a little further north, is more upmarket – you obviously pay for luxuries such as gleaming tiles, TV and your own bathroom. For slightly more you can get a beautiful room with an American breakfast bar at the **Hôtel La Détente** (Map p146; ☎ 820 3975; contact@hotel -ladentente.com; Rte des Almadies; s/d from CFA39,000/ 47,000), which overlooks a pretty garden. **Le Lodge des Almadies** (Map p146; ☎ 869 0345; hotelle lodge@sentoo.sn; Rte des Almadies; r CFA35,000) tops the list. It's a hotel with a personal touch – the tastefully decorated rooms and luxurious, mosaic-decorated bathrooms ooze character and loving attention. And it's got one of Dakar's best restaurants to boot.

DRINKING & ENTERTAINMENT

This is an area to go out rather than stay in – just compare the number of hotels to that of bars. The **Monte Christo** (Map p146; Rte des Almadies) is a classy bar-restaurant with a subdued atmosphere, a good selection of cocktails and fine French cuisine. The trendy **Koch B.** (Map p146; ☎ 820 8671; Rte des Almadies; ⏰ 12pm-3am) next door is a nicely laid-out bar with comfy armchairs. It regularly attracts the Dakarois in-crowd. Across the road, the **Blue Note** (Map p146; Rte des Almadies) with its multiple bar spaces is great for live music. The **News Café** (Map p146;

Rte des Almadies) is a cosy place for some mean cocktails at night and a sumptuous pancake breakfast (CFA2900) the morning after.

Hidden in the *quartier* is **Alma City** (Map p146; ☎ 820 2410), one of the most discreetly fabulous developments of modern Dakar. The small complex off Rte des Almadies houses a tiny but colourful restaurant as well as a recording studio and concert and theatre space. And it's one of the city's few wireless spots.

Clubbers are well catered for with the **Casino du Cap Vert** (Map p146; ☎ 820 0974), one of city's busiest nightspots. But its thunder has recently been stolen by the **Senat** (Map p146) at Le Meridien President, which is now the magnet for Dakar's flashy young crowd. To spot famous footballers, singers and the like, head here.

Pointe des Almadies

This understated cape is the *quartier*'s liveliest spot, framed by several good restaurants, groups of women roasting fish on the street and an unassuming artisans market.

SLEEPING & EATING

Opposite Club Med (Map p146), the palatial **Le Meridien President** (Map p146; ☎ 869 6969; www .lemeridien-dakar.com; r from CFA90,000) overlooks the Pointe des Almadies. It's undeniably the finest hotel in and around Dakar and has every facility you could possibly want (including its own golf club and heliport) and prices to match – rates go much, much higher than that listed here.

The bustling community of small restaurants huddled together at the Pointe stands in complete contrast to such refined luxury. You can either have your fish grilled by one of the women who have put up their stalls near the stony beach or go for something with a roof. **La Pointe des Almadies** (Map p146; ☎ 820 0140; mains around CFA3500; ☼ Tue-Sun) is an enduring institution, with good food, including Vietnamese specialities, in a wide setting complete with flower garden and swimming pool. More Vietnamese is served at the nearby **La Récif des Almadies** (Map p146; ☎ 820 1160; dishes around CFA2800-5000; ☼ lunch & dinner Thu-Tue), an airy sea-view place that gets good reviews. For ambience, **La Crêpe Bretonne** (Map p146; crêpes from CFA1500) is unbeatable. It gets particularly lively on Sunday afternoons, when Dakar's youth comes out to play. **Le Dionewar** (Map p146; meals around CFA5000) keeps locals coming back for its seafood.

N'GOR

East of the point, the sheltered **Plage N'Gor** (N'Gor Beach; Map p146) tastes of carefree beach holidays. You can swim here or indulge in one of several restaurants. A short boat ride (CFA500 return) across the bay takes you to Île de N'Gor (Map p146), a tiny island with more fine beaches and a couple of relaxed hotels.

Sleeping & Eating

PLAGE N'GOR

The **Hotel N'Gor Diarama** (Map p146; ☎ 820 1005; fax 820 2723; r CFA45,000) is the monolith on the headland to the east. A touch more informal is **La Madrague** (Map p146; ☎ 820 0364; ☒), one of the nicest places on Plage N'Gor, though the seaview rooms tend to get booked up quickly. A few steps along, **La Brazzérade** (Map p146; ☎ 820 0364; www.labrazzerade.com; d/ste CFA20,000/35,000; ☒ ☐) has transformed itself from one of the best grilled-food places in Dakar into a cosy, affordable, sea-view hotel with solar-powered hot water and, of course, great grilled food. Seafood lovers mustn't miss a dinner at the **Cabane des Pêcheurs** (Map p146; meals around CFA6000-9000; ☼ 11am-11pm), where freshly caught, prepared and heavenly spiced fish is served with real fisherman's insight.

ÎLE DE N'GOR

Chez Carla (Map p146; ☎ 820 1586; d with/without breakfast CFA20,000/15,000), on the western beach, has long been a N'Gor favourite – both for its cosy rooms and its fine Italian food (dishes cost about CFA3000). The **Sunu Ma Kan** (Map p146; ☎ 647 8166; r CFA10,000) on the other side of the island is another decent choice, with clean, comfortable rooms and a lively beach restaurant. The **Oasis de la Petite Plage** (Map p146; meals around CFA3000-5000) is an overpriced little eatery, though the beachside setting is appealing.

Getting There & Away

To reach Pointe des Almadies or N'Gor you can take a No 8 bus from central Dakar out towards the airport, and then a taxi from there for about CFA700. Ndiaga Ndiayes run along Av Cheikh Anta Diop all the way to N'Gor. A taxi from central Dakar will cost about CFA2000.

GREATER DAKAR & CAP VERT PENINSULA

YOFF

A short distance east of N'Gor, but contrasting sharply in feel, is the town of Yoff. On the map it may look like just another suburb, but there's a vital sense of community here that singles it out from other places around Dakar. The people of Yoff are almost exclusively Lebu, renowned fishermen who have inhabited this area for many centuries. Despite, or because of, their relatively small population (they number a few thousand, whereas the Wolof are counted in millions) they have remained culturally intact and retain a great spirit of independence. The town itself is self-administering, with no government officials, no police force and, apparently, no crime. In fact, it was regarded as a separate state by the French colonial authorities before Senegal itself became independent.

The Lebu of Yoff are nearly all members of the Layen, one of the brotherhoods that dominate life in Senegal (for more details see p45). The founder of the brotherhood, Saidi Limamou Laye, is believed to be a reincarnation of the Prophet Mohammed, and his large **Layen Mausoleum** (Map p146), an impressive 1950 construction, is a highly revered place of pilgrimage for Muslims. The mausoleum is the gleaming white building topped with a green onion-shaped dome on the beach at the eastern end of town.

About 1km northwest of the mausoleum is the main fishing beach, where large pirogues are launched into the giant rollers and the day's catch is sold straight from the sand. The Lebu fishermen have a healthy respect for the sea and a belief in the spirit it contains, which is represented by a large snake. If the waves are too large, the boats stay on the beach.

Even if the waves weren't so dangerously large and the beach wasn't covered in the town's rubbish, Yoff Plage is no place for swimming or sunbathing: skimpy clothing is inappropriate in this close-knit Muslim community. Forget about 'entertainment', too – there are no clubs or bars, drunkenness is frowned upon and smoking is prohibited in Yoff village. This is a place to come and wander around respectfully, simply taking it all in.

Sights & Activities

Yoff village life and the impressive Layen Mausoleum hold plenty of interest for visitors. Art fans should invest a day doing a tour of Yoff's wider surroundings. The fabulous **Village des Arts** (Map p146; Rte de l'Aéroport) is a bubble of creativity, squeezed between the busy Rte VDN (Voie Dégagement Nord) and the imposing national stadium, Stade Léopold Sédar Senghor. It houses the ateliers of some of Senegal's finest artists, including the sculptor Alpha Sow and painters Kebé and Moussa Mbaye. A stroll through their workshops feels like a personalised tour through the world's most informal art gallery. Around the corner, in

---

YOFF HEALERS

One of the most interesting aspects of life in Yoff is the traditional *ndeup* ceremonies, where people with a mental illness are treated and healed. People come to be cured from all over Senegal and Gambia and even from neighbouring countries such as Mali and Guinea-Bissau. Despite the town's Islamic heritage, the ceremonies are totally animist and based on a belief that psychological sickness is the result of possession by spirits. The leaders of the Layen brotherhood turn a blind eye to these 'pagan' ceremonies, allowing the two beliefs to comfortably coexist.

The healing ceremonies, which usually last one day but may last longer for serious illnesses, take place about twice a month. The traditional healers sacrifice animals (a chicken or cow, depending on the seriousness of the illness) to invoke intervention from guardian spirits, and place the sick people into a trance-like state that allows malevolent spirits to be drawn out. Some observers have noted that the process is similar to voodoo ceremonies that take place in other parts of West Africa. The healers' services are not cheap; families of people who need treatment reportedly pay large sums (the equivalent of many years' salary), and often several sufferers are treated at the same time.

The ceremonies take place in the centre of Yoff and can attract large crowds of local people. Tourists are tolerated, but watching can be a disturbing experience. It's best to go with a local and keep to the sidelines. Waving a zoom lens around would be the height of insensitivity.

the neighbourhood Nord Foire, you'll see the colourful **Yengoulene** (Map p146; ☎ 869 0710; Nord Foire) sign overlooking the street. This vibrant bar, restaurant and live-music complex is best visited in party mode at night (and especially on weekends when it holds frequent star-studded concerts), but it's also a good place to stop for a coffee during the day. Near Yoff Virage (Yoff bend) is the personally decorated **Atelier Ousmane Sow** (Map p146), the working and living space of Senegal's most famous sculptor.

Sleeping & Eating

Via Via (Map p146; ☎ 820 5475; viavia@sentoo.sn; Rte des Cimetières; s/d incl breakfast CFA9600/17,200) This backpacker favourite at the eastern end of Yoff has been consistently friendly, clean and welcoming for years. People head here for instant peace when fresh off the plane, or to learn to play some *djembe* (a short, goat hide–covered drum) in a relaxed space.

L'Océan (Map p146; ☎ 820 0047; hotelocean@sentoo .sn; Rue de l'Océan; s CFA12,000, d CFA14,000-30,000; ☎) This is a fairly upmarket place overlooking the sea on the western side of Yoff. Rooms are spacious, and the restaurant (with mains around CFA4500) does a mean Sunday

---

THE AUTHOR'S CHOICE

Hôtel Cap Ouest (Map p146; ☎ 820 2469; capouest@arc.sn; Yoff Virage; s/d CFA16,000/19,000) Just when you thought there was no such thing as a good, affordable room in greater Dakar, you stumble across this cosy place right at the wide bend of Yoff Virage. You can get a large, nicely furnished room here for the price of a downtown brothel, and that's just the beginning. The restaurant features changing wall displays of quality contemporary art and opens onto a small beach, perfect for a sunset drink sipped to the sound of waves lapping on the shore. Don't think that the owners just haven't caught up on current room rates in Senegal's capital – they know exactly what excellent value they're offering, as they've got direct comparisons – the fantastic website au-senegal.com is another one of their products, as is the cultural magazine *221*. So if you want to travel upcountry, you won't get more up-to-date or in-depth advice anywhere.

---

buffet (CFA9500). At high tide waves break into the swimming pool jutting into the sea.

Le Toucan (Map p146; ☎ /fax 820 9039; meals CFA3000) Follow the signs from the main road to this rooftop restaurant, where the Senegalese fare takes a while to come but is worth the wait.

La Terrasse d'Anvers (Map p146; ☎ 688 0000; Yoff Virage) Beer drinkers rejoice: the name evokes Belgium and this is indeed Dakar's most reliable address for a Belgian brew. It's also an excellent restaurant serving, you guessed it, Belgian food, as well as a wide range of quality international cuisine.

Getting There & Away

Yoff is near the airport and the places to stay listed here are most easily reached from there by taxi – the fare is CFA1500. From Dakar's city centre, a taxi to Yoff should cost around CFA2000. By public transport, take DDD bus No 8. Buses loop through one part of the village, but in order to reach either L'Océan or Via Via you have to get off on the main road and walk down a street towards the beach. All places are signposted.

MALIKA

Only a few years ago the tiny village of Malika, 15km east of Yoff, used to be a favourite weekend hideout for young Dakarois couples. But the once wide and unspoilt beaches are gradually disappearing, due to intensive sand mining close by. Some of its formerly popular *campements* (hostels) have already been claimed by the sea, together with the trees that once surrounded them.

At the moment, it's still a good place to go for a peaceful day away from the inner city. You might be allowed to visit the town's famous Quranic school, you can simply chill out at the beach or, if you're feeling energetic, attempt the three-hour walk along the coast to **Lac Rose** (p174). The beach is pounded by some pretty stunning waves – warning enough not to enter the water. Several people have drowned here in recent years.

Sleeping & Eating

The youth-run **Campement Touristique** (☎ 658 4867; r CFA5000) is pretty run down, but a good option if you don't mind roughing it in exchange for kora and drumming lessons. Right behind, the **Campement Les Dunes** (☎ 650 0254; r CFA5000) looks like an extension of the Campement Touristique. The two places enjoy friendly relations and agree on all prices, all the way down to a plate of chicken with rice (CFA1750). They both look equally dire but try to make up for that with a warm welcome. The **Complexe Nabou** (Keur Guila; ☎ 595 3860; d/apt incl breakfast CFA13,000/16,000) looks like a weather-beaten palace in the wilderness. It's run by an ex-dancer with the group Touré Kunda and has a slightly artistic touch.

Getting There & Away

DDD bus No 16 takes you straight from Dakar centre to Malika. To get to the hotels, follow the sand track from the bus stop all the way to the ocean (look for the small sign to the *campements* or ask the locals). A hire taxi from Dakar is around CFA15,000. If you're driving, the most direct route is to turn left off the main road between Dakar and Rufisque at Thiaroye-sur-Mer, which will take you straight there.

LE VILLAGE DES TORTUES

On the Rte de Bayakh just north of the village of Sangalkam is the fascinating **Village des Tortues** (Turtle Village; ☎ 658 9984; adult/child CFA3000/2000; ◷ 9am-5.30pm). This 'village' is a sanctuary for more than 400 injured and neglected turtles. There are several species of land and sea turtles, but the main attractions are the giant African spurred tortoise (*Geochelone sulcata*). This is the largest continental tortoise on earth, and the neatly kept reserve has got scores of them, ranging from newly hatched ones to a 92kg giant.

The wide turtle enclosures are spread across a large botanical garden, full of local medicinal plants, and the turtle tours conducted by passionate staff are packed with information on tortoises and trees.

There's also a small boutique where you can purchase locally made craft work, and a pretty café to sip a *bissap* (a deep-purple drink made from hibiscus, sugar and water) with your packed picnic. People interested in volunteering should call the village, as it regularly hires volunteer workers.

To get here, take DDD bus No 15 or a Ndiaga Ndiaye to Rufisque and then another Ndiaga Ndiaye heading for Kayar; ask to be let off at the village (you'll see the huge sign on your left). Alternatively, a taxi

from Rufisque will cost about CFA2000, or CFA12,000 from Dakar.

LAC ROSE

Also known as Lac Retba, Lac Rose is a shallow lagoon surrounded by dunes, mainly famous for being the final destination of the annual Paris–Dakar rally.

Water here is 10 times saltier than the ocean, and the high concentration of minerals causes the lake to shimmer with a pink light when the sun is high. The spectacle isn't always visible; your best chances of seeing it are in the dry season, but even if nature lets you down, you can still swim here, buoyed by the salt. On the southern side of the lake, the small-scale salt-collecting industry is worth a glimpse (see opposite).

The lake makes an enjoyable day trip from Dakar but the Dead Sea it ain't, whatever tour operators tell you. The saleability of the faint hue together with the rally have spurred a massive tourist industry at the lake edge – be prepared to be hassled by tourist hustlers, souvenir traders etc. Better still, take it head-on and come here for the noisy arrival of the rally.

Most of the hotels listed here organise activities for similar prices (listed rates are approximate). They include 4WD tours around the lake (CFA15,000), beach-buggy (in French, quad) tours (CFA25,000) and camel riding (CFA15,000 per hour). **Chevaux du Lac** (☎ 630 0241) offers horse riding to beginners and advanced riders (two hours/six days CFA6000/400,000).

Sleeping & Eating

The cluster of hotels on the lake get busy with busloads of tourist groups, and the village artisanal that's developed can be a hassle to get through with traders trying to lure you into their shops. There are slightly more secluded options near the salt village and on the opposite side of the lake.

All the *campements* do food, and there's little difference in quality or menu. A promising restaurant was about to open at the Résidence Lac Rose near the salt village when we visited.

Bonaba Café (☎ 638 7538; r per person CFA5000; ☻) Hidden away on the far side of the lake, this café has been a favourite with independent travellers for years. Rooms are simple and the bathrooms shared; the inviting dunes are good for walks and also provide shelter from the more touristy zones. You get here either by walking 2km from the main hotel cluster through the dunes or by pirogue (CFA3000 to CFA5000) from the salt village.

Ker Djinné (☎ 634 0468; d CFA20,000; ⊛) The prettiest of the touristy places, this open-spaced *campement* has round-hut accommodation and a recommended restaurant where a griot usually strums his kora.

Chez Salim (☎ 638 1019; d/tr CFA20,000/25,000; ℗ ✕ ⊛) This large *campement* is one of the more upmarket ones, with a wide range of activities and accommodation in comfortable huts.

Niwa Oasis (☎ 532 2023; r CFA17,000; ⊛) This place en route to the salt collectors only gets really busy when the rally arrives – the winner collects his trophy right opposite, and observers are invited to chill out in the Mauritanian tents on the hotel grounds, where drinks can be purchased. At any other time it's at a pleasant distance from the more crowded corners. The management also operates a small, rustic *campement* nearby.

Ma Petite Camargue (☎ 511 2745; s/d CFA15,000/ 20,000) This cute *campement* on the Rte de Bombilor sits at a relaxing distance from the tourist bubble. Basic accommodation has shared bathrooms, but is adequate. The enterprising French couple managing this place has also taken over Le Jardin du Lac in Niaga-Peul, and there's little doubt they'll turn it from a run-down shell into a stylish hotel-cum-restaurant in no time. Absolutely worth checking out.

Also recommended:

Le Palal (☎ 633 5477; s/d CFA15,000/17750; ⊛) Busy, soulless beach hotel, at the busiest corner of the lake.

L'Étoile du Lac (☎ 822 2016; www.etoiledulac.sn) A promising new construction, with accommodation in pretty, thatched-roof huts. It had just been completed at the time of research (rates weren't available yet).

Getting There & Away

Trying to get here by public transport is nigh on impossible, involving a journey by Ndi-aga Ndiaye (CFA200), *car rapide* (CFA200), DDD bus No 11 to Keur Massar, a taxi trip (CFA1000) or minibus (CFA100) to Niaga-Peul village, then a 5km walk to the lake.

Don't do it. Hire a taxi (return trip with an afternoon wait costs around CFA20,000). Or join an organised excursion from Dakar (see p156).

SALT-COLLECTING AT LAC ROSE

On the southern side of Lac Rose is a village called Niaga-Peul, from where local people go out to collect salt from the lake. The lake is shallow, so they wade up to their waists and use digging tools to scrape the salt off the lake bed and load it into flat-bottomed pirogues. When the canoe is full, and the water only millimetres below the rim, it is punted back to the shore and the salt carried onto the bank in buckets. Each salt collector builds his own pile of salt – marked by his initials – and members of the family are also involved; the women do most of the carrying work. The good-quality salt is put straight into 25kg sacks and sold to middlemen from Dakar who come each morning with trucks and pick-ups. The poorer-quality salt gets loaded in bulk and is taken elsewhere for processing. The workers get paid less than CFA400 for each 25kg sack, and even less for the low-grade salt.

If you're driving from Dakar, take the main road towards Rufisque and, about 6km beyond Thiaroye-sur-Mer, turn left on the tar road 6km beyond Thiaroye-sur-Mer, which takes you to Keur Massar. About 3km beyond the village, in Niakoul Rap, turn left for Niaga-Peul and Lac Rose. Alternatively, go to Bambilor, shortly behind the Village de Tortues, and take the dirt road (apparently soon to be sealed) past a farm that sells fresh milk and juice, directly to the southern end of Lac Rose.

RUFISQUE

Rufisque was one of the first and most important French settlements during colonial days, and the crumbling buildings along the transit town's dusty main road still tell the story of the town's former glory. It's worth stopping here for an hour or so, checking out the architecture and perhaps taking a ride on a horse cart, Rufisque's main mode of public transport. Otherwise do as the locals do – pass through.

If you want to spend the night, the cosy **Oustal de l'Agenais** (☎ 836 1648; Rte de Rufisque; r from CFA11,000) is a good option with clean, comfortable rooms, a cosy restaurant and friendly management.

Getting There & Away

Rufisque is on the main road out of Dakar and there's plenty of transport, including DDD bus No 15, frequent Ndiaga Ndiayes and *cars rapides*. The road is notoriously congested, so the trip can take up to two hours during the rush hour. The best time to get out is early in the morning, before 7am.

KEUR MOUSSA MONASTERY

About 12km southeast of Lac Rose and 50km from Dakar on the road to Kayar, Keur Moussa Monastery is a great place to spend a reflective Sunday morning. The building itself is pretty unremarkable, apart from altar paintings that evoke the ancient Coptic Christian art of Ethiopia. But the real reason to visit is the 10am mass, famous for its unique music – a stunning mixture of kora playing and Gregorian chants in Wolof. The monks sell CDs after the service (CFA10,000), as well as homemade goat's cheese, prayer books and various other items. If you can't make it to the monastery, try Dakar's bookshops for copies of the CDs.

Getting There & Away

Take bus No 15 to Rufisque and change for a minibus to Bayakh or Kayar (CFA100). Tell the driver where you're headed and you'll be dropped off at a junction, from where it's a 1.5km walk to the monastery. It's signposted and all the drivers know it. Getting a lift back to Dakar shouldn't be

difficult, as many people will be going that way after the mass.

If you are driving, take the Rte de Rufisque from Dakar, turn left at Rufisque in the direction of Kayar, drive for 21km to Bayakh and then turn left (south) and continue for 5km to the monastery.

KAYAR

The pretty fishing village of Kayar marks the point where the coast swings from the east towards the north – the beginning of Senegal's Grande Côte. It is framed by a wide sandy beach, where the whole cycle of a fisherman's day can be observed: rolling out to sea, coming home, emptying the nets and gutting the fish.

The northern beaches aren't particularly recommended for swimming, as the current here is very strong. But the coastline is an impressive sight and a great place to relax. Pirogue trips, as well as walks to the sand dune behind the village, fill a day nicely, and watching pirogue makers at work is fascinating. Kayar isn't far from Lac Rose, and the two destinations can easily be combined in a weekend excursion.

The **Auberge de l'Océan Bleu** (☎ 953 5058, 507 9125; r CFA7000-10,000) is a relaxed, simple, solar-powered place right behind the beach (you can't drive here). The manager, David, can arrange pretty much any excursion around the country, and also had a great plan for a pirogue shuttle service between Yoff airport and Kayar. Phone to ask if that's happening.

Petite Côte & Siné-Saloum Delta

Petite Côte means 'small coast' – a name that aptly describes this stretch of seashore, which is indeed short compared to the Grande Côte that leads north from Dakar. In terms of tourism, however, this sheltered shoreline is anything but petite. This is where the industry's monetary hopes reside – in the concentration of seaside centres and classy hotels around Saly, the ever-expanding resort zone halfway down the coast from Dakar.

But there's more to the Petite Côte than your average tour operator will show you. Just a few kilometres away from the built-up hotel zones, small fishing villages tempt with a real-life attitude and calmer beaches.

South of the twin villages Joal and Fadiout, where your footsteps resound to the crunching of seashells, the Saloum River cuts into the coast, opening up a vast maze of mangroves and marshes. This region is astoundingly rich in wildlife, with huge flocks of wading birds making for particularly spectacular sights. But it's not all about nature – this region is also of strong historical interest. At the southern edge of Siné-Saloum, the ancient shell mound Diorom Boumag gives evidence of West Africa's most ancient civilisations. Physical legacies of the area's powerful empires, including the 17th-century kingdom of Cayor, are harder to find. But stay in a village, and local residents will be proud to relate the legendary stories of the illustrious leader Lat Dior and his fierce anticolonial struggle to you.

PETITE CÔTE & SINÉ-SALOUM DELTA

HIGHLIGHTS

- Meander along the coast and enjoy fishing-village life in **Toubab Dialao** (p178)
- Walk the wooden bridge from **Joal** to **Fadiout** (p184), the island where everything is made of shells
- Venture into the maze of mangrove creeks and forest islands that is the vast **Siné-Saloum Delta** (p185)
- Watch dozens of colourful fishing pirogues roll in with their glistening catch at **Mbour** (p183)
- Indulge in lazy beach life at **Saly** (p181), Senegal's largest sea-resort zone

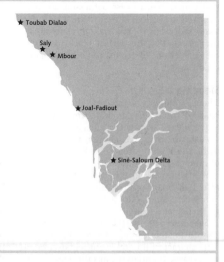

★ Toubab Dialao
Saly ★
★ Mbour
★ Joal-Fadiout
★ Siné-Saloum Delta

- POPULATION: 2.3 MILLION

PETITE CÔTE

This is where Senegal greets the Atlantic with kilometres of sandy coast. Safe swimming beaches attract large numbers of tourists, and cause the flashy holiday village of Saly to spill over its boundaries. If you like your holiday more low-key and your beach body slightly less exposed, the villages Toubab Dialao, Popenguine and La Somone in the north, as well as Mbodiène, Nianing, Joal and Fadiout in the south have white strands that still swing to the local rhythm.

TOUBAB DIALAO

pop about 2000

A tiny fishing village, Toubab Dialao is a pretty hide-out close to Dakar, with beaches that aren't yet haunted by mass tourism. It's great for swimming, walks and horse riding. **Les Cavaliers de la Savane** (☎ 836 7876) offers guided tours on horseback to beginners and advanced riders in the surroundings of the village (two hours CFA10,000), and staff is very knowledgeable about the region. Senegal's famous dance school **L'École des Sables** (☎ 839 8090; www.jant-bi-acogny.com), run by famous dancer and choreographer Germaine Acogny, is situated a short drive along a dirt track out of town. International dance courses and rehearsals often take place here and can sometimes be witnessed. Even if deserted the school is well worth a visit. Its main space has a breathtaking view out to the sea, and is the perfect place to watch the sun set or see groups of flamingos land on the water.

Sleeping & Eating

There are three auberges (small hotels) in the heart of Toubab Dialao that form a Tolkienesque village within the village. The trend was started by a Frenchman, Gérard, who owns the highly rated Sobo-Bade, the hub of much activity in the village.

All the hotels have restaurants and most offer half-board options. In town, the small Senegalese eatery Niougop is unbeatable for ambience and taste.

Sobo-Bade (☎ /fax 836 0356; www.espacesobobade .com; dm per person CFA4000, s/d from CFA10,000/12,000) This characterful hotel is entirely decorated with seashells and overlooks the ocean from its position on a small cliff. The artistic decor is complemented by workshops in dance, batik, percussion and sculpture, and you can hire bikes (two hours CFA5000) or go horse riding (two hours CFA10,000).

La Source Ndiambalane (☎ 836 1703; ndiambalan@ sentoo.sn; d/tr CFA12,000/15,000) Next door to Sobo-Bade, in the heart of town, this place continues the shell-art theme to such perfection that it looks almost like an extension of Sobo-Bade.

Auberge La Mimosa (☎ /fax 826 7326; mimosa@ sentoo.com; d CFA10,000, 🏠) Just across from La Source, this auberge doesn't have a view but does have comfortable rooms and an Internet café, and serves excellent local fruit punches.

Iris Hotel (☎ 836 2969; www.irishotel.net; 🏠 💻 🏠) Follow the dirt track out of town, and the multiple signposts, and you get to this place, the grandest address in town. Unashamedly upmarket, this hotel has luxurious, tastefully decorated rooms and a spectacular sea-view terrace.

L'Escale (☎ 836 3595; meals around CFA4000; 🕙 11am-10pm) If you feel like something different, try this place, which sits a short walk off the main road between Yenne and Toubab Dialao. It has good food and a view. It has a good selection of European food (plus the usual assortment of local dishes) and a view. There are also a couple of rooms for stranded travellers – inquire about rates.

Chez Paolo (☎ 658 7594; pizzas from CFA3500-10,000; 🕙 11am – 10pm) A bit further on, Paolo's is the place to enjoy a proper Italian pizza – phone first, and opening hours will be adapted to your presence.

For some solitude, head for one of the two *campements* (lodges) in Ndayane on the dirt track leading to Popenguine. **Terre d'Afrique** (☎ 957 7155; s/d CFA20,000/30,000) is one of them, yet the better option is the stunning **La Pierre de Lisse** (☎ 957 7148; pierredelisse@sentoo .sn; s/d CFA20,000/30,000), run by the friendly and knowledgeable Bab Mbengue, who's an excellent guide to the region.

Getting There & Away

To get here from Dakar, take any transport headed for Mbour and get off at Diam Niadia junction. Minibuses run from here to Toubab Dialao (CFA300). Or go to Rufisque, take a taxi to garage de Yène and change there for a taxi to Toubab Dialao. A hire taxi from Dakar should cost around CFA15,000.

PETITE CÔTE & SINÉ-SALOUM DELTA

RÉSERVE DE BANDIA

This small **wildlife reserve** (☎ 685 5886; admission adult/child CFA7000/3500; ☯ 8am-6pm) sits 65km from Dakar on the road to Mbour, about 5km south of Sindia. It's well managed and crowded with wildlife, including species indigenous to Senegal as well as rhinos, giraffes, buffaloes, ostriches and other animals more at home in East Africa. In that sense it's more of a zoo, but an amazingly beautiful one with not a cage in sight. And because of its compact size you're almost guaranteed animal sightings.

For those more interested in human tradition than beasts, the Serer burial mounds and giant baobab, once used to bury griots, may be an enticement to visit.

Walking isn't allowed here, but you can normally enter with your own car or hire taxi. During or shortly after the rainy season you may have to hire one of the reserve's own 4WDs (CFA30,000), as many routes will be impassable to smaller vehicles. Tours take two to three hours.

Even if you don't want to visit the park, the fantastic restaurant overlooking a pond is worth a visit. You can normally spot buffaloes, monkeys, birds and crocodiles from here, and the food is good too (dishes CFA4000 to CFA6000).

Across the Dakar–Mbour main road, the fantastic **Accrobaobab** (Xavier Larcher ☎ 637 1428; www.accro-baobab.com; adult/child CFA15,000/10,000) is where you can climb, glide and clamber your way around mighty baobab trees – all with safety nets and trained staff. Huge fun.

POPENGUINE

pop around 1700

This calm village has an ambience all of its own, perhaps because it's a famous Pentecostal pilgrimage site, ever since an apparition of the black Madonna was seen here in 1986 (check www.sanctuaire-poponguine .sn for details on the annual event). A church built here in 1988, **Eglise Notre Dame de Délivrance**, is an impressive modern building featuring contemporary altar paintings, coloured-glass windows and a statue of the black Madonna.

Popenguine lies on the edge of a small **nature reserve** (see the boxed text, right) that is home to plenty of bird life.

Sleeping & Eating

Popenguine's most original accommodation options are at the end of a dirt road that leads right through the village.

Campement Ker Cupaam (☎ 956 4951; dm/d CFA5000/12,000) Unbeatable for character. It's run by a boisterous environmental womens cooperative that looks after the nature reserve next door, and has a highly knowledgeable guide for ornithological tours on site. The food is as good as homecooked.

Keur de Sable (☎ 957 7164; s/d CFA7500/12,000, studio CFA25,000, house CFA20,000). Signposted as a cultural centre on the opposite side of the dirt road, this is mainly a guesthouse with accommodation in basic rooms or houses on the beachside. It's a young and vibrant place that runs a cosy cocktail bar and often has dance and music performances.

Métisse Daguirane (☎ 957 7153; s/d CFA16,850/ 18,850) is in the village centre; the biggest but not best place in town. **Campement Coupru Sur Mer** (☎ 957 7166; r incl breakfast CFA12,000) consists of four well-maintained huts with a kitchen corner in a shaded courtyard. The restaurant does good à la carte meals (CFA3500). **L'écho-Côtier** (☎ 637 8772; meals CFA5000) is a decent beach restaurant behind Keur de Sable.

Back towards the village, the friendly bar-restaurant **Balafon Café** (snacks around CFA2000, ☽ 11am-8pm) overlooks the sea. The rustic beach bar **Chez Ginette** (☎ 957 7110; ☽ Wed-Mon) near the town centre is the place to sip a beer while waves lap at your feet.

TWITCHER TIPS: RÉSERVES DE POPENGUINE & DE LA SOMONE

Less known than Senegal's large national parks, these two tiny reserves are home to some 150 different species. The Réserve de Popenguine was declared a protected zone in 1986, after the blue rock-thrush was spotted here. Excursions to see this, and plenty of other species, can be organised by the Campement Keur Cupaam in Popenguine, whose women's collective looks after the reserve and also has resident ornithological guides from the National Parks Authority. The adjacent Réserve de la Somone is very different in character. It was created by the local community in 1999, and remains independently maintained. The park headquarters are situated at the edge of the reserve (ask locals to show you the way there), but for guided birding tours you are better off booking a combined tour at Popenguine, which has the better-trained staff. The protected zone of La Somone has a stunning lagoon where pelicans and flamingos are the most prominent feathered residents, though with a bit of patience you'll spot rarer species too. At Popenguine you'll pay CFA5000 for a half-day tour around both reserves.

Getting There & Away

From Dakar, head for Mbour and get off at Sindia, from where infrequent bush taxis run to Popenguine for CFA300.

LA SOMONE

pop around 13,000

Some 80km from Dakar, La Somone is the gentle medium between the mass tourism of Saly-Portugal and the village intimacy of Toubab-Dialao. The town sits right on a stunning lagoon, whose extraordinary landscape and rich bird life are protected (see the boxed text, above).

La Somone has many good accommodation choices – the following is only a tiny selection of what's on offer. All of the following places are on the main road in the heart of town.

The nicest place is **Canda** (☎ 958 5054; tening@ sentoo.sn; d CFA18,500; ☒ ☒), a small family-style hotel with pretty rooms and Belgian beer on the drinks menu.

The **Hôtel Sorong** (☎ 958 5175; www.sorong.sn; s/d CFA21,000/30,000; ✹ ☛) is a low-key hotel with a good restaurant (meals around CFA5000, open lunch and dinner), and **Le Phenix** (☎ 957 7517; www.phenix-senegal.sn, in French; villa CFA40,000) has gleaming, spacious villas on the beach that accommodate families. **Le Bassari** (☎ 957 7464; d/tr/q CFA17,000/25,000/34,000) is a beach-view *campement* decorated with masks and artefacts. **Africa Queen** (☎ 957 7435; www.africaqueen .com; d CFA25,000; ✹ ☛) is an unremarkable resort hotel catering mainly to groups, while the luxurious **Club Baobab** (☎ 957 7402; h2131@ accor.com), near the lagoon, only accepts independent travellers in the low season.

A recommended restaurant outside the hotels is the cute **Café Creole** (☎ 958 5191; sylvie creole@hotmail.com; dishes CFA2500-3000; ✹ lunch & dinner), near the junction between Ngaparou and La Somone – the place for tasty Senegalese and European cuisine, with live music on Thursday evenings.

To get to La Somone take a Mbour-bound taxi; get off at Nguékokh where taxis leave for Ngaparou and La Somone (CFA300).

SALY

pop around 20,000

The French call Saly Senegal's Côte d'Azur, and they're not far off. It's easy to forget you're in Africa in Saly. This is the sort of coastal holiday destination found all over the world: palm-lined beaches, dozens of big hotels, nightclubs, bars and souvenir shops. The main tourist strip is in Saly-Portugal. North of town, Saly-Niakhniakhale is only a short drive away, but has an entirely different character. Here you find small hotels and guesthouses in local *quartiers* (areas) and beaches where you can still see the sand between the people.

Saly-Portugal

Depending on your personal taste, this is either Saly's 'burnt zone', as locals like to put it, or the fun part of town. It's certainly where you'll be headed to withdraw cash from either BICIS or SGBS near King Karaoke, and check your emails in one of several Internet cafés.

ACTIVITIES

Saly is all about lazing at the beach, but if that gets too much, or rather too little, there's plenty on offer in the form of water sports,

fishing and excursions. Most of the hotels offer plenty of activities, ranging from sports fishing and jet skiing to pampering sessions in massage parlours.

Fishing & Watersports

The hotel Espadon has one of the best fishing clubs in town. Also recommended are **Saly Fishing Club** (☎ 957 2862; www.salyfishingclub .com) at the Lamantin Beach Hotel and **Marlin Club** (☎ 957 2477; marlinclub@arc.sn) in the heart of Saly's tourist zone. **Diabar Plongee** (☎ 958 5049; diabarplongée@yahoo.fr), near La Somone, and Arcandia run a whole range of activities including diving and fishing.

Beach-Buggy Tours

Riding along the Petite Côte in a big-wheeled beach buggy is a favourite with Saly tourists. Buggies (in French *quads*) can be hired at **Buggyland** (☎ 957 4917; buggyland@sentoo.sn), **Afriquad** (☎ 957 2293) and **Quadrousel** (☎ 957 0787; www.quadrousel.com), all found near the beach in Saly-Sud.

Golf

Golf de Saly (☎ 957 2488; www.golfsaly.com) is Saly's best-known golf club, at the exit towards La Somone.

SLEEPING

This is a tiny selection of the dozens of hotels and self-contained apartments in Saly. Most are in walking distance from one another, and close to the beach.

Les Flamboyants (☎ 957 0770; www.hotelsenegal flamboyant.com; s/d from CFA24,600/25,000; ✹ ☛) For Saly-Portugal, this is a nicely understated place. It's all about forged iron it seems, from the room furnishings to the tables of the green outdoor restaurant. The house cocktails are benign.

Espadon (☎ 957 1949; fax 957 2000; half board per person CFA36,600; ✹ ▢ ☛) This smoothly decorated place provides luxury with an African flavour. Accommodation is in spacious bungalows – each with its private, sunny terrace – that are tucked away in a lush garden. The attached fishing centre enjoys a good reputation.

Lamantin Beach Hotel (☎ 957 0777; www .lelamantin.com; half board s/d/ste CFA82,000/131,000/ 210,000; ✹ ▢ ☛) This five-star establishment calls itself the paradise on earth, and if your idea of heaven involves being pampered in a spa, relaxing in a *hammam* (bathhouse) or on a private beach, than you'll probably agree with them.

Also recommended:

Les Bougainvillées (☎ 957 2222; bougainvilleesaly@ sentoo.sn; r CFA41,200; 🅿 🖳 🖳) With comfortable bungalows set in a spacious garden, this is prettier than your standard resort hotel. It's near the Saly roundabout.

Savana Saly (☎ 939 5800; www.savana.sn; s/d CFA45,000/55,100) Not as refined as its Dakarois sister, but still a good top-end option.

Royam (☎ 957 2070; www.royam-senegal.com; 🅿 🖳 🖳) A classy four-star establishment; individual travellers are only accepted during the low season.

Les Filaos (☎ 957 1180; nffilaos@sentoo.sn; r per person CFA35,600) An enormous holiday complex made up of two parts: Les Calaos and the prettier Les Hibiscus.

EATING & DRINKING

Saly-Portugal's restaurant scene leaves you spoilt for choice, though many serve similar fare. The following are among the most interesting ones.

La Riviéra (☎ 957 0724; Place du Coursel; meals from CFA5000; 🕑 10am-11pm) A large swimming pool is the heart piece of this classy restaurant. It's the frequent site of concerts, shows and the bikini parades of aspiring Miss Salys. The European and African food served here is excellent, but doesn't come cheap.

Le Marlin (☎ 554 2808; Résidences du Port; meals from CFA6000; 🕑 10am-11pm) This refined eatery sits in one of Saly's biggest and brashest entertainment complexes. The seafood here gets good reviews.

El Paséo (Saly junction; meals around CFA5000; 🕑 11am-11pm) This lively place is the right address for sumptuous Spanish meals and other European food in a relaxed environment.

Le Manguier (route de la Somone; dishes around CFA4000; 🕑 lunch & dinner) This tastefully decorated place is a gem, both for its excellent international cuisine and the pleasant courtyard where giant mango trees shade a collection of African masks and statues.

Habana Café (☎ 957 0724; Saly-Sud; dishes around CFA5000; 🕑 11am-midnight) This fairly new place is fast becoming one of Saly's mightiest magnets, thanks to its beautiful beach location, excellent service and its delicious French cuisine.

Rolls Club (☎ 631 1578) There are plenty of bars and clubs in Saly but this place, right in the heart of Saly's tourist zone, is the dance floor everybody heads to at some point of the night. With a wide mix of musical styles (plenty of techno and R&B when we visited), its powerful sound system caters to almost every musical taste.

Self-caterers find all they need at **Supermarché Plein Sud** (☎ 957 3347).

GETTING THERE & AWAY

Saly-Portugal's hotels are 3km off the main road, about 5km north of Mbour. There is no public transport, and taxis charge CFA1500 from the main road to the hotels and other facilities at the beachfront.

Saly-Niakhniakhale

For a little bit of the 'real' Senegal just south of the big hotels, visit this borough, which begins at Les Cocotiers hotel and stretches south from there.

SLEEPING

Auberge Khady (☎ /fax 957 2518; auberge_khady@ hotmail.com; s/d incl breakfast CFA13,800/20,700) This simple but vibrant place 200m from the sea is rightly highly rated. The terrace restaurant is brilliant, and gets lively with dance and music performances on Friday nights.

Ferme de Saly (☎ 957 5006; farmsaly@yahoo.fr; r per person CFA16,500) This place has gradually turned from a farm with rooms for rent into a *campement* with some farming activity. Slightly rundown huts sit on large, overgrown terrain, and most of the food in the beach restaurant is locally grown.

Au Petit Jura (☎ 957 3767; www.aupetitjura.ch; d CFA19,500; 🅿 🖳 🖳 🖳) This pretty little retreat has spotless huts in a half-circle around a swimming pool. The beach is only steps away in this mostly quiet corner of Saly.

Gite Tolosa (☎ 658 7197; apt CFA12,500; 🖳) This place is a bargain for self-caterers. Each of the basic, spacious apartments has a kitchen corner, and there are good weekly rates for those who stay longer. Get a 1st-floor room; they're much nicer.

La Medina (☎ 957 4993; lamedina@sentoo.sn; s/d 13,000/17,000; 🖳) This Mediterranean-style place stretches over three floors surrounding a green courtyard. It's a stunning oasis of peace in the heart of Saly village.

EATING

Most of the hotels listed do food; the restaurants at Auberge Khady and Ferme de Saly are particularly recommended.

Chez Poulo (☎ 659 6331; dishes around CFA1000; ☺ 11am-midnight) A hugely popular eatery about 1km from Saly Village, in the heart of Saly-Niakhniakhale. It's small and informal, but has some of the best Senegalese and European food in the area, as well as local juices.

Baracouda (dishes around CFA2000; ☺ lunch & dinner) Sits right where Saly-Niakhniakhale turns into Saly-Portugal. The perfect spot to enjoy a relaxed plate of *yassa poulet* (grilled chicken marinated in a thick onion-and-lemon sauce) before hitting the night scene.

MBOUR

pop around 150,000

Five kilometres south of Saly, Mbour has a different vibe. The beach isn't so much a sunshine spot for tanning tourists as a place where hundreds of pirogues launch into the sea daily. This is a major fishing centre and the town's 200m-long beach market, plus all the surrounding marine-related commerce, is a sight to behold.

The *gare routière* (bus station) is near the exit towards Dakar, behind a wide gate. Mbour has a BICIS with ATM, several Internet cafés, a post office and hospital, all in the heart of town, near the port.

Sleeping & Eating

There are a few places to stay scattered around town, all of them south of the fishing market.

Village Petit Eden (☎ 957 4477; www.petit-eden .de; d CFA17,000) This cosy place on the Route de Dakar is hugely popular with locals and independent travellers, and for good reason. Management is great, rooms are cosy and there's a good range of excursions on offer.

Les Citronniers (☎ 957 2457; dm/d CFA6000/ 15,000) This slightly run-down auberge in the heart of town has good-value rooms, friendly management and a restaurant that serves a mean *thiéboudienne* (rice baked in a thick sauce of fish and vegetables).

Le Bounty (☎ /fax 957 2951; bounty@sentoo.sn; d CFA9500; ☒) This long-standing favourite is packed with all sorts of kitsch knickknacks, and has rooms that try hard to look like apartments. The restaurant serves a good zebu steak and a variety of excursions can be arranged.

Coco Beach (☎ 957 1004; fax 957 1077; d CFA15,000; ☒ ☒) This beach hotel is Mbour's biggest,

though not its best establishment. It's friendly and packed with activities, but the rooms disappoint.

Hôtel Club Safari (☎ 957 1991; fax 957 3838; s/d incl breakfast CFA16,000/20,000; ☒ ☒) Five blocks south of Le Bounty, this seashell-decorated place has spacious, comfortable rooms set around a pool.

Tama Lodge (☎ /fax 957 0040; www.tamalodge .com; s CFA30,000-60,000, d CFA40,000-80,000) Right on the Plage des Cocotiers (Cocotiers Beach), Tama Lodge is something of a piece of art and, run by a fervent antique collector, as unique as a hotel can get – you sleep in modern mud huts surrounded by some amazing wooden sculptures. The restaurant serves imaginative variations of French and African cuisine – even chips taste somewhat refined here – and a dinner on the beach terrace by candlelight is a fine night out indeed. Half- and full-board options are also available.

Le Kassoumaye (☎ 957 3524; dishes CFA3000; ☺ 9am-11pm Thu-Tue) Good European fare can be found on the beach behind Le Bounty at this restaurant. Dishes are huge and there is an impressive range of desserts.

Chez Paolo (☎ 957 1310; dishes from CFA2000; ☺ 11am-11pm) Anyone in town can show you the way to this favourite local eatery, right on the main road. It may look unpretentious, but the Senegalese food here is divine – the high number of regular locals is proof to its popularity.

WARANG

pop around 5000

Just outside Mbour lies the village of Warang, where a range of excellent, slightly secluded accommodation options invite travellers in search of solitude.

The white bungalows that sit in a well-kept garden at **Les Manguiers de Warang** (☎ 957 5174; lesmanguiers@sentoo.sn; s/d CFA13,500/16,000) are a cross between an African hut and a Mediterranean building. The fusion works, and you can even choose the mosquito-protected outdoor option on the rooftop.

Impressively located between the sea and a small lake, **Warang Hôtel** (☎ 957 2010; lewarang hotel@yahoo.fr; half board CFA19,500) offers good accommodation in simple huts.

Staying at **Mbégeel** (☎ 957 5177; www.mbegeel .com; hut CFA39,500, ste CFA59,000, house CFA98,000; ☒ ☒) is something of an experience. The place was handcrafted by owner Marie-Hélène Le Grand, who lovingly placed every piece of mosaic and mirror-glass into the floor and walls of the cosy huts, arranged soft lighting to enhance the themed interiors, and chose every table, chair and cushion in the green terrain.

Domaine de Samba (☎ 957 5217; www.domainede samba.com; d incl breakfast CFA21,615; villa CFA51,745; **P** **X** 🖵 🕿)) is a resort-style place with accommodation choices ranging from basic rooms to lush villas, and offers the whole pot of activities including horse riding, buggy tours and tennis. The cybercafé is definitely an asset.

Getting There & Away
There's frequent public transport between Mbour and Dakar (minibus CFA1000, *sept-place* taxis CFA1300). Mbour–Joal transport is a little less regular (minibus CFA500, *sept-place* taxis CFA600). Hiring a taxi from Mbour to Warang is a timesaving option (CFA1000). Hire taxis cost around CFA15,000 from Dakar to Mbour or Warang, CFA20,000 all the way to Joal.

NIANING
pop around 2000
The beach is beautiful anywhere along the Petite Côte, and sleepy Nianing is one of the quieter places along the coast, perfect if you like to dip your toes in without anyone stepping on them.

Le Ben'Tenier (☎ 957 1420; bentenier@telecomplus .sn; r per person CFA8630) on the entry to Nianing represents excellent value. It's got a youthful ambience, with friendly, English-speaking management and large bungalows in a spacious garden. **Auberge des Coquillages** (☎ /fax 957 1428; tidiane@telecomplus.sn; s/d CFA26,000/28,100; 🕿), a couple of blocks further along the main road, is much brighter and prettier but you pay for it, too. **Le Girafon** (☎ 957 5266; s/d CFA10,000/ 15,000) is another good option. It's a tiny *campement* in the heart of the village (just follow the signposts) with a relaxed family feel that also organises local excursions.

The restaurant scene is limited to tiny eateries. **Les Bourgain Villees** (☎ 957 5241) is a small family-run place on the main road, which serves simple African meals (around CFA1500) and also has some rooms for rent. Chez Annick and Chez Aicha are the recommended Senegalese restaurants in

town – the grilled fish (around CFA2000) at both is fantastic. The Franco-Senegalese place Le Nianing, in the heart of the village, presents itself as a little more upmarket and nearby L'Oasis, owned by a Sicilian expat, serves exquisite Italian food.

Nianing is on the main road between Mbour and Joal and all public transport stops here.

MBODIÈNE
pop around 3000
The small village of Mbodiène is on the coast about halfway between Nianing and Joal. It sits right on a beautiful lagoon, perfect for bird-watching and bathing. The huge resort hotel **Laguna Beach** (☎ 957 8811; www.lagunabeach.sn; half board per person CFA27,500; **X** 🖵 🕿) seems strangely out of place in this tiny village, but offers accommodation in attractive, 2nd-floor bungalows and an impressive range of activities to those who like being pampered. Along a dirt road that follows the coast, the **Gîte d'Étape de la Fasna** (☎ 957 8817; fax 957 8815) was being completely renovated at the time of writing – the work being done on the spacious huts looked promising. Inquire for rates. A few metres further down, the highly recommended **Plein Soleil** (☎ /fax 957 8823; d/ste CFA21,000/35,000; **X** 🖵 🕿) is a relaxed, family-friendly place in a beautiful location. The welcoming owners also operate **La Maison de la Mer** (☎ 957 8813; d/ste CFA21,000/35,000), a cosy guesthouse right on the beach. Lovingly decorated and furnished with an extensive library, video collection and bar, this is one of the most homely places anywhere in Senegal. For a completely carefree holiday, you can book yourself in on the all-inclusive rate (singles/ doubles CFA492,000/857,000) that contains everything from airport pick-up to activities, food and bottomless drinks.

JOAL-FADIOUT
pop around 38,000
Follow the winding coastal road from Dakar 110km southwards and you reach the twin villages Joal and Fadiout. Joal, the birthplace of former president Léopold Senghor, is on the mainland. Its pretty sister Fadiout sits on a century-old island composed entirely of oyster and clamshells that's reached via a long wooden bridge from Joal. Everything is shells here – they are embedded

Roots Homecoming Festival (p264), Gambia

On the streets of Île de Gorée, Senegal
(p167)

At Parc National de la Langue de Barbarie (p214),
Senegal

On Kololi beach, Atlantic coast (p98), Gambia

A red-cheeked cordon-bleu (p71), Gambia

DAVID TIPLING

ARIADNE VAN ZANDB

A Senegal parrot in Parc National de
Niokolo-Koba (p223), Senegal

Pelicans, Parc National de la Lange de Barbarie (p214), Senegal

ARIADNE VAN ZANDB

in houses and streets, as well as the shared Muslim and Christian cemetery, reached by another bridge crossing.

The citizens of Joal and Fadiout are proud of their religious tolerance: Christians and Muslims live in harmony, with Fadiout's impressive church and shrines to the Virgin Mary near an equally large mosque. Life seems peaceful and relaxed, particularly in Fadiout's maze of narrow alleyways; it's more tranquil the further you get from the colourful artisan market spreading along the roadside from the bridge into town.

There are plenty of pirogue trips on offer here, taking you to the cemetery; a nearby oyster cultivation; and a set of stilt-balanced granaries, modelled on ancient originals that were destroyed when a blaze tore through Fadiout. The trips make for a great day out; just don't let the guides near the Joal side of the bridge talk you into overpriced rides. You're better off relying on the badge-bearing employees of the Syndicat de Tourisme. Guides also hover around the bridge, or can be found at the Hôtel le Finio.

Sleeping & Eating

JOAL
Le Thiouraye (☎ 515 6064; s/d/tr CFA10,000/12,000/ 14,000) This relaxed little auberge on the riverside is a great budget option. Rooms are basic but good value, and you can leap straight from the brilliant terrace restaurant (meals CFA2900 to CFA3800) into a pirogue to Fadiout – useful to avoid the hustlers near the bridge. Ask the owner to arrange this for you.

Hôtel de la Plage (☎ 957 6677; hakim@yahoo.fr; d/tr CFA25,000/28,000; P ⚐) This fairly new place has bright, large rooms at reasonable rates, and a restaurant that's highly recommended (meals CFA5000).

Relais 114 (☎ 957 6178; r incl breakfast with/without bathroom CFA10,000/7500) This colourful place is pretty run down, though the larger-than-life owner Mamadou Balde and his performing pelicans give some character. The rustic Senegalese meals are pretty good (CFA5000).

Hôtel le Finio (☎ /fax 957 6112; r per person CFA6500-9500) This is still Joal's best-known but not necessarily best address. The smallest rooms really don't have much breathing space.

Le Sénégaulois (☎ /fax 957 6241; r CFA14,000) At the end of the bridge to Fadiout you find this bawdy bar that has a few clean but overpriced rooms upstairs. Owner Olivier can also change money.

FADIOUT
Campement les Paletuviers (☎ /fax 957 6205; r per person CFA5000) Walk through the island's narrow alleyways to this no-frills *campement* with basic rooms and shared bathrooms.

Getting There & Away
A minibus to/from Mbour is CFA600. If you're heading on down the coast, it costs CFA1000 from Joal to Palmarin. A *sept-place* taxi goes directly to Dakar most mornings (without changing at Mbour) for CFA1800.

THE SINÉ-SALOUM DELTA

Even a stretch of the finest white beach doesn't last forever. About 60km south of Mbour the Petite Côte is cut by the mouth of the Saloum River, and sand strands give way to a maze of mangrove swamps and creeks. This is the 180,000-hectare zone of the Siné-Saloum Delta, one of Senegal's most beautiful areas. In the delta landscape, shimmering flat lands dotted with palm groves sit next to salt marshes and savannah woodlands, while the coastline is framed by lush greens, long sand banks and lagoons.

Part of the area is included in the Parc National du Delta du Saloum. You won't see large mammals here, apart from the occasional warthog and perhaps a sea cow in the lagoons, but the area abounds with several monkey species, including the rare red colobus, and the range of habitats makes it particularly good for birding.

PALMARIN
pop around 5000
Some 20km south of Joal-Fadiout, Palmarin is an expansive area encompassing four villages, the place where the beaches of the Petite Côte merge with the labyrinthine creeks of the Siné-Saloum Delta. It's a breathtaking spot, where dots of bush grass and tall palm groves, salty plains and patches of gleaming water line the series of causeways leading south from Sambadia.

At the time of writing, the arrival of electricity to the villages was said to be imminent – be prepared though and bring a torch (flashlight).

PETITE CÔTE & SINÉ-SALOUM DELTA

Sleeping & Eating

Palmarin's quickly multiplying *campements* are among the country's classiest, and nestle peacefully on the beach-bound end of sandy side roads. The area is best explored by pirogue or *charette* (horse-drawn cart) – all the *campements* organise reasonably priced tours.

Royal Lodge (☎ 949 1150; www.le-royal-lodge.com; Palmarin; s/d incl breakfast from CFA98,000/130,000) If you're blessed with a bottomless bank account then give this utterly luxurious place a try. Each of its stylish, warmly tinted and carefully crafted apartments comes with DVD, satellite TV and – wait for it – its own Jacuzzi. But the hotel's biggest asset, its lagoon pool with floating bar, is accessible to all who are at least rich enough to invest in a drink.

Lodge des Collines de Niassam (☎ 669 6343; www.niassam.com; half board per person CFA37,000-57,000; 🍽 🐾) Who said that the hotel business couldn't be creative or sophisticated? This place offers accommodation in classy tree houses that cling to the mighty branches of baobabs, or sit on stilts in the shallow waters of the delta. The views are breathtaking, and the home-mixed fruity rums something to get addicted to. Very fine indeed.

Yokam (☎ 936 3974; yokam@teranga-horizon.com; per person incl breakfast CFA7000) This lively *campement* is run by a young and enthusiastic bunch; the bungalows, decorated in traditional straw-hut style, are comfy and spotless.

Lodge de Diakhamor (☎ 644 9491, 957 1256; www.lesenegal.info; half board s/d CFA23,000/41,000) With its red, mud-walled bungalows, this place feels like a cross between a medieval fort and a Fula village, and is apparently modelled on ancient local architecture. The decor is quite a sight and the restaurant (meals around CFA5000) excellent – and best of all, pirogue excursions, horse riding, bicycle and fishing trips are all included in the price.

Djidjack (☎ 949 9619; www.djidjack.com; d/q CFA20,0000/30,000) Sitting in a wonderfully varied and lovingly maintained garden, this Swiss-owned *campement* offers accommodation in appealing large and uberlarge huts. Its heart piece – a huge *case à impluvium* housing a restaurant, bar and library – invites lingering. Camping costs CFA2000 per night.

Campement Villageois de Sessene (☎ 669 0365; r per person incl breakfast CFA6500) This large *campement* is perhaps not the prettiest, but it's run by the local population, and if you wish to spend your holiday cash locally, this is the place to stay.

Getting There & Away

Palmarin is most easily reached from Mbour, via Joal-Fadiout and Sambadia (where you may have to change). The fare from Joal to Sambadia is CFA500 in a Ndiaga Ndiaye, and from Sambadia to Palmarin it's CFA400.

DJIFER

pop around 2000

The fishing village of Djifer is 10km south of Palmarin on the tip of the peninsula separating the Atlantic Ocean from the Saloum River. It's a major jumping-off point for trips into the Siné-Saloum Delta. Most people only come here to get onto a pirogue and explore the region – there's little else that's attractive about Djifer itself. The town has a sewage problem, and the beaches are largely strewn with litter, though some efforts are being made to clear things up.

Palmarin's **Yokam** (☎ 936 3752; r per person CFA3000) has a second branch here, though a much more basic, slightly windblown affair. **La Pointe de Sangomar** (☎ /fax 835 6191; d with/without bathroom CFA12,600/8600), right on the rugged beach, is slightly more upmarket and Djifer's most popular place. About 2km north of Djifer is the **Campement la Mangrove** (☎ 956 4232; hut per person CFA6000), a fairly run-down affair in the centre, though one with camping facilities.

Eating options are restricted to the *campements*, basic *gargottes* (small, simple, local-style eating houses) or self-catering.

Getting There & Away

Djifer can be reached from Mbour, via Joal-Fadiout and Sambadia – see above for details. Another option is by pirogue to or from Ndangane (p188) or Foundiougne (p189).

If you're heading to Gambia, cramped, uncomfortable and notoriously unsafe pirogues occasionally go from Djifer to Banjul (CFA5000 per person). The trip takes about five hours, but may involve an overnight stop on a midway island. You have been warned! On arrival in Banjul go to the immigration office at the port to get your passport stamped.

Another option is a trip to beautiful Îles des Bétanti in the south of the Siné-Saloum

Delta. Pirogues leave from Djifer every afternoon (CFA1500, three to five hours). From there, you can then continue on to Banjul by public pirogue the next morning (CFA1500, three hours).

AROUND DJIFER

Several islands of the Siné-Saloum Delta can be explored on day trips from Djifer. The closest is the pretty, deserted **Pointe de Sangomar** island, a great place for swimming, picnics or camping in solitude. Much more interesting, however, are the beautiful and tranquil islands **Guior** and **Guissanor** across the river mouth. The villages **Dionewar** and **Falia**, the oldest settlements on Guior, nestle right in the web of *bolongs* (creeks), and exploring the labyrinthine paths of the mangroves with a small pirogue or wandering through the forest of Dionewar are unmissable experiences.

In Dionewar you can spend the night in the luxury of the plush **Delta Niominka** (☎ 948 9935; www.deltaniominka.com; r per person incl breakfast CFA25,000), from where several pirogue excursions, as well as transport to and from Djifer can be arranged. Otherwise, it's usually possible to find a room with a welcoming local family.

Boat trips can be arranged directly by haggling with the pirogue owners at the port of Djifer, though you might as well use the services of the two *campements*. For half-day trips, you'll be charged about CFA20,000 to CFA25,000, up to twice that for the whole day. Make sure that the negotiated price includes the cost of the *petite* pirogue on the island and all local tourist taxes. There's a daily public boat that runs between Djifer and Dionewar (per person CFA500). It only goes once a day in each direction though, leaving Djifer around 3pm every day, and returning the morning of the next day. (Exact departure times depend on the tide).

NDANGANE & MAR LODJ

pop around 2500

Ndangane (ndan-gan) is on the northern side of the Siné-Saloum Delta, on a branch of the Saloum River. Once a sleepy backwater, this has now become a thriving tourist centre. Ndangane has two parts: the touristy area, where the tar road from Dakar ends by the boat jetty, and the village proper, a short distance to the west. From

either area, you can get boats across the river to the village of Mar Lodj (also spelt Mar Lothie), a peaceful haven cut off from mainland by the delta. Several local-style *campements* make this a great place to relax for a while. There's no bank here, but Internet connections are available at a couple of places along the road.

Fishing trips and bird-watching boat rides can be arranged at most of the hotels and *campements*, with pirogue trips to Mar Lodj and Île des Oiseaux costing about CFA10,000 a head, with a minimum of four. If you're in the mood for being hassled, head for the pirogue landing and you'll be pounced upon by eager pirogue owners offering you to take you to Mar Lodj. Note that several readers have reported trouble with these guys, overpriced journeys being the most harmless, actual swindles and trips to less exciting destinations as promised (for more cash) being more serious. You're likely to have an easier time booking trips through the hotels.

Sleeping & Eating
NDANGANE

Most of the accommodation and eating options are located around the end of the road to Fimela, which is also where most boat trips depart from.

Le Barracuda (Chez Mbacke; ☎ 6585794; s/d CFA9000/ 12,000) Cheap and very cheerful – this family-run place is right near the stretch of beach where you catch your pirogue for Mar Lodj.

La Palangrotte (☎ 949 9321; lapalang@sentoo.sn; s/d incl breakfast CFA9750/13,000) One of the best choices in Ndangane, no doubt. This place at the exit of town is not only very welcoming and well kept, but also invests 10% of all profits into local development projects. Apparently even Wolof courses are on offer.

Le Cormoran (☎ /fax 949 9316; www.lecormoran .net; s/d/tr CFA13,000/19,000/24,000, all incl breakfast; ⊠ ⊛) Once a fishermen's favourite, this hospitable place now tries to attract more families into its spotless quarters. Not a bad choice by any means.

Les Cordons Bleus (☎ 949 9312; cordons-bleus@ sentoo.sn; s/d/tr CFA25,000/32,000/42,000; P ⊠ ⊡ ⊛) Classy indeed, this establishment has a whole array of activities on offer, ranging from minigolf to a variety of excursions. The rooms are welcoming, too.

All the hotels do food and there are several restaurants.

Le Petit Paradis (dishes from CFA800; ⊙ lunch & dinner) This place along the main mile serves cheap local and considerably more expensive international meals, all spiced up with inspiring conversation (in English) from the dignified and erudite owners.

Le Baobab (☎ 653 4073; dishes around CFA4000; ⊙ 11am-10pm) Past Cordons Bleus, this is excellent for seafood and pizzas in a village-style setting.

Le Tamarko (dishes from CFA3000; ⊙ 11am-10pm) Right opposite the pirogue landing to Mar Lodj, this is a good place to watch the coming and going and haggling and negotiating from a safe distance. The menu is varied, with a good selection of European meals.

Good, cheap local eateries include Le Picboeuf, which is usually packed – a good indicator of its popularity – and La Maroise.

Also recommended:

Chez Madeleine (☎ 949 9313; s/d incl breakfast CFA11,660/22,020; 🞲 🞲) Not exactly thrilling, but decent value for money.

Le Pélican du Saloum (☎ 949 9320; snpelican@sentoo .sn; half board CFA29,600) Part of the Senegal Hôtel chain, this is typical resort-hotel fare.

MAR LODJ

There aren't vast differences in quality between the *campements* on Mar Lodj, just in quality and price. All places offer a pick-up by pirogue from Ndangane, though costs differ widely. Inquire beforehand. There's no electricity on Mar Lodj, but most *campements* either have solar panels or generators. It's still a good idea to bring a torch.

Le Limboko (☎ 641 2253) Definitely worth a visit. At the time of writing, accommodation was being redone and only the excellent restaurant was open (three-course meals CFA6000). The friendly owner Amadou 'Thomas' Ba, the local representative of the Syndicat d'Initiative, is full of useful info and advice, and speaks fluent German and English. Inquire about room rates.

Campement Essamaye (☎ 555 36 67; www.senega lia.com; r per person incl full board CFA17,500) This stunning place stands a good chance of being voted the friendliest on the island. It has simple, but welcoming rooms in a giant Casamance-style *case à impluvium* and excellent excursions on offer. Transport from Ndangane is included in the rate.

Mbine Diam (☎ 636 9199; s/d/tr CFA9000/16,000/ 21,000) One of the simplest *campements* on the island, reflected in the adequate prices.

Le Bazouk (☎ 820 4125; lebazoudusaloum@sentoo.sn; per person CFA12,000) Slightly more welcoming than Mbine Diam, and has a free transfer to and from Ndangane twice daily.

Nouvelle Vague (☎ 634 0723; s/d/tr CFA15,600/ 23,200/25,800) Prices are a little steeper at this place but the accommodation is nicer, too. The transfer to Ndangane here costs CFA7500.

Marsetal (☎ 637 2531; s CFA20,000) On the other side of the island you find this upmarket spot. A short *calèche* (horse-drawn taxi) ride through the village takes you there from the main beach, or you can hire a direct pirogue from Ndangane.

Getting There & Away

Take any bus between Kaolack and Mbour and get off at Ndiosomone, from where bush taxis shuttle back and forth to Ndangane. You can go directly by bush taxi from Dakar to Ndangane for CFA1800, and from Mbour bush taxis go via Sambadia and Fimela.

To reach Mar Lodj from Ndangane there's an occasional public boat charging CFA300 one way. Otherwise, you have to charter. This can cost anything between CFA10,000 and 30,000 return.

You can charter a pirogue between Ndangane and Djifer for about CFA25,000. To or from Foundiougne is about CFA40,000.

FIMELA & SIMAL
pop around 1500

The two villages Fimela and Simal lie just north of Ndangane, past the tourist trail in lush natural settings overlooking the Saloum River. **Le Domaine des Cajous** (☎ 513 6125; www.cajous.com; Fimela; s/d CFA10,000/15,000; 🞲) has cosy bungalows and a welcoming restaurant with magnificent views across the river. In Simal, 2km from Dioffor, the **Gîte de Simal** (☎ 644 9491, 957 1256; www.lesenegal.info; half board s/d CFA21,000/37,000), part of the imaginative TPA chain, invites riverside lingering. Accommodation is in simple but pretty straw huts, with colourful, roofless toilets and showers attached. All activities such as *charette* tours and pirogue and fishing trips around the mangroves are included in the half-board rate.

There are fairly frequent bush taxis from Ndangane to Fimela (CFA200), from where you can hire a taxi to either place for about CFA1000 to CFA2000. Taxis from Fimela to Ndiosomone cost CFA400.

FOUNDIOUGNE

pop around 5000

At the northwestern edge of the delta, where a ferry crosses the Saloum River, the onetime French colonial outpost of Foundiougne (foun-dune) attracts mainly keen anglers, and though it's perhaps not the prettiest corner of the delta, it's a good place to arrange pirogue trips. Most *campements* listed have boat tours on offer, and prices tend to be similar (pirogue day trips around CFA20,000 to CFA30,000, transfer to Djifer CFA40,000).

This area has notoriously bad drinking water – stick to bottled mineral.

Sleeping

West from the ferry pier, there's a string of *campements*. They're numerous, but overall quality standards are pretty low.

La Pirogue (☎ 516 7102; per person CFA8000, half/full board CFA13,000/16,000) Tiny it may be, but it's the finest budget option by far. Rooms are pretty and spotless – not necessarily standard in Foundiougne – and breakfast is served with fresh bread baked on-site.

Le Baobab sur Mer (Chez Anne Marie; ☎ 948 1262; s/d/tr incl breakfast CFA8500/16,000/20,000) Right on the river, this place run by the boisterous Anne Marie is booming. The bar often gets lively in the evenings.

Le Baobab sur Terre (Chez Ismail; ☎ /fax 948 1108; s/d incl breakfast CFA6500/13,000) Opposite the other Baobab, this is the cheapest place in town. It is really very basic, but fair value, and the pirogue tours are recommended.

Indiana Club (☎ /fax 948 1213; www.indianaclub.net; half/full board per person CFA15,000/19,000; 🖳 🍴) A slight cowboy theme gives this place some curious character, and the restaurant serving European and Senegalese food has a good reputation. Add CFA5000 for air-con.

Foundiougne Hôtel (☎ 948 1212; fax 948 1310; s/d/tr CFA21,600/35,200/40,800, all incl breakfast; 🖳 🍴) Proud to call itself a hotel, this place slaps on the costs. Rooms and meals are over-priced but the range of activities, including tennis, volleyball, horse riding, fishing and pirogue trips, is excellent.

Also recommended:

Les Bolongs (☎ /fax 948 1110; www.lesbolongs.com; r CFA10,000) Spacious bungalows sleeping one to four people sit in a lush garden.

Saloum Saloum (☎ 534 8370; saloumsaloum@sentoo .sn; s/d/tr CFA8500/16,000/19,000; 🖳) This community-run place has decent rooms and sluggish service.

Campement Ibou Fall (☎ 544 4244; d CFA10,000) Basic rooms come with kitchen corner and fridge.

Eating

Apart from the hotel restaurants and the *gargottes* grouped around the ferry pier and market, there's really only one other place worth mentioning.

La Cloche (☎ 544 4242; meals CFA3500) This Italian restaurant is right near the jetty. It takes deserved pride in the sparkling cleanliness of its kitchen, as well as its river view and fully fledged Italian menu.

Getting There & Away

By road, Foundiougne is reached from Passi, which is on the potholed tarmac road between Kaolack and Sokone.

By minibus Kaolack–Foundiougne is CFA700. There aren't many direct buses, so you might have to change at Passi. Kaolack–Passi is CFA950, Passi–Foundiougne is CFA600.

Alternatively you can reach Foundiougne from Fatick. Take a bush taxi to Dakhonga, where you take a ferry across to Foundiougne.

Most *campements* can arrange pirogue transfers between Foundiougne and Ndangane, Djifer, Toubakouta or Missirah, but the boat journey is long (around four hours) and expensive (around CFA40,000).

THE FOUNDIOUGNE FERRY TIMETABLE	
Foundiougne	**Dakhonga**
7.30am	8.30am
9.30am	10.30am
11.30am	12.30pm
3pm (except Wed)	3.30pm (except Wed)
5pm	6.30pm

The ferry fare is CFA100 per passenger; CFA1200 per vehicle. A ride across by pirogue (if the ferry isn't running) is negotiable, but at least CFA3000 for the boat.

TOUBAKOUTA

pop around 9500

Nestled among mazes of mangroves, tropical forest and islands that float on myriad waterways, the tiny town of Toubakouta is easily one of the most beautiful spots of the Siné-Saloum Delta. It's an excellent base for excursions to the nearby Parc National du Delta du Saloum and the stunning Aire Marine Protégée de Bamboung (see the boxed text, p67), Senegal's only functioning area of protected sea.

The whole area teems with wildlife and sea birds, and watching flamingos, fish eagles, herons and egrets prepare to roost on the shore at nightfall is fascinating, even if you're not a keen bird-watcher.

Toubakouta has a couple of cybercafés, télécentres and a post office, but no bank. The Paletuviers Hôtel has cash-withdrawal facilities, though access is exclusively granted to guests.

Sleeping

Keur Bamboung (☎ 510 8013; www.oceanium .org; half/full board CFA17,000/22,000) *Campements* rarely come more remote than this village-run ecolodge, stunningly located on the edge of a mangrove-lined island. And remote *campements* rarely come more lovingly done up. Its six individualised huts are all equipped with a water tank, solar-powered lights, impeccable bathroom and the most comfortable mattresses and sheets around. All profits go to the villages, which use it to pay for the patrols of the marine reserve – so spend and feel good. Contact Keur Bamboung before arrival, and they arrange your pirogue pick-up from Toubakouta and 2km donkey-cart ride to the camp. Transport and all activities (mangrove walks, pirogue trips, canoeing, birding) are included in the price.

Keur Youssou (☎ /fax 948 7728; d/tr CFA12,000/ 15,000; 🈺) Rare are the budget places that offer such quality and comfort. The beautifully furnished rooms are a bargain, and the atmosphere friendly and relaxed.

Les Coquillages du Niombatto (☎ 645 3036; layoum@hotmail.com; d incl breakfast CFA12,500) Rooms are basic but impeccable, the restaurant gets good reviews and the management is incredibly forthcoming and knowledgeable.

Hôtel Keur Saloum (☎ 948 7715; www.keursaloum .com; half board s/d CFA36,000/58,000; 🈺 🈴) This is the pick of the top-range places. Tastefully decorated and comfortable bungalows sit in a large garden terrain, and the restaurant serves excellent meals (around CFA7000) on a terrace with a view. Once an anglers' favourite, it now increasingly attracts families, and has a wide range of excursions on offer.

Hôtel les Palétuviers (☎ 948 7776; www.paletuviers .com; half board s/d CFA47,000/63,000; 🈺 🈴) This expansive hotel offers a range of activities and likes to think of itself as a plush holiday haven – but the rooms disappoint, and the atmosphere isn't all that welcoming. The management also operates Île des Palétuviers on Îles des Bétanti, west of Toubakouta, and

---

TWITCHER TIPS: BIRDING IN THE SOUTH OF THE SINÉ-SALOUM DELTA

Toubakouta offers enough bird life to have keen spotters stay here for days and return every year. It's mostly an area for sea birds and waders, though the nearby forest areas also house some other species, including hornbills and sunbirds. A good place to start a birding tour is Diorom Boumag, an impressive, man-made island that evolved from ancient seashell burying mounds, where giant baobabs have taken root. In their branches nestle numerous Senegalese parrots and rose-ringed parakeets. It's best to visit this place by pirogue in the late afternoon, and move further along the river to arrive around dusk at the Reposoir des Oiseaux, where you can watch swarms of pelicans, cormorants, egrets and plenty of other species prepare noisily for the night.

Île de Bamboung is much less visited, and a perfect place for independent travellers to observe birds in a peaceful environment.

A trip to Île des Oiseaux takes up an entire, thoroughly worthwhile, day. Near Îles des Bétanti in the south of Toubakouta, this small islet houses impressive colonies of Caspian sterns, royal sterns, herons, grey-headed gulls, slender-billed gulls and flamingos. With a bit of luck, you might even spot a sacred ibis.

Most of Toubakouta's hotels offer birding trips, the ones run by Hôtel Keur Saloum are particularly recommended. For trips to Île de Bamboung, the *campement* Keur Bamboung is your best option.

Plage d'Or on the Senegalese side of Ginak Island.

Also recommended:

Chez L'Epicier (☎ 936 3424; assenghor@hotmail.com; d CFA12,500) Good-value rooms at the grocery store and fast-food place.

Africa Strike (☎ 948 7740; www.africastrike.com; r per person CFA15,000, half/full board CFA21,500/25,500; ✕ ✕) A fishermen's favourite.

Getting There & Away

Toubakouta is just off the main road between Kaolack and Karang (the Gambian border), about 70km from Kaolack. A bush taxi from Kaolack to Barra via Karang is CFA3000, but you won't get any discount for getting off early. It's cheaper to go by Ndiaga Ndiaye; the fare to Toubakouta is around CFA1300.

PARC NATIONAL DU DELTA DU SALOUM

The **Parc National du Delta du Saloum** (admission CFA2000) is Senegal's second-largest national park. Its 76,000 hectares encompass the dry savannah woodland of the Forêt de Fathala, wide stretches of mangrove swamps, and a maritime part that stretches from the creeks surrounding the Îles des Bétanti all the way up to Pointe de Sangomar. The forest section of the reserve is much better looked after than the ocean area, and is rich in wildlife. Red colobus monkeys, colobus bais, patas, sylvicarpes, phacochers and hyenas all inhabit the woods, though you're unlikely to see the rarer species. The sea parts allow mainly for bird-watching, though sea turtles and dolphins can occasionally be spotted.

The main entrance to the park is in the village of Missirah, though the park headquarters are another 6km away. You pay your admission charge at the office of the **ecoguards** (☎ 936 3431; ⊙ 9am-4pm), which is on your left as you enter the village from the north. The guards will show you around,

and take you to the park headquarters – they are professional guides, and their company a great help, as it's easy to get lost in the park. Note that the number is that of the local *télécentre*; you'll have to leave a message and arrange for them to call you back. It's usually easy enough to show up without prior notice.

Missirah itself is famous for the enormous *fromager* (kapok) tree on the banks of the river, variously estimated at between 200 and 1000 years old. It's also home to the peaceful and welcoming **Gîte de Bandiala** (☎ 948 7735; www.gite.bandiala.com; half/full board per person CFA15,400/21,100), which lies about 2km east of Missirah. A sand path turns off the main road just before you get to the village.

The *gîte* (small hotel) on the edge of the park is full of character and a great base for exploring this part of the delta. The friendly management can make suggestions for forest walks, and give guided tours. It also has a waterhole where monkeys, warthogs and other animals come to drink. Tours by pirogue on the nearby creeks and lagoons cost CFA5500 per person for half a day (minimum four people), and fishing can be arranged (two people CFA50,000).

Getting There & Away

From Kaolack take any vehicle going along the main road towards Karang, get off at Santhiou el Haji (about 80km from Kaolack) and walk 8km west through the forest. Less strenuous would be to get off at Toubakouta and take a bush taxi for CFA400, if you can find one there. Public transport from Toubakouta is rare and only comes in the form of pick-up trucks – but if you ask around in town you will usually find someone willing to hire their car for the trip (around CFA5000).

Another option is to get a private taxi all the way from Kaolack – this will cost between CFA20,000 and CFA40,000.

West-Central Senegal

The route from Dakar to Touba may not exactly be the road to paradise, but it's a straight journey to Senegal's religious and economic core. Past the urban sprawl of Thiès, home to a world-famous tapestry factory, lie the triplet towns of Diourbel, Mbaké and Touba – the heartland of Senegal's Mouride brotherhood. The towns themselves seem fairly unremarkable, with the grand exception of the giant mosque of Touba and its smaller but more beautiful counterpart in Diourbel. But don't let this deceive you: spiritual strength and monetary power form an invincible alliance here that quietly contributes to most of the gradual changes in Senegal's culture, prosperity and politics. Travel here during Grand Magal, the annual religious pilgrimage – provided you can find a seat in a bush taxi; a staggering two million people are Touba bound during the event – and the sheer number and devotion of followers will give you more than just a glimpse of the importance this religious region has nationwide.

If this axis provides for Senegal's economic and religious needs, Kaolack to the south is the city that gets the country moving. Lifted by the accelerated ambience of several *gares routières* (bus and taxi stations), this busy urban centre is the hub that links all four corners of the country. It's the place for the latest news from remote corners and a good base for more remote destinations. Its spectacular round market, one of the largest covered markets in the whole of Africa, heaves with shimmering fabrics, sweet-scented incense, clothes, food and other wares carried here from The Gambia, Mali and Mauritania.

HIGHLIGHTS

- See the fruits of religious devotion and raw capitalism working hand in hand in **Touba** (p196), the centre of the Mouride Muslim brotherhood

- Weave your way around the world-famous tapestry factory in **Thiès** (opposite)

- Sip sweet tea with the vendors in the covered market at **Kaolack** (p197) – the second-largest in Africa

- POPULATION: 1.3 MILLION

THIÈS

pop 1,360,000

Thiès is a place that barely featured in the collective imagination of Senegal until it became the heated focus of a major political scandal in 2006. The phrase *'chantiers de Thiès'* (building sites of Thiès) was on everyone's lips then, referring to the alleged embezzlement of a huge sum of money that had been earmarked for the beautification and modernisation of Senegal's third-largest city. Even though most of the building money is thought to have disappeared in private Swiss bank accounts, vast construction efforts are still apparent in and around town – just check the modern bypass, the street lights and various proudly erected office blocks.

Despite all these efforts, Thiès remains of marginal interest to travellers, and the modern bypass is the only thing most people see of this slow-moving town. But it's worth stepping off the bush taxi for a day or two if only for a surprisingly good string of restaurants and nightclubs, and its world-famous tapestry factory.

Orientation & Information

'The main artery of town is Av Léopold Senghor, where you find a string of good restaurants. It leads north to the train station, and another small cluster of restaurants and bars. But recently its southern end is turning into a more animated centre – you find the town hall here and several banks. And with

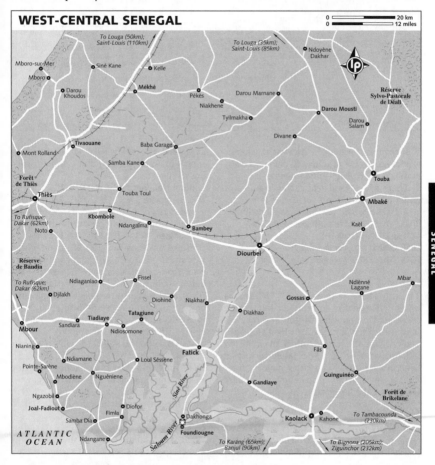

WEST-CENTRAL SENEGAL

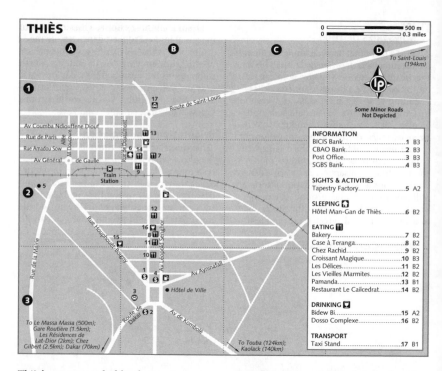

THIÈS

To Saint-Louis (194km)

Some Minor Roads Not Depicted

Route de Saint-Louis

Av Coumba Ndiouffene Diouf
Rue de Paris
Rue Amadou Sow
Av Général de Gaulle

Train Station

Rue Houphouët-Boigny

Rue de la Maire

Route de Dakar

Av Aynina Fall

Hôtel de Ville

Av de Kombolé

To Le Massa Massa (500m);
Gare Routière (1.5km);
Les Résidences de
Lat-Dior (2km); Chez
Gilbert (2.5km); Dakar (70km)

To Touba (124km);
Kaolack (140km)

INFORMATION	
BICIS Bank	1 B3
CBAO Bank	2 B3
Post Office	3 B3
SGBS Bank	4 B3
SIGHTS & ACTIVITIES	
Tapestry Factory	5 A2
SLEEPING	
Hôtel Man-Gan de Thiès	6 B2
EATING	
Bakery	7 B2
Case à Teranga	8 B2
Chez Rachid	9 B2
Croissant Magique	10 B3
Les Délices	11 B2
Les Vieilles Marmites	12 B2
Pamanda	13 B1
Restaurant Le Cailcedrat	14 B2
DRINKING	
Bidew Bi	15 A2
Dosso Complexe	16 B2
TRANSPORT	
Taxi Stand	17 B1

Thiès' current speed of development, you can expect more new restaurants, bars and clubs at the southern end of the town centre.

There are several *télécentres*, cybercafés and a post office in the centre of town.

All these banks have withdrawal facilities:

BICIS (☎ 951 8339; Place de France; ⏱ 7.45am-12.15pm & 1.40-3.45pm)

CBAO (☎ 952 0505; Rue Nationale 2)

SGBS (☎ 951 8225; Av Léopold Sédar Senghor)

Sights

The tiny **Musée de Thiès** (☎ 951 1520; admission CFA500; ⏱ 9am-6pm) is surprisingly interesting. It's housed in a building within a fort that was built as the French garrison in 1864 and, once you've found the staff to unlock the museum building, you'll find a fascinating history of Senegal's railways. The city's major attraction, however, is the world-renowned **Tapestry Factory** (see the boxed text, opposite).

Sleeping

Chez Gilbert (☎ 546 7438; Rte de Dakar; r CFA10,000, with air-con CFA15,000; ❄ ☎) One of the cheapest places in town, this simple auberge, 2.5km

along the Rte to Dakar, has basic, clean rooms in an airy setting and camping space out the back.

Hôtel Man-Gan de Thiès (☎ 951 1526; fax 951 2532; Rue Amadou Sow; s/d CFA15,000/18,000; ❄) Not a bad option – this place has a pleasant garden courtyard and clean rooms.

Le Massa Massa (☎ 952 1244; Cité Malick Sy; r CFA12,600, with air-con CFA20,600; ❄) Hidden in a side street off the Rte to Dakar, a 20-minute walk from town, this place is a gem – the perfect combination of simple and tasteful. It's run by a charming Belgian couple and, best of all, has one of the best restaurants in town, serving fine French and Belgian cuisine (dishes around CFA4000).

Les Résidences de Lat-Dior (☎ 952 0777; residence latdior@hotmail.com; s/d CFA27,600/35,200; Ⓟ ❄ ▯ ☎) Thiès' multistar place is an all-singing all-dancing hotel with a fitness centre, wi-fi access and even its own mosque. It's 2km from the town centre, on the Rte de Dakar.

Eating

What Thiès might lack in soul, it wholly makes up with its restaurant scene – there's

---

TAPESTRIES OF THIÈS

The factory of the **Manufactures Sénégalaises des Arts Décoratifs** (☎/fax 951 1131; admission CFA1000; ✆ exhibition room 8am-12.30pm daily & 3-6.30pm Mon-Fri), off Rue de la Mairie, was one of many artistic endeavours inspired by President Senghor during the 1960s. Today the factory is run as a cooperative, with designs for the brightly coloured, cotton tapestries chosen from paintings submitted by Senegalese artists.

All of the weaving is done on manual looms, and two weavers complete about 1 sq metre per month. Only eight tapestries are made of each design. Most find their way around the world as gifts from the government to foreign dignitaries; there's a huge tapestry hanging in Atlanta airport and another in Buckingham Palace. Others are for sale, but at CFA500,000 per square metre, most of us will be content to admire them in the exhibition room.

---

a string of good-quality eateries here, serving a good range of food from Lebanese *shwarmas* to three-course French meals.

Restaurant Le Cailcedrat (☎ 951 1130; Av Général de Gaulle; meals CFA1500-4000; ✆ 7am-midnight) This place leads the route upmarket, with excellent kofta and Middle Eastern dishes in pleasant surroundings.

Les Vieilles Marmites (☎ 951 4440; dishes around CFA3000; ✆ 11am-2pm & 6pm-midnight) Proof of the quality of its French and Senegalese food, this excellent restaurant off Av Léopold Senghor has been popular for years – the packed tables are proof of the quality of its food.

Case à Teranga (☎ 611 5125; Escale; meals CFA1000-5000) Though slightly more expensive, this restaurant's delicious choice of West Indian, Indian and French cuisine is worth paying for. Come on weekend nights and you can enjoy live music with your meals; come for a weekday lunch and the forthcoming owner Véronique will personally go to the *shwarma* place down the road and get you simple snacks to go with your beer.

Lebanese fast-food joints – good ones – loom large on the local restaurant scene. **Chez Rachid** (☎ 951 1878; Av Général de Gaulle; ✆ noon-midnight) does good *shwarmas* for CFA850. The **Croissant Magique** (☎ 951 1878; dishes around 2000) is popular, though pizzas are better at

Pamanda (☎ 952 1550; Rue de Paris; dishes CFA1000-5000; ✆ 9am-2am). **Les Délices** (☎ 951 7516; Av Léopold Senghor; ✆ 7.30am-2am) has the added attraction of a tea house that serves good ice creams and coffee on a pretty terrace space.

There's a good bakery off Av Général de Gaulle in the route towards the main taxi stand for breakfast stuff, and several small shops for groceries and other items.

Drinking & Entertainment

The town's liveliest places are the mighty entertainment complex **Bidew Bi** (☎ 639 8554; Rue Houphouët-Boigny, Escale; ✆ 7pm-4am), which comprises a busy nightclub and stylish bar, and its rival **Dosso Complexe** (☎ 951 2640; www.dossonight.com; ✆ Tue-Sun; ⬛), where families and romance-seeking couples come for weekend lunches around the pool, and party animals for a night out in such style that even Dakar's city folks have been known to dance here on weekends. (admission CFA2500). It's off Av Léopold Senghor.

Getting There & Away
BUSH TAXI & MINIBUS

Bush taxis and minibuses leave from the *gare routière* on the southern outskirts, 3km/1.5km from the northern/southern centre. There are frequent *sept-place* taxis also from the *gare routière* to Dakar (CFA1200, one hour, 70km), Kaolack (CFA1900, two hours, 140km) and Saint-Louis (CFA2600, four hours, 196km).

TRAIN

The train station and ticket office is on Av Général de Gaulle. The express trains en route to Bamako (Mali) normally come through Thiès every Wednesday and Saturday morning. Thiès–Tambacounda is around CFA10,000/6000 in 1st/2nd class. Thiès to Tambacounda, Kayes (Mali) or Bamako is about CFA6000 in 2nd class. Thiès–Bamako is CFA30,000/20,000 in 1st/2nd class.

Tickets are hard to get in Thiès because most people travel from Dakar and few get off in Thiès so the train is often full. For more details see p283.

A commuter train runs less frequently than it should to Dakar (CFA800) via Rufisque (CFA400) every morning, in theory around 7am Monday to Saturday. The train service is hardly reliable, with frequent derailments and delays.

Getting Around

Any taxi trip around town should cost CFA400, including the *gare routière*–centre trip. A taxi stand is in the north of town.

DIOURBEL

pop 98,000

The steaming hot, sand-blown town of Diourbel (jur-bell) is of enormous significance to the Mourides as it was home to Cheikh Amadou Bamba (opposite), the founder of the Mouride Sufi brotherhood from 1912 until his death in 1927. The colonial government held him here under house arrest, and forbade him to enter the holy city of Touba, 48km to the northeast.

The Bamba family still lives in the town, in a palatial compound that is said to have walls 313m long (313 is the number of prophets in the Quran and a mystical number for Muslims). Nearby is the town's main mosque, built between 1919 and 1925; it's smaller, neater and more aesthetically pleasing than the vast structure at Touba.

You are allowed to visit the mosque outside prayer times (prayers take 10 to 15 minutes). Ask someone to find you the *responsable* (a sort of caretaker figure) and he'll show you around. A small fee for his trouble is appropriate. Remember to take your shoes off at the gate. Men should wear long trousers and women, a long skirt and a scarf to cover their head and shoulders.

The small, simple *campement* **Keur Déthié Caty** (☎ 9715190; P ⚡) is the only place to stay in town, unless you knock on the doors of the locals. There are a few cheap restaurants on the main street and around the *gare routière*.

Getting There & Away

Plenty of traffic runs through Diourbel on its way to Dakar or Touba. Two bus stations are a 10-minute walk apart, one serving Thiès and Dakar, the other Touba and Kaolack. *Sept-place* taxis go to Dakar (CFA1720, three hours, 146km), Thiès (CFA900, 80 minutes, 76km) and Touba (CFA700, one hour, 50km).

TOUBA

pop 452,000

Seeing the combined forces of religion, the economy and politics at work is fascinating anywhere. In Touba, their triple strength overwhelms with its complexity and sheer impact. The black market, one of Senegal's biggest markets, with all its en masse trading and a whole range of undercover activity, sits next to the country's biggest mosque and most important spiritual focus – that's the most obvious sign of this impact. Dubbed the Holy City, Touba is the sacred focus of the Mouride Sufi brotherhood (see p45), the place where their spiritual leader, Cheikh Amadou Bamba, lived, worked and died. He is buried in the grand mosque of Touba, an awe-inspiring building whose minaret dominates the town and much of its surrounding plains.

The construction of the mosque started in 1936 under Bamba's son, who became caliph (brotherhood leader) on his father's death. It houses an impressive Quranic library containing the complete works of Cheikh Amadou Bamba and many of his students. Take a close look at the building and you'll notice the architectural signs of various phases of construction, ranging from vast concrete columns to detailed plaster decorations. Since its foundation, the structure has been constantly enlarged, improved and refined, and this process continues today.

And it's not only the mosque that is swelling in size. The whole of Touba is under permanent construction, with new houses, streets and entire neighbourhoods extending the city's sprawl in ever-larger circles. If you consider that the entire town literally belongs totally to the descendants of Cheikh Amadou Bamba, you'll begin to get an inkling of the brotherhood's immense wealth, all generated from donations of followers, wise investment and, most importantly, ownership of large parts of Senegal's groundnut economy.

Not surprisingly, then, this is a place of pilgrimage for believers and merchants alike, a place whose monument to Mouridism, the grand mosque, attracts as many visitors as does its huge market, a monument to ruthless capitalism (with a healthy dose of illegal

The best time (or the worst, depending on your inclination) is the time of the **Grand Magal**, a pilgrimage that takes place 48 days after the Islamic New Year (for details see the boxed text Islamic Holidays, p46). This celebrates Bamba's return from exile in 1907 after having been banished for 20 years by the French authorities and over the years has turned into a mass event, by now attracting two million or more followers. It's

---

BAMBA – A SENEGALESE ICON

Cheikh Amadou Bamba, the founder of the Mouride brotherhood (1887), is without doubt Senegal's most iconic religious figure. His veiled portrait looks down earnestly on the population from thousands of paintings spread across walls, shop signs, cars, stickers and even T-shirts. Born in 1950 as a relative of the powerful Wolof leader Lat Dior, and member of the wealthy Mbacke clan, he initially renounced his noble heritage and chose a path of religious devotion. His preachings attracted an increasingly large following, the most famous disciple being the eccentric Cheikh Ibra Fall, leader of the Baye Fall, an offshoot of the Mouridiya (the local name of the Mouride brotherhood). Both branches emphasise the importance of physical labour as a path to spiritual salvation. This initially fitted in neatly with the French administration's attempts to improve its territory's economic output, but Bamba's anticolonial stance and the colonialists' fear of his growing Islamic power base led them to exile the charismatic leader in 1895. Bamba returned to Senegal in 1907 and, despite his continued anticolonial rhetoric, entered into hushed negotiations with the French.

Long after his death, the influence of Bamba and his teachings keeps growing, the ever-increasing masses of people descending on Touba for the Magal being proof of the immense popularity the Mouridiya enjoys.

---

an impressive sight, to put it mildly, but not one without risks. Be early if you want to find a place in a taxi before – you'll be fighting for your *car rapide* seat with half the population – and keep your wits about you once there. Crowds, even devoted ones, tend to attract a sizable clientele of criminals, and you don't want to fall prey to them. There are no places to stay in Touba, but on the day of the Magal local families open their homes for visitors, and you'll find a bed and plate of food anywhere in town. Donations of money are of course welcome, and sometimes expected. Just think what you would normally have paid for the service, and give the same amount.

Getting There & Away

To reach Touba from Dakar (165km, 2.5 hours) costs CFA3200 in a *sept-place* taxi and CFA1500 by Ndiaga Ndiaye. Seeing that you're going to the heartland of the Mourides, you might as well go by *car mouride* (bus service financed by the Mouridiya; CFA1500). A day trip to Touba is possible, but you'd do the place more justice by going to Mbaké, staying there for two nights and visiting Touba for the day.

MBAKÉ

pop 40,000

This unremarkable town makes a good base from which to visit Touba. The **Campement Touristique le Baol** (☎ 976 5505; fax 976 7254; s/d CFA11,600/13,000; 🕿) has spartan rooms with

private bathrooms in a homely setting. The English-speaking staff can arrange guides to Touba and other religious sites in the region (inquire about costs). The *campement* has local meals, or you can head for the market where you'll find a few *gargottes* (simple eateries) and *dibiteries* (grilled-meat stalls). There's an SGBS bank past the turn-off to Touba, which is about 10km away.

KAOLACK

pop 179,000

The city of Kaolack sees a lot of visitors that pass through, but only few that stay. Well, they're all making a mistake. Kaolack isn't attractive or picturesque, has neither a thriving tourist industry nor stunning natural surroundings. But as a quieter place, cosmopolitan, fairly hassle-free and a little rugged, it's got a unique urban charm that lies somewhere between the frenzied drive of Dakar and the steady pulse of Tambacounda. Plus, its central position and excellent transport connections make it a great base for exploring pretty much the entire country.

Information

Banks include CBAO and SGBS, both of which have Visa-welcoming ATMs. There are many places to connect to the Net; the Internet Café on Rue Cheikh Tidiane Cherif has a fairly speedy service for only CFA150 per hour. Kaolack also has a relatively well-equipped and -staffed **hospital** (☎ 941 10 29; Ave Valdiodio Ndiaye).

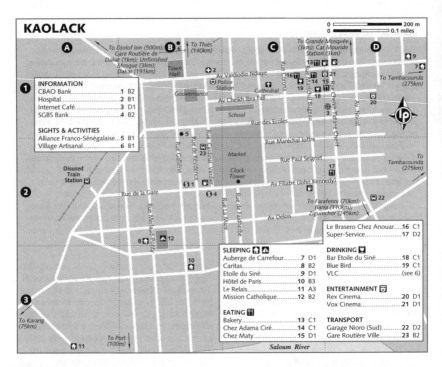

KAOLACK

INFORMATION
CBAO Bank..........................1 B2
Hospital...............................2 B1
Internet Café........................3 D1
SGBS Bank...........................4 B2

SIGHTS & ACTIVITIES
Alliance Franco-Sénégalaise...5 B1
Village Artisanal....................6 B1

SLEEPING
Auberge de Carrefour..........7 D1
Caritas.................................8 B2
Etoile du Siné......................9 D1
Hôtel de Paris....................10 B3
Le Relais...........................11 A3
Mission Catholique............12 B2

EATING
Bakery...............................13 C1
Chez Adama Ciré...............14 C1
Chez Maty.........................15 D1

Le Brasero Chez Anouar....16 C1
Super-Service....................17 D2

DRINKING
Bar Etoile du Siné..............18 C1
Blue Bird...........................19 C1
VLC................................(see 6)

ENTERTAINMENT
Rex Cinema.......................20 D1
Vox Cinema.......................21 D1

TRANSPORT
Garage Nioro (Sud)............22 D2
Gare Routière Ville............23 B1

Saloum River

Sights & Activities

City life literally revolves around the town's large market, a huge conglomeration of rickety stalls, oriental arches and tiny arcades, all presided over by a grand entrance and even grander clock tower, and grouped around a wide patio. It's apparently the second-biggest covered market in Africa after Marrakech, and sells anything from hair products and lengths of cloth to fruits, electrical items and handmade shoes. If you still need to buy the obligatory Senegalese woodcarving, head for the *village artisanal* on the route to Thiès.

Kaolack's famous **Grande Mosquée**, a Moroccan-style building, is in the north of town about 3.5km from the town centre. Its construction was financed by members of the Baye Niass brotherhood, an interesting *confrérie* whose vision finds plenty of support among the Senegalese youth. Near Kaolack's Gare Routière de Dakar, you'll see another **mosque**, a curious modern construction that was built by the illustrious Senegalese millionaire Ndiouga Kébé as part of an ambitious 'future city' project

that never quite left the drawing board. Not even the mosque has been completed, and it's never been used for prayer, but it is admittedly an impressive sight.

The **Alliance Franco-Sénégalaise** (☎ 941 1061; Rue Galliène) is also absolutely worth a visit, either to admire its fantastic decor of colourfully painted walls adorned with mosaic designs, to take in one of the frequent exhibitions and events, or just have a tranquil cup of coffee.

Sleeping

Le Relais (☎ 941 1000; fax 941 1002; Plage de Kundam; s/d CFA22,000/27,000; ✖ ☐ ☒) Southwest of town and right on the river, this stylish place surprises after many unglamorous options. Spacious rooms have TV, phone and even an Internet connection.

Djolof Inn (Rte to Dakar; r CFA10,000; ✖) Just out of town, this is the friendliest, most welcoming of the cheapest. Rooms are basic but impeccable, and for only CFA500, you get a filling, fried-egg breakfast.

Auberge de Carrefour (☎ 941 9000; Av Valdiodio Ndiaye; s/d CFA8500/13,000) This clean auberge is

---

MARCHÉ TOUBA

That travelling salesmen, middlemen and beggars vie for space at the Touba market should be no surprise – the town's role as a spiritual centre does not disguise the fact that it has long been one of the biggest cogs in Senegal's political and economic machinery. Though part of Senegal, Touba has unofficially retained its autonomy. Senegalese police are rarely seen, and the Mourides run their own welfare services. They also enjoy extensive trading relations with other towns and cities within Senegal and abroad. In New York police reckon 90% of the street merchants illegally peddling watches, handbags and the like are Mourides, and current estimates are that every month more than US$1 million is repatriated from small businesses offshore.

There are no tax collectors in Touba as its revenues come from the donations of followers, and no-one is sure exactly how much is bought, sold or bartered within the city, or how much of Senegal's economy is built on Touba's 'shadow' economy. What is certain is that Touba's economic contribution is sizable, and its market is the cheapest place in the country to buy just about anything, from the latest hi-fi gear and jewellery to computers and Russian arms. As you wander through the streets around the mosque, the most obvious sign of the city's prosperity is that every space is being used to display goods for sale. And between the shops and stalls roam salesmen peddling everything from fruit and fake Rolexes to Bamba icons and skin-whitening creams.

---

a decent choice for shoestring travellers. Rooms are spacious and well maintained, and management is friendly and so enthusiastic, they might just turn you into a Kaolack fan.

Caritas (☎ 941 2030; Rue Merlaud-Ponty; s/d CFA10,000/15,000; 🔀) Opposite the mission, this is more upmarket with luxuries such as bathrooms and doors that actually close.

Mission Catholique (☎ 941 2526; Rue Merlaud-Ponty; dm CFA2000, s CFA5000) Staying here must be hilarious if you're 16 and travelling with your clique – the place is packed with youngsters. For anyone else it's just cheap; a bed is about the only luxury the bare rooms hold.

Also recommended:

Etoile du Siné (☎ 941 4458; Av Valdiodio Ndiaye; s/d from CFA6500/9500) A less-than-spotless low-budget option.

Hôtel de Paris (☎ 941 1019; fax 941 1017; Rue Gallliène; s/d CFA24,000/30,000; 🔀 🛋) Has a worn-out charm, but is slightly overpriced.

Eating

If good-quality food is important to you, you should probably cook for yourself. The cheap *gargottes* around the *gares routières* are better for people-watching than for their food, and other good options are rare.

Le Brasero Chez Anouar (☎ 941 1608; Av Valdiodio Ndiaye; meals about CFA3000; 🕑 7am-11pm) This place is close to achieving cult status among travellers. It's a bustling oasis in an urban desert, and the place most cross-country travellers tend to seek out first. The food served is

mainly European cuisine, with a few Senegalese dishes thrown in. It's all about simple, good food – and the friendly atmosphere makes the meals taste even better.

Chez Maty (☎ 941 9000; Rue Cheikh Tidiane Cherif; mains around CF2500; 🕑 11am-2pm & 7pm-midnight Mon-Sat) For cheap *shwarmas* or decent meals, this simple but buzzing place is a good choice. It's one of the cheapies with a good standard of cleanliness – and that's always good to know.

Chez Adama Ciré (☎ 945 0790; Rue Maréchal Bugeau; meals around CFA750) Luckily the generous platters of Senegalese food served in this run-down motel are more presentable than the rooms – if only slightly.

Self-caterers are fairly well served, with the well-stocked **Super-Service** (Av Filiatre), several other small shops and supermarkets, a giant sprawl of a market selling fresh produce and a **bakery** (Av Valdiodio Ndiaye) that's so good you'll just want to live on bread alone.

Drinking & Entertainment

VLC (Village Artisanal; admission CFA2000; 🕑 9pm-3am Thu-Sun) The three letters stand for Village Loisir Club, which is utterly misleading as this is the closest Kaolack gets to urbane entertainment. The music is bass-heavy as it should be, the dance floors crammed. A perfect Saturday night.

Blue Bird (☎ 941 5350; Rue Maréchal Bugeau; 🕑 8am-3am Mon-Sat, 6pm-2am Sun) This place gets busy on weekends, when a dinner for two can be followed by dancing in the adjacent raucous nightclub.

Bar Etoile du Siné (☎ 936 45 93; Av Cheikh Ibra Fall; ☽ 9am-2am) Just over the road is this boisterous bar, a not-so-spotless but entertaining place. It's one for those who take their drink seriously, not one for lone female guests though.

Film-lovers have a choice between the downtrodden **Rex Cinema** (Av Cheikh Ibra Fall) and the downtrodden **Vox Cinema** (Av Valdiodio Ndiaye). Both show American B-grade movies and the occasional quality film from 9pm every night. Admission is CFA1000.

Getting There & Away

The town has three *gares routières:* Gare Routière de Dakar, on the northwestern side of town, for western and northern destinations including Dakar; Garage Nioro (Sud), on the southeast side of the city centre, for Ziguinchor, Gambia and Tambacounda; and Gare Routière Ville for local taxis.

You can travel to Dakar by *sept-place* taxi (CFA2600, three hours).

Minibuses and Ndiaga Ndiayes do the journey for a little less money and a lot more time.

A *sept-place* to the Gambian border at Karang is CFA2300 (two hours, 70km) and to Tambacounda CFA5000 (five hours).

If you're brave, you can save money by taking a *car mouride* (CFA1500, about eight hours). They leave from an unmarked place near the Grande Mosquée – ask your way there.

Getting Around

Kaolack has shared taxis (from the Gare Routière Ville, or just hail them) to take passengers around town (CFA500). They also connect the northern and southern *gares routières* (CFA150).

Otherwise, you can hop on the back of a taxi-*mobylette* (CFA200 to CFA300) or take a horse-drawn *calèche* (cart, CFA300).

Northern Senegal

Senegal's long northern border is defined by the Senegal River, flowing in a great arc westwards from the Futa Jallon highlands in Guinea, through Mali and continuing for some 600km between Senegal and Mauritania. The river and its adjoining creeks and floodplains are a lifeline, but only a short distance away the landscape is dry and vegetation is sparse. North of the river, the deserts of Mauritania mark the southern edge of the Sahara. To the south, the barely accessible Ferlo Plains, home to cattle-herding Fula, stretch into central Senegal.

The river region is the homeland of the Tukulor people, a branch of the Fula, who established here the 16th-century Fouta Toro kingdom, which expanded in the mid-19th century into a vast Muslim empire under the leadership of El Hajj Omar Tall. An immediate sense of history seems to pervade the region. The vast open spaces dotted with the beautiful *banco* (mudbrick) houses of small Tukulor villages seem to be steeped in ancient times, and a chain of 18th-century French forts and the stunning Sudanese architecture of Omarian mosques tell the story of colonial battles. Few travellers come here, making the river route a lonely yet utterly rewarding stretch to follow.

In contrast the gateway to the region, the historic city of Saint-Louis, is a fixed point on most tourist itineraries – and for good reason. This first French settlement in West Africa features stunning 19th-century architecture and a relaxed and friendly ambience that few other places can match. Podor to its northeast is the place to hear Fula music, perhaps during Baaba Maal's Festival du Fleuve.

HIGHLIGHTS

- Soak up history on a stroll through the colonial old town of **Saint-Louis** (p207), with live jazz as background music

- Spot pelicans in flight, as well as hundreds of other species of birds, at the **Parc National des Oiseaux du Djoudj** (p214)

- Follow the historic river route to **Île à Morphil** (p218), passing ancient French forts and stunning Sudanese-style mosques

- Get into the desert spirit at the vast dunes of **Lompoul** (p214)

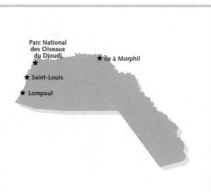

■ POPULATION: 2 MILLION

NORTHERN SENEGAL

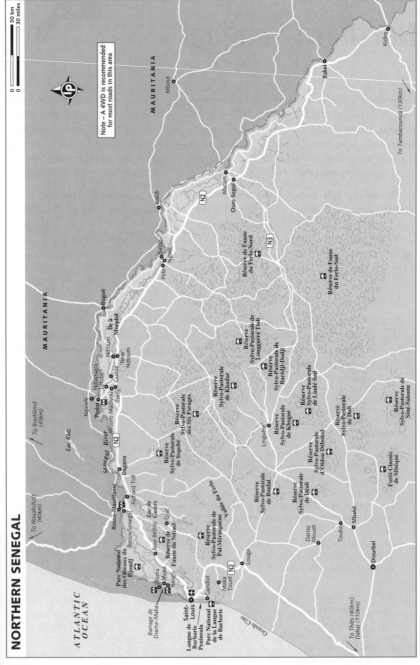

Note – A 4WD is recommended for most roads in this area

MAURITANIA

ATLANTIC OCEAN

Senegal River

To Nouakchott (40km)

To Boutilimit (45km)

To Thiès (40km); Dakar (110km)

To Tambacounda (130km)

Parc National des Oiseaux du Djoudj

Barrage de Diama-Maka

Langue de Saint-Barbarie Peninsula

Parc National de la Langue de Barbarie

Rosso-Mauritanie

Rosso-Senegal

Richard Toll

Ross Béthio

Réserve de Faune du Ndiaël

Lac de Guiers

Dagana

Gandiol

Diama

Maka

Gnit

Grande Côte

Maka Touré

Louga

Darou Moussi

Touba

Mbaké

Diourbel

Réserve Sylvo-Pastorale de Pal-Méringhuène

Vallée au Ferlo

Réserve Sylvo-Pastorale de Sogobé

Réserve Sylvo-Pastorale des Six Forages

Réserve Sylvo-Pastorale de Khadar

Réserve Sylvo-Pastorale de Naolé

Réserve Sylvo-Pastorale de Doali

Réserve Sylvo-Pastorale d'Ouldou Débokol

Réserve Sylvo-Pastorale de Khogné

Réserve Sylvo-Pastorale de Bareidji-Dodji

Réserve Sylvo-Pastorale de Longuguère Tioli

Réserve Sylvo-Pastorale de Linde Sud

Réserve Sylvo-Pastorale de Doli

Réserve Sylvo-Pastorale de Siné-Saloum

Forêt Classée de Mbégué

Réserve de Faune du Ferlo-Nord

Réserve de Faune du Ferlo-Sud

Linguère

Ngawlé

Podor

Wouro Madiyou

Tred

Guédé

Ndioum

New Ndioum

Ngaoura

Dodel

Bogué

Île à Morphil

Ndioum

Peté

Salde

Ngoui

Kaédi

Matam

Ouro Sogui

Mbout

Bakel

Kidira

Lac Rkiz

N2

N3

MAURITANIA

0 50 km
0 30 miles

SAINT-LOUIS & AROUND

The Senegal River flows westwards towards the Atlantic Ocean, but currents and winds have pushed sand across its mouth for thousands of years, changing its course. Now the final section of the river runs south, separated from the ocean by a long narrow peninsula – the Langue de Barbarie. The original city of Saint-Louis was founded in the 17th century on a strategic island near the river's mouth, although it has expanded to cover a much larger area today.

Saint-Louis makes a good base from which to explore northwest Senegal, and several wildlife reserves lie within an easy day's travel – including Parc National de la Langue de Barbarie, at the southern tip of the eponymous peninsula, and Parc National des Oiseaux du Djoudj, the world-famous bird sanctuary.

SAINT-LOUIS

pop 147,100

When you consider the enormous impact the French had on this continent it's fascinating to think that the place where it all began has barely changed for more than a century.

History

Founded in 1659 by Louis Caullier on the easily accessible, inundation-proof Île de N'Dar, Saint-Louis was the first French settlement in Africa. By the 1790s, the town named after the French King Louis XIV was a busy port and centre for the trade of goods and slaves, and was home to a racially diverse population of 10,000. Most notable among the residents at this time were the *signares* – women of mixed race who married wealthy European merchants temporarily based in the city, and thereby earned aristocratic status and great wealth.

By 1885, when the town was connected to the growing urban centre of Dakar by rail (the current train station dates only from 1908), Saint-Louis was at its bustling height. Its symmetrical road system had long been created, and most of the town's characteristic colourful buildings with their shady patios, wrought-iron balconies and large magazine doors had already been built.

With the creation of l'Afrique Occidentale Française (French West Africa) in 1895, Saint-Louis became the capital of the French colonial empire, spanning today's Senegal, Sudan, Guinea and Côte d'Ivoire. When capital status was conferred on Dakar in 1902, Saint-Louis' prestige faded. It remained capital of Senegal and Mauritania until 1958, when all Senegalese administration was moved to Dakar (Nouakchott became the Mauritanian capital in 1960).

Over the years Saint-Louis expanded beyond the confines of the island, covering part of the mainland (Sor) and the Langue de Barbarie Peninsula, where most of the Senegalese inhabitants lived. Yet the island itself barely changed in the 20th century. This policy of neglect led unwittingly to the conservation of the classic architecture, and the island was named a Unesco World Heritage site in 2000. Still, today only a handful of the old buildings have been privately restored to their former magnificence. Others are being gradually worn down by the hands of time, and a stroll through the ancient city can sometimes feel like a walk through an abandoned film set (Saint-Louis has indeed been the site of several French and American cinema productions).

Orientation

The city of Saint-Louis straddles part of the Langue de Barbarie Peninsula, Île de N'Dar and the mainland. From the mainland you reach the island via the 500m-long Pont Faidherbe; two smaller bridges – the almost-derelict Pont Mustapha Malick Gaye and the safer Pont Geôle – link the island to the peninsula. The island was formerly the European quarter, with many grand old houses, a few of which still retain their gracious wrought-iron balconies, while others are gradually crumbling to pieces. The peninsula was the African quarter, previously inhabited by freed slaves; today it's a thriving fishing community called Guet N'Dar.

MAPS

The map *Saint-Louis et la Region du Fleuve Senegal* (CFA3000) a cross between a cartoon and an aerial photograph, is available in bookshops and hotels. It was slightly outdated at the time of writing, though an update may have been published. The leaflet, *Saint-Louis de Senegal – Ville d'Art et d'Histoire* is very useful, containing a map outlining historic buildings.

NORTHERN SENEGAL

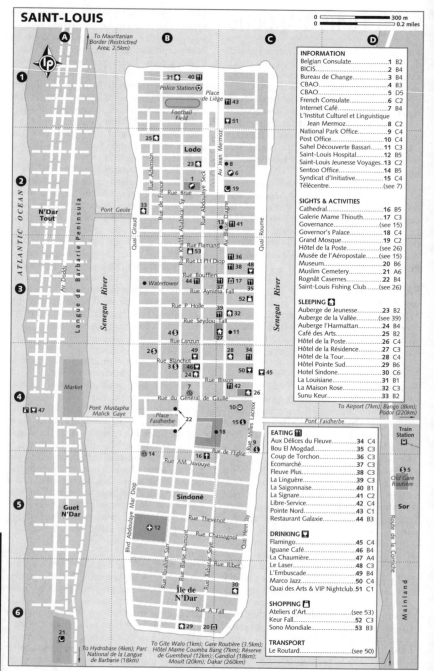

SAINT-LOUIS

0 ————— 300 m
0 ————— 0.2 miles

INFORMATION
Belgian Consulate...................1 B2
BICIS.....................................2 B4
Bureau de Change...................3 B4
CBAO....................................4 B3
CBAO....................................5 D5
French Consulate.....................6 C2
Internet Café.........................7 B4
L'Institut Culturel et Linguistique
Jean Mermoz........................8 C2
National Park Office.................9 C4
Post Office............................10 C4
Sahel Découverte Bassari.......11 C3
Saint-Louis Hospital...............12 B5
Saint-Louis Jeunesse Voyages..13 C2
Sentoo Office.......................14 B5
Syndicat d'Initiative...............15 C4
Télécentre.........................(see 7)

SIGHTS & ACTIVITIES
Cathedral............................16 B5
Galerie Mame Thiouth...........17 C3
Governance.......................(see 15)
Governor's Palace.................18 C4
Grand Mosque......................19 C2
Hôtel de la Poste................(see 26)
Musée de l'Aéropostale.......(see 15)
Museum..............................20 B6
Muslim Cemetery.................21 A6
Rognât Casernes...................22 B4
Saint-Louis Fishing Club......(see 26)

SLEEPING
Auberge de Jeunesse............23 B2
Auberge de la Vallée.........(see 39)
Auberge l'Harmattan............24 B4
Café des Arts.......................25 B2
Hôtel de la Poste..................26 C4
Hôtel de la Résidence...........27 C3
Hôtel de la Tour...................28 C4
Hôtel Pointe Sud..................29 B6
Hotel Sindone......................30 C6
La Louisiane........................31 B1
La Maison Rose....................32 C3
Sunu Keur............................33 B2

EATING
Aux Délices du Fleuve...........34 C4
Bou El Mogdad.....................35 C3
Coup de Torchon..................36 C3
Ecomarché..........................37 C3
Fleuve Plus..........................38 C3
La Linguère.........................39 C3
La Saigonnaise.....................40 B1
La Signare...........................41 C2
Libre-Service........................42 C3
Pointe Nord.........................43 C1
Restaurant Galaxie...............44 B3

DRINKING
Flamingo.............................45 C4
Iguane Café.........................46 B4
La Chaumière.......................47 A4
Le Laser..............................48 C3
L'Embuscade........................49 B4
Marco Jazz..........................50 C4
Quai des Arts & VIP Nightclub..51 C1

SHOPPING
Ateliers d'Art....................(see 53)
Keur Fall..............................52 C3
Sono Mondiale.....................53 B3

TRANSPORT
Le Routard........................(see 50)

To Mauritanian
Border (Restricted
Area; 2.5km)

Police Station
Place
de Liège

Football
Field

Lodo

N'Dar
Tout

ATLANTIC OCEAN

Langue de Barbarie Peninsula

Av Dodds

Senegal River

Pont Geole

Quai Giraud

Rue Adamson

Rue de France

Rue Brue

Rue Abdoulaye Seck

Av Jean Mermoz

Rue Khalifa Ababacar Sy

Rue Blaise Diagne

Quai Roume

Senegal River

Rue Flamand

Rue Lt PH Diop

Rue Boufflers

Watertower

Rue Aynina Fall

Rue P Holle

Rue Seydou Tall

Rue Lanzun

Rue Blanchot

Rue Bisson

Rue du Général de Gaulle

Market

Pont Mustapha
Malick Gaye

Place
Faidherbe

Rue Milles Lacroix

Pont Faidherbe

To Airport (7km); Bango (8km);
Podor (220km)

Rue de l'Eglise

Rue AM Javouye

Sindoné

Blvd Abdoulaye Mar Diop

Rue Thevenot

Rue Chassagnol

Rue Ribet

Guet
N'Dar

Rue Ibrahim Sarr

Rue Blaise Dumont

Rue Babacar Seye

Quai Henri Jay

Île de
N'Dar

Rue A Fall

To Hydrobase (4km); Parc
National de la Langue
de Barbarie (18km)

To Gite Walo (1km); Gare Routière (3.5km);
Hôtel Mame Coumba Bang (7km); Réserve
de Guembeul (12km); Gandiol (18km);
Mouit (20km); Dakar (260km)

Train
Station

Old Gare
Routière

Sor

Route de la Corniche

Mainland

NORTHERN SENEGAL

Information

The website www.saintlouisdusenegal.com contains also plenty of useful information and has links to all major hotels and restaurants.

CULTURAL CENTRES

L'Institut Culturel et Linguistique Jean Mermoz (☎ 938 2626; www.ccfsi.sn; Av Jean Mermoz; ☒ 8.30am-12.30pm & 3-6.30pm Mon-Fri) It has a library and café, publishes a regular guide to events in Saint-Louis, and hosts films, concerts and art exhibitions.

EMERGENCY

Saint-Louis Hospital (☎ 961 1059; Blvd Abdoulaye Mar Diop) Has an Accident & Emergency department.

INTERNET ACCESS

Internet Café (Rue du Général de Gaulle; per hr CFA500; ☒ 8am-11pm) Decent terminals and several phone booths.

Sentoo Office (Blvd Abdoulaye Mar Diop; per hr CFA500; ☒ 9am-1pm & 3-8pm)

MONEY

Both BICIS and CBAO change money, and theoretically travellers cheques (though some travellers have reported difficulties), and have ATMs (Visa only). Receptions at the larger hotels will also change cash, though they might accept euros only.

BICIS (☎ 961 1053; Rue de France; ☒ 7.45am-12.15pm & 1.40-3.45pm Mon-Thu, 7.45am-1pm & 2.40-3.45pm Fri)

Bureau de Change (Rue Calipha Ababacar Sy; ☒ 7.30am-1pm & 2.30-7.30pm)

CBAO (☎ 964 1454; ☒ 8.15am-5.15pm) Sor branch, near the old *gare routière.*

CBAO (Rue Calipha Ababacar Sy; ☒ 8.15am-5.15pm Mon-Fri) Also has a Western Union office.

POST

Post office (Rue du Général de Gaulle) The Art Deco–style building opposite the Hôtel de la Poste.

TELEPHONE

You can make phone calls from any hotel. There's a large **télécentre** (☒ 8am-midnight) on Rue du Général de Gaulle, and numerous others on the island and across the bridge in Sor.

TOURIST INFORMATION

National Park Office (Quai Henri Jay; ☒ 8am-1.30pm & 3-7pm) Can help with information on the national parks of the region, though you might have to show some persistence to get staff to part with leaflets and printouts.

Syndicat d'Initiative (☎ 961 2455; sltourisme@sentoo .sn; Governance; ☒ 9am-noon & 2.30-5pm) This tourist office opposite Pont Faidherbe is a haven of information, and publishes an excellent range of booklets, brochures and maps. Staff will be able to advise you on activities around town, including tours in horse-drawn carts and excursions to the nearby nature reserves. The centre is also particularly involved in developing tourism in the region of Podor.

TRAVEL AGENCIES

Sahel Découverte Bassari (☎ 961 5689, 961 4263; www.saheldecouverte.com; Av Blaise Diagne) This is the mogul of Saint-Louis' travel agencies, with roots in the region as deep as a baobab. It really knows the area, and offers a range of insightful tours in and around Saint-Louis (see p208).

Saint-Louis JV (Jeunesse Voyages; ☎ 961 5152; www .saintlouisjv.com; Av Blaise Diagne) A much smaller operation with an interesting range of tours.

Sights

Originally built to cross the Danube, the Gustave Eiffel–designed **Pont Faidherbe** (Map p204), linking the mainland and island, was transferred to Saint-Louis in 1897. The bridge is a grand piece of 19th-century engineering – 507m long with a section that once rotated for ships to steam up the Senegal River. The public saw it open in 2005 when the bridge was parted to facilitate the return of the *Bou el Mogdad*.

Right opposite the bridge, your view is blocked by a building usually referred to as **Governance**. It's built on the ruins of the 18th-century colonial fort, and a tour around the backrooms of the Syndicat d'Initiative still grants a glimpse of the ancient walls. In the back of the building, you can also visit the **Musée de l'Aéropostale** (☎ 961 2455; admission CFA1000; ☒ 9am-noon & 2-6pm) showing displays about the colonial airmail service that played an important historical role in the development of Saint-Louis. This is the place to read up on the life and achievements of famous pilot Jean Mermoz, who spent plenty of nights in the **Hôtel de la Poste** (☎ 961 1118; www.hotel-poste.com; Rue du Général de Gaulle) diagonally opposite the governance. The hotel is the oldest in town and has been beautifully restored. It was the place all the daring postal pilots used to stay in when they were delivering their precious mail from France.

Place Faidherbe (Map p204), with its statue of the famous French colonial governor, is in front of the **Governor's Palace**

(Map p204). It's flanked north and south by the 1837 **Rognât Casernes** (Map p204) as well as by other essentially intact 19th-century houses. This central space is where Saint-Louis splits into its southern part (Sindoné) and northern part (Lodo); the former was the old Christian town, the latter was home to the town's Muslim population.

In the south, next to the governor's palace you find the **Cathedral** (Map p204), an 1828 building with a neoclassical facade that is one of the oldest operating churches in Senegal. The Maghreb-style building of the **Grand Mosque** (Map p204; Av Jean Mermoz) in the north was constructed in 1847 on order of the colonial administration to appease the growing Muslim population. The oddity of an attached clock tower betrays the designers' religious affiliation.

The island has plenty of other historical buildings, most of them in a semiruinous state, yet still recognisable with their typical balconies and two-storey layout surrounding a small courtyard (see the Saint-Louis walking tour opposite).

At the southern tip of the island is **museum** (☎ 961 1050; Quai Henri Jay; admission CFA500; ✆ 9amnoon & 3-6pm), contains some fascinating old photos of Saint-Louis and other exhibits relating to northern Senegal. It also houses a contemporary art gallery. **Galerie Mame Thiouth** (☎ 961 3611; Av Blaise Diagne; ✆ 8am-7pm) tends to have the more interesting contemporary exhibitions, and they are beautifully displayed under the arched ceilings of a carefully restored house.

The mainland parts of Saint-Louis have less to offer in historical architecture, but more in contemporary life. **Guet N'Dar** (Map p204), with its lighthouse and the beach, is a fantastically busy fishing town, where you can watch some 200 pirogues being launched into the sea every morning. The boats return in the late afternoon – surfing spectacularly on the waves – to unload their fish on the sand. A line of trucks waits to transport most of the catch to Dakar, while some fish are instantly gutted, dried and smoked by local women.

At the southern end of Guet N'Dar is the **Muslim cemetery** (Map p204) where each fisherman's grave is covered with a fishing net, and the **Hydrobase** (Map p213) from where Jean Mermoz took off on his numerous flights.

Activities
ADVENTURE SPORTS
Saint-Louis Quad (Map p213; ☎ 538 5165; www.saint louisquad.com; Gandiol) organises beach buggy tours around the area. Its offices are in Gandiol, but if you call, staff can meet you elsewhere. For wind-and-kite surfing, contact **Vent Tropical** (Map p213; ☎ 575 7600; info@vent -tropical.com) in Bango.

SWIMMING
Several hotels and bars have swimming pools that nonguests can use for a bite at the bar or a small fee. The most central one is the pool at Flamingo (p212). Beach-bound travellers should head straight for the Hydrobase on Langue de Barbarie. Swimming is usually possible, but always ask about conditions as currents can sometimes get strong.

Festivals & Events
The annual **Saint-Louis International Jazz Festival** (below) is an event of international renown that regularly attracts jazz greats from around the world. It takes place in early May, and lasts for about a week. Its

---

SAINT-LOUIS JAZZ

Jazz is a big thing here – and it's not just the shared name with St Louis, Missouri in the USA, where blues and jazz originated. Way back in the 1940s jazz bands from Saint-Louis (Senegal) were playing in Paris and elsewhere in Europe. Worldwide interest was revived in the early 1990s when the Saint-Louis Jazz Festival was first held, with mainly local bands performing. Now renamed the Saint-Louis International Jazz Festival, this annual event is held the second weekend of May, and attracts performers and audiences from all over the world. At most other times, the stages of the city's many concert venues and jazz bars remain empty. For more background, have a look at *St-Louis Jazz*, a book by Hervé Lenormond (French text, published by Éditions Joca Seria, Nantes, France), which outlines the history of jazz in Senegal and has some wonderful photos of musicians from Africa, America and Europe performing in Saint-Louis.

Programmes and dates can be checked on www.saintlouisjazz.com (in French), or with the Syndicat d'Initiative.

fringe events take place all over town, some around Place Faidherbe, others in the bars of the inner city. The main events usually happen at the Quai des Arts (see p212) or on an open-air stage on Place Faidherbe.

If you pass through town in October, you might see the impressive **Regatta of Guet-N'Dar**, a lively boat race that passes through the river arm between Saint-Louis and Guet-N'Dar. The entire population of Guet-N'Dar participates – women sing to encourage the packed pirogues to go faster, sellers shout to encourage buyers and the young fishermen paddle in unison to win the race. Seeing the huge number of colourfully painted boats chasing one another along the river and back is an extraordinary sight. You can find out the race dates from the Syndicat d'Initiative.

Les Fanals, historic processions with decorated lanterns (not the handheld kind, but lanterns so big they resemble carnival floats), are a tradition unique to Saint-Louis. They were initiated by the *signares* and have their roots in the lanternlit marches to midnight Mass. Today, the Fanals are held around Christmas, and sometimes during the jazz festival, to evoke Saint-Louisian history and reaffirm the town's identity.

Walking Tour

A leisurely walk around the chequered pattern of straight streets and colourfully painted buildings of Saint-Louis feels like a voyage back in time. The town's colonial past is present in the dusty corners and leafy patios of its dignified 19th-century houses; some worn down, others restored to new shine. The colonial features of Saint-Louis are imbued with an utterly contemporary and cosmopolitan spirit by the town's arts scene, its vibrant jazz clubs and the hum of working life in the fishing village of Guet N'Dar.

Saint-Louis' preferred postcard image, the elegant iron construction of **Pont Faidherbe (1**; p205) is the best starting point for a trip around town. Opposite, you see the majestic building of the **Governance (2**; p205), and diagonally opposite, the **Hôtel de la Poste (3**; p211), whose cosy café nods nostalgically to the days of the Aéropostale, the colonial airmail service and its hero Jean Mermoz.

Pass the hotel and turn into Av Blaise Diagne, Saint-Louis' pulsating artery, where tiny arts shops, galleries and restaurants

breathe new life into ancient buildings. Around the corner, the mighty warehouses **Maurel** and **Prom (4)** are patiently waiting for new commerce to arrive, perhaps in the form of a smart hotel, such as the **Hôtel de la Résidence (5**; p211), whose restaurant houses a carefully assembled collection of Saint-Louis memorabilia, or **La Maison Rose (6**; p210), where the musty scent of old stairways and

WALK FACTS

Start Pont Faidherbe
Finish Pont Faidherbe
Distance 6km to 7km
Duration half a day

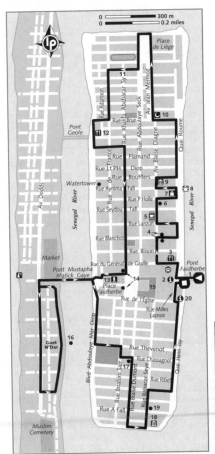

antique furniture hangs over a proud collection of contemporary art.

Along Quai Roume, a proud line of restored warehouses such as **Keur Fall** (7; p212) looks out onto the river, as does the 'grandmother' of all Senegalese boats – the historic **Bou El Mogdad** (8; opposite).

Back on Rue Blaise Diagne, arts fans must take a stroll around the **Galerie Mame Thiouth** (9; p206) before heading back to the Quai for a riverside promenade.

Continuing northwards, the **Grand Mosque** (10; p206) announces the old Muslim quarters (both with the call to prayer and the ringing of bells), and a short walk along the neem tree–lined Av Jean Mermoz takes you to the island's northern point, where you look out onto colourful pirogues and just about glimpse Île Bop Thior – the island where many of the Saint-Louisian bricks were made.

Past the football field, invariably taken over by youths aspiring to Europe's major leagues, a right turn takes you through a scattering of **army quarters (11)**, housed by old military buildings. Another block further west, you hit the western shore. Opposite the Pont Geôle, the pretty hotel **Sunu Keur** (12; p210), yet another charming Saint-Louisian facade, is a good place for a drink or a bite to eat, before setting off for a promenade along the animated Rue Calipha Ababacar Sy. Float through the atmosphere of busy normality all the way to **Place Faidherbe** (13; p205), where **Rognât Casernes** (14; p206) and the **Governor's Palace** (15; p205) replace popular vibrancy with military pomp.

The 1856 Pont Mustapha Malick Gaye takes you from the island onto the Langue de Barbarie Peninsula. The scent of history stays behind as you plunge headfirst into the colourful vitality of the Guet N'Dar. Children play in the sandy streets, and the women cook the fish their husbands have brought home. Dozens of **pirogues (16)** roll in on the eastern shore, unloading their daily catch, and fish are gutted and smoked along the rows of wooden stalls that line the coastal road.

Crossing the bridge to return to the island, turn south (right) for a tour around the ancient Christian quarters of the island's southern tip. Opposite the hospital, the **Ancienne Maison des Soeurs de Saint-Joseph-de-Cluny** (17) with its unique, heart-shaped staircase is in a sad state of neglect.

Walk south down Rue Blaise Dumont, then east around the southern tip of the island and turn left (north) up Rue Babacar Seye. You'll pass the **museum** (18; p206) and the **Lycée Ameth Fall (19)**. Built in 1840 on the site of the old Christian cemetery, the Lycée has housed a hospital and a college. Today, the laughter of school children rings from its leafy courtyard. Walking back towards Pont Faidherbe, don't miss the pretty building of the **National Park Office (20)**, one of the town's oldest houses.

Tours

There are plenty of excellent organised tours on offer in around Saint-Louis. The leading tour operator is **Sahel Découverte Bassari** (☎ 961 5689, 961 4263; www.saheldecouverte.com; Av Blaise Diagne). Its proudest offer is the luxury cruise in the historic ship *Bou El Mogdad* (six-day cruise CFA275,500 or €420; see also opposite), upriver from Saint-Louis to Podor, with various stops at villages and the Parc National des Oiseaux du Djoudj. The company's tours to the dunes of Lompoul (one/two days CFA25,000/35,000) are also recommended.

The **Syndicat d'Initiative** (☎ 961 2455; sltourisme@ sentoo.sn; Governance) also has a range of excellent tours; its two-day trips tracing the river valley from Saint-Louis over Podor to Bakel are particularly good (two days including accommodation CFA60,000). **Saint-Louis JV** (☎ 961 5152; www.saintlouisjv.com; Rue Abdoulaye Seck) has a more modest catalogue, with excellent trips around the Fouta Toro.

Below is a selection of tours run by most operators:

Broussarde (bush tour; around CFA20,000)
La Réserve de Guembeul (around CFA7000; 3hr)
Lac de Guiers (around CFA60,000; 1 day)
Mauritania (around CFA50,000; 1 day)
Parc National de la Langue de Barbarie (around CFA20,000)
Parc National des Oiseaux du Djoudj (around CFA25,000; 1 day)
Saint-Louis (around CFA5000-6000; 2-3hr) Guided tours are either done on foot or by horse-drawn cart.

We've found most of these tours to be excellent value; they include accommodation (if they are overnight trips), transport and entry fees. Some include also meals. Prices quoted are for a minimum of four people; independent travellers may be able to join a larger group.

THE BOU EL MOGDAD – SENEGAL'S CLASSIC CRUISE SHIP

It's hard to estimate how much the presence of the historic cruise liner *Bou El Mogdad* means to the communities living along the Senegal River. But the moved expressions on the faces of those who watched its glorious return in 2005 tell a story of fond reminiscence. Built in the 1950s, the boat chugged regularly up and down the river, connecting villages and facilitating trade. With the construction of the Maka Diama Dam in the mid-'80s it left the northern waters, but it didn't leave the mind of Jean-Jacques Bancal, head of Sahel Découverte Bassari travel agency, who had grown up in the region. He decided to bring the vessel back home. In November 2005, the boat returned in its former glory, and for the first time in decades, the classic Pont Faidherbe was creaked open, while onlookers watched with bated breath and sweaty palms, fearing for Saint-Louis' symbolic iron construction. Now back where it belongs, the boat does a leisurely cruise tour to the ancient town of Podor with stops at some of the river's most beautiful villages. See www.saheldecouverte.com and www.compagniedufleuve.com for details on the cruise.

FISHING & BOAT TOURS

Several hotels and *campements* (inns) offer fishing tours; the best-known, the **Saint-Louis Fishing Club** (☎ 961 1118; www.hotel-poste.com), is run by the Hôtel de la Poste. It offers surfcasting (full day CFA15,000) and angling (full day CFA120,000) excursions. Half-day tours are also available. The **Ranch de Bango** (Map p213; ☎ 961 1981; www.ranchdebango.com), 7km from Saint-Louis, is also good. **Catamaran Saint Louis** (☎ 561 2765; catamaransaintlouis@ yahoo.fr) offers one-day catamaran trips around the Langue de Barbarie (adults/children under eight CFA25,000/10,000) and other excursions leaving from Pont Faidherbe; phone to arrange a trip and staff'll pick you up at your hotel.

Sleeping

Saint-Louis offers accommodation for all budgets, of all types, and in any surrounding. You can either stay on the island in walking distance to all bars, restaurants and the town's historic architecture or move to the busy mainland for a touch of local ambience. The hotels on Langue de Barbarie Peninsula are clustered around Hydrobase, and all have easy access to the beach.

BUDGET
Mainland
Gîte Walo (☎ 961 4407; clem.mathieu@voila.fr; d from CFA10,000) You're bound to pass this place if heading for the centre of Saint-Louis on the way from Dakar, and might as well stop here. It offers an amazing bundle of little niceties for the amount you pay: a wide terrace, shaded courtyard and spacious, spotless rooms. You pay extra for a private bathroom.

Island
Auberge de Jeunesse (☎ 961 2409; pisdiallo@yahoo.fr; Rue Abdoulaye Seck; dm/d CFA5500/10,000) Yes, it's possible: a spotless, cheap, mosquito-netted, ventilated place to spend the night sleeping comfortably, having spent the evening chatting to the friendly host.

Café des Arts (☎ 961 6078; Rue de France; dm/d CFA4500/9000) Rooms are basic, but the family atmosphere of this colourful little place more than makes up for it. An excellent option for those on a peanut budget.

Auberge de la Vallée (☎ 961 4722; Av Blaise Diagne; dm/d CFA5000/10,000) An unspectacular place in the heart of the city, this isn't too bad for the price you pay, though it would be better if it were a touch cleaner.

Auberge l'Harmattan (☎ 961 8253; auberge harmattan@yahoo.fr; Rue Abdoulaye Seck; d/tr CFA15,000/ 20,000;) What started as a restaurant has expanded into this auberge (small hotel). Rooms in the historic building are enormous, but suffer slightly from neglect. The patio is a fine place to relax.

Langue de Barbarie
Hotel Dior (Map p213; ☎ 961 3118; fax 961 5784; www .hotel-dior.com; s CFA12,600-18,100, d CFA18,700-24,200) This is a good-value option at the Hydrobase. You can also camp here (per person CFA2500) and there are even tents for hire (fee and daily charge per person CFA3500).

MIDRANGE
Mainland
Hôtel Mame Coumba Bang (Map p213; ☎ 961 1850; www.hotelcoumba.com; s/d CFA28,000/35,000;) It's named after a water spirit and calls itself 'lover's wood' – the large swimming

---

THE AUTHOR'S CHOICE

La Louisiane (☎ 961 4221; www.aubergela louisiane.com; Point Nord; d/tr CFA18,400/24,300) This isn't Saint-Louis' prettiest place, nor its most prestigious address. But this peaceful little auberge doesn't have to fight for attention among the hotel royalty of Saint-Louis. With three top ingredients – simple, spacious rooms, a prime location overlooking the river and friendly management – it has carved out a solid reputation of its own: that of offering excellent value for money for travellers on slightly tighter budgets.

---

pool and the tranquil riverside garden explain the choice of names. It's 7km from town just off the road to Dakar. If you're really brave and ready to rise early, you can hike to Langue de Barbarie from here. Taxis from town charge from CFA500 to CFA1500 for the trip here.

Island

Sunu Keur (☎ 961 8800; chaffoisjeanjacques@yahoo.fr; Quai Giraud; s/d from CFA15,000/20,000) This calm guesthouse has beautifully decorated rooms overlooking the river in a carefully restored colonial building. The homely ambience is thrown in at no extra cost.

Hôtel de la Tour (☎ 961 6767; fax 961 6767; Rue Blanchot; s/d incl breakfast CFA20,100/28,200; ❸) This relatively new place consists of a maze of rooms that hide behind a humble entrance. Absolutely spotless, it tries its best to be upmarket, but is a little soulless. The oval TV lounge is pretty, though.

Hôtel Pointe Sud (☎ 961 5878; hotelpointesud@ yahoo.fr; Rue Ibrahim Sarr; d CFA28,000) This southern place has a polite living-room charm. Studios and suites have cooking facilities, and the rooftop bar-restaurant is the perfect place for breakfast (CFA2500).

Langue de Barbarie

All of the following hotels are based on the Hydrobase on Lange de Barbarie. Taxis from Saint-Louis charge CFA500 to take you there.

Hôtel Cap Saint-Louis (Map p213; ☎ 961 3909; www.hotelcapsaintlouis.com; s with/without bathroom CFA12,600/10,400, d with/without bathroom CFA32,200/ 14,800; ❿ ❸ ❷) What looks like another resort-type hotel is in fact a very *sympa* (and-

child-friendly) place run by four brothers. It's tastefully done up, sits right on the sea, and has one of the best swimming pools around. If you can afford it, forget about the cheap rooms and head straight for the sublime huts on the seafront. Large groups or families can rent five-bed bungalows (CFA43,400), where the privacy is so perfect you'll forget you're in a hotel.

Hôtel l'Oasis (Map p213; ☎ /fax 961 4232; http:// hoteloasis.free.fr; s/d CFA15,000/21,000; ❸ ❷) This simple and pretty place has long been a favourite with travellers – small, unpretentious huts are decked out in busy African prints and spotless bungalows house up to three people, though that leaves little breathing space.

Hôtel Mermoz (Map p213; ☎ 961 3668; www .hotelmermoz.com; s/d/tr from CFA13,000/18,000/23,000; ❸ ❷) This has more character than many of the large hotels. Huts and bungalows are spaced out in a large, sandy garden, and all buildings are connected by meandering, wheelchair-accessible paths. Larger rooms with bathroom and air-con cost about twice the minimum rate. It has free bikes for guest use, offers a range of seaside excursions and sports, and you can go horse riding at CFA5000 per hour. Stressed-out parents: there's a baby-sitting service available, and children don't pay if they share a room with their parents.

Résid Hôtel Diamarek (Map p213; ☎ 961 5781; www.hoteldiamarek.com; d from CFA22,000) It's another resort hotel clone, but a pretty one. Spacious, spotless bungalows sit in a sandy garden right next to the beach. Rates climb steeply over Christmas.

TOP END
Island

La Maison Rose (☎ 938 2222; www.lamaisonrose .net; Av Blaise Diagne; s/d from CFA45,000/55,000, ste from CFA77,500) As far as uniqueness and style go, this palatial address beats them all. The house is one of Saint-Louis' most famous old buildings, and one of the few that has been decorated with love and taste. Every room and suite is unique, though all exude old-time comfort. The classic furniture and wonderful art works are all part of the extensive collections of the daughter of Senegal's former president, who owns the place.

Hotel Sindone (☎ 961 4244; www.hotelsindone.com; Quai Henri Jay; s/d from CFA26,500/29,300; ❸) A faint rose-'n'-fluffy honeymoon feel scents the air of this stylish and airy hotel on the island's south side. Half the rooms have stunning views over the river, for which you'll pay about CFA3000 extra.

Hôtel de la Résidence (☎ 961 1260; hotresid@sentoo .sn; Av Blaise Diagne; s/d CFA27,600/34,200; 🏊) This is one of Saint-Louis' oldest hotels, and the owners (an established Saint-Louisian family who've been here at least as long as the hotel) have done a great job of evoking that sense of history. Every item and picture in the patio-style restaurant has a meaningful link to Saint-Louis' colourful past (ask and you'll get the explanations). Rooms are pretty and comfortable, and the restaurant is one of the town's very best. Bikes are available for hire, and parents rejoice – there's even a baby-sitting service. Book ahead, as the place is usually packed.

Hôtel de la Poste (☎ 961 1118; www.hotel-poste .com; Rue du Général de Gaulle; s/d/tr CFA30,000/36,000/ 43,000; 🏊) Another Saint-Louis classic; from the 1850s, Saint-Louis' oldest hotel was the historical point of call for the pilots of the colonial air-mail service. Celebrated pilot Jean Mermoz used to stay in room 219 – and the numerous images on the wall won't let you forget that. The hotel's Safari Bar is full of colonial flashbacks, balding animal heads and all. Up to you to decide if historical surrounds are something worth spending your hard-earned cash on.

Eating

There's a growing choice of good restaurants in Saint-Louis. Most hotels also do food – the Hôtel de Résidence leads the pack with a menu that leaves you spoilt for choice.

BUDGET

La Linguère (☎ 961 3949; Av Blaise Diagne; meals around CFA2000) The shoddy interior of the place doesn't do the food served here any justice at all. It's one of the best places in town for generous platters of Senegalese food – the yassa poulet (grilled chicken in an onion-and-lemon sauce) is almost unbeatable.

Pointe Nord (☎ 961 4221; Av Jean Mermoz; dishes from CFA1500; ⏰ 11am-9pm) This humble eatery on the northern tip of the island gets often overlooked. But that's just due to location, rather than food; you can eat an amazing grilled fish here for a fraction of the cost the more established restaurants charge.

For fast food, try one of the *shwarma* (grilled meat and salad in pita bread) joints on and near Av Blaise Diagne. They all serve pretty standard fare, but it does the job.

Self-caterers will save money and have more fun shopping in the market just north of Pont Mustapha Malick Gaye in Guet N'Dar. For European goods and French wine, head for the **Libre-Service** (Av Blaise Diagne) or the **Ecomarché** (Av Blaise Diagne).

MIDRANGE & TOP END

Aux Délices du Fleuve (☎ 961 4251; Quai Roume; pastries around CFA500; ⏰ lunch & dinner) Saint-Louis' famous patisserie serves delicious pastries, ice creams and milky coffees.

La Saigonnaise (☎ 961 6481; Rue Abdoulaye Seck; mains CFA5000; ⏰ noon-midnight) For a taste of Asia, this Vietnamese restaurant at the north end of Rue Abdoulaye Seck complements its great location (looking to Mauritania) with traditional and very tasty Saigonnaise fare (the owner and the chef are from Saigon). Prices are a little hefty.

Coup de Torchon (☎ 518 5408; Ave Blaise Diagne. meals CFA3500-5000; ⏰ 11am-1am) This friendly little restaurant is the perfect place to spend long evenings chatting over huge plates of food. It has live music on Thursdays.

Also recommended:

Fleuve Plus (☎ 961 4152; Rue Blaise Diagne; meals around CFA1500-2000; ⏰ lunch & dinner)

Bou El Mogdad (☎ 961 3611; Quai Rome; meals around CFA3000-5000; ⏰ lunch & dinner)

Restaurant Galaxie (☎ 961 2468; Rue Abdoulaye Seck; meals around CFA2000-4000; ⏰ lunch & dinner)

NORTHERN SENEGAL

Drinking & Entertainment

Saint-Louis has a fine selection of bars, pubs and live-music clubs.

Le Laser (☎ 961 5398; www.casinolaser.com; admission from CFA2000; ☺ 7pm-3am Wed-Sun) For a taste of how Senegal's bright young things let their hair down, head here, part of the Saint-Louis Casino complex on the Quai Roume.

Marco Jazz (☎ 654 2442; Quai Roume) A little north of Pont Faidherbe, this intimate venue is where big jazz names tend to give impromptu concerts during the jazz festival.

La Chaumière (%961 1980; Pointe à Pitre, Guet N'Dar) In Guet N'Dar, this is the nightclub that attracts the most stylish local crowd. It's a place where you'll see more sweat and less make-up. Admission varies.

Flamingo (☎ 961 1118; Quai de Roume) Part of the Hôtel de la Poste empire, this classy restaurant turns into an upmarket bar at night, and frequently has good live bands playing on a small stage near the swimming pool.

Quai des Arts & VIP Nightclub (☎ 961 5656; Av Jean Mermoz) This is where the main action happens during the jazz festival. The rest of the year the place stays fairly calm, though the nightclub attracts a stylish crowd.

Also recommended:

L'Embuscade (☎ 961 7741; Rue Blanchot) Popular beer and tapas place.

Iguane Café (☎ 558 0879; Rue Abdoulaye Seck) Cuba-themed bar.

Le Papayer (Map p213; ☎ 961 8687; Carrefour de l'Hydrobase; ☺ noon-midnight) The best club on the Langue de Barbarie.

Shopping

Sono Mondiale (☎ 577 3076; Rue Flamand; ☺ 8.30am-1pm & 3-8.30pm) This brilliant little shop has a better selection than some of the music shops in Dakar. It has a good variety of African (and not only Senegalese) music on offer – both on CD and cassette – and, oddly, a quirky vinyl collection of old salsa.

Ateliers d'Art (Rue Flamand) In the same building as Sono Mondiale, this is a great place to rummage for fabrics. You can even watch the weavers working on the gigantic, patterned cotton-rugs on sale here – and seeing the work that's involved in making them almost makes you willing to pay the steep prices charged for them.

Keur Fall (☎ 961 6238; keurfall@yahoo.fr; Quai Rome; ☺ 9am-1pm & 3-8pm) On a nicely brushed-up ground floor of one of the old buildings,

Keur Fall sells a wide range of pretty children's and adult clothes, shoes and toys – all made by women in a nearby village and sold under fairtrade conditions.

Getting There & Away

AIR

Saint-Louis has its own airport, 7km out of town (Map p213); a hire taxi from there into Saint-Louis costs around CFA5000. Air Sénégal operates a regular flight from Saint-Louis, which connects to Paris and Dakar every Wednesday. You can book directly, or through Sahel Découverte Bassari (p205). **Air Saint Louis** (☎ 644 8629; www.airsaintlouis.com) can fly you from Dakar at your request.

TAXI

The *gare routière* (bus and bush-taxi station) sits on the mainland at 4.5km from town, south of the Pont Faidherbe. A taxi from here to the city centre on the island costs CFA500. The fare to or from Dakar is CFA3500 by seven-seat *sept-place* taxi.

The Saint-Louis–Richard Toll trip by *sept-place* taxi costs CFA1600. A *sept-place* taxi to Gandiol, from where boats to the Parc National de la Langue de Barbarie leave, costs CFA500.

TRAIN

There is a train station just south of Pont Faidherbe, but despite being World Heritage listed, it's closed and in serious need of repair. Train services between Saint-Louis and Dakar have been suspended.

Getting Around

BICYCLE

Saint-Louis and its surroundings are good biking areas. **Le Routard** (☎ 608 9444; Quai de Roume) opposite the Flamingo hires VTTs (Vélo Tout Terrain or mountain bikes) for CFA5000 per day. Most are in good condition, and child seats are available. Otherwise, several hotels have also bikes for hire.

TAXI

Taxi prices in Saint-Louis are fixed (CFA350 at the time of writing), so there's no need to negotiate for trips around the city. Prices to any destination in the surroundings depend on your negotiating skills. You can either hire private taxis at the *gare routière*, or stop any driver in town and negotiate.

AROUND SAINT-LOUIS
Bango
pop around 2000

Bango is a tiny village north of Saint-Louis, mainly known to travellers for being home to the popular **Ranch de Bango** (Map p213; ☎ 961 1981; www.ranchdebango.com; s/d/tr CFA30,600/ 32,200/35,800; 🚫 🔲). This spacious *campement* sits where the town's urban atmosphere has given way to village tranquillity. Accommodation is in tastefully decorated bungalows set in a large, tropical garden. Activities on offer include pirogue river excursions and fishing.

Based on the Île Thiolette near Bango and the airport, **Vent Tropical** (Map p213; ☎ 575 7600; info@vent-tropical.com) is the best address for windsurfing, kite-surfing and kayak tours.

Gandiol & Mouit
pop around 2300

Gandiol is a small village on the mainland, about 18km south of Saint-Louis. During the rainy season large areas of the surrounding flat landscape are covered by shallow seawater lagoons. In the dry season, the waters recede to leave pans of white mud and salt.

The lighthouse just before Gandiol is the place you want to remember; from there, pirogues cross to the two *campements* on the southern end of the Langue de Barbarie, and it is also the starting point for organised boat tours of the Parc National de la Langue de Barbarie (some boats also leave from the village). If you stay in Saint-Louis, you're probably best off relying on tours of the park organised by the Syndicat d'Initiative (p205) or Sahel Découverte Bassari (p205) – it's quite a trek out here by taxi, and negotiating boats and taxis yourself is unlikely to get you a better rate than the official ones offered.

About 2km south of Gandiol is the smaller village of Mouit, where you will find the national park headquarters. Another 500m further, on the edge of the river, is **Zebrabar** (Map p213; ☎ 638 1862; www.come.to /zebrabar; camping per person CFA2500, s CFA4000-15,000, d CFA7000-18,000), an excellent *campement* in a secluded spot – perfect for excursions into Parc National de la Langue de Barbarie. Accommodation is available in simple huts (and even the cut-off cabin of an old truck) and spacious bungalows. The *campement* sits on a large lot and is a great place to stay

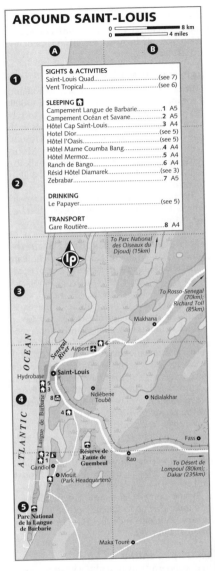

AROUND SAINT-LOUIS

0 — 8 km
0 — 4 miles

SIGHTS & ACTIVITIES
Saint-Louis Quad	(see 7)
Vent Tropical	(see 6)

SLEEPING 🛏
Campement Langue de Barbarie	1 A5
Campement Océan et Savane	2 A5
Hôtel Cap Saint-Louis	3 A4
Hotel Dior	(see 5)
Hôtel l'Oasis	(see 5)
Hôtel Mame Coumba Bang	4 A4
Hôtel Mermoz	5 A4
Ranch de Bango	6 A4
Résid Hôtel Diamarek	(see 3)
Zebrabar	7 A5

DRINKING
Le Papayer	(see 5)

TRANSPORT
Gare Routière	8 A4

with children – there's a miniplayground and plenty of space for little explorers, and the friendly Swiss couple that runs the place makes families feel very welcome indeed. Zebrabar also has kayaks and canoes for hire (free for overnight guests) and can arrange canoe tours and bird-watching excursions with the local fishermen (CFA2500 per person). If you make contact before arrival, they can collect you from Saint-Louis, and drop you off in town for city visits or on departure.

GETTING THERE & AWAY

Hiring a taxi from Saint-Louis to Mouit and Zebrabar should cost you around CFA3000. If you have a lot of time, you can also rely on the bush taxis that run a few times each day from Saint-Louis to Gandiol (CFA500). Sometimes this taxi continues to Mouit (CFA700), otherwise you'll have to walk the last 2km from Gandiol to Mouit and 2.5km to Zebrabar.

If you're driving, turn off the tar road where it swings a sharp right (west) just before Mouit.

Parc National de la Langue de Barbarie

Some 25km south of Saint-Louis, the **Parc National de la Langue de Barbarie** (Map p213; admission CFA2000; pirogue for 1 or 2 people CFA7500, each extra person CFA2500; ☺ 7am-7pm). It includes the far southern tip of the Langue de Barbarie Peninsula, the estuary of the Senegal River (which contains two small islands) and a section of the mainland on the other side of the estuary. The park covers a total area of 2000 hectares, and is home to numerous sea birds and waders – notably flamingos, pelicans, cormorants, herons, egrets and ducks. From November to April bird numbers are swelled by the arrival of migrants from Europe.

You can walk on the sandy peninsula of the Langue, but to explore the whole park and bird-watch you'll need to take a pirogue, which can cruise slowly past the mud flats, inlets and islands where they feed, roost and nest.

If you come to the park independently, you must first go to the park office at Mouit to pay your entrance fee. Pirogues can be hired at the river.

SLEEPING & EATING

In a wonderful position at the southern end of the Langue de Barbarie, about 20km from the Saint-Louis and across the river from Gandiol, are two *campements*. The first, **Campement Langue de Barbarie** (Map p213; ☎ 961 1118; s/d CFA10,000/15,000, half board CFA27,000) is by Hôtel de la Poste. Most people take the half-board option, otherwise breakfast is CFA2000 and meals à la carte cost CFA5000.

Relaxed **Campement Océan et Savane** (Map p213; ☎ 637 4790; r per person CFA6600, half/full board CFA15,200/21,200) is run by Hôtel de la Résidence and has plenty of character. You can stay in low-roofed Mauritanian-style bungalows or, if you want more comfort, in pretty log cabins that house one to five people (CFA30,000) and sit on stilts on the river. The place has electricity, warm water, and a fine restaurant under a huge Mauritanian tent that alone is worth a visit (meals cost CFA6000).

Both places offer boat transfers and opportunities for fishing and windsurfing, kayaking and bird-watching. You can either make a reservation through the appropriate hotel in Saint-Louis, or get directly in touch with the *campement*.

GETTING THERE & AWAY

A taxi from Saint-Louis to the park entrance costs around CFA7000. Once there the usual approach is by pirogue from the mainland, normally from the lighthouse north of Gandiol or Mouit. Organised tours (p208) from Saint-Louis are an option.

Désert de Lompoul

West of Kébémer, Lompoul surprises with the kind of landscape more commonly associated with Mauritania or northern Mali. Huge sand dunes stretch from the coast far into the country's interior.

The enterprising Tourisme Plus Afrique (TPA) agency has established an impressive *campement* in the heart of the dunes. **Le Lodge de Lompoul** (☎ 644 9194; 957 1256; www.lesenegal .info; s/d half board CFA21,000/37,000) offers accommodation in desert-suited Mauritanian tents, with large, comfortable, mosquito net–sheltered mattresses and outdoor toilets. As with all TPA camps, all activities including camel tours, picnics in the dunes and pick-up from Lompoul village are included.

Most people get here by organised tour from Saint-Louis (see p208). If you're in your own car or hire taxi, take the route from Saint-Louis to Dakar, turn off at Kébémer and follow the smooth road to Lompoul village, from where *campement* staff can pick you up in 4WDs.

Parc National des Oiseaux du Djoudj

On a great bend in the Senegal River, this 16,000-hectare **park** (☎ 968 8708; admission CFA2000, plus pirogue CFA3500; ☺ 7am-dusk) is 60km north of Saint-Louis. It incorporates a stretch of the main river with its numerous channels, creeks, lakes, ponds, marshes, reed beds and mud flats, as well as surrounding areas of woodland savannah. This, along with the fact that it's one of the first places with permanent water south of the Sahara, means that a great many bird species are attracted here, making it the third-most important bird sanctuary worldwide (see below for bird-watching tips). It is a Unesco World Heritage site, and the wetlands have been listed as a Ramsar (the international wetland conservation convention) site.

Even if you're not a keen ornithologist, it's hard to escape the impact of seeing vast colonies of pelicans and flamingos in such stunning surroundings. Experienced bird-watchers will recognise many of the European species, and the sheer numbers that assemble here are impressive indeed. Around three million birds pass through the park annually, and more than 350 separate species have been recorded here.

There are also a few mammals and reptiles in the park, most notably populations of warthogs and mongooses, serpents and crocodiles (you're unlikely to spot the latter though). Other mammals include jackals, hyenas, monkeys and gazelles.

Trips around the park are best done by pirogue. The park is officially open from 1 November to 30 April, though the best time for bird-watching is from December to January. During those months you'll be greeted by vast colonies of birds before you've even entered your boat.

SLEEPING

Hôtel du Djoudj (☎ 963 8702; fax 963 8703; huts d/tr CFA15,000/20,000, d/tr CFA27,000/34,500; ◷ rooms only 1 Nov-31 May; ⊠) This friendly, grand place sits near the park headquarters and main entrance. Rooms are comfortable and staff could hardly be friendlier or more helpful. The swimming pool is open to nonguests who eat at the hotel. You can arrange boat rides around the park (adults/children over two CFA3500/2500) and hire bicycles (half-/full day CFA3000/6000).

Station Biologique (☎ 968 8708; dpnsbpnod@sentoo.sn; full board per person CFA15,000) Situated at the park headquarters and main entrance, this low-key camp with clean rooms is mainly intended for research groups and students, though tourists can be accommodated if spaces are available. Camping is allowed.

Campement le Njagabaar (☎ 963 8708; s/d CFA10,000/13,000) In the village, close to the park entrance, this *campement* is a decent alternative for those who find the rates at the Hôtel du Djoudj a little too steep. It only has a handful of rooms though, and might well get filled up during the main tourist season.

GETTING THERE & AWAY

There's no public transport to Djoudj, so you have to negotiate your own private taxi. Expect to pay around CFA20,000. You're likely to be better off on an organised tour (see p208). If you're driving from Saint-Louis, take the paved highway towards Rosso for about 25km. Near Ross-Béthio you'll see a sign pointing to the park, from where it's another 25km along a dirt road.

TWITCHER TIPS: TOURING THE PARC NATIONAL DES OISEAUX DU DJOUDJ

The Parc National des Oiseaux du Djoudj is a protected and internationally renowned bird sanctuary, and bird-watchers flock to the protected area to observe spur-winged geese, purple herons, egrets, spoonbills, jaçanas, cormorants, harriers and a multitude of European migrants that settle here during November to April. The park is most famous for its impressive flocks of pelicans and flamingos, and all tours offered by agencies, hotels and guides focus on these birds.

Tours usually leave Saint-Louis at 7am to reach the park by 8.30am. They start with a two-hour boat ride through the creeks, the highlight and sole purpose of which is to get a view of the enormous pelican colony. After lunch you drive to see flamingo flocks on the lake's edge.

You'll be able to spot other species, no doubt, but if it's the rarer varieties you're after, a tourist trip might not be satisfying. Keen bird-watchers are better off coming with their own guide or contacting the **Station Biologique** (☎ 542 4472; dpnsbpnod@sentoo.sn) and explaining their interest to park director Ablaye Diop or the head of the station, Assane Ndoye, who should be able to put you in touch with a trained ornithological guide, and will have up-to-date research findings about the park.

NORTHERN SENEGAL

SENEGAL RIVER ROUTE

From Saint-Louis, the urban heart of French expansion, the route along the valley of the Senegal River reveals the French conquest of the interior, as well the signs of its opposition – a string of mid-19th-century forts in Dagana, Podor, Matam and Bakel, some in near-complete ruins, others in the early stages of restoration.

The French fortifications were military and administrative centres, around which busy trading towns developed. But their primary purpose was to serve as battle stations in the clashes with the army of El Hajj Omar Tall, who put up fierce resistance to the colonial efforts.

Tall had plenty to defend. His Islamic empire reached across West Africa to Timbuktu (in today's Mali) at its height. Omarian mosques in the river region (notably in Alwar) date from the second half of the 18th century, and still seem to oppose the French forts in a silent, architectural battle.

Where other areas in Senegal lure visitors with lush vegetation and rich wildlife, the hot and arid north is all about history and cultural pride. One of the most fascinating things to do here is to visit the small, sand-blown Tukulor villages spread across the Fouta Toro region. Smooth, earthen *banco* houses seem to rise naturally from the soil, and would blend almost completely with their desert surroundings were it not for the local Tukulor custom of decorating the outer walls in bold stripes of red, brown and yellow.

ROSSO-SENEGAL
pop around 10,000

The fly-blown frontier town of Rosso-Senegal is around 100km northeast of Saint-Louis on the Senegal River, where a ferry crosses to Rosso-Mauritania. In January 2006, it was announced that a bridge is to be constructed to replace the ferry service, yet so far the twice daily boat is the main connection between the two countries. It's also about the only reason you might want to visit Rosso.

If you get stuck, your only choice of accommodation is **Auberge du Walo** (d CFA10,000), 2km from the ferry. Basic double huts come with bathroom, and the restaurant can prepare meals on order.

The journey from Rosso-Senegal to Dakar costs CFA5100 by *sept-place* taxi, to Saint-Louis the fare is CFA1900. A local bush taxi to Richard Toll costs CFA500. For information on crossing the border see p286.

RICHARD TOLL
pop around 70,000

About 20km by road from Rosso is the town of Richard Toll, once a colonial administrative centre. It was home to an agricultural experiment by the French, who tested the tropical adaptability of European plants (hence the name Richard Toll, meaning 'Richard's Garden'). Today, it's the centre of Senegal's sugar industry. You'll pass great cane plantations as you come into town from the west, and, if you're tempted, might be able to arrange a visit to the local sugarcane factory.

The CBAO and BCIS banks have branches here; both are equipped with Visa-friendly ATMs. There's also a Western Union office and several Internet cafés (CFA300 per hour) All of these places are located in the centre, along the main road.

Thanks to the agricultural activity of the area, the region around Richard Toll is irrigated and is a welcoming spot of green amid arid lands. Tours around town in *calèches* (horse-drawn cart), which function as taxis here, are an entertaining way of taking in the ambience.

If you stay overnight, an evening stroll to the **Château de Baron Roger** (see the boxed text, opposite) at the eastern end of town, across the bridge, whiles away an hour or two.

Richard Toll is reasonably well served for accommodation. The cheapest and most basic option is the **Auberge de la Cité** (☎ 641 7581; r CFA10,600) on the main road near the entry to town. The **Hotel la Taouey** (☎ 531 4010; s/d CFA13,600/16,800; ⓟ 🏊) on the river, north of the main street, is slightly better. Rooms are adequate, though a little bare; the management is very helpful; and the bar a great place for a peaceful drink. The **Gîte d'Étape** (☎ /fax 963 3240; s/d CFA25,400/28,800; 🏊 📶), down a dirt road opposite the *gare* (station), is surprisingly well appointed.

For food, **Hotel la Taouey** (meals around CFA3000; ☼ lunch & dinner) is your best option – call in advance; Gîte d'Étape disappoints for what you pay. Otherwise, it's down to the *gargottes* (local eating houses) along the main road.

PODOR & ÎLE À MORPHIL

The ancient town of Podor (population around 7500), once the heart of the ancient kingdom of Tekrour, has been a busy trading centre since the first encounters between Arabs and the Tukulor of Fouta Toro. It's home to an ancient fort, first built in 1744, then reconstructed by Louis Faidherbe in 1854, who hoped to turn Podor into another strategic northern settlement inland from Saint-Louis. A chain of colonial warehouses along the riverfront also bears witness to the era. When we visited, restoration works had just begun at the ancient fort, which should turn the large ruin into quite an impressive sight. There are also plans for a museum here.

Podor is the gateway to excursions to the historic sites of the Île à Morphil (population around 6000, p218) and Wouro Madiyou, home to the unique, mosaic-ornamented brick mausoleum of Cheikh Ahmadou Madiyou (a celebrated contemporary of El Hajj Omar Tall). Only a short drive from Podor, the inhabitants of picturesque *banco* villages such as Ngawlé might invite you for couscous and milk if you arrive showing due respect – ask to greet the head of the village first, explaining what brought you. Learning (and using) a couple of basic Fula greetings will earn you lots of kudos.

Festivals & Events

The Festival du Fleuve is the brainchild of famous singer Baaba Maal, who created it to draw attention to the rich musical heritage and contemporary creations of his home region, the Fouta Toro. Launched in 2006, it's held annually in early March.

Sleeping & Eating

All the places listed below are in Podor.

Maison de la Femme (☎ 965 1234; r 5000) Mme Diop, Mme Barry and the women's collective who run this tiny guesthouse will make you feel truly at home and help you around the region. It's *the* place to stay in town. Ask locals for directions here.

Gîte d'Étape (☎ 965 1642; d incl breakfast CFA6600) Opposite the *gare routière*, this is the only 'proper' guesthouse in Podor. It's owned by the famous musician Baaba Maal who hails from Podor, but unfortunately is not as refined as his singing. The restaurant serves excellent Senegalese food (meals around

---

LA FOLIE DE BARON ROGER

The crumbling facade of the imposing Château de Baron Roger gives a glimpse into the most ambitious periods of French colonialism. Baron Jacques Roger was the governor of Senegal from 1822 to 1827, and built this private palace as his week-end retreat on the banks of the Taouey River, some 100km upstream from the busy colonial capital Saint-Louis. The symmetrical construction was once surrounded by an ornamental park (it's now more like a jungle), which was created by Claude Richard – the man who is responsible for the town's name. When Richard wasn't looking after the introduction of the groundnut to the region, he devoted some time to growing European ornamental plants around the governor's royal home.

The chateau was later inhabited by Baron Roger's successor, Louis Faidherbe, and was at some stage used as a monastery and school. Today it stands as a ruin, and a monument to colonial aspiration.

CFA 3000; you have to order in advance), and the staff is fantastic.

Catholic Mission (Av El Hajj Omar Tall; r CFA5000) The mission has a couple of dusty rooms for stranded tourists. Bring a few beers or a good bottle of red wine, and the talkative Père Mohiss will bless you with his kindness.

If it's nightlife you're after, you're in the wrong place. But for a cold beer and some local contact try the bar-disco Monaco Fleuve right on the river behind the Catholic Mission, or head for the Gîte d'Étape.

Getting There & Away

Sept-place taxis travel fairly regularly between Podor and Saint-Louis (CFA3000, four hours, 262km) sometimes continuing all the way to Dakar (CFA3500). If you're heading west, a *sept-place* taxi to Ouro Sogui (CFA4500, five hours, 222km) is best; a minibus costs CFA2500 but takes twice as long. Hiring a taxi from Saint-Louis to Podor can cost up to CFA40,000.

MATAM & OURO SOGUI

The 230km from Podor to Ouro Sogui lead through the dry, flat lands of Fouta Toro, where acacia trees are about the only vegetation. Matam is another 11km drive from Ouro Sogui along a causeway lined either side with plains and marshes. Matam (population around 11,000) is the administrative centre, yet it has strongly declined in importance and several of its ancient buildings have been gnawed on by frequent flooding, while Ouro Sogui (population around 9000) has grown from an insignificant village into a busy trading centre and transport hub for the Ferlo plains.

Ouro Sogui has two banks with ATMs (don't rely too much on them), a hospital, post office and an aerodrome. Matam has a waterfront lined with several colonial warehouses – testimony of busy days gone by.

In Ouro Sogui, the cheapest accommodation is the **Auberge Sogui** (☎ 966 1198; s/d CFA8500/10,000;) opposite the market, which has just-passable rooms, though the shared bathrooms are grubby. Don't confuse this with the **Hotel Auberge Sogui** (☎ 966 1536; cobasse@hotmail.com; s/d/tr CFA15,000/18,000/21,000;), a huge white monolith that's not as grand as first impressions make you believe. Your best choice here is the **Oasis du Fouta** (☎ 966 1294; seftop@hotmail.com; s/d incl breakfast CFA13,500/15,000;), which has comfortable rooms with TV, an Internet café and a staff that tries to accommodate your every excursion wish, from pirogue journeys to trips into the mountains where El Hajj Omar Tall once battled French forces.

Food outside your hotel is pretty much limited to the cheap eateries and *dibiteries* (grilled-meat stalls) spread across town. The best of these is probably Le Teddungal, where grilled lamb skewers only cost a handful of CFA.

Ouro Sogui's *gare routière* is on the northern side of town, on the road towards Matam. Battered *sept-place* taxis run to Dakar (CFA10,500) and Bakel (CFA2000, two hours, 148km).

On the map of Senegal a road leads from Ouro Sogui southwards across the Ferlo plains to Linguère. At the time of research, this was still one of the country's worst roads, only feasible to take on in a sturdy 4WD. Roadwork along this tired stretch of dusty track was announced, and might well be underway by the time you visit.

BAKEL
pop around 9800

Peacefully perched among a scattering of rocky hills, Bakel is a picturesque spot. Any traveller persistent enough to follow the northern road to this tucked-away village is rewarded with the sight of the most beautiful place along the River Senegal.

Like all the northern towns it's hot, dry and sandy, but it's prettier than most. Its colonial architecture blossomed from the profits of the rubber and peanut trade and is still intact. Its 1854 **fort**, another ambitious Faidherbe endeavour, is well maintained and now houses the local government.

Bakel's second obligatory sight is the **Pavillon René Caillé**, once temporary home to the famous French explorer. It sits on top of a hill from where you get great views over Bakel's old town.

Sleeping & Eating

Bakel sits off any tourist trail, which means that no-one has endeavoured to place any decent sort of accommodation here.

ÎLE À MORPHIL

Between the main Senegal River and a major channel that runs parallel to it for over 100km, Île à Morphil is a long, thin island with Podor at its western end. About 2km after the bridge on the road into town, a dirt road turns off right (east), and a signpost indicates distances to a string of villages along Île à Morphil, all the way to Saldé at its eastern end. From Saldé a ferry crosses over to Ngoui on the mainland, from where you can reach Pete, on the main road.

This is one of the most fascinating areas of the north, with small routes that wind through the dry land and around beautiful banco villages. Guédé, the ancient capital of Fouta Toro, is found here; it has a refined Omarian mosque. The oldest mosque in the area is further east in Alwar, the birthplace of El Hajj Omar Tall. It's amazing to think that the historic leader used to pray in this 18th-century building.

When visiting any of the tiny villages, remember to show respect to the local residents and, if possible, pay a visit to the *chef de village* (village chief).

Hôtel Islam (r per person CFA10,000; ❄) About 500m east of the *gare routière*, this barely held-together place is about your only choice. It has spartan rooms, and not very inviting shared toilets.

For food, it's a trip to the market for fresh produce, or ready-made sandwiches and skewered meat at the *gargottes* next door.

Getting There & Away

If you come from Ouro Sogui on a vehicle bound for Kidira you might be dropped off at the junction 5km south of Bakel, from where local bush taxis shuttle into town. A minibus goes daily (except Fridays) from Bakel to Tambacounda (CFA3500, four hours, 184km) via Kidira (CFA1500, one hour, 60km). Be there early, or you won't get a seat.

KIDIRA

pop around 6000

The main crossing point between Senegal and Mali is the border town of Kidira, where the main road and the railway between Dakar and Bamako cross the Falene River into Mali. Crossing here is quite a task whether you come by train, which is unreliable, or by road, which has been severely washed out on the Malian side. For more details see p286.

Eastern Senegal

It takes some courage to brave the seemingly endless stretch of potholed tarred road that connects Dakar to Tambacounda in the east, but the road that leads through flat savannah lands specked with shrubs and baobabs takes you to one of Senegal's best-kept secrets – the hilly Bassari lands of the southeast. With its craggy mountain plateaus, tucked-away waterfalls and lush forests, this region forms a striking contrast to the even plains that stretch throughout the rest of the country. And the region differs not only in its landscape, but also in its cultural make-up. Among the hills nestle tiny Bassari, Bédik and Fula villages – remote hamlets that adhere strongly to traditional lifestyles and are best visited with a knowledgeable guide. These communities are particularly known for their stunning initiation ceremonies, and with a bit of luck and a good local introduction, you might be lucky enough to watch this colourful display of masked dances.

Eastern Senegal is also home to Senegal's main wildlife reserve, the gigantic Parc National de Niokolo-Koba. It's one of the few parks in West Africa featuring lions, elephants and plenty of other large mammals, though your chances of spotting them are rather slim. You're almost more likely to come across a dozing lion on an early-morning drive through the park than on an organised tour. Bird-watchers are bound to find a trip here rewarding – there are enough spectacular species to see that even reluctant birders will soon be wielding binoculars and scanning treetops for shimmering tail feathers.

HIGHLIGHTS

- Go lion-spotting in the **Parc National de Niokolo-Koba** (p223), Senegal's largest protected reserve
- Cool off under the deep drop of the **Dindefelo** (p227) waterfall
- Go for solitary hikes around the forests of the **Bassari country** (p227) and visit tiny, half-hidden Bédik villages

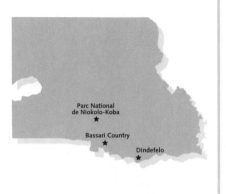

Parc National
de Niokolo-Koba
★

Bassari Country
★

Dindefelo
★

- POPULATION: 800,000

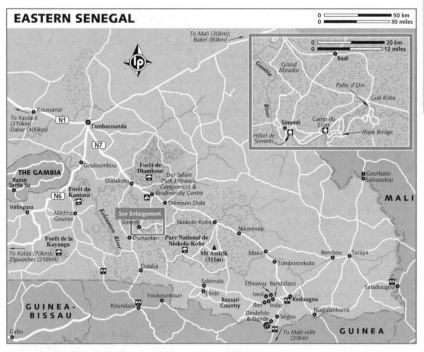

TAMBACOUNDA

The eastern town of Tambacounda, or 'Tamba', as the locals affectionately call it, is all about dust, sand, sizzling temperatures and lines of traffic heading out in every direction of the country. Tamba is a major junction of routes leading eastwards to Mali, south to Guinea, west to Dakar and Gambia, and southwest to Ziguinchor. The hectic heat of the permanent loading and unloading of taxis, coming and going of people, the shouting and deal-making, joyful greeting and tearful leaving is worth taking in for a day or so. Apart from that, there's little to see here, unless you've got a penchant for old, colonial railway stations, and once-grand villas and their expansive gardens.

Orientation & Information

The town has two main streets: Blvd Demba Diop runs east–west, parallel with the train tracks, while Av Léopold Senghor runs north–south. The latter has shops, an Internet café, a well-stocked pharmacy and a SGBS bank, which can exchange cash and give advances on credit cards. In the north of town, there's the busy market, a great place to rummage for Malian batiks, and the post office.

The Syndicat d'Initiative isn't particularly active here, but it does have a local representative at **Hôtel Niji** (☎ 981 1250; nijihotel@sentoo .sn; quartier abattoirs), near the pharmacy, who can help out with information about the region. Staff at the **Headquarters of Parc National de Niokolo-Koba** (☎ 981 1097; ☼ 7.30am-5pm) can help with inquiries about the park, and they also have 4WDs for hire.

Sleeping

Most places also run tours to the Parc National de Niokolo-Koba (see p224).

Bloc Gadec (☎ 531 8931; d, q per person CFA3000) Not bad at all for a budget place, this friendly little hostel in the centre of town near the *gare routière* (bus and bush-taxi station) has spacious, clean rooms with shared toilets.

Hôtel Keur Khoudia (☎ /fax 981 1102; Blvd Demba Diop; s/d CFA11,700/16,000; ❄) With spotless bungalows at decent prices and helpful management, this popular hotel is an excellent choice for those travelling on a budget.

The Hôtel de Simenti in Niokolo-Koba is run by the same family, so you're in perfect hands if you intend to visit the park.

Hôtel Niji (☎ 981 1250; nijihotel@sentoo.sn; s/d/tr CFA11,200/14,00/16,700; ✹) This well-known place has a rather basic main section that has seen better days. The adjacent Hôtel Niji Annexe, with thatch-roofed round houses in a shady garden compound, is a slightly better choice, and a more upmarket section was being built when we visited.

Le Relais de Tamba (☎ 981 1000; www.relaishorizons .net; Rte National; s/d/tr CFA22,200/27,200/36,600; P ✹ ✹) The Relais hotel chain has a reputation for classy simplicity, and this branch has all the niceties of their other places. For those who like a certain level of comfort, this hotel, 1km from Tamba, is the best option in town.

Oasis Oriental Club (☎ 981 1824; rgueguen@sentoo .sn; Rte National; s/d/tr CFA25,000/32,000/40,000; P ✹ ✹) They may not be cheap, but the large huts of this top-level *campement* (hostel) are welcoming. With tasteful, minimalist décor and inviting bathrooms they might just be worth paying slightly exaggerated rates for.

Also worth considering:

Complex Leggal Pont (☎ 981 1756; legalpont2003@ yahoo.fr; Blvd Demba Diop; s/d from CFA8800/10,200; ✹) Part of Tamba's main entertainment hub; the rooms are much nicer than the bleak corridors suggest. Weekend crowds mean the rooms at the back get noisy.

Hôtel Asta Kébé (☎ 981 1250; fax 981 1744; s/d CFA21,600/26,200; ✹ ✹) Once the best address in town, this place is now slightly neglected and hoping for better days.

Eating & Drinking

Tambacounda isn't exactly blessed with great culinary choices, but there are a number of decent *gargottes* (small, simple, local-style eating houses) and other cheap eateries in the centre of town.

Le Relais du Rais (dishes from CFA500; ✹ noon-2.30pm & 6-11pm) It may look unremarkable, but this little eatery serves excellent local dishes, including a mean *thiébouthienne* (Senegalese rice and fish dish), and generous plates of *yassa*.

Bar-Restaurant Chez Francis (☎ 643 1231; Av Léopold Senghor; meals around CFA4000; ✹ 11am-2am) Popular because of the hearty meals, and because it's got a reputation for attracting expats, this place has meals and cheap, ice-cold beer.

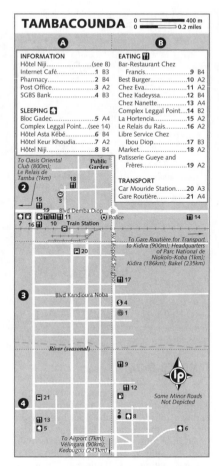

TAMBACOUNDA	0 — 400 m / 0 — 0.2 miles
A	**B**
INFORMATION	**EATING**
Hôtel Niji.........................(see 8)	Bar-Restaurant Chez
Internet Café.........................1 B3	Francis.......................9 B4
Pharmacy..............................2 B4	Best Burger.................10 A2
Post Office............................3 A2	Chez Eva....................11 A2
SGBS Bank............................4 B3	Chez Kadeyssa...........12 B4
	Chez Nanette..............13 A4
SLEEPING	Complex Leggal Point...14 B2
Bloc Gadec..........................5 A4	La Hortencia...............15 A2
Complex Leggal Point....(see 14)	Le Relais du Rais.........16 A2
Hôtel Asta Kébé..................6 B4	Libre Service Chez
Hôtel Keur Khoudia...........7 A2	Ibou Diop..................17 B3
Hôtel Niji............................8 B4	Market.......................18 A2
	Patisserie Gueye and
	Frères......................19 A2
	TRANSPORT
	Car Mouride Station......20 A3
	Gare Routière..............21 A4

Eating & Drinking

Tambacounda isn't exactly blessed with great culinary choices, but there are a number of decent *gargottes* (small, simple, local-style eating houses) and other cheap eateries in the centre of town.

Complex Leggal Pont (☎ 981 1756; Blvd Demba Diop; ✹ restaurant 8am-midnight, bar & nightclub 11pm-4am) This may be a slightly rundown version of an entertainment complex, but it's nevertheless very popular. The nightclub and bar attract crowds on weekends.

Best Burger (☎ 981 3203; Blvd Demba Diop; ✹ 9am-2am) A popular hangout for Tamba's youth, this places serves proper meals and pizzas as well as the biggest burgers ever encountered.

Self-caterers will find all the fruit, veg and bags of rice they need at the local market. In the centre of town, the **Libre Service Chez Ibou Diop** (Av Léopold Senghor) is not only a good place to find European foods, but also a good spot to meet and mingle in the evenings. The

Pâtisserie Guèye & Frères (Blvd Demba Diop), next to Best Burger, is the place to get your bread and croissants in the morning.

Also recommended:

Chez Eva (Blvd Demba Diop) One of several reasonable *gargottes* (basic eateries) on Blvd Demba Diop.

Chez Nanette (meals about CFA1500; ☺ 8am-midnight) Opposite the *gare routière*; serves local and international fare.

La Hortencia (Blvd Demba Diop) Does the best salads in town.

Getting Around

All taxi trips around town cost CFA300 – no need to bargain.

Getting There & Away

AIR

Tambacounda Airport is 8.5km out of town, on the road to Kedougou. A taxi from the airport should cost around CFA3000. In theory **Air Sénégal** (☎ info line 804 0404) flies from Dakar to Tambacounda (1¼ hours) twice every Saturday from November to March. Contact the airline first, though, as flights can be quite irregular.

BUS & BUSH TAXI

From the *gare routière* on the eastern side of town vehicles go to the Mali border at Kidira (CFA5000 by *sept-place* taxi, three hours; CFA3500 by minibus). Vehicles to most other destinations go from the *gare routière* on the southern side of town.

Vélingara is well served by minibuses (CFA1400) and *sept-place* taxis (CFA1650), as it's a popular place to cross into Gambia. A *sept-place* journey from Dakar to Tamba is CFA7500, or CFA5000 by Ndiaga Ndiaye. Tamba to Kedougou is CFA4800 by *sept-place,* or CFA3500 by Ndiaga Ndiaye; Tamba to Kaolack is CFA4000.

The *car mouride* (a long-distance bus service) leaves from outside the *car mouride* station (just south of the train station) daily at 4.30am for Dakar (CFA5000, eight hours). You have to reserve your place in advance at the office. There are also *cars mourides* from here to Kedougou (CFA3000, three hours) and Bakel (CFA3500, five hours).

TRAIN

The train between Dakar and Bamako (Mali) passes through Tambacounda twice a week – once in each direction (see p283) provided there hasn't been a derailment or other impediment. Normally, the eastbound train passes through on Wednesday and Saturday evening, but you always need to check at the station, as the service is notoriously unreliable. The ticket office opens a few hours before the train arrives, but tickets can be bought the day before. First/2nd-class fares from Tambacounda are CFA10,995/8060 to Kayes, CFA14,710/10,995 to Kita and CFA19,320/14,165 to Bamako.

PARC NATIONAL DE NIOKOLO-KOBA

The World Heritage site of Niokolo-Koba, a vast biosphere reserve spanning about 9000 sq km, is Senegal's major national park. The landscape is relatively flat, with plains, marshes and a few hills – the highest is Mt Assirik (311m) in the southeast. The vegetation is spectacularly varied, with savannah woodland and grassland, patches of bamboo and gallery forest along the rivers.

The Gambia River and its two tributaries, the Niokolo-Koba and the Koulountou, cross the vast wildeness and are crucial sources of water for the 80 species of mammals and 350 bird species that inhabit the park.

African classics such as lions live in the park, along with waterbucks, bushbucks, kobs, duikers, roan antelopes, giant derby elands, hartebeests, baboons, monkeys (green and patas), warthogs and buffaloes. Hippos and three types of crocodiles – the Nile, the slender-snouted and the dwarf – live in the rivers, and chimpanzee troops inhabit parts of the eastern and southern areas, though you'll be lucky to spot them.

Not all of Niokolo-Koba's enormous area is equally well maintained, and visitors to the more far-flung corners have reported woodcuttings and an eerie absence of wildlife. The best part for animal spotting is the area of Simenti.

If you take the Tambacounda–Kedougou route, you're likely to see monkeys, birds, porcupines and other animals crossing the road or lying on the tarred road – be careful if you're driving. Just before dawn, the road is particularly full of animals, and there's a good chance you might spot a lion stretching out on the roadside.

The park was neglected until the early 1990s, and poaching has also been a problem, but international funding for its development as part of the Parc Transfrontalier Niokolo-Badiar transnational ecosystem (which includes areas in neighbouring Guinea) has improved the situation slightly. Several NGOs are also working directly with the surrounding populations to help conserve the resources found in the park, such as ronier palms and bamboo.

Information

Dar Salam is the main park entrance for tourists on the main road between Tambacounda and Kedougou. The Dar Salam Biodiversity Centre, which does a lot of educational work with the local population, houses a small exhibition and is a good source of information. About an hour's drive south of Dar Salam lies Simenti, the park's main focus, where many animals are concentrated. There's also a park office, visitors centre and the large Hôtel de Simenti.

Details about track conditions and other aspects of the park can be obtained from the park **headquarters** (☎ 981 1097; ☒ 7.30am-5pm) in Tambacounda, on the road to Kidira. A glossy visitor guide (in French; CFA6000), including a park map and illustrations of some of the wildlife you might see, is also available at the park entrance.

WHEN TO GO

Parc National de Niokolo-Koba is officially open from 15 December to 30 April – the park centres, biodiversity centre, even Hotel Simenti, are closed for the rest of the year – though you can visit at any time. During the rains, and until late November, most park tracks are impassable without a 4WD. In December and January conditions are pleasantly cool, but the best viewing time for wildlife is during the hot season (April to May) when the vegetation has withered and animals congregate at water holes. The park gates are open from 7am to 6pm daily.

ACCESS

You must have a vehicle to enter the park, as walking is not allowed except near accommodation sites or in the company of a park ranger. Travellers without a car can visit the park using public transport or *sept-place* taxis or on an organised tour. All tracks, except those between the park gate and the Simenti area, require a 4WD, even in the dry season.

FEES & GUIDES

The entrance fee (adults/children under 10 CFA2000/free, vehicle CFA5000) gives you access for 24 hours. Trained, approved and English-speaking guides can be hired at the gate or in Simenti (CFA6000 per day).

Tours

Four or five-day all-inclusive tours from Dakar to Niokolo-Koba range from about CFA150,000 to CFA200,000 per person, with a minimum of four to six people (see p294).

Several of Tambacounda's hotels, including Hôtels Niji, Asta Kébé and Keur Khoudia can arrange 4WD tours (CFA70,000 to CFA90,000). Rates usually include fuel, a driver/guide and park admission for the car, but you pay separately for your park fees, food and accommodation.

Sleeping & Eating

Dar Salam Campement (☎ 981 2575; Dar Salam; d/tr CFA7000/8000, camping per tent CFA3500) At the park entrance, this *campement* has clean bungalows with private bathroom and a good restaurant (dishes cost CFA3500). Camping is permitted, but there are no facilities. You need to be fully self-sufficient and that includes having your own wheels.

Hôtel de Simenti (☎ 982 3650; Simenti; s/d CFA15,000/20,000; ☒) This concrete monstrosity may not look in touch with its surroundings, but it sits in a prime spot in the park overlooking the river. The busiest animal sites are close to here, and you can see many animals drinking and grazing from a nearby hide.

Camp du Lion (r CFA7000, camping CFA3500) This tiny *campement* about 10km east of Simenti has simple huts in a beautiful spot beside the Gambia River. It can be reached in an ordinary car and has a 4WD for excursions (half-day per person CFA6000). You can also walk to the nearby *pointe de vue* (lookout), where hippos and other animals drink on the opposite bank of the river.

Getting There & Away

You're best off hiring a taxi (around CFA35,000 to CFA40,000 per day) or 4WD (around CFA60,000 to CFA70,000 per day) in Tamba. There's also an official transfer between Hôtel Keur Khoudia in Tamba and Hôtel de Simenti (CFA60,000).

If you do rely on public transport, take a Kedougou minibus from Tamba (CFA4500) and get off at the Dar Salam park entrance. From there, you can call Hôtel de Simenti and they'll pick you up (CFA25,000). If you have a lot of time you can wait for a passing park vehicle, but those are few and far between.

Getting Around

Without wheels, Simenti is the best base for walking tours in the immediate surroundings. From the visitors centre, a path leads for a few hundred metres to a hide overlooking a water hole-grazing area (depending on the season). It's likely you'll see as many animals here as from the back of a 4WD.

The visitors centre or Hôtel Simenti can organise your guide. They both also offer pirogue tours (per person CFA3500).

LOCAL TAXI & FOUR-WHEEL-DRIVE HIRE

You can hire *sept-place* taxis at Tamba's main *gare routière* in town (CFA35,000 to CFA50,000). Make sure the car's condition is good enough to get you into the park, and remember to allow for all the other costs involved (admission, guides etc). The driver should pay for his own food and accommodation (the *campement* doesn't charge drivers).

A well-maintained *sept-place* taxi is likely to get you the necessary clearance for Simenti, the Camp du Lion and the main central area. If the rains have recently finished, it's a good idea to call in at the park headquarters to ensure the track to Simenti is passable without a 4WD.

You can hire 4WDs at the park headquarters in Tamba (CFA70,000 per day, including fuel); with **Malaw Diouf** (☎ 539 6840; Hôtel Asta Kébé; per day CFA40,000-50,000) at or through most other hotels. Staff at the Hôtel de Simenti recommend **Mr Timeri** (☎ 981 1348, 646 4152).

BASSARI COUNTRY

The far southeast corner of Senegal is often called Bassari country after the largest tribal group, whose traditional way of life gives this region its particular character. This is the only place in Senegal where you can go mountain climbing. The striking landscape, with its cragged mountain paths, forests, plateaus and steep waterfalls has much in common with the adjacent Futa Jallon region in neighbouring Guinea.

It's perfect for extended hiking tours along solitary paths that pass through bushland and occasionally a tiny village. It's advisable to walk with an experienced guide who knows the area and local people well. Bring some small gifts of money, tea, coffee and kola nuts, as a gesture of appreciation for being allowed to visit the local villages.

Specialist tour companies in Dakar arrange extended hiking trips here (see p149) and ever-growing numbers of adventurous travellers have started to come this way.

Kedougou

Kedougou is the largest town in southeast Senegal, though this seems hard to believe when you walk along the red, dusty roads lined by lush greenery and traditional huts.

The colourful market is famous for its indigo fabrics, imported from Guinea. Other facilities include a petrol station, *télécentres* (privately owned telephone bureaus), a Western Union office and Internet access (a whopping CFA1500 per hour) at the Kedougou Multi-Service.

Alimentation de Dioubo in the town centre is a well-stocked grocery and a popular gathering ground in the evening for Kedougou's youth. English-speaking 'Darryl' who runs the place is also a mine of local information.

SLEEPING

These places all arrange tours in the surrounding area or to Parc National de Niokolo-Koba and have cars for hire. Note that in most *campements* prices double for air-con rooms.

Campement Bantamba (Chez Moulaye; ☎ 558 0154; s/d CFA8300; P ❄) Set in a large garden by the river on the edge of town, this youth-run *campement* feels wonderfully remote; the restaurant is also good, and has a well-deserved reputation for serving up the best spaghetti Bolognese.

Chez Diao (☎ 985 1124; d CFA5400; ❄) This relaxed, leafy place in the centre of Kedougou has clean bungalows with shared toilets. Breakfast costs CFA1000 and meals, usually a choice of chicken and chips or Senegalese food (CFA3000) are available to nonguests too.

Le Nieriko (☎ 985 1459; d/tr CFA8600/12,600; ❄) On the edge of town, Le Nieriko has well-kept bungalows in a spacious garden setting, and satellite TV in the lounge for the bored.

Le Bedik (☎ 985 1000; s/d/tr with breakfast 22,200/ 27,000/36,600; P ⊠ ⊠) Kedougou's most up-market accommodation, this place has comfortable, TV-equipped bungalows, a tennis court and friendly management.

Other options:

Campement Dioulaba (☎ 985 1278; d CFA9000; ⊠) In the centre of town, opposite Chez Diao and with similar facilities.

Campement Moïse (☎ 985 1139; d/tr CFA6000/9600; ⊠) Another typical Kedougou *campement* with thatched-roof huts, basic rooms and shared bathrooms.

Relais de Kedougou (☎ 985 1062; lerelais@sentoo.sn; s/d from CFA11,600/14,200; P ⊠ ⊠) A hunter's favourite, opposite Le Bedik. The restaurant has great river views.

EATING & DRINKING

All the *campements* serve food, though most only do so on request. Otherwise it's down to the cheap eateries around the market, such as **Keur Niasse** (meals around CFA1500; ⊠ 10am-10pm), near Campement Diao. The most upmarket restaurant is **Nieta** (meals around CFA1000-2500; ⊠ 11am-2.30pm & 7pm-11pm), on the route to Tamba, with simple meals and drinks in a spacious, pretty round hut.

For an evening drink, try the **Tour de Babel** (admission around CFA1000; ⊠ 9pm-2am) or **Black & White** (admission around CFA1000; ⊠ 8pm-2am), both lively bar-nightclubs. 'Grown folks' are said to prefer the dance floors of La Popotte at the military camp.

GETTING AROUND

Almost all *campements* have one or more 4WDs with a driver for hire (CFA40,000 to CFA50,000 per day), and some rent bicycles (CFA3000), which are good for town trips, but often too clapped-out for trips into the hills.

GETTING THERE & AWAY

There's plenty of traffic between Tamba and Kedougou (*sept-place* taxi CFA4800, Ndiaga Ndiagye CFA3500, four hours). There's no regular public transport to Mali, but intrepid overland drivers occasionally go this way. Complete all your exit formalities in Kedougou, as the border post on the route to Kéniéba is unreliable.

In contrast Guinea is well served by public transport (*sept-place* taxi to Labe CFA15,000; minibus CFA12,000, 24 to 48 hours). Taxis

supposedly leave every day, but the best day to set off is Friday.

Around Kedougou

Kedougou is a pretty town, but mainly it's the starting point for visits to the hills of Bassari country. The best way to explore Kedougou's stunning surroundings is a combination of driving (a 4WD) and hiking – best done in the company of a good guide (see opposite).

THE KEDOUGOU–SALÉMATA ROUTE

The washed-out westbound road from Kedougou towards Salémata is lined with small roadside villages, typically inhabited by Fula and Bassari people and other tribal groups up in the mountains, and accessible by tiny mountain paths. These are the hamlets of the Bédik, seminomadic people who adhere strongly to traditional lifestyles and are keen to preserve their relative isolation.

One of the nearest villages is **Bandafassi**, the capital of Kedougou district. The inhabitants are mainly Fula and Bassari, and the village is renowned for its basket makers. In Indar, a part of Bandafassi, is the wonderfully welcoming *campement* **Chez Léontine** (☎ 554 9915; d CFA6000), with solar-powered lights and delicious meals prepared by the charming owner. It's a great base for hikes up the hill to the Bédik village of **Ethiowar**, from where you get wonderful views over the surrounding savannah.

Ibel, a Fula village, lies another 7km up the road from Bandafassi. Here you'll find the slightly neglected **Campement Baobab** (d CFA6000). Visits are usually combined with a steep hike up to **Iwol**, a stunningly beautiful community stretched out between a giant *fromager* (kapok tree) and a sacred baobab. Plenty of legends are associated with this place, and the local teacher will share them with you for a donation (CFA1000). The local women make beautiful pottery – tiny Bassari statuettes and small incense burners (CFA300 per piece).

Continuing west from Ibel, you reach **Salémata**, 83km west of Kedougou. This is a regional hub, with a health centre, small boutiques and the friendly *campement* **Chez Gilbert** (☎ 985 5009; d/tr CFA8000/9000). In April and May, the entire region surrounding Salémata is plunged into weeklong festivities during the annual initiation ceremonies of the Bassari. Observers are accepted, but keep a respectful distance, so as not to turn a local celebration into a tourist event. Gilbert can invite Bassari dancers to perform some of their spectacular masked and costumed dances outside this season.

The best day to visit is Tuesday, when the *lumo* (weekly market) brings the vil-lage to life, and with it a better chance of public transport (minibus from Kedougou CFA2250, four hours), for those who really can't afford a hired 4WD – a good invest-ment, considering the dreadful state of the road.

Don't leave Salémata without taking the 15km trip to **Ethiolo**, either on foot or by car.

The road leads mainly through forest and bushland, and there's a good chance of spot-ting chimpanzees in the trees (some of the few wild chimps left in Senegal). Ethiolo's brilliant **Campement Chez Balingo** (☎ 985 1401) has accommodation in traditional Bassari stone huts, and is run by the enthusiastic and knowledgeable Balingo, who can take you on exciting tours of Ethiolo's surroundings.

DINDEFELO & DANDE
One of the most popular destinations from Kedougou is Dindefelo, famous for its im-pressive 100m **waterfall** with a deep, green pool suitable for swimming. It's a 2km hike through lush forest from Dindefelo village to the cascade. The starting point is the **campe-ment villageois** (☎ 658 8707; r per person CFA3000), a great place with accommodation in basic, well-kept huts and tasty Senegalese food. You pay CFA500 waterfall admission at the *campement*; the money goes to the village – just check the solar-powered streetlights.

Much less visited is the village of **Dande**, on the hill above Dindefelo, but if you love steep climbs, don't miss out on this spectacular hike. From here, you can visit the source of the waterfall and stand scarily close to the top edge (don't go here without a guide, as the deep drop is hidden by some innocent-looking shrubs). Nearby there's also an impressive natural cave – gigantic, and so smoothly hollowed out as if manmade or shaped by water – a striking sight. Watch out for the beehives in the bushes.

If you rely on public transport, go to Din-defelo on Sunday, the day of the *lumo*. The minibus costs CFA700 and takes two hours, but a hired 4WD really is the better option: the road is no fun, and a punctured minibus wheel much less so. It can eat an entire day.

Casamance

CASAMANCE

News from Casamance has frequently been of the negative kind, but forget the region's troubles for one minute – there isn't a more beautiful region in the whole of Senegal. Lush tropical landscapes, fertile soils, myriad waterways and the unique culture of the Diola – the largest tribe of the Casamance – give the expansive zone its distinctive flavour.

The mighty Casamance River winds its way through the region in a maze of picturesque creeks and lagoons. Small islands, areas of palm grove, forest, mangrove swamp and abundant estuary vegetation accompany its picturesque course. The pirogue is the ideal means of exploring the waterways, though the surrounding area provides plenty of potential for extensive walking or bicycle tours. On the western coast, Senegal's finest beaches spread in a wide strip of white sand from Cap Skiring towards the 'hip' villages of Kafountine and Abéné, broken by a mangrove-lined delta where the Casamance River spills into the Atlantic. Ziguinchor, the region's gateway, is an atmospheric regional capital where elegant colonial houses and cheap hotels line majestic avenues bordered by flowering trees.

Over the last few decades the region has unfortunately become better known for an ongoing separatist rebellion than for its attractive landscape. At the time of writing, a 2004 peace deal between the Senegalese government and insurgents had calmed things down and tourists were returning. The most exciting sign was the renovation of several *campements villageois,* the rural, village-managed lodgings typical of the Casamance.

HIGHLIGHTS

- Swim by day and party by night at **Cap Skiring** (p242), home to the best beaches in Senegal
- On foot or bicycle, trace the small forest paths and wide shorelines around **Oussouye** (p239)
- Admire original local architecture and get a taste of rural life from the *campement villageois* at **Affiniam** (p246)
- Feel like you've been sent back in time on the peaceful **Île de Karabane** (p240), and admire dozens of bird species on your pirogue trip there
- Drum up a reggae beat and relax in the hammock at **Kafountine** (p247)

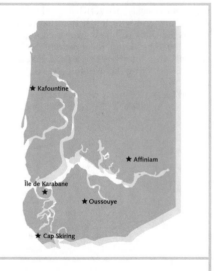

- POPULATION: 1.5 MILLION

HISTORY

The Diola people of Casamance have a long history of resisting the rule of outsiders. It's a sentiment that underlined their outright rejection of slavery (both European and African), their refusal to accept France's colonial administration and the bloody war being waged by those seeking secession from Senegal.

In the 19th and early 20th centuries, the French colonial authorities controlled their territory through local chiefs. In Casamance, however, the Diola people do not have a hierarchical society and thus had no recognised leaders. The French installed Mandinka chiefs to administer the Diola, but they were resented as much as the Europeans, and Diola resistance against foreign interference remained extremely strong well into the 1930s.

In 1943, the last Diola rebellion against the French was led by a traditional priestess called Aline Sitoe Diatta, from Kabrousse. The rebellion was stopped and Aline Sitoe was imprisoned at the remote outpost of Timbuktu in neighbouring Mali, where she eventually died.

The conflict that has plagued the region for the last 20 years originated from a pro-independence demonstration held in Ziguinchor in 1982, after which the leaders of the Mouvement des Forces Démocratiques de la Casamance (MFDC) were arrested and jailed. Over the next few years the army clamped down with increasing severity, but this only galvanised the local people's anti-Dakar feelings and spurred the movement into taking more action.

In 1990, the MFDC went on the offensive and attacked military posts. The army responded by attacking MFDC bases in southern Casamance and over the border in Guinea-Bissau, which had been giving covert support to the rebels following a coastal territorial dispute with Senegal. As always it was local civilians who came off the worst, with both the Senegalese army and the MFDC accused of committing

TO GO OR NOT TO GO?

It's the nature of news that you hear more about killing than about living, and in the case of Casamance good news is hard to find. This means that the vast majority of Senegalese know little more than outsiders about the current situation in the Casamance.

Everybody we spoke to in the Casamance assured us that travelling to the area was perfectly safe, but it pays to be extra careful. Don't travel on the roads at night, particularly in the areas near Guinea-Bissau and the route from Ziguinchor to Kafountine via Bignona. There have been occasional car hijackings and ambushes at roadblocks, usually put up by armed bandits rather than separatists defending the rebel cause. Alarm bells rang when, in 2006, the deputy prefect of Diouloulou was assaulted at one of these roadblocks and later lost his life. Attacks are rare, but they do occur, so make sure you give yourself enough time to arrive at your destination before nightfall.

At the time of writing, conflicts between rebel forces and Bissau-Guinean military had just flared up in a small area near the Guinea-Bissau border. This resulted in the temporary suspension of public transport and the closure of the border crossing in São Domingo. These kinds of confrontations have become very rare since 2004, but you always need to check the latest security advice, listen to the locals, and give conflict areas a wide berth. In Ziguinchor you can ask at your hotel, but a more grass-roots picture may be gleaned by talking to bush-taxi drivers: if they are reluctant to go, you should be, too.

During the two weeks we travelled through the Casamance, visiting remote villages as well as major tourist centres, we didn't experience any difficulties whatsoever. By contrast, the hospitality of the people, their eagerness to welcome foreign visitors back into their region and help tourists to travel safely were impressive and moving. Casamance used to be one of Senegal's major tourist destinations, and for most people, the suffering is greater for the lack of tourists and tourist dollars than any direct confrontation with separatist fighters.

The only real permanent no-go zone is the Parc National de Basse-Casamance, which has been closed for years because of suspected land mines. Rest assured that unless you just wander off on your own accord, people will simply not allow you to get too close to trouble.

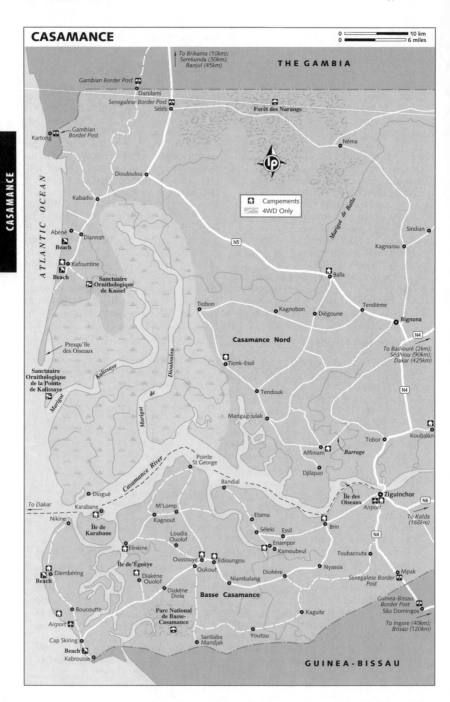

CASAMANCE

CASAMANCE

| 0 | 10 km |
| 0 | 6 miles |

THE GAMBIA

To Brikama (10km);
Serekunda (30km);
Banjul (45km)

Gambian Border Post

Darsilami

Senegalese Border Post

Séléti

Forêt des Narangs

Néma

Kartong

Gambian
Border Post

ATLANTIC OCEAN

Diouloulou

Kabadio

Campements
4WD Only

N5

Sindian

Kagnarou

Abéné
Beach

Diannah

Kafountine

Beach

Baïla

Sanctuaire
Ornithologique
de Kassel

Tiobon

Kagnobon

Diégoune

Tendième

Bignona

N4

Casamance Nord

To Badiouré (2km);
Sédhiou (90km);
Dakar (425km)

N4

Presqu'île
des Oiseaux

Sanctuaire
Ornithologique
de la Pointe
de Kalissaye

Kalissaye

Dioulouou

Tionk-Essil

Tendouk

Mangagoulak

Tobor

Koubalan

Marigot de

Affiniam

Barrage

Djilapao

Casamance River

Pointe
St George

Bandial

Île des
Oiseaux

Ziguinchor

N6

Dıogué

Karabane

M'Lomp

Etama

Essil

Brin

To Kolda
(188km)

N4

To Dakar

Nikine

Île de
Karabane

Kagnout

Séleki

Enampor

Kamoubeul

Toubacouta

Loudia
Ouolof

Elinkine

Île d'Égueye

Oussouyé

Ediougou

Nyassia

Mpak

Senegalese Border
Post

Diembéring
Beach

Diakène
Ouolof

Oukout

Diohère

Diakène
Diola

Niambalang

Basse Casamance

Guinea-Bissau
Border Post
São Domingos

Boucoutte

Parc National
de Basse-
Casamance

Kaguite

To Ingore (40km);
Bissau (120km)

Airport

Cap Skiring
Beach

Santiaba
Mandjak

Youtou

Kabrousse

GUINEA-BISSAU

atrocities against people who were thought to be sympathetic to the opposite side.

As the '90s wore on, ceasefire agreements were signed and broken as periods of peace repeatedly ended in violence. In 1995 four French people touring in Casamance went missing. The Senegalese government blamed the MFDC while Father Diamacoune Senghor, the MFDC's leader, accused the army of trying to turn international opinion against the rebels. Peace talks continued but following the government's refusal to consider independence for Casamance, a group of hardliners broke away from the MFDC and resumed fighting.

Meanwhile Father Diamacoune urged his supporters to continue the search for reconciliation with the government. A new ceasefire was agreed upon in late 1997 but it did little to slow the mounting death toll, and during the following three years about 500 people were reported killed. His authority fading, Father Diamacoune unexpectedly signed a peace deal in March 2001. While the agreement provided for the release of prisoners, the return of refugees and the clearance of landmines, it fell short of the full autonomy many rebels sought. Divisions within the MFDC deepened; a bloody battle was fought between two opposing factions and many in Casamance begun referring to some of the rebels as bandits, or common thieves. Things have since become calmer, and the latest peace deal (agreed in 2004) appears to be effective, though occasional uprisings and street ambushes still occur.

INFORMATION

For information – from the political situation to hotel bookings – try the websites www .casamance.net and www.casamance.info (both run by Philip Chiche from Le Flamboyant hotel in Ziguinchor).

DANGERS & ANNOYANCES

Most tourists visit the Casamance without experiencing any problems, but given the precarious political situation, caution is advisable (see p229).

Along the region's main arteries and near major settlements you will come across military checkpoints manned by government forces. You'll be asked to show identification; as long as all papers are in order, these checks tend to be swift and painless.

GETTING THERE & AWAY
Air

There are airports at Ziguinchor and Cap Skiring. Air Sénégal International flies every day between Ziguinchor and Dakar (one way CFA50,000); from November to May it flies twice a week from Dakar to Ziguinchor (one way CFA59,000).

Boat

At the time we visited, the boat service between Dakar and Ziguinchor was so good, reliable, safe and comfortable that the other options – relatively expensive airfares or a tedious taxi journey via Gambia – somewhat lost their appeal. The boat travels mainly through the night; you can get sleeper seats or a bed in a cabin, and arrive relaxed in the morning (see also p291).

There's a sad background for all this unexpected comfort. In 2005 the current boat *Le Willis* took over the journey previously made by the MS *Joola*, which had tragically capsized in 2002 in the worst catastrophe Senegal had ever experienced. Almost 2000 people perished (only 64 passengers were rescued), caused by dangerous overloading.

This shocking wake-up call has now made the *Joola*'s successor one of the safest passenger boats of the region. Passenger numbers are strictly respected, baggage is weighed before getting onboard, and all essential safety measures, including permanent radio contact, life vests and satellite surveillance, are in place. You have to book your place on the overnight trip in advance.

In Dakar the **Somat ticket office** (Map p150; ☎ 889 8009, 889 8060/51) is next to the Gorée ferry pier; in Ziguinchor it's at the port. The boat departs Dakar every Tuesday and Friday at 7pm, returning from Ziguinchor every Sunday and Thursday at 2pm. In Dakar, you need to arrive at least 1½ hours in advance; in Ziguinchor at least one hour. Tickets cost CFA15,500/23,500/28,500 for an armchair/sleeper seat/cabin bed (cabins sleep four people). Residents pay CFA5000 less, children under 12 travel for half price, and children under four are free.

Bush Taxi

The road from Dakar past Kaolack and down the Trans-Gambia Hwy looks relatively short and straight on the map, and is in a good state, too (with the exception of a few wobbly kilometres in Gambia). But having to cross The Gambia can be a pain, to say the least. Gambian border posts can be hard work to deal with: payments are asked for and visas and vaccination certificates demanded, when in fact none of this is required if you're in transit. Then there's the ferry from Farafenni to Soma, a boat that almost deserves the title 'antique' and is frequently out of service. All of this makes journey times unpredictable. Some drivers claim to do Ziguinchor–Dakar in seven hours, but 10 or more is more likely.

Ziguinchor–Dakar costs CFA7500 by *sept-place* taxi (a seven-seater Peugeot) and CFA5500 by Ndiaga Ndiaye; several cars leave every morning from the *gare routière* (bus and bush-taxi station) in Ziguinchor – it's best to get there early as most drivers like to leave no later than 7am. From Ziguinchor you get connections to all other Casamance destinations. On the Gambian border, you might be asked to pay CFA2500 tax (payable in CFA), sometimes more, and other 'extras' depending on the mood of the Gambian officers. Stay calm and smiling if faced with red-tape tedium.

GETTING AROUND

Casamance can be toured by car, public transport, pirogue, bicycle or on foot. In Ziguinchor and Cap Skiring you can hire

---

LOCAL GUIDES

If you want to leave the roads and main tracks to explore quieter areas on foot or by bike or pirogue, a local guide is recommended. As well as showing you the way (a maze of paths and trails crosses the region and there are very few signposts), guides can introduce you to aspects of religious practice and culture in the Casamance that you might otherwise miss.

The best way to find a guide is by asking around at your hotel. Some of the best guides of the region are those of the *campement villageois* in Oussouye. The Relais de Santhiaba and Le Flamboyant hotels in Ziguinchor, and Diatta Tour International in Ziguinchor and Cap Skiring are all able to recommend reliable, enthusiastic and knowledgeable guides. Rates start at about CFA5000 per day.

---

cars, and hiring a taxi with a driver should cost around CFA20,000 for the day.

Cap Skiring, Ziguinchor, Affiniam, Elinkine and Île de Karabane all have pirogues to take travellers on tours, or just from A to B. See individual sections for more details.

For cycling the smaller tracks are often too sandy, even for fat-tyred mountain bikes, but there are several good dirt roads in the Casamance that are rideable, such as the route to Enampor, several tracks around Oussouye and Cap Skiring. The main tar roads are also OK on a bike, although you need to keep your eyes and ears open; what little traffic there is tends to go quite fast, and there's no room for error. For specialised hiking and biking tours, contact **Casamance VTT** (☎ /fax 993 1004; casavtt@ yahoo.fr) in Oussouye.

ZIGUINCHOR

pop 217,000

Ziguinchor (zig-an-shor) is the largest town in southern Senegal, as well as the main access point for travel in the Casamance region. It's hard to imagine a more laid-back town than this regional capital – just don't call it sleepy. Unlike other 'junction towns', Ziguinchor has real atmosphere, couched among the majestic houses, leafy streets and busy markets of this old colonial administrative centre. It's worth spending a couple of days here, just soaking up the calm ambience of the town.

ORIENTATION

Ziguinchor's suburbs sprawl into the surrounding bush, but the central area is quite compact and can easily be covered on foot.

The focal point of the town is the traffic circle Rond-Point Jean-Paul II from which many streets radiate, including Rue Javelier, a bus road with shops, restaurants and a bank. It leads past the covered Marché Escale to the Rue du Commerce, which runs along the southern bank of the Casamance River. This is where you find the ferry terminal.

Leading east from Rond-Point Jean-Paul II is Av Carvalho, which links the centre to the *gare routière*. From a roundabout near the *gare routière*, the wide Rte 54 leads south to Guinea-Bissau and north, via the bridge

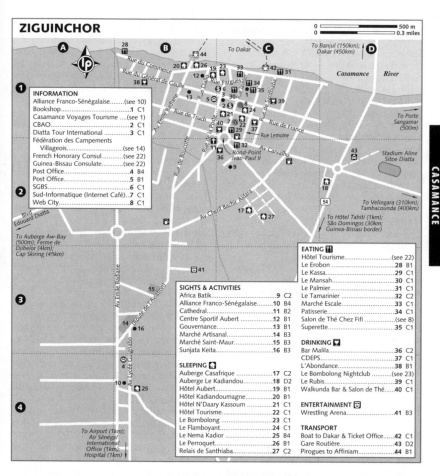

ZIGUINCHOR

0 ——— 500 m
0 ——— 0.3 miles

To Dakar
To Banjul (150km);
Dakar (450km)

Casamance River

To Porte
Sangamar
(500m)

INFORMATION
Alliance Franco-Sénégalaise........(see 10)
Bookshop...1 C1
Casamance Voyages Tourisme ....(see 1)
CBAO..2 C1
Diatta Tour International 3 C1
Fédération des Campements
  Villageois.................................(see 14)
French Honorary Consul...........(see 22)
Guinea-Bissau Consulate..........(see 22)
Post Office......................................4 B4
Post Office......................................5 B1
SGBS...6 C1
Sud-Informatique (Internet Café).7 C1
Web City...8 C1

Stadium Aline
Sitoe Diatta

To Velingara (310km);
Tambacounda (400km)

To Hôtel Tahiti (1km);
São Domingos (30km);
Guinea-Bissau border)

To Auberge Aw-Bay
(500m); Ferme de
Djibelor (4km);
Cap Skiring (45km)

EATING
Hôtel Tourisme.........................(see 22)
Le Erobon....................................28 B1
Le Kassa......................................29 C1
Le Mansah...................................30 C1
Le Palmier...................................31 C1
Le Tamarinier 32 C2
Marché Escale.............................33 C1
Patisserie....................................34 C1
Salon de Thé Chez Fifi...............(see 8)
Superette....................................35 C1

SIGHTS & ACTIVITIES
Africa Batik...9 C2
Alliance Franco-Sénégalaise.........10 B4
Cathedral..11 B2
Centre Sportif Aubert 12 B1
Gouvernance.....................................13 B1
Marché Artisanal..............................14 B3
Marché Saint-Maur...........................15 B3
Sunjata Keita.....................................16 B3

DRINKING
Bar Malila....................................36 C2
CDEPS...37 C1
L'Abondance...............................38 B1
Le Bombolong Nightclub ....(see 23)
Le Rubis......................................39 C1
Walkunda Bar & Salon de Thé....40 C1

SLEEPING
Auberge Casafrique 17 C2
Auberge Le Kadiandou.....................18 D2
Hôtel Aubert.....................................19 B1
Hôtel Kadiandoumagne....................20 B1
Hôtel N'Daary Kassoum 21 C1
Hôtel Tourisme.................................22 C1
Le Bombolong 23 C1
Le Flamboyant..................................24 C1
Le Nema Kadior 25 B4
Le Perroquet....................................26 B1
Relais de Santhiaba.........................27 C2

ENTERTAINMENT
Wrestling Arena.........................41 B3

TRANSPORT
Boat to Dakar & Ticket Office......42 C1
Gare Routière.............................43 D2
Pirogues to Affiniam..................44 B1

CASAMANCE

crossing the Casamance River, to Banjul and Dakar.

The road heading southwest from the Rond-Point Jean-Paul II passes the cathedral and becomes Av Lycée Guignabo (or Route de l'Aviation), passing Marché Saint-Maur and the Marché Artisanal before reaching the airport, which is 3.5km from the centre.

INFORMATION
Bookshops
The best bookshop in town is on the northern end of Rue Javelier, with a good selection of titles on Senegal and Casamance (mostly in French), as well as some English-language magazines.

Cultural Centre
Alliance Franco-Sénégalaise (☎ 991 2823; Av Lycée Guignabo; ◷ 9.15am-noon & 3-7.15pm Mon-Sat) This is easily Ziguinchor's most stunning building – a giant *case à impluvium* (large, round traditional house), decorated with blindingly busy South African Ndebele and Casamance patterns, at the southern end of Av Lycée Guignabo. Inside there are exhibitions, a large concert hall where shows take place at least once a week, and a welcoming restaurant and bar. Tourists are expected to make a donation of CFA750 when visiting the centre, and are given a postcard of the centre in exchange.

Internet Access
There are plenty of Internet cafés, including the two in the following list. Le Flamboyant and Hôtel Kadiandoumagne are both wi-fi

spaces, and the Alliance Franco-Sénégalaise has a speedy Internet café.

Sud-Informatique (☎ 991 1573; www.sudinfo.sn; Rue Javelier; per hr CFA1000; ✆ 9am-midnight) Has fast machines and good facilities, including satellite TV tuned to European football.

Web City (☎ 991 1044; Rue Javelier; per hr CFA1000; ✆ 10am-midnight) Offers a reasonable service.

Medical Services

Véronique Chiche at Le Flamboyant hotel can recommend reliable doctors in town.

Hospital (☎ 991 1154) Ziguinchor's regional hospital is located next door to the airport. It has an Accident & Emergency department, but it's not well equipped.

Money

The following banks change money, give advances on credit cards and have ATMs taking Visa and MasterCard.

CBAO (Rue de France; ✆ 7.45am-noon & 1.15-2.30pm Mon-Thu, 7.45am-1pm & 2.45-3.45pm Fri)

SGBS (Rue du Général de Gaulle; ✆ 7.45am-noon & 1.15-2.30pm Mon-Thu, 7.45am-1pm & 2.45-3.45pm Fri)

Post

Post office (Av Emile Badiane) South of the Marché Artisanal. Best for parcels.

Post office (Rue du Général de Gaulle)

Telephone

There are plenty of private *télécentres* along Rue Javelier and in the surrounding streets.

Tourist Information

Véronique and Philip at Le Flamboyant hotel on Rue de France will share their knowledge with anybody there for a drink or meal. Véronique speaks English and can help set up excursions or hire local guides.

Fédération des Campements Villageois (Fecav; ☎ 991 1268, 558 1421; Marché Artisanal) Mr Sane at the FECAV can help you with the latest information on the *campements villageois*, recent openings, state of repairs and travel.

Travel Agencies

Casamance Voyages Tourisme (☎ 991 4362; casamancevoyagestourisme@yahoo.fr; Rue Javelier) A good option for purchasing tickets and arranging tours.

Diatta Tour International (☎ 991 2781; aessibye@yahoo.fr; Rue du Général de Gaulle) An excellent agency that can arrange air tickets, tours, hotel and *campement* (hotel) reservations and car hire and fishing trips. It also has a subsidiary branch in Cap Skiring. In Ziguinchor, this is also the DHL agent.

SIGHTS

Central Ziguinchor, with its colourful colonial buildings and wide streets overlooked by mighty trees, is well worth exploring for an afternoon. Interesting buildings include the central **post office** on Rue du Général de Gaulle (there are occasional open days, on which you can visit all those parts of the structure you don't normally get to see), the office of **Diatta Tour International** next door, a pink-tinted house with a wide courtyard, the **Gouvernance** (Rue du Général de Gaulle) and, of course, the stunning **cathedral** (Rond-Point Jean-Paul II). Still on the architectural side, the huge *case à impluvium* of the **Alliance Franco-Sénégalaise** (☎ 991 2823; ✆ 9.15am-noon & 3-7.15pm Mon-Sat) offers plenty of interest – from the mosaic floors to the Ndebele patterns painted all across the walls and ceiling. Not far from there, the Marché Artisanal and the Marché Saint-Maur, both on Av Lycée Guignabo, tempt with woodcarvings, fabrics and, more ordinarily, fresh fruit and vegetables.

Any day around town should also take you along **Rue du Commerce**, which runs parallel to the river – not only for the stunning view, but for the impressive sight of dozens of pirogue makers and painters, fishermen and women cleaning mussels. The best place to see them at work is the stretch of coast between the Hôtel Kadiandoumagne and the restaurant Le Erobon.

Heading 5km west out of town, you can walk through the vast greenness of the **Ferme de Djibelor** (☎ 991 1701; admission CFA2000; ✆ 9am-6pm), which has a large, tropical fruit and flower garden to enjoy (and from which to purchase fresh produce). It also has a rather bizarre crocodile farm at the back, where you can get close to Nile crocs in all ages and sizes – from tiny babies to 'granddads', though knowing that they're kept to be one day slaughtered for their meat and skin spoils the fun a little (the crocodile products from the farm can be exported legally, as they're not taken from wild animals).

ACTIVITIES
Pirogue Excursions

The standard day trip from Ziguinchor includes a pirogue trip to Affiniam and Djilapao on the northern side of the Casamance River and a trip to Île des Oiseaux. These three places are set in beautiful surrounding. Affiniam has a stunning *case à impluvium* (the *campement villageois*), and in Djilapao, you can see some beautiful *cases à étages* (traditional two-storey mud houses). Île des Oiseaux is great for bird-lovers; with very little effort you can see pelicans, flamingos, kingfishers, storks and sunbirds as well as many more species.

Many hotels offer trips to these destinations including Le Flamboyant, the Hôtel Kadiandoumagne and the Relais de Santhiaba. Prices vary slightly but are usually around CFA15,000 per person, with a minimum of four travellers. Alternatively, you can just hire the whole pirogue for CFA50,000 per day. A final option to consider is the public ferry to Affiniam – for more details see p246.

Sports

Ziguinchor is in theory a great base for bicycle excursions, though you'll probably need to bring your own two wheels; all the previously existing bike hire facilities have closed due to the difficult maintenance of bikes forced daily along Ziguinchor's sandy roads.

If a lack of pedal power means you're not getting your legs moving enough, try the **Centre Sportif Aubert** (☎ 938 8020; Rue Diallo; per hr CFA500), opposite of the hotel of the same name, where you can work out on the latest fitness equipment, use the pool or participate in a range of courses from aerobics to weight workouts.

COURSES

Africa Batik (☎ 9911 2689) Near Rond-Point Jean-Paul II, it offers batik-making courses of varying duration. Inquire for rates.

Alliance Franco-Sénégalaise (☎ 991 2823; ⏰ 9.15am-noon & 3-7.15pm Mon-Sat) And if you want to learn French, try here.

Sunjata Keita (Av Lycée Guignabo) This small percussion boutique can arrange drumming courses.

FESTIVALS & EVENTS

The annual **Ziguinchor carnival**, held during carnival season in February, features plenty of local drumming and dancing groups, as well as wrestling matches and impressive parades. Check www.casamance.net and www.casamance.info for dates.

SLEEPING
Budget

Hôtel Tourisme (☎ 991 2223; Rue de France; s/d CFA6600/8200) Four simple, clean rooms, in the heart of town, and above a great restaurant – it's a bargain. It's managed by the owners of Le Flamboyant, and benefits from their good kitchen and vast regional knowledge.

Le Bombolong (☎ 938 8001; r CFA8000) This simple place with a leafy courtyard is best known for its nightclub. Off Rue de Commerce, it is a relaxed place to stay unless you're a light sleeper.

Relais de Santhiaba (☎ 991 1199; s with/without bathroom CFA9000/5000, d with/without bathroom CFA13,000/8000; ✷) This simple place, in a side-street off Ave Cherif Bachir Aidara, is a good pick among the cheapies. Looks drab from the outside, but rooms are surprisingly welcoming and facilities are clean.

Porte Sangamar (☎ 653 9728; r from CFA8000) This place tells a story of mismanagement. It's wonderfully set on the river, and the scrubbed white walls promise simple charm – but rooms are dark and soulless, though well maintained.

Auberge Casafrique (☎ 991 4122; casafrique@yahoo.fr; s with/without bathroom CFA8000/5000, d with/without bathroom CFA10,000/7000; ✷) This basic auberge near Relais de Santhiaba has spartan rooms set in a leafy garden. Several comfy chill-out spaces (including a sofa-TV combination) make it sure to appeal to young travellers, and it was full every time we visited – always a good sign.

Auberge Aw-Bay (☎ 936 8076; r per person CFA3600) This pretty auberge west of town was worryingly empty when we visited – despite its good-value rooms, very clean shared toilets and a mango-tree garden with ready hammocks.

Auberge Le Kadiandou (☎ 991 1071; off Route 54; s/d/tr CFA5000/6000/8000) This small guesthouse near the *gare routière* has performed a steep descent over the last few years. The mere sight inspires bug paranoia.

Midrange & Top End

Le Flamboyant (☎ 991 2223; flamboyant@casamance .net; Rue de France; s/d CFA15,000/17,000; ✷ 🖳 🖥) This classy place is possibly the best value in the country! The tranquil rooms with their red-brick floors and comfy mattresses come with phone, satellite TV, fridge bar and soothing spotlighting, and are set in a quiet garden. The French couple that runs Le Flamboyant is absolutely forthcoming and knowledgeable, and oh yes, the whole place is a wi-fi zone. Bliss.

Le Perroquet (☎ 991 2329; perroquet@sentoo.sn; Rue du Commerce; s/d CFA10,000/12,000) This simple place right on the river and beside the pirogue pier is excellent value. For 1st-floor rooms with balcony you pay an extra CFA1000, a small investment for stunning river views.

Hôtel Kadiandoumagne (☎ 938 8000; www.hotel -kadiandoumagne.com; Rue du Commerce; s/d CFA22,000/ 25,000; 🍴 🖥 🛗) Stunningly located right on the river, the top-quality and tongue-twisting Kadiandoumagne (kaj-an-dou-man) has good rooms, wi-fi access in the restaurant, and stunning views from the spacious restaurant terrace. It's also one of the few places in the country that is equipped for wheelchair users, and even has a chair for hire. Ask about the excellent range of pirogue excursions.

Hôtel Aubert (☎ 938 8020; hotelaubert@sentoo.sn; Rue Fargues; d/tr CFA22,000/30,000; 🍴 🖥 🛗) Part of Ziguinchor's upper class of hotels, this is a tastefully laid-out place, complete with a sports centre and jazz bar. The comfortable rooms have satellite TV and minibar.

Le Nema Kadior (☎ 9911052; controlenema@senegal -hotel.com; Av Lycée Guignabo; s/d CFA18,500/20,000; 🍴 🛗) Part of the Senegal Hôtel chain, this somewhat dated resort hotel has spacious, nicely laid-out rooms, though the dusty bungalow fronts and overgrown garden lend the setting an atmosphere of slight abandon.

Hôtel Tahiti (☎ 991 5949; tahitimotel@sentoo.sn; s/d incl breakfast CFA15,600/18,200; 🍴) It's placed in a strangely unattractive location on the roadside, in front of a military camp. But its well-kept rooms equipped with TV, fridge and phone make this a viable option.

Hôtel N'Daary Kassoum (☎ 991 1472; ndaary@ hotmail.com; Rue de France; d CFA12,000; 🍴) This place has more statues than visitors in its gloomy lounge. Rooms don't feel welcoming with dark decor and rattling air-con, but then again, they're fairly cheap, too.

EATING

The best restaurants, and those with the widest range of choices, are the hotel restaurants – Le Flamboyant and Hôtel Aubert are good, and the restaurant of the Kadiandoumagne and Le Perroquet are unbeatable for views.

Le Erobon (☎ 991 2788; Rue du Commerce; meals around CFA2000; 🕐 10am-1am) This humble outdoor eatery is highly recommended. You can come here any time of day for grilled fish,

carefully spiced and served with a sea view. The ambience is wonderfully relaxed.

Hôtel Tourisme (☎ 991 2223; Rue de France; mains around CFA3000; 🕐 noon-2.30pm & 7-10pm) It doesn't look much during the day but after dark the lighting lends this place some style. Great for seafood dishes and *al dente* spaghetti.

Le Palmier (☎ 936 8181; Rue du Commerce; dishes from CFA1000; 🕐 24hr) Not the best address, but this near-port cheapie serves Senegalese, Guinean and Casamance specialities.

Le Mansah (☎ 936 8146; Rue Javelier; dishes around CFA2000; 🕐 8am-midnight) It looks so shady you'd be forgiven if you were too shy to enter. But the food, including prawns grilled on a skewer with hot sauce, is tasty.

Le Kassa (☎ 936 8300; Rond-point Jean-Paul II; meals around CFA1500-2500; 🕐 8am-2am) This is the most inviting of the local-style places – a spacious restaurant-cum-bar with a fairly wide menu and frequent live shows on weekends.

Also recommended:

Salon de Thé Chez Fifi (Rue Javelier; dishes around CFA1500; 🕐 10am-11pm) A great place to sip a cup of milky coffee watching the bustle of Ziguinchor's most animated street.

Le Tamarinier (Av Carvalho; meals around CFA1500-2500; 🕐 lunch & dinner) Good Senegalese meals and standard international cuisine (think chicken and chips).

Self-caterers can buy all the fresh fruit and vegetables they can carry on **Marché Escale** (Rue Javelier), right in the heart of town. There's also a small **superette** (Rue Lemoine), as well as a good **patisserie** (Rue Javelier) opposite the restaurant Le Mansah.

DRINKING & ENTERTAINMENT
Bars & Nightclubs

There are plenty of *buvettes* (roughly translated as drinking holes) along Ziguinchor's central streets. Some of the less intimidating options include the following.

Walkunda Bar & Salon de Thé (☎ 991 1845; 🕐 9am-1am) This pretty place near the Rond-Point Jean-Paul II serves drinks at very reasonable rates, as well as filling meals.

Bar Malila (near Rond-Point Jean-Paul II) It's tiny, and if it weren't for the smart bar chairs and red-blue lighting it would be like any other drinking spot. It gets going around 2am.

L'Abondance (Rue du Général de Gaulle; 🕐 5pm-2am) This is really a *dibiterie* (grilled-meat place) rather than a bar, but it's also the final stop after a night dancing.

Le Rubis (Rue de Santhiaba; admission CFA1000-2000) Under new owners this was Ziguinchor's most fashionable dance floor when we visited, with salsa on Fridays and a global punch of hip-hop, R&B and *mbalax* (a mixture of Cuban beats and traditional *sabar* drumming) on Wednesdays and Saturdays.

Le Bombolong Nightclub (Rue du Commerce; admission CFA1000-2000) Another busy club downtown following the same rules as Le Rubis – 'grown-ups' sway to salsa on Fridays, while Saturday is younger and hipper with heavier bass and faster rhythms.

The youth centre CDEPS near Rue de France is frequently hired for public dance soirees on weekends.

Wrestling

During the dry season (November to May), you stand a good chance of seeing wrestling matches, usually held on late Sunday afternoons at the wrestling arena (really just a dusty field), east of Av Lycée Guignabo.

GETTING THERE & AWAY
Air

Air Sénégal International (☎ 991 1081) has an office at the airport. See p231 for details of flights to and from Ziguinchor.

Boat

See p231 for information on the boat service between Dakar and Ziguinchor.

Bush Taxi

Ziguinchor's extremely well organised *gare routière* is 1km east of the centre. If you want to get all the way to Dakar, get there early, around 6am or even earlier, to catch a taxi that'll take you all the way.

Traffic goes via the Trans-Gambia Hwy, crossing the Gambia River on a ferry between Soma and Farafenni.

Sample fares (in CFA) include the following:

Destination	Sept-place taxi	Minibus	N'Diaga N'Diaye
Bissau	5000	-	-
Cap Skiring	1400	1100	1000
Dakar	7500	5500	5000
Elinkine	1300	850	-
Kafountine	2500	1700	1600
Kaolack	5500	3800	-
Kolda	3500	-	-
Séléti	2200	-	-
Soma	2500	-	-
Tambacounda	7500	-	-

CASAMANCE

CAMPEMENTS VILLAGEOIS

Among Casamance's attractions are its *campements villageois*, traditional-style lodgings, often in remote locations, that are built by local residents, integrated in the village and best of all, benefit the local community. The *campements* have existed since the 1970s, when Adama Goudiaby and Christian Saglio initiated them as a way of counteracting rural exodus and offering perspectives to local youth. Ten were built originally, but during the years of conflict, many were left in ruins. Over the last few years, the Fédération des Campements Villageois (FECAV) has with financial help from the French and German Cooperations been able to begin an ambitious renovation programme.

At the time this book was researched, the *campements* of Oussouye, Enampor, Baïla, Koubalan and Affiniam had been fully restored, so spectacularly, that some of them exceed any competing private ventures in quality and service. All of them are built in traditional architectural styles (the *case à impluvium* in Enampor and *case à étage* in Oussouye are particularly impressive), and offer insightful excursions into the immediate surroundings led by knowledgeable local guides. Integrated and respectful rural tourism rarely comes more enjoyably.

The prices of all Campements Villageois are standardised, with only small variations:

- bed (with mosquito net) – CFA3000
- breakfast – CFA1500 to CFA1800
- 3-course lunch or dinner – CFA2500 to CFA3500
- beer – CFA800
- soft drink – CFA500

For more information, particularly regarding renovation progress of other *campements*, contact Mr Sane at the **Fédération des Campements Villageois** (FECAV; ☎ 991 1268, 558 1421).

CASAMANCE

GETTING AROUND

Car

The setup for hiring cars in Ziguinchor is quite informal, but **Diatta Tour International** (☎ 991 2781; aessibye@yahoo.fr; Rue du Général de Gaulle) and most hotels will be able to help. Cars usually come with a driver, which cuts the hassle with paperwork or deposits. Expect to pay around CFA25,000 per day plus fuel. Another option is to hire a taxi; if you pay for fuel, the daily rate should be around CFA20,000. It's best to get going early, especially if you're taking a long trip – you don't want to be on the road after dark, and neither does your driver if he has to get back to Ziguinchor.

Taxi

The official rate for a taxi around town or to the *gare routière* is CFA400. It's supposed to be the same price between the centre and the airport (3.5km), and even between the *gare routière* and Auberge Aw-Bay on the west side of town (3km), but for these longer rides you'll probably have to pay from CFA500 to CFA750. The main taxi rank is at Rond-Point Jean-Paul II.

BASSE CASAMANCE

It's hardly an overstatement to claim that this region has got it all. Small Diola villages hide among the lush greens, and make great bases for walks and bike rides (preferably with local guidance). At the end of the road that leads west from Ziguinchor lie the stunning beaches of Cap Skiring, and the sparkling nightlife this understated holiday zone proudly calls its own. One of the finest excursions anywhere in Senegal is taking a pirogue from there to the laid-back Île de Karabane, an island seemingly lost in time, then travelling from there to the busy fishing village of Elinkine and back to beautiful Oussouye. This circuit can be done in a few days, though you might be forgiven for wanting to take a couple of weeks. Some visitors have been known to settle in the region, lured by the tranquil scenery, friendly people and unique architecture.

ENAMPOR

Enampor is 19km from Brin, and a bicycle ride (only for the brave) along the deserted red-dirt road makes you understand the meaning of heading into the middle of nowhere.

But the reward is sweet. The **Campement Villageois** (☎ 441 4484, 936 9160; r per person CFA3000) is a huge *case à impluvium*, one of the most beautiful examples around. All around the *case* there's a photo exhibition on display, showing images of the most recent Diola initiation ceremony held in the region in 2004 (the first one in more than 30 years). The photos aren't that great in quality, but still give an amazing insight into a defining local tradition.

The staff at the *campement* are happy to show you the sights, including a sacred royal site and forest. The surroundings are also great for leisurely walks and pirogue trips.

In theory there are two minibuses per day from Ziguinchor to Enampor and nearby Séleki (CFA500).

Hiring a private taxi will set you back CFA7000 to CFA9000. Other than that, it's a bush taxi to Brin and a long walk or bicycle ride to Enampor (you take the left, or southerly, fork at Essil).

Moving on from Enampor, it's possible to go by hire pirogue from Enampor to Ziguinchor, or just about anywhere else in Casamance – ask around in the village.

CASES À IMPLUVIUM

Across Casamance there has traditionally been at least one *case à impluvium* in most Diola villages. The *impluvium* is in effect a huge, round mud house made using beams of ronier palm and mangrove wood (both of which are impervious to termites), and has a thatched-grass roof.

Historically, during wartime villagers would shut themselves inside the *impluvium* for safety. Rainwater was funnelled into a large tank in the centre of the house through a hole in the roof (which also admits a wonderful diffused light). The largest *impluviums* could hold 40 villagers and their cattle.

With mud and thatch proving useless against modern weapons, there are few *impluviums* left. Two of the better examples are the village *campements* in Enampor and Affiniam, while the fanciest of all is the Alliance Franco-Sénégalaise in Ziguinchor.

OUSSOUYE

Roughly halfway between Ziguinchor and Cap Skiring, Oussouye (oo-soo-yeh) is the main town in the Basse Casamance area. It swings to its own relaxed rhythm, and makes a great base for trips around the region. For the local Diola population this town is of significance, as it's home to an animist king who is often sought for advice.

Oussouye is home to **Casamance VTT** (Chez Benjamin; ☎ /fax 993 1004; http://casavtt.free.fr), an inspirational little company that specialises in area tours and organises the annual semimarathon (see right). Benjamin, the English- and Spanish-speaking owner, rents mountain bikes for CFA4000/7500 a half/full day, and organises guided cycling, hiking and pirogue tours from CFA10,500 per day (CFA14,500 with meals). During the dry season (November to May), longer tours can also be arranged at similar per-day rates.

It's worth making some time to visit a humble shop called **Kalaamisoo**, a workshop in the centre of the village for disabled people who make and sell beautiful woven hats, baskets and other items. It's usually open all day – just turn up and knock on the door.

Sleeping

Oussouye has some of the prettiest *campements* in the whole of Casamance – another reason for including a couple of days here into your itinerary. In addition to the options below, a new, French-run *campement* (Chez Françis) was very near completion at the time of research. The organic brick structure promised plenty of character – it's worth checking if the place is open.

Campement Villageois d'Oussouye (☎ 993 0015; http://campement.oussouye.org; s/d CFA4500/6000) This stunning and well-run *campement villageois* is one of the great success stories of the rekindling of the regional tourist industry. Accommodation is in a beautifully restored *case à étages*, built entirely in the stunning, heat-busting mud-architecture once typical of the region. Another big plus: the resident guide Jean Baptiste, a calm force of a tourist guide who has a deep knowledge of the region and is all too happy to share it.

Campement Emanaye (☎ 993 1004; emanaye@yahoo.fr; s/d CFA4500/6000) The striking two-storey mud dwelling that houses good quality en suite rooms gives great views over the local rice fields.

Auberge du Routard (☎ 993 1025; r per person CFA3000) This is a jovial place where the ladies of the hut can be found making batiks in the centre of a small *case à impluvium* – an art they will teach you for a small fee. Rooms are basic but clean, and bathrooms are shared.

Eating & Drinking

There are plenty of little eateries in town.

Le Kassa (☎ 563 7186; Route Nationale; dishes around CFA1000; ✆ lunch & dinner) This small local eatery is worth a visit, especially if you like the taste of deer, a speciality in the region. The place is as welcoming as a rough hug, and portions are huge.

Le Passager (☎ 512 0243; meals around CFA1500) Restaurants near *gare routières* are usually busy places, waiting rooms for travellers as they are. This one is no exception. It's about as buzzing as it gets in Oussouye, and serves enormous portions of local and international food – with deer as its speciality.

The Télécentre et Buvette du Rond-Point is an ideal place for a quiet drink and any urgent phone calls you may need to make.

Getting There & Away

All bush taxis between Ziguinchor and Cap Skiring pass through Oussouye. Most continue to the Cap, and rates to Oussouye are usually around CFA1000.

EDIOUNGOU

A short bike ride or pleasant walk from Oussouye lies the small village of Edioungou, famous for its pottery (see right). You can watch the local women create their pretty wares, and purchase some during the day, but if you want to spend the night there's the ambitiously sized (and priced) **Campement Les Bolongs** (☎ 993 1041; s/d CFA10,000/13,000). Even if you don't intend to spend the night, you should come here for a meal (around CFA2000 to CFA4000, open from 9am to 10pm) with a view – the spacious restaurant terrace overlooks a particularly beautiful part of the mangroves.

M'LOMP

On what is allegedly a tarred road between Oussouye and Elinkine you'll pass through the village of M'Lomp, the best place to admire the local *cases étages* that are unique to this part of West Africa. The old lady who lives in the largest *case étage* near the main road will show you around her place for a small fee. The tour will undoubtedly include the enormous *fromager* (kapok) tree, at least 400 years old and sacred in the village, that towers above the first *case étage*.

Decent food in a welcoming setting can be found at **Les Six Palmiers** (☎ 569 9058; meals CFA500-1000; ☺ 8am-11pm). To get here, ask for Chez Brigitte, and any local can give you directions.

POINTE ST GEORGE

To the north of M'Lomp and Oussouye, on a large bend in the Casamance River, lies Pointe St George. If you've got a 4WD, this beautiful spot is well worth a visit. Plans exist for the creation of a maritime reserve in the region, and the reopening of the *campement villageois*. Contact the Océanium (p154) in Dakar and the FECAV (p234) in Ziguinchor for the latest information.

ELINKINE

The busy fishing village Elinkine is the best jumping-off point for Île de Karabane. Hundreds of fishermen and their families have moved to Elinkine from all over West Africa in recent years, adding to the bustle of a beach that's lined with colourfully painted pirogues. This isn't so much a place to laze and sunbathe, but a great destination for those keen to gain a glimpse of day-to-day

---

POTTERY IN THE MAKING

Edioungou, a small village just east of Oussouye, has been a centre of pottery-making for many years. Until recently, customers were local people from other parts of Casamance, but the women who make the pots have been assisted by a development organisation to sell their wares to tourists.

Items range from spherical bowls and jugs, which have a pleasing purity of design and organic simplicity, to more elaborate cups and candle holders. The work is distinctive because the potters add a mixture of soil and crushed shells to their clay and when fired the pots take on the look of burnished leather. You can buy the pots in Edioungou, Oussouye and at stalls and markets elsewhere in Casamance.

If you don't feel like lugging your precious new pots around for your entire holiday, you can try posting them from the Oussouye post office – though there's no knowing how safe that would be. The DHL in Ziguinchor (p234) is a safer but infinitely more expensive option.

---

life in a dynamic community of fishermen. The simple but charming **Campement Le Fromager** (☎ 525 6401; s/d CFA3000/6000) has been rebuilt after having been burnt to the ground a few years ago, and now offers good, basic accommodation and a vast range of excursions. Mammadou Ndiaye, the welcoming manager, has spent several decades in the local tourist industry – use your chance to tap into his vast regional knowledge.

There are normally several Ndiaga Ndiayes each day from Ziguinchor to Elinkine via Oussouye for CFA850, or from Oussouye for CFA300. The timetable for transport from Elinkine is less predictable. A seat in one of the occasional *sept-place* taxis that cover this route is CFA1250 to Ziguinchor. Hiring a taxi from Elinkine to Oussouye will cost you between CFA6000 and CFA10,000.

ÎLE DE KARABANE

The perfect address for those determined to pass a few hours or days doing little and not feeling an inch of guilt is Île de Karabane. It's hard to believe that this tranquil island near the mouth of the Casamance River used to be home to the first French trading stations in the region (1836–1900). The French legacy is now largely ruins, but you can still see the crumbling remains of a tall Breton-style church and a school. Along the beach lies the so-called Catholic Cemetery with the graves of French settlers and sailors including a Capitaine Aristide Protet, who apparently died when he was hit with a poison arrow during a Diola uprising in 1836, and was buried with his dog. The beach is good for swimming, and the mangroves surrounding the island are great for relaxed boat tours. A pirogue trip to the Île des Oiseaux offers effortless viewing of pelicans, herons, cormorants and plenty of other sea birds. Angling, oyster plucking and visits to local fishing villages can all be organised – and there's a pretty realistic chance of spotting dolphins on the way.

There are no landline phones on Karabane and mobile coverage isn't great. Always leave a message if you don't get an answer on any of the numbers given – you will be called back.

Sleeping & Eating

The following places are listed by location from east to west. All serve food.

Campement Le Barracuda (☎ 659 6001; r CFA3000, half board CFA7300) With its pretty en suite rooms, forthcoming management and excellent restaurant, this is probably the most commendable place on the island. It's definitely the best address for birdwatching and angling excursions, whether you're an experienced fisherman or first-time rod-holder.

Hôtel Carabane (☎ 569 0284; hotelcarabane@yahoo.fr; s/d CFA13,000/18,000) This delightful and well-maintained hotel is set in a lush and shady tropical garden. You'll have the honour of staying in what used to be the colonial governance, and enjoying your drink in the former Catholic mission. Plenty of pirogue excursions can be arranged from here.

Chez Helena (☎ 654 1772; s/d CFA4000/6000) If the rooms were as pretty as the gleaming restaurant terrace, this would be a fantastic place to stay. Well they're not, but boisterous manager Helena will try to make you forget the ugly lino floors and curious assembly of furniture by wrapping you up in sparkling conversation.

SHARK'S FIN SOUP

Elinkine is a pretty fishing village, and a great place to watch the whole humdrum surrounding this industry. Yet in the minds of many it's forever associated with the ruthless fishing of sharks. Many fishermen have been drawn to town by the presence of sharks in the surrounding waters, and the willingness of many Asian restaurantgoers to pay stacks of money for the privilege of eating their tasteless cartilage. Shark fishing is carried out almost exclusively by Ghanaians. The local Diola people understand the value of the fins, but apparently find the meat less than appetising, and can't sell it to the Muslim community as they won't eat it. But while the Ghanaians sell thousands of fins a year, they seem to have little idea of their end use. One fisherman asked: 'What do they do with the shark fins?' When told they were eaten in soup he replied in amazement: 'What, they don't even make anything out of them? Just soup?'

Badji Kunda (☎ 556 2856; r per person CFA3000) Littered with small statues and colourful wall paintings, this place has a decidedly carefree and arty ambience. The owner, Malang Badji, is a renowned sculptor and painter; his works are on display and for sale here. If you're staying for a few days and you don't mind paying for materials, you can try your hand at local glass painting or pottery.

Leliba (☎ 544 5108; r per person CFA4000) Furthest along the beach, this busy little *campement* offers workshops in dance, music and crafts, and even houses a small recording studio. It will appeal to those keen to learn about and assimilate some local culture. Basic accommodation is in huts scattered around a large *case à impluvium*.

If you've grown tired of your hotel food, try the **Kaaty** (dishes CFA2500; 6am-midnight), a laid-back bar-restaurant where seafood and other simple dishes are on offer. Or down a drink at Africando, a cute bar set up by an enterprising mind in the expansive roots of a large *fromager*.

Getting There & Away

Île de Karabane is best reached by motorised pirogue from Elinkine. A fairly regular boat (*navette*) leaves Elinkine daily at 2.30pm and 5pm, reaching Île de Karabane half an hour later before continuing to the village of Diogé on the north bank of the Casamance River. It returns at 10am the next day. The fare is CFA1000. Alternatively, you can charter a boat for about CFA10,000 each way – just ask at the harbour. If you know where you'll be staying, your *campement* can also arrange to pick you up for a fee. A hired pirogue from Cap Skiring will cost you around CFA30,000 to CFA40,000.

ÎLE D'ÉGUEYE

This corner, at about 17km from Oussouye, is still something of a travellers' secret, thanks to its secluded position between two small branches of the Casamance River, which enclose this 'island'. The surroundings of the island are quite simply breathtaking, and that's certainly what the owners of the pretty **Campement de l'Île d'Egueye** (☎ 544 8080; r incl full board CFA11,000) thought. If you want to hide from the world, this is where you do it. You get here by pirogue from Diakène Ouolof, an excursion-worthy village in itself, between Oussouye and Cap Skiring. Phone the *campement* to see if you can get picked up, or talk to Benjamin at Casamance VTT in Oussouye (p239).

CAP SKIRING

Considering the awesome beauty of Cap Skiring's beaches, the tourism industry of the area is still surprisingly low-key. A handful of resort-style hotels attracts European package tourists, but all along the beachfront you also find small *campements* appealing to independent travellers. Off the beaten track this ain't, but if you want a few easy days of sun and sand, with the option of a bit of partying after hours, this is the place.

Orientation

The village of Cap Skiring is 1km north of the junction where the main road from Ziguinchor joins the north–south coast road. It's a busy little place with plenty of shops, restaurants, bars and nightclubs, a market and the *gare routière*. Following the main road through the village, you'll come to a junction, where the *village artisanal* (craft market) lies on your right, and the high walls of the Club Med complex on your left. The airport is another 4km along the road that goes past the Club.

There are some places to stay in the centre itself, but most hotels and *campements* sit on the beach south of Cap Skiring village, 5km along the coast road towards Kabrousse.

Information

Cap Skiring has a small hospital, a post office and several *télécentres* in the centre of the village. The CBAO bank in the village has an ATM that accepts Visa cards.

Diatta Tour International (☎ 991 2781; aessibye@yahoo.fr) Opposite Auberge le Palmier, this busy little touring agency arranges a variety of excursions, including bird-watching and fishing trips around the region. In the absence of a local tourist information office, this is a great place to ask questions and get your planning straight. And, of course, to arrange car and bike hire.

Net's Cap (☎ 993 5371; net-s-cap@sentoo.sn; per hr CFA300; ☼ 9am-10pm) This is one of the fastest and best-equipped Internet cafés in the entire country. Come here to surf the Net with speed, send your emails, print your digital images and do any other Web-related stuff you might have been putting off for weeks.

Sleeping

You'll find accommodation for all budgets in Cap Skiring, most of it overlooking the beach and offering all the associated facilities and activities you'd expect, though with greatly differing quality and price. Half- and full-board deals are available everywhere, and in some of the bigger hotels they are all that's available. Tours and day trips can be arranged at most hotels.

BUDGET

Just south of the junction is a sandy track that stretches along the beach. All the *campements* listed here are situated there.

Campement Chez M'Ballo (☎ 936 9102; r with/without bathroom CFA7500/4000) Possibly the pick of the cheap places on this strip, M'Ballo is a good-value option with a relaxed and friendly atmosphere. Palm trees fight for space in this pretty plot of green, and the restaurant gives great views across the beach.

Campement Paradise (☎ 993 5129; r with/without bathroom CFA12,000/6000; ☒) If you're spending your holiday on a beachfront, you're unlikely to spend much time in your room – so who cares that it's basic? The garden around the bungalows invites lounging and accesses the beach. A great budget option.

Auberge Le Palmier (☎ 993 5109; d with bathroom CFA10,000; ☒) Opposite the Club Med, this long-standing favourite with independent travellers masters the art of tasteful understatement. Rooms are as welcoming as the friendly management, and the restaurant gets good reviews, too. For an extra CFA2000 per night you even get hot water.

Noopalou Coussene (Chez Bruno Diatta; ☎ /fax 993 5130; www.casamance-peche.org; half board per person CFA15,000) This is a simple but excellent place, specialising in fishing excursions. Accommodation is in sparkling rooms or self-contained bungalows.

Auberge de la Paix (☎ 993 5145; aubergedelapaix@ yahoo.fr; s/d CFA6000/10,000) This is a friendly place with a family feel and a chilled-out restaurant with hammocks to laze a day away.

Le Falafu (☎ 513 3185; falafu@gmx.net; s/d from CFA8000/10,000) This laid-back place calls itself the 'house of friendship and culture', probably for the hairdressing, dancing and batik courses it can arrange. It looks a tad dreary, though, and the potential sea view is unfortunately blocked by a bungalow – for an extra CFA4000 you can book a room in there and watch the sunset.

Le Mussuwam (☎ /fax 993 5184; s/d incl half board from CFA11,500/15,500; ✖) What this place has in size, it lacks in inspiration. It's not the prettiest option around, nor the cheapest – but it does have hot water, if that's something to entice you.

Le Buhanor (☎ 993 5270; r per person CFA6000) This is probably the oddest of the lot. Accommodation is in amply decorated, though slightly neglected mudbrick bungalows. It's potentially really nice, but at the time of research, the ambience was marred by extensive building works that could possibly have gone on for a long time. Check the status and let us know.

MIDRANGE

Villa des Pêcheurs (☎ 993 5253; www.villadespecheurs .com; s/d from CFA13,000/15,000; ✖) On the same beachfront strip as the *campements,* this is a wonderful place. Stylish rooms and the renowned restaurant are all done in wooden decor, and overlook a tranquil stretch of beach. Fishing trips including surf casting and angling can be arranged, but nonanglers must not fear – this place appeals also to those that have no interest in casting nets.

Les Paletuviers (☎ 993 5210; www.hotel-kaloa .com; r incl breakfast CFA15,000; ✖ ✆) This freshly polished hotel in the centre of Cap Skiring

village offers quite possibly the best value for money in the whole of Cap Skiring. It looks out onto a beautiful stretch of mangroves, and offers all the quality and comfort of a top-end place at a much better rate.

Hôtel Diattakunda (s/d CFA15,000/18,000; ✖ ✆) At the time we visited, this place right next to Les Paletuviers was so new, it didn't even have a telephone number yet. It looked impressive though, with impeccable, inviting bungalows spread out around the swimming pool.

Les Bougainvilliers (☎ 993 5129; d CFA20,000; ✖ ✆) At the time of research this was still a popular restaurant-bar with eight nearly finished rooms at the back. If the character and quality of the eatery are anything to go by, this will be very nice indeed. Plans were also for a fully equipped studio flat to rent out for a weekly rate.

Hôtel Résidence Kacissa (☎ /fax 993 5258; www .kacissa.com; s/d CFA20,000/30,000, villa per week CFA225,000) On a quiet stretch of beach north of Cap Skiring, this place surprises with comfort and a variety of accommodation for most budgets. The fully equipped, two-storey villas are the best pick, and house five to seven people.

TOP END

La Maison Bleue (☎ 993 5161; www.lamaisonbleu.sn; r per person CFA30,8000) As styled as a supermodel strutting down the catwalk, this luxurious place oozes sophisticated chic. Rooms have individual colour schemes, and shades of blue are tastefully dotted around the Moroccan-style lounge, the mosaic-decorated swimming pools and the airy terrace restaurant. Massages and beauty treatments are on offer, too – but much more interesting are the weekend trips to Guinea-Bissau's archipelago. During low season, prices drop by almost 50%.

Hôtel La Paillote (☎ 993 5151; www.paillote.sn; s/d CFA52,000/74,000; ✖ ✆ ✆) This is the charming grandmother of Cap Skiring's hotels. It's been here the longest, and spoils visitors the best. For a luxurious stay with access to a supreme variety of activities and services – including tailoring, golf, tennis, beauty treatments and, crucially, baby-sitting – alongside the obligatory pirogue excursions and water sports. This is your ideal holiday home.

Les Hibiscus (☎ 993 5136; hibiscus@sentoo.sn; s/d incl breakfast CFA19,900/28,800) Right on the border of

Guinea-Bissau near Kabrousse is this classy hotel in lush gardens on the beach, where comfortable bungalows are decorated with stunning murals and local fabrics.

Résidences Les Alizés (☎ 993 5288; www.residences -les-alizes.com; d per week CFA280,000, villa per week CFA1.6 million; 🔀 🖭) You'll be beautifully wrapped up during your stay here, and yet the tall, three-storey villas don't have the soul of some of the other top-end places. There's a minimum stay of one week, and if your pockets are well lined, you can even buy the villa after your holiday…

Eating
Besides the hotel restaurants, Cap Skiring has a whole range of eateries to choose from. Most of them sit along the main road in the village, and are really hard to miss. The following is only a selection.

Le Kassala (☎ 653 0382; roast meat per kg CFA5000; 🕙 8pm-4am) This lively *dibiterie* is what the Senegalese call a *terminus* (a final halt). Why? It's the almost obligatory 3am food stop for rumpled clubbers before heading home. It's also a fine and friendly place to hang out in the evenings, savour some delicious roast meat and catch up on local gossip.

Le Terazza (Chez Gnima; ☎ 993 5110; pizza around CFA2000-3000) This is where to buy your bread and croissants in the morning and to enjoy the best pizza in town in the evening. Apart from the excellent food, it's energetic Gnima and her mainly female staff who give this place its warm and welcoming character.

Les Bolongs (☎ 936 9104; meals CFA2000-5000; 🕙 9am-4am) Right opposite the CBAO bank, this terrace restaurant is the place to enjoy a simple, solid meal while watching the bustle of the street below.

Le Salima (☎ 936 9127; meals from CFA500; 🕙 lunch & dinner) This unpretentious little eatery in the heart of the village serves generous Senegalese dishes.

Le Carpe Rouge (☎ 993 5250; 🕙 lunch & dinner) You guessed it, red carp is the speciality of this pretty Senegalese restaurant. Right next to Le Salima, this is a little more upmarket and offers a more varied menu.

Le Djembe (Chez Nadine & Patrick; ☎ 533 7692; le -djembe@voila.fr) This colourful place continues the musical theme way beyond the name – you can enjoy live jazz here on Fridays while relishing mouthwatering French and Italian dishes. A great place for family meals.

Drinking & Entertainment
There's certainly no lack of partying options in Cap Skiring – you don't need the privilege of a Club Med membership to have a good time here. All the places listed below sit almost on top of one another along the main street in the village.

Case Bambou (☎ 993 5178; moise_dasylva@yahoo.fr; admission CFA1000; 🕙 10.30pm-4am) This has held down a solid reputation as Cap Skiring's hottest and most elegant nightspot for years, and still attracts a groomed and trimmed crowd of well-to-do folk and youngsters at weekends.

Les Paletuviers (admission CFA1000; 🕙 9pm-3am) Part of the Paletuviers hotel, this is one of Cap Skiring's most enduring venues. It serves up a reliably good mixture of Senegalese and international grooves.

Savane Café (admission CFA3000; 🕙 9pm-3am) The most expensive place of the lot promises *soirées de classe* and is indeed a waxed-and-shined place for a night out in style. The only drawback – the prices keep all but the most affluent locals out, so it can get quite tourist-heavy.

Kassoumaye (admission CFA500-1000; 🕙 10pm-4am) Those who can't afford Case Bambou tend to shake their leg at Kassoumaye – hence the largely local crowd at this down-to-earth nightclub.

Black & White Bar (🕙 10am-3am) A small place playing reggae music in a mellow atmosphere.

Getting There & Away
AIR
See p231 for details of Air Sénégal International flights to Dakar. **Air CM** (☎ in France 01 53 41 00 50; mail.aircom@wannadoo.fr) has a twice-weekly connection between Paris and the Cap. It also does a lot of special deals including flights and discount accommodation with some of Cap Skiring's top-end hotels.

BOAT
Pirogues from Cap Skiring leave from the beach opposite the Hôtel Katakalousse, some 3km south of Cap Skiring on the main road. Two reliable and experienced *piroguiers* are **Jean Baptiste & Philippe Gomis** (☎ 555 2415). They can accommodate about any boat excursion in the area, including fishing trips (half-/full day CFA13,500/30,500), bird-watching tours to Île des Oiseaux (CFA20,000) and a

highly recommended tour to Île de Karabane (CFA30,000). Staff can arrange a taxi pick-up from Cap Skiring.

BUSH TAXI
Sept-place taxis (CFA1400) and minibuses (CFA1100) run regularly throughout the day between Ziguinchor and Cap Skiring, although there's more traffic in the morning.

Getting Around
It's quite a trek from the main *campement* area to Cap Skiring village. You can hail a taxi for around CFA600. Bicycles are another good option – most hotels, *campements* and Diatta Tour International have them for hire. Day trips by pirogue start at around CFA25,000.

Auto Cap4 (☎ 993 5265; autocap4@sentoo.sn) has an eclectic mix of 4WDs for hire starting at CFA30,000 a day.

BOUCOTTE
This tiny village lies halfway between Cap Skiring and Diembéring, on the escape route from the tourist bustle. The beach at Cap Skiring will seem unremarkable compared with the seemingly endless stretch of white sand and blue waves at Boucotte beach. Augustin Diatta, founder of Diatta Tours, recognised this too and put up the pretty **Oudja Hôtel** (☎ 991 2781, 517 5895; s/d/tr CFA10,000/12,000/15,000) right behind the shoreline. It's a charming *campement* set on a huge terrain with accommodation in spacious bungalows. At the time of writing, a family suite housing four people was under construction.

Also in the making was Diatta's ambitious project of building a **botanical garden** near Boucotte. Plenty of digging and planting had already been done when we visited – it's definitely worth phoning Oudja Hôtel to check whether work has been completed. Once in the village, you absolutely should pay a visit to the **Boucotte Museum** (ask any local to take you there). It's a low-key exhibition of Diola artefacts and objects along the roots of some giant *fromager* (kapok) trees.

Hiring a taxi from Cap Skiring to Boucotte should cost around CFA2000 to CFA3000; if you call before setting out a pick-up can be arranged. A seat in one of the regular but rare (once or twice a day) bush taxis costs

CFA500 – but careful, you'll be dropped off on the main road, from where it's still a long trek down a sand track to Oudja Hôtel. Alternatively, you can walk along the beach, or take the environmentally unfriendly option of driving along the seashore in your 4WD when the sea is low.

DIEMBÉRING
Away from the hustle and bustle of Cap Skiring, Diembéring tempts independent travellers with a taste of village life and a quiet beach.

The place to stay is **Campement Asseb** (☎ 993 3106; r per person CFA3000), a spacious and peaceful *campement* near the big *fromager* tree at the entrance to town. The rooms are a bit rough around the edges, but fair value. On a hill in the centre of the village is another *campement*, **Aten-Elou**, which was completely derelict at the time we visited. Even if you find it closed, the stroll through Diembéring (check the slit drums on the market) and the short climb are worth doing – you get an amazing view across the village and its surroundings from the *campement* site.

The local *groupement de femmes* (womens collective) was looking into renovating the site at the time we visited, and whether they succeeded or not, it's worth checking out the collective. They make cute toys and other souvenirs from colourful African fabrics and sell them at reasonable prices – and who knows, your purchase might buy another brick for the *campement* near the central square of Djembéring.

Diembéring can be reached by bicycle, though the road is sandy and hard work in the heat. Rates for private taxis to/from Cap Skiring vary enormously depending on season and state of the roads. Expect to pay between CFA4000 to CFA6000 each way. The daily minibus from Ziguinchor passes through Cap Skiring around 5pm and returns early next morning; the seat costs CFA600 to CFA700 from Cap Skiring to Djembéring.

PARC NATIONAL DE BASSE-CASAMANCE
This national park has been closed for several years now and, with no-one quite sure whether land mines have been laid in the area or what fauna remains, it looks certain to remain closed for the foreseeable future.

The park measures about 7km by 5km and there are several vegetation zones: tropical forest and dense undergrowth give way to open grassland, tidal mud flats and mangrove swamps. Before it was closed there were quite a few animals, especially red colobus monkeys and duikers, as well as a herd of forest buffaloes and populations of bushbucks, porcupines, mongooses, crocodiles and leopard. The park had a good network of trails, plus several miradors (lookouts) for viewing birds and animals.

If and when the park reopens, the best option is to stay in Oussouye and visit the park for the day by bike or taxi. Make sure you ask about the latest security situation before setting off.

Getting There & Away

From Oussouye go 2km west on the main road towards Cap Skiring, and turn left (south) at the signpost for the park. The park entrance is 8km down the sandy road towards Santiaba Mandjak. Once you enter the park, keep heading south for half a kilometre, then take the first right to reach the park headquarters.

CASAMANCE NORD

The route northwards from Ziguinchor is best explored with plenty of time available, as several *campements villageois* will tempt you to leave the main road and venture along sandy tracks to tiny settlements.

KOUBALAN

Koubalan is a small village, 22km northeast of Ziguinchor. Its **campement villageois** (☎ 578 2091, télécentre 936 9473; badianepap@hotmail.com) was created in 1979, and recently restored. Accommodation is in a beautifully decorated, spacious round hut. Ask the staff to take you on excursions; there's plenty to do here: visits to a sacred forest, pirogue trips through the mangroves (some just being reforested) to nearby bird habitats, trips to local artisans' workshops and much more. A tour around Koubalan leads to several other *campements* further east that stay in close contact with Koubalan. Keen walkers can ask to be taken on a guided tour to those villages.

Getting There & Away

You reach Koubalan by bush taxi from Ziguinchor (CFA500, 45 minutes). It's on a dirt road off the Ziguinchor–Bignona road. You can also get here by pirogue from Ziguinchor, but there's no regular service, so you need to negotiate private hire.

AFFINIAM

A few kilometres north of the river, Affiniam is stunningly located between forest and river, and easily reached from Ziguinchor by boat.

The **campement villageois** (☎ 508 8025, télécentre 936 9619) is in a beautiful *case à impluvium* (see the boxed text, p238) on the edge of the village, shaded by giant *fromager* trees, and in close distance to the pirogue point. The village itself has an interesting *artisanal* centre, where you can buy locally produced soap, marmalade and juice, and sometimes watch batiks being made. Otherwise, Affiniam is in a good location for pirogue trips to bird habitats and the *case à étage* in Djilapao.

Getting There & Away

The best way of visiting Affiniam is by pirogue. There's a public boat once a day between Affiniam and Ziguinchor (CFA400, departing from Ziguinchor at 3.30pm or from Affiniam at 9.30am, 1½ hours, daily except Thursday and Sunday). Hiring a boat will cost around CFA25,000; hiring a taxi from Ziguinchor costs CFA15,000 (one hour, 30km).

BIGNONA

Bignona is a crossroads town, where the main route to/from Banjul joins the Trans-Gambia Hwy 30km north of Ziguinchor. What looks like a sleepy place full of crumbling colonial buildings was also a core area of the separatist movement. At the time we researched this book, this was the only area where we were advised to be careful, which mainly means not venturing too far off the beaten track and not travelling after nightfall.

A short drive out of town, the **Hôtel Le Palmier** (☎ 994 1258; r CFA7000) has adequate facilities in an old, colonial-style building. In Badiouré 11km from Bignona on the road towards Séléti, you find the **Relais Fleuri** (☎ 994 3002; fax 994 3219; s/d CFA12,000/14,000; 🌀 🛌), which is as pretty as its name, but caters almost exclusively to hunters. Just avoid the main season (January to April).

BAÏLA

On the route from Bignona to Diouloulou, Baïla tempts with another pretty **campement villageois** (☎ 544 8035, télécentre 936 9516). The large, round hut with its 30 rooms is modelled on the local prefect's house, and the welcoming staff will treat you like a dignitary. The area is great for walks, there are some giant *fromagers* and baobabs to see, and pirogue tours can be organised. It's best to go with a guide, and don't venture out on lonely paths late at night.

Ziguinchor to Baïla takes around 45 minutes along the tarmac main road. A bush taxi costs CFA1500, a hire taxi around CFA20,000.

KAFOUNTINE & ABÉNÉ

Kafountine and Abéné are the hip face of tourism in Senegal. The two villages on the coast just south of Gambia have spawned more than 20 guesthouses, often the sort of places where dreadlocked staff seem happy to drum the day away and everything is 'cool, mon'. The villages are separated from the rest of Casamance Nord by a large branch of the River Casamance called Marigot Diouloulou.

This isolation has meant the area has largely avoided the conflict of the separatist movement, although there was a brief clash here in April 2002. It also means the area looks more to the north than to the south: if you travel here from Gambia, the reggae-vibing tourist scene will seem familiar.

Several Senegalese and European artists have settled here, *djembe* (a short, goat hide–covered drum) clutched between their knees and tie-dye kit in hand, and have tuned the area into the laid-back rhythms of 'baba cool' – a West African version of relaxed reggae culture. You don't have to look far for your introductory drumming, batik or dance workshop.

If this is your scene, come here over Christmas and New Year, when the area buzzes with aspiring and competent drummers who travel here from Europe and around West Africa to participate in the Dutch-run **Abéné Festivalo** (www.alnaniking.co.uk/senegal/festival). This annual event is something of a mini-pilgrimage of *djembe* drummers – from one-rhythm amateurs to fully fledged

professionals. It's mainly about informal settings and participative drumming rather than mighty stages and big names. For details see the website.

KAFOUNTINE

Kafountine village is spread out near the end of the potholed tarred road leading in from Diouloulou. It's reasonably well equipped, with a **télécentre** (☎ 9369492; Kafountine Village), a slowish cybercafé, a hospital and a post office but no bank. Most hotels and *campements* are scattered along a wide, sandy beach that divides into two areas: the northern strip, reached by turning right on the sandy road as it leads west from the village, and the southern strip that lies on the main road south of Kafountine village. The beachfront is a taxi- or bicycle-worthy 1km from the village. To reach the southern strip, you pass the fishing village, a busy settlement with lines of shacks where fish is dried and smoked, and a beach from where the boats are launched.

Sights & Activities

The typical Kafountine tourist does as the locals do – very little. A day fills nicely

---

TWITCHER TIPS: BIRDING SITES AROUND KAFOUNTINE

The creeks and lagoons around Kafountine are wonderful areas for watching birds, especially waders and shore birds. You can start your excursions right in town, at the small pool near the Campement Sitokoto, or at the bar of the *campement* Esperanto, where you can gaze across the *bolongs* (creeks) while imbibing a soothing sunset drink. Esperanto and several other lodgings organise trips to the famous birding sites further afield, including the Sanctuaire Ornithologique de la Pointe de Kalissaye, a group of sandy islands (usually hidden by the waters), at the mouth of the Marigot Kalissaye, and the highly rated Sanctuaire Ornithologique de Kassel, some 5km southeast of Kafountine. Another place is the Presqu'île des Oiseaux, a narrow spit of land between the ocean and a creek, noted for its huge populations of Caspian terns. It lies south of the Kafountine fishing village – most *campements* organise excursions.

CASAMANCE

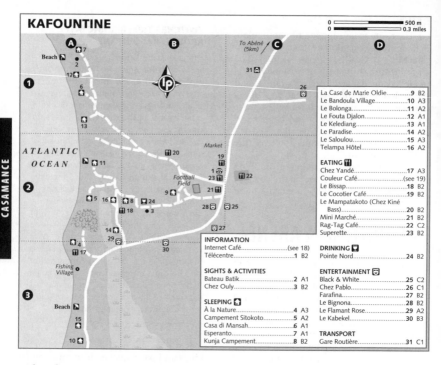

with relaxing swims, some hammock-lounging and a spell of *djembe* drumming in the evening. But don't get sucked into Kafountinian apathy before trying some of the excellent pirogue tours, and the birding and fishing trips that you can do here. Most hotels offer these; the tours organised by Esperanto are particularly recommended.

At the southern end of town, it's worth checking out the **fishing village** for some real Kafountine life. Fishing times depend on the tide, but try to visit when the boats are being launched or, more spectacular still, when they come back after a long day at sea, surfing in on the rollers. And don't miss a stroll past the area near the hotel À la Nature, where pirogue makers carve and paint the typically colourful boats.

If you're interested in crafts, **Bateau Batik** (☎ 936 9520; bateaubatik@hotmail.com) is your place. Near Le Fouta Djalon *campement,* this is a relaxed café and, surprise, a batik workshop. Making your own batiks costs CFA3000 for four- to six-hour sessions, or you can just come and check out the batiks on exhibition while sipping a coffee.

To relax from all the relaxing try Chez Ouly, a recommended massage parlour, all fine-smelling essential oils, opposite Pointe Nord bar.

Sleeping
NORTHERN STRIP

Esperanto (Chez Eric & Antonella; ☎ 635 6280; esperanto@arc.sn; d CFA10,000, incl half board CFA16,500) This relaxed place on the river is a real gem – you might be tempted not to leave the hotel at all if you choose to stay here. Bungalows (some family-sized) are large and pretty, but it's the landscaped garden with its palm trees and bamboo bridges, and the location between river and sea (and the bird life this attracts) that hold the greatest appeal. Or is it the tasty Moroccan food served in the restaurant?

Le Kelediang (☎ 542 5385; www.senegambia.net; r per person CFA3200) Enter the forest, and soak up the free-spirited, close-to-nature atmosphere of this relaxed Dutch-run establishment. Accommodation is in deliberately basic but comfy bungalows and the restaurant near the beach serves delicious lunch and dinner.

Ask about pirogue excursions with Fela the Rasta griot.

La Case de Marie Oldie (☎ 936 9710, 539 2379; s/d CFA3000/4500) This red-brick *case à impluvium* construction is a treat in close proximity to Kafountine village. Sunny, clean and friendly – and the rates are unbeatable.

Le Fouta Djalon (☎ 936 9494; www.casamance.net /foutadjalon; s/d CFA12,000/20,000) The hotel's extensive garden begins right behind a small dune that leads to the beach. The red-brick huts are comfortable and the cosy bar invites relaxed evening drinks.

Le Bolonga (☎ 994 8515; s/d CFA7500/10,000) This quality place really is as warm and welcoming as the bar-reception in the wide brick building at the entrance suggests. The young staff goes to great lengths to put you at ease and appease all your excursion or workshop wishes.

Campement Sitokoto (☎ 994 8512; per person incl breakfast CFA4500) Kafountine's *campement villageois* has basic rooms with clean, shared bathrooms right near the river.

Casa di Mansah (☎ 542 5623; r per person CFA3000) This place has been a work in progress for several years now, and still only a couple of the 16 bungalows are completed. No matter, if you want to feel integrated in local family life, and take up some drumming lessons with Momo the young master (per hour CFA2500), this is your kind of place.

Le Paradise (télécentre ☎ 936 9492; r CFA4000) 'Very Jah', is the going description of this phlegmatic little *campement*. Drumming, smoking, hanging about and philosoph- ising – voilà the ambience of this self- declared paradise. The drumming courses here get good reviews.

Telampa Hôtel (☎ 936 9608; telampa@net-up.com; r per person CFA6000) Telampa was another work in progress when we visited, with spacious, half-finished rooms available for rent. If it gets finished, this two-storey hotel overlooking a shady courtyard could be very nice indeed. (As long as it gets rid of the musty carpets in the rooms.)

Kunja Campement (☎ 512 0251; r per person CFA3000) This tired-looking *campement* had new management with great-sounding plans of turning this into an ecofriendly, organic- food place with community involvement. If it works to regular Kafountine-speed its realisation could still take a while, but there's no harm in checking.

SOUTHERN STRIP

À la Nature (☎ 994 8524; alanature@arc.sn; r per person incl breakfast CFA4500) Past the fishing village and pirogue-makers and just above the high- water line, this is Kafountine's famous beachfront venture with a decidedly Rasta feel. Drumming workshops and hammock- lounging are obligatory.

Other options on the southern strip:

Le Saloulou (☎ /fax 994 8514; r per person CFA6000) It might not be fancy, but it's just seconds from the surf and offers fishing trips in the sea or *bolongs* (creeks).

Le Bandoula Village (☎ 994 8511; s/d CFA13,000/ 15,000) A few steps down from Le Saloulou, this place is slightly more upmarket, as the fair rates suggest. Not a bad option.

Eating & Drinking

Kafountine isn't a gourmet's paradise, and the hotel restaurants are still your safest bet. Esperanto, Fouta Djalon, Le Keledian and Bandoula Village are among the most reliable. Other good options:

Le Bissap (☎ 994 8512; dishes CFA2000-3000; ☺ 8am-midnight) A cute eatery near Kunja Campement that advertises a unique *cuisine de métissage* (fusion cuisine). Food is tasty, and you can check your emails and buy your own groceries there, too.

Le Mampatakoto (Chez Kiné Basse; ☎ 575 1688) At the time we visited, Le Mampatakoto had just been completed and was still awaiting the big opening ceremony. It looked promising though, and owner and head chef Kiné Basse is something of a local institution, renowned for her love of parties as well as, reassuringly, her cookery skills.

Alternatively, there are a few cheap eater- ies in the market offering similar local fare for little money; the Rag-Tag Café in town is popular, though the local favourite seems to be Chez Yandé, near À la Nature. Le Cocotier Café and **Couleur Café** (☎ 936 9520) both serve simple Senegalese meals (around CFA750 to CFA1500, open 8am to midnight) as well as liquids, and the tiny but popular **Pointe Nord** (☺ 11am-2am) doesn't even bother with the food.

Self-caterers can stock up in the centre of the village. The **Mini Marché** (☺ 9am-11pm) sells a good variety of foodstuffs and is a popular hangout for local youth. A few metres along, the Superette has a good selection of wines, thanks to French management, as well as food.

Entertainment

This is a town full of party-ready inhabitants. The nightclubs are usually packed with dreadlocked youngsters, and often get rowdy as the night wears on. The **Farafina** (admission CFA1500-2000), halfway between Kafountine centre and the Fishing Village, enjoys the reputation of being the most upmarket and most expensive place of the lot. **Black & White** (admission CFA1000) in Kafountine village and **Chez Pablo** (admission CFA500-1000), situated on a side street near the *gare routière* off the road to Abéné, are the cheaper alternatives. Additionally, there's a set of bars that have live bands on rotation. They include Le Kabekel, Le Flamant Rose and Le Bignona. The music can be anything from drumming troupes to local *mbalax* outfits to the occasional visiting group. Entry is usually CFA500, or free with obligatory drinks purchase.

Getting There & Away

From Ziguinchor, *sept-place* taxis (CFA2200) and minibuses (CFA1700) run directly to Kafountine. Alternatively, take any vehicle to Diouloulou, from where local bush taxis take the holed-tarmac road to Kafountine for CFA600.

You can also get bush taxis from Serekunda or Brikama in Gambia, although direct traffic usually goes via the back roads and the sleepy Darsilami border rather than the main crossing at Séléti, so you won't get your passport stamped on the Senegal side (see the boxed text, opposite). Brikama to Kafountine is CFA1300.

A rarely used option is to cross the border just south of Kartong, which involves a river crossing by pirogue (see p121).

Getting Around

It's quite a walk from the hotel-lined beach-front to the village centre, and while you can hope for a ride with a friendly local, you're unlikely to come across a taxi. Ask your hotel to call you a cab; it'll set you back around CFA1000 to CFA2000. If you're headed towards the southern strip, you'll find an occasional taxi shuttling up and down between Kafountine centre and the fishing village.

Bikes aren't a bad option, if you've got the leg muscle to negotiate sandy roads. There's a shop in the market that hires them, as do some of the *campements*. Rates are standardised at CFA2500 per day, but may be negotiable depending on the quality of the bike.

ABÉNÉ

Abéné, a slightly quieter version of Kafountine, lies 6km north just off the route to Diouloulou. There's a selection of accommodation, either in the village itself or a couple of kilometres away on the shore. From the village it's a 2km-long walk along a sandy track to the beach, past a small craft village near the junction where a track goes off to the upmarket Village-Hôtel Kalissai.

If cycling is more your thing, try the Campement la Belle Danielle in the village centre, where bikes can be hired for CFA2000 per day. The friendly owner is full of suggestions for interesting day trips.

Sleeping

Campement La Belle Danielle (☎ 936 9542; r per person CFA2500, half board CFA6000) Contrary to the name this isn't the most beautiful *campement* in town, but the one that offers the deepest insider knowledge. Manager Mammadou Konta is the local representative of the tourist board, and can organise pretty much any pick-up and excursion around Casamance. Besides bicycles, you can also hire 4WDs (around CFA40,000 per full day), and approach Konta with any other worry, idea or suggestion.

Black Sofa (☎ 506 1973; r per person CFA2500) This spacious *campement* looked like either a recently abandoned ship at the time we visited, or it was just dormant waiting for its seasonal occupants. It's a tranquil place close to the beach that is reputed for its dance and drumming courses and musical soirees. Phone to see if it's been dusted and brought to life before you visit.

The following three *campements* are all at the end of the road leading from the village to the beach.

Maison Sunjata (☎ /fax 994 8610; info@senegambia .de; s/d CFA7500/15,000) Set in a well-tended garden, this small German-run place has clean, comfortable rooms with bathroom shared between two bungalows.

Le Kossey (☎ 994 8609; r per person CFA5000) The beach begins where the lush garden with its inviting bungalows stops. This place is particularly famous for its Rasta drumming parties on New Year's Eve.

O'Dunbeye Land École de Danse (Chez Thomas; ☎ 524 9600; www.odunbeyeland.com/fr; r per person CFA2600) There are plenty of drumming and dancing courses going around in Abéné, and this place offers some of the best-quality ones. The ambience is expectedly artistic, accommodation basic and the food delicious.

Le Kalissai (☎ 994 8600; www.kalissai.com; s/d CFA28,000/32,000; 🔀 🖭) You won't find anything more polished than this luxury establishment anywhere near. Bungalows and surroundings are as welcoming as you want them to be for the price, and you can even fly here in your privately hired plane (see right). Class.

Eating

Chez Vero (☎ 617 1714; meals around CFA3000; 🕙 10am-10pm-ish) Near the town centre, on the way to the beach, the much-loved auntie of Abéné's restaurant scene. Food has been consistently good for many years now, and lunch and dinner only are served on a semicircle terrace, under the watchful eyes of gaudy Madonnas and griots gazing off the walls.

Seymi (snacks from CFA700) This chilled-out eatery was described by one local as a 'shop with people hanging about', and by another as '*alimentation avec animation*', meaning 'dinner with a show'. The 'shows' are rather spontaneous affairs, depending on the mind-state of the beer-sipping youngsters who populate this joint.

THE DARSILAMI BORDER

Bush taxis from Brikama to Kafountine often go via the remote Darsilami border. The taxi (usually a minibus or Ndiaga Ndiaye) will stop at Darsilami so you can be stamped out of Gambia. However, the area on the Senegal side has long been controlled by antigovernment groups so while armed men may look at your passport, there won't be any stamp. If you arrive in Abéné or Kafountine without a stamp, don't panic. The usual procedure is to head up to Séléti the following day, chat with the border police, perhaps offer them a cigarette, and get the stamp. A simpler alternative is to get your hotel to do this for you. In Abéné, the guys from the Campement La Belle Danielle will do it for about CFA2000, no sweat.

The unpretentious **Afad Snackbar** (snacks from CFA700) opposite the Village Artisanal and the nearby **Bistro Café** (☎ 634 3532) both serve reasonable fast food. Bistro Café is the more upmarket of the two, with decent pizzas on the menu (CFA1000 to CFA2000), a well-stocked boutique selling batiks and clothes, and the occasional drumming soiree.

Getting There & Away

All public transport to and from Kafountine stops at the turnoff to Abéné, near a place called Diannah. The village is 2km off the main road and the beach is a further 2km that you'll have to walk. A private taxi will cost CFA2500 to CFA3500. Abéné also has its own aerodrome, with flights to and from Dakar. Hiring a three-seater aircraft will cost around CFA280,000 one way. Plane hire is arranged at Le Kalissai hotel.

HAUTE CASAMANCE

SÉDHIOU

Some 100km east of Ziguinchor, Sédhiou lies just north of the Casamance River. It's the largest town in this part of Casamance, a tranquil place that sleepwalks through an existence that's rarely disturbed by visitors. From 1900 to 1909, this was the main trading post of the French colonial administration, though this moment in the political spotlight has left few marks.

The **Hôtel La Palmeraie** (☎ 995 1102; philippe .bertrand@apicus.net; s/d CFA20,000/28,000; 🔀) is the place you should be staying in Sédhiou. It's a large and well-maintained hotel that sits beautifully in an impressive palm garden right on the river. It caters mainly to hunters, and though the manager apologetically shrugged her shoulders, maintaining that there was little else to do in Sédhiou, it's easy to spend a relaxing couple of days exploring the town and its surroundings even if you're not chasing wildebeest.

Budget-bound travellers can head for the **Centre Touristique** (☎ 995 1646; d CFA6500), a no-frills bed-and-roof option.

A short diversion off the smooth tarmac road from Kolda to Carrefour Diaroumé takes you to Sédhiou (bush taxi CFA3500); the turnoff is signposted. There are also bush taxis between Sédhiou and Bounkiling on the Trans-Gambia Hwy (CFA2000).

KOLDA

Kolda's glory lies all in its past, the time when this second-largest city of the Casamance used to be the capital of Fouladou, the historical 19th-century Fula kingdom led by the illustrious kings Alpha Molo and his son Musa Molo. The legacy of this grand past is a large Fula population – whose culture and language predominate in Kolda and its surrounding villages – plenty of proud retellings of classic lore (just mingle with the locals for a while), and an enduring reputation for mystic powers associated with the area.

Today, Kolda is an unspectacular place, where life centres on the three blocks opposite the post office in the centre of town (this is where you'll probably be dropped if you're coming from Ziguinchor). As you cross the bridge the first left is Rue Elhadji Demba Koita, where you find the drab **Hôtel Moya** (☎ 996 1175; fax 996 13 57; s/d from CFA9800/10,800; ✖).

Rooms here are overpriced, and the management is uniquely unforthcoming. If you must stay here, go for the bungalows with fan, they're much better than the pricier air-con rooms. A couple of blocks further down is the impressively sized **Hôtel Hobbe** (☎ 996 1170; www.hobbe-kolda.com; s/d CFA18,100/22,000; ✖ ▢ ✉), which caters mainly to hunters and often gets booked up during the main hunting season from January to April. Rooms are enormous and come with cable TV and beds that would make an '80s porn star blush. Just out of town on the route to Bignona sits the hotel **Le Firdou** (☎ 996 1780; fax 996 1782; s/d CFA14,100/18,700; ⓟ ▢ ✉), doubtlessly the pick of the lot. Attractive bungalows sit right on the river in a spacious garden, where palm trees fight for space.

Kolda isn't exactly blessed with a thriving restaurant scene or nightlife. Simple meals can be found at Chez Koumba, Chez Bintou, La Terrasse and Darou Salam (meals are around CFA700 to CFA1500 and all are open for lunch and dinner). The latter is the most upmarket of the lot, which isn't saying much – the town's culinary choices are mainly between your regular Senegalese dishes and *brochettes* (cubes of meat or fish grilled on a stick) with bread. Most places are open until their food stocks are depleted – a hot meal after hours can be tricky to obtain.

For entertainment head for the Moya Nightclub at Hôtel Moya or the Badaala; both get packed with local youth at weekends. If dance floors intimidate you, the Fouladou Bar is a popular drinking hole; it's slightly on the grubby side, though.

Where the town of Kolda threatens to let you down, the surroundings offer ample compensations. During the rainy season, you can enjoy beautiful hikes along the swelling Casamance River, watching pelicans land on small river islands and spotting monkeys. On a Wednesday, a day trip to the gigantic market of Diaobé (38km from Kolda on the route to Vélingara) is a must – traders from all across the Casamance, Gambia and Guinea come here to peddle their wares, transforming the humble village into a bustling hub of activity.

Kolda is well served by public transport. If you head to Ziguinchor, make sure you get into a *sept-place* taxi that takes the route Kolda–Carrefour Diaroumé–Ziguinchor, rather than Kolda–Tanaf–Ziguinchor. The former is a motorist's tarmac dream, the latter a potholed promise of breakdown. The price is the same – CFA3500 – the travelling time about seven hours for the first option, at least three to four hours more for the second. A *sept-place* taxi to Vélingara costs CFA2300, to Tambacounda CFA3000. All bush taxis leave from the *gare routière* about 2km outside town on the road to Sédhiou.

The Gambia & Senegal Directory

CONTENTS

ACCOMMODATION

In both Gambia and Senegal, there's a huge discrepancy between tourist facilities available in the coastal areas and cities, and those inland. This is most strongly felt in Gambia, where a highly built-up and developed resort zone at the Atlantic coast contrasts with a near absence of facilities upcountry. There's the occasional upmarket or run-down camp (Georgetown has a good selection) or guesthouse in the country, but especially if you travel at the luxury end of the market, your choices will be severely limited. In Senegal, some very well-appointed camps have opened in the remote regions, but most areas, particularly the villages in the north, have only few, lesser-quality choices.

Travellers on tighter budgets are better catered for, although there are not as many backpacker lodges or cheap and cheerful safaris as there are elsewhere on the continent. Generally speaking, the cost of accommodation here is higher than in East or Southern Africa, and noticeably more than most parts of Asia, although it's cheaper than Europe.

Overall, Gambia and Senegal have a wide range of places to stay, from international-type hotels in the capitals, through to comfortable midrange establishments, and down to the most basic lodgings in the rough end of town. Generally, price reflects quality, although Dakar and Gambia's Atlantic coastal resorts are culprits of overpricing.

Top-end hotels have clean, well-appointed rooms with private bathrooms and hot showers, 24-hour electricity and air-conditioning. They are normally equipped with satellite TV and telephone, and many of them have a minibar and safe. Rates frequently include breakfast. Apart from a handful of notable exceptions, service can be pretty lousy, even in the most expensive places.

Rooms in the midrange section have a private bathroom, but not always hot water (not necessarily essential in a tropical climate, but an asset in the winter months, when nights can get quite chilly). They will have fans and most probably even air-con, though you sometimes might have to pay extra for it (in places where electricity depends on generator power, this can push up prices quite dramatically).

Budget places can sometimes be real bargains, with good, clean midrange-type rooms for much better rates. However, they aren't necessarily spotless and may be downright filthy. Bathrooms are often shared, and sometimes in an appalling state. Some budget places will provide a fan, while others won't have any relief from the heat.

Many places, especially those in the top-end and midrange brackets, have high and low-season rates. This book quotes high-season rates throughout, applicable from November to April. During low season (May to October) you can often get rooms

---

PRACTICALITIES

■ The following English-language magazines cover the region and are mostly published monthly. *African Business* (IC Publications) has economic reports, finance and company news. *Africa Today* (Afro Media) has good political and economic news, plus business, sport and tourism. *Focus on Africa* (BBC) has excellent news stories, accessible reports and a concise run down of recent political events. *Focus on Africa* is the easiest to find in Gambia and Senegal. *New African* (IC Publications) has a reputation for accurate and balanced reporting, with a mix of politics, financial and economic analysis. It has features on social and cultural affairs, sport, art, health and recreation. *West Africa* (West Africa Publishing) is a long-standing and respected weekly focusing on political and economic news. In Western countries, some titles are stocked in larger mainstream newspaper shops; others can only be tracked down at specialist suppliers or libraries. There are many more periodicals produced in French. The most widely available are *Jeune Afrique* and *l'Intelligent,* popular monthly magazines covering regional and world events.

■ The electricity supply in both Gambia and Senegal is 220V. Plugs in Senegal usually have two round pins, like those in France and continental Europe. This plug type is also used in Gambia, but you'll also find plugs with three square pins, as used in Britain.

■ The metric system is used in both Gambia and Senegal. To convert between metric and imperial units refer to the conversion chart on the inside front cover of this book.

---

about 25% to 50% cheaper. Even hotels that don't offer discounts are usually open to negotiation, most preferring to rent a room for marginal profit than staying empty. Note that some, though few, hotels close entirely during low season. If you travel over Christmas and New Year you can expect price hikes in some hotels, usually the top-end places.

Hotel managers in both Gambia and Senegal tend to be more creative in the labelling of their places, than in raising standards. At time of writing it was fashionable to rename former camps as 'lodges', a title supposed to imply better quality. Ecolodge is another favourite, appealing to travellers' sense of environmental consciousness – but beware, some hotels claiming ecofriendliness take the idea no further than using biodegradable washing powder.

In Senegal, you'll find the occasional auberge and *gîte* – something like a hostel or inn, and varying widely in quality. A *maison d'hôte* is a guesthouse, usually a small, family-like place. A *maison de charme* is similar to a *maison d'hôte*, often with a welcoming decor. An *hotel de passe* is always on the low end of basic, generally implying the availability of rooms by the hour.

The best website is www.ausenegal.com – it lists almost every hotel in the country, with online booking facilities for the most established ones.

Apart from the *campements villageois* (rural village-managed lodgings) in Casamance, all accommodation places in Senegal charge a tourist tax of CFA600 per person per day. Some, usually the more upmarket places, include this in the rate they charge, but most don't, and will add the tax to your final bill. Throughout this book, tourist tax usually isn't included in the rates given.

Campements

Campements are common in Senegal. The name implies a hotel or lodge with accommodation in bungalows or, frequently, round huts. They exist in all price ranges, from very basic to all-dancing luxury versions, though the majority sit in the midrange bracket.

Camping

There are not many camping grounds in Gambia and Senegal, and those that do exist cater mainly for overlanders in their own vehicle. However, some hotels and *campements* allow camping, or provide an area where tents can be pitched. Grassy sites are very rare – you often have to force pegs through hard-packed gravel.

Hotels

Hotels come in all shapes and sizes, from cheap *hotels de passe* to glittering five-star palaces. Even the top-end versions can double as brothels; the room standard merely reflects the wealth of the clients. Some male tourists travelling to the busy tourist zones of Gambia have reported prostitutes being sent up to their rooms without request. Be wary and complain if this happens to you.

If breakfast is included it's usually on a par with the standard of accommodation: a full buffet in more expensive places, coffee and bread further down the scale.

Some hotels charge by the room, so whether you are alone or with somebody makes no difference to the price, though most places have single and double rates, the rate for two people sharing being cheaper than that of two singles added up.

Resorts
You can spend your entire holiday at resort hotels without venturing out. They are usually large complexes with several restaurants, bars, a nightclub, possibly hair salons, massage parlours, souvenir shops and bike- or car-hire facilities. They also tend to have a wide range of activities on offer. In Senegal, most resort hotels are clustered around Saly, with a few places in Cap Skiring and Dakar. In Gambia, you find them all along the Atlantic coast.

Book Accommodation Online
For more accommodation reviews and recommendations by Lonely Planet authors, check out the online booking service at www.lonelyplanet.com. You'll find the true, insider lowdown on the best places to stay. Reviews are thorough and independent. Best of all, you can book online.

ACTIVITIES
Most tourist activities in Senegal and Gambia tend to be related to the sea, beach tourism being an important slice of the holiday industry. Upcountry it's all about the scenery and wildlife, with bird-watching, tours around the national parks and hiking among favourite pursuits.

Bird-Watching
Senegal and Gambia are among West Africa's best bird-watching destinations. In Gambia, tourists interested in birding benefit from a well-organised network of trained guides, tours and camps. Senegal

---

LAUNDRY

Throughout Gambia and Senegal, finding someone to wash your clothes is fairly simple. The top-end and midrange hotels charge per item. At cheaper hotels, a staff member will do the job, or find you somebody else who can. The charge at cheap hotels is usually per item, but the price is lower than at the big hotels and often negotiable. If you do hand your washing over, never include your underwear. No-one washes anyone else's briefs and handing your dirty drawers to the laundry lady will cause her embarrassment.

---

has equally interesting bird-watching sites, but no comparable set-up. While some national parks have ornithological guides, bird-watchers will mainly have to organise their own excursions. See p71 for details on birding sites, species that can be seen, and contact details for birding associations.

Boat Trips
Boat trips are a great way of exploring regions of Senegal and Gambia. Gambia is almost more river than land, and going upcountry by boat is infinitely more rewarding than braving the roads. You can go from the coast all the way to Basse Santa Su in the east, but smaller excursions in the coastal area are also possible. In Senegal, the myriad mangrove-lined waterways of the Siné-Saloum and Casamance are best explored by boat.

Most trips are done by small, brightly painted wooden boats (pirogues) usually equipped with a motor. Motorised pirogues require a lot of petrol to run, the cost of which is carried by the person who hires the boat. This can make pirogue trips expensive. As the amount of petrol needed is the same for one person or a group of 10, you always have to hire the boat, and are hence better off if you're travelling with a group.

On the Senegal River, you also have the possibility to travel by cruise ship, the *Bou El Mogdad,* an old, dignified boat, which has a real historical importance in Senegal. See p209 for more information.

Cycling
Senegal and Gambia are good for the off-road, dirt-track variant of cycling. If you can

bear the heat it can be a great way of exploring the countryside. The best-organised cycling organisation in Senegal is **Casamance VTT** (☎ /fax 993 1004; casavtt@yahoo.fr) in Oussouye, Casamance.

Diving & Other Water Sports

In Senegal, the places for diving and water sports are Dakar, Saint-Louis and the Petite Côte; in Gambia, the Atlantic coastal resorts are your best bet. The large resort hotels usually have water-sports equipment for hire, or make it available at no cost to guests. The most popular activities include kayaking, water skiing, parasailing and jet skiing. Below is a list of other organisers; see individual regional chapters for more details.

THE GAMBIA

Watersports Centre (Map p92; ☎ 7765765; Denton Bridge, Banjul) Between Banjul and Bakau; offers the whole range of water sports, from jet skiing to surfing and parasailing.

SENEGAL

Arcandia (☎ 958 5055; olepepe@sentoo.sn) One of the biggest water-sports centres on Senegal's Petite Côte.
Atlantic Evasion (Map p146; ☎ 820 7675; www .atlantic-evasion.com; N'Gor) Based in Dakar, at Plage de N'Gor, with a wide range of water sports.
Diabar Plongée (☎ 958 5049; www.diabarplongee.com) Diving centre at the Petite Côte.
L'Océanium (Map p148; ☎ 822 2441; www.oceanium .org; Dakar) Dakar-based and ecoconscious. Organises spectacular diving tours to the Île de la Madeleine.

Fishing

Deep-sea sport fishing can be arranged in Dakar and Saly in Senegal and in the hotel resorts at the Atlantic coast in Gambia. More relaxed outings in creeks, rivers and mangroves are possible all along the Petite Côte, Cap Skiring, the Siné-Saloum region in Senegal and on the Gambian coast. Most *campements* organise such trips, either in small, wooden pirogues or motorised boats. Depending on the season, ocean catches include barracuda, tuna, sailfish, blue marlin, swordfish, sea bass and wahoo. See regional chapters for more details, and check www .au-senegal.com.

THE GAMBIA

Several fishing companies are based at the Sportsfishing Centre at **Denton Bridge** (Map p92), 3km from Banjul. They include the following:
Gambia Fishing (☎ 7721228; www.gambiafishing.com) Small but fantastic little company specialising in lure and anchored-bottom fishing.
Greenies Gamefishing (☎ 9907073; greenies@gambia fishing.freeserve.co.uk) Specialises in blue-water fishing.

SENEGAL

Atlantic Evasion and L'Océanium in Dakar, and Diabar Plongée and Arcandia in Saly organise fishing (see left for details).
Le Marlin-Club de Katakalousse (☎ 993 5282; marlin@sudinfo.sn) Organises fishing excursions around Cap Skiring. You can also bargain with the pirogue owners based opposite the hotel; ask for Jean-Philippe.
L'Espadon (☎ 957 2066; www.espadon-hotel.com) This hotel-based fishing club in Saly gets good reviews.
Ranch de Bango (Map p213; ☎ 961 1981; www.ranch bango.com) One of the major fishing centres near Saint-Louis.
Saly Fishing (☎ 957 2862; www.salyfishingclub.com) A major Saly-based operation.

Hiking

The single most interesting region for hiking is southeastern Senegal, the only area in Senegal and Gambia where you find mountains. Walks lead along small, steep paths, through tiny villages and occasionally through thick forest. It's best to go with a guide, not so much to prevent getting lost, but mainly to find the best spots and ensure a welcoming reception in the villages. See also the boxed text, p227.

Swimming

In the tourist areas of Senegal and Gambia most major hotels have pools that nonguests are able to use for a fee or a small consumption at the hotel restaurant/bar. If you like your swim less chlorine and more saline, you've got a long stretch of coast from where to jump in. Best are the Gambian coast and Senegal's Cap Skiring and Petite Côte; the Grand Côte and Cap Vert Island are too dangerous due to strong undertows. Always seek local advice before swimming in the ocean and respect any warning signs put up.

BUSINESS HOURS

The further you're away from the city, the more flexible opening times seem to get. Note that Friday afternoon is never a good time to try to find people in their offices –

for Muslims, this is the holy day of the week, and many take a longer break for the afternoon prayers, or simply go home.

The Gambia

Government offices are open from 8am to 3pm or 4pm Monday to Thursday, and 8am to 12.30pm Friday. Banks, shops and businesses usually open 8.30am to noon and 2.30pm to 5.30pm Monday to Thursday, and 8am to noon Friday and Saturday. Restaurants tend to serve lunch from around 11am to 2.30pm and dinner from 6pm onwards. Most restaurants in the cities stay open until the last guest leaves, though in smaller towns and villages many close around 10pm, or whenever the food runs out. Bars usually open around 8pm, tend to get going from 11pm onwards, and close around 3am or 4am.

Senegal

In Senegal, businesses and government offices are open from 8am to noon and 2.30pm to 6pm Monday to Friday, and some open from 8am to noon on Saturday. Most banks are open from 8.30am to noon and 2.30pm to 4.30pm Monday to Friday. Some banks also open until 11am on Saturday mornings. The bank at Léopold Sédar Senghor International Airport is open until midnight daily. Shops are usually open from 9am to noon, and from 2.30pm to 7pm Monday to Saturday, and very few open from 9am to noon on Sunday. Some shops are open all day, but they are still in the minority.

The larger restaurants in the urban centres may serve food all day, but it's more common for places to offer lunch (noon to 2.30pm) and dinner (7pm onwards). Most restaurants in Dakar are closed on Sunday. Many places that serve food in the day turn into bars at night, and can stay open (guised in a new ambience) until 3am or 4am. For a night out in Dakar, don't even think of leaving the house before midnight; most places only get going around 1am.

CHILDREN

With an average of five children per mother, you may guess that Senegal and Gambia are places where children are very welcome. No-one will be surprised to see travelling families and people will generally be happy to accommodate children.

However, you need to bring a certain amount of courage and sense of adventure. If you're an easily worried parent, you might not want to brave some journeys upcountry, and even if you are happy to take certain, sensible risks, you should come prepared, having done some reading on the country, investigated facilities and the state of roads.

Practicalities

Travel with older children, from about the age of five, is fairly straightforward. Most hotels and *campements* offer the option of adding an extra bed to a room, usually at a very reasonable rate, and many have family rooms, with a double bed and a single, either in the same, or in a second room. Children under two normally don't pay; in some places this extends to children of five or more years if they share a room with their parents. Most hotels offer at least a discount for under-12-year-olds.

Child-minding facilities are only available in a few hotels, most of them in the upper midrange or top-end bracket, and there's little in the way of professional babysitting agencies.

Other extra provisions for kids, such as high chairs, hire cots and nappy-changing facilities, are generally only found in top-end, and some midrange places. All of the major supermarkets in urban areas, and even some smaller boutiques, stock throwaway nappies, though they're usually even more expensive than in Europe. In smaller places less frequented by tourists or expats, you might not find them so readily, muslin cloths and plastic wraps being the locally used variant. If you're still feeding formula, you're better off taking as much with you as you need; you might not find the same variety, or may have to pay extortionate rates for it. Breastfeeders, by contrast, have it much easier. Most local kids are breastfed way beyond the age of one, and breastfeeding in public isn't frowned upon – though foreign women invariably attract more stares than local women; covering up with a cloth keeps them away.

Safety while travelling is a problem. Most bush taxis don't have seatbelts, let alone child seats. However, if you hire the whole taxi for the trip, or a day (usually by paying for all the seats), you can mount your own child seat, if you've brought it. That's absolutely recommended – the dangers of road travel in the two countries are very real, and it's a good idea to avoid unnecessary risks, particularly if travelling to remote areas where hospital facilities are limited.

Leave your pram behind! Trying to push a buggy around sandy footpaths, performing a slalom around beggars and parked cars is frustrating to say the least. A baby rucksack is much, much more useful – or you can just learn to strap your little one on your back, local style.

On public transport you'll have to pay for your child if they have their own seat. If they are young enough to sit on your lap, they travel for free. Kids usually love Dakar's battered, though fantastically painted *cars rapides* (a form of bush taxi, often decrepit; cheaper than an Ndiaga Ndiaye).

If you travel with children, a well-stocked first-aid kit is absolutely essential, as is malaria medication, sunscreen, a sun hat and a mosquito net.

Throughout the book, particularly child-friendly features have been highlighted in individual reviews. Lonely Planet's *Travel with Children* provides more detailed advice, as well as ideas for games on the bus.

Sights & Activities

While Senegal and Gambia offer little in the way of child-dedicated facilities, such as playgrounds or theme parks, there are plenty of activities that will excite children – you just need a little bit of imagination. Of the urban centres, Dakar is the one with the biggest kids' scene, complete with theme park, kids' theatre shows, workshops and film projections (see p155). In Gambia, many of the resort hotels along the coast cater well for children, with shallow kids' pools, board games and the occasional slide and swing.

Saint-Louis in Senegal is a calm city with fairly safe streets, where pelican- and flamingo-watching tours around the Langue de Barbarie and the Parc de Djoudj lie in close proximity.

Some of the national parks can be pretty boring for little ones, as animals aren't always easily spotted; Senegal's Reserve de Bandia being a notable exception, with almost guaranteed sightings of buffaloes, monkeys, rhino, crocodiles and other African 'classics' (see p179).

Pirogue tours are usually a hit, as are trips on a horse or donkey cart. The latter are possible in many places, but particularly in Senegal's Siné-Saloum region, Rufisque and the north.

CLIMATE CHARTS

In Gambia, the coolest period is from December to mid-February, with average daytime maximums around 24°C (75°F). In October and November, and from mid-February to April, the average daytime maximums rise to 26°C (79°F), rising further through May and June to sit around 30°C (86°F) from July to September. Senegal has a wider range. In Dakar average daytime maximums are around 24°C (75°F) from January to March, and between 25°C and 27°C (77°F and 81°F) in April, May and December. From June to October they rise to around 30°C (86°F). In southern Senegal, though, temperature patterns are similar to those in Gambia. Temperatures along the coast are generally lower than these averages, while inland they are higher. The northern and eastern parts of Senegal, bordering on Mauritania and Mali, generally have the highest temperatures.

Rainfall is a more significant factor than temperature in the climate of Gambia and Senegal. The wet season is shorter (with lower total rainfall) in the north. The rainy period also gets shorter, and the amount of rainfall

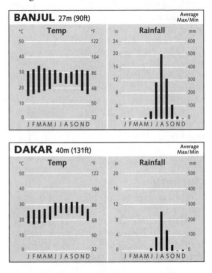

decreases, as you go inland. For example, in the far north of Senegal, the average annual rainfall is just 300mm, while in the far south it can top 1500mm. Dakar, about halfway down the country on the coast, gets around 600mm annually, while inland Tambacounda, at approximately the same latitude, normally gets half of this or less.

CUSTOMS
The Gambia
There are no restrictions on the import of local or foreign currencies, or on the export of foreign currency, but you cannot export more than D100. The usual limits apply to alcohol (1L of spirits, 1L of wine) and tobacco (200 cigarettes).

Senegal
There are no limits on the import of foreign currency; CFA200,000 is the maximum amount of local currency foreigners may export. Duty must be paid on some electrical and electronic items, such as computers and VCRs.

DANGERS & ANNOYANCES
On a world scale Gambia and Senegal are fairly safe places to visit. Outside Dakar violent crime is almost unheard of. Even in Dakar, relatively few people report being robbed, and only a tiny percentage of those suffer any physical harm. Still, be on your guard, especially in downtown Dakar – which doesn't mean treating everyone you meet as a potential assailant.

For specific threats to women, see p277.

Begging
In most of Africa there is no government welfare for the unemployed, sick, disabled, homeless or old. If such people have no family to help, they are forced to beg, and you will undoubtedly encounter this during your trip.

Especially in Dakar, groups of beggars squat near traffic lights or junctions, and will walk up to your car once it's come to a stop. This can be intimidating and annoying, but while you certainly can't help everyone, you don't have to refuse to give completely.

You'll see plenty of locals who are worse off than you digging into their pockets – helping the needy is a fundamental part of

Islam – and even small coins will be appreciated. Just pick the right situation. If there are 20 street kids grouped around your car, don't even start, or you'll cause so much excitement you'll have trouble closing your car window.

Bribery
Throughout Africa bribery is a way of life and you'll probably encounter the problem, especially in Gambia. Put simply, poorly paid officials may use 'rich' tourists to top up their salaries. For example, at an airport or border, a customs official may go through your belongings, find a (possibly fictitious) fault, and start involving you in a lengthy discussion, all intended to extract some money from you.

Travellers have different ways of dealing with this kind of situation. The best method is to feign ignorance, bluff your way through and always, always stay polite – officials love to see people being humble in response to their authority. Some 'bribe-hunters' might go as far as threatening to take you to the police station, deny you access into the country etc, but that's usually a bluff, provided that you're really not breaking any law.

Sometimes you have to play the system. For example if officials are slow in processing a visa request, offering a small *cadeau* (literally 'gift') may be your only option. But tread very carefully; never simply offer to pay. Wait to see whether the official hints for something extra. Ask whether any 'special fee' is required to speed up the process.

Civil Unrest
This mainly concerns the Casamance region in Senegal. Though officially at peace with Dakar since 2004, the area isn't entirely safe, largely due to common robbers profiting from the precarious political situation. You're unlikely to experience any problems if you respect some basic rules.

Don't venture off the beaten track, specially if you're on your own, and don't travel at night. Especially on the road from Ziguinchor to Abéné there have been occasional car hijackings, where tourists have been robbed of their possessions, and kidnappings (of local officials). These have happened after dark; daytime travel is generally safe.

At the time of research, there were frequent violent clashes between the police and Dakar students. Confrontations always took place near the university campus, mainly on the Av Cheikh Anta Diop. Avoid the zone if you hear of such occurrences – you don't want to find yourself in the middle of a stone-throwing, tear gas–spraying exchange.

Gifts

One great annoyance for visitors to Africa is local people (not beggars) asking for gifts. 'Do you have something for me?' ('Donnez-moi un cadeau') becomes familiar everywhere you go, usually from young children, but also from youths and even adults. Part of this expectation comes from a belief that anyone God has been good to should be willing to spread some wealth around. Because non-African foreigners are thought to be rich (which, relatively speaking, they are), generosity is generally expected. The usual gift asked for is, of course, money, but people may request your hat, shoes, camera or bicycle, all within a couple of minutes of meeting you. In this kind of situation you are not really expected to give anything. It's a 'worth a try' situation, and your polite refusal will rarely offend.

The situation changes when the gift is given in return for service, in which case it becomes more like a tip. There are no hard-and-fast rules when deciding whether to give. Simply pointing out the way to the bus station would not be seen as a significant service, whereas helping you for 10 minutes to find a hotel probably would be. When deciding how much to give, think how much a bottle of Coke or beer costs. Giving your helper enough 'to have a drink' is usually sufficient. If you're not prepared to offer a tip, don't ask for significant favours. In tourist areas you'll encounter locals who make a living by talking to foreigners, then providing 'friendly' services (from information and postcards to hard drugs and sex) for money. Avoid them unless you really need something and do not mind paying. (See also the boxed text, p39.)

Mugging

The danger of robbery is much more prevalent in cities and larger towns than in rural or wilderness areas. The riskiest place is Dakar, where plenty of pickpockets and street hustlers roam the inner city (see p151 for more details). In the resorts near Banjul attacks are slightly rarer but not unknown; tourists have on occasion been pushed to the ground and had bags or cameras stolen, but they haven't been knifed or otherwise seriously injured (see p103). Gun crime is virtually unheard of.

Police Checks

In Senegal, police checks are usually brief and polite – you're likely to be let off with a smile if your papers are in order. Not so in Gambia. You'll encounter police and military stops all across the country that seem to exist primarily for the purpose of extracting bribes. They'll take their time checking your passport, then probably ask for your vaccination certificate, and if you've provided all that with a smile, they may engineer some other mysterious fault on your part. Keep calm, keep smiling, don't be intimidated and don't offer any money quickly. Most importantly, never ever drive past a stop (some can be hard to spot, watch out for them near larger settlements), as this will always result in you having to pay a bribe, possibly after a slow bag search and some shouting.

Precautions

Taking some simple precautions will hopefully ensure your journey to Senegal or Gambia is trouble-free. Remember that many thousands of travellers enjoy trips without any problems whatsoever, usually because they were careful. Most of the precautions that we have suggested below are particularly relevant to cities, although some of them might apply in towns and other places too.

- Don't make yourself a target. Carry around as little as possible; leave your day-pack, camera, credit card and personal stereo in your hotel room – provided you feel safe about the place. In Senegal, even passports can usually be left behind, though it's a good idea to make a copy of it and keep that with you. An exception is the Casamance, where you'll encounter police checkpoints. In Gambia, you need to keep your passport and vaccination certificate with you at all times.

- Don't display your money and other symbols of wealth. Don't wear jewellery or watches, however cheap they actually are,

---

REALITY CHECK

Lest you get too paranoid, remember this. Considering the wealth of most tourists and the unimaginable poverty of most locals, the incidence of robbery or theft in most of Gambia and Senegal is incredibly low. Even a shoestring traveller's daily budget of about US$12 a day is what many Gambians make in a month. When you sit in a bus station sipping a soft drink that costs half a US dollar, look around you. You'll see an old man selling fans carefully woven from palm leaves for about half this price, or a teenage youth trying to earn that amount by offering to clean your shoes. It reminds you with a jolt that the vast majority of local people are decent and hardworking and want from you only respect and the chance to make an honest living.

---

unless you're prepared to lose them. Use a separate wallet for day-to-day purchases, and keep the bulk of your cash out of sight, hidden in a pouch under loose-fitting clothing.

- Never look as though you're lost (even if you are), and try not to look like a tourist! Remember to walk purposefully and confidently. If you need to keep your bearings, tear out the map you need from this guidebook, or photocopy it, and use that as your reference. If you need to consult the map, step into a shop or some other place where your disorientation is not so obvious. Or just forget about the map and ask someone, it's usually quicker and raises far less suspicion (it's the way locals get around).
- Don't walk in the backstreets, or even on some of the main streets, at night. Take a taxi. A dollar or two for the fare might save you a lot of trouble.
- Take someone you trust with you if you tend to travel to a risky area of town. It's usually not too difficult to find someone – ask at your hotel reception – who wouldn't mind earning a few dollars for the task of guiding you safely around the streets.

Scams

The hustlers of Dakar and Banjul, and some other places frequented by tourists, have perfected a dazzling array of scams and con tricks. Some are imaginative and amusing; others are serious and cause for concern. Their aim is always to get some (or all) of your money.

A NICE WELCOME

You may be invited to stay in someone's house, in exchange for a meal and drinks, but your new friend's appetite for food and beer may make this deal more expensive than staying at a hotel. More seriously, while you are entertaining, someone will be at the house of your 'friend' going through your bag. This scam is only likely in tourist areas – we heard about it in Saint-Louis – but remember in remote or rural areas you'll come across genuine hospitality.

POLICE & THIEVES

If you buy grass or other drugs from a dealer, don't be surprised if he's in cahoots with the local police who then come to your hotel or stop you in the street and find you 'in possession'. Large bribes will be required to avoid arrest or imprisonment. The solution is very easy – do not buy grass.

REMEMBER ME?

A popular trick in the tourist areas involves local lads approaching you in the street with the words 'Hello, it's me, from the hotel, don't you recognise me?' You're not sure. You don't really remember him, but you don't want to seem like the white person who can't tell the difference between one black man and another. So you stop for a chat. Can he walk with you for a while? Sure. Nice day. A few more pleasantries. Then comes the crunch: how about a visit to his brother's souvenir shop? Or do you want to buy some grass? Need a taxi? A tour? By this time you're hooked, and you probably end up buying or arranging something. A variation involves the con-artist pretending to be a hotel employee or 'son of the owner' out to get supplies for the bar or restaurant. There's been a mix-up in the shop, or he's just out of petrol and needs to get the food stock back. Can you lend him some money? You can take it off the hotel bill later. And there's more. Once you've passed him some bank notes (or even if you haven't), and he's gone, a couple of guys approach you, introducing themselves as tourist guards (with ID cards and all), out to protect visitors to their country from the low-down con-artists, such as the one you've just fallen for. They explain his trick, will accompany you for a while, and, grateful for their help and understanding, you'll make a small donation to their fund.

The way to avoid the trap is to be polite but firm. Anyone calling you 'my friend', *'mon frère'*, or just hissing at you without knowing your name is probably a stranger, so just walk on. Tell people confidently you're not staying in any hotel, you've spent years living here; that'll probably put them off, too.

SOCK SELLERS

A youth approaches you in the street with a couple of pairs of socks for sale. Even though you make it clear you don't want them he follows you for several minutes – checking you out. Then his buddy approaches you from the other side and he also tries to persuade you to buy the socks. He bends down and starts playing with your trousers and shoes, supposedly to show you how well the socks would go with what you're wearing. You are irritated and distracted, and while you bend down to fend him off, whoosh, the other guy comes in from the other side and goes straight for the wallet in your pocket.

The solution? Be firm, walk purposefully, stay cool, and don't be distracted. And don't carry your wallet in your back pocket.

THE VISITORS BOOK

In both Gambia and Senegal, the 'visitors book' has become one of the most popular and definitely the most effective means of extracting cash from tourists. There are several variations, but the following scenario is a classic of the genre. You're in the market, carrying your camera, when a man approaches telling you he has a newborn child. Could you please, if it's no problem at all, come to his compound and take a photo of him and the child. It's not far away, it won't take long, and it would mean the world to him and his sick wife. When you get to the compound you meet his sick 'wife' but the baby is nowhere to be seen. Dad explains that his child is also unwell and has been taken back to the hospital, but seeing as you're here would you like a Coke – it's free! 'It is our duty to be hospitable,' he says. 'We have lots of tourists here, and we never

take money for a drink.' As there is no baby around you have had your suspicions for a while – but you feel too rude to walk out as they bombard you with a string of questions about your country. When you get up to leave, the 'visitors book' appears, listing the names of dozens of other Western tourists who've allegedly donated money to the family to help pay for rice – D500 being the average 'donation'. When it gets to this stage few are able to escape. Your only chance is to leave as soon as you see the baby is not there, or better, to say at the outset that you don't want to give money.

Security

To keep your money and other valuables (such as passport and air ticket) safe from pickpockets, the best place is out of sight under a shirt or skirt or inside your trousers. Some travellers use a pouch or money belt that goes around their necks or waists, while others go for invisible pockets and other imaginative devices.

DISABLED TRAVELLERS

Neither Senegal nor Gambia are easily accessible to disabled travellers. Hotels that make provisions, such as wheelchair access etc, are few and far between. The sandy, and obstacle-ridden pavements can be hard to negotiate for the visually or mobility impaired. However, if you stick to the large, established (and unfortunately expensive) hotels you can expect help, a general awareness, and things such as disabled toilets and wheel-chair access. If you plan to travel upcountry, you're best off travelling with a tour company, and explaining to them your special requirements beforehand.

EMBASSIES & CONSULATES

For practical purposes, the term 'embassy' in this chapter encompasses consulates and high commissions as well as embassies. In some parts of Africa, countries are represented by an honorary consul (not a full-time diplomat, but usually an expatriate working in a local business or aid project who performs limited diplomatic duties on behalf of citizens).

Gambian Embassies & Consulates

Belgium (☎ 02 640 1049; 126 Ave Franklin-Roosevelt, Brussels 1050)

France (☎ 01 42 94 09 30; 117, Rue Saint-Lazare, 75008 Paris)
Germany (☎ 030 892 31 21; fax 891 14 01; Kurfürstendamm 103, Berlin)
Guinea-Bissau (☎ 0203928; Avenida de 14 Novembro, Bissau) Located 1km northwest of Mercado de Bandim.
Nigeria (☎ 0682 192; 162 Awolowo Rd, Ikoyi, Lagos)
Senegal (☎ 821 44 76; 11 Rue de Thiong, Dakar)
Sierra Leone (☎ 225191; 6 Wilberforce St, Freetown)
UK (☎ 020 7937 6316; 57 Kensington Ct, London W8 5DH)
USA (☎ 0202-785 1399; gamembdc@gambia.com; Suite 1000, 1155 15th St NW, Washington, DC 20005)

Gambia is also represented in Austria, Canada, Italy, Japan, the Netherlands, Norway, Spain and Switzerland. For a complete list, www.embassy.org is supposed to list every embassy, though last time we checked the site was slightly outdated. It's worth a try though.

Embassies & Consulates in The Gambia

The following list includes embassies of some 'home' countries and of neighbouring countries for which you might have to get a visa. Most are open 9am to 1pm and 2pm to 4pm Monday to Friday. Opening times different from these appear in the list. It's always best to go at the beginning of the morning session, as lunch hours can be very flexible. Note that for every visa application you need to provide between one and four (usually two) passport photos.

Some embassies and consulates are in Banjul, and others are scattered along the Atlantic coast. For details of embassies in Gambia not listed here, check in the phone book (most Gamtel offices have one).

Guinea (Map p92; ☎ 226862, 909964; top fl, 78A Daniel Goddard St, Banjul; ◷ 9am-4pm Mon-Thu, to 1.30pm & 2.30-4pm Fri)
Guinea-Bissau (Map pp100-1; ☎ 4494854; Atlantic Rd, Bakau; ◷ 9am-2pm Mon-Fri, to 1pm Sat)
Mali (Map p92; ☎ 226942; VM Company Ltd, Cherno Adama Bah St, Banjul)
Mauritania (Map pp100-1; ☎ 461086; Badala Park Way, Kololi; ◷ 8am-4pm Mon-Fri)
Senegal (Map pp100-1; ☎ 373752; fax 373 750; ◷ 8am-2pm & 2.30-5pm Mon-Fri) Off Kairaba Ave.
Sierra Leone (Map p92; ☎ 228206; 67 Daniel Goddard St, Banjul; ◷ 8.30am-4.30pm Mon-Thu, to 1.30pm Fri)
UK (Map pp100-1; ☎ 495133/4; fax 496134; 48 Atlantic Rd, Fajara; ◷ 8am-3pm Mon-Thu, to 1pm Fri)
USA (Map pp100-1; ☎ 392856/8, 391971; fax 392475; Kairaba Ave, Fajara)

Several European countries have honorary consuls in Gambia, including Belgium (at the Kairaba Hotel, Kololi); and Germany, Denmark, Sweden and Norway (above Tina's Grill, Saitmatty Rd, Bakau). These people have limited diplomatic powers, and are mainly there to assist holidaymakers who run into difficulties. If you need either of these consuls, you can get information about them from one of the holiday reps working for the German and Scandinavian tour companies, usually contactable through the larger hotels. French diplomatic affairs are dealt with by the French embassy in Dakar, Senegal.

Senegalese Embassies & Consulates

If you are outside of West Africa, you'll find Senegalese embassies here:

Belgium (☎ 06730097; senegal.ambassade@coditel.net; 196 Av Franklin-Roosevelt, Brussels 1050)
Canada (☎ 0238 6392; www.ambassenecanada.org; 57 Marlborough Ave, Ottawa ON K1N)
France (☎ 01 44 05 38 69; www.ambassenparis.com; 22 Rue Hamelin, 75016 Paris)
Germany (☎ 0228-21 80 08; Argelanderstrasse 3, 53115 Bonn)
Guinea (☎ 224 46 29 30; Corniche Sud, Coléah, Conakry; ◷ 9am-12.30pm & 1.30-5pm Mon-Fri)
Guinea-Bissau (☎ 245 212944; 43 Rue Omar Torrijhos, Bissau; ◷ 8am-5pm Mon-Fri)
Japan (☎ 0464 8451; fax 464 8452; 1-3-4 Aobadai, Meguro-ku Tokyo 153)
Mali (☎ 223 218273/4; fax 211780; 341 Rue 287 X Av Nelson Mandela, Bamako; ◷ 7.30am-1pm & 1.30-4pm Mon-Fri)
Mauritania (☎ 222 525 72 90; Av de l'Ambassade du Sénégal, Nouakchott)
Morocco (☎ 07754171; 17 Cadi Ben Hamadi Benhadj, BP 365 Rabat)
UK (☎ 020 7938 4048; www.senegalembassy.co.uk; 39 Marloes Rd, London W8 6LA)
USA (☎ 02234 0540; 2112 Wyoming Ave NW, Washington, DC 20008)

In West Africa, Senegal also has embassies in Banjul (see left), Abidjan (Côte d'Ivoire), Freetown (Sierra Leone), Lagos (Nigeria), Niamey (Niger) and Praia (Cape Verde).

Embassies & Consulates in Senegal

The following is a list of some embassies, consulates and diplomatic missions in Senegal. You usually need to provide between one and four passport photos when applying for a visa for a neighbouring country.

INTERNATIONAL ROOTS FESTIVAL

On the back of Alex Haley's book *Roots* and its success, the Gambian government initiated the **Roots Homecoming Festival** (www .rootsgambia.gm), a biennial event last held in June 2006, featuring concerts, talks, commemorative walks and workshops across the country. The climax is a big celebration in Jufureh with dance displays and concerts by local troupes and stars from the African diaspora. Registration for the full weeklong programme costs US$250, though it's perfectly possible to participate only in a few events (some are free, others like the 'Jufureh pilgrimage' cost up to US$100).

Many embassies are in or near central Dakar, but there is a steady movement of the diplomatic corps towards the Point E and Mermoz areas, about 5km northwest of the centre. If you need to find an embassy that is not listed here, check the phone book, one of the listings magazines, or www .ausenegal.com/practique_en/ambassad .htm. Most embassies are open from 8am to noon, and in theory from 2.30pm to 5pm, though you're always better off seeking a morning 'appointment.'

Belgium (Map p148; ☎ 822 4720; Route de la Corniche-Est)
Burkina Faso (Map p146; ☎ 827 9509/8; Lot 1, Liberty VI Extension; ☼ 8am-3pm Mon-Fri)
Canada (Map p148; ☎ 889 4700; Immeuble Sorano, 4th fl, 45-47 Blvd de la République)
Cape Verde (Map p150; ☎ 821 1873; 3 Blvd el Haji Djily Mbaye; ☼ 8.30am-3pm Mon-Fri)
Côte d'Ivoire (Map p152; ☎ 869 02 70; Allées Seydou Nourou Tall cnr Rue G, Point E; ☼ 9am-12.30pm & 3-5pm Mon-Fri)
France (Map p150; ☎ 839 5100; 1 Rue Assane Ndoye)
Gambia (Map p150; ☎ 821 7230; 11 Rue de Thiong; ☼ 9am-3pm Mon-Thu & to 1pm Fri)
Germany (Map p148; ☎ 889 4884; 20 Av Pasteur)
Ghana (Map p152; ☎ 869 4053; Rue 6,Point E)
Guinea (Map p152; ☎ 824 8606; Rue 7, Point E; ☼ 9.30am-2pm Mon-Fri) Directly opposite Ker Jaraaf.
Guinea-Bissau Dakar (Map p152; ☎ 824 5922; Rue 6, Point E, Dakar; ☼ 8am-12.30pm Mon-Fri); Ziguinchor (☎ 991 1046; ☼ 8am-2pm Mon-Fri)
Italy (Map p148; ☎ 822 0076; Rue Seydou Nourou Tall)
Mali (Map p146; ☎ 824 6252; 23 Route de la Corniche Ouest, Fann; ☼ 8am-11am Mon-Fri)
Mauritania (Map p146; ☎ 822 6238; Rue 37, Kolobane; ☼ 8am-2pm Mon-Fri)

Morocco (Map p152; ☎ 824 6927; Av Cheikh Anta Diop, Mermoz) Near the Total petrol station where all the *cars rapides* wait.
Netherlands (Map p150; ☎ 849 0360; 37 Rue Kléber)
Spain (Map p148; ☎ 842 6408; 18-20 Av Nelson Mandela)
Switzerland (Map p148; ☎ 823 0590; Rue René Ndiaye)
UK (Map p148; ☎ 823 7392; 20 Rue du Dr Guillet) One block north of Hôpital Le Dantec.
USA (Map p150; ☎ 823 4296; Av Jean XXIII)

FESTIVALS & EVENTS

There's always a festival on somewhere in the region: some so small and informal that you'll hardly hear about them; others huge, international events. Here's a selection.

Abéné Festivalo Informal event, mainly featuring drumming troupes of varying standards. Happens every New Year.
Dak'Art Biennale (☎ 823 0918; www.dakart.org) Fantastic biennial arts festival, held in Dakar.
Festival International du Film de Quartier (www .festivaldufilmdequartier.com) Dakar Film Festival with excellent fringe shows.
International Roots Festival Biennial festival held all across Gambia in June, with a focus on the village of Jufureh, made famous by Alex Haley's book *Roots*. Features mainly traditional music, as well as debates.
Kaay Fecc (☎ 826 4950; www.ausenegal.com/kaayfecc) One of Africa's best dance festivals.
Kartong Festival (☎ 8900411, 7730535; peterborshik@ hotmail.com; www.kartongfestival.com) Village festival in Gambia. Features stunning local, largely traditional groups.
Saint-Louis International Jazz Festival (www.saint louisjazz.com, in French) Renowned international jazz festival in a historical setting.

FOOD

The availability and quality of restaurants differs enormously between the urban and rural areas of the region. The best place by far to go out for a meal is Dakar, home to hundreds of restaurants, serving all kinds of food, from simple rice dishes to several course dinners. Upcountry, your choice is more often between hotel food and that served in the local *gargotte* (eating house), usually found near the taxi ranks or along the market. And if you arrive late in the evening (after 11pm), even the *gargotte* may have run out of food, and you'll be forced to hunt for bread and sardines at the local corner store.

Also note that in smaller towns, restaurants and hotels may only serve food on request, so you have to order in advance.

Prices for meals vary enormously (as does the standard of food). Local rice dishes are always the cheapest, and you can find them in small eateries from CFA1000 or D25. A classy restaurant will charge around CFA5000 to CFA70000 or D200 to D250 for a dish – but beware, the stylishness of the surroundings doesn't necessarily reflect the quality of food. Hotels, as with pretty much anywhere around the world, tend to overcharge, though some have surprisingly good restaurants (if that's the case, we have tried to highlight this in this guidebook). See also the Food & Drink chapter (p79).

GAY & LESBIAN TRAVELLERS

Most people in both Gambia and Senegal, especially the older generation, are conservative in their attitudes towards gays and lesbians, and gay sexual relationships are both a cultural taboo and (officially) very rare among locals. Strictly speaking, being gay or lesbian is illegal in Senegal. Some parts of the predominantly Muslim community are actively antigay – some villagers have prevented gays being buried in the village cemetery. Most locals, though, have a fairly 'live and let live' attitude. Flirting from Westerners is more often met with embarrassment than with anger.

Among the expat community, which is pretty much confined to the Atlantic coast resorts in Gambia, and Dakar and the resort zones around Saly and Cap Skiring in Senegal, there is a percentage who are gay (as in any Western community), but there are no established regular meeting places or 'scenes', so it is usually quite difficult for visitors to make contact. In most places in Senegal and Gambia, any open displays of affection are generally frowned upon, whatever your orientation.

HOLIDAYS

Senegal and Gambia don't exactly lack in public holidays, and especially in Senegal you'll be forgiven for thinking that the country enjoys a near uninterrupted chain of public celebrations. Both Christian and Islamic events are celebrated. The Muslim holidays, such as Korité, Tabaski, Tamkharit and Maoulid, are determined by the lunar calendar, and occur on different dates each year (for more details, see the boxed text p46). The exact dates of these holidays are only announced just before they occur, as they depend on the sightings of the moon.

And occasionally, experts differ in their readings of the moon, which can result in a two-day celebration.

Governmental departments shut on public holidays, as do many businesses and shops, though there'll always be a boutique open where you can get your bread and coffee. Public transport can be less frequent, and taxis usually increase their prices, sometimes quite drastically.

The Gambia

Holidays include the following:
New Year's Day 1 January
Independence Day 18 February
Good Friday March/April
Easter Monday March/April
Workers' Day 1 May
Anniversary of the Second Republic 22 July
Christmas 25 December

Senegal

Holidays include the following:
New Year's Day 1 January
Independence Day 4 April
Easter Monday March/April
Whit Sunday/Pentecost Seventh Sunday after Easter
Whit Monday Day after Whit Sunday
Ascension 40th day after Easter
Workers Day 1 May
Assumption August 15
Christmas Day 25 December

Other annual festivals include the Grand Magal pilgrimage and celebration, held in Touba 48 days after the Islamic New Year to celebrate the return from exile of the founder of the Mouride Islamic brotherhood; and the Paris–Dakar Rally, which ends at Lac Rose in mid-January.

INSURANCE

An insurance policy covering you for medical expenses and an emergency flight home is essential. Hospitals in Senegal and Gambia are not free, and the good ones are not cheap, particularly for foreigners, who may have to pay up to three times the price charged to locals. Air ambulances and international medical evacuation (medivac) flights are frighteningly expensive, so you need to be fully covered.

Most travel insurance also covers your baggage in case of loss, and cancellation or hijack. (It's important to read the small print, but some aspects they cover are enough to put you off flying!) It's possible to get medical travel insurance only; however, in our experience there is generally little difference in price for such policies covering Africa.

If your travel agent, insurance broker or credit-card company can't help you with a good policy, try a student travel service. It's preferable to get a policy from an insurance company that will directly pay any costs you incur, rather than reimburse you after you pay your bills.

Worldwide cover to travellers from over 44 countries is available online at www .lonelyplanet.com/travel_services.

INTERNET ACCESS

Access to the Internet is becoming increasingly easy and cheap in Gambia and Senegal; in Dakar, Senegal, and the tourist areas of the Atlantic coast in Gambia, the service is world-class. See the Information sections in the destination chapters for locations of Internet cafés.

Unless you're planning on staying in expensive hotels there's not much point in bringing your notebook or palmtop computer with you as you'll need to be very lucky indeed to find a phone jack. Even if there is a jack, at the time of writing none of the major ISPs (Internet Service Providers) had local dial-in numbers, meaning connecting to the Net could be both very slow and very expensive. If you do bring a computer, invest in a universal AC adaptor, a plug adaptor for each country you visit, and a reputable 'global' modem. Telephone sockets will probably be different too, so bring at least a US RJ-11 adaptor that works with your modem. Especially in Senegal, wi-fi access is rising fast, and several hotels and restaurants around the country now offer free wi-fi access – perfect for connecting your laptop. See particular reviews for places with wi-fi access.

If your Internet email account is hosted by a smaller ISP or your office or school network, your best option is to rely on cybercafés and other public access points to collect your mail. To do this, you'll need to carry three pieces of information: your incoming (POP or IMAP) mail server name, your account name and your password. Your ISP or network supervisor will be able to give you these. Armed with this information,

you should be able to access your Internet mail account from any Internet-connected machine in the world, provided it runs some kind of email software (Netscape and Internet Explorer both have mail modules).

The Gambia

Internet cafés are common in Banjul and on the Atlantic coast, and there's usually some place to log on in the larger upcountry towns, too. There are three operators whose signs can be seen fairly frequently: Cyber-World, Quantumnet (www.qanet.gm) and Gamtel. All charge about D30 an hour as a base rate. The service is generally reasonably fast, with newish terminals and extras such as microphones and cameras standard. However, frequent power cuts have the potential to ruin your whole day, so it's wise to ask whether the café has a back-up generator, or at the very least a surge protector, before logging on.

Away from the coast and all the cashed-up tourists, Net access is harder to find, slower and more expensive, and the power cuts are more frequent, too.

Senegal

Senegal is the third-best place in Africa for Web services, and you'll have no problem logging on. Cybercafés are plentiful, though not all are equally speedy. All major towns upcountry are connected, and some of the smaller places, too, though the more remote you get, the more you have to pay.

In Dakar, Internet phone and video facilities are common, and you normally pay CFA300 per hour. In Kedougou, this price is a staggering CFA1500, and in most other places you'll pay something in-between.

LEGAL MATTERS

While marijuana is widely available in both Gambia and Senegal, its use is illegal in both countries. If you're caught in possession you could face up to two years in an African jail; a less-than-attractive proposition. However, unless you're caught by an unusually straight cop, or are carrying a particularly large quantity of the drug, it's more likely you'll be 'persuaded' to buy your way out of trouble, which usually results in a very one-sided bargaining session. Either way, you are in deep shit if you get caught.

COPIES

Photocopies of all your important documents, plus airline tickets and credit cards, will help speed up replacement if they are lost or stolen. Keep these records and a list of travellers cheque numbers separate from other valuables, and also leave copies with someone at home so they can be faxed to you in an emergency.

MAPS

Most maps of Senegal also show Gambia, but the level of detail on the smaller country is generally poor.

Macmillan's *Traveller's Map of Gambia* (at a scale of 1:400,000) is by far the best – clear and easy to read, with most roads, tourist sights and places of interest marked – but can be hard to find.

The most widely available map of Gambia is the 1:350,000 effort by Canadian group International Travel Maps. This is not bad, but there are several errors that can be frustrating. For Senegal, the locally produced *Carte du Senegal* (1:912,000) is the best and cheapest available and includes a basic street map of Dakar; this map is hard to find outside Senegal though.

Also good for country coverage is the *Senegal Carte Routière* (1:1,000,000) produced by the Institut Géographique National (IGN). Not as good, but more widely available internationally, is ITMB's *Senegal, Including Gambia* (1:800,000).

If your journey through Gambia and Senegal is part of wider travels in West Africa, the Michelin map *Africa – North & West* (sheet number 953, formerly number 153) is one of the few maps in the world to have achieved something like classic status. The detail is incredible, given the limitations of scale (1:4,000,000), and the map is regularly updated (check the date on the back cover to make sure you buy a recent version). You should expect a few discrepancies between the map and reality, particularly with regard to roads, as old tracks get upgraded and once-smooth highways become potholed disasters. However, no overland driver would be without this map. There's even a **153 Club** (www.manntaylor.com/153.html) for those people who have driven across the Sahara and around West Africa.

MONEY
The Gambia

Gambia's unit of currency is the dalasi (da-la-see). This is abbreviated to D or d, and is written before or after the numbers. Throughout this book, we have put it before, eg D200. The dalasi is not fixed and floats against other international currencies, although locals will tell you it's been drowning for years. When this book was written, the dalasi had just become fairly stable; check the situation when you travel, and bear value-decrease in mind when considering prices listed in this book.

The dalasi is divided into 100 bututs, and there are coins for five, 10, 25 and 50 bututs, although apart from the 50 these are rarely seen. Notes in circulation are D5, D10, D25, D50 and D100. There is also a D1 coin.

Gambia's main banks are Standard Chartered, Trust Bank and IBC, all of which have branches in Banjul, Serekunda and the Atlantic coast resorts. Upcountry, only Basse Santa Su and Brikama have bank branches.

Senegal

The currency of Senegal is the West African CFA franc, called the 'franc CFA' in French (pronounced franc seh-eff-ahh). CFA stands for Communauté Financière Africaine, and is also the official currency of Benin, Burkina Faso, Côte d'Ivoire, Guinea-Bissau, Mali, Niger and Togo.

There are 100 centimes in one CFA franc and they come in 5, 10, 25 and 50 denominations. There are coins for CFA5, CFA10, CFA50, CFA100 and CFA250 and there are notes for CFA500, CFA1000, CFA5000 and CFA10,000.

The value of the CFA is tied to the euro at a fixed rate of 1 euro to 655.957CFA.

The main banks are BICIS (which is affiliated with and accepts cheques from BNP in France), SGBS and CBAO. The first two have the largest number of branches; at least one of them tends to be present in the larger towns.

ATMs

There are ATMs at several banks (notably Standard Chartered) and a couple of petrol stations in Banjul and around the Atlantic coast. Senegal is amazingly well served, with ATMs in all major and some minor towns, and all across Dakar. Still, even in

NEW CURRENCIES

There are plans to unite Gambia, Senegal and 13 other West African countries in a joint monetary zone. In theory, this united currency was supposed to replace all existing ones by 2004, but it hasn't. The hugely ambitious project was launched by the Economic Community of West African States (Ecowas), which argues that a single currency, combined with common customs laws, common tariff levels and open borders, will help achieve regional economic integration and eventually prosperity in this, the poorest region on earth.

The initial plan was to bring Gambia together with Ghana, Guinea, Liberia, Nigeria and Sierra Leone in a currency labelled the West Africa Second Monetary Zone (WAMZ). Then, just as these countries get used to the WAMZ, they'd be expected to go through the whole process again when their new currency merges with the CFA, which is already used in eight West African states.

At the time this book went to press, no news was available about the progress of the project, and locals didn't seem to know anything about it at all. Whether it's been scrapped, thrown into the too hard basket or simply been given more time to mature isn't quite certain. But who knows, perhaps you will be asked to change your dollars into WAMZ by the time you travel. Keep an ear out for the latest news before you head off.

Senegal it's not wise to rely on their presence if you travel upcountry, as a broken or empty teller can leave you stranded.

In theory ATMs accept credit and debit cards from banks with reciprocal agreements. In Senegal SGBS and CBAO ATMs normally take Visa and MasterCard, but BICIS accepts only Visa. In Gambia you're stranded with anything but Visa, and the Cirrus, Maestro and Plus networks displayed at some ATMs aren't generally accepted.

Banks and card companies often use fair exchange rates, which can make drawing money from the wall cheaper than changing travellers cheques.

In Senegal, your typical withdrawal limit is CFA300,000, though some bank branches only allow up to CFA150,000. In Gambia, limits can be ridiculously tight, with some banks only allowing withdrawal of up to D2000.

Black Market

Until a few years ago, Gambia had a thriving black market, where many tourists changed money for slightly better rates, though at hugely higher risks (of theft and of being arrested or fined). These days, as the dalasi has become more stable and the police tougher, the black market is more insignificant. You can still find people changing cash in shady restaurants, near the Barra ferry and in other places, but they will rarely offer you a better rate than the bank (sometimes it's worse), and you run a very real risk of being conned out of your money.

If you travel overland from Senegal, money changers will probably crowd around your taxi as you enter Gambia. Don't feel pressured, many places and most taxis in Gambia also accept CFA, so that you can get by without changing money before you reach Banjul or the coastal resorts.

Cash

In Senegal and Gambia, major international currencies such as euros, US dollars and British pounds can be changed in banks in the capital cities, major towns and tourist areas. In urban areas, you can usually change money at hotel reception desks, although rates are often lousy or commissions high. Another option is to try asking discreetly at a shop selling imported items. Saying something like 'The banks are closed and I have US dollars – do you know anyone who can help me…?' is better than 'Do you change money?'

Try to do all your changing in the cities before heading upcountry. And if you do take foreign currencies into the more remote areas, try to make it euros rather than pounds or dollars or you risk getting stuck.

Because of counterfeiting, old US$100 notes and some other older notes are not accepted at places that don't have a light machine for checking watermarks.

Credit Cards

The use of credit cards is mainly limited to midrange and top-end hotels and restaurants, car-rental outfits, purchasing air tickets and some tours. Visa is the most widely accepted. You won't usually be able to use them in supermarkets and only in very few shops (such as Senegal's large bookshops).

Certainly don't rely on plastic when travelling upcountry, not even for use in ATMs. Some banks in the interior of Senegal and Gambia can give cash advances on credit cards, though readers have reported this being too much hassle to try.

Your card company will tell you which banks in Gambia and Senegal will accept your card. You'll also need to ask your bank or card company about charges, and arrange a way to pay card bills if you're travelling for more than a month or so. Debit cards can be used to draw cash and because there's no bill to pay off they are good for longer journeys.

International Transfers

Unless you've got a bank account with a major bank in France, it's highly unlikely that your bank will accept international wire transfers. And even if it does, chances are it'll take longer than your holiday and cost you almost as much.

Faster and a lot simpler than banks is Western Union Money Transfer, where all you need to do is phone someone with money, get them to send their cash and tell you the password, and you can pick up the cash at a branch the next day. This doesn't come cheap either, but if you're really stuck for cash in a small village in the sticks of Gambia or Senegal, this might sometimes be your only option. Western Union offices are springing up quicker than potholes in Gambia's tarmac, and even small towns often have a branch.

Moneychangers

All the major bank branches change money, as do exchange bureaus, which are mostly present in the tourist zones. The airports in both countries have bank branches; if they are closed, you can try the bookshop at Dakar airport, or, failing that, change a small amount with the guys lurking around outside for just that purpose – at least to get you into town where you have better options.

In Gambia, moneychanging bureaus tend to give a slightly better rate for cash than banks, and a slightly worse rate for travellers cheques, but as rates and commissions can vary, it might be worth shopping around.

BANK CHARGES & COMMISSIONS

Generally, whenever you change money you have to pay something to the bank – that's how it makes its profit. The charge can be a flat fee (of around US$2), but sometimes it's a commission quoted as a percentage of the amount you change (usually between 1% and 2%). Sometimes you have to pay a charge in addition to a commission.

Alternatively there may be no charge or commission at all, but this doesn't necessarily mean it's a better deal, as the bank may instead make its money from the lower rate it offers you. For example, Bank A may give you CFA500 to the US dollar, and charge a commission of 2%. Over the street, Bank B may not charge any commission but only give you CFA480 per US dollar. Keep this in mind when looking around.

If you're dealing with CFA francs and euros, much of this is academic. The rate is fixed at 656:1 and all you need to compare between banks is the charge or commission.

Tipping

Tipping in Gambia and Senegal is only expected from the wealthy. This means well-to-do locals and nearly all foreign visitors. Anyone staying in an upmarket hotel is expected to tip porters and other staff, but not a backpacker in a cheap hotel.

At the better restaurants, you're expected to tip around 10%, though many places include this in the bill. At the other end of the scale are the more basic restaurants and eating-houses where no tipping is expected from anyone. There's a grey area between these two classes of restaurants, where tipping is rarely expected from locals, but may be expected of wealthy-looking foreigners.

No-one tips taxi drivers.

Travellers Cheques

Travellers cheques can be a safer alternative to cash – you can get a refund or replacement if they get stolen. But changing them isn't easy in either country. The major city banks accept them grudgingly but charge high commissions, and you'll be stuck with them in the smaller branches upcountry.

Only Amex cheques are considered, and the best currency for travellers cheques (as for cash) is the euro.

PHOTOGRAPHY & VIDEO
Film & Accessories

Film is relatively expensive in Gambia and Senegal because it has to be imported. Outside the major cities only standard print film is available; in Gambia slide film is almost impossible to find. Even if the expiry date has not yet been reached, the film may have been damaged by heat. It's best to bring all you need with you.

The sunlight is frequently strong, so most people find 100 ASA perfectly adequate, with possibly 200 ASA or 400 ASA for long-lens shots. Useful photographic accessories might include a small flash, a cable or remote shutter release, filters and a cleaning kit. Also remember to take spare batteries.

The old X-ray machines at some airports may not be safe for film. Even newer film-safe models can damage high-speed film (1000 ASA plus), especially if the film goes through several checks, so use a protective lead bag. Alternatively, carry film in your pocket and have it checked manually by officials.

The main photo laboratories in the cities of Gambia and Senegal, as well as some clued-up Internet cafés, have facilities for printing digital images, but you're better off waiting until you get home, where it's cheaper.

Photographing Animals

To score excellent wildlife shots, a long lens helps, although you'll need a tripod for anything over 200mm. If your subject is nothing but a speck in the distance, resist wasting film but keep the camera ready.

Photographing People

Taking pictures of strangers is a sensitive issue, especially if a relatively affluent photographer takes pictures of poorer people. What you might consider a great, typical Gambian scene, they may find humiliating, feeling uncomfortable being photographed in a day-to-day situation and poverty. Pictures by locals are usually only taken at ceremonies, parties, in bars and restaurants, when people are dressed their best.

Approach people photography with respect. Some tourists go for discreet shots with long lenses. Others ask permission first. If you get 'no' for an answer, accept it. Some local people may agree to be photographed if you give them a picture for themselves. Take their address and make it clear that you'll post the photo. Your promise will be taken seriously, so never say you'll send a photo unless you intend to.

Restrictions

In Senegal and Gambia no permit is required for photography. You'll mostly have no problem with a camera (providing, of course, you observe the usual rules of politeness). Note that you should avoid taking photos of military installations, airports, ferries, harbours and government buildings. This is particularly pertinent in Gambia, where there's a good chance you'll have your film and camera confiscated; you might even get arrested. Things are more relaxed in Senegal, though you could still get into trouble. Always ask before taking pictures of places of worship or a natural feature with traditional religious significance.

Technical Tips
CAMERA CARE

Heat and humidity can take a toll on your camera, but the biggest danger is the all-pervading dust that accompanies almost every trip out of town. If you don't take precautions, grit will soon find its way into lenses and camera bodies. Try to find a camera bag that closes with a zip or some other form of seal – the traditional top-opening shoulder bags are hopeless at keeping dust out. Carry snap-lock or zip-lock bags to put lenses into when they're not in use. The worst time of year for dust is during the harmattan (the light winds from the north that carry tiny particles of sand from the desert, causing hazy skies from December to February).

EXPOSURE

When photographing animals or people, take light readings from the subject and not the brilliant African background, or your shots will turn out underexposed.

TIMING

The best times to take photographs on sunny days are the first two hours after sunrise and the last two before sunset. This takes advantage of the colour-enhancing rays cast by a low sun. A polarising filter can help to cut out glare, which is especially useful during hazy periods before the rainy season.

For further tips, check out Lonely Planet's *Travel Photography*.

Video

A properly used video camera can give a fascinating record of your holiday. As well as obvious things – sunsets, spectacular views – remember to record some of the ordinary everyday details of life in the country.

One good rule to follow is to film in long takes, and don't move the camera around too much. Otherwise, your video could well make your viewers seasick! If your camera has a stabiliser, you can use it to obtain good footage while travelling – even on bumpy roads. Video cameras often have sensitive microphones, which can be a problem if there is a lot of ambient noise.

While travelling, you can recharge batteries in hotels as you go along, so take the necessary charger, plugs and transformer.

You should follow the guidelines outlined under Photographing People (opposite) regarding people's sensitivities; many locals find video cameras even more annoying and offensive than still cameras. Always ask permission first. And remember, you're on holiday – don't let the video take over your life.

POST

Senegal has one of the most reliable postal services in the whole of Africa, and Gambia isn't doing too badly either. Telephone networks are good, too, both for mobile phones and landlines. Post is much quicker and more reliable from the main centres.

In both countries the postal services are relatively cheap. For postcards or any sort of stationery or packaging materials, the cheapest places are almost always located outside the post office.

Receiving Mail

If you need to receive mail, you can use the poste restante service, where letters are sent to a post office (usually in a capital city) for you to collect. In Gambia, the best place for poste restante is the main post office in Banjul; mail should be addressed as follows: Your name/Poste Restante/General Post Office/Banjul/The Gambia.

In Senegal, the main postal branch in Dakar is the place for poste restante. You send letters to: Your name/Poste Restante/PTT/Dakar/Senegal. Note that some travellers have reported negative experiences using this service.

Letters usually take about a week to arrive from Europe, and twice as long from North America or Australasia. However, they can take much longer to work through the system once in Senegal or Gambia. If they've arrived in the country, they'll be registered on the computer system, and you can track their whereabouts. (Parcels and large envelopes are usually stuck at customs). To collect your mail, go to the main post office and show your passport; always bring some money with you in case of unexpected customs charges.

It's essential to write your name clearly in capital letters. If you can't find mail you're expecting, check under your other names. Ask people writing to you to use just your family name and initials. If your family name is common, it should be underlined and your given name written in lower case.

Sending Mail

Letters sent from Dakar or Banjul take about a week to reach most parts of Europe, and eight to 15 days to reach North America or Australasia. Don't rely on this – sometimes it can take three times longer for a letter to arrive. If speed is important, you're better off using a DHL service – especially in Senegal, where they have a number of offices.

SHOPPING

Keen shoppers can spend many hours browsing in the shops, stalls and markets of Gambia and Senegal, hunting for that rare souvenir.

Wherever there are tourists, you will find stalls full of wooden carvings of variable quality, the same designs endlessly repeated. It is easy to be disdainful of hastily made 'airport art', but if you look hard you may well find something that catches your eye. Many wooden carvings are stained brown or black, and shoe polish seems to be the dye of choice.

If it's jewellery you're after, the numerous, tiny boutiques of inner-city Dakar or Gambia's coastal area will soon catch your eye. It's best to shop here with someone who knows the difference between a skilled goldsmith selling real items, and one that shifts only mass-produced fakes. Mauritanian silversmiths have a tradition of creating delicate, silver filigree jewellery. You'll find them near Marché Sandaga in Dakar.

FUNKY SOUVENIRS

You're the type of traveller who steers clear of 'tourist trash' but still wants to bring home something special? Try the following:

- a lamp shade or CD shelf made from old cans, craftily welded together by Baba Diawara and sold in his fabulous little workshop opposite Marché Soumbédioune in Dakar

- an Afro-funky jeans outfit made by the young-people's label **Sigil** (☎ 864 7705; www.keur-gui.com; Villa 988, Sicap Rue 10, Dakar)

- a *sous-verre* (glass painting) in the full-colour style of Dakar's *cars rapides,* sold in **Michèle Ka's hair salon** (☎ 824 7033) in Dakar's Point E, near the big swimming pool

- a book by Dakar's leading cartoonist Mohiss, sold in all the big Dakar bookshops. No-one teases the Senegalese better

- a length of cloth printed with the face of Gambia's president, sold in markets all across the country (election time is a good moment to find these)

- an intricately decorated incense burner (the ones made in the Bassari lands are particularly beautiful) together with a bag of *thiouraye* (a mixture of seed and fragrant wood) to burn in it – it'll do wonders for your love life

- a pair of sandals made to fit at the Moroccan workshops in Dakar's Rue Mohammed V

- a wall hanging made from stitched-together lengths of hand-woven indigo fabric – Kedougou market is your best bet

- a batik painting by a leading Gambian artist, try the Lemonfish Gallery in Kartong and the African Heritage Centre in Bakau

- a scrap-material bird made by Dhiedhiou Tall, on sale at the Institut Français in Dakar

Fabrics are another shopper's favourite, and you'll find a wide selection of locally dyed or imported fabrics in every large market. If it's Malian-style *bazins* (dyed fabrics that are beaten to shine with wooden clubs) you're after, it's again advisable to go with someone who knows their stuff – these fabrics range from expensive, rustling, rich *bazin* destined for the affluent classes and first quality (still shimmering) to second quality, usually used for table cloths and bedspreads. You can take your fabrics to a local tailor and have them made into a perfectly fitting outfit. Alternatively, you can buy ready-made clothing. Brightly coloured baggy trousers and shirts are popular. These are cheap and likely to fall apart at a moment's notice, though. The shops selling this type of clothing usually also have a range of batik paintings, which are just as quickly churned out.

For lovers of West African music, there is an enormous supply of locally produced CDs and cassettes, usually sold in markets or by merchants on the street. International artists such as Youssou N'Dour frequently produce albums for the local market that never reach Europe. You take your chances on quality, with prices around US$2 per tape and US$10 for the CD.

Many people come to this region to learn drumming. If you really want to purchase an instrument to play, go with your drumming teacher, they'll have their reliable drum maker. If you are just looking for a souvenir, you can go to any market and haggle. But you might want to consider the fact that the Western love of *djembe* (a short, goat hide–covered drum) has caused such an increase in production that the *dimb* tree they are made from has become almost extinct in some areas, causing all the usual problems associated with deforestation.

Genuine collectors of African art are likely to be more interested in the wooden sculptures, particularly masks, headdresses and stools that have found their way from all over West and Central Africa to the galleries of Dakar, and to a few stalls in the markets of Banjul and Brikama in Gambia. Some of the dusty pieces are genuine, which raises questions about whether travellers should encourage the people of Africa to sell off the best parts of their cultural inheritance, while others are replicas made specifically for sale.

For contemporary art, it's best to seek out your artist of choice and purchase directly from them. Dakar and Gorée are among the best places for this, details are included in the relevant regional chapters.

At some market stalls you may see ivory for sale. While it's not illegal to buy ivory within Gambia or Senegal, it is illegal to export it in any quantity, so if you carry it home to Europe (or wherever) and it's discovered in your luggage you face arrest, fines or imprisonment. By buying ivory, you'll also be supporting the poaching of elephants.

Bargaining

As soon as you flag down your first taxi in Dakar, you'll be introduced to the art of bargaining, an aspect of daily life in this part of the world. Bargaining accompanies almost every purchase, with the exception of supermarkets, some fixed-prices boutiques (usually created to provide relief for haggle-shy tourists) and pharmacies. In terms of public transport, taxi prices are always open to negotiation, while bus rates aren't.

Some tourists are put off purchasing altogether by the practice of bargaining, haunted by the fear of being overcharged. You may be, but this shouldn't worry you

PLAYING THE MARKET

The markets in Gambia and Senegal are large, vibrant, colourful and always fascinating, and well worth a visit even if you don't want to buy anything. There are markets with ramshackle stalls, where women sell carefully arranged fruits and vegetables, and those made of lines of boutiques crammed with cheaply imported electrical items, clothes and shoes, endless rolls of gaudy fabrics and pretty much anything else anyone might want. Most larger towns also have crafts markets ('villages artisanals' in Senegal), where carved masks, statues and other items are sold mainly to tourists.

The biggest markets are in large towns such as Banjul, Serekunda, Dakar and Kaolack, but the markets in smaller places are also well worth a visit.

In rural areas, many villages hold a weekly market called *lumo*. It always takes place on a particular day of the week, and it's possible to explore an entire region by travelling from the *lumo* of one village to the next. This is not only a great option because you'll see the villages from their liveliest side, but also because in remote areas, the day of the *lumo* is often the only one you will find relatively frequent bush taxis.

Some *lumos* can be major events, attracting traders and customers from the surrounding area, and from as far away as Mauritania, Mali, Guinea and Guinea-Bissau. The market in Diaoubé, near Kolda in northern Casamance, is one of the largest *lumos* in Gambia and Senegal, and absolutely worth a visit.

Most travellers love to visit markets, but dealing with overeager traders requires a particular cool and self-control. The Senegalese are famous for their skill of selling anything to anyone, so you need to be equally clever if you don't want to return home with bags full of unwanted stuff.

The first rule is to feign utter disinterest. Show curiosity, and you'll have a hard time shaking the vendor off. The second is keeping a sense of humour. Getting cross will only decrease your own pleasure, while a witty remark or a calm 'I'm not interested' will get you off without spoiling the fun. If you really want something, casually ask for the price, then put on your best shock-expression and enter the almost compulsory process of negotiation.

Walking around town (especially the inner city of Dakar), you'll often be approached by walking traders, decorated by their wares like Christmas trees. Red traffic lights are another favourite sales spot. Walking past at a fast pace, looking straight ahead is the best way of ridding yourself of the keen salesman. A confident 'bakhna' (meaning ' it's OK) or 'après' (literally, 'later', intended to mean 'I'm pretending to come back later but never will') should shake them off. If that doesn't work, keep looking straight past them, and keep walking on.

In particularly busy spots, such as Dakar's Marché Sandaga, the hassle can verge on danger, as pickpockets work the crowds, and gangs of youths posing as merchants can surround tourists and snatch bags and cameras. For information on precautions to take, see Dangers & Annoyances (p259).

too much. Treat bargaining as a simple aspect of travel in the region, and indulge in the pleasure of rehearsing your own mock-expressions of outrage at a perfectly reasonable price. Simply accepting the first price quoted (even though it may be utterly affordable to you) means setting standards that might subsequently outprice locals or other, poorer travellers.

Confidence in bargaining comes from knowing the going rate. You'll find this out easily if you know locals (who'll probably end up bargaining for you, if they realise you're keen on purchasing), and you'll get a feel for it once you've spent some time in the countries.

There are two hard-and-fast rules to bargaining: theatrical skills are a huge asset and exaggerated seriousness won't get you anywhere. Treat this as a game, and don't be afraid of losing (or be vexed if you do). You show interest in an item, the vendor will name a price (anything from the real rate to twice or more that – hence the importance of local knowledge), you pretend to faint with shock and make your first offer. Now the vendor's jaw drops. He'll probably feign indignation, indicating a clear no. You plead abject poverty, insisting on your first rate for a bit, and he'll come down. Then you go up a little. This carries on until you've found a mutually agreeable price. And that's the crux – mutually agreeable. You hear travellers all the time moaning about how they were 'overcharged' by souvenir sellers. When things have no fixed price, nobody really gets overcharged. If you don't like the price, it's simple – don't pay it.

If sellers won't come down to a price you feel is fair (or that you can afford), it either means that they really aren't making any profit, or that if you don't pay their prices, they know somebody else will. Remember the sellers are no more obliged to sell to you than you are to buy from them. You can go elsewhere or, if you really want the item, accept the price. This is the raw edge of capitalism! And don't forget that prices can change depending on where you buy. For example, a soft drink in a city may be a third of the price you'll pay in a remote rural area, where additional transport costs have to be paid for. Conversely, fruit and vegetables are cheaper in the areas where they're grown.

SOLO TRAVELLERS

It's perfectly possible to explore Senegal and Gambia on your own, but you probably won't spend much time alone anyway, as people start talking to you, take you out for drinks and chat to you in the bush taxi. There's none of the embarrassed staring at the ceiling here that frustrates Westerners on their daily schlep to work – people talk to one another.

Travelling single can get a lot more expensive, though.

Many hotels charge by the room, whether it's inhabited by one or two people (though if that's the case, you should always try negotiating), and on boat trips, you'll be paying for the entire boat, when it can actually hold a dozen others (it's always worth trying to gather an improvised circle of friends for that purpose).

Women travelling alone will have to put up with a lot of unwanted attention from men; see Women Travellers (p277) for details.

TELEPHONE & FAX

Very few Gambian and Senegalese households have their own private line, hence the flourishing scene of public telephone offices, from where you can make local, national and international calls, and sometimes even send faxes.

Even the tiniest towns tend to have at least one telecentre, either run by the national company (Gamtel in Gambia, Sonatel in Senegal), or privately owned.

Connections to and from Europe and America are usually very good, but calling other African countries takes a lot of patience – calls may be relayed through Europe, which means bad reception or possibly none.

Calling abroad from Africa isn't cheap by any means. Calls are charged by the unit, and those add up fast on a call abroad. In Gambia, you're likely to pay around D50 per minute, in Senegal CFA600 to CFA800. In Senegal, a 20% reduction applies between 8pm and 7am, in Gambia you get 33% off between 11pm and 7am.

Making reverse-charge (collect) calls is possible, but it's much easier – and far less expensive for your caller – to get the number of the telecentre you're calling from and then get someone to ring you back.

Mobile Phones

Mobile phones are booming in both Senegal and Gambia, completely overtaking land-lines in importance. In Senegal, Alizé, Sentel and Tigo are the main operators; in Gambia you'll come across the names Gamcel and Africell.

Senegal has almost complete mobile cover-age. All major and minor towns are covered, and even in remote villages, there's usually one spot where you get reception. Alizé is the most widely extended network and your best bet travelling upcountry. Gambia is almost equally as well served, Africell seeming to have the widest coverage. Along some border stretches in Gambia, you'll find that Senega-lese numbers function better than Gambian ones – but note that this means you're effec-tively making an international call.

If you stay for a while, it's a good idea to get a mobile. You can buy handsets almost anywhere, from the simplest first-generation phone to the latest camera-video gizmo. If you bring your own phone, make sure you're able to insert any other SIM card (though unlocking contract phones is a flourishing business in Senegal and Gam-bia), and bear in mind that dust resistance is more important than chic. Connecting is easy. You buy a SIM card (D500 at Gamcel in Gambia, CFA25,000 at Alizé in Senegal), and top up with prepaid cards, which sell in units of D50, D100, D150 and D300 in Gambia and CFA2500, CFA5000 and CFA10,000 in Senegal.

Calls from mobile to mobile are fairly cheap, while mobile-landline costs almost the same as an international call.

Phonecards

In Senegal, the widely available prepaid Nopale phonecard allows you to call from any phone at a loca rate – the cost of the call gets taken off the amount you purchased the card for.

Phone Codes

To phone Senegal or Gambia from another country, you need to dial your country's in-ternational access code (for example, ☎ 00 or ☎ 010), then the country code: ☎ 220 for Gambia, or ☎ 221 for Senegal. There are no area codes in Gambia or Senegal; the first three figures of a phone number allow you to identify what region a call comes from.

To phone overseas from either Gambia or Senegal, first dial the international access code (☎ 00 for both Gambia and Senegal), then the code of the country you want to reach, then the city code (omitting the first zero if applicable), and then, finally, the number.

In Gambia, the number for directory as-sistance is ☎ 151; in Senegal it's ☎ 12.

TIME

Gambia and Senegal are at GMT/UTC, which for most European visitors means there is no or very little time difference. The time is the same all year; neither country has daylight-saving time. When it's noon in Gambia or Senegal, it's 7am in New York, noon in London, 1pm in Paris and 10pm in Sydney.

TOILETS

There are two main types of toilet in Africa: the Western style, with a bowl and seat; and the African one – a hole in the floor, over which you squat. Standards for both vary tremendously, ranging from the pristine to the unusable. Some travellers complain that African toilets are difficult to use, or that you have to remove half your clothing to use them. This is not so, and it only takes a small degree of practice to master a comfortable squatting technique.

In rural areas squat toilets are built over a deep hole in the ground. These are called 'long drops', and the crap just decomposes naturally, as long as the hole isn't filled with too much other rubbish (such as paper or synthetic materials, including tampons, which should be disposed of separately).

In remote wilderness areas, there may be no toilets at all, and you have to find a quiet bush or rock to relieve yourself behind.

Some Western toilets are not plumbed in, but just balanced over a long drop, and sometimes seats are constructed to assist those who can't squat. The lack of running water usually makes such cross-cultural mechanisms a disaster. A noncontact squat loo is better than a filthy box to hover over any day.

A couple of clued-up eco-lodges in Gam-bia have installed compost toilets – a great, nonsmelling, biodegradable solution, espe-cially for areas close to the coast. They just haven't caught on widely yet.

There's little in the way of public toilets, and you've got to muster some courage to enter one of the booths that are occasionally available in Dakar. Restaurants will usually be kind enough to allow you relief, though you might have to purchase a soft drink or something. Long journeys can be problematic. Buses don't have toilets, and there are no comfy service stations on the way. On several-hour trips, drivers will put in a piss-stop, usually near an empty field – easy for men, tough for women (that's where the sarong or wrap-skirt comes in really handy). Some petrol stations have toilets at the back – don't be shy to ask.

TOURIST INFORMATION

Gambia is represented in Britain by the **Gambia National Tourist Office** (☎ 020 7376 0093; www .gambiatourism.info) based at the Gambian high commission. This office has a decent website, responds promptly to calls, faxes and emails and will send a useful colour brochure anywhere in the world. The newly formed Gambia Tourist Authority plans to open information booths in the coastal resorts.

In Gambia the **Association of Small Scale Enterprises in Tourism** (ASSET; www.asset-gambia.com) is a great umbrella organisation that tries to help small businesses, mainly by assisting local entrepreneurs to get a foot in a market that's almost entirely dominated by big tour operators and the government. In Kartong, the local **Kartong Association for Responsible Tourism** (KART; ☎ 4495887; www.safarigarden.com) is good, especially for independent travellers.

Senegal's Syndicat d'Initiative has an office in each of the regions. However, they vary greatly in how active they are. The main branch is in Saint-Louis, a busy office and excellent resource for tourists. The Gorée office is also good, while the ones in Tambacounda, Joal and Sokone are mainly one-man operations that don't even have their own offices (still, try calling them, you just never know).

You'll find Syndicat d'Initiatives in the following locations:

Gorée (☎ 823 9177; methiourseye@hotmail.com)
Lac Rose (☎ 836 5517; kerkanni@tpsnet.sn)
Saint Louis (☎ 961 2455; sltourisme@sentoo.sn)
Saly (☎ 957 2222; bgvsn@yahoo.fr)
Siné-Saloum (☎ 948 3140; www.tourismesinesaloum.sn)
Tambacounda (☎ 981 1250; nijihotel@sentoo.sn)
Ziguinchor (☎ 993 5151; paillote@sentoo.sn)

VISAS

Depending on your nationality, you could need to buy a visa and have it stamped in your passport in order to enter one or both countries. Some information is given below, but it's best to phone your nearest Senegalese or Gambian embassy before travel. Don't forget to ask how long it takes to issue the visa, and whether you need to enter the country within a certain period. Websites such as www.lonelyplanet.com, or the governmental webpages of each country can also be useful.

Multiple-entry visas can be handy if you're flying into Senegal and then visiting Gambia before returning to Senegal for your return flight (or vice versa).

VISAS AT BORDERS & AIRPORTS

Most travellers arriving in Gambia from Senegal just used to get their visa at the border. That's no longer recommended, as border officials have frequently been reported to be difficult, refuse visas or charge extortionate rates. You can ultimately save yourself a lot of hassle and probably money sorting out your visa before you head off.

If you don't need a visa to visit Gambia, you might be asked to get a tourist stamp on arrival, usually from the nearest immigration post. This should be free, so watch out for fictitious charges.

The Gambia

Visas are not needed by nationals of Commonwealth countries, Belgium, Germany, Italy, Luxembourg, the Netherlands, Ecowas or Scandinavian countries for stays of up to 90 days. For those needing one, visas are normally valid for one month and are issued in two to three days for the equivalent of about US$45; you'll need to provide two photos. You can find out whether you need a visa by emailing enquiries@gambiatourism .info. An application form can be printed out from www.gambia.com, but if you're applying by snail mail in the USA allow at least two weeks for the process.

Last-minute travellers can sometimes be allowed to enter and obtain a proper visa by submitting their passport to the **Immigration Office** (Map p92; ☎ 4228611; OAU Blvd, Banjul; 🕑 8am-4pm) and making a demand. However, it's obviously much safer to arrive with all your papers in order. The Immigration

Office also handles requests for extensions (D250).

Senegal

Visas are not needed by citizens of the EU, Canada, South Africa, Japan, Israel, USA and several other (mainly African) countries. Tourist visas for one to three months cost about US$15 to US$20. Australians, New Zealanders and Norwegians definitely do need a visa. For extensions, you submit a demand to the **Ministère de l'Intérieur** (Map p150; Place de l'Indépendance, Dakar), who'll give you a receipt, which already gives you right to an extended stay until your official prolongation arrives some two weeks later.

WOMEN TRAVELLERS

While it's not exactly dangerous to travel on your own as a woman in Gambia and Senegal, you do need to know how to live with a grinding background noise of constant pestering (which can be anything on a sleazy scale from near-stalking to whistling), develop a thick skin and a repertoire of ripostes to offers of marriage and be able to bear occasional disrespect with a grin.

Unwarranted and usually unwanted interest is a pretty steady travel companion of lone female travellers. There are several reasons for this. In this part of the world, it's unusual for women to travel alone, particularly if you leave your husband in another country, or, God beware, don't even have one. Western women are also widely perceived as 'easy prey'. That's partly due to the portrayal of women and sex in Hollywood movies and TV series, and partly because there's a considerable number of female travellers who continue to confirm the stereotype. A third reason is a general flirtatiousness that frequently colours conversations between young people. Guys won't hesitate to approach you, and see how far they can go. It's up to you to set the boundaries.

Dress Code

Dress code can make a difference to how you are regarded to a certain extent. In urban areas, tight jeans and tops are perfectly acceptable – young Senegalese women dress that way and you can too, without causing distress to anyone. In nightclubs, female dress code tends to be staggeringly sexy, though you might choose not to take the

---

SAI-SAIS

In Senegal, a *sai-sai* is a womaniser, a smooth operator, charming hustler, conman or a dodgy mixture of all of these. These guys are usually young, often good-looking men, who approach women, sometimes bluntly, sometimes with astonishing verbal skills in towns, nightclubs, bars and particularly on beaches. While some of these guys are fairly harmless (just don't get your heart broken), others can pull some pretty sly jobs, involving sexual advances, tricking you out of money or downright stealing. Women beware. Use the same yardsticks you would at home before getting involved with men. Anyone who approaches you out of the blue claiming undying love a little too quickly isn't serious. Don't fall for their games.

---

theme as far as some punters unless you really want to get laid. Things are a little different when you travel through rural areas or visit someone's house (especially for the first time). That's when a little more modesty is recommended; go for a below-knee skirt or long trousers, T-Shirts are fine. Miniskirts are only worn by very young women, and then rarely (mainly in bars and nightclubs) – you'll notice that even the most sensual Senegalese dress code typically involves figure-hugging trousers and tops, rather than short skirts.

Sexual Harassment

Especially if walking on your own around inner city Dakar, Banjul or the coastal areas, you are bound to be chatted up, possibly followed and asked for your phone number. The best way of showing disinterest and shaking off hangers-on is to ignore them and keep walking. If that doesn't work, state firmly that you're not interested and make sure you look as though you're heading to meet friends (or better still, your husband).

Avoid getting involved in conversation, but keep it cool – chilly politeness is more effective than anger. Some of the most relentless guys might call you racist if you refuse to answer their advances – don't be intimidated and just keep walking.

Inventing a husband is a pretty good strategy, and can help ward off suitors. On the same note, it's always better to refer to serious partners as husbands – the fact that you might have a boyfriend usually doesn't deter (and will possibly awaken some sort of male competitive instinct – the last thing you want).

Beaches are prime hassle zones, and the areas where female readers report the most irritating, sometimes downright threatening advances. It's not a good idea for women to take solitary strolls along the beach.

Harassment is a pretty wide term, and while it's certainly annoying to be the object of so much uncalled-for attention, and to have your ears ring with constant smooth talking, it's worth remembering that very few women become the victims of physical harm or rape. And if you follow some common-sense ground rules – don't stroll along deserted beaches or dark city roads alone, don't hitch-hike or accept rides in cars full of drunken men – you're unlikely to get into serious trouble.

On the upside of this, the more conservative male-female relationships of society also mean that such niceties like getting help carrying a bag, having doors held open, drinks bought, and being asked to dance, still exist.

Tampons

Tampons (usually imported from Europe) are only available at supermarkets and pharmacies in large towns such as Dakar and Banjul, and generally only in the smallest size. They're quite expensive, too, so you might want to take a sufficient supply with you. In Senegal, a tampon is usually called a *tampon hygiénique*. By simply asking for a tampon you'll be requesting a stamp, as in a passport stamp, which just won't suffice.

Transport in The Gambia & Senegal

CONTENTS

THINGS CHANGE

The information in this chapter is particularly vulnerable to change: prices for international travel are volatile, routes are introduced and cancelled, schedules change, special deals come and go, and rules and visa requirements are amended. Airlines and governments seem to take a perverse pleasure in making price structures and regulations as complicated as possible. You should check directly with the airline or a travel agent to make sure you understand how a fare (and ticket you may buy) works. In addition, the travel industry is highly competitive and there are many lurks and perks.

The upshot of this is that you should get opinions, quotes and advice from as many airlines and travel agents as possible before you part with your hard-earned cash. The details given in this chapter should be regarded as pointers and are not a substitute for your own careful, up-to-date research.

GETTING THERE & AWAY

ENTERING THE GAMBIA & SENEGAL
Passports

A full passport is essential for entering both Gambia and Senegal. Some officials prefer passports that expire at least three months after your trip ends, so change yours if it's near the end of its life. Senegalese border officials are notably easier to deal with than their Gambian counterparts, and passport checks are usually quick and polite. If you enter The Gambia from Senegal, you might encounter some red-tape tedium at the border, especially if you're travelling on a French or Senegalese passport. It's important that your papers are in complete order, meaning you've got a passport with a valid visa (if you need one) and your vaccination certificate (see p295).

No issues have been reported regarding entry problems due to particular stamps in passports. French and Senegalese travellers might experience slight hassles when entering The Gambia, but as long as all papers are in order, it's highly unlikely that entry will be denied.

AIR

West Africa isn't particularly cheap to reach from other parts of the world, and the best connections still follow the old colonial ties. For cheap flights to Senegal, you're best off checking websites and travel agents in France. For those to Gambia, the UK is a better address. Charter flights are popular for both countries; contact details of the major operators are given below.

Airports & Airlines
THE GAMBIA

The Gambia's main airport is **Banjul International Airport** (BJL; ☎ 4473117; www.gambia.gm/gcaa) at Yundum, about 20km from the city centre, and about 15km from the Atlantic coast resorts. The most impressive thing about it is its architecture (conceived by a Senegalese architect). It's very small scale, with few facilities. There is no airport bus – see p97.

At the time of research, the former national carrier, Gambia International Airways, wasn't operating; Gambian airspace is mainly used by charter flights.

The closest Gambia had to a national airline at the time of research was **Slok Air** (in Gambia ☎ 4377782), a Nigerian company that had its licence revoked and then moved to The Gambia. It's extremely unreliable, with flight cancellations, reroutings and delays being frequent.

Air Guinée (☎ in Banjul 412907; www.mirinet.com/airguinee; airline code 2U; hub Conakry Airport, Conakry)

Air Sénégal International (☎ in Banjul 4202117; www.air-senegal-international.com; airline code V7; hub Airport International Léopold Sédar Senghor, Dakar)

Slok Air (☎ in Fajara 4377782; www.slokair.com; airline code SO; hub Banjul International Airport, Banjul)

SN Brussels (☎ in Kololi 027232323; www.flysn.be; airline code SN; hub Brussels Airport, Brussels)

West Coast Airways (☎ in Banjul 7767666; airline code WCG; hub Accra Airport, Accra)

SENEGAL

Senegal's main airport is the **Aéroport International Léopold Sédar Senghor** (DKR; ☎ 869 5050; 24hr information line ☎ 628 1010; www.aeroportdakar.com) in Yoff, 30 minutes from central Dakar. It's a well-organised airport, with a bank, exchange facilities, car-hire companies and several tour operators.

At the time of research, planning for a new airport, to be created near Thiès, had begun, though its realisation is likely to take some time. The airports of Saint-Louis (☎ 961 1490) and Cap Skiring (☎ 993 5177) also have international connections to France.

The national carrier is **Air Sénégal International** (☎ 804 0404; in France ☎ 0820 202123; www.air-senegal-international.com), which forms part of the Royal Air Maroc group, and is one of the most reliable airlines in Africa. It has an excellent safety record, and serious delays, cancellations or reroutings are infrequent.

Air Algérie (in Dakar ☎ 823 2964; www.airalgerie.dz; airline code AH; hub Algiers Airport, Algeria)

Air France (in Dakar ☎ 823 2964; www.airfrance.fr; airline code AF; hub Airport Charles de Gaulle, Paris)

Air Guinée (in Dakar ☎ 821 4442; www.mirinet.com/airguinee; airline code 2U; hub Conakry Airport, Conakry)

Air Ivoire (in Dakar ☎ 889 0280; www.airivoire.com; airline code VU; hub Abidjan Airport, Abidjan)

Air Mali (in Dakar ☎ 823 2461; airline code XG; hub Bamako Airport, Bamako)

Air Portugal (in Dakar ☎ 821 5460; www.tap.pt; airline code TP; hub Lisbon Airport, Lisbon)

Air Sénégal International (in Dakar ☎ 804 0404; www.air-senegal-international.com; airline code V7; hub Airport International Léopold Sédar Senghor, Dakar)

Alitalia (in Dakar ☎ 823 3129; www.alitalia.it; airline code AZ; hub Rome Airport, Rome)

Iberia (in Dakar ☎ 889 0050; www.iberia.com; airline code IB; hub Madrid Airport, Madrid)

Royal Air Maroc (in Dakar ☎ 849 4747; www.royalairmaroc.com; airline code AT; hub Casablanca Airport, Casablanca)

SN Brussels (in Dakar ☎ 823 0460; www.flysn.be; airline code SN; hub Brussels Airport, Brussels)

South African Airways (in Dakar ☎ 823 0151; www.flysaa.com; airline code SA; hub Johannesburg Airport, Johannesburg)

TACV Cabo Verde Airlines (in Dakar ☎ 821 3968; www.tacv.com; airline code VR; hub Praia Airport, Cape Verde)

Virgin Nigeria (in Lagos ☎ 460 0505; www.virginnigeria.com; airline code VK; hub Lagos Airport, Lagos)

There's a couple of airlines who have just started flying to Dakar, but are very important for East–West Africa connections.

Ethiopian Airlines (ET; in Senegal ☎ 821 32 98; www.flyethiopian.com; 16 Av Léopold Sédar Senghor; hub Addis Ababa)

Kenya Airways (KQ; in Nairobi ☎ 020 3274747; www.kenya-airways.com; hub Nairobi Airport, Nairobi) No Dakar office.

Tickets

Regular flights to both Senegal and Gambia tend to be comparatively expensive, and rising petrol prices keep pushing ticket rates up. Furthermore, airport tax can be surprisingly steep; on flights from Paris to Dakar, for instance, airport tax amounts to about €150. But there are occasional good deals, you just need to invest some time in doing your research.

It's worth checking the websites of airlines, though they sometimes don't offer the discounted tickets you might find advertised on 'cheap flight' sites. the website www.lastminute.com and its French equivalent www.lastminute.fr occasionally have good deals. To Senegal, Air Sénégal usually has the cheapest scheduled flights.

Especially in larger towns, it's worth seeking out the help of a travel agent who knows about special deals, has strategies for avoiding layovers and can offer advice on everything from which airline has the best vegetarian food to the best travel insurance to bundle with your ticket. You might find the cheapest flights advertised by obscure 'bucket shops'. Many such firms are honest, but there are a few who will take your money and disappear. If you feel suspicious, only pay a small deposit. Once you have your ticket, ring the airline to confirm you are booked onto the flight before paying the balance. If the agent insists on cash in advance, go elsewhere.

Several airlines offer 'youth' or 'student' tickets, with discounts for people under 26 (sometimes 23) or in full-time education. If you're eligible, ask the travel agent if any student fares are available – they might 'forget' to tell you. Regulations vary, but you'll need to prove your age or student status.

INTERCONTINENTAL (RTW) TICKETS

The cheapest way of getting to/from Gambia and Senegal is usually on a round-the-world (RTW) ticket, which sells for around A$3000; you'll probably have to look hard to find one routing through West Africa.

Africa

There are plenty of connections to other West African capitals, though not all airlines are in a particularly good state, and delays, cancellations and reroutings are common.

East and Southern Africa are more difficult to reach. There are some intra-African flights to more far-flung destinations, but these often involve multiple changes, long waiting times and can be very expensive. Most long-haul destinations within Africa are more commonly, and cheaply, reached via Europe. But things are gradually beginning to improve. From Dakar, there are now direct daily flights from Dakar to Johannesburg in South Africa (from CFA494,000 to CFA784,000) and Kenyan Airways was rumoured to be starting a regular route between Dakar and Nairobi.

THE GAMBIA

The best African airline with Gambia flights is Air Sénégal International, flying daily to and from Dakar from where you can connect to other destinations. Return fares are around CFA150,000 – why most people do the Banjul–Dakar journey by bus or taxi. Slokair is the second major operator, theoretically with flights to Dakar, Freetown and Accra, but it isn't reliable, with frequent cancellations and spontaneous reroutings of flights. Air Guinée is another tiny operator (dubbed Air 'Maybe' among West Africans) that has flights between Banjul and Conakry that go via Labé in Futa Jallon. West Coast Airways flies to Lagos, Freetown and Accra, should it still exist by the time you read this. Bellview used to be reputed to

have the safest and most reliable flights between Anglophone West Africa, until one of its planes crashed in Nigeria in October 2005, leaving over 100 passengers dead. It still has twice-weekly flights to Lagos via Freetown (around US$350 one way). All of these airlines have ticket offices in Banjul (p96) or along the Atlantic Coast.

SENEGAL

Air Sénégal International has excellent connections to Benin, Burkina Faso, Cape Verde, Côte d'Ivoire, The Gambia, Ghana, Guinea, Guinea-Bissau, Mali, Mauritania, Morocco and Niger; check the homepage for prices and frequency. Air Mali flies twice a week to Bamako, TACV Cabo Verde Airlines flies three times a week to Praïa and Air Guinée goes to Conakry via Labe and Banju. You can reach Banjul by Slokair, if you're brave. Abidjan is reliably reached by Air Ivoire, which often has good deals.

Many travellers fly from Dakar to Casablanca (Morocco) to avoid the difficult overland section through Mauritania and the Western Sahara. Royal Air Maroc has two flights a week.

Most tickets within the West African region are in the range of US$250 to US$350, and can be bought at the airline offices in Dakar or via a travel agency. Dakar also has a direct daily connection to South Africa with South Africa Airways.

The young company Virgin Nigeria Airways started regular flights between Dakar and Lagos in March 2006; though the initial flight had to be withdrawn due to technical difficulties, this could be promising.

Asia

Some people travelling from Asia come to Senegal via Dubai, and East Africa. Kenya has better Asia connections – and is linked directly to Senegal by Kenya Airways flights. For Gambia, you have to travel via Europe, and even for travel from Asia to Senegal, this is almost always the quicker and cheaper option.

Australia & New Zealand

There are not many route options from Australia and New Zealand to Gambia and Senegal. Most people fly via Europe or, occasionally, East Africa, using several different airlines. Recommended ticket agencies:

STA Travel Australia (☎ 1300 360 960; www.statravel .com.au)

STA Travel New Zealand (☎ 0800 100 677; www .statravel.co.nz) Usually has the cheapest deals. Phone ☎ 131 776 to find your nearest branch.

Continental Europe

THE GAMBIA

The only airline serving Gambia from Europe is SN Brussels Airlines. Most visitors come on charter flights as these are cheaper and usually direct. The leading charter holiday operator is The Gambia Experience (p102), which has good-value 'no-frills' offers, sometimes from around UK£400. Flights depart from Gatwick, Manchester and Bristol. There's plenty of competition in the tourist season, with Thomson Holidays, Airtours, Cosmos, First Choice, TUI and plenty of other operators organising regular tours and flights.

To check what's on offer in the Netherlands and Germany start with Sunair and Olympia; in Belgium Xenior Tours and Sunsnacks; and from Scandinavia try Scandinavian Leisure Group (DLG).

SENEGAL

Senegal has good direct connections to European countries including Belgium (SN Air Brussels), Italy (Alitalia), Portugal (Tap Air Portugal), Spain (Iberia Airways) and, of course, France (Air France, Air Sénégal).

To France, there are several daily flights; Air Sénégal tends to be the cheapest, even when booking directly with the airline. Alitalia flies twice or four times a week, depending on the season, between Milan and Dakar (from about €600 return), while Iberia flies from Madrid and TAP Air Portugal has several flights a week from Lisbon (starting at about €600 return). Fares on scheduled flights from London, via Europe, to Dakar start at about UK£550, if you're lucky.

There are plenty of charter flights to Senegal with French and Belgian package-tour companies, all of them a lot cheaper than the scheduled flights. In Senegal, the best agency for charter flights is Nouvelles Frontières (p151) in Dakar.

BELGIUM

Recommended agencies:

Joker Toerisme (☎ 02-502 1937; brussels@joker.be; Blvd Lemonnier 37, 1000 Bruxelles) Is affiliated with the Via Via travellers lodge in Yoff.

Nouvelles Frontières (☎ 02-547 4444; www.nouvelles -frontieres.be; Blvd Lemonnier 2, 1000 Bruxelles)

FRANCE

Recommended agencies:

Anyway.com (☎ 0825 84 84 83; www.anyway.com)

Dakar Voyages (☎ 01 72 38 69 65, 0811 03 43 50; www.dakarvoyages.com)

Lastminute (☎ 0892 705 555; www.lastminute.fr)

Nouvelles Frontières (☎ 08 25 00 08 25, 01-45 68 70 00; www.nouvelles-frontieres.fr; 87 blvd de Grenelle, 75015 Paris)

OTU Voyages (☎ 0 820 817 817, 01-44 41 38 50; www.otu.fr; 39 av Georges-Bernanos, 75005 Paris) Offers special deals to students and young people.

Voyageurs du Monde (☎ 01-42 86 16 00; www.vdm .com; 55 rue Ste-Anne, 75002 Paris)

GERMANY

Recommended agencies:

Condor (☎ 0180 5 767 757; www.condor.de) Often has cheap flights between October and April.

Lastminute (☎ 01805 284 366; www.lastminute.de)

STA Travel (☎ 030 311 0950; Goethesttrasse 73, 10625 Berlin) Has branches in most major cities.

ITALY

Recommended agencies:

CTS Viaggi (☎ 06-462 0431; 16 Via Genova, Rome) Specialises in youth fares.

Passagi (☎ 06-474 0923; Stazione Termini FS, Galleria di Tesla, Rome)

THE NETHERLANDS

Recommended agencies:

Budget Air (☎ 020-627 1251; www.nbbs.nl; Rokin 34, Amsterdam)

Holland International (☎ 070-307 6307) Has offices in most cities.

SPAIN

Recommended agencies:

Barcelo Viajes (☎ 91-559 1819; Princesa 3, 28008 Madrid) Branches in most major cities.

Nouvelles Frontières (☎ 91-547 42 00; www.tuiviages .com; Plaza de España 18, 28008 Madrid) Has branches in major cities.

UK & Ireland

Advertisements for many travel agencies appear in the travel pages of the weekend broadsheet newspapers, in *Time Out*, the *Evening Standard* and in the free magazine *TNT*. There are plenty of cheap charter deals to The Gambia. If you're going to Senegal, you can save money taking a cheap flight to Paris, and get on a French charter or scheduled flight from there. Other travellers take the charter to Banjul, and go overland to Dakar from there.

Recommended agencies:

Africa Travel Centre (☎ 020-7387 1211; www .africatravel.co.uk; 21 Leigh St, London WC1H 9QX) Often has good deals.

STA Travel (☎ 020-7361 6262, www.statravel.co.uk; 86 Old Brompton Rd, London SW7)

Gambia Experience (☎ 0845 330 4567; www.gambia .co.uk) Offers tours and usually has the cheapest flights.

USA & Canada

No flights are scheduled from the USA to The Gambia, but Senegal is connected by a daily direct flight between Dakar and New York (tickets start at US$800). All other flights from North America go on European airlines via Europe, so it may be cheaper to fly to London or Paris and buy a discounted ticket onwards from there.

Citizens of Canada will also probably find the best deals travelling via Europe, especially London (although there are some very cheap flights from Montreal to Paris). Contact some of the travel agents listed in the Britain or France sections earlier.

Discount travel agents in the USA and Canada are known as consolidators. San Francisco is the ticket consolidator capital of America, although some good deals can be found in Los Angeles, New York and other big cities. Agencies also tend to advertise in the travel sections of main newspapers, such as those in the *New York Times, Los Angeles Times, Chicago Tribune* and *San Francisco Examiner*.

Recommended agencies:

Council Travel (☎ 800-226 8624; www.counciltravel.com) Has offices throughout the USA.

STA Travel (☎ 800-777 0112; www.statravel.com) Has offices throughout the USA.

Travel CUTS (☎ 800-667-2887; www.travelcuts.com) Canada's national student-travel agency.

LAND & RIVER
Car & Motorcycle

Driving your own car or motorbike to Senegal requires plenty of research and planning. See p15 for manuals covering the many issues to be dealt with.

For Senegal, it's important to note that no vehicles older than five years may be imported. If your car is older and you are just trying to cross Senegal to reach The Gambia, you're likely to experience some problems at the border, and might be accompanied by a border official all the way to The Gambia.

If you want to travel around Senegal and Gambia using your own car or motorcycle but don't fancy the Sahara crossing, another option is to ship your vehicle. The usual way of doing this is to load your car or motorcycle on board at a port in Europe and take it off again at either Dakar or Banjul.

Freight costs range from US$500 to US$1000 depending on the vehicle size and final destination. However, apart from the cost your biggest problem is likely to be security. Many drivers report theft of items from the inside and outside (such as lights and mirrors) of their car. Vehicles are usually left unlocked during the crossing and when in storage at the destination port – so chain or lock all equipment into fixed boxes inside the vehicle.

Getting a vehicle out of a port is almost always a nightmare, requiring visits to several different offices where stamps must be obtained and mysterious fees paid at every turn. Consider using an official handling agent or an unofficial 'fixer' to take you through this process. In Gambia, Sukuta Camping (www .campingsukuta.de) can help with all sorts of overland information. For Senegal, try the Dakar Rally (www.dakar.com).

For sending motorcycles out of Senegal, we heard of one biker who avoided these pitfalls by sending his bike 'air mail' from Dakar to Paris using **Air France Cargo** (☎ 820 0743) for what seems like a pretty good price. He went to the Air France Cargo office at Léopold Sédar Senghor International Airport, at Yoff; filled out forms with the assistance of a local 'transiter' (recommended by Air France); loaded his bike (about 200kg) onto a bike stand; and took photos of it for security; all in less than a day for just over US$500. If you are considering this option from the UK to Senegal, **Allied Pickfords** (☎ 020-8219 8000, 0800-289 229; www.allied-pickfords .co.uk) is not the cheapest, but has been recommended.

Train

The only functioning passenger train in the region is the one linking Dakar with Bamako, with several stops on the way. In theory, trains

---

OVERLAND THROUGH THE WESTERN SAHARA

There are three main routes across the Sahara leading to West Africa: the Route de Hoggar (through Algeria and Niger); the Route de Tanezrouft (through Algeria and Mali); and the Atlantic Route through the Western Sahara (through Morocco and Mauritania).

With the decade-long fundamentalist insurgency in Algeria seemingly finished, regular traffic ran in both directions along the Route de Hoggar in 2001 for the first time since the late 1980s. However, news of the peace and love in Algeria has apparently not reached the smugglers (or bandits, depending who you talk to) who are still taking advantage of whomever they can along the northern Mali section of the once-popular Tanezrouft route.

Therefore, at the time of writing the Atlantic Route is still the most popular for tourists. It's also the most direct overland route to Senegal.

It would be almost criminal negligence to travel through the Sahara without first checking the excellent, up-to-date and entertaining website put together by desert specialist Chris Scott at www.sahara-overland.com.

Other decent websites include that of the 153 Club (named after the old Michelin map of North West Africa) at www.manntaylor.com/153.html; the thorough www.sahara-info.ch (in German); the Dakar Rally site www.dakar.com; and www.sahara.it (in Italian).

The Atlantic Route – Northbound

It is now legal to travel north through Mauritania along this route, but because so much of the southbound traffic is on a one-way journey to the vehicle purgatory that is West Africa, going north without your own transport can be pretty tough. It's probably best to try and arrange your transport before you leave Nouakchott.

From Nouâdhibou northbound transport can be hard to find. Your best bets are the camping grounds.

If you have your own vehicle, head north and have your passport stamped at the small post, then drive on to Fort Guergarrat to complete the border formalities for Morocco. Despite this being far easier than it once was, it's still advisable to wait in Nouâdhibou for other vehicles to form a mini convoy for the trip to Dakhla. It's also worth noting that inexperienced drivers will probably need a guide to get between Nouâdhibou and Nouakchott.

---

run between Dakar and Bamako twice a week in each direction and the trip takes 35 hours. In practice, this almost never occurs – one train is often out of action; the trip usually takes 40 hours or longer; the train has lots of thieves; and derailments are frequent. If it's adventure you're after, do the journey by all means, but if you just want to get from Dakar to Bamako, the road is a better option.

Tickets are available at all the stations the train passes, during office hours. You're always at an advantage buying your ticket in, and travelling from, Dakar – the train is often full on leaving the capital.

Seats are numbered, although for 2nd class you should get to the train two hours before departure. The 1st-class seats are large and reasonably comfortable, while 2nd class is more crowded. Sleepers (couchettes) are basic but adequate. You can get cheap food at stations along the way, and will find people reaching into the train with bags of peanuts, fruit, cakes and boiled eggs at every stop. The *Mistral International* (Senegalese) train has a restaurant car, but don't count on it; bring your own provisions.

At each border post you have a short hike to the immigration office. Foreigners sometimes have their passport taken by an immigration inspector on the train, but you still have to collect it yourself by getting off at the border post. Nobody tells you this so if your passport is taken, ask where and when you have to go to get it back.

Theft can be a problem on this train. Keep all valuables with you and be sure to carry a torch; if you leave your seat, especially at night, ask a fellow passenger to watch your gear; and expect to become a target when the lights go out (often in the train and the station) as the train pulls into Kayes and Bamako. Good luck!

The Atlantic Route – Southbound

Travel through Morocco is pretty straightforward (see Lonely Planet's *Morocco* guide). About 500km south of Agadir you enter the disputed territory of Western Sahara, but the road continues along the coast all the way to Dakhla.

Dakhla has some cheap hotels and a decent camping ground (which also has some rooms to rent) where all the overlanders stay, and this is the best place to find other vehicles to team up and travel with.

If you are hitching, drivers taking second-hand cars from Europe (especially from France and Germany) to sell in West Africa may occasionally offer lifts, but you would be expected to share fuel and paperwork costs. Hitchers are not allowed in Mauritanian vehicles, and there have been occasional scams where hitchers with local drivers are threatened with abandonment in the desert unless they pay a large 'fee'.

For years a twice-weekly convoy headed south from Dakhla, but as of 2002 this is no more. All immigration and customs facilities have moved south to the border at Fort Guergarrat, from where you cross into Mauritania and the last 100km to Nouâdhibou. It's important to take supplies for at least two days on this leg, and for inexperienced or 2WD drivers to go in a group in case someone gets stuck. The route is clearly marked and no matter how bad the road gets, do not stray – twisted wrecks are proof of how near landmines can be.

From Nouâdhibou, most cars go south down the coast to Nouakchott, through the Banc d'Arguin National Park (including a 160km stretch along the beach at low tide, with soft sand on one side and waves breaking over your windscreen on the other). Some cars, and most bikes and hitchers, go east on the iron-ore train to Choûm and then take the route via Atar and Akjout to Nouakchott. The train heads east from Nouâdhibou to Choum on Monday and returns on Saturday, and you'll need to be at either end the day before to guarantee a space.

From Nouakchott to Rosso, the southern border is a straightforward run on a good tarred road. Rosso is a hustlers' paradise, but for those with their own vehicle there is a less bothersome way into Senegal. Turn right (west) along a sandy track just as you enter Rosso and follow the Senegal River for 97km to Maka Diama. There are border posts on both sides of the river and crossing will cost you CFA5000/10,000 in winter/summer, landing you just a short drive from the comforts and cold beer of Saint-Louis. Remember to stock a few packets of cigarettes before you set off as they are the best 'bribe' – cheap and usually enough to keep the official happy.

Guinea

Nearly all traffic between Senegal and Guinea goes to/from Labé, a large town in northwestern Guinea.

The busiest route is via Koundara, but some transport also goes via Kedougou (in the far southeast of Senegal) and the small town of Mali (usually called Mali-ville, to distinguish it from the country of the same name).

If you're leaving Senegal, there are several places you can get a frighteningly packed *sept-place* (seven-seater) taxi. Tambacounda has connections almost every day, which go via Medina Gounas and Sambaïlo (where you may have to change). From Kedougou, your best chance to find transport is on Friday, though at least one car might leave on most other days.

Another popular jumping-off point is Diaoubé near Kolda. Wednesday, the day of the Diaoubé *lumo* (market) is the best day to get transport here. Fares to Guinea are around CFA15,000 from all these places, and the trip can take up to 48 hours, as routes are bad and Guinean roadblocks tedious to pass.

Guinea-Bissau

Bush taxis run several times daily between Ziguinchor and Bissau (CFA6000, 147km) via São Domingos (the border) and Ingore. The road is in fairly good condition, but the ferries on the stretch between Ingore and Bissau can make the trip take anything from four to eight hours.

Occasionally the São Domingos border closes unexpectedly, apparently on the whim of the guards, but this doesn't usually last too long. Other options are to go from Tanaf to Farim or from Tambacounda via Vélingara to Gabú.

Mali

Travellers have traditionally taken the train from Dakar to Bamako, but train services have deteriorated at the same time that road have improved, so that the bush taxi option is becoming much more attractive. From Dakar to Tambacounda it's a slow slog, while Tambacounda to the border crossing in Kidira (three hours, 184km) is excellent. From Kidira to Kayes in Mali, road quality worsens drastically, making actual travelling times unpredictable. Tamba to Kidira by *sept-place* taxi costs CFA5000. In Kidira, you cross the road bridge to Diboli, from where bush taxis go to Kayes for CFA3000. From Kayes to Bamako, both train and taxi are equally good (or bad) options.

Mauritania

The main border point is at Rosso, where a ferry crosses the Senegal River. It's been announced that a bridge is supposed to replace the boat service within the next few years, but work hadn't started at the time of research.

You can go direct to Rosso from Dakar in a *sept-place* taxi (CFA4500, six hours, 384km), but most travellers stop off at Saint-Louis, from where a *sept-place* to Rosso (two hours, 106km) is CFA2000. Crossing the Senegal River is done on a large ferry (free/CFA2000/3000 for passengers/cars/4WDs, twice daily). You can also cross by pirogue (canoe) for CFA1000. Visas can be obtained at the border. From the Mauritanian immigration post it's 500m to the *gare routière* (bus and bush-taxi station), from where bush taxis go to Nouakchott.

Rosso has a reputation for being a bothersome place, and travellers usually return with stories of extortion and frustration, but it's about the only place where you can cross with a vehicle. The only other option is the Maka Diama barrage, 97km southwest of Rosso and just north of Saint-Louis, although the track between the barrage and the main road on the Mauritanian side is soft sand. The crossing here costs CFA5000/10,000 in winter/summer, and there is a theoretical maximum weight for vehicles of 2.8 tonnes. The smaller crossings along the border are pirogue-worthy only.

SEA

The days of working for your passage on commercial boats have long gone, although a few lucky travellers do manage to hitch rides on private yachts sailing from Spain, Morocco or the Canary Islands to Senegal, Gambia and beyond.

Another nautical option available is taking a cabin on a freighter. Several cargo ships run from European ports, such as London-Tilbury, Bordeaux, Hamburg or Rotterdam, to various West African ports (including Dakar) with comfortable officer-style cabins available to the public.

A typical voyage from Europe to Dakar takes about eight days, and costs vary according to the quality of the ship. Don't take this option if you want to save money – single fares from Europe to Dakar are around US$1500 to US$1800 per person in a double cabin.

For more information see *Travel by Cargo Ship*, a handy book written by Hugo Verlomme, or contact a specialist agent.

Associated Oceanic Agencies Ltd (☎ 020-7930 5683; fax 7839 1961; 103 Jermyn St, London SW1Y 6EE UK)
Freighter World Cruises (☎ 626 449 3106; toll-free 1-800 531 7774; fax 449 9573; www.freighterworld.com; 180 South Lake Ave, No 335-1, Pasadena, CA 91101 USA) Publishers of Freighter Space Advisory. Excellent website with listings of freighter trips worldwide, including to Dakar and Banjul.
Maris Freighter Cruises (☎ 1-800 996 2747, 203 222 1500; 215 Main St, Westport, CT 06880 USA)
Strand Voyages (☎ 020-7836 6363; fax 7497 0078; voyages@strandtravel.com.au; Charing Cross Shopping Concourse, Strand, London WC2N 4HZ UK)

GETTING AROUND

TRAVELLING BETWEEN THE GAMBIA & SENEGAL

Air

The main airlines flying between Gambia and Senegal are Slokair (see p279) and Air Sénégal International (see p280). Few travellers fly between Gambia and Senegal, as flights tend to be expensive, and can be so unreliable that they don't save much time.

Boat

There's nothing in the way of scheduled boat services between the two countries. However, if you're very brave, you can take one of the pirogues from various places in the Siné-Saloum region to Banjul. Note that these aren't particularly safe, can often be overfilled and have to venture out of the shelter of the Siné-Saloum Delta and into the ocean for a bit, meaning that things can get pretty rough. It's an adventure, certainly, but not for the faint-hearted.

The most common departure points are in and around Djifer, you have to ask around when the next boat might be leaving (usually when enough people have registered an interest). A place in an often overcharged pirogue costs CFA5000, and the trip takes around six hours. From Betenti, there's an almost daily pirogue to Banjul (CFA1500, three hours), which leaves around 8am.

Alternatively, you can always hire a pirogue, but that will set you back around CFA150,000 to CFA200,000.

Bush Taxi

TO/FROM DAKAR

Sept-place taxis run frequently between Dakar and Banjul, and in theory, the trip should be fairly quick and painless. In practice, crossings between Senegal and Gambia can be time consuming, as Gambian officials tend to be deeply suspicious of Senegalese vehicles and their passengers, and like to make border crossings as tedious as possible.

The main route from Gambia to Senegal takes you via the Barra ferry (p96) to Karang at the border, then to Kaolack and Dakar. On the Barra side of the Gambia River there's plenty of transport to the border at Karang where you complete border formalities. From there you change into a minibus that goes to the Senegalese border post, and from there into a bush taxi to Dakar or Kaolack.

The road to Dakar is tarred most of the way, the stretch from Sokone to Kaolack being the only really tricky bit. Once you've crossed on the ferry, the drive to Dakar takes a minimum of five hours, possibly a lot longer.

A second option takes you from Banjul to Soma in eastern Gambia, where you cross the Gambia River to Farafenni, then continue along the Trans-Gambia Hwy to Kaolack and Dakar. It's an interesting journey, but you'll have to put up with some terrible roads. The stretch from Brikama to Soma counts among the worst roads of the region.

Most Senegal-bound drivers accept dalasi, but prefer to charge fares in CFA. There's no bank in Barra or Karang, so you should change dalasi into CFA in Banjul before starting this journey.

If you're coming from Dakar and think you might miss the last ferry across to Banjul (it leaves at 7pm), accommodation in Barra is limited to a couple of sleazy hotels. You'd be far better off staying in Toubacouta and getting the ferry from Barra to Banjul the next morning.

TO/FROM TAMBACOUNDA & KOLDA

From Basse Santa Su bush taxis go through Sabi to Vélingara (CFA1000, 45 minutes, 27km). The bush taxis leave when they fill up, which can mean several hours of waiting, but there's usually one early in the morning. This is one of the few borders where you don't have to change vehicles, making the trip pretty straightforward. Your transport arrives in Vélingara at a small garage on the western side of town. Vehicles for Tambacounda go from another garage on the northern side of Vélingara and *calèches* (horse-drawn taxis) shuttle between the two for CFA250 per person. Vélingara to Tambacounda is CFA1650 by *sept-place* taxi, CFA1400 by minibus.

Another tiny crossing is the one at Pata, from where a smooth dirt road takes you to Kolda. This isn't very frequented, and there isn't always a post at the Senegalese border, but it's the most direct route from Georgetown to Kolda. If you're coming from the Senegalese side and hope to hire a taxi for the brief stretch from Pata to Georgetown, be prepared for some reluctance and inflated pricing on behalf of the Senegalese taxi drivers, who generally aren't keen to face the Gambian police posts.

TO/FROM ZIGUINCHOR & KAFOUNTINE

To get to Ziguinchor you must take a bush taxi from the garage near Serekunda market to the Gambian border at Giboro (D50). From here it's about 3km to the Senegalese border post at Séléti, where a bush taxi to Ziguinchor is CFA2200. You can also get to Giboro from Brikama via bush taxi.

If you're heading for Kafountine, you could get yourself to Diouloulou via Giboro, then change for Kafountine. It's also possible to go from Brikama to Kafountine via the tiny border town of Darsilami. This route isn't frequently used by public transport, but perfectly possible in a hire taxi.

The short hop from Kartong to Kafountine that you see on the map isn't that time-saving if you consider the pirogue crossing of the Allahein River involves a 10km walk on the Senegalese side, as well as the absence of border posts to complete your formalities (see p121). It's possible, but most people tend to take the longer routes via Brikama.

Car & Motorcycle

Taking a rental car across a border in this region is usually forbidden, although the rules about going between Gambia and Senegal are less stringent. Driving from northern to southern Senegal will almost always take you through Gambia anyway, and most Senegalese companies accept this. However, driving with a Senegalese number plate through Gambia can be less than fun – Gambian police points love to check Senegalese cars, so make absolutely sure you've got all your papers in order. For this reason, Senegalese drivers usually don't like going into The Gambia. If you've hired a *sept-place* taxi in Senegal, you're better off letting the driver return, and hire a Gambian car to take you around the country. Senegalese taxi drivers are always looked at with suspicion by the Gambian posts, and the delays can be excruciating.

THE GAMBIA
Air

There are no internal flights in Gambia.

Bicycle

Cycling is a cheap, convenient, healthy, environmentally sound and fun way to travel and gives you a deeper insight into Senegal and Gambia, as you often stay in small towns and villages, interact with the local people and eat African food more frequently. In general, the more remote the areas you visit, the more serious the conditions, but the better the experience.

If you've never cycled in Africa before, Gambia and parts of Senegal provide a good starting point. The landscape is flat and the distances between major points of interest are not so large.

A mountain bike or fat-tyred urban hybrid is most suitable to the dirt-and-sand roads and tracks. However, some tracks are so sandy that no tyre is ever thick enough, and you will have to push. Generally speaking, away from urban areas the main tarred routes are relatively quiet and don't get too much traffic.

When you do encounter traffic, however, drivers are more cause for alarm than any road surface. Cyclists are regarded as second-class citizens in Africa, so make sure you know what's coming behind you and be prepared to take evasive action onto the verge, as locals are often forced to do. A small helmet-mounted rear-view mirror is worth considering.

The best time to bike is the relatively cool period from mid-November to the end of February. Even so, you'll need to carry at least 4L of water and smother yourself with sunscreen. If you get hot, tired, or simply want to cut out the boring bits, bikes can easily be carried on buses and bush taxis for a small luggage fee. If you're camping near settlements in rural areas, ask the village headman each night where you can pitch. Even if you don't have a tent, he'll find you a place to stay.

It's important to carry sufficient spares, and have a good working knowledge of bike repair and maintenance – punctures will be frequent. Take at least four spare inner tubes, some tyre patching material and a spare tyre. Consider the number of tube patches you might need, triple it, and pack those too.

Anyone considering doing some serious cycling in Senegal and Gambia should contact their national cycling association. The following associations also have useful information.

Cyclists' Touring Club (☎ 087-0873 0060; cycling@ctc .org.uk; www.ctc.org.uk) Based in Britain, provides members with route details and information for many parts of the world.

International Bicycle Fund (☎ /fax 206-767 0848; www.ibike.org/bikeafrica) A US-based, low-budget, socially conscious organisation that organises tours, provides information and has an excellent website with information on cycling in West Africa, a huge range of links and a list of cyclist-friendly airlines.

Boat

Seeing that The Gambia consists mainly of a waterway, with a few kilometres of land on each shore, it's surprising how little the river is used as a means of transport. There are no scheduled passenger boats, which is a shame as a picturesque river journey sounds a lot more enticing than a long trip along potholed tarred road, squeezed into a battered passenger taxi.

Trips upriver are organised by only a handful of private tour operators (see p290). They are absolutely worth checking out, and even spending some money on – the river is only rarely seen from the side of the road, and a leisurely boat trip with occasional stops in small villages and shore-side camps might just be the best thing you'll do on your holiday. Note that some river tours are mainly suited to groups of at least four (which will also bring the price down). If you travel alone, check with the company if it's possible to join a group.

If you want to stay close to the Atlantic coast, you can take part in pirogue day trips around the mangroves between Banjul and Lamin, the best place to book these is Denton Bridge (see p103).

All along the river, there are several ferry crossings connecting the north and south bank. The main ones are the *Barra Ferry* (see p96), a slow beast of a boat that travels between Barra and Banjul, and the one connecting Farafenni and Soma (see p132). Other north–south connections are the pirogues that cross the river at various points, though these can only carry people.

Bus

The Gambia Public Transport Corporation (GPTC) bus network was once the envy of many West African nations. Its fleet comprised several high-standard express buses that regularly connected even the most far-flung destinations. But the state of the roads and the lack of continued funding have taken a heavy toll, so the GPTC buses are no longer a viable option for travellers. We found the main bus stop completely deserted, and were repeatedly told that buses had stopped running. Occasional buses go upcountry, all the way to Basse, but they are not reliable and can take a very long time to arrive. Even bush taxis can sometimes spend up to 12 hours on the 360km – think again if you want to take the bus.

Bush Taxi

There are two main routes though Gambia: the potholed dirt road along the northern bank of the river, and the potholed tarred road along the southern bank. The north side was long considered the last choice, but

---

LUGGAGE FEES

Wherever you travel by bush taxi there is always an extra fee for luggage, which varies according to the size of the baggage. The baggage charge is partly because bush-taxi fares are fixed by the government and may not reflect true costs. So the only way the driver can earn a bit extra is to charge for luggage. Local people accept this, so travellers should too, unless of course the amount is beyond reason.

The fee for a medium-sized backpack is usually around 10% of the fare, though you'll usually have to bargain hard to get away for less than 20%. Fares tend to rise with the size of the luggage, or if the item is likely to dirty the vehicle.

If you think you're being overcharged, stand your ground politely and the price will soon fall.

---

as the tarred road deteriorated further in the south, it suddenly gained immensely in appeal – washed-out dirt is still much better to drive on than perforated asphalt.

Roads are fine up to Brikama, and again from Georgetown to Basse, all other stretches are anything from bearable to barely existent. This is supposed to change, however, with road funding programmes in place, so keep an ear out for any updates.

It's becoming increasingly popular to take the ferry to Barra, follow the northern stretch via Kerewan to Farafenni before heading south for the last leg between Soma and Basse. The southern stretch is better served by public transport than the north.

Bush taxis on the southern route go from Serekunda, but usually only as far as Soma (about halfway up the country), where you must change vehicles for onward travel.

Other public transport routes include the fantastically smooth tarmac that parallels the coastline all the way to Kartong, and the good dirt track from Brikama to the southern borders.

Car & Motorcycle

It's possible to hire a car or motorbike in Gambia's resort areas (see p114) and Serekunda, but before doing this read the boxed text on p293. Most hire agencies are small operators, Hertz being the only big name represented.

Cars can often be hired with a driver, though in this case you're likely to be much better off just negotiating a daily rate with a bush-taxi driver. You'll need to have an international driving licence, and be at least 23 years of age (some hire agencies demand a minimum of 24 years) to hire a car. Deposits are required, but vary between agencies. See the Atlantic Coast (p114) and Dakar (p165) chapters for details of hire agencies.

Despite the British heritage, people in Gambia drive on the right, in line with Senegal and most other countries in West Africa.

At the time of writing, petrol prices were CFA500/D30 per litre, and were steadily on the rise.

For minor repair works, there are improvised garages all along major roads, and every village has someone who can weld your oil tank back together. Car parts are harder to find – unless you happen to drive a Peugeot 405…generally: the less fancy your car, the more likely you are to get it repaired.

Local Transport

TOWN TAXIS

Town taxis operate in the Atlantic coast resorts, particularly along Kairaba Av linking Serekunda to Fajara. They are painted yellow with green stripes. They operate as shared taxis, with people getting in and out as they like along set routes. Fares are usually just a few dalasis and are not negotiable. Town taxis can also be hired in a more traditional manner (where you are the only passenger/s): this is called a 'town trip'. The cost of a town trip should be D25, but can be more (especially late at night), but it's always cheaper than the same trip in a tourist taxi.

TOURIST TAXIS

Tourist taxis, painted green with a white diamond on the door, are specifically for tourists and can go anywhere in the country, though they mainly operate in the tourist resorts, along the coastal road and are rarely seen further inland than Brikama. Tourist taxis can be found at ranks near large hotels, and drivers offer rides to all the places of interest in Gambia. A list of rates is on display outside most hotels and at the airport. They are considerably more expensive than local cabs, though tariffs are negotiable within reason.

Tours

Nearly all places of interest in Gambia can be reached by public transport, but taking an organised tour can be a good way to get around the country if you want to avoid the hassles of travelling on public transport or if money is not a primary concern.

There are several large companies based in the Atlantic coast resort area that run organised tours. Most cater specifically for groups of tourists at the big hotels, but many of the excursions are open to independent travellers, too.

Gambia River Experience (☎ 4494360; gambiariver@ yahoo.com; www.gambiariver.com) An inspired little company with offices in Fajara and at Lamin Lodge does trips from Denton Bridge or Banjul, all the way up to Georgetown. Trips are either done by motorised pirogue or large boat. One of their offers includes a weeklong cruise along the river. Check the website for more details.

Gambia Sport Fishing (☎ 4495683, 908577; www .gambiafishing.com) These guys have a good reputation and offer beach- and river-fishing excursions. Some sample trips include inshore or creek fishing for UK£45 per person; beach fishing for UK£35 per person; or a four-day upriver freshwater-fishing trip for UK£290 per person including accommodation. Costs for all trips are based on a minimum of three anglers per boat and include transport to and from Denton Bridge, bait, tackle, soft drinks, an experienced skipper and fuel, but not lunch.

Gambia Tours (☎ 4462601/2; fax 462603; www.gambia tours.gm) A family enterprise with a good range of tours around the country.

Hidden Gambia (in UK ☎ 01527 576239; www.hidden gambia.com) This company has an excellent set of excursions, including twice-weekly trips between Bintang and Farafenni, and tours around the Georgetown area (including trips to the River Gambia National Park). It also offers 'Discover the River' trips that take you all the way from the coast to upcountry (seven-/14-day trips £425/575).

Mr Musa Bah (☎ 9914630) He does upcountry tours in his own car, and has been consistently recommended by travellers over the years.

Mr Saiko Demba (☎ 4497186; www.leybato.abc.gm; Leybato, Fajara) The manager of the Leybato guesthouse (p106) has a car and minibus (both with driver) available. He charges per vehicle, so it's cheaper if you get a group together. He can arrange anything from local tours to long excursions around Gambia and into Senegal.

Olympic Travel (olympictravel@gambinet.gm) An efficient operator with a range of tours on offer.

Wally Faal (☎ 3372103; wallyfaal@yahoo.com; www .geocities.com/birdinggambia) This is one of the friendliest, best-informed bird guides around. Highly recommended. See also p71.

SENEGAL

Air

Of the several airlines that used to serve Senegal's regional airports, **Air Sénégal International** (☎ 804 0404; www.airsenegalinternational.sn) is the only one still working at press time. It has flights to Saint-Louis, Ziguinchor, Cap Skiring and Tambacounda, though only those to Ziguinchor (once or twice daily, return CFA80,600) operate with regularity. Flights to Cap Skiring (Friday and Sunday, return CFA110,600) and Saint-Louis (Wednesday, return CFA70,000) operate only from November to April, and the two flights that fly from Dakar to Tambacounda every Saturday seem pretty irregular.

Flights are particularly worth considering to Ziguinchor or Cap Skiring, as reaching the Casamance by road involves either tedious border crossings in The Gambia, or a seemingly endless tour via Tambacounda around The Gambia. Saint-Louis is fairly comfortably reached by road. Generally, services tend to be good and reliable, though there can be delays.

If you're in a group, you might consider plane charter. Most charter companies specialise in particular destinations.

Air CM (in France ☎ 01 53 41 00 50; mail.aircom@wannadoo.fr) Have a twice-weekly connection between Paris and the Cap and plenty of good package deals.

Air Saint Louis (☎ 644 8629; www.airsaintlouis.com) Flights from Dakar to Saint-Louis.

Hôtel Kalissai (☎ 994 8600; www.kalissai.com) Arranges flights from the aerodrome in Abéné to Dakar.

Senegalair Avion Taxis (☎ 821 3425) Flies mainly to Simenti in Parc National du Niokolo-Koba, though it can also arrange flights elsewhere.

Bicycle

Please see p288 for information on travelling by bicycle in this region.

Boat

The most important boat service in Senegal is *Le Willis,* which connects Dakar twice weekly to Ziguinchor in the Casamance – possibly the easiest way of reaching southern Senegal (if flying is too expensive). See the Casamance chapter (p231) for more details.

If it's a trip on the Senegal River you're after, you can travel with the *Bou El Mogdad* (p209), a stunning old boat with a long historical connection to the region. This is not a public transport alternative to road

travel though, but a cruise ship that chugs leisurely from Saint-Louis to Podor over several days.

For cruise trips around the Petite Côte, and all the way to Guinea-Bissau, the *Africa Queen* is the most famous option.

Various towns and islands in Senegal can be reached by regular ferry services, including Gorée Island (see p169) and Foundiougne (see p189). Regular pirogues connect Dakar and Île de N'Gor (see p171), Dakar and Île de la Madeleine (see p170), Ndangane and Mar Lodj (p188) and various places in the Siné-Saloum region. Note that only the regular, ferry-type pirogues are equipped with life vests; self-hired boats don't necessarily come with the requisite features.

Africa Queen (West Africa Sportsfishing; ☎ 957 7435; Saly)

Bou El Mogdad (☎ 961 5689; www.saheldecouverte .com) One- to four-day trips can be booked through Sahel Découverte Bassari in Saint-Louis (see p205).

Gorée Ferry (☎ 24hr info line 628 1111, 849 7961)

Le Willis (☎ 889 8009, 889 8060/51; tickets from CFA15,500) Departs from Dakar every Tuesday and Friday at 7pm, returns from Ziguinchor every Sunday and Thursday at 2pm.

Bus

Senegal's long-distance bus network stands up fairly well compared to those of other countries in the region. The blue buses (some routes are also served by yellow American school buses) are owned and run by members of the Mouride brotherhood, hence they're known to everyone as *cars mourides. Cars mourides* go from Dakar to most major towns in the country. They leave from the Shell station at Av Malick Sy near *gare routière* Sapeurs-Pompiers (usually just referred to as Pompiers), usually in the middle of the night. You have to book your seat in advance. There's no central phone number, and the best thing is to go to the Shell station (every taxi driver knows it), ask for the person responsible for the *cars mourides,* let them know the direction you're going and they should, in theory, book you on the bus.

Even though most *cars mourides* are in good quality, some even have air-con, travelling by bus can be very tedious, and is always time consuming. The advantage of the prebooking system is that buses are fairly punctual. But sharing a vehicle with tens of others and their usually substantial luggage always means enduring many stops for people to get off on the way, waiting for them to untie their bags from the roof, watching smaller cars pass you by. Punctured tyres take longer to repair, too.

Bush Taxi

Bush taxi is the term for all public transport smaller than a big bus. They leave once they are full; this might take half an hour, or several days if you're out in the sticks.

The best time for catching bush taxis is usually from 6.30am to 8.30am. In remote locations, your best chance for transport are the market days, when people will be heading to the market town (or village) in the early morning and returning in the evening.

Tickets are sold by seat, so if you want extra leg room or want to speed up the process, you can purchase two seats or more. This is also the best way to calculate taxi hire. If you want to hire the whole vehicle, take the cost of a ticket and multiply it by the number of seats to get the amount you should be paying. You might get the driver to reduce that price a little, but shouldn't have to pay much more than that.

Though public transport prices are fixed, they frequently increase in line with rising petrol prices. To give a bit of an idea, *sept-place* bush taxi prices from Dakar include Kaolack (CFA2500, three to four hours), Saint-Louis (CFA3100, four to five hours) and Ziguinchor (CFA6500, nine to 10 hours). Minibuses are typically about 20% to 25% cheaper than *sept-place* taxis, and Ndiaga Ndiayes about 30% to 35% cheaper.

MINIBUS

With a capacity of about 20 people these are smaller versions of the Ndiaga Ndiaye (most of them are Nissan Urvans). They are sometimes also referred to as *petit car*. These mainly operate on rural roads, and cost about the same as the Ndiaga Ndiaye.

NDIAGA NDIAYE

These Mercedes minibuses, named after the first entrepreneur that introduced them to Senegal, are usually the cheapest though slowest form of transport. The ubiquitous 32-seaters, also known as car or grand car, are recognisable by their white colour, and the word *Alhamdoulilahi* (Thanks to God) painted across most vehicles.

They have no timetables, and usually set off when they're full, or when the driver feels like it. They also stop every few hundred metres to drop or collect passengers, which is why they can take almost twice as long for a short journey than a *sept-place* taxi. Or was that because of frequent punctures, engine failures or the occasional accident? It all sounds grim, but in the more remote regions, they'll probably be your only choice of transport, and – the big plus – they're always very social and if you're not in a rush can be a great place to meet the locals.

PICK-UP

Leaving the city and heading for the rather remote regions, you'll occasionally encounter covered pick-up trucks on the street (called *bâchés* in Senegal). These battered vehicles, crammed with people, chickens, sacks of rice and live goats, are sometimes the only type of bush taxi you'll find in the very remote regions.

SEPT-PLACE TAXI

Sept-place taxis (also sometimes referred to as brake or *cinq-cent-quatre*) are Peugeot 504s, used as a slightly more comfortable means of transport.

The quality varies. Some drivers are safe and considerate, others verge on insanity. Some cars are quite new and well maintained with comfortable seats while others are reduced to chassis, body and engine. With three rows of seats, Peugeot taxis are built to take the driver plus seven passengers (hence the name *sept-place*). On the main routes in Gambia and Senegal this limit is observed. But as you get into more remote areas it's often flouted: you might be jammed in with a dozen adults plus children and bags, with more luggage and a couple of extra passengers riding on the roof. These cars do hundreds of thousands of kilometres on some of the worst roads in the world – a credit to the manufacturer and the ingenuity of local mechanics.

Car & Motorcycle

Some general points about driving your own vehicle to and around the region are covered on p283 and p289. Most car-rental companies are based in Dakar; for rates, conditions, and company addresses see p165.

WARNING

Unless you're very familiar with the state of the streets in Senegal and Gambia, driving around the two countries is not something that should be taken lightly.

Road conditions inland are often terrible. What looks like a promising stretch of racing tarmac on the map, may in reality turn out to be a string of large potholes, vaguely connected by tired asphalt. If you don't want to bust a tyre here, you'll have to perform that careful slalom around the cracks and obstacles you'll see the local taxi drivers perform - and sometimes even leave the route entirely to drive beside it. A straight dirt road can be easier to drive on than perforated asphalt, but you also have to get used to it. Keep the speed down, and watch out in bends, as it's easy to slide off the road.

Other dangers involve cars and animals moving unexpectedly into your path. Cows in particular never give way to a car. If you see a herd approach, take your foot off the gas, and keep moving along slowly, careful not to touch the animals. Don't come to a full stop, they might feel tempted to do the same. Take particular care if driving through Senegal's national park of Niokolo-Koba, especially in the early morning hours. Many wild animals sleep on the warm tarmac at night, and you really don't want to risk hitting a lion.

If you want to hire a car - it's worth considering getting one with a driver (many agencies only rent with drivers for long-distance travel), as he'll be familiar with the territory, and any mechanical problems that arise will be his responsibility, rather than yours. Neither country has automobile associations to assist you in case of an accident.

DRIVING LICENCE

You need an international driving licence to drive or hire a car in Senegal, most hire companies request a minimum age of 23.

HIRE

Car hire is generally expensive. By the time you've added up the cost of the car, the distance travelled, plus insurance and tax, you can easily end up paying over US$1000 per week.

Hiring 4WDs is even more expensive and hire rates often shoot up if you want to go upcountry, where bad road conditions increase the risk of accidents. Some hire companies can provide a chauffeur at very little extra cost – sometimes it's cheaper because you pay less for insurance.

You will also need a credit card to pay the large deposit. For those still interested, there are car-rental agencies in the capitals and main tourist areas. In Senegal all the international names (Hertz, Avis, Budget etc) are represented, and there are also smaller independent operators.

It usually works out better renting a *sept-place* or other taxi with its driver. To hire a car for a day or longer, negotiate a daily rate (let the driver know where you want to go, as a day around Dakar doesn't go for the same rate as outings over washed-out dirt roads), fill the tank (make sure you've

made clear who pays for petrol) and head off. Even if the daily rate you arrive at is similar to that of a hire car, the great advantage of using a taxi with driver is that all repairs that might need to be undertaken will be his responsibility rather than yours. If you want to hire a taxi with driver for a journey, multiply the number of seats by the fare and you should be paying about the same amount.

Hitching

Hitching in the Western sense (because you don't want to get the bus, or more specifically because you don't want to pay) is also possible, but may take a very long time. Most people with space in their car are likely to want a payment – usually on a par with what a bus costs. The most common vehicles for lifts of this sort are nearly-new white Toyota Land Cruisers driven by locals working for government bodies, international agencies or aid organisations.

Remember though, as in any other part of the world, hitching is never entirely safe, and we don't recommend it. Travellers who decide to hitch should understand that they are taking a small but potentially serious risk. If you're planning to travel this way, take advice from other hitchers (locals or travellers) first. Hitching in pairs is obviously safer.

Local Transport

CALÈCHE & CHARETTE

You have herewith left the world of the motorised vehicle. Horse-drawn *charettes* and their 'upmarket' counterpart *calèches* are used as means of public transport in places such as Rufisque, Richard Toll and Dagana. A *charette* is little more than a simple board attached to a wheel and strapped behind a horse, and it's more typically used to transport bags of sand and bricks. The *calèche* actually has seats and a sunroof, and can be a fun means of strolling around town (especially if you've got kids), provided that you're not pressed for time.

CAR RAPIDE

This colourfully decorated, blue-and-yellow Dakar minibus is one of Senegal's symbols; you'll see it on postcards and as souvenirs. While it really is cute to look at, it's not a great way to get around unless random stops, daredevil overtaking manoeuvres and crammed seats are your thing. *Car rapides* only really operate in Dakar and pretty much cover any journey you can imagine, though not always as directly or quickly as you might hope. You pay CFA50 for a short hop, CFA100 for slightly further, and never more than CFA150.

MOBYLETTE

The only place *mobylettes* (mopeds) are used as regular means of public transport is in Kaolack. You pay for the passenger seat, hang on, and be patient while the driver gets you from A to B, either at the speed of a slow motorbike or a battered bicycle, depending on his and your combined bodyweight.

SENBUS

These brand new minibuses are one day supposed to replace *cars rapides* completely,

which would be a shame, seeing that the cars really characterise Dakar. The Senbuses aren't as imaginatively decorated, but they are a great means of getting from A to B, with predetermined stops, one seat per person and other such luxuries. Routes are displayed in front of the vehicle, and rates are the same as *cars rapides*.

Tours

Most places of interest in Senegal can be reached by either public transport or car, but if you're short on time you could get around the country on an organised tour.

A small selection of tour operators based in and around the Dakar area is included here.

M'boup Voyages (☎ 821 8163; mboup@telecomplus.sn; Place de l'Indépendance) One of the most enduring agencies with tours to the major destinations.

Origin Africa (Map p152; ☎ 860 1578; origin@sentoo .sn; Cité Africa, Ouakam) One of the more interesting tour operators in Senegal, with plenty of tours to destinations less frequently covered.

Pain de Singe (Map p150; ☎ 824 2484; paindesinge@ arc.sn) Absolutely original, this tiny operation runs excellent, eco-oriented tours, including trips to the marine reserve at Bamboung, to Casamance and plenty of other off-the-beaten-track destinations.

Sahel dEcouverte Bassari (Map p150; ☎ 842 8751; bassari@bassarisenegal.com, carresahel@sentoo.sn; 7 rue Masclary) Its tours in northern Senegal are particularly good. It caters well for Spanish speakers.

Senegal Tours (Map p150; ☎ 839 9900; fax 823 2644; 5 Place de l'Indépendance) This is of the largest operators in the country.

TPA (☎ 644 9491; 957 1256; tpa@sentoo.sn; www .lesenegal.info) A tour operator with a difference, TPA is the leading agency for 'bush tourism', with excellent tours around the lesser travelled routes, including trips to its remote *campements* (hotels with accommodation in huts or bungalows) in Lompoul, Simal and Palmarin (Siné-Saloum).

Health

CONTENTS

Travel health depends on your predeparture preparations, your daily health care while travelling and how you handle any medical problem that does develop. While the potential dangers can seem quite frightening, in reality few travellers experience anything more than an upset stomach.

BEFORE YOU GO

If you wear glasses take a spare pair and your prescription. If you require a particular medication take an adequate supply, as it may not be available locally. Take part of the packaging showing the generic name rather than the brand, which will make getting replacements easier, but be sure to remove or black out the price you paid at home, or you could encounter a sudden dose of hyperinflation. It's a good idea to have a legible prescription or letter from your doctor showing that you legally use the medication.

RECOMMENDED VACCINATIONS

Plan ahead for getting your vaccinations: Some require more than one injection, while some vaccinations should not be given together. Note that some vaccinations should not be given during pregnancy or to people with allergies – discuss with your doctor.

It is recommended you seek medical advice at least six weeks before travel. Be aware that there is often a greater risk of disease for children and during pregnancy.

Discuss your requirements with your doctor, but vaccinations you should consider for a trip to Gambia or Senegal are listed here (for more details about the diseases themselves, see the individual disease entries later in this chapter). Carry proof of your vaccinations on an international health certificate, especially for yellow fever, as this is sometimes needed to enter some countries.

In both Senegal and The Gambia you will need a yellow-fever vaccination certificate if you're coming from a yellow fever–infected area.

INTERNET RESOURCES

There is a wealth of travel-health advice on the Internet. For further information, the Lonely Planet website at www.lonelyplanet .com is a good place to start. The World Health Organization publishes a superb book called *International Travel and Health*, which is revised annually and is available online at no cost at www.who.int/ith. Other websites of general interest are MD Travel Health at www.mdtravelhealth.com, which provides complete travel health recommendations for every country, updated daily, also at no cost; the Centers for Disease Control and Prevention at www.cdc.gov; and Fit for Travel at www.fitfortravel.scot.nhs .uk, which has up-to-date information about outbreaks and is very user-friendly.

It's also a good idea to consult your government's travel-health website, if one is available, before departure:

Australia (www.dfat.gov.au/travel)
Canada (www.hc-sc.gc.ca/english/index.html)
UK (www.doh.gov.uk/traveladvice/index.htm)
USA (www.cdc.gov/travel)

FURTHER READING

Lonely Planet's *Healthy Travel Africa* is a handy pocket size and packed with useful information on pretrip planning, emergency first aid, immunisation and disease information, and what to do if you get sick on the road. *Travel with Children* from Lonely Planet also includes advice on travel health for younger children.

HEALTH

HEALTH

REQUIRED & RECOMMENDED VACCINATIONS

It is essential to have a vaccination certificate to show you've been jabbed for yellow fever.

Diphtheria & Tetanus Vaccinations for these two diseases are usually combined and are recommended for every-one. After an initial course of three injections (usually given in childhood), boosters are necessary every 10 years.

Hepatitis A Vaccine for Hepatitis A (eg Avaxim, Havrix 1440 or VAQTA) provides long-term immunity (possibly more than 10 years) after an initial injection and a booster at six to 12 months. Alternatively an injection of gamma globulin can provide short-term protection against hepatitis A – two to six months, depending on the dose given. It is not a vaccine, but a ready-made antibody collected from blood donations. It is reasonably effective and, unlike the vaccine, it is protective immediately, but because it is a blood product there are concerns about its long-term safety. Hepatitis A vaccine is also available in a combined form, Twinrix, with hepatitis B vaccine. Three injections over a six-month period are required; the first two provide substantial protection against hepatitis A.

Hepatitis B Travellers who should consider vaccination against hepatitis B include those visiting countries where there are high levels of hepatitis B infection, where blood transfusions may not be adequately screened or where sexual contact or needle sharing is a possibility. Vaccination involves three injections, with a booster at 12 months. More rapid courses are available if necessary.

Meningococcal Meningitis Vaccination is recommended, especially during the dry season from November to June. A single injection gives good protection against the major epidemic forms of the disease for three years. Protection may be less effective in children under two years.

Polio This is still prevalent in The Gambia and Senegal, so everyone should keep up-to-date with this vaccination, which is normally given in childhood. A booster every 10 years maintains immunity.

Rabies Vaccination should be considered by those who will spend a month or longer in a country where rabies is common, especially if they are cycling, handling animals, caving or travelling to remote areas, and for children (who may not report a bite). Pretravel rabies vaccination involves having three injections over 21 to 28 days. If someone who has been vaccinated is bitten or scratched by an animal, they will require two booster injections of vaccine; those not vaccinated require more.

Tuberculosis The risk of TB to travellers is usually very low, except for those living with or closely associated with local people. Vaccination against TB (BCG) is recommended for children and young adults living in these areas for three months or more.

Typhoid Vaccination against typhoid may be required if you are travelling for more than a couple of weeks. It is available either as an injection or as capsules to be taken orally.

Yellow Fever A yellow-fever vaccine is now the only vaccine that is a legal requirement for entry into Gambia and Senegal, usually only enforced when coming from an infected area. At the time of research, yellow fever was still affecting small numbers in Senegal. For immunisation you may have to go to a special yellow-fever vaccination centre.

For those planning on being away for a while or working abroad (eg as a Peace Corps worker), *Where There Is No Doctor* by David Werner is a very detailed guide ideal for self-diagnosing almost anything.

IN TRANSIT

JET LAG & MOTION SICKNESS

Eating lightly before and during a trip will reduce the chances of motion sickness. If you are prone to motion sickness try to find a place that minimises movement – near the wing on aircraft, close to midships on boats, near the centre on buses. Fresh air usually helps; reading and cigarette smoke don't. Commercial motion-sickness preparations, which can cause drowsiness, have to be taken before the trip commences. Ginger (available in capsule form) and peppermint (including mint-flavoured sweets) are natural preventatives.

IN THE GAMBIA & SENEGAL

AVAILABILITY & COST OF HEALTH CARE

The Gambia's main government-run hospital is in Banjul, but there is a better selection of private clinics and doctors in the area around the Atlantic coast resorts. If you're upcountry, there are hospitals in Bansang and Farafenni.

In Senegal you'll find the country's main hospitals as well as many private clinics and doctors in Dakar. Around the country, most large towns have hospitals, doctors and clinics; if you need to find any of these, ask at an upmarket hotel.

INFECTIOUS DISEASES

Self-diagnosis and treatment can be risky, so you should always attempt to seek medical help. Your embassy or consulate usually has a list of doctors in the area that speak your language, and good hotels should be able to recommend a local doctor or clinic. Although we do give drug dosages in this section, they are for emergency use only. Correct diagnosis is vital. In this section we have used the generic names for medications – check with a pharmacist for brands available locally.

Note that antibiotics should ideally be administered only under medical supervision. Take only the recommended dose at the prescribed intervals and use the whole course, even if the illness seems to be cured earlier. Stop immediately if there are any serious reactions and don't use the antibiotic at all if you are unsure that you have the correct one. Some people are allergic to commonly prescribed antibiotics such as penicillin; carry this information (eg on a bracelet) when travelling.

Cholera

This is the worst of the watery diarrhoeas and medical help should be sought.

Cholera is mostly transmitted via contaminated human excrements. This might sound like a rather unlikely source of infection – but beware, an infected person preparing meals without having washed their hands properly might transmit the disease. Infection is unlikely outside known problem areas, but if you really want to be safe, prepare your own food and choose restaurants with excellent standards of cleanliness.

Note that in Senegal, cholera outbreaks are frequently reported after the annual mass pilgrimage.

Fluid replacement is the most vital treatment – the risk of dehydration is severe as you may lose up to 20L a day. If there is a delay in getting to hospital, then begin taking tetracycline. The adult dose is 250mg four times daily. It is not recommended for children under nine years or for pregnant women. Tetracycline may help shorten the illness, but adequate fluids are required to save lives.

Dengue

This viral disease is transmitted by mosquitoes and is fast becoming one of the top public-health problems in the tropical world. The disease has been reported in small numbers in both Gambia and Senegal. The *Aedes aegypti* mosquito, which transmits the dengue virus, is most active during the day (unlike the malaria-carrying mosquito), and is found mainly in urban areas, in and around human dwellings. Symptoms of dengue fever include a sudden onset of high fever, headache, joint and muscle pains (hence its old name, breakbone fever) and nausea and vomiting. A rash of small red spots sometimes appears three to four days after the onset of fever. In the early phase of illness, dengue may be mistaken for other infectious diseases including malaria and influenza. Minor bleeding such as nose bleeds may occur in the course of the illness, but this does not necessarily mean that you have progressed to the potentially fatal dengue haemorrhagic fever (DHF). This is a severe illness, characterised by heavy bleeding, which is thought to be a result of secondary infection due to a different strain (there are four major strains) and usually affects residents of the country rather than travellers. Recovery even from simple dengue fever may be prolonged, with tiredness lasting for several weeks.

There is no vaccine against and no specific treatment for dengue. Aspirin should be avoided, as it increases the risk of haemorrhaging. The best prevention is to avoid mosquito bites – see p299.

Filariasis

This mosquito-transmitted parasitic infection is found in many parts of Africa, including Gambia and Senegal. Possible symptoms include fever, pain and swelling of the lymph glands; inflammation of lymph drainage areas; swelling of a limb or the scrotum; skin rashes; and blindness. Treatment can eliminate the parasites from the body, but some of the damage caused may not be reversible. Prompt medical advice should be obtained if the infection is suspected.

Fungal Infections

These occur more commonly in hot weather and are usually found on the scalp, between the toes (athlete's foot) or fingers, in the

HEALTH

MEDICAL KIT CHECKLIST

Following is a list of items you should consider including in your medical kit – consult your pharmacist for brands available in your country.

- antibiotics – consider including these if you're travelling well off the beaten track; see your doctor as they must be prescribed, and carry the prescription with you
- antihistamine – for allergies, eg hay fever; to ease the itch from insect bites or stings; and to prevent motion sickness
- antifungal cream or powder – for fungal skin infections and thrush
- antiseptic (such as povidone-iodine) – for cuts and grazes
- aspirin or paracetamol (acetaminophen in the USA) – for pain or fever
- bandages, Band-Aids (plasters) and other wound dressings
- basic set of children's medication – if you're travelling with children
- calamine lotion, sting-relief spray or aloe vera – to ease irritation from sunburn and insect bites or stings
- cold and flu tablets, throat lozenges and nasal decongestant
- insect repellent, sunscreen, lip balm and eye drops
- loperamide or diphenoxylate – known as 'blockers' for diarrhoea
- multivitamins – consider for long trips, when dietary vitamin intake may be inadequate
- prochlorperazine or metaclopramide – for nausea and vomiting
- rehydration mixture – to prevent dehydration, which may occur, for example during bouts of diarrhoea; particularly important when travelling with children
- scissors, tweezers and a thermometer – note that mercury thermometers are prohibited by airlines
- sterile kit – in case you need injections in a country with medical hygiene problems; discuss with your doctor
- water-purification tablets or iodine

groin and on the body (ringworm). You get ringworm (a fungal infection, not a worm) from infected animals or other people. Moisture encourages these infections.

To prevent fungal infections wear loose, comfortable clothes, avoid artificial fibres, wash frequently and dry yourself carefully. If you do get an infection, wash the infected area at least daily with a disinfectant or medicated soap and water, and rinse and dry well. Apply an antifungal cream or powder such as tolnaftate. Try to expose the infected area to air or sunlight as much as possible. Wash all towels and underwear in hot water, change them often and let them dry in the sun.

Hepatitis

This is a general term for inflammation of the liver, a common disease worldwide. Several different viruses cause hepatitis, and differ in the way they are transmitted. Similar symptoms in all forms include fever, chills, headache, fatigue, feelings of weakness and aches and pains, followed by loss of appetite, nausea, vomiting, abdominal pain, dark urine, light-coloured faeces, jaundiced (yellow) skin and yellowing of the whites of the eyes. People who have had hepatitis should avoid alcohol for some time afterwards; the liver needs time to recover.

Hepatitis A is transmitted by contaminated food and drinking water. You should seek medical advice, but there is not much you can do apart from resting, drinking lots of fluids, eating lightly and avoiding fatty foods. Hepatitis E is transmitted in the same way as hepatitis A; it can be particularly serious in pregnant women.

There are almost 300 million chronic carriers of hepatitis B in the world. It is spread through contact with infected blood, blood products or body fluids; for example through sexual contact, unsterilised needles and blood transfusions, or through contact with blood via small breaks in the skin. Other risk situations include shaving, tattooing or body piercing with contaminated equipment. The symptoms of hepatitis B may be more severe than those of type A and the disease can lead to long-term problems such as chronic liver damage, liver cancer or a long-term carrier state. Hepatitis C and D are spread in the same way as hepatitis B and can also lead to long-term complications.

There are vaccines against hepatitis A and B, but there are currently no vaccines against the other types of hepatitis.

HIV & AIDS

Infection with the human immunodeficiency virus (HIV) may lead to acquired immune deficiency syndrome (AIDS), which is a fatal disease. With an HIV prevalence rate of 0.8% (44,000 people) according to a 2003 estimate, Senegal has one of the lowest HIV/AIDS rates in Africa, and the prevalence in The Gambia is also relatively low. Still, that's no reason for taking risks. Any exposure to blood, blood products or body fluids may put the individual at risk. The disease is often transmitted through sexual contact or dirty needles – vaccinations, acupuncture, tattooing and body piercing are potentially as dangerous as intravenous drug use. HIV/AIDS can also be spread through infected blood transfusions; some developing countries cannot afford to screen blood used for transfusions. If you do need an injection, ask to see the syringe unwrapped in front of you, or take a needle and syringe pack with you.

There are two types of HIV, and both are fairly common in West Africa. Unfortunately, many HIV tests do not test for both variations. What this means is that unprotected sex with someone who has tested negative for the virus might not be as safe as it sounds. Fear of HIV infection should never discourage treatment for serious conditions.

Leishmaniasis

This is a group of parasitic diseases transmitted by sandflies, which are found in many parts of the Middle East, Africa, India, Central and South America and the Mediterranean. Cutaneous leishmaniasis affects the skin tissue causing ulceration and disfigurement, and visceral leishmaniasis affects the internal organs. Seek medical advice, as laboratory testing is required for diagnosis and correct treatment. Avoiding sandfly bites is the best precaution. Bites are usually painless, itchy and are yet another reason to cover up and apply repellent.

Malaria

This serious and potentially fatal disease is spread by mosquito bites. Nowhere in Gambia and Senegal is completely free of malaria so it's extremely important to avoid mosquito bites and to take tablets to ensure a good degree of protection.

Symptoms range from fever, chills and sweating, headache, diarrhoea and abdominal pains to a vague feeling of ill-health. Seek medical help immediately if malaria is suspected. Without treatment the disease can rapidly become more serious and can be fatal.

Antimalarial drugs do not prevent you from being infected, but kill the malaria parasites during an early stage in their development and significantly reduce your risk of becoming very ill or dying. Expert advice on medication should be sought as there are many factors to consider including the area to be visited, the risk of exposure to malaria-carrying mosquitoes, the side effects of medication, your medical history and whether you are a child or an adult or pregnant. Travellers to isolated areas in high-risk countries may like to carry a treatment dose of medication for use if symptoms occur.

If medical care is not available, malaria tablets can be used for treatment. You need to use a malaria tablet different from the one you were taking when you contracted malaria. The standard treatment dose of mefloquine (Larium) is two 250mg tablets and a further two six hours later. For Fansidar, it's a single dose of three tablets. If you were previously taking mefloquine and cannot obtain Fansidar, then other alternatives are Malarone (atovaquone-proguanil; four tablets once daily for three days), halofantrine (three doses of two 250mg tablets every six hours) or quinine sulphate (600mg every six hours). There is a greater risk of side effects with these dosages than in normal use if used with mefloquine, so medical advice is preferable. Be aware also that halofantrine is no longer recommended by the WHO as emergency standby treatment because of side effects, and should only be used if no other drugs are available.

Travellers are advised to prevent mosquito bites at all times. The main messages:
- Wear light-coloured clothing.
- Wear long trousers and long-sleeved shirts.
- Use mosquito repellents containing the compound DEET on exposed areas (prolonged overuse of DEET may be harmful, especially to children, but using it

is preferable to being bitten by disease-transmitting mosquitoes).

■ Avoid perfume and aftershave.
■ Use a mosquito net impregnated with mosquito repellent (permethrin) – it may be worth taking your own.
■ Impregnating your clothes with permethrin effectively deters mosquitoes and other insects.

In the Gambia you absolutely need to take precautions against malaria.

Malaria is a killer and exists year-round throughout Senegal. It is essential that you take appropriate precautions, especially if you're heading out of Dakar.

Meningococcal Meningitis

This is a serious disease that attacks the brain and can be fatal. There are recurring epidemics in various parts of the world, including the interior regions of Gambia and Senegal.

A fever, severe headache, sensitivity to light and neck stiffness that prevents forward bending of the head are the first symptoms. There may also be purple patches on the skin. Death can occur within a few hours, so urgent medical treatment is required.

Treatment is large doses of penicillin given intravenously, or chloramphenicol injections.

Rabies

This fatal viral infection is found in many countries. Many animals can be infected (such as dogs, cats, bats and monkeys) and their saliva is infectious. Any bite, scratch or even lick from an animal should be cleaned immediately and thoroughly. Scrub with soap and running water, then apply alcohol or iodine solution. Seek medical help promptly to receive a course of injections to prevent the onset of symptoms and death.

Schistosomiasis

Also known as bilharzia, this disease is common in Gambia and Senegal. It is transmitted by minute worms that infect certain varieties of freshwater snails found in rivers, streams, lakes and particularly behind dams. The worms multiply and are eventually discharged into the water.

The worm enters through the skin and attaches itself to your intestines or bladder.

The first symptom may be a general feeling of being unwell, or a tingling and sometimes a light rash around the area where it entered. Weeks later a high fever may develop. Once the disease is established, abdominal pain and blood in the urine are other signs. The infection often causes no symptoms until the disease is well established (several months to years after exposure) and damage to internal organs irreversible.

Avoiding swimming or bathing in fresh water where schistosomiasis is present is the main method of preventing the disease. Even deep water can be infected. If you do get wet, dry off quickly and dry your clothes as well.

A blood test is the best way to diagnose the disease, but the test will not show positive for some weeks after exposure.

Sexually Transmitted Diseases (STDs)

HIV/AIDS and hepatitis B can be transmitted through sexual contact – see the relevant sections earlier for more details. Other STDs include gonorrhoea, herpes and syphilis. Sores, blisters or rashes around the genitals and discharges or pain when urinating are common symptoms. With STDs such as the wart virus or chlamydia (both common in Gambia and Senegal), symptoms may be less marked or not observed at all, especially in women. Chlamydia infection can cause infertility in men and women before any symptoms have been noticed. Syphilis symptoms eventually disappear completely but the disease continues and can cause severe problems in later years. While abstaining from sexual contact is the only 100% effective prevention, using condoms is also effective. Gonorrhoea and syphilis are treated with antibiotics. The different STDs each require specific antibiotics.

Sleeping Sickness

In parts of tropical Africa tsetse flies can carry trypanosomiasis, or sleeping sickness; however it is seldom seen in Gambia and Senegal. The tsetse fly is about twice the size of a housefly and recognisable by the scissorlike way it folds its wings when at rest. Only a small proportion of tsetse flies carry the disease, but it is a serious disease. No protection is available except avoiding the tsetse fly bites. The flies are attracted to large moving objects such as safari buses, to perfume and aftershave and particularly to the colours purple and dark blue (avoid dark blue hire cars). Swelling at the site of the bite, five or more days later, is the first sign of infection; this is followed within two to three weeks by fever.

Tetanus

This disease is caused by a germ that lives in soil and in the faeces of horses and other animals. It enters the body via breaks in the skin. The first symptom may be discomfort in swallowing, or stiffening of the jaw and neck; this is followed by painful convulsions of the jaw and whole body. The disease can be fatal. It can be prevented by vaccination.

Tuberculosis (TB)

This bacterial infection is usually transmitted from person to person by coughing but may be transmitted through consumption of unpasteurised milk. Milk that has been boiled is safe to drink, and the souring of milk to make yogurt or cheese also kills the bacilli. TB is quite a problem in parts of Gambia, though travellers are usually not at great risk as close household contact with the infected person is usually required before the disease is passed on.

Typhoid

This is a dangerous gut infection caused by contaminated water and food. While it's seldom seen in Gambia and Senegal, if you suspect you have typhoid seek medical help immediately.

In its early stages sufferers may feel they have a bad cold or flu on the way, with headache, body aches and a fever that rises a little each day until it is around 40°C (104°F) or more. The victim's pulse is often slow relative to the degree of fever present – unlike a normal fever where the pulse increases. There may also be abdominal pain, vomiting, diarrhoea or constipation.

In the second week the high fever and slow pulse continue and a few pink spots may appear on the body; trembling, delirium, weakness, weight loss and dehydration may occur. Complications such as pneumonia, perforated bowel or meningitis may occur.

Typhus

This disease is spread by ticks, mites or lice. It begins with fever, chills, headache and

muscle pains followed a few days later by a body rash. There is often a large painful sore at the site of the bite and nearby lymph nodes are swollen and painful. Typhus can be treated under medical supervision. Seek local advice on areas where ticks pose a danger and always check your skin carefully for ticks after walking in areas that may harbour ticks, such as tropical forests. An insect repellent can help, and walkers in tick-infested areas should consider having their boots and trousers impregnated with benzyl benzoate and dibutylphthalate.

Yellow Fever

This viral disease is endemic in many African and South American countries and is transmitted by mosquitoes. The initial symptoms are fever, headache, abdominal pain and vomiting. Seek medical care urgently and drink lots of fluids.

TRAVELLER'S DIARRHOEA

Simple things such as a change of water, food or climate can all cause a mild bout of diarrhoea, and many people experience a few rushed toilet trips soon after arriving in Africa. If there are no other symptoms then don't worry, this is just your body dealing with the change – it doesn't mean you've got dysentery!

Dehydration is the main danger with any diarrhoea, particularly in children or the elderly as dehydration can occur quite quickly. In all circumstances fluid replacement is the most important thing to remember. Weak black tea with a little sugar, soda water, or flat soft drinks diluted 50% with clean water are all good. With severe diarrhoea, a rehydrating solution is preferable to replace minerals and salts lost. Commercially available oral rehydration salts (ORS) are very useful; add them to boiled or bottled water. In an emergency you can make up a solution of six teaspoons of sugar and half a teaspoon of salt to a litre of boiled or bottled water. You need to drink at least the same volume of fluid that you are losing in bowel movements and vomiting. Urine is the best guide to the adequacy of replacement – if you have small amounts of concentrated urine, you need to drink more. Keep drinking small amounts often. Stick to a bland, fat-free diet as you recover.

Gut-paralysing drugs such as loperamide (Imodium) or diphenoxylate (Lomotil) can be used to bring relief from the symptoms, although they do not actually cure the problem. Only use these drugs if you do not have access to toilets, eg if you must travel. Note that these drugs are not recommended for children under 12 years.

In certain situations antibiotics may be required: diarrhoea with blood or mucus (dysentery), any diarrhoea with fever, profuse watery diarrhoea, persistent diarrhoea not improving after 48 hours and severe diarrhoea. These suggest a more serious cause of diarrhoea and, in these situations, gut-paralysing drugs should be avoided. A stool test may be necessary to diagnose what bug is causing your diarrhoea, so you should seek medical help urgently.

Where this is not possible the recommended drugs for bacterial diarrhoea (the most likely cause of severe diarrhoea in travellers) are norfloxacin 400mg twice daily for three days or ciprofloxacin 500mg twice daily for five days. These are not recommended for children or pregnant women. The drug of choice for children would be co-trimoxazole with dosage dependent on weight. A five-day course is given. Ampicillin or amoxycillin may be given in pregnancy, but medical care is necessary.

Two other causes of persistent diarrhoea in travellers are giardiasis and amoebic dysentery. You should seek medical advice if you think you have either, but where this is not possible tinidazole (Fasigyn) or metronidazole (Flagyl) are the recommended drugs. Treatment is a 2g single dose of tinidazole or 250mg of metronidazole three times daily for five to 10 days.

Amoebic Dysentery

Caused by the protozoan *Entamoeba histolytica*, amoebic dysentery, is characterised by a gradual onset of low-grade diarrhoea, often with blood and mucus. Cramping abdominal pain and vomiting are less likely than in other types of diarrhoea, and fever may not be present. It will persist until treated and can recur and cause other health problems.

Giardiasis

A common parasite, *Giardia lamblia*, causes giardiasis. Symptoms include stomach cramps, nausea, a bloated stomach, watery, foul-smelling diarrhoea and frequent gas. Giardiasis can appear several weeks after you have been exposed to the parasite. The symptoms may disappear for a few days, then return; this can go on for several weeks.

ENVIRONMENTAL HAZARDS
Food

There is an old colonial adage that says: 'If you can cook it, boil it or peel it you can eat it...otherwise forget it'. Vegetables and fruit should be washed with purified water or peeled where possible. Beware of ice cream sold on the streets of Banjul or Dakar or anywhere it might have been melted and refrozen. Seafood is generally some of the safest food available in Senegal and Gambia, but shellfish such as mussels, oysters and clams should be treated with caution, while undercooked meat, particularly in the form of mince, should be avoided. If a place looks clean and well run and the vendor also looks clean and healthy, then the food is probably safe. In general, places that are packed with travellers or locals will be fine, while empty restaurants are questionable. The food in busy restaurants is cooked and eaten quite quickly with little standing around, and is probably not reheated.

Heat Exhaustion

Dehydration and salt deficiency can cause heat exhaustion. Take time to acclimatise to high temperatures, drink sufficient liquids and do not do anything too physically demanding.

Salt deficiency is characterised by fatigue, lethargy, headaches, giddiness and muscle cramps; salt tablets may help, but adding extra salt to your food is better.

Anhidrotic heat exhaustion is a rare form of heat exhaustion that is caused by an inability to sweat. It tends to affect people who have been in a hot climate for some time, rather than newcomers. It can progress to heatstroke. Treatment involves removal to a cooler climate.

Heatstroke

This serious, occasionally fatal, condition can occur if the body's heat-regulating mechanism breaks down and the temperature rises to dangerous levels. Long, continuous exposure to high temperatures and insufficient fluids can leave you vulnerable.

The symptoms are feeling unwell, not sweating very much (or at all) and a high body temperature (39°C to 41°C or 102°F to 106°F). Where sweating has ceased, the skin becomes flushed and red. Severe, throbbing headaches and lack of coordination will also occur, and the sufferer may be confused or aggressive. Eventually the victim will become delirious or convulse. Hospitalisation is essential, but in the interim get victims out of the sun, remove their clothing, cover them with a wet sheet or towel, then fan continually. Give fluids if they are conscious.

Insect Bites & Stings

Filariasis, leishmaniasis, sleeping sickness, typhus and yellow fever are all insect-borne diseases, but they do not pose a great risk to travellers.

Bed bugs are a particular problem in the budget-accommodation places of Gambia and Senegal. These evil little bastards live in various places but are found particularly in dirty mattresses and bedding, and are evidenced by spots of blood on bedclothes or on the wall. Bedbugs leave itchy bites in neat rows, often along a line where your body touched the mattress. They won't kill you but bites often itch for days, making sleep difficult. Calamine lotion or a sting-relief spray may help, but your best bet is to just find another hotel.

Parasites

You should always check all over your body if you have been walking through a potentially tick-infested area as ticks can cause skin infections and other, more serious diseases. If you find a tick attached, press down around its head with tweezers, grab the head and gently pull upwards. Avoid pulling the rear of the body as this may squeeze the tick's gut contents through the attached mouth parts into the skin, increasing the risk of infection and disease. Smearing chemicals on the tick will not make it let go and is not recommended.

Water

The number one rule is be careful of the water and especially of ice. If you don't know for certain that the water is safe, assume the worst. Having said that, we travelled throughout Senegal and Gambia and in most towns the tap water was OK to drink. However, people respond differently, and water that's fine for some might spark a marathon

session on the throne for others – you'll soon know where you stand (or sit).

Bottled water and soft drinks are generally fine and are widely available, although in some places bottles may be refilled with tap water – check the seals. Take care with fruit juice, particularly if water may have been added. Milk should be treated with suspicion as it is often unpasteurised, though boiled milk is fine if it is kept hygienically. Tea or coffee should also be OK, since the water should have been boiled.

The simplest way to purify water is to boil it thoroughly. Alternatively, you could buy a water filter for a long trip. There are two main kinds of filter. Total filters take out all parasites, bacteria and viruses and make water safe to drink. They are often expensive, but they can be more cost effective than buying lots of bottled water. Simple filters (which can even be a nylon mesh bag) take out dirt and larger foreign bodies from the water so that chemical solutions work much more effectively; if water is dirty, chemical solutions may not work at all. It's very important when buying a filter to read the specifications, so that you know exactly what it removes from the water and what it doesn't. Simple filtering will not remove all dangerous organisms, so if you cannot boil water it should be treated chemically. Chlorine tablets will kill many pathogens, but not some parasites such as giardia and amoebic cysts. Iodine is more effective in purifying water and is available in tablet form. Follow the directions carefully and remember that too much iodine can be harmful.

WOMEN'S HEALTH
Gynaecological Problems

Antibiotic use, synthetic underwear, sweating and contraceptive pills can lead to fungal vaginal infections, especially when travelling in hot climates. Fungal infections are characterised by a rash, itch and discharge and are usually treated with Nystatin, miconazole or clotrimazole pessaries or vaginal cream. Maintaining good personal hygiene and wearing loose-fitting clothes and cotton underwear may help prevent these infections.

Sexually transmitted diseases are a major cause of gynaecological problems. Symptoms include a smelly discharge, painful intercourse and sometimes a burning sensation when urinating. Medical attention

HEALTH

should be sought and sexual partners must also be treated. For more details see p300. Besides abstinence, the best thing is to practise safe sex.

Both in Gambia and Senegal, tampons and the tiny, discreet and comfortable types of hygienic pads are only available in the supermarkets and service stations of the larger towns – and they tend to be comparatively expensive. Upcountry, it'll all be less-than-sexy towels. Best bring a good supply with you.

Pregnancy

It is not advisable to travel to some places while pregnant as some vaccinations against serious diseases (eg yellow fever) are not advisable during pregnancy. In addition, some diseases are much more serious for the mother during pregnancy (eg malaria) and may increase the risk of a stillborn child.

Most miscarriages occur during the first three months of pregnancy. Miscarriage is not uncommon and occasionally leads to severe bleeding. The last three months of pregnancy should be spent within reasonable distance of good medical care. A baby born as early as 24 weeks stands a chance of survival, but only in a good modern hospital. Pregnant women should avoid medication, although vaccinations and malarial prophylactics should be taken where needed.

Language

CONTENTS

COLONIAL LANGUAGES

The sheer number of indigenous tongues spoken in Gambia and Senegal means that a common language is essential. Whereas Swahili developed in East Africa as a way for all the tribes to communicate, in West Africa the languages of the former colonial powers – French in Senegal and English in Gambia – have become each country's common language (or 'lingua franca').

We assume most readers of this book have a comfortable grasp of English, but some pointers for survival in French are provided here. Note that the French of France often differs from the French of Africa: for starters the French of Africa is pronounced with an accent that makes it easier to understand for English ears. Conversely the French you speak with an *accent terrible* is more likely to be understood in *les marchés de Dakar* than on *les boulevards de Paris*.

FRENCH

Though we've generally only included the polite form of address with the following phrases – *vous* (you) – the informal mode *tu* is used much more commonly in West Africa; you'll hear less *s'il vous plaît* and more *s'il te plaît* (which may be considered impolite in France unless spoken between good friends). If in doubt in Africa (when dealing with border officials or any older people) it's always safer to use the polite *vous* form.

If you fancy getting stuck into your *français* to a greater extent than is possible with what we include here, Lonely Planet's compact *French Phrasebook* offers a handy, pocket-sized guide to the language that will cover all your travel needs and more.

Pronunciation

Most of letters in the French alphabet are pronounced more or less the same as their English counterparts. Here are a few that may cause confusion:

j	**zh** in the pronunciation guides; as the 's' in 'leisure', eg *jour,* zhoor (day)
c	before **e** and **i**, as the 's' in 'sit'; before **a**, **o** and **u** it's pronounced as English 'k'. When undescored with a 'cedilla' (**ç**) it's always pronounced as the 's' in 'sit'.
r	pronounced from the back of the throat while constricting the muscles to restrict the flow of air
n, m	where a syllable ends in a single **n** or **m**, these letters are not pronounced, but the preceding vowel is given a nasal pronunciation

The pronunciation guides included with each French phrase should help you in getting your message across.

Accommodation

I'm looking for a ...
Je cherche ...	zher shersh ...
camping ground	
un camping	un kom·peeng
guesthouse	
une pension (de famille)	ewn pon·syon (der fa·mee·ler)
hotel	
un hôtel	un o·tel
youth hostel	
une auberge de jeunesse	ewn o·berzh der zher·nes

Where is a cheap hotel?
Où est-ce qu'on peut trouver un hôtel pas cher?
oo es·kon per troo·vay un o·tel pa shair
What is the address?
Quelle est l'adresse?
kel e la·dres
Could you write the address, please?
Est-ce que vous pourriez écrire l'adresse, s'il vous plaît?
e·sker voo poo·ryay ay·kreer la·dres seel voo play

LANGUAGE

```
SIGNS
Entrée              Entrance
Fermé               Closed
Interdit            Prohibited
Ouvert              Open
Renseignements      Information
Sortie              Exit
Toilettes/WC        Toilets
  Femmes               Women
  Hommes               Men
```

Do you have any rooms available?
Est-ce que vous avez des chambres libres?
e-sker voo-za-vay day shom-brer lee-brer

I'd like (a) ...
Je voudrais ...   zher voo-dray ...
  single room
  une chambre à un lit   ewn shom-brer a un lee
  double-bed room
  une chambre avec un   ewn shom-brer a-vek
  grand lit   un gron lee
  room with two beds
  une chambre avec des   ewn shom-brer a-vek day
  lits jumeaux   lee zhew-mo

How much is it ...?
Quel est le prix ...?   kel e ler pree ...
  per night
  par nuit   par nwee
  per person
  par personne   par per-son

May I see it?
Est-ce que je peux voir   es-ker zher per vwa
  la chambre?   la shom-brer
Where is the bathroom?
Où est la salle de bains? oo e la sal der bun
Where is the toilet?
Où sont les toilettes?   oo-son lay twa-let
air-conditioning
climatisation   klee-ma-tee-za-syon
bed
lit   lee
blanket
couverture   koo-vair-tewr
hot water
eau chaude   leeo shod
key
clef/clé   klef/klay
sheet
drap   drap
shower
douche   doosh

toilet
les toilettes   lay twa-let

Conversation & Essentials
In common with many other predominantly Muslim groups, the Wolof and Mandinka use the traditional Arabic Islamic greetings: *salaam aleikum* (Peace be with you); the response is: *aleikum asalaam* (And peace be with you).

Hello.	*Bonjour.*	bon-zhoor
Goodbye.	*Au revoir.*	o-rer-vwa
Yes.	*Oui.*	wee
No.	*Non.*	no
Please.	*S'il vous plaît.*	seel voo play
	S'il te plaît. (inf)	seel ter play
Thank you.	*Merci.*	mair-see
You're welcome.	*Je vous en prie.*	zher voo-zon pree
	De rien. (inf)	der ree-en
Excuse me.	*Excusez-moi.*	ek-skew-zay-mwa
Sorry. (forgive me)	*Pardon.*	par-don

(Have a) good evening.
Bonne soirée.   bon swa-ray
What's your name?
Comment vous   ko-mon voo-za-pay-lay voo
  appelez-vous?
Comment tu   ko-mon tew ta-pel
  t'appelles? (inf)
My name is ...
Je m'appelle ...   zher ma-pel ...
Where are you from?
De quel pays êtes-vous? der kel pay-ee et-voo
De quel pays es-tu? (inf) der kel pay-ee e-tew
I'm from ...
Je viens de ...   zher vyen der ...
I like ...
J'aime ...   zhem ...
I don't like ...
Je n'aime pas ...   zher nem pa ...

Directions
Where is ...?
Où est ...?   oo e ...
Go straight ahead.
Continuez tout droit.   kon-teen-way too drwa
Turn left.
Tournez à gauche.   toor-nay a gosh
Turn right.
Tournez à droite.   toor-nay a drwat
How many kilometres is ...?
À combien de kilomètres a kom-byun der kee-lo-me-trer
  est ...?   e ...

Emergencies

Help!
Au secours!   o skoor
There's been an accident!
Il y a eu un accident!   eel ya ew un ak·see·don
I'm lost.
Je me suis égaré/e. (m/f) zhe me swee·zay·ga·ray
Leave me alone!
Fichez-moi la paix!   fee·shay·mwa la pay

Call ...!	*Appelez ...!*	a·play ...
a doctor	*un médecin*	un mayd·sun
the police	*la police*	la po·lees

Health

I'm ill.	*Je suis malade.*	zher swee ma·lad
antiseptic	*l'antiseptique*	lon·tee·sep·teek
aspirin	*l'aspirine*	las·pee·reen
condoms	*des préservatifs*	day pray·zair·va·teef
contraceptive	*le contraceptif*	ler kon·tra·sep·teef
diarrhoea	*la diarrhée*	la dya·ray
medicine	*le médicament*	ler may·dee·ka·mon
nausea	*la nausée*	la no·zay
sunblock cream	*la crème solaire*	la krem so·lair
tampons	*des tampons*	day tom·pon
	hygiéniques	ee·zhen·eek

I'm ...	*Je suis ...*	zher swee ...
asthmatic	*asthmatique*	(z)as·ma·teek
diabetic	*diabétique*	dee·a·bay·teek
epileptic	*épileptique*	(z)ay·pee·lep·teek

I'm allergic	*Je suis*	zher swee
to ...	*allergique ...*	za·lair·zheek ...
antibiotics	*aux antibiotiques*	o zon·tee·byo·teek
nuts	*aux noix*	o nwa
peanuts	*aux cacahuètes*	o ka·ka·wet
penicillin	*à la pénicilline*	a la pay·nee·see·leen

Language Difficulties

Do you speak English?
Parlez-vous anglais?
par·lay·voo zong·lay
Does anyone here speak English?
Y a-t-il quelqu'un qui parle anglais?
ya·teel kel·kung kee par long·glay
I don't understand.
Je ne comprends pas.
zher ner kom·pron pa
Could you write it down, please?
Est-ce que vous pourriez l'écrire, s'il vous plaît?
es·ker voo poo·ryay lay·kreer seel voo play

Can you show me (on the map)?
Pouvez-vous m'indiquer (sur la carte)?
poo·vay·voo mun·dee·kay (sewr la kart)

Numbers

0	*zero*	zay·ro
1	*un*	un
2	*deux*	der
3	*trois*	trwa
4	*quatre*	ka·trer
5	*cinq*	sungk
6	*six*	sees
7	*sept*	set
8	*huit*	weet
9	*neuf*	nerf
10	*dix*	dees
11	*onze*	onz
12	*douze*	dooz
13	*treize*	trez
14	*quatorze*	ka·torz
15	*quinze*	kunz
16	*seize*	sez
17	*dix-sept*	dee·set
18	*dix-huit*	dee·zweet
19	*dix-neuf*	deez·nerf
20	*vingt*	vung
21	*vingt et un*	vung tay un
22	*vingt-deux*	vung·der
30	*trente*	tront
40	*quarante*	ka·ront
50	*cinquante*	sung·kont
60	*soixante*	swa·sont
70	*soixante-dix*	swa·son·dees
80	*quatre-vingts*	ka·trer·vung
90	*quatre-vingt-dix*	ka·trer·vung·dees
100	*cent*	son
1000	*mille*	meel

Question Words

Who?	*Qui?*	kee
What?	*Quoi?*	kwa
What is it?	*Qu'est-ce que c'est?*	kes·ker say
When?	*Quand?*	kon
Where?	*Où?*	oo
Which?	*Quel/Quelle?*	kel
Why?	*Pourquoi?*	poor·kwa
How?	*Comment?*	ko·mon

Shopping & Services

I'd like to buy ...
Je voudrais acheter ...   zher voo·dray ash·tay ...
How much is it?
C'est combien?   say kom·byun

I don't like it.
Cela ne me plaît pas.   ser·la ner mer play pa
May I look at it?
Est-ce que je peux le voir?   es·ker zher per ler vwar
I'm just looking.
Je regarde.   zher rer·gard
It's cheap.
Ce n'est pas cher.   ser nay pa shair
It's too expensive.
C'est trop cher.   say tro shair
I'll take it.
Je le prends.   zher ler pron

Can I pay by ...?   *Est-ce que je peux*   es·ker zher per
                         payer avec ...?   pay·yay a·vek ...
  credit card   *ma carte de*   ma kart der
                     crédit   kray·dee
  travellers   *des chèques*   day shek
  cheques   *de voyage*   der vwa·yazh

more   *plus*   plew
less   *moins*   mwa
smaller   *plus petit*   plew per·tee
bigger   *plus grand*   plew gron

I'm looking   *Je cherche ...*   zhe shersh ...
for ...
  a bank   *une banque*   ewn bonk
  the ... embassy   *l'ambassade*   lam·ba·sahd
                         de ...   der ...
  the hospital   *l'hôpital*   lo·pee·tal
  the market   *le marché*   ler mar·shay
  the police   *la police*   la po·lees
  the post office   *le bureau de*   ler bew·ro der
                         poste   post
  a public phone   *une cabine*   ewn ka·been
                        téléphonique   tay·lay·fo·neek
  a public toilet   *les toilettes*   lay twa·let
  the telephone   *la centrale*   la san·tral
  centre   *téléphonique*   tay·lay·fo·neek
  the tourist   *l'office de*   lo·fees der
  office   *tourisme*   too·rees·mer

Time & Dates
What time is it?
Quelle heure est-il?   kel er e til
It's (8) o'clock.
Il est (huit) heures.   il e (weet) er
It's half past ...
Il est (...) heures et   il e (...) er e
demie.   day·mee

in the morning   *du matin*   dew ma·tun
in the afternoon   *de l'après-midi*   der la·pray·mee·dee

in the evening   *du soir*   dew swar
today   *aujourd'hui*   o·zhoor·dwee
tomorrow   *demain*   der·mun
yesterday   *hier*   yair

Monday   *lundi*   lun·dee
Tuesday   *mardi*   mar·dee
Wednesday   *mercredi*   mair·krer·dee
Thursday   *jeudi*   zher·dee
Friday   *vendredi*   von·drer·dee
Saturday   *samedi*   sam·dee
Sunday   *dimanche*   dee·monsh

January   *janvier*   zhon·vyay
February   *février*   fayv·ryay
March   *mars*   mars
April   *avril*   a·vreel
May   *mai*   may
June   *juin*   zhwun
July   *juillet*   zhwee·yay
August   *août*   oot
September   *septembre*   sep·tom·brer
October   *octobre*   ok·to·brer
November   *novembre*   no·vom·brer
December   *décembre*   day·som·brer

Transport
What time does ... leave/arrive?
À quelle heure part/arrive ...?
a kel er par/a·reev ...
  boat
  le bateau   ler ba·to
  bus
  le bus   ler bews
  train
  le train   ler trun

I'd like a ticket to ...
Je voudrais un billet à ...
zher voo·dray un bee·yay a ...
I want to go to ...
Je voudrais aller à ...
zher voo·dray a·lay a ...
Which bus goes to ...?
Quel autobus/car part pour ...?
kel o·to·boos/ka par poor ...
Does this bus go to ...?
Ce car-là va-t-il à ...?
ser ka·la va·til a ...
Please tell me when we arrive in ...
Dîtes-moi quand on arrive à ... s'il vous plaît.
deet·mwa kon·don a·reev a ... seel voo play
Stop here, please.
Arrêtez ici, s'il vous plaît.
a·ray·tay ee·see seel voo play

the first	le premier (m)	ler prer·myay
	la première (f)	la prer·mayir
the last	le dernier (m)	ler dair·nyay
	la dernière (f)	la dair·nyair
ticket	billet	bee·yay
ticket office	le guichet	ler gee·shay
timetable	l'horaire	lo·rair
train station	la gare	la gar
daily	chaque jour	shak zhoor
early	tôt	to
late	tard	tar
on time	à l'heure	a ler

I'd like to hire	Je voudrais	zher voo·dray
a/an ...	louer ...	loo·way ...
car	une voiture	ewn vwa·tewr
4WD	un quatre-quatre	un kat·kat
motorbike	une moto	ewn mo·to
bicycle	un vélo	un vay·lo
petrol/gas	essence	ay·sons
diesel	diesel	dyay·zel

Is this the road to ...?
C'est la route pour ...?   say la root poor ...
Where's a service station?
Où est-ce qu'il y a   oo es·keel ya
une station-service?   ewn sta·syon·ser·vees
Please fill it up.
Le plein, s'il vous plaît.   ler plun seel voo play
I need a mechanic.
J'ai besoin d'un   zhay ber·zwun dun
mécanicien.   may·ka·nee·syun

AFRICAN LANGUAGES

The diverse tribes and ethnic groups of Gambia and Senegal are spread across the national boundaries, and each has their own language or dialect. According to the Summer Institute of Linguistics Ethnologue there are up to 50 distinct languages spoken in the region, at least 15 of which have over 15,000 speakers. Some of the native tongues spoken as a first language by a significant proportion of people are listed here (although many people speak at least two indigenous languages). Note that the phrases reflect pronunciation and not correct spelling.

DIOLA

The Diola people inhabit the Casamance region of Senegal, and also southwestern Gambia, where their name is spelt Jola.

Their language is Diola or Jola, not to be confused with the Dioula or Dyola spoken in Burkina Faso and Côte d'Ivoire. Diola society is segmented and very flexible, so several dialects have developed which may not be mutually intelligible between groups even though the area inhabited by the Diola is relatively small.

Hello/Welcome.	kah·sou·mai·kep
Greetings. (reply)	kah·sou·mai·kep
Goodbye.	ou·kah·to·rrah

FULA (FULFULDE/PULAAR)

The Fula people are found across West Africa, from northern Senegal to as far east as Sudan and as far south as Ghana and Nigeria. The Fula are known as Peul in Senegal, and are also called Fulani and Fulbe. There are two main languages in the Fulani group:

- Fulfulde/Pulaar, spoken mainly in northern and southern Senegal; includes Tukulor and Fulakunda dialects
- Futa Fula (aka Futa Djalon), one of the main indigenous languages of Guinea, also spoken in eastern Senegal

These far-flung languages have numerous regional dialects and variants that aren't always mutually intelligible between different groups.

The following phrases in Pulaar should be understood through most parts of Senegal. Note that **ng** is pronounced as one sound (like the 'ng' in 'sing'); practise isolating this sound and using it at the beginning of a word. The letter **ñ** represents the 'ni' sound in 'onion'.

Hello.	no ngoolu daa (sg)
	no ngoolu dong (pl)
Goodbye.	ñalleen e jamm (lit. 'Have a good day.')
	mbaaleen e jamm ('Have a good night.')
Please.	njaafodaa
Thank you.	a jaaraamah (sg)
	on jaaraama (pl)
You're welcome.	enen ndendidum
Sorry/Pardon.	yaafo or achanam hakke
Yes.	eey
No.	alaa
How are you?	no mbaddaa?
I'm fine.	mbe de sellee

Can you help me please?	*ada waawi wallude mi, njaafodaa?*
Do you speak English/French?	*ada faama engale/faranse?*
I speak only English.	*ko engale tan kaala mi*
I speak a little French.	*mi nani faranse seeda*
I don't understand.	*mi faamaani*
What's your name?	*no mbiyeteedaa?*
My name is ...	*ko ... mbiyetee mi*
Where are you from?	*to njeyedaa?*
I'm from ...	*ko ... njeyaa mi*
Where is ...?	*hoto woni?*
Is it far?	*no woddi?*
straight ahead	*ko yeesu*
left	*nano bang-ge*
right	*nano ñaamo*
How much is this?	*dum no foti jarata?*
That's too much.	*e ne tiidi no feewu*
Leave me alone!	*accam!* or *oppam mi deeja!*

1	*go-o*
2	*didi*
3	*tati*
4	*nayi*
5	*joyi*
6	*jeego*
7	*jeedidi*
8	*jeetati*
9	*jeenayi*
10	*sappo*
11	*sappoygoo*
12	*sappoydidi*
20	*noogaas*
30	*chappantati*
100	*temedere*
1000	*wujenere*

MALINKÉ

Malinké is spoken in Senegal's east. With speakers numbering over 250,000 it is recognised as one of the country's six national languages. While it is similar in some respects to Mandinka, the two are classed as separate languages.

Good morning.	*nee·so·ma*
Good evening.	*nee·woo·la*
How are you?	*tan·as·te?*
Thank you.	*nee·kay*
Goodbye.	*m·ba·ra·wa*

MANDINKA

Mandinka, a national language of Senegal, is the language of the Mandinka people found largely in central and northern Gambia, and in parts of southern Senegal. The people and their language are also called Mandingo and they're closely related to other Manding-speaking groups such as the Bambara of Mali, where they originate.

In this guide, **ng** should be pronounced as in 'sing' and **ñ** represents the 'ni' sound in 'onion'.

Hello.	*i/al be ñaading* (sg/pl)
Goodbye.	*fo tuma doo*
Please.	*dukare*
Thank you.	*i/al ning bara* (sg/pl)
You're welcome.	*mbee le dentaala/ wo teng fengti* (lit. 'It's nothing.')
Sorry/Pardon.	*hakko tuñe*
Yes.	*haa*
No.	*hani*
How are you?	*i/al be kayrato?* (sg/pl)
I'm fine.	*tana tenna* (lit. 'I am out of trouble')
	kayra dorong (lit. 'Peace only')
What's your name?	*i too dung?*
My name is ...	*ntoo mu ... leti*
Where are you from?	*i/al bota munto?* (sg/pl)
I'm from ...	*mbota ...*
Can you help me please?	*i/al seng maakoy noo, dukare?* (sg/pl)
Do you speak English/ French?	*ye angkale/faranse kango moyle?*
I speak only English.	*nga angkale kango damma le moy*
I speak a little French.	*nga faranse kango domonding le moy*
I don't understand.	*mmaa kalamuta/mmaa fahaam*
Where is ...?	*... be munto?*
Is it far?	*faa jamfata?*
Go straight ahead.	*sila tiling jan kilingo*
left	*maraa*
right	*bulu baa*
How much is this?	*ñing mu jelu leti?*
That's too much.	*a daa koleyaata baake*
Leave me alone!	*mbula!*

1	*kiling*
2	*fula*
3	*saba*
4	*naani*
5	*luulu*
6	*wooro*
7	*woorowula*
8	*sey*

LANGUAGE

9	kononto
10	tang
11	tang ning kiling
12	tang ning fula
20	muwaa
30	tang saba
100	keme
1000	wili kiling

WOLOF

Wolof (spelt *ouolof* in French) is the language of the Wolof people, who are found in Senegal, particularly in the central area north and east of Dakar, along the coast, and in the western regions of Gambia. The Wolof spoken in Gambia is slightly different to the Wolof spoken in Senegal; the Gambian Wolof people living on the north bank of the Gambia River speak the Senegalese variety. Wolof is used as a common language in many parts of Senegal and Gambia, often instead of either French or English, and some smaller groups complain about the increasing 'Wolofisation' of their culture.

In this guide, **ng** should be pronounced as in 'sing' and **ñ** represents the 'ni' sound in 'onion'.

Hello.	na nga def (sg)
	na ngeen def (pl)
Good morning.	jaam nga fanane
Good afternoon.	jaam nga yendoo
Goodnight.	fanaanal jaam
Goodbye.	ba beneen
Please.	su la nexee
Thank you.	jai-rruh-jef
You're welcome.	agsil/agsileen ak jaam (sg/pl)
Sorry/Pardon.	baal ma
Yes.	wau
No.	deh-det

Also available from Lonely Planet:
French Phrasebook

How are you?	jaam nga am? (lit. 'Have you peace?')
I'm fine.	jaam rek
And you?	yow nag?
What's your (first) name?	naka-nga sant?
My name is ...	maa ngi tudd ...
Where do you live?	fan nga dahk?
Where are you from?	fan nga joghe? (sg)
	fan ngeen joghe? (pl)
I'm from ...	maa ngi joghe ...
Do you speak English/ French?	deg nga angale/faranse?
I speak only English.	angale rekk laa degg
I speak a little French.	degg naa tuuti faranse
I don't speak Wolof/ French.	mahn deggumah wolof/ faranse
I don't undestand.	degguma
I'd like ...	dama bahggoon ..
Where is ...?	fahn la ...?
Is it far?	soreh na?
straight ahead	cha kanam
left	chammooñ
right	ndeyjoor
Get in!	dugghal waay!
How much is this?	lii ñaata?
It's too much.	seer na torob
Leave me alone!	may ma jaam!

Monday	altine
Tuesday	talaata
Wednesday	allarba
Thursday	alkhyama
Friday	ajuma
Saturday	gaawu
Sunday	dibeer

0	tus
1	benn
2	ñaar
3	ñett
4	ñeent
5	juroom
6	juroom·benn
7	juroom·ñaar
8	juroom·ñett
9	juroom·ñeent
10	fuk
11	fuk·ak·benn
12	fuk·ak· ñaar
20	ñaar·fuk
30	fanweer
100	teemeer
1000	junneh

Glossary

Items marked G or S are used only in The Gambia or Senegal respectively.

auberge – hostel or small hotel

balafon – wooden xylophone typically played by griots
bazin – dyed fabrics that are beaten to a shine with wooden clubs
bolong (G) – literally 'river' in Mandinka; when used in an English context it means creek or small river
boubou – common name for the elaborate robelike outfit worn by men and women (also called *grand boubou*)
bumsters (G) – 'beach boys' who usually loiter around the coastal resort zones of The Gambia, trying to make a living by hustling tourists

cadeau (S) – gift, tip, bribe or hand-out
calèche – horse-drawn cart used to carry goods and people, particularly in the rural regions of Senegal
campement (S) – could be loosely translated as 'hostel', 'inn' or 'lodge', or even 'motel'; it is not a camping ground
campement villageois (S) – rural, village-managed lodgings typical of the Casamance
car mourides – long-distance bus service financed by the Sufi brotherhood of the Mourides
car rapide (S) – usually decrepit yellow-blue minibus, popular public transport of Dakar and symbol of Senegal
case (S) – hut
case à étages (S) – two-storey mud house
case à impluvium (S) – large round traditional house, with roof constructed to collect rainwater in a central tank or bowl
chambres de passage (S) – very basic place to sleep, often near bus stations; with a bed or mat on the floor and little else, and nearly always doubling as a brothel; also called *maison de passage*
climatisée – air-conditioned (often shortened to 'clim')
commissariat (S) – police station
compteurs (S) – meters (usually in taxis and *télécentres*)
confrérie – brotherhood

dash (G) – bribe (noun); also used as a verb 'You dash me something…'
demi-pension (S) – half board (dinner, bed and breakfast); see also *pension complète/simple*
dibiterie – grilled-meat stall
djembe – short, goat hide–covered drum

Ecowas – Economic Community of West African States
essence (S) – petrol (gas) for car

factory – fortified slaving station
fanals – large lanterns; also the processions during which the lanterns are carried through the streets
fête (S) – festival
fromager (S) – kapok tree; also known as silk-cotton tree

garage (G) – bus and bush-taxi station
gare routière (S) – bus and bush-taxi station; also called *autogare* and *gare voiture*
gargotte (S) – basic eating house or stall
gasoil – diesel fuel
gendarmerie (S) – police station/post
gîte (S) – used interchangeably with 'auberge' and *campement*
grigri – charm or amulet worn to ward off evil (pronounced gree-gree); also written as *grisgris* or *grisgri*
griot – traditional musician or minstrel who also acts as historian for a village, clan or tribe
groupement de femmes – women's cooperative

harmattan – light winds from the north that carry tiny particles of sand from the desert, causing skies to become hazy from December to February
hôtel de ville (S) – town hall

IMF – International Monetary Fund
Inch' Allah – God willing, ie hopefully (Arabic, but used by Muslims in Africa)

kora – 21-string harp-lute

lumo – weekly market, usually in border areas

mairie (S) – town hall; mayor's office
maison de passage see *chambres de passage*
marabout – Muslim holy man
marigot (S) – creek (S)
mbalax – mixture of Cuban beats and traditional *sabar* drumming; the heart and soul of Senegalese music
MFDC – Mouvement des Forces Démocratiques de la Casamance
mobylette – moped

ndeup (S) – ceremonies in which people with a mental illness are treated and healed (S)
Ndiaga Ndiaye (S) – white Mercedes bus, used as public transport (S)

occasion (S) – lift (noun), or place in a car or bus (pronounced oc-cars-ee-on, often shortened to *occas*)

pagne (S) – length of cloth worn around the waist as a skirt

paillote (S) – shelter with thatched roof and walls; usually on the beach or around an open-air bar-restaurant

palava – meeting place

paletuviers (S) – mangroves

patron (S) – owner, boss

pension (S) – simple hotel or hostel, or 'board'

pension complète (S) – full board (lunch, dinner, bed and breakfast)

pension simple (S) – B&B

pétrole (S) – kerosene

pirogue – traditional wooden canoe, either a small dugout or long, narrow sea-going fishing boat

préfecture (S) – police headquarters

quatre-quatre (S) – literally, '4x4' (4WD car)

quartier – area

Quran – Islamic holy book (also called the Koran)

Ramsar – an international convention concerned with the conservation of wetland habitats and associated wildlife

sabar – tall, thin, hourglass drum

sai-sai – Wolof term for a womaniser; also used for youngsters smooth-talking women, usually with sexual but sometimes criminal intentions

sous-verre (S) – reverse-glass painting; technique in which images are drawn onto the back of a glass surface, particularly in Saint-Louis/Senegal

Sentram (S) – Senegal's maritime-transport organisation

sept-place – usually a Peugeot 504 or 505, with seven seats

serviette (S) – towel (in bathroom)

serviette hygiénique (S) – sanitary pad (see also *tampon hygiénique*)

serviette de table (S) – table napkin, serviette

signares – women of mixed race who married wealthy European merchants during colonial times, particularly in Saint-Louis/Senegal

Sonatel (S) – Senegal's phone company

syndicat d'initiative (S) – tourist office

tampon (S) – stamp (eg in passport)

tampon hygiénique (S) – tampon (also *tampon périodique* and *serviette hygiénique*)

taxi-brousse (S) – bush taxi

telecentre (G) or **télécentre** (S) – privately owned telephone bureau

toubab – white person

ventilé (S) – room with a fan

village artisanal (S) – craft market

zouk – style of music, originally from Guadeloupe, that mixes African and Latin-American rhythms

Behind the Scenes

THIS BOOK

This 3rd edition of *The Gambia & Senegal* was written and researched by Katharina Kane. The 1st edition was written by David Else and the 2nd by Andrew Burke. This guidebook was commissioned in Lonely Planet's Melbourne office, and produced by the following:

Commissioning Editors Stefanie Di Trocchio, Will Gourlay, Jane Thompson, Margaret Toohey
Coordinating Editors Adrienne Costanzo, Jackey Coyle
Coordinating Cartographer James Ellis
Coordinating Layout Designer Steven Cann
Managing Cartographer Shahara Ahmed
Assisting Editors David Carroll, Barbara Delissen, Kate Evans, Charlotte Harrison, Craig Kilburn, Martine Lleonart
Assisting Cartographers Diana Duggan, Matthew Kelly, Amanda Sierp, Simon Tillema, Natasha Velleley
Assisting Layout Designers Laura Jane, Carlos Solarte, Wibowo Rusli
Cover Designer James Hardy
Project Manager Nancy Ianni
Language Content Coordinator Quentin Frayne

Thanks to Helen Christinis, Sally Darmody, Jennifer Garrett, Stephanie Pearson, Raphael Richards, Celia Wood

THANKS
KATHARINA KANE

Big thanks to Souleymane Kane for being patient enough to see his fiancée bent over manuscripts until the day before the wedding. Thanks also go out to his entire family, particularly to Yeya Sy for taking up endless baby-sitting duties.

My parents, brothers and sisters – you've been amazingly patient.

In Dakar, thanks go out to Romuauld Taylor, Mady Kane and Cherif Bojang at the 221. Jean at the Océanium – your enthusiasm is infectious! Hélène, thanks for introducing me to Angélique Dhiedhiou. Still in Dakar, thanks to Stephanie and Baba, Sandrine and Marcus for friendship and advice, as well as Nounou and his entire, wonderful team for far too many things that can be listed here. For accompanying me on my many travels, I'd like to thank Djiby Pene, Modou the taxi driver, and particularly Daby Ba, for staying cool during the car accident. Thanks to the hospital staff in Dakar, and particularly Idy Faye for late-hour consultations. In Thiès, thanks to Beuz, you're doing an amazing job! In Saint-Louis, I'm grateful to Jean-Jacques Bancal, Bamba and Amadou Cissé. Thanks to Anthony in Palmarin, Bouba with the *mobylette* in Toubakouta and Ousmane with the *mobylette* in Foundiougne. In Eastern Senegal, I could only complete my work thanks to Pape Samba and his mum, Pape Moussa, Modou Senn and his amazing driver, and Numu Diallo, for his amazing insights into the region. Jean-Baptiste, Augustin Diatta, Véronique Chiche and Dr Teneng – greatest respect for all your amazing work in the Casamance! Sandy Haessner – you're an amazing photographer, let's build projects! And Maurice Phillips, Peter Borshik, Astrid Bojang, Nina, EJ and the Egalitarian – you've been incredibly helpful in The Gambia. Thanks to Kathy Joyce for her brilliant Banjul suggestions, and to Sarah Gelpke for chats about bumsters.

THE LONELY PLANET STORY

The story begins with a classic travel adventure: Tony and Maureen Wheeler's 1972 journey across Europe and Asia to Australia. There was no useful information about the overland trail then, so Tony and Maureen published the first Lonely Planet guidebook to meet a growing need.

From a kitchen table, Lonely Planet has grown to become the largest independent travel publisher in the world, with offices in Melbourne (Australia), Oakland (USA) and London (UK). Today Lonely Planet guidebooks cover the globe. There is an ever-growing list of books and information in a variety of media. Some things haven't changed. The main aim is still to make it possible for adventurous travellers to get out there – to explore and better understand the world.

At Lonely Planet we believe travellers can make a positive contribution to the countries they visit – if they respect their host communities and spend their money wisely. Every year 5% of company profit is donated to charities around the world.

All my close ones that are far, thanks for everything and apologies should I have forgotten anyone in writing – I haven't in thought.

OUR READERS

Many thanks to the travellers who used the last edition and wrote to us with helpful hints, useful advice and interesting anecdotes:

A Ronald Ariesen, Jeffrey Austin **B** Diane Bah, Michele Bain, Gisa Becker, Eva-Maria Bengtson, Françoise Benkemoun, Arnaud Bocquier, Gilbert Boerekamp, Ellen Bork, Erica Borremans, Jill Buckler **C** Douglas Calhoun, Nigel Canavan, Jackie Church, Bryan Cooper, Sistah Coyle, Roberto Antonio Cusato **D** Chris Darby, Alexander Davies, Anthony De Lannoy, Jeremy Devereux-Hickman, Aart Dijkzeul, Clare Donnelly, Priscilla Dorresteijn, Ursula Duerig, Yan Dufour, Claire Duiker **F** Hanne Finholt **G** Alexander Garcia, Mike Giles, Guido Giorgetti, Conni Gunsser **H** Andy Hards, Alex Hare, Alton & Petra Hartley, Martin Holland, Mike Hood, Paul Hoskins **J** Alison Jaap, Tanja Jaarsveld, Abdou Jallow, Evan Jones, Marianne Jonker, **K** Merle Kamarik, Claire Kelly, GS Kingston, Reinoud Koeman, Paul Kramer, Jennifer Krischer **L** Maarten Lambrechts, Peter Langfield, Mariken Lenaerts, Debbie Ling **M** Mark Mansi, Aly Marroun, Nick Massey, Vincent Mattelaer, Clodagh McCloskey, Andre Meerkerk, Thierry Michilsen, Charlotte Miran, Phil Mitchell, Domenico Monacelli, Claudia Montulet **N** Emma Nesper, Eric Nicholson **O** Bengt Ohlson, Rita van Oosterhoud **P** Bjvrn Parmentier, Robert Patterson, Karl Ivan Pedersen, Judith Beggs Pierson, Evelyn Pijl, Kirsten Platten, Robert Pospiech, Bjorn Prevaas, Marcus Probst **R** Samantha Reid, Bas Renes, Anna Renner, Anton Rijsdijk, Steven Riley, Derek Rosen, Elke Rosiers, Hans Rossel, Shawn Rubin **S** J Sabharwal, K Sabharwal, Leigh Salmon, Silvia Sanchez, Camiel & Rosemar Schuurman, Lynne Scragg, Sharon D'Arcy Searle, Brant Sextro, Owen Shahadah, Lior Shamir, Angela Shanely, René Smit, Jo Smith, Jonathan Smith, Wietske Spoelstra, Tom Suter **T** Carolyn Taylor, Alex Thomson

SEND US YOUR FEEDBACK

We love to hear from travellers – your comments keep us on our toes and help make our books better. Our well-travelled team reads every word on what you loved or loathed about this book. Although we cannot reply individually to postal submissions, we always guarantee that your feedback goes straight to the appropriate authors, in time for the next edition. Each person who sends us information is thanked in the next edition – and the most useful submissions are rewarded with a free book.

To send us your updates – and find out about Lonely Planet events, newsletters and travel news – visit our award-winning website: **www.lonelyplanet.com/feedback**.

Note: we may edit, reproduce and incorporate your comments in Lonely Planet products such as guidebooks, websites and digital products, so let us know if you don't want your comments reproduced or your name acknowledged. For a copy of our privacy policy visit www.lonelyplanet.com/privacy.

V Anthony Vandyk, C Vare, Erwin van Veen **W** Christian Wejse, Laura Westberg, Alan White, Christiane White, Errol Williams, Martin Willoughby-Thomas, Robert Winshall

ACKNOWLEDGMENTS

Many thanks to the following for the use of content:

Globe on back cover ©Mountain High Maps 1993 Digital Wisdom, Inc.

Index

000 Map pages
000 Photograph pages

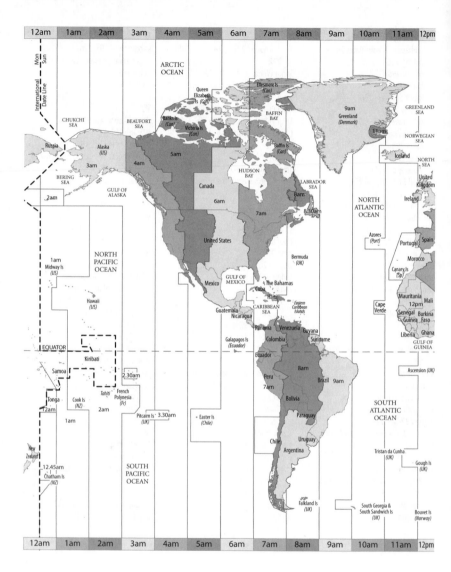

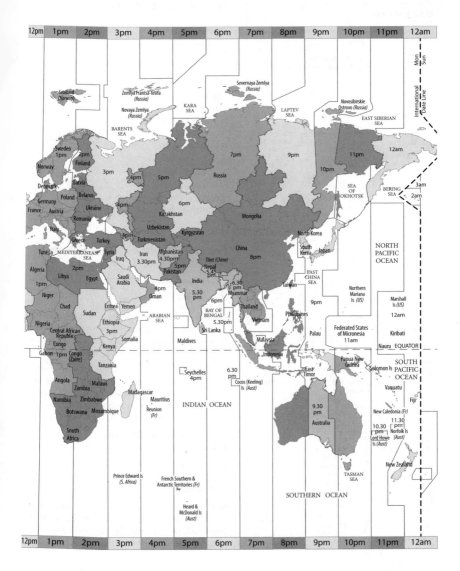

328

MAP LEGEND

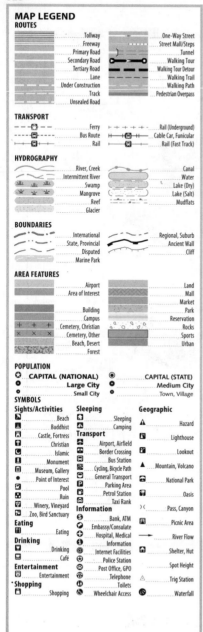

LONELY PLANET OFFICES

Australia
Head Office
Locked Bag 1, Footscray, Victoria 3011
☎ 03 8379 8000, fax 03 8379 8111
talk2us@lonelyplanet.com.au

USA
150 Linden St, Oakland, CA 94607
☎ 510 893 8555, toll free 800 275 8555
fax 510 893 8572
info@lonelyplanet.com

UK
72–82 Rosebery Ave,
Clerkenwell, London EC1R 4RW
☎ 020 7841 9000, fax 020 7841 9001
go@lonelyplanet.co.uk

Published by Lonely Planet Publications Pty Ltd
ABN 36 005 607 983

© Lonely Planet Publications Pty Ltd 2006

© photographers as indicated 2006

Cover photographs: Gambian men on the beach, Caroline Penn/APL/
Corbis (front); Hands beating drums, David Tipling/Lonely Planet Images
(back). Many of the images in this guide are available for licensing
from Lonely Planet Images: www.lonelyplanetimages.com.

Printed through Colorcraft Ltd, Hong Kong
Printed in China